WITHDRAWN

Dictionary of Feminist Theologies

BIRMINGHAM UNIVERSITY LIBRARY

Dictionary of Feminist Theologies

Edited by
LETTY M. RUSSELL
and
J. SHANNON CLARKSON

MOWBRAY

© 1996 Westminster John Knox Press

Published in Great Britain by Mowbray
A Cassell imprint
Wellington House, 125 Strand, London WC2R 0BB

Published in the United States by Westminster John Knox Press, 100 Witherspoon Street, Louisville, KY 40202-1396

All rights reserved. No part of this publication may be reproduced or transmitted in any form or by any means, electronic or mechanical, including photocopying, recording, or by any information storage or retrieval system, without permission in writing from the publishers.

Unless otherwise noted, scripture quotations are from the New Revised Standard Version of the Bible, copyright © 1989 by the Division of Christian Education of the National Council of the Churches of Christ in the U.S.A., and are used by permission.

Book design by Publishers' WorkGroup
Cover design by Alec Bartsch

First edition

This book is printed on acid-free paper.

PRINTED AND BOUND IN THE UNITED STATES OF AMERICA
BY R. R. DONNELLEY & SONS COMPANY

9 8 7 6 5 4 3 2 1

British Library Cataloguing-in-Publication Data

A catalogue record for this book is available from the British Library.

ISBN 0-264-67387-5

1974322X

The Women's World Wide Web

Contents

Preface

We were sitting at dinner with Cynthia Thompson in San Francisco in November 1992. This was an hour-long respite in the middle of a harried schedule at the annual meetings of the American Academy of Religion and the Society of Biblical Literature. As guests of Cynthia Thompson and Westminster John Knox Press, we were prepared for some business conversation but not for what we heard. "Why don't you two edit a feminist theological dictionary?" Cynthia asked. Shannon thought it was a great idea, because she likes computer challenges and long lists of phone calls. Letty thought it was impossible. She had another book in mind, and neither she nor Shannon knew anything about editing dictionaries.

There were a lot of impossibilities built into this project. First, there was the problem of getting feminist scholars in religion to agree that this dictionary was needed and that it would be possible for us to edit it. Second, there was the problem of getting any agreement on the title of the dictionary or on the words that should be included. Third, there was the problem of finding the writers and of including as many and as diverse a group as possible. Last, there was the sinking feeling that there would always be people who would look at the entries and think, I could do that one better!

We did, however, find a number of reasons to say yes to this team effort on behalf of women in religion. The opportunity for networking and exchange with the advisers and writers was truly exciting. Each entry that came in was like a special letter to be rejoiced over and pondered. The opportunity to contribute to the growing field of womanist, *mujerista*, and feminist studies inspired us to take the risks involved in moving into the double unknowns of dictionary editing and feminist theological dictionary editing. After all, we thought, this is a book we would like to have and use, so why not do it?

Scholarly work in feminist studies in religion has been developing since the late 1960s, and a wealth of research and writing has been carried out in religious studies. It would seem that the time has come for a dictionary that will assist both students and interested readers in the search for study and reference materials. In the more limited field of feminist theological studies, there is also a great wealth of material. This *Dictionary of Feminist Theologies* seeks to provide guidance to readers who are interested in all areas of Christian theology as they relate to feminism, as well as in theologies of other religions as developed by feminists. Entries include topics of international interest and articles written by international scholars, but the majority of the writers are from North America and have written in English; 21 percent of the writers are women of color.

This *Dictionary* is an aid to feminist scholarship and teaching, and it will also be helpful to students in seminary and in religious studies departments. An important readership would be the large number of women and men, both clergy and lay, interested in feminist theologies and looking for information that could lead them to further understanding of a particular topic. No other dictionary of this kind exists in English. The entries are intended to be intelligible to educated laypersons as well as to clergy and religious professionals. Together, the *Dictionary* and *The Women's Bible Commentary* published by Westminster John Knox Press in 1992 make available an important area of contemporary theology and church renewal for church members interested in learning about the insights of feminist theory and theologies.

The *Dictionary* covers standard topics of Christian theological studies, as well as topics of other religions that are important for the continuing feminist dialogue among many different religious, cultural, and racial groups. There are also entries on topics of particular interest to those engaged in feminist studies. There are no entries on persons, but there is a listing of all the contributors. As an aid to those who would like an overview of current work in feminist theologies, there are slightly longer introductory articles on Feminist Theories; Theologies, Contemporary; Justice and Social Change; Spirituality, Women's; Ethics and Moral Theologies; Biblical Studies; Church Ministries and Worship; Theologies, Historical; and Church Histories. The extensive Bibliography provides a key to further resources on all the topics covered in the *Dictionary.* It is also a resource for those seeking a comprehensive bibliography of English-language publications on feminist theologies in the U.S. context.

The work of writing and editing the *Dictionary of Feminist Theologies* fell into three overlapping phases. The 1993 phase included the important work of designing the book, selecting its title, and working with the editorial advisory groups to select the words and recruit writers. In this phase the Yale Advisory Group, made up of women teaching in the Feminist Studies program at Yale Divinity School at that time, assisted in finalizing the design, selecting areas of study, and suggesting words in group members' areas of specialization. In addition, the International Advisory Group submitted suggestions for the design, title, entries, and writers from all parts of the world. The names of the participants in the advisory groups are listed in a separate section of this volume.

Those editorial advisers who were able met in November 1993 to discuss the plan and suggestions for the title. No title was adequate for the book, because no one title describes all of the work being done by women in the study of religion today. The decision to call the book a *Dictionary of Feminist Theologies* was based in the need for some way to speak about the work that we do in common. Even though the focus is Christian theology, Jewish feminists and post-Christian and post-Jewish feminists, as well as women of many other faiths and ideologies, are constantly sharing in the discussion and were welcomed as contributors. Because "feminist" so often has been identified with "white feminist," many women theologians of color speak of their work in reference to their own context. For instance, many of the African-American writers, such as Katie Cannon, speak of themselves as "womanist" theologians, while writers such as Ada María Isasi-Díaz speak of Hispanic women's liberation theology as *mujerista* theology. Discussion of the diversity of feminist theologies is found in the Introduction, as well as throughout this volume in entries by women from many different contexts.

The 1994 phase of the writing consisted of finding the writers and then doing everything in our power to get the entries sent in! The computers stayed busy with all the details of working with 185 authors. With the able help of Stephanie Egnotovich, our second editor at Westminster John Knox Press, we began to shape the entries and the book and to confer with the authors about their entries. Many times the writers were in the midst of crises in their own lives but were trying to keep up with the demands of their academic work, including the *Dictionary.* Ultimately, the number of those unable to finish was two.

In 1995, the final editing phase, our Yale Advisory Group continued to help us with names and to advise us on entries. In particular, Susan Garrett worked with us on the biblical entries, and Margaret Farley and Serene Jones advised us on the ethical, theological, and historical entries. Sharon Ringe of the International Advisory Group provided a crucial service in translating the Spanish entries. In addition, we received wonderful and patient support from Barbara Blodgett, Karen Mabee, Maria Malkiewicz, and Connie Reinhardt, and Elizabeth Russell Collins in the preparation of the Bibliography and the manuscript. To these women and to all the women in the editorial advisory groups, we owe special thanks. A real gift of this phase was the way so many writers thanked *us* for the opportunity to share in the project! But it was we who were thankful every time we could read their entries with interest and excitement.

Although Letty said at the beginning that a dictionary was a pretty impossible project, she discovered that she was in very familiar territory. It was familiar not because it was like writing a book but because, as Katherine Gill, a Yale adviser, pointed out, it was like *teaching.* The *Dictionary* was interactive and required flexible responses up to the very end. Each day the shape changed and the challenges were different, according to which entries did or did not appear. This *Dictionary of Feminist Theologies* is itself a conversation among a *women's world wide web* of people who joined together for one brief time to give reports on where they are in feminist theologies. We hope you enjoy reading the entries and that you will enter into the conversation as it continues to evolve among all who join in this adventure of learning and teaching!

Introduction

It would seem that those who read the *Dictionary of Feminist Theologies* would just use it like other dictionaries, to look up definitions of words that are listed in alphabetical order. Yet this is only one of many uses for this particular dictionary. Just as feminist theologies are plural, so are the needs of those who want to learn about these theologies. This volume provides a pluralistic approach to feminist theologies so that the reader can look for entries from different contexts or different theological disciplines. The bibliographies and the list of contributors provide an opportunity for further reading and research, and the more general, area entries provide an overview of the field. It is hoped that the entries and the reader's interest will overlap sufficiently so that the *Dictionary* will continue to spark new ideas and questions among us all.

In this volume it is generally understood that feminist theologies are a reflection of the meaning of God's self-revelation in our lives from the perspective of advocacy for the full humanity of women of all races, classes, sexual orientations, abilities, and nationalities. In the Preface, however, we indicated that a dictionary about feminist theologies is almost impossible because there are so many different points of view and perspectives that are emerging both within and beyond the Christian tradition. Even the word *feminist* is suspect as a general designation, because its use is associated with the dominant perspectives of white, middle-class, Western women.

Theologies is also suspect, because it has been associated with the dominance of white, Western Christianity and with patriarchal images of God. Some women indicate that their discussion on God/Goddess moves beyond male images of God by speaking of "thealogy." Others want to move beyond the structures of institutional religions and speak of spirituality instead of religion or theology. *Weaving the Visions: New Patterns in Feminist Spirituality*, edited by Judith Plaskow and Carol P. Christ in 1989, is a good example of a religious and theological pluralism that is also reflected in the many entries on spirituality in this volume.

In our title, the plural *theologies* is very appropriate. In an emerging field, there is no one corner on the current explorations. This is what makes the *Dictionary* so exciting! We can find entries from many different perspectives, depending on the racial, economic, national, sexual, and political background of the writer. To introduce the reader to feminist theologies from many different contexts, there are entries from different regions: Africa, Asia, Europe, Latin America, North America, the Pacific Islands, and

South Asia. There are also entries on Jewish theologies and Buddhism, Hinduism, Islam, Shintoism, and Wicca. Women speaking out of their racial oppression are heard from through indigenous, womanist, and *mujerista* theologies, as are those writing lesbian theologies.

A dramatic difference of perspective arises from the varied theological disciplines of the authors. Sacraments, for instance, is covered by a variety of entries: a historical view from Fredrica Thompsett, an African view of sacrifice from Elizabeth Amoah, a biblical view of sacrifice and Christology from Joanna Dewey, a liturgical view of Eucharist from Janet Walton, and a biblical view of baptism from Sharon Ringe. The differences in theological fields are increased further by the way the authors draw from related fields of social analysis, psychology, economics, history, and literature. For these reasons, it is very important to note the cross-references that are marked in each entry with asterisks (*), indicating where the reader can find other information on a particular topic. The reader can use this additional information to take part in the continuing dialogue and discussion of the definitions.

Two other helps for the reader confronting such a diverse feast of definitions are the Bibliography and the introductory entries on different areas in feminist and liberation theologies. The Bibliography provides a major resource for the reader. In such short entries the authors can offer only an aperitif, not a full meal. However, through the entry bibliographies they can direct readers to further sources. The authors' names and dates at the end of each entry are keyed to the long Bibliography in the back of the book, where everything is listed alphabetically, by author and date, so that the reader can find the complete reference all in one place. Readers can also use the Bibliography to look up books written by a particular author whose entries they find useful for their own learning.

The area entries are listed alphabetically with the other entries and are marked with a double asterisk (**). Readers who have never read feminist theologies will have an easier time knowing what to look up and how things fit together if they read all of the introductory area articles first, as an introduction to the field. The area entries include Biblical Studies; Church Histories; Church Ministries and Worship; Theologies, Contemporary; Ethics and Moral Theologies; Feminist Theories; Theologies, Historical; Justice and Social Change; and Spirituality, Women's. As the Yale Editorial Advisory Group tried to plan the areas of the book, we found ourselves surprised at how far we had to go beyond the traditional Christian theological categories to include the feminist scholarship in religion that is crucial to the shaping of this new field. We are confident that the entries will be part of the continuing work of reshaping and transforming theological scholarship.

Inclusive language is used in the entries, but the scripture texts cited are not necessarily inclusive, especially in God language. Unless otherwise noted, quotations and chapter and verse references are from the *New Revised Standard Version of the Bible* (NRSV, 1989). The Older Testament is referred to as Hebrew Scriptures, Old Testament, or First Testament, depending on the preference of the author. The Younger Testament is referred to as the Greek Testament, the New Testament, or the Second Testament. Again, the different terms both remind us of the differences in the canon of the Bible among Jews, Catholics, Orthodox, and Protestants and make us aware of the pluralism of biblical perspectives found among the theological entries.

Overall, the *Dictionary* contains a feast of information and an invitation to join in the continuing dialogue about what constitutes feminist theologies. The format of the entries tries to shape that dialogue both by giving attention to the traditional meaning of a term and by then expanding on its meaning from a feminist perspective. Many entries close with questions and issues that are posed for further study and reflection. There are still many questions, so use the *Dictionary of Feminist Theologies* with caution, because these questions may become *your* questions. It doesn't have "all the answers," but it does invite us all to reflect on the transformations that are happening within and among us and to name these transformations as gifts in our lives.

Editorial Advisory Groups

Yale Advisory Group

Marilyn Adams, *Historical Theology and Philosophy*
M. Shawn Copeland, *Theology and Black Studies*
Margaret A. Farley, *Ethics*
Susan R. Garrett, *New Testament*
Katherine Gill, *Church History*
Serene Jones, *Historical Theology*
Lee McGee, *Pastoral Counseling*
Letty M. Russell, *Contemporary Theology*
Victoria R. Sirota, *Church Music and Liturgy*
Kathryn Tanner, *Historical Theology*
Lee Palmer Wandel, *History and Religious Studies*
Jann Cather Weaver, *Religion and the Arts*

International Advisory Group

Maria Clara Bingemer, *Latin American Theology*
Rita Nakashima Brock, *Theology*
Katie Geneva Cannon, *Womanist Ethics*
Francine Cardman, *Church History*
Chung Hyun Kyung, *Korean Theology*
Mary Rose D'Angelo, *New Testament*
Diana Eck, *Comparative Religion*
Marcia Falk, *Jewish Liturgical Studies*
Ivone Gebara, *Latin American Theology*
Mary C. Grey, *European Theology*
Beverly Wildung Harrison, *Ethics*
Mary E. Hunt, *Ethics*
Ada María Isasi-Díaz, *Ethics*
Musimbi R. A. Kanyoro, *African Theology and Linguistics*
Ursula King, *Theology and Religious Studies*
Hisako Kinukawa, *Japanese Theology and Biblical Studies*
Kwok Pui-lan, *Chinese Theology and Ethics*
Adair T. Lummis, *Sociology of Religion*
Mary John Mananzan, *Philippine Theology*
Mercy Amba Oduyoye, *African Church History*
Judith Plaskow, *Jewish Theology*
Nancy D. Richardson, *Ethics and Ministerial Studies*
Sharon H. Ringe, *New Testament*
Rosemary Radford Ruether, *Theology and Church History*
Katharine Doob Sakenfeld, *Old Testament*
Elisabeth Schüssler Fiorenza, *New Testament*
Elsa Tamez, *Biblical Studies*
Susan Brooks Thistlethwaite, *Theology*
Emilie M. Townes, *Womanist Theology and Ethics*
Phyllis Trible, *Old Testament*

Contributors

Denise M. Ackermann
Professor of Practical Theology, University of the Western Cape, Cape Town, South Africa
power

Carol J. Adams
Independent scholar, Richardson, Texas
battering; rights, animal; vegetarianism

Elizabeth Amoah
Lecturer, Department of the Study of Religions, University of Ghana, Legon-Accra, Ghana
rituals, African; sacrifice/self-negation

Barbara Hilkert Andolsen
Helen Bennett McMurray Professor of Social Ethics, Monmouth College, West Long Branch, New Jersey
rights, reproductive

María Pilar Aquino
Assistant professor of Theological and Religious Studies, University of San Diego, San Diego, California
colonization; feminist theology, Latin American

Ellen T. Armour
Assistant professor of Religous Studies, Rhodes College, Memphis, Tennessee
essentialism

Karen Baker-Fletcher
Assistant professor of Theology and Culture, School of Theology at Claremont; Assistant professor of Religion, Claremont Graduate School, Claremont, California
difference; womanist voice

Angela Bauer
Assistant professor of Hebrew Bible, Episcopal Divinity School, Cambridge, Massachusetts
heterosexism in biblical interpretation; servant/slave; shalom/peace

Lyn M. Bechtel
Assistant professor of Hebrew Scripture, Moravian Theological Seminary, Bethlehem, Pennsylvania
shame

Dianne Bergant
Professor of Old Testament Studies, Catholic Theological Union, Chicago, Illinois
canon

Donna Berman
Rabbi Emerita of Port Jewish Center, Port Washington, New York; doctoral candidate, Drew University, Madison, New Jersey
bat mitzvah; midrash

Elizabeth Bettenhausen
Women's Theological Center, Boston, Massachusetts
evil; free will; rights, human

Phyllis A. Bird
Associate professor of Old Testament Interpretation, Garrett-Evangelical

Theological Seminary, Evanston, Illinois
harlot

Donna Bivens
Women's Theological Center, Boston, Massachusetts
race

Kathleen M. Black
Associate professor of Homiletics and Liturgics, School of Theology at Claremont, Claremont, California
church ministries and worship

Barbara J. Blodgett
Doctoral candidate, Department of Religious Studies, Yale University, New Haven, Connecticut
religion; responsibility

Riet Bons-Storm
Professor of Practical Theology and of Pastoral Theology and Care, University of Groningen, Netherlands
pastoral care

Wendy Sue Boring
Doctoral candidate, Yale University, New Haven, Connecticut
reason/passion

Elizabeth M. Bounds
Assistant professor, Religious Studies Program, Virginia Polytechnic Institute and State University, Blacksburg, Virginia
economics of class; politics; working poor

Rita Nakashima Brock
Associate professor in the Endowed Chair in Humanities, Hamline University, St. Paul, Minnesota
feminist theories

Cheryl Anne Brown
Adjunct assistant professor of Biblical Studies, Fuller Theological Seminary, Pasadena, California
wilderness

Pamela K. Brubaker
Assistant professor of Religious Studies, California Lutheran University, Thousand Oaks, California
stereotypes; work

Lisa Sowle Cahill
Professor of Christian Ethics, Department of Theology, Boston College, Chestnut Hill, Massachusetts
marriage; objectivity

Claudia V. Camp
Associate professor of Religion, Texas Christian University, Fort Worth, Texas
Sophia/Wisdom

Margaret M. Campbell
Associate professor of Religious Studies, Holy Names College, Oakland, California
resurrection

Katie Geneva Cannon
Associate professor of Religion, Temple University, Philadelphia, Pennsylvania
emancipatory historiography; virtue, womanist

Francine Cardman
Associate professor of Historical Theology, Weston Jesuit School of Theology, Cambridge, Massachusetts
Christology; church histories

Charlotte Caron
Co-president, St. Andrew's College, Saskatoon, Saskatchewan, Canada
thealogy

Nancy A. Carter
Consultant for Health and Welfare Ministries, General Board of Global Ministries, United Methodist Church
AIDS

Rebecca S. Chopp
Professor of Theology, Dean of the faculty, Candler School of Theology, Emory University, Atlanta, Georgia
methodologies; praxis

Sook Ja Chung
Pastor, Womanchurch, Seoul, Korea
minjung

Linda J. Clark
James R. Houghton Scholar of Sacred Music, Boston University School of Theology, Boston, Massachusetts
rituals, women's

J. Shannon Clarkson
Assistant professor, Quinnipiac College, Hamden, Connecticut
parasitic reference; third world

Sheila D. Collins
Associate professor of Political Science, William Paterson College, Wayne, New Jersey
classism; domination; social analysis

Mary T. Condren
Lecturer in Women's Studies and Religion, Trinity College, Dublin, and University College, Dublin, Ireland
gendered representation; spirituality, Celtic female

Paula M. Cooey
Professor of Modern and Contemporary Religious Thought, Trinity University, San Antonio, Texas
kenōsis; *pluralism: theological responses; popular religiosity*

M. Shawn Copeland
Associate professor in Theology, Marquette University, Milwaukee, Wisconsin
theologies, contemporary

Pamela D. Couture
Assistant professor of Pastoral Care, Candler School of Theology, Emory University, Atlanta, Georgia
feminization of poverty

Toni Craven
Professor of Hebrew Bible, Brite Divinity School, Texas Christian University, Fort Worth, Texas
Apocrypha; creation story

Mary Rose D'Angelo
Associate professor, Department of Theology, University of Notre Dame, Notre Dame, Indiana
abba/*Father;* diakonia

Susan E. Davies
Jonathan Fisher Professor of Christian Education, professor of Pastoral Theology, Bangor Theological Seminary, Bangor, Maine
education; heresy

Ellen F. Davis
Associate professor of Old Testament, Yale University Divinity School, New Haven, Connecticut
land

Betty A. DeBerg
Associate professor of Theology, Valparaiso University, Valparaiso, Indiana
women's organizations

Joanna Dewey
Associate professor of New Testament Studies, Episcopal Divinity School, Cambridge, Massachusetts
sacrifice, the Bible, and Christ

Susan Dolan-Henderson
Assistant professor of Christian Ethics and Moral Theology, Episcopal Theological Seminary, Austin, Texas
care; postmodernism

Kelly Brown Douglas
Associate professor of Theology, Howard University, Washington, D.C.
Christ, Jesus; freedom

Elizabeth A. Dreyer
Associate professor, Department of Ecclesiastical History, Washington Theological Union, Silver Spring, Maryland
asceticism; spirituality, medieval

Ruth C. Duck
Associate professor of Worship, Dean of chapel, Garrett-Evangelical Theological Seminary, Evanston, Illinois
inclusive language

Nancy J. Duff
Associate professor of Theological Ethics, Princeton Theological Seminary, Princeton, New Jersey
call/vocation; mothers/motherhood

Mitzi N. Eilts
Coordinator of Church-College Relations, Education & Publication, United Church Board for Homeland Ministries, Cleveland, Ohio
story

Cynthia Eller
Associate editor, Continuum Publishers, New York, New York
Goddess; matriarchy; spirituality, women's; Wicca/neopaganism

Victoria Erickson
University chaplain, Associate professor of Sociology of Religion, Drew University, Madison, New Jersey
ethnography, liberationist; social construct

Toinette M. Eugene
Associate professor of Social Ethics, Garrett-Evangelical Theological Seminary, Evanston, Illinois
appropriation/reciprocity; redemption/salvation

Virginia Fabella
Academic dean, Institute of Formation and Religious Studies, Quezon City, Philippines
dialogue, theological

Margaret A. Farley
Gilbert L. Stark Professor of Christian Ethics, Yale University Divinity School, New Haven, Connecticut
ethics and moral theologies; relationships

Marie M. Fortune
Executive director, Center for the Prevention of Sexual and Domestic Violence, Seattle, Washington
pastoral misconduct; violence, sexual

Susan R. Garrett
Professor of New Testament, Louisville Presbyterian Theological Seminary, Louisville, Kentucky
apostles; new creation

Ivone Gebara
Professor, Centro Ecumenico de Servico a Ecucação Popular, São Paulo, Brazil
ecofeminism; poverty

Marie J. Giblin
Assistant professor, Xavier University, Cincinnati, Ohio
dualism; empowerment; hierarchy

Katherine Gill
Assistant professor of European Christianity, Yale University Divinity School, New Haven, Connecticut
martyr

Anne Bathurst Gilson
Visiting scholar, Episcopal Divinity School, Cambridge, Massachusetts
embodiment; incarnation

Aruna Gnanadason
Women's Desk, World Council of Churches, Geneva, Switzerland
dowry (India); feminist theologies, South Asian

Deirdre J. Good
Professor of New Testament, General Theological Seminary, New York, New York
meek; son of God; Son of man

Elaine L. Graham
Lecturer in Social and Pastoral Theology, Victoria University of Manchester, Manchester, England
psychology of women

Mary C. Grey
Professor of Contemporary Theology, University of Southampton, Southampton, England
feminist theologies, European; guilt; revelation

Leslie Griffin
Assistant professor, School of Law, Santa Clara University, Santa Clara, California
interdependence; legal theory

Rita M. Gross
Professor of Comparative Studies in Religion, University of Wisconsin–Eau Claire, Eau Claire, Wisconsin
Buddhism; dialogue, interfaith

Christine Gudorf
Professor of Religious Studies, Florida International University, Miami, Florida
development; rights, children's; theologies, liberation

Amy Laura Hall
Doctoral candidate in Religious Studies, Yale University, New Haven, Connecticut
agapē

Daphne Hampson
Senior lecturer in Divinity, University of St. Andrews, St. Andrews, Scotland
monotheism; post-Christian

Han Kuk Yom,
Pastor, Seoul, South Korea
Mariology

Eleanor H. Haney
Chair of Liberal Arts Department, Maine College of Art, Portland, Maine
character; cosmos

Nancy A. Hardesty
Visiting associate professor of Philosophy and Religion, Clemson University, Clemson, South Carolina
healing; theologies, evangelical

Beverly Wildung Harrison
Professor of Christian Ethics, Union Theological Seminary, New York, New York
anger/wrath; socialism–capitalism

Susannah Heschel
Abba Hillel Silver Associate Professor of Jewish Studies, Department of Religion, Case Western Reserve University, Cleveland, Ohio
anti-Judaism/anti-Semitism

Carter Heyward
Howard Chandler Robbins Professor of Theology, Episcopal Divinity School, Cambridge, Massachusetts
Christa; desire; eros

Christine Firer Hinze
Assistant professor, Department of Theology, Marquette University, Milwaukee, Wisconsin
conscience

Mary E. Hobgood
Assistant professor of Religious Studies, College of the Holy Cross, Worcester, Massachusetts
Marxism

Valerie J. Hoffman
Assistant professor of Religion, University of Illinois at Urbana-Champaign, Urbana-Champaign, Illinois
Islam

Amy Hollywood
Assistant professor of Religion, Dartmouth College, Hanover, New Hampshire
deconstruction

Mary E. Hunt
Adjunct associate professor, Department of Women's Studies, Georgetown University, Washington, D.C.
androcentrism; friendship; theology, queer

Ada María Isasi-Díaz
Assistant professor of Theology, Drew University, Madison, New Jersey
experiences; justice and social change; preferential option; solidarity; theology, mujerista

Janet R. Jakobsen
Assistant professor of Women's Studies and Religious Studies, University of Arizona, Tuscon, Arizona
ideology

Grace M. Jantzen
John Rylands Senior Research Fellow, University of Manchester, Manchester, England
autonomy; idolatry; philosophy

Elizabeth A. Johnson
Professor of Theology, Fordham University, Bronx, New York
God; image of God

Penelope D. Johnson
Professor of History, New York University, New York, New York
mystics, medieval

Serene Jones
Assistant professor of Systematic Theology, Yale University Divinity School, New Haven, Connecticut
theology, historical

Patricia Beattie Jung
Associate professor of Theological Ethics, Wartburg Theological Seminary, Dubuque, Iowa
emotion

Kang Nam-Soon
Instructor of Constructive Theology, Methodist Theological Seminary, Seoul, South Korea
androgyny; han; *misogyny*

Musimbi R. A. Kanyoro
Executive secretary for Women and Church in Society, Lutheran World Federation, Geneva, Switzerland
naming; polygamy; translation

Judith Webb Kay
Assistant professor of Religion and Dean of students, University of Puget Sound, Tacoma, Washington
natural law

Catherine Keller
Associate professor of Constructive Theology, Drew Theological School, Madison, New Jersey
eschatology

Flora A. Keshgegian
Associate university chaplain, Brown University, Providence, Rhode Island
memory; suffering

Ursula King
Professor and head of Department of Theology and Religious Studies, University of Bristol, Bristol, England
Hinduism; paradigm shift; world religions and Christianity

Hannah W. Kinoti
Senior lecturer, Department of Religious Studies, University of Nairobi, Kenya
culture

Hisako Kinukawa
Lecturer, Tokyo Women's Christian University, Tokyo, Japan
purity–impurity; Shintoism

Cynthia Briggs Kittredge
Doctoral candidate, Harvard Divinity School, Cambridge, Massachusetts
Pauline texts

Kristen E. Kvam
Assistant professor of Theology, Saint Paul School of Theology, Kansas City, Missouri
anthropology, theological

Kwok Pui-lan
Associate professor of Theology, Episcopal Divinity School, Cambridge, Massachusetts
feminist theologies, Asian; mission

Nadia M. Lahutsky
Associate professor of Religion, Texas Christian University, Fort Worth, Texas
Gnosticism; widows

Karen Lebacqz
Professor of Christian Ethics, McGill University, Montreal, Canada
bioethics; justice

Marilyn J. Legge
McDougald Professor of Systematic Theology, St. Andrew's College, Saskatoon, Saskatchewan, Canada
contextualization; imperialism

Amy-Jill Levine
Professor of New Testament Interpretation, Vanderbilt University, Nashville, Tennessee
hermeneutics of suspicion

Adair T. Lummis
Faculty research associate, Hartford Seminary, Hartford, Connecticut
anthroplogy, cultural; gendered institutions; pluralism, religious

Mary Ann Lundy
Deputy general secretary, World Council of Churches, Geneva, Switzerland
unity and diversity

Mary John Mananzan
Director, Institute of Women's Studies, St. Scholastica's College, Manila, Philippines
prostitution

Joan M. Martin
Assistant professor of Christian Social Ethics, Episcopal Divinity School, Cambridge, Massachusetts
sisterhood; work, womanist

E. Ann Matter
Professor and chair, Department of Religious Studies, University of Pennsylvania, Philadelphia, Pennsylvania
mystics/interior journeys; mythologies

Melanie A. May
Dean of the program in the Study of Women and Gender in Church and Society; professor of Theology, Colgate Rochester Divinity School/Bexley

Hall/Crozer Theological Seminary, Rochester, New York
doxology; ecumenism; feminist theologies, North American

Sallie McFague
Carpenter Professor of Theology, Vanderbilt University, Nashville, Tennessee
creation; Holy Spirit

Lee McGee
Roger Squire Assistant Professor of Pastoral Counseling, Yale University Divinity School, New Haven, Connecticut
conflict; family

Lisa Meo
Coordinator, The Weavers, Suva, Fiji
feminist theologies, Pacific Island

Linda A. Mercadante
Professor of Theology, Methodist Theological School in Ohio, Delaware, Ohio
addiction

Joyce Ann Mercer
Doctoral candidate in Practical Theology, Emory University, Atlanta, Georgia
faith; liberation

Carol Meyers
Professor, Department of Religion, Duke University, Durham, North Carolina
archaeology

Virginia Ramey Mollenkott
Professor of English and Women's Studies, William Paterson College, Wayne, New Jersey
ageism; lesbian; metaphor

Marianne Blickenstaff Mosiman
Teaching assistant, United Theological Seminary, Dayton, Ohio
election; prophets, biblical women

Greer Anne Wenh-In Ng
Associate professor of Christian Education, Emmanuel College, Toronto School of Theology, Toronto, Ontario, Canada
cognitive dissonance

Vivian-Lee Nyitray
Assistant professor, Departments of Religious Studies and Literature and Languages; director, Asian Languages and Civilizations Program, Univerisity of California, Riverside, California
Confucianism; tao; yin–yang

Mercy Amba Oduyoye
Former deputy general secretary of the World Council of Churches, former faculty member of University of Ibadan, Nigeria
conversion; feminist theology, African; inculturation; pagan

Ofelia Ortega
Executive secretary, Ecumenical Theological Education, Unit on Unity and Renewal of the World Council of Churches, Geneva, Switzerland
theological education

Marta Palma
Executive secretary for Latin America and the Caribbean, World Council of Churches, Geneva, Switzerland
prophecy, church women's

Sun Ai Lee Park
Editor, *In God's Image,* Seoul, South Korea
minjung

Amy Plantinga Pauw
Associate professor of Doctrinal Theology, Louisville Presbyterian Theological Seminary, Louisville, Kentucky
doctrine

Margarita Pintos
Professor in the Academy of the German Republic in Madrid; member of the Feminist Theology Seminar of the Instituto Fe y Secularidad of Madrid, Spain
pride; truthfulness

Tina Pippin
Associate professor of Religious Studies, Agnes Scott College, Decatur, Georgia
judgment; whore of Babylon

Judith Plaskow
Professor of Religious Studies, Manhattan College, Bronx, New York
covenant; feminist theologies, Jewish

Carolyn J. Pressler
Associate professor of Old Testament, United Theological Seminary of the Twin Cities, New Brighton, Minnesota
biblical criticism

Anne Primavesi
Lecturer in Theology, Bristol University, Bristol, England
pantheism

Marjorie Procter-Smith
Associate professor of Liturgy and Worship, Perkins School of Theology, Dallas, Texas
lectionary; liturgy

Sally B. Purvis
Independent scholar, Atlanta, Georgia
community; compassion; cross; gender construction

Nancy J. Ramsay
Professor of Pastoral Theology, Louisville Presbyterian Theological Seminary, Louisville, Kentucky
counseling

Mary Judith Ress
Maryknoll lay missioner, editor/member of *Con-Spirando*, Santiago, Chile
conscientization

Lynn N. Rhodes
Associate professor of Ministry and Field Education, Pacific School of Religion, Berkeley, California
church ministries and worship

Nancy D. Richardson
Associate dean for Ministry, Harvard Divinity School, Cambridge, Massachusetts
racism

Marcia Y. Riggs
Associate professor of Christian Ethics, Columbia Theological Seminary, Decatur, Georgia
equality

Sharon H. Ringe
Professor of New Testament, Wesley Theological Seminary, Washington, D.C.
baptism; gospel; jubilee

Carol S. Robb
Professor of Christian Social Ethics, San Francisco Theological Seminary, San Anselmo, California
sexuality

Maria José F. Rosado Nunes
Professor of Sociology of Religion, chair of Feminist Studies, Instituto Metodista de Ensino Superior and Pontificia Universidade Catolica, São Paulo, Brazil
materialism; nationalism; oppression

Rosetta E. Ross
Assistant professor of Ethics, Interdenominational Theological Center, Atlanta, Georgia
grace

Susan A. Ross
Associate professor of Theology, Loyola University, Chicago, Illinois
body

Rosemary Radford Ruether
Georgia Harkness Professor of Applied Theology, Garrett-Evangelical Theological Seminary, Evanston, Illinois
Gaia; patriarchy; sexism

Letty M. Russell
Professor of Theology, Yale University Divinity School, New Haven, Connecticut
authority; ecclesiology; partnership; predestination

Maura A. Ryan
Assistant professor of Christian Ethics, University of Notre Dame, Notre Dame, Indiana
abortion; agency; virtue

Susan M. St. Ville
Instructor, Department of Religious Studies, St. Lawrence University, Canton, New York
epistemological privilege; French feminism

Katharine Doob Sakenfeld
William Albright Eisenberger Professor of Old Testament Literature and Exegesis, Princeton Theological Seminary, Princeton, New Jersey
biblical studies

Linda Schearing
Assistant professor of Hebrew Scriptures, Department of Religion, Gonzaga University, Spokane, Washington
depatriarchalization

Sandra M. Schneiders
Professor of New Testament Studies and Christian Spirituality, Jesuit School of Theology/Graduate Theological Union, Berkeley, California
kerygma

Luise Schottroff
Professor for New Testament, University of Kassel, Kassel, Germany
authority of scripture; virgin birth

Eileen M. Schuller
Associate professor of Religious Studies, McMaster University, Hamilton, Ontario, Canada
biblical translation

Elisabeth Schüssler Fiorenza
Krister Stendahl Professor of Divinity, Harvard University Divinity School, Cambridge, Massachusetts
discipleship of equals; feminist hermeneutics

Janet Silman
Teacher of Biblical Studies, Dr. Jessie Saulteaux Resource Center, Manitoba, Canada
spirituality, aboriginal; theology, indigenous women's

Victoria R. Sirota
Assistant professor of Church Music, Yale University Divinity School Institute of Sacred Music, New Haven, Connecticut
immanence

Moshe Sluhovsky
Instructor in History, Division of the Humanities and Social Sciences, California Institute of Technology, Pasadena, California
exorcism; witchcraft

Christine M. Smith
Associate professor of Worship and Preaching, United Theological Seminary of the Twin Cities, New Brighton, Minnesota
preaching

Marti Steussy
Associate professor of Old Testament, Christian Theological Seminary, Indianapolis, Indiana
righteousness

Jeanne Stevenson-Moessner
Adjunct assistant professor of Practical Theology, Columbia Theological Seminary, Decatur, Georgia
priesthood of all believers

Allison Stokes
Founding director, Women's Interfaith Institute in the Berkshires, West Stockbridge, Massachusetts
spirituality groups

Marjorie Hewitt Suchocki
Vice president for Academic Affairs and Dean, Claremont School of Theology, Claremont, California
metaphysics; sin; theology, process; Trinity

Elsa Tamez
President and professor of Theology, Seminario Bíblico Latinoamericano, Costa Rica
justification by faith

Susan Brooks Thistlethwaite
Professor of Theology and Culture; director of Center for Theology, Ethics and the Human Sciences, Chicago Theological School, Chicago, Illinois
pornography; violence, institutionalized

Fredrica Harris Thompsett
Academic dean and Mary Wolfe Professor of Historical Theology, Episcopal Divinity School, Cambridge, Massachusetts
sacraments; transcendence

Deanna A. Thompson
Doctoral candidate in Theology, Vanderbilt University, Nashville, Tennessee
reality, women's; relativism

Bonnie Thurston
Associate professor of New Testament, Pittsburgh Theological Seminary, Pittsburgh, Pennsylvania
pastoral epistles

Emilie M. Townes
Associate professor of Christian Social Ethics, St. Paul School of Theology, Kansas City, Missouri
ethics, womanist; hegemony

Phyllis Trible
Baldwin Professor of Sacred Literature, Union Theological Seminary, New York, New York
rhetorical criticism

Gail Lynn Unterberger
Pastoral psychotherapist, Interfaith Counseling Services, Gaithersburg, Maryland
ministry; prayer; soul

Vuadi Vibila
Doctoral candidate, Hamburg University, Hamburg, Germany
marginalization

Katharina von Kellenbach
Assistant professor of Religious Studies, St. Mary's College of Maryland, St. Mary's City, Maryland
Holocaust

Elina Vuola
Researcher at the Institute of Development Studies, University of Helsinki, Finland
order of creation; orthodoxy

Janet R. Walton
Professor of Worship, Union Theological Seminary, New York, New York
Eucharist

Lee Palmer Wandel
Associate professor of History and Religious Studies, Yale University, New Haven, Connecticut
Fall; predestination

Jann Cather Weaver
Associate dean for student life; assistant professor (adjunct) of Religion and the Arts, Yale University Divinity School, New Haven, Connecticut
seeing

Delores S. Williams
Associate professor of Theology and Culture, Union Theological Seminary, New York, New York
atonement; survival; theology, womanist

Miriam Therese Winter
Professor of Liturgy, Worship, Spirituality and Women's Studies, Hartford Seminary, Hartford, Connecticut
religious life; Women-Church

Kathi Wolfe
Freelance writer, contributor to *The Disability Rag/Resource, Mainstream Magazine,* and other publications, Falls Church, Virginia
disability; handicapism

Serinity Young
Visiting scholar, Southern Asian Institute, Columbia University, New York, New York
world religions

Valarie H. Ziegler
Associate professor of Religious Studies, DePauw University, Greencastle, Indiana
heaven; hell; tradition

Barbara Brown Zikmund
President and professor of American Religious History, Hartford Seminary, Hartford, Connecticut
marks of the church; ordination

Abbreviations

ABD	*Anchor Bible Dictionary* (ed. Freedman et al.)
Add.	Addition(s)
AILL	*An Inclusive-Language Lectionary*
BA	*Biblical Archaeologist*
B.C.E.	before the common era
BR	*Biblical Research*
ca.	circa
CBQ	*Catholic Biblical Quarterly*
C/C	*Christianity and Crisis*
CC	*Cross Currents*
CCent	*Christian Century*
C.E.	common era
CTS	*Chicago Theological Seminary Register*
f.	feminine
Gk	Greek
Heb	Hebrew
HS	Hebrew Scriptures (or Old Testament or Older Testament)
HTR	*Harvard Theological Review*
IGI	*In God's Image* (ed. Lee-Park)
Int	*Interpretation*
IRM	*International Review of Mission*
JAAR	*Journal of the American Academy of Religion*
JB	Jerusalem Bible
JBL	*Journal of Biblical Literature*
JFSR	*Journal of Feminist Studies in Religion*
JPSV	Jewish Publication Society Version
JPTS	Jewish Publication Society Version
JSA	*Journal of Studies in Alcohol*
JSOT	*Journal for the Study of the Old Testament*
JWCS	*Journal of Women in Culture & Society*
KJV	King James Version
LXX	Septuagint (Hebrew Scriptures in Greek)
m.	Mishnaic tractate
NEB	New English Bible
NHC	Nag Hammadi Codex
NIB	*New Interpreter's Bible* (ed. Keck)
NIV	New International Version
NJB	New Jerusalem Bible
NRSV	New Revised Standard Version
NT	New Testament (Greek Testament or Younger Testament)
OED	*Oxford English Dictionary*
OT	Old Testament (Hebrew Scriptures or Older Testament)
PG	J. P. Migne, Patrologia graeca
Q	Q source; also Qumran texts
RIBLA	*Revista de interpretação biblica Latinoamericana*
RSV	Revised Standard Version
sg.	singular
TDNT	*Theological Dictionary of the New Testament* (ed. Kittel/Friedrich)
TEV	Today's English Version (Good News)
USQR	*Union Seminary Quarterly Review*

Dictionary of Feminist Theologies

***Abba*/Father** *Abba* is an Aramaic word that has been widely used as the basis for claims that Jesus used the divine title Father in a unique and revelatory fashion. A variety of Christian theologians have fastened on "Jesus' *abba* experience" as a source of *Christology. This idea is based primarily on analyses of *gospel materials by Joachim Jeremias (1967, 11–65). It has been used to privilege Father as a divine title and to reject feminist critiques of exclusively masculine language and imagery for God and of the problematic character of parental language for God. Jeremias's case, which has been modified very little by his followers, relies on a series of interrelated claims: (1) that the word *abba* represents a special use by Jesus that was central to his teaching; (2) that for Jesus it expressed a special kind of intimacy and tenderness, deriving from its supposed origin in baby talk; (3) that Jesus' practice was distinct from the practices of both the early church and Judaism. These claims were formulated under the influence of the patently anti-Jewish article in the *TDNT* by the Nazi scholar Gerhard Kittel.

Some feminist scholars have taken over arguments which accept the claim that Jesus used *abba*/father in a special way, locating that use in the antipatriarchal context of the movement in which Jesus proclaimed God's reign. Claiming a nonpatriarchal sense for Jesus' use, they have attempted to subvert the construct itself and to put it to the service of feminist critique of *patriarchy and its deities. But as Madeline Boucher has pointed out, the evidence for Jesus' use of either *abba* or Father is both slender and problematic, and the anti-Jewish contexts of the original arguments raise serious questions about the potential of feminist reuse. Recent studies and new evidence from early Judaism make it possible to challenge claims that *abba* was both unique and central to Jesus' teaching or even used by Jesus. The Aramaic word *abba* is attributed only once to Jesus in the NT, in a context that is likely to be redactional (Mark 14:36); it is twice attributed to the Spirit (Gal. 4:6; Rom. 8:15). Galatians 4:6 strongly suggests that using this address reflects not baby talk but transition to adulthood in the Spirit (Gal. 3:22–4:8; John Chrysostom, *Commentary on the Epistle to the Galatians* 4, in PG 61:657).

The linguistic arguments Jeremias used to attribute the word to Jesus have been shown to be highly problematic. In addition, newly available texts from Qumran have shown that Jews in the holy *land in the first century B.C.E. were indeed willing to address God as "my father" (4Q*372*, 1; 4Q*460*). Rereading other Greek and Hebrew evidence from Judaism shows that the title evoked divine authority and kinship with God and was particularly important in the contexts of the providence of God, repentance, and persecution of the just Jew, especially by Gentiles.

The title Father for God is placed in the mouth of Jesus in three other passages of Mark (8:38; 11:25; 13:32) and in six passages from Q, including the model *prayer known as the Lord's Prayer (Matt. 6:9 // Luke 11:2). It is much more frequent in the letters and in Matthew, John, and Luke. It also occurs in rabbinic literature and the Jewish *liturgy. Jesus and/or his companions may have used the title Father for God in some form, but it cannot be shown with certainty that they did so. If they did, it was because the title resonated deeply with their Jewish hearers, perhaps to express resistance to the imperial title *pater patriae:* "God's reign (not the emperor's) is near"; "God (not the emperor) is our father." Increased use of the divine title Father in the late first and early second centuries resulted from a complex nexus of forces, including emerging christological speculation, resistance or accommodation to the imperial title *pater patriae,* and a popularized philosophical piety that used Father as a divine title for the deity as utterly transcendent. Along with Madeline Boucher and Mary R. D'Angelo in the United States, Martina Gnadt in Germany continues to work on this issue of *abba* as a divine title.

Boucher, in Withers [1984]; D'Angelo, *JBL* [1992a]; D'Angelo, *HTR* [1992b]; Schuller, *CBQ* [1992]; Strottmann [1991]

MARY ROSE D'ANGELO

Abortion Abortion is the cessation of gestation prior to fetal viability. Common discourse generally uses the term in its narrow sense, to connote the act of electively terminating a pregnancy.

The practice of abortion is almost everywhere subject to social control. Policies governing the availability of and access to surgical or pharmacological abortion typically claim one (or more) of three "centers of gravity": (1) protection of fetal life; (2) maternal health; and (3) reproductive privacy. Interests in protecting fetal life are usually expressed in prohibitions against elective abortion or in restrictions on the practice of abortion as the fetus approaches viability. Regulations aimed at protecting fetal life assume that fetuses enjoy the full panoply of personal rights either from conception or as they achieve statistical viability. Concerns for the safety of women are invoked to support requirements that abortions be performed by medical professionals or within particular institutional settings. Likewise, where elective abortion is otherwise prohibited, exceptions (e.g., in cases involving rape or incest or where pregnancy poses a physical or psychological risk) are often justified on the basis of maternal health interests. Policies centered in reproductive privacy resist placing undue restrictions on a woman's ability to determine whether or not she will continue a pregnancy. Such policies assume that a woman's right to bodily integrity supersedes the rights or interests that could be said to pertain to the pre-viable fetus.

Access to safe and legal abortion has been a key item on the contemporary feminist political agenda. Indeed, for most feminists reproductive liberty is a fundamental tenet of feminism. In the United States, the demand for abortion rights emerged as a feminist issue alongside shifts in women's consciousness of their own *agency and the possibilities for social and professional involvement (Luker, 113–21). As the women's movement of the 1960s and 1970s challenged traditional assumptions concerning women's domestic role, as greater numbers of women began to view motherhood as one among many possible life choices, many increasingly came to see control over fertility and reproduction as preconditional to self-determination. Thus, in the long and acrimonious debate occasioned by the legalization of "abortion on demand" in the United States in 1973, more has been at stake for pro-choice feminists than the unborn fetus's right to birth or the individual's right to the means to terminate an undesired pregnancy. The fight for reproductive *rights (including the right to abortion) has been nothing less than a demand for a new social order, one in which women define rather than are defined by their reproductive contribution.

In addition to identifying relevant ethical principles or values for an analysis of elective abortion, feminist theologians have been concerned with uncovering gender bias in religious teachings regarding reproduction. Recurring themes in feminist theological reflection on abortion include (1) a commitment to bodily integrity as a fundamental feature of respect for the well-being and dignity of women; (2) a view of pregnancy as "a creative moral action to be undertaken with *freedom, intelligently and with forethought," rather than simply a "natural process" (Harrison 1983, 228); (3) an insistence on an adequate description of abortion, i.e., as a genuine moral dilemma encountered under specific socioeconomic, historical, and cultural conditions; and (4) a critique of assumptions concerning "natural" gender roles.

Feminist theologians do not speak in a single voice on the legitimacy of abortion. However, on this much there is wide agreement: an adequate analysis of abortion must draw from all available sources of moral wisdom, most particularly from the lived experience of those who bear (and have always borne) the burdens of reproduction.

Gudorf [1994]; Harrison [1983]; Luker [1984]; Sherwin [1992]

MAURA A. RYAN

Addiction *Addiction* is a generic term describing a fairly wide range of behaviors deemed excessive, compulsive, and destructive, in particular alcohol and drug abuse. It is considered an increasing inability to control consumption, which becomes habitual and progressive. Other characteristics include physical dependency, increased tolerance, craving, withdrawal distress, and rapid reinstatement.

The professional fields dealing with addiction are still in a "pre-paradigm" state. There is vociferous debate over whether addiction is a distinct physical disease or a clinical entity unrelated to other causal factors. The "disease" description is most commonly ascribed to alcoholism.

The usage of the term *addiction* in America first surfaced in the late eighteenth century with regard to uncontrolled alcohol abuse. Previously, habitual drunkenness was generally considered a matter of choice. The term later extended to the abuse of certain drugs. Today it has expanded considerably, with problematic behaviors—such as excessive shopping, sex, or dependence on another person—diagnosed as "process" (rather than "substance") addictions.

Conceiving of addiction as a spiritual, not just a physical, problem helps some persons. But one unfortunate outcome is that addiction can resemble a narrowly conceived version of actual and/or original *sin. When *pride or grandiosity is considered the prime "character defect" of an addict and "admission of powerlessness" is enjoined (as in the twelve steps of Alcoholics Anonymous), women can be encouraged in stereotypical self-denigration and passivity. The diagnosis of "codependency" especially can fault women for conforming to societal requirements, view women's relational sensitivity as pathological, and misinterpret coerced behavior as self-aggrandizing and controlling. The focus on individual sobriety in the various addiction-recovery programs can discourage social action, even against societal forces that advance substance abuse and other self-destructive behaviors.

Donovan, in Donovan/Marlatt [1988]; Haaken, *JWCS* [1993]; Levine, *JSA* [1978]; Mercadante, in Chopp/Taylor [1994].

LINDA A. MERCADANTE

Agapē How is *agapē*, the Greek word for love in the Septuagint and New Testament, related to *friendship and *desire? This question has divided Christians since Jesus reiterated the Mosaic command to love, and we can find the roots of our disagreement in scripture itself. In the Septuagint, *agapē* translates a Hebrew word *('aheb)* that conveys several, possibly disparate facets of love: awakening desire, as in the Song of Songs; desperate longing, as in the Psalms; and resolute fidelity, as in Deuteronomy. The story of the loving Samaritan adds another layer: *agapē* is to be shown universally.

One strand of the Christian *tradition, woven especially by Augustine and Thomas Aquinas, suggests that *agapē* is continuous with a *passionate love* for our creator. These writers thus hold a place for impassioned friendship as flowing from our relationship with a beckoning God. Another thread, discernable in Luther and Kierkegaard, accentuates our sinful inclinations, which hinder both the stability and universality of *agapē*. These writers therefore describe *agapē* as a *willed decision* made in response to an almighty God.

Many feminists have enhanced the former view, suggesting that God actively longs for her children, and that we are in turn called to an attentive, even passionate *agapē* for God's daughters and sons. This interpretation is informed by some women's profound love for their own children, partners, and communities. Yet other feminists continue to suspect our affections and call rather on our sense of duty. These women advise that without a committed resolve to love all persons, we will choose to love only our own. Women holding both perspectives strive to consider the demands of *justice on love and thus agree that our construal of *agapē* must mitigate self-sacrifice, lest some bear the burden of God's command while others choose to ignore it.

Andolsen, *Journal of Religious Ethics* [1981]; Gudorf, in Andolsen/Gudorf/Pellauer [1985]; Fabella/Oduyoye [1988]; Farley [1986]

AMY LAURA HALL

Ageism Ageism is a prejudiced outlook toward (or treatment of) people who are deemed too young or too old to be regarded as fully human. It involves categorizing people into age groups and then responding to them on the basis of *stereotypes rather than seeing their individual differences. For instance, defining old age as a plight or a problem turns elderly people into unfamiliar others, from whom a youth-oriented society shrinks away in *guilt, pity, or fear of contamination. Such a definition erases or obscures the vast majority of people over sixty-five, who, to the degree that they maintain *autonomy and connectedness, remain cognitively alert, physically active, and meaningfully productive until the final few months of their lives.

Whereas traditional society would define counteracting ageism as a matter of competing rights, feminist theologians take a more organic approach by viewing ageism as alienation from a life process that includes aging and death. The cure lies in emphasizing divine *immanence. Because the rule of the "totally other" Father-God has identified *sexuality, woman, and decay with *evil, old women have been particularly despised; as Matilda Joslyn Gage remarked in 1873, when a woman is no longer sexually attractive to men, she is regarded as having forfeited the right to live. It is no accident that old women are the single poorest minority group in the United States.

Ageism is present within feminist communities whenever younger women expect older ones to regard the agendas of adults in their prime as more important than those of children or elderly people, or when media feminists highlight the achievements only of women under sixty-five. Ageism may also help to explain why women's history has been lost, so that women have repeatedly had to "reinvent revolution" instead of profiting from the insights of those who preceded them.

Because everyone is aging, no matter what their current age, it is wise to approach everyone as a person in process, including people in their eighties, nineties, and older.

Friedan [1993]; Kehoe [1989]; Levin/Levin [1980]; MacDonald/Rich [1991]

VIRGINIA RAMEY MOLLENKOTT

Agency Agency is a *power or potentiality for action. In theological *ethics, agency concerns, in particular, the capacity to act in response to God's self-communication or to make free and rational choices vis-à-vis God's demand or invitation. As such, any account of human agency (or moral agency) presupposes a deeper theological setting, i.e., an underlying theory of *revelation and *grace, a view of the nature of consciousness and rationality, an understanding of the relationship between divine law and human *freedom, and a commitment to some description of sinfulness and salvation.

As feminists continue to challenge traditional theological categories, languages, and methods, they recast and reshape understandings of moral agency. Favoring an "embodied and embedded" rationality, feminists generally resist dualistic anthropologies and thus question descriptions of human agency that locate moral knowledge and action primarily in the independence of the will from *emotion or the rational application of universally valid and impartial principles. Emerging in feminist ethics is an autonomous and relational moral subject, constituted within and acting for the sake of concrete *relationships of varying kinds (Farley 1985); moral knowing and acting from this perspective are "part of and informed by the entirety of our experience": emotional, physical, social and historical, cultural, intellectual, and religious (Smith 1985, 248). Here agency is a personal and "political" reality: a capacity for the transformation of selves in, through, and for the transformation of communities.

Attentive to the dimensions of power in the social construction of knowledge and experience, feminist and womanist theologians have questioned traditional assumptions regarding the conditions for free choice and therefore the meaning of moral *responsibility. Katie Geneva Cannon has argued, for example, that moral agency for black women cannot be understood apart from the continuing social matrix (shaped by the legacy of chattel slavery and forced segregation) in which black women find themselves as moral agents (9). Where surviving in the face of persistent powerlessness, i.e., "carving living space out of [an] intricate web of *racism, *sexism and *poverty," is the primary moral and religious challenge, moral *virtue is best described not in terms of responsible uses of power (as in mainstream Christian ethics) but in the sense of developing strategies that allow persons and communities *without* power to persist with dignity. Cannon and others insist that an adequate description of agency must account for the relationship between the choices available to agents and the development of moral consciousness, i.e., to the meanings of *conscience, freedom, and accountability under specific interpersonal and interstructural conditions.

Sensitivity to issues of power and powerlessness has also generated feminist criticism of treatments of *sin in mainstream Christian theological ethics. Theologians such as Valerie Saiving, for example, have questioned the primacy of *pride (in the form of self-assertion or idolatry) in Christian descriptions of sinfulness and hence also of virtue (as self-restraint and fitting self-disposition). While feminists do not disagree that freedom and finitude are moral and religious problems, they question whether, given women's historical situation of unequal or limited social, political, and economic power, "inordinate self-assertion" accurately represents women's existential temptation. They insist, therefore, on understandings of sin that can account for the embeddedness of moral experience and thus the complex nature of moral failure.

Feminists argue that wherever dominant theologies have failed to take seriously the religious and moral experiences of women, they have offered incomplete and distorted descriptions of the "human," of the God–human encounter, and thus of moral agency. Insisting on answers to theological questions that are both true to women's experiences and empowering, feminist critique makes possible (and necessary) more adequate theories of agency.

Cannon [1988]; Farley, in Andolsen/Gudorf/Pellauer [1985]; Saiving, in Christ/Plaskow [1979]; Smith, in Andolsen/Gudorf/Pellauer [1985]

MAURA A. RYAN

AIDS

Global Overview. AIDS (acquired immunodeficiency syndrome) is a global pandemic that exacerbates problems of oppressed groups. Stereotypes of AIDS as a disease of white gay men, Haitians, Africans, drug addicts, and prostitutes have fueled homophobia, *sexism, *racism, and *classism. Some people promote the harmful concept that AIDS is

God's *judgment and classify infected people as either "guilty victims" or "innocent victims." Since the mid-1980s, feminists have been among those countering increased *oppression linked to AIDS and responding to the pandemic in other helpful ways.

AIDS has particularly affected people of color. At the end of 1994, WHO announced that over 4.5 million people are officially reported to have AIDS; another 19.5 are estimated to be infected with HIV (human immunodeficiency virus). Of these people, an overwhelming number are people in Asia and Africa (Women and AIDS: Agenda for Action). In the United States, AIDS affects African Americans, Hispanics, Native Americans, and gay men of all racial backgrounds. Over 80 percent of women with AIDS live in Africa (WHO 1994). Over 77 percent of women with AIDS in the United States are women of color ("Facts about . . . Women and AIDS").

Many people with AIDS do not like to be called AIDS victims and prefer "PLWAs" (Persons Living With AIDS), "HIV positive," or even "HIV challenged." Use of only "HIV positive" to refer to PLWAs sometimes protests the Centers for Disease Control's (CDC's) sexist definition of AIDS. Althoughbroadened in the early 1990s to include some gynecological symptoms, the CDC's definition still discriminates against women, as does the center's recording procedure, which does not track woman-to-woman sexual transmission. HIV-infected women are one-third more likely to die without an AIDS-defining condition than HIV-infected men (Corea, 271–94).

Religious Responses. More and more persons of *faith are responding positively through *education, direct ministries, and opposition to those *preaching *shame and blame. Feminists and womanists have focused on the following concerns, with some emphasizing one area more than another:

*Compassionate *ministry.* Along with many other faithful people, feminists stress nonjudgmental ministry. Examples are hospital visits, spiritual guidance that respects the individual's values and needs, pastoral services for memorial and funeral ceremonies, and bereavement support. Bereavement counseling and other ministries extend to parents, siblings, spouses, committed partners or companions, children, any who identify as "family" of the PLWA.

**Sexuality and sexual identity/orientation.* Many feminists stress full inclusion of lesbians, gays, and bisexuals in the religious community. They contrast the scriptural concept of *purity and holiness with that of hospitality and holiness to give a biblical foundation to HIV/AIDS ministry. Others outline responsible sexual *ethics that also affirm sexuality as a gift from God.

Sexism, racism, classism. Feminists point out that, in the United States, AIDS treatments and services have been aimed at men and that root issues of oppression must be addressed. For example, men with HIV can go to one doctor. Women may have to go to at least three doctors, including their gynecologists and their children's pediatricians. Many women cannot afford one doctor, let alone three or transportation to them. Very often, subsidized housing provided for PLWAs is for adults only, not women with children. Globally, the power differential between women and men increases the burden on women. For example, teaching the mechanics of "safer sex" is useless if a woman is not safe from domestic *violence that results from her request to have safer sex. Women living in *poverty may not even have access to latex condoms. Additionally, a woman's desire for children must be honored, including her choice to have children when she is HIV positive.

The Future. Some feminists give AIDS a low priority, saying they do not want to be drawn away from women's health issues such as breast cancer or to be "caretakers" of men. However, by 2000, HIV may infect 14 million women and ten million babies and create ten million orphans ("Women and Aids: Agenda for Action," 1995). Moreover, most women do care about what happens to the men they love who are or may become infected. AIDS is therefore a women's issue worthy of feminist attention.

ACT UP [1990]; Corea [1992]; Dane/Levine [1994]; Hallman [1989]; *HIV/AIDS Ministries Network Focus Papers* [1989–1995]; Peavey [1990]; Russell [1990]

NANCY A. CARTER

Androcentrism Androcentrism, derived from Greek, is literally "male-centeredness." It considers males to be normative humans, females as derivative and subordinate. It silences women and other marginalized beings in a patriarchal society of which Christianity is a part. This mistaken *anthropology is the product of hierarchical, dualistic thinking and structures that result in unequal *power distribution, distorted perceptions, and systematic injustice. Most feminists reject androcentrism, seeking to replace it with inclusive, holistic patterns rather than with its female equivalent, gynocentrism, of which there are virtually no historical examples. Feminist theologies are the record of this effort.

Androcentrism reflects a methodology in which such binary opposites as male–female, public–private, divine–human are set up, with privilege accruing to one and to the detriment of the other. Differences of *race, class, ability, age, and *sexuality are interwoven into this same unhelpful pattern. The result is an exaggerated focus on and valuing of some, usually white, moneyed males, to the exclusion of others. When used to frame theology, androcentrism erases all but a privileged few perspectives.

Although theologians generally agree that the Divine has no gender, resistance to efforts to eradicate androcentric language about God and/or to substitute female images such as *Goddess reveals the firm grip of androcentrism. Similar problems accrue in biblical interpretation, skewing the Christian *tradition away from what many consider its egalitarian roots. One proposal to overcome androcentrism is to replace it with anthropocentrism, or human-centeredness. This solves the gender problem but maintains a similar false dichotomy that elevates humans over nature. *Ecofeminists reject this strategy because it reinforces damaging dynamics in the name of including women.

Constructive *liberation theologians seek instead to change the pattern by expanding the center. Then the particularity of every starting point, including that of men, can be appreciated without privileging any single one. Doing theology in that expanding center is the task ahead.

Ruether [1983]; Schüssler Fiorenza [1984/1995]; Schüssler Fiorenza [1992]

MARY E. HUNT

Androgyny The term *androgyny* has Greek roots: *andros* means "man" and *gynē*, "woman." *Androgyny* is a synthetic term formed out of the combination of two conceptual qualities previously strictly separated.

In most Chinese thought and religion, the complementary principles of *yin and yang are important. Yin is the dark side, the receptive, the passive, the female; yang is the sunny side, the active, the positive, the male. Especially in *Taoism, the idea of complementarity of yin and yang is fundamental, and the ideal is balance, not the victory of one over the other. This idea of complementarity often leads to the idea of androgyny. Taoist *philosophy resolves the complicated problem of the unity of opposites by claiming that yin and yang are one.

Western theological and philosophical literature has also dealt with androgynous themes. For example, much of Gnostic literature stresses androgyny as a salvation theme. The idea of androgyny is also found in the writings of Plato and of the Renaissance *mystics.

Androgyny has been claimed by some contemporary feminists as an ideal of humanity. They use the term *androgyny* to refer to the state of a single individual who possesses both traditionally masculine and traditionally feminine virtues. Androgyny is thus defined not by physical hermaphroditism but by psychological characteristics.

There are, however, feminists who think that the very concept of androgyny involves misleading presuppositions and the labeling of certain psychic attributes as masculine and others as feminine. Other feminist theologians have also raised objections to the idea of androgyny, criticizing it as "pseudo-wholeness." The real problem is a paradox inherent in the ideal of androgyny: while it claims to eliminate sexual stereotyping of human characteristics, its articulation is based on the conceptions of masculinity and femininity that it rejects.

Daly [1978]; Park [1993]; Ruether [1983]; Vetterling-Braggin et al. [1978]

KANG NAM-SOON

Anger / Wrath In Christian theological discourses prior to the advent of feminist theologies, anger and its near-analogue, wrath, were defined as *hostile dispositions* (combinations of attitude and act) expressing protest, objection, and active dissent. Both divine and human persons' actions expressed anger and, in intensified form, wrath. As with most patriarchal religious logic, these theologies affirmed divine anger (and wrath), using the presumption that God's anger was invariably "righteous" or justified in the face of human religious *idolatry or moral unfaithfulness.

Human anger or wrath, by contrast, was suspect, invariably so if directed toward God but also of dubious value when directed toward humans and their environments. Unless aimed specifically at *sin and *evil, anger was theologically and morally dangerous to the Christian. It was theologically suspect because it threatened what classical Christianity perceived as the chief theological *virtue of unqualified obedience to God. It was morally suspect because it endangered both general human powers of rational discernment and the self-sacrificial love that by the fourth century had become the highest virtue of patriarchal Christianity's vision of the moral life. Because anger itself came to be classified as one of the most "deadly" of sins, the possibility of human righteous anger was all but lost.

All feminist theologies reconfigure both divine–human *relationships and the manner in which human theological and moral virtues are conceived, so the redefinitions of anger implicit or explicit in these theologies are complex and varied. Liberal and radical (or liberationist, including both cultural radical and political-economic radical) feminisms differ considerably on this point. All agree that anger is not only a disposition but a relational dynamic and in no way the deadly sin of classical *tradition. Feminist theologies all but unanimously reject the patriarchal definition of the Christian life as involving "*sacrifice" of self and refuse the notion that the self-assertions involved in the expression of our passions, including anger, are "wrong."

Liberal theologies, however, follow the modernist psychologizing tendency that separates feeling and action. Hence they affirm anger as legitimate chiefly at the emotional level. Because liberal feminism separates love and *justice and privileges care over justice, its theological and moral norms depict the Christian life primarily as one of caretaking or peacemaking. As a result, the intensity of anger that energizes acts, even acts of restraining evil, is viewed more dubiously. Liberal feminism construes assertiveness as a form of aggression or even *violence.

By contrast, radical feminism's moral norms stress active justice making, including, at times, aggressive restraint of social evil. More complex than interpersonal caring, justice requires commutative participation or shared power, redistribution of moral and material goods, and even, in some liberationist feminism, aspects of retributive or compensatory action. Thus active expressions of anger may be morally obligatory in some situations.

Feminist reconstructions of the religious and moral meaning of anger also include insights correlative with the newer, body-centered approaches to human *psychology. Anger is recognized as a way of experiencing our embodied energy as women. It is a body-centered response to our total environment. Anger is a body signal, a response to action upon us. *Oppression or *domination may be seen as a condition that prevents us from fully experiencing our anger. Feminists recognize that abuse deprives us of the ability to read body signals fully and to gain awareness that unjust power is being directed against us. On this reading, discernment of our anger and awareness of its legitimacy as a healthy bodily response is a necessary condition for *survival and capacity to resist oppression. Discerning and processing anger is a basic aspect of "salvo" or *healing. Effectual direction of anger is also synonymous with achieving effective moral *agency.

The feminist redefinition of the dynamics of anger in divine–human interaction is, so far, somewhat less well developed than is feminist *anthropology. It is clear, however, that a strong trend is present in Christian feminism to reappropriate ancient Hebraic and early Jewish themes emphasizing both positive and negative emotional interaction between God and humanity. Feminists encourage deep wrestling with God and call on believers to express and ritualize anger toward God. In the face of human *suffering and the loss of real good that evil entails, we should be angry. Divine mystery does not require passivity. Feminists increasingly see that failure to express anger to God, as when we fail to express it to each other, distorts our piety and makes it a sanctimonious and brittle spirituality of denial.

Anzaldúa [1990]; Brock [1988]; Farley [1986]; Harrison [1985]; Heyward [1995]; Lorde [1984]; Soelle [1995]; Townes [1995]

BEVERLY WILDUNG HARRISON

Anthropology, Cultural Cultural anthropology is divided into three subfields: *archaeology, linguistics, and ethnology. Archaeology is the study of ancient human life through relics left by past *cultures. Linguistics is the study of how language develops through the symbols and layered meanings of words people use to describe their world. Ethnology, the subfield most frequently identified with cultural anthropology, is the study of cultures of various groups over time and how their values and beliefs interrelate and change. Although there have been divisions of emphasis within ethnology, it generally is less concerned with how economics, geography, and social structures affect human life than with how values arise, are transmitted, and influence human conduct.

*Ethnography is the fieldwork research approach generally used by anthropologists in studying contemporary cultures. It involves the researcher becoming a participant-observer in the daily life of another group. Through the eventual ethnographic report, the researcher typically strives to understand the culture from the viewpoint of people in that culture and to highlight differences and similarities between cultures.

Understanding religious *pluralism is expedited by the work of cultural anthropologists. But cultural anthropologists are not themselves free of culture or religious bias. Anthropologists' gender and values are likely to affect what they observe and how they interpret observations. Recently some anthropologists have tried to rectify previous ethnographic work that focused on men in particular cultures and included sexist assumptions in data interpretation. Ethnographic studies focusing on women's lives increase knowledge of women's cultural contributions. These studies provide evidence that gendered experiences can affect women in any cultural setting but underline the fact that women's experiences are also shaped by and filtered through their economic and familial statuses and social affiliations. Such research is important to feminist theologians who attempt to take account of women's multiple experiences in their own reflections.

Bell/Caplan/Karim [1993]; di Leonardo, in Kramarae/Spender [1992]; Fetterman [1989]; Marcus/Fischer [1986]

ADAIR T. LUMMIS

Anthropology, Theological Theological anthropology involves the constellation of religious teachings concerning what it means to be human. The Greek word *anthrōpos,* which signifies "human," provides part of the name for this constellation. The adjective *theological* underscores that this study differs from the study of humanity in anthropology as a social-scientific discipline. Although religious understandings of anthropology have been formulated variously, the term *theological* stresses that this field of study explores religious considerations of what it means to be God's human creatures. Thus theological anthropology considers such questions as: What traits and responsibilities does God give to human persons? What are God's intentions for and interactions with human persons?

For most of the history of Western Christianity, theological anthropology was not a separate topic. Instead, this constellation's "stars" were clustered in other configurations in that anthropological considerations were lodged within other doctrines, such as teachings on *creation or on the person of Jesus Christ. With the modern era's attention to the human subject, theological anthropology has come into its own as a distinct theological topic. Culling relevant points from a variety of sources, it often uses a narrative framework that relates to Western Christianity's reading of the opening chapters of Genesis, which tells the story of humanity as originally created by God and as fallen away from God's intentions. It then sets this trajectory of good-yet-sinful humanity within the larger narrative of God's designs and actions for *healing and renewing creation.

Until recently, English-speaking Christians called this topic the *doctrine of man.* The change to more inclusive terminology is appropriate because the *doctrine attends to the character and activity of human persons. Yet this change can be worrisome when it disguises the fact that gender plays a significant (yet often silent) role in anthropological considerations. Christian theology often overlooks women in its discussions of human beings, relying instead on views that deem males as the paradigm for human personhood. Thus it could be fitting to term a theologian's discussions of human persons a *doctrine of man,* if men's attributes and activities are what that theologian has in mind.

Feminist theologies call for clarity and candor concerning the relations of gender to theological anthropology. While Christian feminists differ in understanding and assessing these relations, they are united in opposing anthropologies that assume or argue that women are inferior to men. Notions of female inferiority pervade traditional Christian discussions of anthropological topics. Three areas where these notions are particularly vivid merit brief examination:

1. Discussions of creation constitute one area that relies frequently on notions of female inferiority. Christian *tradition has used the doctrine of creation to divide humanity into two divergent ranks, assigning different tasks and traits to men and to women. For example, many Christians have interpreted the opening chapters of Genesis in connection with New Testament texts such as the commands concerning women's silence and submission in 1 Tim. 2:11f. The Timothy text claims that one reason for women's silence and submission is that God created Eve after Adam. When this text be-

comes the lens for reading the first chapters of Genesis, it endorses interpreting women's subordination to men as part of God's original and enduring intention for human life. On such a basis, women have been said to be created in God's image only in a partial way, while men have been seen as created in the fullness of the *image of God. Hence, in much of Christian tradition, women's subservient status becomes their natural and God-intended place. This understanding posits what could be termed *perpetual hierarchy* as God's will and intention for gender relations.

2. A second aspect arises out of Christian theology's use of oppositional dualisms. Such dualisms not only posit a *difference between two entities; they also posit that this difference is so great and grave that the two entities diametrically oppose each other. Christian tradition often has understood maleness and femaleness as such a pair of opposites. Moreover, this pair is aligned with an entire series of oppositions: men are categorized with mind, *reason, will, and *transcendence; women are categorized with *body, intuition, *emotion, and *immanence. These *dualisms have long undergirded considerations of why God created women. Because of women's alignment with body, many have asserted that God's primary purpose for women concerns the reproduction of the human species. Thus men and women have two different purposes in life. Men betray God's intentions for men if they become immersed in matters of children and home; such betrayals have been denounced frequently in Christian tradition. Similarly, women can choose not to fulfill their intended role, but Christian tradition has assessed such a choice variously: at times these women are scorned for betraying God's intentions for them; at other times they are praised for "rising above" their natures.

3. Christian understandings of temptation and *sin constitute a third area where traditional assumptions about the inferiority of women can be seen. When female inferiority and subordination are posited as God's design, then any deviation from—or even questioning of—this arrangement becomes a mark of sin. Such views undergird many traditional discussions of the "first" sin in Eden, wherein Eve is blamed for talking with the serpent without having received Adam's permission. Other discussions fault Eve for being prone to sensual desires, warning that all women have similar inclinations. In these ways, Christian tradition has portrayed Eve and all her daughters as both dangerous to men and in need of male control.

Traditional understandings of sin have received feminist scrutiny from another direction, namely, in terms of equating *pride with sin and overlooking the ways in which negating and undervaluing the self might be sinful. Valerie Saiving charted this direction in 1960; Judith Plaskow later explored this thesis more fully. Many feminists have found their linking of self-negation with sin insightful.

Although Saiving's essay forms an early feminist exploration in theological anthropology, there is no one articulation of a feminist theological anthropology. Some consensus among Christian feminists appears, however, in terms of both what to oppose and what to promote. On the critical side, they recognize the need to oppose hierarchies that assign greater value to some groups of persons than to others, attesting that the Christian *faith both assesses whatever dehumanizes other persons as sinful and calls Christians to contend against sin. On the constructive side, Christian feminists call for a new anthropology that portrays different ways of being human and it accents the significance of *relationships that are marked by mutuality and *equality.

Much remains to be explored in the constellation of issues that form the contours of theological anthropology, especially through reconsidering the traits and tasks of the human species as well as the significance of gender. The need to pay attention to both the distinctiveness of and the divergences within women's experiences forms a particular concern. Without the former, feminist theological anthropologies will have difficulty addressing the well-being of women, especially in the context of women's sufferings. Yet gender is but one aspect of identity; attention must be given to all the particularities of women's experience so that differences among and between women are recognized and valued.

Carr/Schüssler Fiorenza [1991]; Miles [1989]; Moltmann-Wendel [1986]; Plaskow [1980]; Russell [1982]; Saiving, in Christ/ Plaskow [1979]; Trible [1978]; Williams [1993a]

KRISTEN E. KVAM

Anti-Judaism/Anti-Semitism Anti-Judaism can be defined as the tendentious denigration of Judaism for the purpose of elevating, through contrast, another religion or an ethnic group. Because of the linkage of nascent Christianity to the Hebrew Bible and Judaism, explanations for the split between the two religions became a necessary component of Christian theology. Those explanations inevitably took the form of assertions of Christian ethical or theological superiority and even charges of divine rejection of the Jews. Negative *stereotypes of Judaism have flourished within Christian writings for two thousand years, fueling and legitimating anti-Semitism, a system of *oppression of Jews, and encouraging the persecution of Jews.

Christian feminism reflects anti-Jewish traditions, although recent efforts to establish a Christian theological *tradition without anti-Judaism have included some feminist participation. Christian feminists have stigmatized Judaism in three ways.

1. *Destruction of preexistent *goddess worship.* Most of the negative depictions of Judaism in Christian feminist writings are inaccurate distortions that draw on age-old stereotypes rather than reliable scholarship. For example, claims that a goddess-worshiping, matriarchal *culture dominated in the ancient Near East prior to the rise of biblical *monotheism are historically unfounded but predominate nonetheless in feminist writings. Judaism is scapegoated in this scenario for the origins of *patriarchy, and patriarchy is defined in historical terms, in opposition to those who claim it is biologically rooted and therefore ineradicable. Concomitant with patriarchy, according to these feminists, came the rise of war and *violence, which are also blamed on the alleged intolerance of the monotheistic deity. Hana Wolff (1981) cites passages in the Hebrew Bible that describe divine *anger to "prove" that the "Old Testament God of wrath" is an image of divinity that leads to "war horrors, concentration camps, and *Holocaust" (162f.). Christians, she advises, should return the Old Testament to Judaism.

Traditional Christian claims that the Jews killed Jesus render plausible arguments that the ancient Israelites killed the goddess. Just as Christian theologians through the centuries have blamed the Jews for the death of Jesus, some feminist theologians blame Jews for the death of the goddess and the introduction of patriarchy. To counter these claims, recent feminist studies have demonstrated that biblical women did have active religious lives (C. Meyers 1988) and that biblical literature itself contains both patriarchal and antipatriarchal strategies (Pardes). Moreover, both textual and archaeological evidence demonstrates that goddess worship continued throughout antiquity and well into the Middle Ages, even alongside the male monotheism of biblical religion (Frymer-Kensky 1992; Freedman 1987).

2. *Judaism as a patriarchal and misogynist culture.* Another popular claim is that Jesus was a feminist who liberated women from Judaism's *misogyny (Swidler; Moltmann-Wendel 1978). His *liberation of women, the argument continues, was thwarted within Christianity by the patriarchal convictions of his earliest

followers, who were Jews imbued with Judaism's *sexism. Again, Jews and Judaism are blamed for the sexism of Western civilization.

Such arguments contrast Jesus' teachings in the Gospels with statements from Jewish texts, particularly the Talmud, that originated in a much later period. The more appropriate evidence from first-century Palestine indicates that women served as synagogue leaders and maintained positions of social and financial importance, suggesting that Jesus' behavior was no different from that of other Jews in his day (Nathanson, in Schüssler Fiorenza, ed., 1993; Kraemer). The very fact that Jesus was a Jew implies that all of his teachings, including those concerning women, should be taken as expressions of Judaism and as a source for Jewish women's history as much as a theological mandate for Christian women.

3. *Blaming Judaism for war and violence.* Finally, the most problematic example of feminist anti-Judaism is blaming Judaism for militarism, violence, and genocide. Carol Christ has suggested that the writings of the prophets constitute a "pervasive prophetic intolerance toward other religions that has produced, among other horrors, a climate in which witches could be put to death in Europe, in which the genocide of Native Americans could be attempted by Europeans, and in which genocide of Jews could be attempted by the Nazis" (78). Christ, who rejects Christianity as a source for women's spirituality, finds Judaism inferior to paganism in its treatment of women. The German Protestant feminist theologian Christa Mulack has argued similarly, drawing an analogy between Judaism, which she defines as a religion of obedience to the commandments of God, and Nazism, which she defines as a system of obedience to the commands of Hitler (155–56; cf. M. Brumlik, *Der Anti-Alt* (Frankfurt am Main: Eichborn, 1991). Both are moralities of obedience to orders, in contrast to Christian and feminist *ethics of *compassion and *responsibility.

Analogies between Judaism and Nazism are repugnant efforts at projection, blaming the victims for their own murder. Because Christians controlled Western European political history for the past two thousand years, it is Christianity's influence that should be measured as a force for provoking or hindering acts of violence carried out at the behest of the rulers and general populace.

Anti-Judaism is not unique to Christian feminists; it is part of the heritage of Christian theology. Although feminists have paid attention to issues of *racism and *classism, significantly less attention has been given to anti-Semitism, often with the claim that Christian theological anti-Judaism is not responsible for anti-Semitism. Given the history of persecution and murder of Jews by Christians, theological traditions that stigmatize Judaism should be taken seriously.

Some feminists have made a concerted effort to criticize and eradicate anti-Judaism along with sexism (Plaskow; Siegele-Wenschewitz, ed., 1988; von Kellenbach). That effort involves accepting Christian responsibility for Western Christian civilization's sexism, acknowledging that sexism is a problem for both Christianity and Judaism, and avoiding claims of superiority or patterns of projection and blame. Recognizing Jesus' Jewishness means attributing his positive teachings about women to Judaism and viewing the sexism that is also present within his message as a heritage that feminist theologians of all *faith traditions must confront and eliminate.

Christ [1987]; Kraemer [1992]; Mulack [1987]; Pardes [1992]; Plaskow, *JSFR* [1991]; Swidler, *Catholic World* [1971]; von Kellenbach [1994]

SUSANNAH HESCHEL

Apocrypha *Apocrypha* (from Gk, "hidden books") describes Jewish noncanonical religious literature included in various Christian Old Testaments. The term refers to books or parts of books not found in the Hebrew but included in the Greek Bible (Septuagint, or LXX). In the sixteenth century these books were denied *canonical status by the Protestant Reformation but accepted by the Roman church (Council of Trent, 1546).

Apocryphal and *deuterocanonical* are variously defined, canon-related terms. Catholic Old Testaments include the twenty-four scrolls of the Hebrew Bible (= the thirty-nine books of the Protestant Bible), seven additional deuterocanonical books from the LXX (Tobit; Judith; Wisdom of Solomon; Sirach; Baruch, with the Letter of Jeremiah; 1 and 2 Maccabees), plus additions to Esther (Add. A–F) and to Daniel (Prayer of Azariah and the Song of the Three Jews, Susanna, Bel and the Dragon). The Greek Orthodox Bible adds 1 Esdras, Prayer of Manasseh, Psalm 151, and 3 Maccabees (with 4 Maccabees as an appendix). The Slavonic Bible includes 3 Esdras (= 2 Esdras in NRSV).

The eighteen books in the NRSV apocrypha (all the books listed above) include three titled by the names of faithful women: Judith, Esther (Additions), Susanna. In all, sixteen women are mentioned in the books by name: Agia, 1 Esd. 5:38; Anna, Tob. 1:9ff.; Antiochis, 2 Macc. 4:30; Apame, 1 Esd. 4:29–31; Arsinoë, 3 Macc. 1:1; Cleopatra, Add. Esth. 11:1, 1 Macc. 10:54–58, 11:9–12; Deborah, Tob. 1:8; Edna, Tob. 7:2–8ff.; Esther, esp. Add. Esth. C, 14:1–19; Eve, Tob. 8:6; Hagar, Bar. 3:23; Judith, Jdt. 8—16; Sarah, Tob. 3:7ff.; Susanna, Sus 2ff.; Vashti, Add. Esth. 1:9–10; and Zosara, Add. Esth. 5:10–14. Women figure as unnamed characters (variously as *servants, community members, brides, *widows, wives, *mothers, daughters, nurses, *prostitutes, worshipers) in all but three books of the Apocrypha (Prayer of Azariah and the Song of the Three Jews, Prayer of Manasseh, and Psalm 151).

Most notable of the unnamed women is the courageous mother martyred with her seven sons (see esp. 2 Macc. 7:1–42 and 4 Macc. 14:11–18:24). Striking female representations include wisdom personified as a woman (Wisd. Sol. 6:12–21ff.; Sir. 4:11; 6:18; 14:20; 15:24; 51:13ff.; Bar. 3:9–4:4); God personified as a mother (2 Esd. 1:28; 2:2), nurse (2 Esd. 1:28), and hen (2 Esd. 1:30); and female personifications of the earth (2 Esd. 7:54, 62), Zion (2 Esd. 9:38–10:54), Babylon and Asia (2 Esd. 15:46–63), *righteousness and iniquity (2 Esd. 16:49–52).

Meurer [1991]; Meyers/Craven/Kraemer [forthcoming]; Nickelsburg [1981]

TONI CRAVEN

Apostles The term *apostle* derives from the Greek word *apostolos,* which originally meant "sent": an apostle is someone "sent" by another. The word is not used in secular Greek to refer to one commissioned and sent by a deity, so it may have first been used with this meaning by members of the earliest Christian communities. In the church today the term is especially associated with the Twelve (i.e., the twelve disciples of Jesus who were specially commissioned by Jesus and sent forth to do mission) and with Paul, "apostle to the Gentiles" (Rom. 11:13). In early Christian usage the term *apostolos* referred to ones specially commissioned and sent forth and thus was never used as widely as, for example, *disciple* (Gk *mathētēs,* literally "learner" or "follower"). *Apostolos* may have had a broader range of referents than modern readers generally suppose. Indeed, some women may have served as apostles in the earliest days of the church. The oversight or suppression of historical evidence for female apostles is symptomatic of the more general tendency of historians down through the ages to write women out of the annals of the church (Schüssler Fiorenza, 160–204) and is one of many factors that have helped to sustain prohibitions against women's leadership in the church.

The earliest evidence for Christian usage of the term comes from the letters of Paul. In Phil. 2:25 and 2 Cor. 8:23, Paul refers to apostles (i.e., envoys or delegates) sent out by particular churches. Elsewhere Paul employs the term *apostolos* to refer to members of a select group of believers who were sent by God to preach and to do the work of the *gospel, empowered to perform special signs, and destined to suffer in an especially acute way (1 Cor. 4:9; 12:28–29; 2 Cor. 12:12). Paul frequently called himself an apostle (Rom. 1:1; 11:13; 1 Cor. 1:1; etc.). Some, however, may have disputed Paul's claim to the title (1 Cor. 9:2; 15:9); moreover, Paul contested others' claim to the designation, calling them (sarcastically) "super-apostles" (2 Cor. 11:5; 12:11) and even "false apostles" (2 Cor. 11:13). Thus one can discern that the definition of the role was still variable in the Pauline era.

In Rom. 16:7, Paul refers to Andronicus and Junia(s) as "prominent among the apostles." Traditionally, the latter figure has been assumed to be a male, whose name, Junias, may have been short for Junianus; but the shortened name is otherwise unattested in ancient sources. Junia, in contrast, was a common Roman name for females; virtually all the church fathers identified the partner of Andronicus as a female (Lampe). Recently scholars have argued that Andronicus and Junia were a husband-and-wife team, like Prisca and Aquila (who are never called apostles in the NT, however; see Rom. 16:3–5; Acts 18:1–3, 18–19, 26; cf. 1 Cor. 9:5). Paul refers to other women leaders in the church, but again, without the title *apostle*. Besides Prisca, these include especially Phoebe, a deacon and benefactor of Paul and others (Rom. 16:1–2), and Euodia and Syntyche, ones who "struggled beside" Paul in the work of the gospel (Phil. 4:2–3). Moreover, second-century legends tell of a woman missionary, Thecla, who, after enduring numerous trials, was commissioned to teach the word of God (Schüssler Fiorenza, 173–74).

Assuming that Matthew and Luke both used Mark as a source, one detects toward the end of the first century an increasing restriction of the term *apostolos* to the twelve disciples of Jesus. Luke in particular introduces the term *apostolos* to characterize the Twelve where it was not present in his source (Luke 17:5; 22: 14; 24:10; cf. 11:49). Luke uses the term with reference to Paul only in Acts 14:4, 14 (where his usage may be dependent on an earlier source). Luke's recounting of the *election of Matthias to replace Judas Iscariot is instructive: the replacement must be "one of the men [*andres*] who have accompanied us" (Acts 1:21–22). One wonders if any of the women mentioned in Luke 8:2–3 would have qualified apart from gender.

Betz, *ABD* [1992]; Brooten, in Swidler/Swidler [1985]; Furnish [1985]; Lampe, *ABD* [1992]; Schüssler Fiorenza [1984/1995]

SUSAN R. GARRETT

Appropriation / Reciprocity Generally speaking, the concept of appropriation has to do with the act of preempting, usurping, confiscating—possessing the power to seize and control a people's resources, without authority or with questionable authority. Within the terms of this critique, the social processes of appropriation mean the taking over of someone else's *culture and/or educational capital or discourse, more or less with a desire beforehand to convert the thing taken over to one's own use.

The particularity of women's lives is the essence of who they are and the substance of their communities. This is "their stuff," and women of differing contexts who approach material as if it can be taken with carte blanche and interpreted through the lens of a different experience, with no attempt to understand the culture it comes from and the lives it represents, not only do *violence to that culture but wreak havoc on measured attempts at scholarship that seek to be truly liberatory as well as ethical.

Is it self-evident that persons or groups are guilty of appropriation only when they have the power to co-opt, seize, and control? Is it reasonable to assume that any process of appropriation is also a process of confiscation? In essence, can there be appropriation without intellectual *domination, particularly in relation to the sociotheological and ethical work of womanists and other women of color who are intellectuals, academicians, and literary authors or scholars? Can reciprocity "make right" appropriation without a concomitant expression of change or transformation in intentional *relationships between women of the dominant culture and womanists and other women of color? The definition and developmental understanding of the linking concept of reciprocity helps to determine the response.

The assumption has been that in a reciprocal process one recognizes the validity of sources and origins in the development of own's own discourse. Generally speaking, reciprocity means giving back in kind and quality, mutually exchanging and being changed by another's data and resources, and paying back what has been received from cooperative work, mutual dependence, action, and influence. Moreover, to engage reciprocally requires a willingness to develop and deepen levels of personal *conversion and vulnerability to the other's perspective as well as social location. Exploring and acknowledging differences are principal methods to be utilized in developing a means of mutual appropriation and reciprocity that has any ethical integrity.

Womanist consciousness does not obscure or deny the existence of *race, sex, and class oppression, but rather, through full, sharp awareness of tridimensional oppression, it presents the liberating possibilities that also exist. Repeatedly in the *dialogue and debate engaged in by feminists and womanists, the ethical issues entailed by expressions of appropriation and reciprocity become central, as in the (ab)use made of womanist materials by those seeking from them support and legitimation for already defined projects. Appropriation and reciprocity observed between feminists and womanists require much more careful engagement than simply changing the epigraphs at the beginnings of essays and the sources listed in bibliographies and cited in footnotes; they usually result in a changed theoretical stance or articulation.

The juxtaposition of the terms *appropriation* and *reciprocity* dictates, of necessity, the claims of accountability. Whether the mutual process begins with paradigms created by mentors of European and Euro-American ancestry or with theoretical constructs emerging from the oral traditions in the African diaspora or with a dialectical, syncretistic interplay between the two, to decline the ethical labor of wrestling with the issues is to cede a future scholarship to conventional, either-or dichotomies. It is to play the game of androcentric, heteropatriarchal academese without understanding it.

Cannon, *Annual of the Society of Christian Ethics* [1993]; Eugene, *JFSR* [1992]; Lugones, in Card [1991]; Townes, *Annual of the Society of Christian Ethics* [1993b]

TOINETTE M. EUGENE

Archaeology The term *archaeology* is derived from the Greek words *archaios* (ancient) and *logos* (knowledge); strictly speaking, it means the study of the past in the broadest sense. The word is popularly used, however, to indicate a particular focus in the study of the past, that is, on the material remains of ancient societies. Archaeology deals with the physical objects of daily life. It examines the tools and vessels that people used, the buildings in which they lived and worked, the objects they used to wage war or to worship gods, the garments they wore, the ways in which they obtained food and sustained life, and the modes in which they buried and remembered their dead. To this list must also be added the written or epigraphic remains of past societies, which have been invaluable—especially for those examining the biblical world and that of early Christianity and Judaism—for understanding human cultures and their religious traditions.

The epigraphic remains have historically been weighted more heavily than the nonepigraphic ones in studying the biblical origins of Judaism and Christianity. Because ancient documents, like the Bible itself, are largely the product of the literary and chronistic activity of elite male scribes, priests, and courtiers, the focus on texts marginalizes women or renders them invisible. The nonepigraphic remnants of antiquity, in contrast, are uniquely situated to redress the bias of texts. The gender-inclusive archaeological remains of daily life allow us to look at women's worlds in a way that written sources never can.

The potential for archaeology to give visibility to the women in ancient societies cannot be realized, however, until the traditional, elitist bias of archaeology itself is overcome. By examining public, monumental, and therefore male-dominated structures and artifacts (e.g., temples, palaces, fortifications, weapons), archaeology, like textual study, has directed most of its energies to the products of male activity. Only by studying the domestic contexts in which most people lived rather than the monumental productions of the few can the gender imbalance in archaeology be redressed. Recent developments in Syro-Palestinian archaeology are moving in just that direction and provide hope that the material context and conditions of the lives of women will become increasingly accessible to those interested in the roles of women in ancient society. Early results of this shift in archaeological focus indicate that women were more powerful shapers and transmitters of *culture, including *religion, than is apparent from the androcentric textual remains alone.

Conkey/Spector, in Schiffer [1984]; Hanes/Kelly, in Embree [1972]; Meyers [1988; 1992]; Seifert [1991]

CAROL MEYERS

Asceticism The term *asceticism* has its origins in the Greek idea of "exercise" or "training." This understanding gradually expanded to include not only physical training but mental, spiritual, and ethical development as well. Through systematic, rigorous disciplines one could achieve excellence in *virtue and holiness.

Some form of spiritual asceticism, a voluntary, systematic program of self-discipline and self-denial, can be found in almost all religions. Practices include fasting, sexual abstinence, inflicting bodily pain, and solitude. Motivations for engaging in such practices might be purification, *atonement for *sin, avoidance of *evil, or gaining access to spiritual realms through visions or extrasensory experiences.

The understanding of asceticism as the harsh denial of all sensual pleasure for the sake of higher spiritual states, motivated by anti-matter, anti-body dispositions, is undergoing reevaluation and transformation. Feminist scholars especially are critical of past dualistic, misogynist understandings of asceticism that connected matter/woman/*body with sin and death and recommended the control and/or suppression of the former in the interests of "higher" spiritual values. The rediscovery, rehabilitation, and integration of the body and spirit from theological, linguistic, spiritual, psychological, and physiological perspectives have been key to this reevaluation.

While some feminist theologians reject asceticism outright because of its dualistic foundations, others have attempted to transform its meaning. Asceticism may be seen as a way to deconstruct harmful, socially conditioned *stereotypes of self as woman or man in the interest of creating new, life-giving self-definition, marked by love, *equality, and mutuality. Ascetic practices can also serve to dismantle compulsive, addictive behaviors in favor of *liberation and a fullness of life (both sensual and intellectual) that has been buried beneath dulling, routinized patterns of living.

Asceticism can also be understood in relational, sociopolitical terms. Self-denial can result in enhanced sensitivity, *compassion, and *solidarity with the oppressed, leading to action on their behalf. In a more general vein, asceticism can be seen as a way to respond creatively to the inevitable *suffering and stripping that are part of daily life. Finally, asceticism can lead one to embrace living simply and acting energetically on behalf of our endangered ecosystem.

Bynum [1987]; Cooey [1994]; McFague [1993]; Miles [1988]

ELIZABETH A. DREYER

Atonement In Christian *tradition, atonement refers to the restoration of relationship between God and humanity through the life and death of Jesus *Christ. The term literally means reconciliation or "at-one-ment." God's action in the death and *resurrection of Jesus Christ is understood to be the source of salvation because it overcomes the power of *sin and *evil in the world and in our lives.

In both feminist and womanist theological circles, the viability of Christian theories of atonement that stress the *sacrifice of Jesus has been questioned. Feminist scholars JoAnne Brown and Rebecca Parker raise the question of divine child abuse in relation to Christian notions that God, the father, intended the death of his innocent son, Jesus, on the *cross in order to redeem humankind from sin. In an article titled "God So Loved the World" in *Christianity, Patriarchy, and Abuse,* Brown and Parker criticize Christian theories of atonement describing God the Father's love as exemplified in the execution of his innocent Son. They suggest that this understanding of God's love can support child abuse in society and can cause children to interpret parental abuse as love.

Womanist theologian Delores S. Williams provides a critique of atonement theory from the perspective of African-American women's *oppression in the context of social-role surrogacy. In *Sisters in the Wilderness,* she defines social-role surrogacy as black women performing tasks in social roles the society has assigned to someone else. Black women thus stand in place of someone else and are meeting other people's needs and goals. Williams sees Jesus as a surrogate standing in the place of sinful humankind when he died on the cross and as put to the service of someone else's goal (e.g., God the Father's). Williams resolves the issue theologically by claiming that Jesus did not come *to die* for humankind; Jesus came *to live* for humankind. Thus it is Jesus' life and his ministerial vision that redeem humans.

This womanist critique of atonement theory came under public attack in 1993 because of Williams's remarks about atonement at a feminist conference in Minneapolis, Minnesota. The Re-Imagining Conference was a celebration of the Ecumenical Decade of the Churches in Solidarity with Women of the World Council of Churches. The group of about two thousand included women from many parts of the world. Conservative elements in some of the mainline denominations in the United States publicized Williams's remarks, as well as other features in the conference that conservatives thought were too radical. The print and TV news media in the United States picked up the conservative critique and thus began a public debate that continues today. The discussion of the meaning of the atonement and of Christ's sacrifice continues as a key point for theological reconstruction.

Brown/Bohn [1989]; Grey [1989]; Williams [1993a]

DELORES S. WILLIAMS

Authority Authority is a crucial theological problem in contemporary society. In the midst of radical social change, traditional sources of authority come into question and new understandings of authority emerge. For feminist theologians this issue is particularly pressing as they confront the authority of patriarchal religious and cultural traditions. Women who question authority are often considered "uppity" by those who live according to the dominant male paradigms of religion.

Authority can be understood as legitimated *power. It is a form of power, or the ability to accomplish desired ends. Authority in a religious community usually includes social power to affect the behavior of another group or individual. Human beings look for guidance and a sense of security and turn to authorities in their lives to fill those needs. Those in authority accomplish their ends by evoking the assent of the respondents. Their power is derived from political, economic, intellectual, and social structures that lead persons to consider that an interpreter of a text or *doctrine, a person, a government, etc., has a legitimate reason to expect acceptance and obedience from the respondents. The problem is that authority, like other forms of power, can be corrupted and used in illegitimate ways to manipulate or even destroy the respondents.

As women find that their authority is questioned when they move out of traditionally stereotyped female roles, they become suspicious of the patriarchal paradigms of authority and seek to create their own paradigm or interpretive framework for the meaning of authority. The prevailing paradigm of authority in male-dominated religions is one of *authority as *domination*. In this framework, all questions of authority are settled with reference to what is considered to be the highest authority. The feminist *liberation paradigm of *authority in *community* seeks to raise questions of legitimacy based on the needs of those who are at the bottom of the patriarchal pyramid of oppressions.

Authority as domination is a constellation of beliefs, values, and methods which reinforce an understanding that reality itself is structured in the form of a *hierarchy or pyramid. Things are assigned a divine order, with God at the top, men next, and so on, down through dogs, plants, and so-called impersonal nature. This paradigm reinforces ideas of authority *over* community and refuses to admit the ideas and the persons who do not fit into the established Western, white, male hierarchies of thought or social structures.

In this framework, Christian theological truth is sought through a hierarchy of biblical and church traditions. The difficulty for women and for *third world groups is that their perspectives often do not fit in the pyramid structure of such a system of interpretation. The price of inclusion in the theological enterprise is loss of their own perspective and *culture in order to do "good theology," as defined by "those at the top." The price of resistance is further *marginalization.

One emerging feminist paradigm that tries to make sense of biblical, theological, and ecclesial truth claims is that of authority in community. In this view, reality is interpreted in the form of circles of *interdependence. Ordering is explored through inclusion of diversity in a rainbow spectrum that requires not that persons submit to the "top" but that they participate in the common task of creating an interdependent community of humanity and nature.

Authority as *partnership is not unrealistic; indeed, it provides an interpretative framework for a much more realistic alternative in a world bent on self-destruction so that some nation or group can claim superiority. Authority can be shared in new ways when the question is no longer "Is it legitimate from the perspective of those on top?" For feminists the question is "Is it legitimate from the perspective of those on the bottom as they struggle for *justice?" To those who say that this is a denial of biblical and church authority, feminists point out that it is at least consistent with Jesus' own welcome to all outsiders (Luke 4:16–30).

Bird, *NIB* [1994]; Janeway [1981]; Russell [1987]; Sennett [1981]; Wink [1984]

LETTY M. RUSSELL

Authority of Scripture Feminist theologies have criticized and redefined scriptural *authority. Criticism is directed against scripture's consistent *androcentrism and its support of *patriarchy, or even against scripture as a whole when it is seen as inherently patriarchal and antiwoman. Feminist redefinition of the authority of scripture understands authority not as a norm determined from without, to which believers must submit, but as emerging from a general rereading as part of the *liberation process. Scriptural authority thus arises "from below," from the community (*ekklēsia*) that works for the liberation of women, men, children, and nature from patriarchal *domination. Feminist interpretation discovers "foremothers" in or behind the biblical texts. There is a lively discussion of these questions within feminism, because the patriarchal character of scripture prevents women from having an independent religious identity. The process of detecting the patriarchal infection of texts is still in full flood. On the other hand, feminist rereading of biblical texts is a vital source of power within parts of the women's movement.

The traditional understanding of scripture in white, Western, male-oriented thinking, which often tries to overturn the feminist process, is typified by two ways of dealing with scriptural authority: (1) fundamentalist reading takes all of scripture to be the word of God and demands its acceptance by believers and recognition of scripture as an indisputable norm; (2) liberal reading distinguishes, for example, between a timeless core and a time-conditioned husk or seeks a *canon within the canon and criticizes certain aspects (e.g., Jesus is used to critique Paul). Both fundamentalist and liberal views of scriptural authority are linked with existing social institutions (church, state, university).

Feminist theologies draw a clear distinction between scripture itself and the history of its interpretation and effects. In particular, the history of Christian interpretation and application is frequently more antiwoman and subject to the interest of patriarchal dominance than scripture itself.

Classifications that collate initiatives in feminist theology according to type may be helpful. Thus Carolyn Osiek distinguishes five responses of feminist women when they recognize that the Bible is being used to sustain *oppression: "rejectionist, loyalist, revisionist, sublimationist, and liberationist" (97). Another approach recently proposed is the pinpointing of feminist theological initiatives within their social context. There is growing recognition that there cannot be *one* correct feminist rereading and feminist-historical exegesis. This *contextualization of rereading and discussion of scriptural authority does not mean that feminist theologies advocate arbitrariness. It is clear that scripture itself is a source of women's visions. The clarity of the feminist vision of a human world committed to right *relationships and love for all living things requires that differences be taken seriously but also that feminist *praxis be clear and unmistakable everywhere. Taking *differences seriously means mutual attention to women's experiences that are determinative for feminist scriptural interpretation. The experience of institutional oppression of women through scripture, which, for example, was crucial for *The Woman's Bible* (1895), is not fundamentally contradictory to women's spiritual experiences with the Bible as a light for women's path and a source of strength for women.

Recognition of different historical and social contexts and their significance for feminist scriptural interpretation has produced a *process of mutual enrichment*. The self-confidence with which Jewish feminists and Christian womanists assert their religious identity as women *and* as Jewish or Christian challenges white Christian women who are uncertain whether they can continue to regard themselves as Christian in light of the patriarchal character of scripture. Confessional differences within Christianity also bring fruitful mutual challenges. The ecclesiological orientation of Catholic women questions Protestant individualism. Protestant struggles with the biblical text as the word of God challenge the relativizing of those texts by the feminist critique of patriarchy. Feminist liberation theologians from the two-thirds world and the marginalized third of Western industrial societies challenge Western-oriented Christian women through their option for poor women and their experiences of *transcendence in interpreting scripture within the process of struggle for *survival and liberation.

Osiek, in Collins [1985]; Russell [1985a]; Schüssler Fiorenza, ed. [1993; 1994]; Stanton [1895]

LUISE SCHOTTROFF

Autonomy The word *autonomy* comes from two Greek words, *autos* (oneself) and *nomos* (law), and literally means "being one's own law." It is contrasted with *heteronomy* (other law), "being subject to the law of another." Jewish and Christian thought has tried to hold these two apparently incompatible ideas together by arguing that while humankind is subject to the law of God, it is nevertheless possible freely to choose that law for oneself and thus be autonomous after all. However, the extent to which autonomy is possible has been a matter of ongoing dispute, especially within the Christian *tradition. An influential strand running from Augustine to Calvin and beyond emphasizes the limitation of human *freedom (*free will) because of sinfulness and stresses divine *grace and even *predestination in human choices.

Within secular philosophical thought since the Enlightenment, autonomy has been seen as necessary for moral choices, in the sense that a person cannot be seen as worthy of moral praise or blame for her actions unless she has freely chosen them: she has no moral *responsibility for what she cannot help. This means that since morality is central to what it is to be human, so also is autonomy. Immanuel Kant held that rationality and autonomy constitute human personhood, and few moral philosophers have disagreed. This has put them at odds with reductionist and determinist science but in line with feminist philosophers who challenge such reductionism.

Feminists have pointed out, however, that the autonomy cherished in both the secular and the religious tradition is too often left abstract. In practice, one person's freedom often depends on another's servitude. For many centuries, and in all but a privileged few contexts today, women have been denied the *education, material conditions, and political right to exercise autonomy and have instead constituted the labor force that enables (some) men to have freedom. Moreover, the chains that bind women can be internal, ideological bonds, fostered by church and society that valorize male aggression and female submission. Feminist efforts for *justice, therefore, are efforts to realize concrete, not abstract, autonomy and *agency for women as well as men, in a mutuality in which the autonomy of one is not built on the servitude of the other.

Gilligan [1982]; Kittay/Meyers [1987]; Welch [1990]

GRACE M. JANTZEN

Baptism Derived from a Greek verb meaning "dip" or "immerse," baptism is one of two *sacraments recognized by most branches of the Christian church. The ritual, involving either immersion or the pouring or sprinkling of water on a person, originated in the *ministry of John the baptizer (Mark 1:4–6), which included a prophetic call to repent, or "turn" from one's former life, and to receive forgiveness of sins and welcome God's reign. Jesus himself was said to undergo this baptism (Matt. 3:13–17 // Mark 1:9–11 // Luke 3:21–22) in an event linked to the descent of the Holy Spirit and God's affirmation of Jesus as God's beloved child. The same ritual ("in the name of" the Trinity; Matt. 28:19) became an entry ritual marking a person's commitment to the Christian community and, often, their reception of the Holy Spirit, as can be seen from the frequent references to baptism in Acts.

In the first century, baptism was related theologically to Israel's crossing of the Sea of Reeds (1 Cor. 10:1–4), to Noah's escape from God's condemnation (1 Peter 3:21), and to new birth (John 3:4–5)—a meaning sustained in the connection of this ritual with the bestowing of a name. The interpretation that has had the greatest influence on Christian theology is that in baptism the Christian is symbolically united with Christ in his death and *resurrection (Rom. 6:1–4).

As a one-time ritual of initiation, baptism differs from other water-related rituals of ablution or purification that are repeated over time. Unlike rituals involving the genitalia (such as circumcision) or events related to procreation (such as the onset of menstruation), baptism is appropriate for both females and males. Church traditions differ on whether infants should be baptized, as a sacrament of their inclusion in God's saving act in Jesus Christ (an act later "confirmed" by the child), or whether only adult "believer's" baptism is valid. Recent concern about gender-inclusive language for God has sparked debates about the acceptability of baptisms performed without the words "Father, Son, and Holy Spirit."

Duck [1991]; LaCugna [1993]; Procter-Smith [1990]; Procter-Smith/Walton [1993]; Ramshaw/Walton [1995]

SHARON H. RINGE

Bat Mitzvah *Bat mitzvah,* literally "daughter of the commandment," is a ceremony that marks a twelve- or thirteen-year-old Jewish girl's entrance into young adulthood. The first bat mitzvah ceremony in North America took place in 1922 and was celebrated by Judith Kaplan, daughter of Rabbi Mordecai Kaplan, founder of the Reconstructionist movement. The ritual was generally patterned after the *bar mitzvah* ceremony (meaning "son of the commandment"). The Talmud states that boys become obligated to live according to Jewish law at age thirteen and girls at age twelve; therefore bar mitzvah and bat mitzvah mark the beginning of a child's full participation in the Jewish community.

Until Judith Kaplan's bat mitzvah, only a boy's Jewish coming of age was publicly celebrated. Today the bat mitzvah ceremony in Reform and Reconstructionist congregations directly parallels the bar mitzvah. Girls lead the service, read from the Torah and haftarah (a selection from one of the prophetic books), and usually give a *dvar Torah,* a short sermon on their Torah portion in which they explore what the text means to them. In some communities the bat mitzvah service may include poetry, music, and artwork written, created, performed, or selected by the child.

The bat mitzvah ceremony varies among Conservative congregations, depending on how egalitarian a particular synagogue is. In Orthodox communities the ceremony is becoming more popular. However, since the Orthodox do not generally allow women to lead public worship, an Orthodox bat mitzvah usually takes the form of a luncheon or dinner during which the child presents a *dvar Torah.*

Many Reform, Reconstructionist, and Conservative synagogues are now offering special courses for women who, as children, were denied a Jewish *education and who yearn for the opportunity to prepare for bat mitzvah. These ceremonies are often particularly moving because they offer women who have been marginalized the opportunity finally to engage and confront their *tradition.

Encyclopaedia Judaica [1971], 4:243–47; Goldin [1995]; Salkin [1991]

DONNA BERMAN

Battering

Definition and Analysis. Battering is the threat or use of physical force to coerce and control an adult intimate partner; it occurs in intimate *relationships regardless of sexual orientation or marital status. Battering is sometimes referred to as domestic *violence, spouse abuse, or wife abuse. In 95 percent of the cases in the United States, the abuser is a man, the victim, a woman (Adams, 7). According to the U.S. Bureau of Justice National Crime survey, in the United States a woman is beaten in her home every fifteen seconds (Adams, 12). Abusive men are the major source of injury to adult women in the United States. According to United States Department of Justice's Bureau of Justice Statistics, "Women are six times more likely than men to be the victim of a violent crime committed by an intimate" (Adams, 12).

Battering is recognized as a method by which an intimate partner establishes coercive control over his partner. "Two key aspects of violence are threat and control. That is, the effects of battering are seen not only in the actual physical assaults, but in how fear of being hurt is used to manipulate and control woman via threats" (Carlin, in Adams, 12). In other words, when a man hits a woman, he has not lost control of himself; he achieves and maintains control of his partner. It is not so much what is done but what is accomplished. Battering is thus defined as "a *pattern* of behavior, not isolated individual events. One form of battering builds on another and sets the stage for the next battering episode" (Ganley, in Adams, 12).

Traditionally, battering was seen as a private problem, and little ethical, theological, or *social analysis was offered until the feminist movement of the 1970s invited the *naming of women's experiences. Until this time, explanations for wife beating identified the problem very individualistically: it was said to occur because the man had lost control or was provoked, that he could not control his *anger, was under extreme stress, or was under the influence of alcohol or drugs. Society at large, like the batterer, denied, minimized, or blamed others (especially his partner) for the batterer's behavior. Often the response of representatives of religious institutions has been to encourage the victim to pray more and forgive the abuser. Rather than focusing on both the physical and the spiritual trauma that battering prompted, this theological response dematerializes the problem.

For assessment purposes, five forms of battering (first developed by Anne Ganley in 1981) have been identified: physical battering, sexual battering, psychological battering, destruction of property, harm to animals (Ganley, 8; Adams, 1995). The strength of these categories is the recognition of the interrelatedness of different kinds of behavior and the identification as battering behavior of phenomena that are not ordinarily perceived as battering. Understanding battering behaviorally (that is, understanding that battering behavior is deliberately chosen by the abuser) transforms the traditional understanding of battering as a private problem to a recognition that it is a community problem. As a community problem, it requires that aversive consequences for the abuser be established and enforced by the community, especially, but not exclusively, by the criminal *justice system. This is only now beginning to be implemented in some communities in the United States.

Theological Issues. Complex theological issues are raised by woman-battering. My focus is on those identified within the battered women's movement in the United States but also discussed in other countries that share Western religious traditions. Some of the concerns are specific to Christianity, others are not. Central to all of them is the premise that ensuring women's safety is the primary practical and theological issue.

Battering is a problem of *evil, of consciously willed violence on the part of the abuser. The community's failure to respond is often consciously willed as well. Victims' experience of violence often raises for them the question of theodicy; in the absence of a community interpretation that focuses on the abuser's choice to be abusive, the answer a victim often provides to the issue of the existence of evil in God's world focuses on her or on God. Either God has abandoned her or God is (rightly) punishing her. The effort to understand the why of one's victimization is a healthy sign. The problem is that traditional theology has not offered a framework that keeps central the batterer's choice to batter.

The question of theodicy is but one of the many theological issues that often deflect the focus from the batterer's behavior. Other theological views that focus on the victim instead of on the batterer's behavior include the following:

1. Premature forgiveness is often urged on the victim, before the batterer's behavior has changed. One feminist theological response is to say that the decision to forgive must always be the victim's, that forgiveness is not always necessary, and that any discussion of forgiveness before she is safe, that is, before the battering behavior is stopped, disregards her safety and therefore is inappropriate.
2. Gender-based notions of proper religious behavior, in which women are to be selfless and self-abnegating, contribute to a woman's confusion about putting her safety first. She may feel that she is committing the *sin of *pride and forsaking her proper role if she prioritizes her own safety over her relationship with her partner. Feminist ethicist Sarah Bentley points out that the creation of safe space for battered women is "symbolic of a deeper reality: a woman's right to have *a separate identity* from that of her husband" (Bentley, 154). Without this recognition, a woman's refusal to be self-abnegating may generate deep *guilt.
3. The *suffering *servant model very likely keeps victims from establishing safety concerns as their first priority. It keeps them distracted from a focus on the abuser's behavior. Christian emphasis on *sacrifice as good matches the way in which girls are taught to consider others rather than themselves, to be self-sacrificing in a social situation. The religious meaning of sacrifice is thus layered on top of the social view of women as sacrificial. Hence, many women believe that they must mediate their abuser's relationship with God, and this role requires staying with the abuser. But the woman's first moral and religious *responsibility is her own safety and that of any children.
4. The traditional theological mind–body *dualism that disowns the *body while equating it with women, that posits women as the fallen, "inferior," bodily half of creation (Bussert, 15), produces the idea that women's bodily suffering is spiritually redemptive. Women's bodies are separated from the idea of worth or integrity. This can contribute to the minimization of a woman's safety needs. Insisting on a theology that emphasizes the sacredness and integrity of women's bodies is an important feminist contribution.
5. Confusion about breaking the *covenant of *marriage contributes to women's dilemma. Traditional theological formulations often condemned the battered wife for breaking up the relationship by leaving and seeking safety. Now, through feminist reformulations, it is understood that the batterer is the one who breaks the covenant by choosing to be violent. The focus is on his behavior, not on her attempt to protect herself from this behavior.
6. *Androcentric images of God that present God as a male protector rather than as a liberator who empowers can contribute to women believing that they should be passive in the face of violence and await God's intervention. In addition, the idea that women's subordination is theologi-

cally justified creates the idea of "just battery," that a man may properly chastise or punish his wife (Engel, 242–61).

A relationship exists between a community's response to violence and one's experience of God. If a community responds to a man's abuse of a woman by immediately saying, "This abuse must stop," and then puts into place the mechanism for ensuring that this happens (such as court-mandated counseling and reinstitution of the charges against the batterer if battering behavior occurs), a caring and responsive God has been made present. But when a community appears uncaring, failing to intercede after beating upon beating, the absence of response echoes on many levels, including the divine level. When a woman wonders where God is in her suffering, she has been forced to ask this question because her community deserted her. It is now understood that one cannot simply say, "God wants you to be safe," or, "Pray." It is necessary to ensure every battered woman's safety and to call every batterer to account for his use of violence.

Adams [1994b]; Adams, in Adams/Donovan [1995]; Bentley, in Adams/Fortune [1995]; Bussert [1986]; Engel, in Adams/Fortune [1995]; Fortune [1987]; Ganley [1985]

CAROL J. ADAMS

Biblical Criticism Biblical criticism refers to scholarly methods used to analyze and understand the Hebrew Scriptures and the New Testament. Such critical analysis of the biblical texts is related to but distinct from biblical hermeneutics, interpretive theories or models used to relate the ancient biblical texts to contemporary theological or ethical reflection.

Traditional Biblical Criticism. Modern biblical criticism has its roots in the interest in history and empiricism that flourished during the Enlightenment. At its inception, biblical criticism was both radical and liberating. Scriptural interpretation had been constrained to the service of religious dogma. Biblical scholars began to treat the Bible as a product of human creativity, subject to investigation like any other text.

From its beginnings in the late eighteenth century until the 1960s, biblical criticism focused almost exclusively on historical study of the texts. Students of the Bible came to recognize that it was neither a unified, atemporal *revelation nor the product of one or a few human authors. Rather, the Hebrew Scriptures and the New Testament are a composite, the end results of centuries of selecting, recording, editing, and reinterpreting the *traditions of ancient Israel and the early church. Scholars developed a range of methods to investigate not only the history described in the text (Did the events happen? What was their significance?) but also the history of the text (Is a given passage derived from a single author or is it composite? How was it compiled, by whom, in what setting, and why?).

Since the 1960s, a greater range of methods has found widespread acceptance within the biblical guild. Some scholars use anthropological and sociological methods to investigate the social structures and processes that shaped biblical texts. Others focus on the Bible as literature with its own fictive world of meaning, examining the plot lines, characters, and outcomes of biblical stories (narrative criticism); articulating the "deep structures" underlying a text as a primary clue to its meaning (structuralism); studying the rhetorical devices used to persuade or move the reader (*rhetorical criticism); or investigating the role of the reader in the creation of meaning (reader-response criticism).

Feminist Use of Biblical Criticism. Feminists use the whole range of biblical-critical methods to reenvision biblical history and retell biblical stories in ways that support the full humanity of women. Feminist biblical historians use historical-critical, anthropological, and archaeological studies to reconstruct the history of women's *agency and women's victimization in ancient Israel, Judaism, and the early church. Feminist literary critics use a variety of "new" methods to uncover androcentric ideologies encoded in biblical texts, to highlight neglected female images of God or neglected stories of women, and to identify women's genres.

Feminist biblical criticism is diverse, reflecting the critics' varying *cultures, training, and interests. Nonetheless, there are characteristics common to the various forms of feminist criticism that distinguish it from traditional biblical scholarship. Women and men using traditional tools of scholarship for feminist purposes have transformed those tools in at least two ways.

First, feminists use gender as a fundamental analytical category. Recognizing that the Bible is a product not of human beings in general but of elite, urban men, feminists use biblical-critical methods to demonstrate the androcentric and patriarchal character of biblical texts. Whereas traditional male scholarship either has ignored gender or has treated "women in the Bible" as a kind of appendix, feminist criticism reconstructs biblical history as a history of women and men and insists that biblical texts, like all texts, are gendered. Womanist, *mujerista,* and Asian women critics have shown that gender as an analytical category cannot be used in isolation from other social factors, including class, ethnicity, and religion. They confront Euro-American feminists' universalization of their experiences and call for more complex analyses of history and text.

Second, feminist biblical scholars have consistently challenged the notion that scholarship can or should be value-neutral. The biblical scholars who developed traditional historical-critical methods were seeking scientific ways to approximate the positivistic historical meaning of the biblical text. Feminists (building on theories of the sociology of knowledge developed in other disciplines) assert that the *race, class, and gender of the interpreter, as well as her training and interests, determine what questions she asks, what data she sees as significant, and what models she uses to interpret that data. The goal of most feminist biblical critics is not to unlock the one right or best interpretation of history or text but to enable a disciplined interpretation that generates new, rich, and plausible meanings.

Ongoing Issues in Feminist Biblical Critics. Among the main problems facing feminist biblical critics is the lack of available data. There are few depictions of women in the texts and those few have more to do with male fears and ideals than with women's experience. Extrabiblical literary and documentary evidence and cross-cultural studies can provide models or support historical hypotheses; nonetheless, in the face of scant data about women, any reconstruction of biblical history is tentative. Similarly, the pervasive *androcentrism of the biblical texts means that feminist literary critics must "read against the grain," lifting up submerged meanings and suppressed voices.

Another ongoing issue facing feminist biblical critics is the question of criteria. If one recognizes that multiple readings of any given text are both inevitable and valuable, then the question arises whether and on what basis one may exclude some readings and prioritize others. Feminist scholars have answered this question in part by affirming traditional criteria (whether the interpretation adequately accounts for textual or historical data; whether it is consistent and coherent) and in part by assessing the ethical consequences of an interpretation; interpretations that support the powerful against the powerless are rejected.

Finally, affirming that biblical-critical methods are usable tools in women's struggles for *liberation does not imply that nonprofessional women's interpretations of the Bible are invalid. Indeed, some professional women biblical scholars and theologians take the way a passage functions within their communities as their starting point. The relationship of professional feminist criticism to the interpretations of one's community—and to its agenda—is a crucial and ongoing challenge for feminist biblical critics.

Bellis [1994]; Cannon/Schüssler Fiorenza [1989]; Hayes/Holladay [1987]; Newsom/Ringe [1992]; Russell [1985a]; Sakenfeld, *Princeton Seminary Bulletin* [1988]; Schüssler Fiorenza [1993]; Weems, in Felder [1991]

CAROLYN J. PRESSLER

Biblical Studies** The term *biblical studies* has traditionally referred to scholarly study of the Hebrew Scriptures and the New Testament as collections of documents from the ancient cultural contexts of Israel in the ancient Near East and early Christianity in the Greco-Roman world. More recently, a focus on literary style and composition has supplemented the older emphasis on historical reconstruction of the background of the texts and efforts to discern authorial intention. The field of biblical studies thus encompasses textual criticism, aspects of ancient history, history of religions, literary criticism, and theological themes of specific biblical texts. The ways in which the Bible can become meaningful for contemporary believers (hermeneutics) may also be included in the term.

In Christian feminist studies, the Bible has come to be recognized as a primary source for *misogynist aspects of the theology and practice of Christian *faith. It is generally agreed that both the Hebrew Scriptures and the New Testament are products of patriarchal religion in patriarchal cultures. Nonetheless, many feminists also view the Bible as a text with liberating potential that can stand in criticism of negative attitudes toward women in Jewish and Christian traditions. Christian feminist biblical interpretation represents an effort first to unmask the patriarchal perspectives in biblical studies and then to seek strategies by which the Bible can be reclaimed for Christian faith.

***Hermeneutic of Suspicion.** Feminist biblical studies thus begin with a hermeneutic of suspicion, expecting that close study asking the right questions will uncover many levels of patriarchal bias, some in the Bible itself, others developed by later interpreters and recorded and perpetuated in theological works, in scholarly biblical commentaries and histories, and in popular devotional literature. Some of these patriarchal biases are easy to identify, such as the interpretation of the Genesis *creation story (promulgated by certain *Pauline texts and passages from the *pastoral epistles) in which it is claimed that woman was "created second and sinned first" and that therefore God intends that women should be subordinate to men. Paul's instruction that women should keep silent in church (1 Corinthians 14) and the various texts in the pastoral epistles subordinating slaves to masters and wives to husbands are also clear examples of texts regarded with suspicion by feminist biblical interpreters. Yet most examples are not so obvious. For instance, is the story of Ruth in the Hebrew Scriptures a story of a woman working in *solidarity with another woman for *survival against incredible odds (a positive image to be celebrated by women)? Or is it a story told by men to portray the ideally obedient wife and daughter-in-law? Feminist commentators are divided, although most recognize that any story may have more than one level of meaning.

Feminists also bring their hermeneutic of suspicion to biblical texts about human beings that make no explicit reference to women, as well as to texts about God. A study of Hebrew Scripture words for the poor, for instance, suggests that these words generally refer to free Israelite males, not to women, children, indentured persons, or slaves. Biblical language about God is overwhelmingly masculine, with extensive use of imagery of God as king (Hebrew Scriptures) and father (New Testament; see *Abba*), with references to Jesus as *Son of man (as traditionally translated), and with the consistent use of masculine pronouns for God in both the Greek and Hebrew languages. Feminist interpreters not only search the text for lesser-known female/feminine or non-gender-specific imagery for God (as, for example, *Sophia/Wisdom, rock of salvation) but also reevaluate and reconceive the significance of the traditional masculine language and imagery (see *Christa, *Inclusive Language).

***Biblical Translation.** *Translation is a critical task in which the patriarchal biases of the text can be confronted and distinguished from the patriarchal biases of previous translators. Many feminists support the use of inclusive English wording to translate generic masculine language for human beings (NRSV) and the use of inclusive language for God (*AILL*). Yet others debate whether such translations are more accurate to the intent of the Bible's ancient writers and hearers or whether they obscure the reality of the patriarchal nature of the original Greek and Hebrew texts. Some argue for the need to distinguish between translations for use in liturgical settings and translations for use in study by persons without knowledge of the original languages.

***Biblical Criticism.** Biblical translation is usually debated in the context of the larger rubric of biblical criticism, which incorporates a whole range of methods developed by modern scholarship to understand texts from times and cultures far removed from the readers' own. While using these methods, feminist criticism does not pretend to be value-neutral or positivistically objective, and it insists that the claims of *objectivity in traditional scholarship are misplaced and cannot be sustained. Feminist biblical criticism includes two main foci: (1) reconstructing the world of women in biblical cultures and (2) literary rereading of the texts with new sensitivity to the roles of women in them.

1. Since the biblical texts tell us relatively little about the place of women, and much of what is presented may be skewed by the *androcentric biases of the ancient authors, *archaeology and extrabiblical sources provide important additional resources for feminist biblical studies. The role of women in *Gnostic Christianity, the evidence for women *apostles, and the role of *widows in the early church are examples of such studies in early Christianity.
2. Literary rereading uses various strategies, the best known of which is *rhetorical criticism. Close attention to stylistic features of a text may open new possibilities of meaning. In the creation story of Genesis 2, for example, it has been suggested that the creation of the woman at the end of the story is intended not to show her subordinate role but rather, by a "ring formation," to show her status as equivalent to the man who is created at the very beginning of the story. Literary analysis gives special attention to gaps or silences in the text and the ways in which readers consciously or unconsciously fill in those gaps.

Special Issues. Feminist biblical scholars generally recognize that *patriarchy is a system that has structurally oppressed many nondominant groups and that has led to misuse of natural resources. Therefore their concerns often go beyond texts specifically about women. Topics such as *ecofeminism, *heterosexism in biblical interpretation, and the relative merits and significance of the English terms **servant* and *slave* in biblical translation are explored as specific aspects of the challenge to patriarchy.

Feminist scholarship, along with biblical scholarship generally, is becoming increasingly aware of the dangers of simplistic comparisons between Christianity and early Judaism that perpetuate the *anti-Judaism/anti-Semitism that has characterized so much Christian theology and history writing. Hence recent feminist study seeks to take account of the anti-Judaistic biases of the New Testament writers and their modern interpreters, including biases about the place of women in Judaism.

Biblical *Authority. Christians generally regard the Bible as foundationally authoritative for faith and practice, although some branches (e.g., Roman Catholicism) grant significant authority to *tradition as well as to scripture, and there are differences in the number of canonical books (see *Apocrypha). While some branches of Protestantism have historically granted a place for reason and experience in comprehending Christian faith, the Bible has generally held the place of privilege. Thus the question of how such a patriarchal document can remain authoritative is central for Christian feminist biblical studies. The question of biblical authority is scarcely new; the church has been debating errors in scientific and historical information in the Bible for centuries. But the feminist emphasis on patriarchal bias is perhaps more radical because such bias so pervades the text as a whole.

Among Christian feminists who wish to reclaim the Bible despite its patriarchal slant, various hermeneutical strategies have been proposed. At one end of the spectrum, some interpreters frankly privilege the category of women's experience, whether individual experience or the experience of women in struggle for *justice, and judge the authoritative potential of biblical passages according to this criterion. Interpreters using this approach may suggest rejecting or discarding any text that cannot be interpreted to affirm full *equality of women and other oppressed groups. Toward the other end of the spectrum are those (sometimes called evangelical) who consider themselves responsible for following the plain sense of the text at all points. Feminists in this tradition focus their efforts on seeking out an alternative, nonsubordinationist meaning for each text that seems to subordinate women. While a hermeneutic of suspicion calls all feminist interpreters to this task, it is of central importance to those who view the Bible as a prescriptive and unchanging *archetype* rather than as a descriptive *prototype* with historical and cultural limitations.

Within the middle range of this spectrum on biblical authority are various other options. Most feminist critics concede that some, even many, texts cannot be reinterpreted to present a nonpatriarchal picture of the role of women. Such passages are often viewed as representing the brokenness of creation, including human society, that is still visible in present-day patriarchy. Those who place themselves in the center of the interpretive spectrum recognize the importance of experience in all biblical interpretation (not just in feminist study) yet are unwilling to establish it as an authoritative criterion external to the text. Recognizing that their experience informs their questions, they continue to look for intrabiblical criteria in judging some passages to represent brokenness but other passages to represent wholeness or opposition to patriarchy that should be affirmed. The criteria for assessment generally focus on one or more biblical themes that can be developed theologically as a counter to patriarchy. These include the concepts of *new creation/reign of God, a *shalom community, **agapē*, the *jubilee year, a *kerygma that is restated to be more inclusive of all people, and principles of more inclusive justice drawn from the *prophets.

Although such an emphasis on liberative themes may lead to a preferential focus on certain texts or a "*canon within the canon" (a usually unadmitted reality of all theological interpretations of the Bible), in principle all biblical material remains subject to continuing consideration in the community of believers. The theological themes selected are noteworthy for their breadth. Some of them (e.g., justice in the prophetic literature) do not even deal directly with the relations between women and men, but rather, an argument is made by extrapolation for a nonpatriarchal attitude toward women. Indeed, all the themes cited presume a broad definition of feminism as concerned not just for women but for women along with all who are oppressed and disempowered by patriarchal structures, thus placing feminist biblical studies into a larger context of hermeneutical and theological reflection.

Bird, in Miller et al. [1987]; Newsom/Ringe [1992]; Perkins, *Int* [1988]; Ringe, *Theology Today* [1987]; Russell [1985a]; Schüssler Fiorenza [1992a]; Trible [1978]

KATHARINE DOOB SAKENFELD

Biblical Translation The task of biblical *translation has been ongoing since various parts of the Hebrew Bible were first put into Greek in the third century B.C.E. Today there are an estimated fourteen hundred projects in process to translate the Bible into all the languages of the world. With regard to translations into English, our generation has experienced what has been called a "rage to translate." This impetus for new translations reflects the discovery of ancient manuscripts (particularly the Dead Sea Scrolls), advances in the study of philology (meanings of words) and in the methodology of textual criticism (what text to translate), and the rapid rate of change in the English language. Some translations are prepared by and serve a specific faith community (NIV, JPSV, NJB) while others draw on translators from a wide variety of backgrounds (NRSV). Some translations attempt to make the Bible accessible to those reading it for the first time or for whom English is not a first language (TEV), and others place the emphasis on academic rigor and historical accuracy.

In the nineteenth century, the first generation of feminist scholars suggested that women needed to study Greek and Hebrew so that they could translate the Bible for themselves, with particular attention to how passages involving women were treated. Today it is widely recognized that there are significant issues of language and gender involved in treating texts that deal with women specifically, texts that speak to the whole community of men and women, and texts about God.

A number of recent biblical translations (including the NRSV) have adopted, as a matter of principle, *inclusive language, that is, the use of expressions such as *people, human being, brothers and sisters* where the original text refers to both women and men. This, in fact, ensures an accurate translation of the Hebrew and Greek, given that in current English usage terms such as *men, mankind,* and *he* are understood not as generic but as referring to males alone or at least as subsuming the female into the male. Sometimes in English, inclusivity requires the use of plural rather than the singular (e.g., "happy are they who . . . " rather than "happy is he who . . . ") or a reformulation and freer treatment of the sentence structure. In addition, careful attention must be paid to the translation of specific terms (e.g., *diakonos*/deacon) so that a distinction prejudicial to women is not introduced into the text where it is not found in the original. Language about God, who is beyond gender, is especially difficult to translate, given that the English language does not have a pronoun for living beings that is not gender-specific.

In many places the Bible itself is androcentric in its fundamental orientation, and there is, at present, considerable discussion among feminist scholars about how to treat such texts. Some suggest that the goal of translation is to make such texts as inclusive as possible by introducing women and female imagery even where they do not appear in the original (e.g., to expand the God of Abraham to the God of Abraham and Sarah; to introduce women explicitly into many of the laws or the wisdom statements; to speak of "God our father and our mother"). Other feminist scholars disallow such a free style of translation, either because they believe in the given nature of the original text as the word of God or because they fear that the very real and dangerous biblical *androcentrism will be only superficially disguised and never confronted directly.

Some of the most creative work and innovative experimentation with options for translating in a way that includes women can be seen not in translations of the Bible as a whole but in translations of the selections of *lectionary readings that are used in various churches and in translations of the Psalms that are used for *prayer and singing.

AILL [1983–85]; Bird, *USQR* [1988]; Castelli et al., *JFSR* [1990]

EILEEN M. SCHULLER

Bioethics The term *bioethics* is relatively new and generally applies to *ethics in medicine, health care, and medical research. Both the scope and the method used by feminists writing on bioethics differ from "malestream" bioethics, which has been dominated by attention to specific practices such as assisted suicide and by a preference for the application of principles to cases.

Feminists examine not only specific practices within medicine but also, and particularly, the structure of the health care system itself and the ways in which it generates and perpetuates *domination of women and other groups. Feminists approach bioethics with a *hermeneutic of suspicion: they analyze oppressive patterns of relationship and the ideologies that foster those patterns. Some feminists offer scathing criticism of the medical establishment, seeing it as the enforcement of a sexual caste system or an empire of patriarchal power. Others accept the basic structures of health care while urging more just access and delivery of services.

Feminists criticize mainstream bioethics for its reliance on principles and for its choice of principles such as *autonomy, which is understood to reflect patriarchal rather than feminist models. Feminist method in bioethics stresses concrete experiences and the development of "thick" cases. Most feminists do not believe that any single ethical approach will suffice to handle all issues.

Feminist bioethicists have paid particular attention to the medicalization of childbirth, the use of mental health diagnoses to subjugate women, the standardization of practices that damage women's health, the role of new reproductive technologies in distributing social power, and inequities in access to and delivery of health care. Beginning with women's experience, stress is given to questions of *embodiment. Dualisms such as a mind–body or nature–culture split are rejected. Feminist bioethicists also stress relationality, mutuality, and "caring," though *care is not seen as inimical to *justice.

Theological feminists have particularly emphasized the interpretation of nature in bioethics: mutuality and *responsibility rather than *rights, the *epistemological privilege of the socially marginalized, a historical and contextual analysis of structures of *oppression, the moral *agency of women and their claim to bodily integrity as a central ethical principle, and a vision of justice as "right relationship." The concrete well-being of the least powerful members of society, usually women, is the litmus test for the justice of health care policies and practices.

Some of the journals that carry discussions of importance in bioethics are: *Hastings Center Report; Hypatia; Philosophy and Medicine; Second Opinion; Signs; Theology and Medicine.*

Daly [1978]; Davis, *Hastings Center Report* [1991]; Farley, in Andolsen/Gudorf/Pellauer [1985]; Gudorf, in Dubose/Hammel/O'Connell [1994]; Harrison [1983]; Holland/Peterson [1993]; Lebacqz, in Lammers/Verhey [1987]; Sanders, in Flack/Pellegrino [1992]; Sherwin [1992]

KAREN LEBACQZ

Body The body is the physical, material dimension of human existence. As understood in the Jewish, Christian, and Muslim traditions, the body, along with the *soul or spirit, constitutes the human person. As created by God, the body is "good"; but under the influence of dualistic Greek thought in Western Christianity, the body came to be understood as inferior to the immaterial soul. Although in orthodox Christian theology the bodiliness of Christ was affirmed against *Gnostic strains of thought, anti-body sentiment has never been far from the surface and has had profound effects on women. More recently, feminist theologies have embraced *embodiment as a woman-centered value.

In the history of *religion and *culture, women traditionally have been associated with the body. The biological processes of menstruation, pregnancy, and lactation have served to define women as "more bodily" than men. When interpreted as lower than the soul, the body is seen as particularly prone to *sin. Women consequently have borne the brunt of the *tradition's unease with and often even hatred of the body. Women and oppressed men have shared this imposed association with the body and *sexuality and have been judged as less rational than dominant men.

Feminist theologies have emphasized that human experience and knowledge are rooted in the body. They have stressed "embodied thinking" that is rooted in concrete circumstances and oriented toward practical results. They have promoted an "embodied morality" that takes *emotion seriously. Along with recent historical and philosophical work on the body, feminist theologies stress the contextual nature of conceptions of the body.

Finally, bodily integrity is a central issue for feminist theologies and *ethics: women have the right to exercise control over their bodies, to enjoy or to refuse sexual intimacy, to be free from surrogacy, harassment, and *violence.

Cooey [1994]; Cooey/Farmer/Ross [1987]; Gilkes, in Townes [1993]; Gudorf [1994]

SUSAN A. ROSS

Buddhism Buddhism, a major world religion, was founded in India in the sixth century B.C.E. by an upper-class and upper-caste male who, by "renouncing the world," left behind his caste and class duties and privileges. His reasons had to do with the basic tenet of the religion he founded, which proclaims that conventional lifestyles inevitably produce *suffering. This religion proclaims with equal conviction that humans can alleviate their suffering by cultivating appropriate mental states and that this possibility is fully within the reach of all human beings. Buddhism became the world's first "portable" religion when it spread to Southeast Asia and later to East Asia, where it is now a prominent religion. Today, Buddhism is rapidly spreading in the Western world, where it is encountering and interacting with Western feminism. Nevertheless, feminist scholarship about and analyses of Buddhism lag behind feminist assessments of *monotheistic religions.

Buddhism is unique among *world religions in many ways. Lacking a transcendent deity, it is thoroughly nondualistic in outlook. Denying personal immortality, it emphasizes impermanence and claims that accommodating impermanence is the only way to tranquillity. Contrary to popular Western *stereotypes, it is not otherworldly but instead emphasizes that the immediate present is our most basic reality. Its major focus is on human perfectibility through the practice of meditation, morality, and wisdom seeking; it views human nature as basically good because all human beings are intrinsically endowed with "Buddha nature," the potential for enlightenment. Furthermore, it has no ontological or religious preference for maleness over femaleness, despite its less than exemplary record historically and socially. Buddhism's traditionally *patriarchal forms seem to exist because it emerged and evolved in cultures that were already patriarchal, aided by the long-standing Buddhist tendency to renounce, rather than seek to change, the world of convention.

In some senses, feminist perspectives are nothing new to Buddhism. Women's involvement in the religion has been at issue from Buddhism's beginnings, and many arguments against male privilege are found in traditional texts. It is also undeniable that, using feminist standards of assessment, Buddhism is in need of feminist transformation. Therefore the encounter between Buddhism and Western feminism is producing new perspectives about how feminists might view Buddhist history, how they analyze the basic doctrines of Buddhism, and how they would construct postpatriarchal Buddhism.

A feminist reading of Buddhist history reveals that from the beginning there have been two dominant views about women. The more popular but less normative view is that being female is an unfortunate rebirth because women suffer more than men and have fewer opportunities. Their misfortune is explained by *karma,* cause and effect from past lives. Clearly, this explanation takes rebirth for granted, a judgment widespread in Asia but not so widespread among Western Buddhists. The more normative but less popular view is that, like all other labels, *male* and *female* are "empty" of any real content, being merely conventional categories that apply to the world of relative truth but have no ultimate value or relevance. In addition, occasionally one finds the opinion that women actually excel at Buddhist spiritual disciplines and have more aptitude for them than do men, on average.

For feminists, a major question concerns whether core Buddhist teachings are sexist. Though many women are not attracted to Buddhism because of its male-dominant forms, most feminists who persevere in their explorations of Buddhism come to the conclusion that Buddhist meditation disciplines and doctrines are genuinely gender-free and gender-neutral. In addition, the sects of Buddhism that recognize the existence of mythological transhuman role models have always portrayed these models as both female and male. In fact, feminist Buddhists often find a deep affinity between Buddhism and feminism in that both seek *freedom from deeply ingrained habitual patterns that cause suffering. Furthermore, these two paths to freedom are complementary, each providing what the other has overlooked. Buddhism seeks spiritual detachment that brings ultimate tranquillity, while feminism seeks freedom from conventional sex roles and male gender privilege.

For Buddhist feminists, the most pressing agenda is reconstruction of Buddhist institutional life. This is a difficult task since, as in all other world religions, men have controlled Buddhist institutional life for a long time and have done so in ways that seriously shortchange women, despite the fact that nothing in Buddhism's *ethics or worldview can legitimately be used to justify such behavior.

For many Buddhist women, the most serious and obvious issue is the *renewal of the nuns' order* in those forms of Buddhism that have lost it. Because monasticism has been so important to Buddhism's survival historically, this is a central issue. Currently, Chinese, Korean, and Vietnamese forms of Buddhism have preserved their orders for fully ordained nuns, but these orders have been lost in Sri Lankan, Thai, Burmese, and Tibetan forms of Buddhism, which have only a novice ordination for women. Restoring the nuns' order is probably the most conservative aspect of the Buddhist feminist agenda and the one on which there would be the least disagreement. Some feminists would want not only to restore the nuns' ordination but to delete some of the more patriarchal forms of Buddhist monastic practice, such as the rules that formally subordinate all nuns to all monks without regard for seniority or attainments.

For many Western Buddhist women, more critical issues have to do with the *lay householder lifestyle,* because most Western Buddhists are not taking monastic vows. Nevertheless, many of these Western Buddhists have taken up meditation and study programs that in Asia were usually done only by monastics. This development of serious lay meditation is something of an innovation in Buddhism. However, for this innovation to succeed, lay Buddhist life must be transformed along the lines envisioned by transformative feminism, which seeks to undo the current conventional gender-role system and to bring traditionally feminine values into the center of public life and policy. In sum, since serious Buddhist study and practice are time-consuming and difficult, both economic production and physiological reproduction must be properly limited. Too many hours worked overtime and too many babies are equally counterproductive to serious Buddhist practice, which is why monasticism was the traditionally preferred lifestyle. The innovation feminism brings to this volatile situation is the insistence that women take their proper places in the meditation halls and men take their proper places in the kitchens and nurseries while constructing a householder lifestyle that includes serious study and practice.

Everywhere in the Buddhist world, the most central and important feminist agenda is *thorough *education of women* in both Buddhist meditative and scholarly disciplines. For its survival, Buddhism depends on the transmission of its core teachings about enlightenment from teacher to student, throughout the generations. In too many cases, because of conventional expectations surrounding gender, women have had to struggle unduly to take their place in that lineage of transmission and have not become revered, respected, and widely known teachers. In the feminist future of Buddhism, well-educated women who take on the teaching role that is so central to the religion and traditionally so largely reserved to men will be the leaders in the development of postpatriarchal Buddhism.

Allione [1984]; Boucher [1993]; Gross [1993]; Klein [1994]; Okoshi et al. [1990]; Paul [1979]; Shaw [1994]; Tsomo [1988]

RITA M. GROSS

Call / Vocation

Call / Vocation The *doctrine of vocation affirms that every individual life with its unique combination of gifts and limitations has divinely appointed purpose and that we are called to glorify God in all that we do. So understood, the doctrine of vocation addresses the feminist understanding of *sin, preserves the integrity of vocational differences, and encourages participation in social and political change.

The Doctrine of Sin. The doctrine of vocation claims that limitations as well as gifts lend positive meaning to our lives. It condemns, therefore, every attempt to be more than whom God calls us to be (e.g., through oppressive behavior) and guards against any tendency to be less than whom God intends us to be. Hence vocation encompasses the feminist understanding of sin as overextension of *power as well as sin understood as passivity.

Vocational Differences. The doctrine of vocation challenges arguments that deny the freedom of God to call people to different identities and tasks. For instance, ruling homosexuality out of bounds by an argument from nature (male and female bodies were created exclusively to complement each other) refutes the freedom of God to call individuals into different types of *relationships. Likewise, identical roles cannot be assigned to all members of any one *race, class, *culture, or gender. For instance, not all women are called to be *mothers or all men to be fathers; some women are called to the ordained *ministry, some men into full-time child care, etc.

Participation in Social and Political Change. Although the doctrine of vocation can be misused to counsel tolerance for oppressive situations, if rightly interpreted it challenges oppressive conditions. The church is commissioned to change those situations and structures that prevent people from glorifying God or from fulfilling their divine vocation.

Miller-McLemore [1994]; Rhodes [1987]; Russell [1979]

NANCY J. DUFF

Canon A biblical canon is an approved collection of books considered inspired and believed to be a source of *revelation. Both ancient Israel and early Christianity preserved certain traditions as normative, against which subsequent religious *tradition and the lives of believers were and continue to be measured. The Jewish community decided on the contents of its canon after the destruction of the second temple (circa 70 C.E.). Beginning in the second or third century C.E., and down through the centuries, different Christian communions (Catholic, Greek Orthodox, Ethiopic, Slavonic, Protestant) made decisions about which writings to include in their respective canons.

The question of canon is a question of *authority. Who decides what is authoritative? Many feminists question the value of traditional biblical canons because it was within *patriarchal, *androcentric societies that the traditions they contain originated and were shaped, were later transmitted, and finally were canonically constituted. These feminists maintain that the interests and insights of women were not only routinely misrepresented by these traditions but also systematically disregarded by the same traditions or outrightly expunged from them. This belief has led feminists such as Mary Daly and Carol Christ simply to reject the biblical tradition as having no redeeming qualities or revelatory value for women.

Other feminists, frequently referred to as revisionists, have retained traditional canons but have developed various critical ways of interpreting them from feminist perspectives. Their methods employ both standard historical and literary approaches and newer hermeneutical techniques, as well as the findings of the social sciences. The decisive feature of all of these interpretive approaches is the critical feminist perspective.

Several feminist approaches include a systematic unmasking of the androcentric bias of traditional historical-critical analysis itself. Their starting point is the conviction that the reconstructed view of biblical history promoted by this approach misrepresents women and their importance in ancient society. They propose that one way to correct this distortion is to go beyond the canonical writings, long considered the primary, even exclusive, source of historical information. They complement this source with the writings and *archaeological artifacts of the broader ancient world to reconstruct a more accurate picture of that world (Schüssler Fiorenza 1983; Ackerman). Then, by comparison, this revised view of history can uncover the biases within the biblical story. It can enlighten both the roles that women play in the story and the ways in which they have been minimized and excluded there.

Methods and insights gleaned from the social sciences have also opened the canonical biblical texts in new and fascinating ways. Cross-cultural studies of the social structures and the gender-related customs of contemporary traditional societies have been invaluable in throwing light on some of the customs presumed by and referred to in the biblical material.

In addition to historical approaches, feminists have employed literary methods that open the canonical texts to meanings not considered by the biblical authors. While these approaches respect the integrity of the canons that prove to be so troublesome, they have produced interpretations that are both critical of the canons' biases and constructive of critical feminist theology (Trible 1984; Camp).

Finally, the development of various forms of feminist hermeneutics moves biblical interpretation far beyond the confines of androcentric canons. Whether the preferred approach is Rosemary Radford Ruether's "liberating-prophetic critique," Letty Russell's model of the liberating action of God, Elisabeth Schüssler Fiorenza's feminist theological hermeneutics, or Sally McFague's elaboration of *metaphor (see Camp), the goal of feminist interpretation is liberation of the word of God from the androcentric biases that permeate its canonical articulation.

Ackerman, in Day [1989]; Bird [1982]; Bird, *NIB* [1994]; Camp, in Schüssler Fiorenza, ed. [1993]

DIANNE BERGANT

Care The terms *care* and *care ethic* have become principal representatives of feminist *ethics. The concept of care in its present form can be traced back to the work of Carol Gilligan in moral *psychology. Gilligan, whose work began in the 1970s and continues into the present, saw a male bias within developmental theories, and her work to correct this has changed the face of psychology and provoked an explosion in the field of feminist ethics. However, it has been misused for some antifeminist purposes as well.

Gilligan realized that most developmental psychology evaluated women negatively. Starting with Freud, and continuing with Jean Piaget and Lawrence Kohlberg, women were considered morally deficient. We were seen as caring too much about *relationships or as "narcissistically" involved with our children and not capable of "higher" moral considerations such as *justice and other more abstract "goods." This reinforced the prevailing patriarchal notion that women were fit only for the "private" sphere and should be restricted from the "public" sphere of work and government.

Gilligan immediately saw that the problem for women could be found in the very design of the investigations. Both Piaget and Kohlberg used only boys in their original studies; girls' were an afterthought. With boys as the standard, girls' differences were interpreted as deviance and moral inadequacy. Gilligan also found that the study questions were hypothetical, concerned with male issues, and designed to elicit a more abstract response.

In Kohlberg's theory, moral development was set out in six stages. Gilligan saw that the higher stages were characterized by what males considered valuable and did not take into account that morality might be characterized in other ways. In doing her studies she used women who were caught in real-life moral dilemmas, such as the decision to have an *abortion. She found that women made their decisions not from abstract principles but within the context of relational concerns and caring. Gilligan describes development in terms of three modes: (1) egocentric concern with the self, (2) consideration of others and (3) relationships strengthened by working through *conflict.

A great deal of feminist theory comes from the ideas found in Gilligan's care ethic. Women's experience becomes essential; sensuality, relationality, and mothering all become important factors in creating feminist ethics. Women's ability to connect to others becomes an antidote to the ills caused by ethics done from a removed and falsely impartial perspective. Gilligan herself maintained that the ethics of justice and care belonged together, but some feminist theory began to put forward the ethic of care as *the* women's morality, equal to, if not superior to, male morality. The ethic of care was sometimes contrasted with justice, *autonomy, separation, and abstract forms of *reason considered "male."

While the original impulse behind this was to elevate women's morality, it at times had undesired consequences for women. It increased a kind of *dualism and made caring and justice appear separate. It was largely attractive to white women who were not employing ethical analysis that begins with *race, gender, and class. It led to some other potential problems: for example, should a woman stay connected to her abuser? Would not separation be more appropriate in that and other cases? Questions were also raised concerning whether the care ethic fed into *stereotypes about women, from the Victorian "angel in the house" to the present-day "codependent," who gives up her own needs for the needs of others. Worse, the care ethic was used by antifeminists to say that they had been right all along, that women did care more than men, and that mothering and home life were what was best for women.

Further psychological studies have shown that there is not a strict gender split between care and justice. James Rest and others have found that both women and men use a mixture of care and justice considerations when making moral decisions, depending on a variety of factors. Womanist, *mujerista*, and other ethicists stress justice with relationship, beginning with structures of *oppression. In feminist theology and ethics, care and justice are not considered mutually exclusive virtues. Rather, most theorists consider them important aspects of any ethic. Moreover, consideration of the importance of care and connection have influenced ideas about God, informing feminists in creating theology with a more immanent, intimate God rather than the aloof God of classical theism. Despite some of its problems, the care ethic has been an important impetus in feminist ethics to create ethics that support and encourage the experience and well-being of women.

Andolsen/Gudorf/Pellauer [1985]; Brown/Gilligan [1992]; Cannon, in Daly [1994]; Gilligan [1982]; Isasi-Díaz, in Daly [1994]; Rest [1979]

SUSAN DOLAN-HENDERSON

Character The Christian understanding of character has traditionally been developed around the concept of *virtue. Theologians appropriated Greek and Latin excellences of the male citizen (*vir* is the Latin word for "man" and the root of *virility* as well as *virtue*) and added to them or transformed them with valued Christian traits of character. Justice, wisdom, temperance, and courage were identified by Plato as necessary for the ideal *polis;* these were appropriated and transformed into theological virtues. More current theological interest in virtue serves to shift moral reflection away from reliance on laws to be obeyed and toward reliance on the good person to make appropriate decisions (the good tree brings forth good fruit).

A feminist critique of this ethical construction of character includes rejection of the existence of a double standard regarding which character traits are valued. While the above are presumably the virtues of a "good person" and "a Christian," they remain the excellences of men, and other virtues are expected of women, including humility and patience. Further, because the norm of the human is elite, Eurocentric, and male, other groups cannot be either good or human.

Feminists also reject the assumption of an *abstract human essence* that ultimately denies the ethical significance of our historical and social differences. In many instances, the assumption is also that the good Christian has the resources and responsibilities appropriate to the social location of elite, white men. In addition, the use of the language of character is a *language of control*, a disciplining of one's emotions, one's bodily impulses, and one's mind in obedience to or conformity with Christ. The assumption is that the self is essentially out of control, its yearnings and passions to be distrusted. Thus if love is to be a virtue, it must become something else (supernatural gift, **agapē*, or *caritas*), and not simply our earthly *eros directed to God and the neighbor.

Feminists have not addressed character in any comprehensive way, but several possibilities have emerged. One follows the writings of psychologists Jean Baker Miller and Carol Gilligan, suggesting that there is a feminine way of being in the world that might become the basis of new theories of character or virtue. Some feminist ethicists have suggested "an ethic of care," in which care is both a norm for decision making and a virtue.

Writing in the context of an ethic of *survival and resistance, African-American womanists identify distinctive character traits. M. Shawn Copeland speaks of sass, along with courage and mother wit (Townes, 124), that enabled slaves to resist. Delores Williams implicitly suggests struggle, survival, and mothering-as-resistance. These are more than activities; they are *valued characteristics* of African-American women. And many speak of love (the love of oneself, the love of one's *body, so despised, caricatured, and defiled by the dominant society) as absolutely essential to survival and resistance.

Among European Americans, Beverly Harrison writes of *anger as a virtue. Carter Heyward draws on Audre Lorde to lift up eros, a passion that unites, as an excellence as well as an intrinsic dimension of our selfhood that can, and indeed should, be trusted. She writes of the four qualities of "wisdom, passion, *justice and *prayer" (24). Still others have reclaimed *friendship.

Third-world feminists in general value *community and commitment to the struggle and to the community. Community is the context of both survival and resistance. It is implicitly also a foreshadowing of a new, just society. Further development of an ethic of character would thus be rooted in a relational, communal, embodied, historically and socially distinct understanding of selfhood.

Andolsen/Gudorf/Pellauer [1985]; Harrison [1985]; Heyward [1984]; Townes, ed. [1993]

ELEANOR H. HANEY

Christ, Jesus Christian communities of every generation have to discern the significance of Jesus Christ for their own lives, because their affirmations of Jesus Christ are contextual. They must answer for themselves what it means for Jesus, the first-century Jew from Nazareth, to be Christ (i.e., the Messiah, the bearer of God's salvation). Moreover, the community's historical, cultural, social, and political contexts inevitably shape their christological answers. It is essential, therefore, to identify the context out of which any *Christology or theological definition of Jesus Christ emerges.

The following definition derives from a womanist context. It reflects the meaning of Jesus Christ for African-American women as they struggle for life and wholeness for themselves and their community/family. This definition also reflects the *faith of the wider African-American community, male and female, given the life situation of resistance to *oppression that African-American women share with African-American men. From a womanist perspective, *Jesus Christ means that God is real.* Christ brings God down to earth. Christ is God's actual presence in the daily lives of African-American women. Christ is a living being with whom African-American women have an intimate relationship. This relationship has several dimensions that clarify the womanist meaning of Jesus Christ.

First, *Christ is a friend and confidant.* African-American women are certain that Christ knows intrinsically the complex reality associated with being black and female in a society that is hostile to both blackness and femaleness. Christ is one to whom African-American women can cry, talk, and share their pains and sorrows. Refrains such as "Jesus is my bosom friend" and "A little talk with Jesus makes it right" echo through their songs. African-American women's confidence in Christ as a friend and confidant is based on their knowledge of Jesus' relationship to the poor and oppressed in his own time. Luke's birth narrative provides them with the needed evidence that Jesus experienced from the moment of his birth what it meant to be on the margins of society. African-American women testify in song: "Poor little Jesus boy / Made him to be born in a manger / World treats him so mean / Treats me mean too."

Second, *Christ is a co-sufferer.* African-American women believe that Christ is one with them in their peculiar *suffering. Sojourner Truth, in her speech at the 1851 Women's Rights Convention, captured this aspect of Christ's meaning for African-American women when she testified, "I have borne thirteen children, and seen them most all sold off into slavery, and when I cried out with my mother's grief, none but Jesus heard me!" (Foner, 103). Jesus' crucifixion is the event that most clearly demonstrates to African-American women Christ's *solidarity with them in their suffering. The pain of the *cross poignantly confirms that Christ existentially knows their painful struggles to make it through each day.

Third, *Christ is a healer and provider.* African-American women are sure that Christ will help them take care of their needs. They call to Christ in song: "Feed me, Jesus, feed me," or "Clothe me, Jesus, clothe me." Again, this assurance that Christ will respond to their needs is based on their knowledge of Jesus' *ministry. They reason that if Jesus helped the oppressed of his own time, he will surely do the same for them. They have sung, "Jesus make de dumb to speak. / Jesus make de cripple to walk. / Jesus give de blind his sight. / Jesus do most anything."

Fourth, *Christ is a liberator.* African-American women believe that Christ is working through, for, and with them to liberate the African-American community from its complex oppression. They believe Christ is stridently against all that is hostile to the life and wholeness of African-American women and men. They also believe that Christ will help them to defeat that which oppresses. The *resurrection provides the foundation of this belief. It reveals that oppression and death are not the last word; wholeness and life are.

Essentially, the life, ministry, and actions of Jesus provide the vital keys to a womanist definition of what it means for Jesus to be Christ. A womanist meaning of Jesus Christ is revealed, therefore, in who Christ is and through what Christ does in the life of the African-American community. The meaning of Christ is found in the relationship that Christ shares with African-American women and men. This rich relationship primarily shows that Jesus Christ means life, *freedom, and wholeness.

Brock [1988]; Douglas [1994]; Foner [1972]; Grant [1989]; Heyward [1989a]; Johnson [1990]; Ruether [1981]; Wilson-Kastner [1983]

KELLY BROWN DOUGLAS

Christa *Christa* is the name of a sculpture by English artist Edwina Sandys. On April 19, 1984, this four-foot-tall bronze of a crucified woman was put on exhibit in the Cathedral Church of St. John the Divine in New York City. Eleven days later, it was removed in a storm of controversy. The term *Christa* subsequently emerged as a christological image among some Christian feminists, where it also has been controversial.

Some theologians have used Christa to represent the creative, liberating Spirit of God/dess. Attempting in their Christologies to differentiate many women's experiences of salvation from the church's traditional teachings about Jesus Christ, Rita Nakashima Brock and Carter Heyward employ the term *Christa* for the Spirit that is sacred, vulnerable, deeply embedded in women's lives, and erotic (source of creative power and sexual pleasure; cf. *eros).

Emphasizing her collective and erotic character, Brock describes "Christa/ Community" as "a revelatory and redemptive witness of God/dess's work in history . . . the church's imaginative witness to its experiences of brokenness and [the] sacredness of erotic power in human existence" (69). Citing Christa as the "eternal resource of nourishment on the sacred journey toward *justice," Heyward writes, "There is no greater delight than to celebrate and share the body of Christa," which she locates "in the power between us, in our relation, as well as in the persons we are and are becoming" (117).

By contrast, other women have criticized Christa as an icon that too readily can be used to glorify women's *suffering. They contend that feminists who wish to celebrate either women's vulnerability or the erotic power in women's lives risk colluding with the massive social, political, and economic systems that violate women. Using Christa to signify redemptive power requires distinguishing the christological significance of the Jesus story from the man himself. In this way, Christa can be an iconoclastic image that shatters the maleness of Christ.

Brock [1988]; Dyke [1991]; Heyward [1989b]

CARTER HEYWARD

Christology

Classical Christology. The person and work of Jesus *Christ, particularly as defined by the ecumenical councils of the early church, has traditionally been the subject matter of Christology. Jesus Christ was understood as the "only begotten *Son of God" who "for us [humans] and for our salvation became human" (Creed of Nicaea, 325 C.E.); he was "truly God, truly human" (Definition of Chalcedon, 451 C.E.). God the Son or Word (Logos) was incarnate in Jesus of Nazareth; having taken on human nature, he saved humankind from *sin, death, and the consequences of the *Fall by his death and *resurrection, through which he was also made known to be the Christ (God's anointed One, the Messiah). Classical Christology's concentration on the *metaphysics of divine–human relation in Jesus (one person, two natures) tended to obscure the underlying concerns about salvation that motivated these early debates. The weight of christological thought came to rest on the divine nature of Jesus Christ, overshadowing the significance of his humanity.

Doctrinal decision making through councils, intended to define or delimit the *faith of all Christians, became possible only after the emperor Constantine took an interest in the Christian God and the affairs of the church (311 C.E. and afterward) and put imperial resources toward the resolution of theological controversies that were socially as well as ecclesiastically disruptive. In addition to changing the way in which doctrinal authority was exercised, the trinitarian and christological controversies tied the interests of church and empire more closely together; in both theology and art, the portrait of Jesus often took on imperial outlines.

Contemporary Developments. Since the Enlightenment, biblical scholars and systematic theologians have undertaken various "quests" for the historical Jesus, seeking the man behind the christological doctrines and even behind the Gospels themselves. Social-political or theological agendas (often unacknowledged) have inevitably accompanied these quests and their resultant portraits of Jesus. With the emergence of black theology in the United States in the 1960s and Latin American and other liberation *theologies in the 1970s, classical Christology increasingly came to be regarded as either irrelevant metaphysically or dangerous politically, as a legitimation of dominating *power relations. Instead, these new theologies focused on the historical Jesus as liberator and source of *empowerment for those struggling against injustice and *oppression.

Black and liberation theologies and Christologies emphasized the sociol-political context of faith and the centrality of liberating *praxis for Christian life. But their analyses of *race and class oppression often failed to attend to the presence and experience of women. Feminist theology, with its explicit commitment to the full humanity and well-being of women, offered a corrective to this myopia but suffered from short-sightedness of its own: the assumption that the experience of the relatively privileged white women who predominated in feminist movements was an adequate description of all women's experience and the basis for doing theology.

Confronted by the realities of *difference and the increasingly strong voices of womanist, *mujerista,* and Asian, African, and Latin American women theologians, white feminists have come to recognize the limitations of their own experience, the particularity of women's lives, and the complexity of analyzing the interconnection of oppressions within which *sexism is a multivalent factor. A multiplicity of feminist theologies has developed in the past decade, sharing some common foundations and goals but specified in the context of concrete communities of struggle and accountability. When these theologies turn their attention to the subject of Christology, they do so in relation to the historical issues of classical Christology; the developments of black, liberation, and other contemporary theologies; and the particularities of women's experiences of oppression and resistance. There are a variety of approaches to feminist-womanist Christologies.

Decentering the Classical *Tradition

The Maleness of Jesus. Mary Daly's (1973) *naming of "christolatry" and denial of women's need for a savior and Rosemary Radford Ruether's (1981) pointed posing of the question "Can a male savior help women?" were early defining moments in the feminist discussion of Christology. Daly rejected classical Christology as damaging to women, and she found no value in attempting to reconstruct the male symbol of Jesus. Ruether (1983) refocused the issues of classical Christology and redirected attention to the historical Jesus, understood as a messianic prophet who critiqued structures of oppression, including *patriarchy, and whose praxis was liberating and socially transformative. She regarded Jesus' maleness as non-normative, but did not resolve the methodological issue of how to construct a nonsexist Christology, suggesting androgynous or spirit Christologies as alternative possibilities. Jesus is the Christ, but he is not the exclusive or final *revelation of redeemed and redeeming humanity.

Jesus-Sophia. Elisabeth Schüssler Fiorenza offered a feminist theological reconstruction of Christian origins (hence of christological beginnings) in *In Memory of Her* (1983). Jesus was *Sophia's prophet, proclaiming a vision of the *basileia* (kingdom/reign) of God that engendered a *discipleship of equals; the community's praxis of inclusive wholeness subverted patriarchal relations of *domination in empire and household. Despite the subsequent repatriarchalization of Christianity, Schüssler Fiorenza sees Jesus and the movement gathered around him as a possible prototype for women struggling for *liberation today. In *Jesus: Miriam's Child, Sophia's Prophet* (1994), she further develops the issues and implications of Sophia Christology for a feminist critical practice of transformation.

Wisdom/Sophia traditions are also a source for Elizabeth Johnson's reconceptualizing of the triune God in *She Who Is.* Jesus-Sophia is Wisdom made flesh, the compassionate presence of God in the words and deeds of Jesus as he teaches, heals, and calls women and men into inclusive table community. After his death and resurrection, he is known to be the Christ and the community continues his redeeming and liberating work. Returning to Sophia as the interpretive symbol of Jesus the Christ overcomes sexist Christology, Johnson claims, by shattering the connection between maleness and divinity in the mystery of God, the humanity of Jesus, and the reality of Christ.

Contextualizing Women's Experience of Jesus

Black Women's Experience. While acknowledging the feminist critique of classical Christology, Jacquelyn Grant took feminist theology and Christology to task in *White Women's Christ and Black Women's Jesus* (1989) for being white and racist, inadequate for black women. Instead she proposed a womanist Christology beginning from a tridimensional analysis of black women's experience of race, sex, and class oppression and the meaning of Jesus in their lives. In the womanist tradition, Jesus is divine co-sufferer who identifies with the sufferings of black women; Jesus is God, hence white people are not; Jesus Christ is black, and as "least among the least" Christ is a black woman.

Kelly Brown Douglas further develops womanist Christology in *The Black Christ* (1994). Her multidimensional analysis of black people's experience includes sexual orientation; her bifocal vision considers the effects of oppressions on the black community and the ways in which the community nurtures oppressions within itself. Both affirming and challenging, the black Christ is found wherever the community is engaged in the struggle for wholeness and is seen particularly in the faces of the poorest black women. His maleness is not essential; he is Christ because of what he did, not because of who he was.

Third-world women from Africa, Asia, and Latin America approach Christology from the dual context of their particular community's history and struggle for liberation and from their experience as women in that community. Although there are differences among them, most of the theologians whose writings are available in the English-speaking world (e.g., in Fabella/Oduyoye) tend to focus on the historical Jesus as liberating in his *ministry, egalitarian in his *relationships with women, and *suffering in *solidarity with the people in each situation of oppression. They emphasize what Jesus does and where Jesus is, not who he is. Western (i.e., white North American/European) feminist critiques of Christology are acknowledged, but neither the questions nor the answers are taken for granted as applicable to non-Western contexts.

Relocating Christology: Christic Community. Any notion of Jesus as savior or hero (including liberator) is rejected by Rita Nakashima Brock in *Journeys by Heart: A Christology of Erotic Power* (1988). Neither does she consider Jesus to be the Christ. Rather, Christology is centered in community and relationship. Jesus is but one participant in the revelation or *embodiment of redemptive community that Brock terms *Christa/Community.* There is no exclusive locus to this redemptive community; wherever the erotic power of "heart" flows in mutual relation, there Christa/Community engenders wholeness, the *healing of brokenheartedness that is salvation.

Shifting the understanding of Jesus' historical context by locating him in the Spirit-driven reign-of-God movement, Mary Rose D'Angelo views Jesus as a prophet in a community of shared prophecy that resists imperial rule and expects the establishment of *justice for the impoverished and marginalized of Israel.

In addition to the issues and approaches noted here, two concerns are of particular importance for the ongoing work of feminist, womanist, and liberation Christologies: Christian *anti-Judaism's classical christological roots and its feminist manifestations, and religious *pluralism and christological exclusivism.

Brock [1988]; D'Angelo [1992]; Douglas [1994]; Fabella/Oduyoye [1988]; Grant [1989]; Johnson [1992]; Ruether [1983];

Schüssler Fiorenza [1983]; Schüssler Fiorenza [1994]

FRANCINE CARDMAN

Church Histories** Church history as a historical and theological discipline in the European and North American contexts has traditionally organized itself around a standard periodization (early, medieval, Reformation, modern, and American) and a narrative structure largely determined by denominational or confessional identities. Wherever the story began (e.g., with conflicting claims about the early period, for Roman Catholic and Orthodox churches; with the Reformation, for mainline Protestant churches), it led to the present institutional reality through varying degrees of continuity or discontinuity with other periods and churches.

Despite particular variations, elements of a master narrative were at work in all versions. The story moved quickly from its Jewish origins (usually ignoring the significance of its setting in Roman-occupied Palestine), through the Gentile* mission and the encounter with Greco-Roman culture (conceived of as the universalization of the *Gospel), to a focus on Western Christianity separated from the Orthodox and other (generally unmentioned) churches of the East, through the Middle Ages (a golden age of faith or a period of decadence and decline) and the Reformation (the recovery of the gospel or the shattering of church unity), and to the present via the Enlightenment, the age of revolutions, and the rapid missionary expansion of both Catholic and Protestant Christianity to the New World, Africa, and Asia (the success of evangelization or, more recently, a means of colonial imperialism). The ideas, institutions, and personalities of dominant males were key to the narrative's telling.

Changing Historiographies. Recent changes in the meaning and practice of both "history" and "church" have begun to challenge the plausibility and even the possibility of such a master narrative and to lay the groundwork for feminist revisionings of church history.

In "secular" historiography, the increasing influence of social history and the emergence of women's history and gender studies have shifted the focus from a relatively limited range of experience determined by dominant males to the wide-ranging description and analysis of the everyday experiences of nonelites and women, the silenced and *marginalized. Because it demands attention to particularity and context, social history leads to a multiplicity of local and nontotalizing histories. Women's history likewise interrupts master narratives, though initially it tended to repeat the patterns of *androcentric historiography through its "compensatory" efforts to retrieve the history of notable or exceptional women. Now it looks for the historical roots of "feminist consciousness" in women's awareness of themselves as a subordinate group and in their efforts at emancipation (Lerner); examines the historical development and social construction of gender and the *power dynamics of gender relations; analyzes women's experience through a multifaceted lens of *race, class, sex, and sexual orientation; contests and destabilizes the categories of historiography.

The changing historical circumstances of contemporary Christianity have begun to alter the meaning and locus of "church" in the writing of church history. The ongoing shift in the center of gravity from "first world" to "third world" Christianity makes it impossible to continue writing church history from a presumed Euro-American center. At the same time, *third world churches are beginning to write histories of their own that are not simply a history of missions or of Western cultural expansion and in which the classical debates and historical divisions of first-world churches are not the central or defining questions (EATWOT). Globally, Christianity is a minority religion. These realities, coupled with advances in the intra-Christian theological discussion, are shaping the beginnings of an ecumenical church historiography (Vischer). "Church" in these emerging histories is identified as the people (rather than clergy or institutional leadership), particularly the poor and the oppressed, including women; "history" is local, regional, contextual, and takes into account social, political, and economic as well as religious factors. In each of these cases, the standard periodization is inadequate, and a new interpretive chronological framework must be engendered from within the new perspectives.

Feminist Church Histories. Feminist (re)writings of church history take place in the context of the developments in general historiography and the changing circumstances of contemporary churches outlined above. They are related as well to the emergence of feminist *historical theology. Presuppositions of feminist church historiography include its global and *ecumenical orientation, its local and contextual embodiment, and its commitment to a multifaceted analysis of sex and gender in relation to class, race, and sexual orientation. Periodization is an open question even when the standard categories are resorted to for the sake of convenience (as they are below). The rapidly increasing number of studies focused on particular experiences and practices (e.g., *asceticism, the regulation of *marriage) in specific places and times, especially in relation to women and nonelites, makes for a complexity that challenges any attempt at reconstructing an overarching master narrative. Here it is possible to give only an indication of some of the advances and achievements of feminist church historiography in the past two decades.

1. *Christian Origins/Late Antiquity.* In contrast to the androcentric church history that considers only males as *apostles and disciples of Jesus, Elisabeth Schüssler Fiorenza (1983) offers a reconstruction of Christian origins in which women play a central role as apostles, *prophets, and leaders in a *discipleship of equals. This egalitarianism was lost as Christianity expanded into the Greco-Roman world and conformed itself to patriarchal social norms, restricting the public role of women and constructing a theology of women's subordination to men. In the early stages of compensatory women's history, the fourth-century ascetic movement was often looked to as a counterpoint to the patriarchalizing of Christianity because it offered women the opportunity for spiritual *equality with men, including equality in martyrdom. Extensive research on women's experience of asceticism by Elizabeth Clark (1986) and others has since revised this optimistic estimate. A more nuanced understanding reflects on the ambiguity of women's advancement through adherence to male-defined norms of virginity and of the role of class privilege in allowing some women to achieve considerable *freedom through asceticism. Ross Kraemer's (1992) study of women's religions in the Greco-Roman world makes possible comparisons among pagan, Jewish, and Christian women.

2. *Medieval Christianity.* Women's religious communities and notable figures within them (e.g., Hildegard of Bingen, the Beguines) have been obvious subjects for feminist historical scholarship. The three volumes of *Medieval Religious Women* (Nichols/Shank) include essays on a variety of communities, locales, and forms of religious life. The bibliography in this area is extensive and still growing. Caroline Bynum goes beyond the history of institutions and exceptional women in this period to explore the gendered meaning of the *body, particularly the female body, in medieval religion. In *Fragmentation and Redemption* (1991), as in her earlier works, she studies texts (the use of maternal and other female imagery in medieval religious writings), religious practices (women's experience of fasting and eucharistic devotion), and artistic representations (of the body of Christ, of female bodies).

Looking at another kind of bodily experience, Clarissa Atkinson investigates the construction of motherhood as *ideology and institution in *The Oldest Vocation: Christian Motherhood in the Middle Ages* (1991). She argues that the social and theological meaning of motherhood changed repeatedly in conjunction with changing emphases on the motherhood of Mary and the humanity of Jesus, the importance of spiritual versus physical motherhood, the recognition of women saints who were also *mothers, and the role of the *family in the religious and social agendas of both Protestantism and Catholicism. Other historians are pursuing aspects of the everyday life of medieval Christians, such as *work, the household economy, family structure, and the regulation of *sexuality.

3. *Reformations: Protestant and Catholic.* In a pioneering and now classic essay, the late Joan Kelly pointedly asked, "Did women have a renaissance?" and concluded that they did not (1984, 19–50). She argued that in relation to the increased opportunities for men, women's freedom and status actually declined during this period. Feminist historians of the church have begun to ask similar questions in regard to women and the Reformation: Did ideas about women, marriage, family, and society change? Did women's actual situation change? Did women play a role in the Reformation? Revising earlier estimates of the positive changes in women's status wrought by the Reformation, the historians represented in *Women in Reformation and Counter-Reformation Europe* (Marshall) come to more mixed conclusions. The new note of positive valuation of marriage and family life in the Reformers' theologies was muted by the patriarchal model of domesticity they put into practice; public and private spheres were more sharply delineated and economic opportunities for women declined. Any improvements in women's actual status were more often brought about by the institutional and political changes set in motion by the Reformation than by its theology. New forms of charitable institutions offered both Protestant and Catholic women opportunities for activism, and Catholic women especially found new expressions of spirituality or deepened old ones.

4. *American Religious History.* The extensive selection of primary sources and the accompanying interpretive introductions in the three volumes of *Women and Religion in America* (Ruether/Keller) provide a documentary history of women's involvement in religious bodies and expressions in North America from the colonial period to the twentieth century. The definition of religion is broad, and the range of communities and experiences represented is wide: mainline, radical, and marginalized traditions; Protestant, Catholic, Jewish, white ethnic, black, and Native American communities; Holiness, Pentecostal, Wesleyan, Puritan, and revivalist churches; movements for women's right to preach and be ordained, to teach, and to exercise lay leadership; utopian and social reform movements. Ruether and Keller's work calls attention to the manifold sources and materials available for the writing of multicultural, feminist church histories in the North American context.

Women's history is not in itself feminist history but an essential basis for it. As feminists continue to study women's historical experiences of Christianity, the dominant narrative diminishes and is replaced by multiple narratives that are shaped by the fundamental questions of feminist historiography: Who are the subjects writing (church) history? What are its appropriate sources and contents? How should its development through time be punctuated? Out of the one, there will be many feminist church histories.

Atkinson [1991]; Bynum [1991]; Clark [1986]; EATWOT [1985]; Kraemer [1992]; Lerner [1993]; Marshall [1989]; Nichols/Shank [1984–87]; Ruether/Keller [1981–86]; Vischer [1982]

FRANCINE CARDMAN

Church Ministries and Worship**

Historically, the church has been a *hierarchical institution whose leadership has been in the hands of males, with male control of the language, space, and functions of church life. A patriarchal system of thought and social organization permeated the functions of ministry. Traditionally, these ministries included maintaining *faith and *doctrines, educating the faithful, converting the nonbelievers, conducting worship, preaching the *gospel, and serving the needy. In different church traditions and in different periods, some of these ministries have been more important than others.

Today the ministries of the church include religious *education, *pastoral care and nurture, service, worship (*liturgy and ritual, *preaching, *sacraments), church leadership, *mission, and evangelism. Within specific communities of faith, feminists are examining these functions of *ministry, how they should be carried out, and what new forms of church life need to be developed. Feminists call for a diversity of forms of worship and church ministries. *Contextualization of form, content, and process is critical in honoring the diverse reality of women's lives.

The unique contribution feminists bring to these ministries of the church is an underlying concern about how these ministries attend to the lived experiences of women, to the oppressions and injustices that women endure, and to the intersection with all *marginalized. Constructing church ministries that empower women to live out their faith is also of key importance.

Feminists are challenging all hierarchical forms of relationship, traditional leadership roles, the distinction between clergy and laity, and the forms, language, and images of worship and spirituality that are not inclusive. Definitions of *family life and gender roles that undergird religious education, the assumption that there is any one set of doctrines that governs true worship, and any exclusive claim to the truth are also being critiqued.

Feminists are constructing church ministries that attend to new models of leadership as *partnership, the formation of women's liturgical and spiritual communities (*Women-Church), and the interconnectedness of human lives with all of creation. Serious attention is also given to the contributions and challenges of diversity in relationship to *race, *culture, age, class, sexual orientation, and physical abilities.

Based on feminists' practice of church ministries, certain commitments are emerging from what actually contributes to *justice and the well-being of women. These commitments have been named in various ways and are often interconnected. Because of the importance of contextualization, the commitments have different forms and different emphases. However, they are beginning to provide insights for church ministries and worship from feminist perspectives.

1. Leadership for the ordering of community life is *nonhierarchical and shared.* It does not reside in one person or one office. Feminists are opposing the clericalism of the church and seek new ways of being in community that are genuinely collegial. Ministry is the work of the whole people and is not relegated to the paid or ordained representatives. Partnership has become an important *metaphor for leadership. It includes the abilities to learn and to be vulnerable, changed, and challenged, as well as the ability to share one's expertise in nondominating ways. It affirms the *priesthood of all believers, including children, and claims that every believer has a *call and vocation. As feminists explore the meaning of the priesthood of all believers, the traditional meanings of *ordination are being challenged. Some feminists are questioning the validity of the office itself.

2. Church ministries and worship attend to the **empowerment of women* through the ordinary, particular and diverse stories of their lives. Educational programs, models of pastoral care, creative worship design, and forms of ser-

vice, etc., are developed to enable women to participate fully, provide leadership, and utilize their gifts and *authority for ministry. Narrative is one of the basic modes of education: telling the stories of our lives and lifting up the "silenced" lives and voices of history. The sacred worth of each person's life is valued and *differences of race, class, physical ability, age, sexual orientation, etc., are seen as positive contributions to the life of the community. To facilitate empowerment, feminists use *inclusive language that involves nonsexist as well as emancipatory language and images.

3. Church ministries and worship arise out of *an embodied faith* that emerges from a theological commitment to an immanent God who dwells within us and the world around us. The transcendent God as "Holy Other" is not totally disregarded, but emphasis is placed on God's *immanence. Embodiment in ministry honors and celebrates our bodily existence in this world. All that we know through our bodies is valued as much as that which we know through our minds. Physical expression and the active participation of our whole selves are encouraged in worship and education. In feminist liturgies the life cycles of women, as well as the abuses that are suffered by women's bodies, are shared in community within sacred, safe space.

Embodiment also involves the visual and physical setting where these ministries take place. Attention is given to countering the messages of *hierarchy and *domination and creating space for mutuality in the environments where we worship, learn, and participate in pastoral care. Embodiment also takes seriously the connection between spirituality and *sexuality, so that the totality of our lives can be present in our ministries.

4. Church ministries and worship *shun the notion that there is only one way*, one "right" religion, one theory that has ultimate "truth." These ministries support a range of theologies and possibilities. Human beings live with the ambiguity that comes when we know that we cannot absolutize particular notions of truth. Most important, we believe in continued *revelation. Feminists critique that which has been handed down to humanity from the past, try to be honest about the messiness of our real lives, and value experimentation as well as self-criticism as we explore new ways of being in our varied ministries.

5. As we embrace theologies and experiences of life that are different from our own, we also *widen what we consider to be the *canon* in many areas. In pastoral care, traditional diagnoses are being reexamined in light of Western culture's *oppression of women and others. Interpretations of the sacraments (particularly the *Eucharist in the Christian church) that have been paramount and beyond critique are now being challenged. Feminists are experimenting with alternative forms of worship and preaching. Exegesis is no longer limited to the commentaries of white, western men. Instead, the writings of women and those whose opinions have long been silenced are becoming authoritative as well. The canon of sacred texts is being broadened to include texts, dramas, and works of art from other cultures and other periods. Feminists are committed to a faith that helps humans live in ambiguity, resist absolutes, and still act courageously.

6. All of creation is included in the work of ministry and worship. This means that humans cannot separate the secular from the sacred, the personal from the political, or other parts of creation from the human. It means that we struggle to understand *the connections of our lives with all of creation.* All old divisions have to be examined to see if connections exist and how the relationality of life informs our concrete ministries and worship. Denominational structures are called into question, and feminists seek ways to honor ecumenical and interfaith work and *dialogue. Church ministries of care and mission seek to understand systemic and institutional forms of oppression that try to separate the material from the spiritual and the sa-

cred from the social and political dimensions of life. Feminists seek ministries that understand that *healing has communal dimensions and that for healing to occur, humans have to confront systemic and institutional forms of oppression in personal and social settings.

7. The service and mission of church ministries and of worship life involve the *power to imagine what is not yet:* a world where justice for women and all of creation is possible. This work is the active engagement in *care and justice for all of creation. It is work that refuses to dichotomize individual pain and structural injustice but seeks to address the interconnections and intersections. Prophetic preaching paints pictures of this new world and calls the community to active ministries that work for just change. Pastoral care is involved in the healing of individuals in relationship. It confronts all that violates lives. It includes nurturing life in community so that individual gifts may be used for communal healing.

The meaning of feminist church ministries and worship is discovered in the concrete action and reflection of communities of faith and struggle who search for justice for all. Every year, more and more resources are published that support and encourage feminist ministries. In the area of worship there are rituals designed for separate feminist liturgy and ritual (Women-Church) groups and liturgical resources for use in traditional worship services. Feminists are creating their own music for liturgical celebrations and writing new, inclusive words to old, familiar hymn tunes. In addition to liturgical resources, the fields of preaching, pastoral care, and religious education have emerging resources that are based in feminist theology.

Elkins [1994]; May [1991]; Procter-Smith [1990]; Procter-Smith/Walton [1993]; Rhodes [1987]; Ruether [1985]; Russell [1993]; Weidman [1985]; Winter/Lummis/Stokes [1994]

LYNN N. RHODES and KATHLEEN M. BLACK

Classism *Classism* describes the practice of hierarchically dividing up human societies on the basis of economic status, rank, caste, or estate and of perpetuating such inequities through the economic, political, symbolic, and discursive levers available to the economically powerful. In feminist theologies, classism, along with *racism, *sexism, *heterosexism, and militarism, is ranked as one of the major forms of systemic *evil to be eradicated through a liberating *praxis and a radical restructuring of the economic, social, and political order.

The term is derived from the concept of *class,* a general term in sociological discourse subsuming a variety of systemic economic distinctions among people. In Marxian theory, from which much feminist theory derived its initial impetus, the term *class* assumed a more technical and pejorative meaning. It referred to the basic antagonistic division in capitalist societies between those who own the means of production (capitalists, or the bourgeoisie) and others (workers, or the proletariat) who are compelled to "sell their labor power" to the capitalists in exchange for a wage or salary. In Marxian theory, as capitalism developed and expanded across the globe, swallowing up traditional societies and altering systems of production and consumption, it transformed more and more of humanity into the proletariat—people condemned to earn their livelihood under the control and direction and at the mercy of the capitalist.

Contemporary Marxian theorists have added intermediary strata to the basic bipolar schema elaborated by Marx, suggesting that those who work in professional, managerial occupations occupy an ambiguous status between owners and workers. Lacking the ultimate control over the production process exercised by capitalists, they nevertheless serve to justify and reinforce the basic class system.

Class divisions are inherently unjust because they allow one group of people ultimately to control and exploit the lives of others—not only economically but also politically, culturally, and even spiritually. The Marxian concept of alienation, fostered by the capitalist system of production through which the industrial worker is estranged from his/her fellow workers, from the process and object of his/her work, and ultimately from his/her own powers of creation, has been likened to the Christian condition of *sin, or radical estrangement from God.

Although Marx traced the origins of all class divisions to the natural division of labor in the family, based on differences of sex and age, feminist theorists have criticized *Marxian theory for reducing all contemporary societal inequity and injustice to the basic class relations of the capitalist production system. In their view, women occupy a unique space in the social world. They share the class conditions of the men (fathers and husbands) to whom they have been historically attached and, as they have moved into the wage-labor force in their own right, the conditions that attach to the particular sector of the labor market in which they find themselves. But they cannot be totally defined by their class status.

Women's lives have been defined and delimited not only by the capitalist mediated system of production but by gendered systems of reproduction, *sexuality, and the socialization of children, inherited from traditional societies but interpenetrated and restructured in differing ways by capitalism. Moreover, because women are found in every *culture and *race, they have also been delimited by a variety of racial and ethnic caste systems. Each of these systems combines with the others in complex ways in differing historical eras and cultures. For example, in contemporary U.S. society, "racial/ethnic oppression and sexism are constitutive elements of class dynamics" (Mud Flower Collective, 77). Thus for feminist theologians, the eradication of classist systems is a necessary, though not sufficient, condition for the emergence of genuine human *equality and *community.

Marx [1977]; Mitchell [1971]; Mud Flower Collective [1985]; Soelle/Cloyes [1984]

SHEILA D. COLLINS

Cognitive Dissonance Cognitive dissonance is a theory in American *psychology, first expounded by Leon Festinger in 1957, that refers to the state of *conflict produced when assumptions, beliefs, or attitudes are contradicted by new information or evidence. To reduce their feeling of discomfort, individuals try to ignore or reconcile the differences, screening out upsetting experiences (one thinks of incest victims) or reinforcing existing beliefs by overzealous assertions.

The discomfort or dissonance produced by feminist and third-world interpretations of scripture for persons hitherto exposed only to traditional (male-centered, first-world) interpretations may result in denying the validity of the former; however, it may also lead to new "ahas." Cognitive-dissonance theory may account for resistance to the use of *inclusive language in church but may also be instrumental in "jarring" persons into realizing why they can no longer sing, "Rise up, O men of God."

While psychology's concern has been to observe and test hypotheses on the phenomenon of dissonance reduction in relation to mental health, feminist theology and the feminist movement make use of cognitive dissonance to raise consciousness in order to critique *patriarchal thought, traditions, and practices in church and society. Confrontation with the discrepancy or dissonance between rhetoric about human worth and rights on the one hand and unjust, sexist social arrangements on the other, combined with the possibility of alternatives, could spur attempts at concrete change even where such conditions for centuries have been only endured and lamented as "natural" and inevitable, as, for instance, in *han*-ridden women of traditional *Confucian societies. As long as the world is patriarchally ordered, there is a need to be critical of all assumptions, values, and definitions (Lerner) and thus to live with and, indeed, invite the tension of cognitive dissonance in the continuing struggle against *sexism, *racism, and all other forms of *oppression that diminish human life.

Bartky [1990]; Goldenson [1970]; Lerner [1986]; Wickland/Brehm [1976]

GREER ANNE WENH-IN NG

Colonization The concept of colonization has been used in theological discourse as a category by which to analyze social constructions of *domination and subordination. Colonization can take place only in the area of social *relationships of *power. Its reference points are the interaction among various social groups in any society and the result of that interaction. An example of colonization can be seen in the massive European invasion of the Americas, which was accomplished by means of genocide against indigenous peoples, the pillaging of lands and properties, the rape and violation of native women, and the destruction of native intellectual creations, in order to impose European symbols, languages, and social institutions.

Critical theologies of *liberation have determined that past and present colonial systems, along with the conceptual models by which they are supported, have been constructed by social elites who occupy positions of power and control, in order to impose their own interests. Christian theology has often been used to impose the normative position of this Eurocentric, white, male *culture. The social organization resulting from these models, in addition to being profoundly unequal and *hierarchical, turns out to be conflictive and violent because it is imposed by force against the interests and needs of other social groups. Historical experience indicates that colonization condemns women, nonwhite races, and indigenous cultures to a position of sustained disadvantage. As a heuristic category, this concept of colonization serves to elaborate theologically an alternative vision of society that supports the self-determination of women, the anthropological equivalence of excluded groups, and the sociopolitical recognition of women of *marginalized races and cultures.

Aquino [1993]; Gutiérrez [1973]; Oduyoye [1986]

MARÍA PILAR AQUINO

Community Inclusive access and egalitarian structure above all characterize the conviction, if not always the practice, of contemporary Euro-American Christian feminist work on and in community. For many Euro-American feminists, Christian and non-Christian, feminism is first experienced in small communities of women marked by mutual respect, *solidarity, and caring. The personal value and political and spiritual *power of such communities for the women who participate in them makes them potentially revolutionary sites of social transformation. For Christian Euro-American feminists, the centrality of community is a point of both connection with and departure from the malestream Christian *tradition from which we emerge.

From New Testament texts and their feminist interpretations, we know that the Jewish community which surrounded Jesus was transformed by the contested decision to admit non-Jews. House churches and other small communities that were loosely associated and whose membership and leadership exhibited egalitarian characteristics were followed by early signs of the formalization of belief interpreted as *doctrine and the *hierarchicalization of leadership roles into offices. Christian community was understood as the locus of the ongoing *incarnation of the risen Christ; Paul's *metaphor of the community as "the body of Christ" prominently expresses the *immanence of Christ in the community. At the same time, disputes regarding the nature and the boundaries of communities are also discernable. Thus, from the beginning, embodied communities have been central to the practice of Christianity, while the concept was, and is, complex, contested, and multivalent.

The European and Euro-American malestream tradition of theology and *ethics consistently identifies *Christian community* and *church,* whatever it may specifically mean by those terms. Euro-American feminists have a much more complex relationship to "the church," since it remains largely a *patriarchal institution. Some women leave the church because they judge it to be essentially incompatible with feminist community. Others stay and attempt to dismantle patriarchal claims regarding Christian community and to reconstitute those communities through and by the values of inclusivity and egalitarianism, values that resonate with and are enfleshed in parts and pieces of the Christian tradition itself. Other persons and groups remain "within the church" and also gather in feminist communities such as *Women-Church to engage in new, specifically women-affirming structural and liturgical practices. It is also the case that some openly *lesbian feminist Christians, such as Carter Heyward, are establishing their place at the margins but within the borders of institutions whose ambivalence about their presence renders that presence itself an act of protest and a catalyst for change in the direction of feminist convictions.

Within this wide range of *relationships between feminist Christians on the one hand and their traditions and contemporary Christian institutions on the other, there is agreement, at least in principle, regarding the necessity of inclusivity and egalitarianism. The commitment to inclusivity often includes discussions of the value of diversity of various sorts as a feature of Christian feminist community itself. Euro-American Christian feminists' difficulty in embodying a commitment to diversity does not dilute that commitment but rather teaches more about its complexity. They are assisted in their analysis of *classism and *racism by the critiques of their sisters of color. Commitments to egalitarian communal structures commonly take the form of a rejection of "clericalism" and the implementation of shared leadership with the rotation of role assignments, so that tendencies toward hierarchical, supremacist structures do not develop into practices.

Finally, convictions regarding inclusivity and egalitarianism as constitutive features of feminist Christian community provide impetus for those values to be embodied by feminist Christians in all personal, social, and political contexts. Christian feminist community is found in the embrace of spirituality and the commitment to and struggle for *justice for all creatures and for *creation itself. The nature of Christian feminist community pushes beyond any communal walls that might exist and toward all those who are excluded and oppressed by social and political structures, of whatever kinds.

Eugene et al., in Daly [1994]; Harrison [1985]; Ruether [1985]; Russell [1993]; Schüssler Fiorenza [1992a]

SALLY B. PURVIS

Compassion Literally "feeling with," compassion's prominence in the theological vocabulary of Christian feminists has several sources. First, feminism operates from an appreciation for *embodiment and with an emphasis on the fecundity of *emotion and passion in feminist theology and *ethics. With its attention to relationality, mutuality, and *solidarity as theological ethical values, Christian feminist theology examines and describes the epistemological richness of emotion. Furthermore, because Christian theology and ethics are concerned with inscribing and supporting right relations in all human interactions, they encourage passionate connection and mutual feeling among humans as agents and instruments of the struggle for *justice. In contrast to some patriarchal construals of justice and knowledge as objective and detached, feminist theology and ethics stress the importance and obligatory nature of our connectedness, and compassion is an important component of that connectedness.

Within this overall framework, compassion is being redescribed by feminists not only as the capacity to be moved by the pain or joy of another; compassion also denotes an important source of the energy we need to respond—to right a wrong, when we can; to protest when we are impotent to effect change; and to support the conditions for flourishing that we observe. Compassion, in this view, is a robust concept that includes not only motivation but movement.

Finally, compassion is at the heart of feminist descriptions of God. In contrast to religious and secular versions of God as an "unmoved mover," religious feminists, including Christians, describe God as being moved by and present in human *suffering and in efforts to alleviate it and the conditions in which it is bred. In part a response to the horrors of contemporary times and in part an outgrowth of experiences of a loving God, compassion is a central feature of a feminist image of the Divine.

Fabella/Oduyoye [1988]; Farley [1990]; Heyward [1984]; Johnson [1993]

SALLY B. PURVIS

Conflict The *Oxford English Dictionary* defines conflict as a fight, a battle, a (prolonged) struggle between opposing forces; fighting strife; the clashing of variant or opposed principles, beliefs, etc. This traditional understanding of conflict always involves a struggle between persons or groups in which the participants seek to overpower one another. In the *patriarchal view, conflict is understood in terms of *domination, submission, and *power *over* others. Each individual or group is encouraged to accrue power and resources for itself. This type of conflict is costly in that one person or group gains and the other loses, gaining nothing. Such conflict entails one who wins and one who loses resources, respect, honor, or life.

Conflict can be beneficial when it corrects an injustice. Most women, however, dislike and avoid conflict because they believe they possess fewer resources and therefore will lose in a conflict. Feminists have proposed other understandings of conflict. In her helpful book *Toward a New Psychology of Women* (1976), Jean Baker Miller states that conflict is not necessarily threatening or destructive. She asserts that within a framework of inequality, the existence of conflict is denied and the means to engage openly in conflict are excluded (125–33).

Feminists have examined the issue of *agency to further define *destructive* and *constructive* conflict. Miller defines agency as "being active, using all of one's resources, but without the connotation of aggression" (120). She proposes defining power as the capacity to produce change, thus replacing the idea of power as dominion or mastery, implying "power over" (116). In this sense, conflict between individuals or groups with equal power may benefit both parties. Feminists are working to shift women and men to this new understanding and practice of conflict. They assert that it is important for women to engage in conflict, rather than avoid it, and to work to function with agency and *equality in conflict.

Harrison [1985]; Haugk [1988]; Jordan et al. [1991]; Miller [1976]

LEE MCGEE

Confucianism Founded by Master K'ung (551–479 B.C.E.), codified and established as state *orthodoxy during the first century C.E., and recodified and expanded over the centuries, Confucianism should not be equated with Chinese *culture. Its accommodation to competing religious traditions, particularly

*Buddhism, and its historic geographical extension beyond Chinese national boundaries to Korea, Japan, and parts of Southeast Asia evince a remarkably adaptable yet conservative cultural system.

The ideal Confucian figure is one who, through a process of *education and critical self-reflection, cultivates the ultimate *virtue of *jen*, "humaneness" or "cohumanity." The perfected person fulfills the five *relationships (ruler–subject, parent–child, husband–wife, older–younger, and between peers) so that all interactions manifest the transformative aesthetic qualities of ritual action and thus "mirror heaven" in harmony, efficacy, and completeness.

Confucius (Master K'ung) said little about women, and early texts do not deny women access to *education or suggest that they cannot cultivate virtue or become ritually refined. It was with the systematic grafting of *yin–yang cosmological theories onto the core of Confucian ideas during the Han dynasty (second century B.C.E. to second century C.E.) that gender *hierarchy suffused the *tradition. Han cosmology hierarchized complementary traits, perhaps to justify the qualities of the yang ruler over the yin ruled; consequently, yang (light, strength, growth, life, male, masculine) was given primacy over yin (shadow, weakness, decay, death, female, feminine). The human heart/mind (*hsin*) had both yang rationality and yin emotionality, but as the latter caused confusion, yang was more highly regarded and morally superior. Pre-Confucian notions of patrilineality and patrilocality thus fused with the imperative to educate, cultivate, and control the self—to the detriment of traits and persons associated with yin. Women are not incapable of cultivating knowledge and virtue, but the *essentializing tendency to associate women with yin facilitated their denigration.

That women cannot be effectively imagined or imaged as "authentically human" renders the ideal figures of the *chün-tzu* ("gentleman" or "superior person") and the *sheng-jen* ("sage" or "completed person") inapplicable to women, a disposition reinforced by covert linguistic marking of these terms as masculine. Rather than "going out" to become "superior persons," women are enjoined to "stay in" and fulfill domestic relationships as virtuous wives and *mothers. From the Han dynasty onward, handbooks for women promulgated the "three obediences" and the "four virtues": the former historically understood as requiring a woman to follow her father before *marriage, her husband when married, and her son if widowed, and the latter demanding of women morality, skill in handcrafts, and attention to personal appearance and language. Despite historical instances wherein women were (posthumously) declared *chün-tzu*, female virtue was typically recognized in terms of chaste *widowhood or filiality toward in-laws.

Whether labeled *traditional values* (Korea, Japan, and Taiwan) or *feudal values* (the People's Republic of China), Confucian concepts of ancestor reverence, *family primacy, and differential labor as defining the spousal relationship form barriers to cultural transformations promoting full and/or equal recognition of women. Confucianism is the omnipresent patriarchal partner. Even in a religiously diverse society such as Korea, where 70 percent of all Christian church members are women, few hold leadership positions, ordained or otherwise.

Current feminist tasks include recovering of women's histories, reinterpreting texts and commentarial traditions, analyzing gender-biased language, and studying childhood socialization in sex-role differences. In dialectical negotiation between increasingly Western-nuanced Confucianism(s) and increasingly indigenized feminism(s), the preservation yet rethinking of certain ideals is underway. Young, educated women, even after marriage, are using their significant economic power to subsidize their brothers' education or parents' retirement, thereby altering the perception of female filiality to the natal family from an obligation diminished by wedding vows to a lifelong possibility.

Feminist transformations of Confucianism will require the separation of centuries of social convention from religious necessity and the reenvisioning of complementary relationships without essentializing images of woman, either as unrestrained and threatening or as bound head, hips, and feet to her "shadowy" nature.

Guisso/Johannessen [1981]; Kelleher, in Sharma [1987]

VIVIAN-LEE NYITRAY

Conscience The Latin word for conscience is *conscientia,* "knowing with, knowing within oneself" (Gk, *syneidēsis*). It denotes a multidimensional, uniquely human capacity for perceiving, judging, and deciding in relation to moral value. In Jewish scriptures the equivalent term (translated into Greek) is *kardia,* "heart." In the NT, *syneidēsis* is used frequently by Paul, the Greek philosophical term synthesized with the Jewish idea of *kardia* to forge a distinctive Christian moral concept.

Christian ethicists understand conscience in three senses: (1) most fundamentally, as an aspect of personhood experienced as an interior "law . . . written on [the] heart" (Rom. 2:15), a personal dynamism and response toward moral value; (2) as the process of analysis and deliberation concerning the right, or good, in particular cases, requiring honest, receptive *dialogue with sources of moral wisdom (scripture, religious traditions, other funds of descriptive and normative insight); (3) as the event of moral *judgment and decision in the concrete. In its third sense, conscience has been considered an absolute subjective guide: one must always follow it, and external authorities may not force a person to violate it. Theologians have disputed the seat of conscience, some locating it in practical reason (Aquinas), others in the will and affections (Duns Scotus). Scholars today argue that *conscience integrates reason and *emotion* to reflect the "heart," or inner core, of the person alluded to in scripture.

Contemporary religious ethicists employ psychological theory to distinguish conscience from Freudian superego. The former is an active interior motivation that seeks out genuine value; the latter is an exterior motivation, a socially inculcated monitor revolving around concern for external approval, motivating by way of *guilt and *shame. Psychological studies of moral development have also shed light on conscience formation and the *care ethic. In both formation and enactment, conscience is revealed as supremely personal and intensely communal.

Feminist *ethics originates in women's awareness of disparity between traditional interpretations of their identities, capabilities, and roles and their own experiences of themselves and their lives (Farley), thereby providing a singular vantage point and agenda. *Solidarity with women means that, for feminist consciences, the litmus test for moral value is the impact of a perception, judgment, or action on women's well-being. The feminist moral ideal is variously described, e.g., as acknowledgment of women's fully human status; as women's enfranchisement in historically male-reserved spheres; as creative *partnership in transformed domestic and public arenas; as *sisterhood at the margins or outside the boundaries of *patriarchy. In every case, feminist ethicists bring critical questions, emphases, and enhancements to standard analyses of conscience.

First, feminists direct a **hermeneutic of suspicion* against gender subtexts lodged in traditional approaches to conscience. *Misogyny is exposed in assumptions concerning women's weaker apprehension of moral value, their less-rational evaluation process, and their greater tendency to err (hence greater need for [male] authorities); in patterns of social formation that conflate superego with conscience and inculcate in women, more than men, feelings of dependence on approval or of responsibility for the continuance of *relationships; in interpretations of Christian values such as self-sacrifice or chastity as pertaining particularly and inordinately to women.

Second, feminists affirm those features of *traditional accounts* ratified by women's history and experiences, such as the deeply relational yet personal nature of the "knowing with and within" of conscience; the crucial role of *community in shaping and nurturing moral sensibility and evaluative competence; *authority's role as companion, not tyrant; and conscience as integrated, embodied feeling and knowing from the heart.

Finally, feminists are making *transformative inroads* on questions concerning women's and men's moral development and decision-making styles, connections between theological doctrines (e.g., the Trinity) and construals of conscience, and the light cast by women's diverse situations and feminist critical-social theory on bogus versus authentic perceptions of moral value.

Andolsen/Gudorf/Pellauer [1985]; Brown/Gilligan [1992]; Cahill, in LaCugna [1993]; Farley [1986]; Harrison [1985]; Saiving, in Christ/Plaskow [1979]

CHRISTINE FIRER HINZE

Conscientization

Conscientization, or consciousness raising, is a term used to describe the learning process in which groups begin to perceive social, political, or economic *oppression and act to eliminate it. The term comes from the Portuguese *conscientização* and was made popular in the late 1950s and early 1960s by Brazilian educator Paulo Freire. Freire's innovative approach to literacy training among poor peasants encouraged them to "decode" their situation of *poverty in a systematic way in order to do something about it. For Freire, conscientization meant learning to *name* and *change* the world. Only by seeing oneself as subject and therefore as separate from the world can one transform it. Freire believes that once the poor come to perceive "limit situations" as the frontier between being and being more human, they will direct increasingly critical actions toward the elimination of dehumanizing oppression.

An essential part of conscientization is impoverished groups' ability to decode their situations. In *Pedagogy of the Oppressed* (1970), Freire says that humans "*are* because they *are* in a situation, and they *will be more* the more they not only critically reflect upon their existence but critically act upon it" (100). Those who become "conscientized" suddenly see through those myths that perpetuate their oppression. When people realize they are oppressed, they also know they can achieve *liberation by transforming the oppressive situation, a process that can happen again and again.

Influence on Liberation Theology. Freire's method of conscientization had a profound influence on Latin American liberation theology. The "Freire method" provided a model of action for progressive church people; since the 1960s, thousands of pastoral workers have gone to live in barrios or rural villages where they work with the poor in articulating their needs and organizing, often working in Christian base communities.

In the fifteenth anniversary edition of *A Theology of Liberation* (1973/1988), theologian Gustavo Gutiérrez points to Freire's influence: "During the 1950's and 60's we saw the first steps being taken in conscientization, and we saw the poor beginning to organize themselves in the defense of their right to life, in the struggle for dignity and social *justice, and in a commitment to their own liberation" (xxix). He also notes, "It is in the conscientization and resultant organization of poor sectors that rouse the greatest fears and the strongest resistance" (xxiv).

Feminist Consciousness Raising. The process of conscientization can be compared to the process through which women grow in feminist awareness. Feminist consciousness is not merely *freedom *from* *marginalization, oppression, discrimination, and *violence but freedom *for* self-definition, self-affirmation, and self-determination; the recognition of their full humanity and the freedom to exercise that personhood in every sphere.

Feminist conscientization begins when women recognize that their oppression is structural and is based on gender: they are women in a system controlled by men for their own advantage. Next, they become aware that they are not isolated victims but members of an oppressed group that can turn its *solidarity in oppression into solidarity in action and transform oppressive structures.

For women, conscientization is the discovery that "the personal is political." What women have been taught to experience as personal problems are not individual or private at all: they are generated by social systems. Women cannot deal with them merely by making adjustments in their personal lives; they must transform sociopolitical systems.

Feminist conscientization has revealed the role of *patriarchy not only as the root of women's oppression but also as the source of all other forms of hierarchical *domination; in this way, women's liberation finds itself related to liberation movements throughout the world.

Berryman [1987]; Freire [1970]; Gutiérrez [1973/1988]; Schneiders [1991]

MARY JUDITH RESS

Contextualization

Contextualization The term *contextualization* was introduced to the theological world in 1972 by the Theological Education Fund of the World Council of Churches. Previously, such terms as **inculturation, adaptation,* and *indigenization* were used to designate ways of reformulating theology in a context other than the dominant Euro–North American. Contextualization has come to signify a shift from abstract and supposedly universal theology to the insistence that theology depends on the *praxis (concrete, partial, and historical) of which it is a part. It can also indicate commitment to analysis of global and local relations that confine affluence and *freedom to a small percentage of peoples worldwide.

Feminist theologies are context-specific, shaped by particular struggles for emancipation and *justice. *Contextualizing theology* in feminist terms means that women's shared experience in their historical, socioeconomic, geopolitical, cultural, ethnic, and religious contexts is the starting point of the theologizing process. It also serves to critique a narrow and distorted framing of feminist theological agenda. For example, if the starting point is shared experience of resistance to *oppression and exploitation (not privatized experience, a priori propositions, or scripture and *tradition), experience signifies persons-in-relation. White feminist theology then must become critical of its tendency to elevate the particular pain and experiences of white, middle-class women into universal female experience. Hence contextualization indicates responsible specifying of experience; analyzing context with attention to social, historical, and other relational particularities of women's existence; and shaping theological images and visions appropriate to the context.

In sum, feminist theological method is contextual. Its theological significance is based on how well it unmasks the historical dynamics of oppression (global and local, internal and external) and offers a vision of abundant life for all, especially for the most oppressed women in that context.

Brown, in Russell [1985b]; Fabella/Oduyoye [1988]; Harrison [1985]; von Wartenberg-Potter [1987]

MARILYN J. LEGGE

Conversion

Conversion The *gospel word *metanoia* denotes a complete change of direction. It begins with a conviction that one's goal and style of life are contrary to the will and intentions of God as seen in *Christ and to a desire to conform to the fullness of humanity presented in Christ. A precondition to conversion is a confrontation with the gospel, the message of God's love; it begins with the *grace of God in offering the gospel. To experience conversion, one must have the opportunity to hear the gospel. It is for this reason that Christianity is intrinsically missionary; it has a message to announce to the whole world.

In the churches' history, many nations have turned to Christ as a result of Christian *preaching. They have adapted their lifestyles to conform to the gospel and, in turn, have undertaken to announce the good news that others may be converted. The change of mind is believed to be effected by the Spirit of God working in and among the people. Nevertheless, conversion has sometimes been forced on people on the analogy of the parable of the wedding feast (Matt. 22:1–10), said to represent a mandate to "compel" people in the streets "to come in." The gospel message can be "compelling," but the methods have not always been in conformity with the mind of Christ. Mass conversions and destruction of cultures raise questions about the nature and fruits of evangelization. What beliefs, practices, attitudes, and *relationships are indicative of a turning in the direction of God's intentions for all *creation?

Feminist theologians raise many questions about the patriarchal mindset that makes use of conversion techniques to dominate others. However, feminist and *liberation movements for *justice also call persons to turn around and see things in a new way. When this conversion happens and people take steps with others to change their societies, the process is called "*conscientization." Just as conversion is a continuing process for Christians, so, too, the need to keep seeing and acting in new ways is a fundamental process of transformation for feminists.

Oduyoye [1986]; Oduyoye [1995]; Potter, *IRM* [1973]; Russell [1974]

MERCY AMBA ODUYOYE

Cosmos The dominant Western Christian understanding of the cosmos, or the nature of the universe, relies primarily on Greek concepts. The result has been a dualistic and essentialist view of the universe. The *dualism is characterized by a subject–object epistemology, an ontology of physical and spiritual essences, and a superior–inferior (and good–bad) ethical framework. The earthly, physical essence is finite, changing, and inferior, indeed fallen, and ultimately less real than the supernatural, eternal, unchanging, and perfect essence of God. The human essence is a combination of spirit and *body; we are also part of a male or female essence, and females have essentially less spirit and more body than men do. Females are also objects to male subjects and inferior in many ways to male superiority.

Feminists charge that this *social construction reflects and supports white male dominance and privileges a certain abstract European intellectual language. White, elite males, who have the more excellent spiritual and intellectual nature, become the gatekeepers of how we are to know God and ourselves. They alone are the subjects of their own lives and interpreters of everyone else's.

Feminists are developing new cosmologies. A major one is relational, sometimes described in ecological terms. In this, there is no essential being; there are relatives. All of us (all creatures, the earth and God) are becoming, in and through *relationships. Body, *soul, nature, spirit are not separate and hierarchically valued substances but dimensions of an ultimately universal web of relatedness.

Some feminists, primarily Euro-Americans, affirm an ontological connection between femaleness and the natural world, perhaps suggesting a new *essentialism.

Others, particularly womanists, suggest a more complex relatedness. In her exploration of *wilderness experience, for instance, Delores Williams recognizes a more political and socially constructed understanding of the woman–nature relation.

Central to such new constructions are stories of women's experience. Different racial and other groups of women explore their own heritages for the "subjugated knowledge" that can lead to alternative cosmologies. Finally, some feminists turn to modern science for constructing the cosmos in religious terms.

Collins [1991]; King [1994]; McFague [1993]; Ruether [1992]; Williams [1993a]

ELEANOR H. HANEY

Counseling In contrast to the broader term *care, counseling* describes in-depth, focused attention to emotional distress with the goal of alleviating or easing that distress. Counseling denotes a *healing intent. For this reason the term *therapy* is often used interchangeably with *counseling*.

Historically, pastoral counseling has a rabbinical and, later, a penitential lineage. With the advent of modern *psychology in the latter part of the nineteenth century and especially in the twentieth century, counseling emerged as a specialized *ministry informed particularly by the disciplines of psychiatry, psychology, and systems theory. In pastoral counseling, the dominance by white men as theorists and practitioners has been thoroughgoing until recent years.

The effects of this dominance by men are pervasive and problematic. Perhaps most striking is the circumscribed focus on individuals or families apart from reflection on the effects of social and historical location, such as gender, *race, class, economics, and *power inequities. Women's experience is variously described as inscrutable, stereotypic (within patriarchal patterns), or indistinguishable from that of men and boys. Issues of power within the counseling relationship often have been ignored.

Feminist theologies have been particularly attentive to issues of social location and inclusion as these impact on the theoretical construction and practice of counseling. They have moved power from the margins of discussion to the center and have assigned normative status to the equitable distribution of power in their theoretical construction and reflections on practice.

Two avenues for exploration and critique have emerged in feminist pastoral theologies: first, the consequences of *sexism, *classism, and *racism in distorting the experience of women and of the human community more broadly; second, the rich particularity of the experiences of women as resources for fuller understanding of human experience and God. Both avenues establish gender as a crucial variable for theory and practice. Feminist pastoral theologians have "mined" such categories as identity and development, *sexuality, spirituality, *ethics, and epistemology for their potential to disclose the significant influence of gender in shaping human experience.

In the first avenue of exploration, feminist pastoral theologians have proposed constructive alternatives in several crucial areas. They have addressed the nature and dynamics of power as grounded in and authorized by *relationships of trust and care. Such a construct envisions mutuality and the *empowerment of others rather than a unilateral and hierarchical exercise of power. They have helped the *tradition recover a broader paradigm for *sin that includes not only the assertion of too much self (*pride) but also the refusal to be a self (hiding). Moreover, they are discerning the more insidious consequences of sin as women internalize the *shame and the subordinate identity that sexist *stereotypes promulgate. They have also addressed the role of sexism in the widespread tolerance of physical and sexual *violence against women and children.

In the second avenue of exploration (the particularity of women's experience), feminist pastoral theologians also have made constructive proposals. They have insisted on an intrinsically relational *anthropology, and they have helped recover *embodiment as a central dimension of human experience. They have developed *metaphors from women's experience, such as labor, birth, and *friendship, to reframe the practice of care. They have also attended to the *interdependence of sexuality and spirituality, with corresponding new insights into the nature and presence of God.

Works in progress extend the gains in both these avenues. They also disclose tensions between modernist and poststructural perspectives, especially as the latter take more seriously the formative significance of social location for such issues as *authority, identity, relationality, and power.

Glaz/Moessner [1991]; Graham [1992]; Jordan et al. [1991]; McGoldrick/Anderson/Walsh [1989]

NANCY J. RAMSAY

Covenant *Covenant* has been a central category of Jewish self-understanding from biblical times to the present. According to the Torah (Gen. 12:1–9; 15; 26:23–24; 28:10–19; Ex. 19:5), God enters into a mutually binding agreement, first with the patriarchs, and then with the entire people of Israel. They promise obedience to God's commandments, and in return, God promises to give them *land and progeny and to make them a "kingdom of priests, a holy nation" (Ex. 19:5, NJB).

Jewish feminist discussions of covenant have focused largely on the question of the extent to which women are included in the covenant community. The original and primary sign of the covenant, circumcision (Gen. 17:10), excludes women by definition. The covenant at Sinai is spoken in male pronouns, and its content assumes male hearers. For example, the Tenth Commandment says, "You shall not covet your neighbor's wife" (Ex. 20:17). In preparing the Israelites for the *revelation at Sinai, Moses addresses the community only as men: "Prepare for the third day," he enjoins the people, "do not go near a woman" (Ex. 19:15). Such passages, combined with the subordinate legal status of women in rabbinic Judaism and the striking absence of women's concerns from many areas of Halakhah (Jewish law), give rise to Rachel Adler's pointed questions: "Have [women] ever had a covenant . . . ? Are women Jews?"

These questions must not be interpreted too literally, for the same sources that can be read as indicating women's exclusion from the community of Israel also presuppose their presence. Women's contributions as *mothers and wives are essential to the fulfillment of covenantal promises. Questions about women's relationship to the covenant are meant to highlight the *marginalization and otherness of women in the covenantal community and to provide the critical foundations for strategies of feminist transformation. One of the earliest Jewish feminist innovations, for example, was the creation of birth ceremonies for girls, paralleling *brit milah* (the covenant of circumcision). The purpose of such ceremonies was precisely to mark and celebrate the incorporation of girls into the covenant.

While women's status in the covenant community has received primary attention, some Jewish feminists have begun to address the concept of covenant itself. Heidi Ravven suggests that, because the Bible and *tradition conceptualize the covenant in erotic as well as political terms, women's experiences in the *family may provide models of covenantal relationship different from those offered by men. Ravven thinks that Carol Gilligan's delineation of a female ethic of caring, in contrast to a male ethic of rights and obligations, might provide an interesting starting point for a new model of covenant. In contrast to Ravven, Laura Levitt uses the feminist critique of patriarchal *marriage as a starting point for criticizing erotic images of covenant. Given the understanding of marriage in the Jewish tradition as male acquisition and possession of female *sexuality, Levitt questions whether the erotic understanding of covenant is salvageable from a feminist perspective, whether it can be disconnected from traditional models of marriage. She argues that while contemporary liberal Jewish theologians tend to prefer a marital to a contractual model of covenant because the former seems more egalitarian, in fact the same inequalities and potential for abuse are built into both the Sinaitic covenant and the marriage relationship.

Adler, *Moment* [1983]; Levitt [1992]; Plaskow [1990]; Ravven, *Anima* [1986]

JUDITH PLASKOW

Creation In the Western Jewish and Christian traditions, creation refers to the Genesis accounts of God's creation of the world. The distinctive notes of the two mythological accounts are *ex nihilo* (creation from nothing, thus underscoring the total dependence of everything on the one God); the aesthetic mode of creation versus a birth mode (the world was created by the "word" or the "hands" of God, thus producing a work of art that God finds "good"); the position of women in the two accounts (one suggesting *equality of the sexes and the other, subordination of woman to man); and the "dominion" of human beings over nature. In Christianity, the *doctrine of creation has taken second place to *redemption, the first Adam being superseded by the second Adam, *Christ.

Feminists of many sorts have objected to various aspects of the Genesis accounts. The strength of the objections is due in part to the prominence and power of Genesis in Western *culture, e.g., the numerous paintings during the Middle Ages and the Renaissance depicting Eve as giving the apple to Adam and thus as responsible for "original *sin."

But feminists have also offered alternative understandings of creation. One set of alternatives focuses on biblical reinterpretations, especially of the Genesis accounts, giving primacy to the woman. Another biblically based alternative is the identification of *Sophia as the divine mediator in creation ("The Lord by wisdom founded the earth"; Prov. 3:19).

A substantial contribution is the work of feminists on various *goddess traditions of creation at historical, mythological, and spiritual levels. The birth of the world from the body of the Great Mother, the sense that all of nature is alive and sacred, and the prominence of women's roles and status suggest a powerful alternative to the traditional Western view of creation. The range of feminist work in this area is wide and deep, from the Virgin Mary and the Virgin of Guadalupe to Hindu's Shiva and ancient fertility goddesses, as well as Wicca traditions.

Yet another view of creation is being offered by *ecofeminists who, again, are varied in background and context. Asian, womanist, Native American, Goddess, *mujerista*, and European-American feminists in different ways are insisting that "salvation" or the good life must be for *all* life-forms, not just human beings. Ecofeminists decry the *dualisms of male over female and human beings over nature that have been prominent in Western patriarchal thought. Creation has suffered in *patriarchy as have women; therefore ecofeminists have insisted on the rights of nature and care for nature in ways few other liberation *theologies have.

Several issues and unresolved questions emerge in this work of feminists on creation. First, for European-American feminists, especially Christians, the stress on creation rather than the traditional emphasis on redemption raises the issue of how the Christian paradigm can be stretched (or reinterpreted) to accommodate this shift. A second concern is the tension between the needs of oppressed human beings, especially women, and the destruction of the natural world. Finally, an intriguing and important area of feminist concern is the test case that nature provides on dealing with *difference. Can the life-forms in the natural world be appreciated in *their* differences from *us?*

Adams [1993]; Gimbutas [1982]; Johnson [1993]; McFague [1993]; Trible [1978]

SALLIE MCFAGUE

Creation Story Two *creation stories open Genesis. In Gen. 1:1–2:4a, the six days of creation climax in the creation of male and female in "the image of God" (1:27). In Gen. 2:4b–3:24, human life begins in an Eden garden where God forms humus into human form (Heb, *'ădāmāh* to *'ādām*). Both creation stories are theological affirmations about the relationship between God, world, and humanity.

In Genesis 1, commonly assigned to the Priestly *tradition, God speaks the world and humanity into existence and this is "good" (a sevenfold judgment in this story—1:4, 10, 12, 18, 21, 25, 31). Transcendent and all-powerful, God creates order out of a primordial chaos of formlessness, darkness, and too much water (1:1, 6, 9) and creates the earth, heavens, and all living things in a six-day process. Rest and a third blessing (see 1:22, 28; 2:3) close the seventh day.

In Genesis 2—3, the Yahwist version, an immanent God creates order out of chaos where there is not enough water, forming dust into humanity and breathing life into it. A garden, work, and a command not to eat of the tree of the knowledge of good and *evil fill out the story. Deciding to make a partner for the human, God creates the animals. Repairing this misfired divine action, God creates woman and human community is born (bone of bones, *'ishshāh* from *'ish*).

*Patriarchal interpretation has read female subordination into both stories. But the Genesis texts describe parity. God gives humankind "dominion" over fish and other living things, not over each other (1:28). God punishes both female (3:16) and male (3:19), cursing the serpent (3:14) and the ground (3:17).

The paradigmatic story in the Hebrew Bible is the exodus from slavery to *freedom, not the creation story. Eve is never mentioned after Gen. 4:1. Only in the *Apocrypha, Pseudepigrapha, New Testament, and rabbinical and Christian writings is Eve held responsible for the "fall from *grace."

Bellis [1994]; Meyers [1988]; Trible [1978]

TONI CRAVEN

Cross As a historical artifact, the cross is the undisputed implement of Jesus of Nazareth's death. Crucifixion was commonly employed by Roman officials as a method of execution in that time and place, and the historical claim that Jesus was crucified is virtually universally accepted. Feminist Christians for the most part have not taken part in Euro-American, male scholarly disputes about the details of the crucifixion, such as the role of the Jewish Sanhedrin, the actual date of the execution, the exact nature of the Roman officials' charges against him, etc. However, the cross *as a symbol* is deeply controversial among Christian feminists, and there is no consensus regarding either its symbolic nature or its symbolic value (or nonvalue) for Christian feminist theology.

Some Euro-American, African-American and Asian-American feminist theologians raise serious concerns about the cross as a symbol of Christian life, and those concerns take several forms that can loosely be categorized into theological objections and ethical objections. In the first group would fall the numerous and growing group of feminist scholars who critique all forms of the classical doctrines of the *atonement from the perspective of what they claim about the nature of God, what they claim about the nature of the human person, and what they claim about the relationship between them. The relational, loving God of Christian feminism, whose reality in the world is incarnate in *solidarity with the poor and oppressed, is not the God who demanded the death of "His son" as restitution for the sins of humanity. Likewise, the ongoing *incarnation of the passion of God in the human passion for *justice is incompatible with the utterly passive, ineffective humanity that is the beneficiary of the atonement. Christian feminism conceives the relationship between God and humans as including mutuality: God is implicated in human *suffering, and human suffering is implicated in God. Thus whatever the details of the various versions of the *doctrines of atonement, they are all incommensurate with key theological insights and teachings of Christian feminism.

Likewise, the ethical objections to the cross as a symbol of Christian life note that in the history of Christianity, the cross as symbol has served to valorize both abuse and suffering. Feminist Christian theological *ethics interrogates the symbols and practices of Christian communities, assesses their impact on groups of people, and specifically attends to their impact on women. When and to the extent that the cross as symbol subverts the protests to and the struggle against human suffering and the *violence in our lives, it is incompatible with a Christian feminist understanding of the nature of God and humans. Insofar as those in power appropriate the cross as an instrument of their oppression of others, it remains a dangerous symbol for all groups, including Christian churches, that are still largely *patriarchal and supremacist.

The cross as a symbol can also be seen as ineluctably tied to the patriarchal exaltation of Jesus as historically male. Reactions to the public display of the **Christa,* a female figure hanging on the cross, were evidence of the inability or unwillingness of many to image the redemptive power of the Christian God as female, as well as of the ongoing need for Christian feminists to articulate and represent female images.

For Christian feminists, then, the cross must be rejected as a symbol for Christian life insofar as it has historically functioned to promote oppressive beliefs and practices. The controversy regarding the cross as a symbol of Christian life has to do as well with whether it ought to be retained and recast. Those in favor of the latter position argue from two related but distinct perspectives. The first, articulated by some Christian feminists who identify themselves as sharing the convictions of Latin American liberation *theologians, relates experiences of the cross as a symbol of God's solidarity with the poor and oppressed. In a dramatic reversal of a Lutheran *theologia crucis,* persons experience the cross as a symbol not of the *absence* of God but of the *presence* of God with and in human suffering. Other feminists argue that the cross is a symbol of creative power, and as such, it functions to figure forth an understanding and practice of *power itself as life and love that do not deny the reality of suffering and pain but move through them to other experiences of life. With this interpretation, the cross moves through crucifixion to *resurrection and symbolizes that love and life are more powerful than *evil and suffering.

From a Christian feminist perspective, the cross, like all symbols, must be contextualized within the material realities of human lives. Insofar as it functions to valorize abuse and *oppression, and insofar as its historical interpretations of atonement and the masculinity of our *redemption remain attached to it like barnacles, it must be put aside. Some accounts testify that the cross is a symbol of redemption, not oppression. Others see the cross primarily as a symbol of violence and innocent suffering and are more wary of its positive power in the lives of the people who invoke it.

From a Euro-American feminist Christian perspective, the cross, like most Christian symbols, is ambiguous, and its meaning and its value must be gleaned from its function in concrete human lives. Like all Christian symbols, it must be understood and embraced as one among many symbols, all of which must be multiplied and juxtaposed lest they become idols.

Aquino [1993]; Brock [1988]; Brown/Bohn [1989]; Heyward [1989a]; Purvis [1993]; Williams [1993a]; Williams [1993b]

SALLY B. PURVIS

Culture Culture is the totality of any given society's way of life. It comprises a people's total social heritage, including language, ideas, habits, beliefs, customs, social organization and traditions, art and symbolism, crafts and artifacts. Undergirding culture is a network of interrelated value systems that is capable of influencing and conditioning perception, judgment, and behavior. Religious values are important in this respect. Most cultures relegate the woman to a secondary position in society for some "curious" reasons, such as the perceived dictates of *religion, her lesser physical strength, or some mystical value allotted to the female versus the male.

Culture is distinguished from nature. It is a human achievement and can be described as the artificial, secondary environment that human beings superimpose on the natural. Hence culture is the evidence of human endeavor and achievement in society. It manifests human purposiveness and effort. Among the characteristics of culture is the human effort exerted to preserve and transmit human achievements from generation to generation. On the whole, women play a vital part in the transmission of culture, due to their traditional roles as *mothers and first teachers of children. Women are therefore culture carriers in a fundamental way. Every individual is a product of a particular culture, some of whose traits are acquired spontaneously from the cultural environment and others through a deliberate system of *education and conditioning.

Culture is not static. Contemporary society is characterized by heightened cross-cultural influences and rapid cultural changes due to improved global communications systems. The flow of communications and cultural influences have dominantly been from north to south, which means that indigenous cultures of the south have tended to assimilate cultural traits of the more dominant cultures of the north and to experience cultural *violence as their own cultures erode.

The contemporary consciousness of gender issues should serve to challenge cultures to improve the lot of women. Some feminist scholars have begun to develop methods of "cultural hermeneutics" (Kanyoro) to analyze the multilayered interaction within a concrete cultural setting as women begin to express their "will to arise" (Oduyoye/ Kanyoro).

Eugene, in Daly [1994]; Kanyoro [1994]; Oduyoye/Kanyoro [1992]; Pobee [1994]; Schüssler Fiorenza/Copeland [1994]; Tamez, in Mananzan/Grey/Russell [1996]

HANNAH W. KINOTI

Deconstruction *Deconstruction* is a central term in the American reception of the work of French philosopher Jacques Derrida. Although Derrida insists that deconstruction names neither a *doctrine nor a method but, rather, an event, it may be provisionally described as a reading, writing, and thinking practice that unsettles the system of binary oppositions on which Western *metaphysics is grounded. Through a process of inversion and displacement, deconstruction shows the *interdependence of apparently opposing elements on each other and uncovers the instabilities in their systematic deployment. Inherently political, deconstruction subverts *hierarchies and the logic of thought that continually reinscribes them, while arguing for the inevitability and inescapability of repeated reifications (regarding an abstract construction as real). The work of deconstruction is, then, ongoing and perhaps even endless.

Although generalizations about the use of the term *deconstruction* are possible, Derrida's writings belie them. His voluminous output includes detailed readings of central texts in the Western philosophical canon, social-scientific texts, modern literature, poetry, and art. Reference to religious thought, always fleetingly present in his work, became more marked in the late 1980s and in the 1990s. Derrida's writings may accurately be understood as a series of events in which *dualistic structures of thought are uncovered, elicited, and shaken, thereby disseminating new forms of writing and knowledge. In this way, the association of the term *deconstruction* with Derrida's work remains justified.

Derrida's critique of Western metaphysics has been influential in the United States among theologians and "a-theologians" (those on the borders of theology) who are attempting to think of the possibility and meaning of religion without a traditional God. The political nature of the deconstructive event has also led to its *appropriation and repetition by feminist thinkers and feminist theologies, although with important concerns about deconstruction's apparent erasure of the subject and elision of woman/women as a category of analysis.

Armour, in Holland [1995]; Derrida [1981]; Derrida, in Jardine/Smith [1987]; Elam [1994]

AMY HOLLYWOOD

Depatriarchalization Depatriarchalization is a hermeneutical (interpretive) process whereby the Bible is reread to free it from the patriarchal bias of the societies that produced and transmitted it. The concept, as applied to *biblical studies, first appeared in Phyllis Trible's 1973 article "Depatriarchalizing in Biblical Interpretation." Responding to the position that *patriarchy had divine sanction, Trible argued that the Bible was neither at war with nor neutral to women's *liberation. Since "the intentionality of biblical faith" was to offer salvation to men and women, the interpretive task was to recover and emphasize the intentionality of the text and to "translate biblical *faith without *sexism." The hermeneutical challenge was to reread (not rewrite) the biblical text (31).

Trible identified two strategies for the rereading she advocated: (1) an emphasis on biblical themes that "disavowed" sexism and (2) a close reading of texts dealing with females and males to expose the ways such texts had been misread and misunderstood. Other feminists, like Trible, were unwilling to abandon the Bible as hopelessly patriarchal. Mary Ann Tolbert (1983) and Adela Yarbro Collins (1985), for example, both edited collections on feminist interpretation. Tolbert compared depatriarchalizing to Bultmann's "demythologizing," saying that both methods face the reality that the "message is inextricably bound to its particularity" (126).

Trible insisted that depatriarchalizing was not an operation imposed on the biblical text but one operating within the text itself. Thus the task of every feminist interpreter is (1) to identify the Bible's depatriarchalizing principle, (2) to recover that principle in the passages and themes where it is found, and (3) to accent it in the final reading (Trible, 48). Critics of the depatriarchalizing process have challenged Trible's axiom "We expose it; we do not impose it" by suggesting that the text is often "irredeemably *androcentric" in spite of wishes that it be otherwise (Clines).

Clines, *JSOT* [1990]; Collins [1985]; Russell [1985a]; Tolbert [1983]; Trible, *JAAR* [1973]

LINDA SCHEARING

Desire In feminist theory, thanks largely to Freud, desire ordinarily means *sexual* desire (Valverde). In feminist theology, desire is addressed more implicitly than directly and, as in the larger corpus of feminist work, normally can be related to "the work of love" (Harrison) or to "the power of the erotic" (Heyward). It is important to note, however, that Beverly Harrison, Carter Heyward, and many other feminist ethicists and theologians understand "love" and "erotic power" as sacred (creative and liberating) *power, not simply as sexual libido. In this sense, for many feminists "desire" denotes not only sexual yearning but also, in a larger sense, a psychospiritual reaching for that which is unrealized. Thus desire plays at least three distinct, sometimes overlapping, roles in feminist theologies: (1) as a primary psychospiritual motive in feminist theology, (2) as a strong erotic yearning for right relation, and (3) as a specifically sexual urge.

As Motive in Feminist Theology. In her 1985 essay "The Power of Anger in the Work of Love," Christian social ethicist Beverly Wildung Harrison identifies love with the making of *justice or right relation and defines *anger as "a feeling-signal that all is not well in our relation to other persons or groups or to the world around us" (14). Predicated throughout Harrison's groundbreaking essay is an assumption that feminists are motivated by passionate desire for right relation. Citing "activity," "*embodiment," and "relationship" as foundational to "love," Harrison represents the feminist experience of desire as an embodied, or erotic, psychospiritual motive that is grounded in actual relationship with others and takes the form of action in the world around us. In this way, desire is foundational to feminism as a political and theological movement.

As Erotic Yearning for Right Relation. Throughout her work, *lesbian feminist theologian Carter Heyward, like Harrison, associates justice or right relation with "mutual relation" and suggests that our "power in mutual relation" is both sacred and erotic (cf. *eros). Implicit in Heyward's theology, as in much Christian, Jewish, and other feminist *liberation theory, is that our sacred power, or God, is the root of our desire for mutual relation, and that such structures of alienation (Marx) as *racism, *classism, and *heterosexism break or twist our desire, thereby generating *evil. In this social framework, the desire for right relation constitutes the basis of a theological *anthropology and soteriology in which human goodness and human moral *agency play central roles.

As Sexual Urge. With few exceptions, feminist theologians are reticent to discuss sex in explicitly "sexual" language. This reticence probably reflects four problems: (1) the (white) *race and (middle-) class bias of most feminist theology; (2) our relatively recent and still tenuous professional standings in religion and the academy; (3) the extent to which, especially for white, class-privileged Christian women, any expression of sexual pleasure has been traditionally taboo; and (4) the degree to which explicitly sexual language in heterosexist, racist *patriarchy is pornographic (violent, especially toward women) in the dominant racist, classist, and heterosexist *culture.

Nonetheless, many feminist theologians are being challenged and stretched by the work of secular feminists for whom desire often refers, in woman-affirming, passionate ways, to the yearning for good sex, hot or cool. In a 1989 essay, Joan Nestle remembers fondly that her mother "liked to fuck" and reminds her readers that her mother's desire was as basic to an authentic feminist agenda as any woman's desire for control of her own body.

In summary, there is no single "theory of desire" among feminists in theology or elsewhere. As Mariana Valverde notes, "Nobody has the monopoly on either the experience or the theory of desire" (176). As is true also of eros, our experiences and understandings of desire are likely to generate disagreement and debate among feminist theologians precisely because the whole area of women's sexuality remains so largely captive to social forces of *violence, exploitation, and fear.

Harrison [1985]; Heyward [1989a]; Nestle, in Snitow et al. [1989]; Valverde [1985]

CARTER HEYWARD

Development In the 1950s the term *development* designated the modernization of nations through industrialization as measured by increases in per capita gross national product. At the 1955 Bandung Conference, poor nations of the world recognized their joint membership in an underdeveloped *third world. By the 1960s development was the theoretical basis for economic policy in much of the world, with poor nations pursuing capital investment from multinational corporations and borrowing heavily from first-world banks and international lending sources to fund the national infrastructure for industrialization.

By the late 1960s, Latin American social scientists had developed a complex critique of both developmentalist policy (*desarrollismo*) and the theory of development that informed it, on the grounds that growth stimulated by these policies had not benefited the poor masses but rather often increased their misery. Popular movements began to insist on *liberation rather than development, invoking *dependency theory* which linked the *poverty of the south to the colonial/neocolonial policies that had created wealth in the north.

By the early 1980s, feminist attention to development policies had assimilated the liberationist critique of development and deepened it, based on the exclusion of women from both rural and urban development strategies and on the effects on poor third-world women of neoliberal austerity plans. These plans were imposed on poor nations that required refinancing of the external debt acquired under developmentalism. The cornerstone of International Monetary Fund and World Bank austerity plans is severe cuts in social spending (e.g., health, *education, and provision of water, electricity, and sewers). Despite some class and *race tensions among feminists and women activists in developing nations, the shared goals of feminist groups include (1) evenly distributed national economic development, (2) integral development of the whole human person for both men and women, (3) social development as requiring participation of all sectors (including networks of women's organizations) in national and local decision making, and (4) forgiveness of external debt as a precondition for effective development.

Frank [1969]; Hinkelammert [1988]; UNICEF [n.d.]; Waring [1988]

CHRISTINE GUDORF

Diakonia The Greek word group *diakonia* (service), *diakonos* (server), and *diakoneō* (serve), whose contexts included both table service (John 2:5, 9) and cultic office, was accommodated in early Christianity to describe forms of *ministry. The words indicate a communal function; the Gospels exploit the *metaphor to inculcate nonauthoritarian Christian leadership (Mark 9:35; 10:43–45; Matt. 20:26–28; 23:11; Luke 22:26–27; John 12:26, 29).

Until recently, translators and most commentators understood these words as referring to Christian ministry when applied to men, to table service when applied to women. But early Christian writers used the words for communal functions of women as well as men. Paul applies *diakonos* to himself (1 Cor. 3:5; 2 Cor. 3:6; 6:4; 11:23), to Christ (Gal. 2:17; Rom. 15:8), to *authority (Rom. 13:4), to Timothy (1 Thess. 3:2). Similarly, he applies *diakonos* to Phoebe, a minister (not a *servant and probably not deacon) of the church at Cenchreae (Rom. 16:1).

The two very different stories about Martha and Mary (Luke 10:38–42 and John 11:1–12:19) appear to testify to early memories of a female missionary pair known as Martha the *diakonos* and Mary the sister. Mark applies the verb *diakoneō* to the many women followers/disciples of Jesus (15:41; cf. 1:30), as does Matthew (27:55; cf. 8:15); the conjunction of "follow" and "minister" makes the reference to Christian functions clear. In both, the women, who alone follow to the *cross, are exemplary.

Luke 8:3 describes women as ministering "from their goods," apparently restricting the ministry of women to benefactions. Acts 6 carefully, but inconsistently, distinguishes the ministry of the word from the ministry of the table (i.e., charity; cf. 11:29; 12:25; Matt. 25:40; 2 Cor. 8:4; 9:1, 12, 13; Rom. 15:31), naming only men in either role. In the early second century, Pliny gives evidence that Christian women used the Latin equivalent *ministrae* as a title (*Letters* 10.96.8). *Diakonos* is paired with *episkopos* in Phil. 1:1 and appears subordinate to the *episkopos* in 1 Tim. 3:1–14, but the technical meaning "deacon" cannot be attributed to the NT with certainty.

D'Angelo, *JFSR* [1990]; Schüssler Fiorenza [1992a], 50–76

MARY ROSE D'ANGELO

Dialogue, Interfaith Interfaith dialogue among the world's major religions is alive and well. Nevertheless, many feminists conclude that often interfaith dialogue is not sufficiently feminist. Women are underrepresented as spokespersons for their religious traditions at all levels of interfaith dialogue. Issues central to feminist transformations of the world's religions are seldom central to interfaith dialogue. Feminist implications of both abstract and practical concerns are neglected unless feminists have been included in the dialogue. Finally, the *patriarchalism common to the world's major religions is glossed over or ignored, even in dialogues that attempt to include a critical element in their analyses. In sum, much interfaith dialogue suffers from the same lacks so glaringly obvious in conventional academic theology.

Since interfaith dialogue is crucial to life in the global village in an age of *pluralism, women and feminism must become ever more involved. Two factors are largely responsible for the lack of strong feminist presence in interfaith dialogues. First, feminist perspectives are much less well developed in most of the world's religions than in Christianity and Judaism. Second, interfaith dialogue has not been a high priority for well-known feminist spokespersons from the major *world religions, including Judaism and Christianity.

One possible tactic to encourage greater feminist presence in interfaith dialogue is to organize more women's dialogues. Gatherings limited to women provide a safe environment and are often energizing. However, such dialogues often do little to redress the balance of *power between women and men in the major religions themselves and would not bring feminist presence into the forefront of interfaith dialogue. Therefore, it is also crucial that interfaith dialogue among the major world religions become a higher priority for feminists, especially for major feminist leaders from the various traditions.

Brock/Cooey/Klein, *JFSR* [1990]; *Buddhist-Christian Studies Journal* [1980]; Eck/Jain [1987]; O'Neill [1990]

RITA M. GROSS

Dialogue, Theological Organized theological dialogue among women, as distinct from interfaith *dialogue, started only in the 1980s. Women of different cultures initiated conversations among themselves to give voice to their theological insights in a world still dominated by male thinking. With the development of contextual theologies and the awareness that theology is influenced not only by gender but also by geography, *culture, *race, religious affiliation, ethnic background, and social location, these conversations are generally *ecumenical, multicultural, and multiracial in character. Without advocating separatism, white feminists from the West, women from the "*third world," and women of color in the "first world" have recognized the value of hearing one another's experiences and wisdom in doing theology. Their goal is not only mutual understanding, respect, and *empowerment but also appreciation of commonalities and *differences and *solidarity building. Collective work or action is often sought, especially against the *oppression and *domination of women in both church and society.

Topics for dialogue range from women's spirituality and traditional theological themes such as Christology reworked from a feminist perspective, to common concerns such as seminary *education for women, to *justice and human rights issues such as *violence against women. Though they may not be formally called dialogues, these theological conversations among women have two distinctive features: the sharing of personal stories and a critical analysis of women's realities. These two features are notably absent in theological meetings of men or those organized by men.

Third-world women have additional goals in the dialogue among themselves, namely, the incorporation of women's perspective in the emerging third-world liberation *theologies, being formulated largely by male theologians, and a new methodology that includes women's experiences and women's ways of knowing.

As all truth is interpreted truth, women engaged in ecumenical theological dialogue believe no one has a monopoly on truth and that it is possible to arrive at new truths through dialogue. Their common hope is for ongoing dialogue among women as a necessary step toward authentic *pluralism in feminist theology.

Fabella [1993]; Fabella/Oduyoye [1988]; Mud Flower Collective [1985]; O'Neill [1990]; Russell et al. [1988]

VIRGINIA FABELLA

Difference In modern Western *culture there has been a tendency to view difference as a problem. Races, genders, sexual preferences, classes, and nature have been viewed dualistically and hierarchically. Women, nature, and people of color have been cast low in the *hierarchy. In dichotomous *dualisms, whiteness has been viewed as morally, ontologically, and aesthetically superior to blackness or color, male to female, heterosexual to homosexual, culture to nature, upper-class to lower-class, etc.

Womanist and feminist theology and *ethics argue for positive, nonhierarchical moral, ontological, and aesthetic valuations of differences among humankind and in all of *creation. They emphasize *solidarity and mutuality among human beings of diverse races, ethnicities, cultures, genders, classes, and sexual preferences. Womanist theologies in particular emphasize a positive valuation of diversity in *race, gender, class, and sexual preference among humankind, rejecting notions of supremacy along racial, gender, class, and *heterosexist and homophobic lines. Womanists build on Alice Walker's (1983) words on difference in her definition of *womanist:* "A woman who loves other women, sexually and/or nonsexually. Appreciates and prefers women's culture, women's emotional flexibility . . . , and women's strength. Sometimes loves individual men, sexually and/or nonsexually. Committed to *survival and wholeness of entire people, male *and* female. Not a separatist, except periodically, for health" (xi).

Walker goes on to observe that a womanist is "traditionally universalist, as in: 'Mama, why are we brown, pink, and yellow, and our cousins are white, beige, and black?' Ans.: Well, you know the colored race is just like a flower garden, with every color flower represented." Womanists envision the human race as one *family, with the colored race being like a flower garden. Just as one appreciates diversity in creation, one must appreciate the different colored skins of people, who are part of creation.

Walker's final definition that "womanist is to feminist as purple to lavender" has to do with the gradations of difference in religio-cultural and social-historical experiences among white women and women of color (xii). While womanists emphasize ontological, aesthetic, and moral positive valuations of difference, they do so in light of the social-historical reality of oppressive *relationships between white women and women of color. As a result of hierarchy, women of color are among the oppressed of the oppressed. While both white women and women of color have experienced *patriarchal *oppression, women of color experience race *and* gender oppression. Women of color experience economic oppression in disproportionate numbers.

Historically, white women have been oppressed in terms of gender but privileged and oppressive in terms of race, making for unequal relations with women of color. Walker's last definition takes difference seriously, noting the importance of race in women's experiences. Womanism and feminism are related but distinct responses to women's experience in contexts of oppression and survival.

Collins [1991]; Grant [1989]; Russell et al. [1988]; Walker [1983]

KAREN BAKER-FLETCHER

Disability A disability is an impairment (such as blindness, polio) that substantially limits one or more major life activities (such as seeing, walking,); or a record of such an impairment (for example, a history of having had cancer or having been hospitalized for mental illness); or the perception of such an impairment (for example, regarding someone with facial disfigurement as "disabled" when no limitations on major life activities exist). (This definition is derived from the Americans with Disabilities Act of 1990.) It is estimated that there are forty-nine million people with disabilities in the United States and half a billion people with disabilities worldwide.

Traditionally, theologians have discussed disability in terms of *suffering and *healing and people with disabilities as those in need of comfort, *compassion, and charity. Clergy and theologians alike have defined disabled people as those who need help and pity—as those who need "to be ministered to." Many feminists and feminist theologians have concurred with this model of thinking about disability. They have held and continue to hold images of people with disabilities that portray them as being frail, incapable, passive, and "sick."

Today, this model of thinking is offensive to most persons with disabilities. The disability community is a diverse entity, consisting of individuals of all *races, genders, sexual orientations, classes, and religions; however, most people with disabilities no longer think of themselves as frail, "infirm," always needing to be healed, passive, or desiring to have clergy minister to them. The disability community now sees individuals with disabilities as whole human beings who are active in their communities (both secular and religious) and society, who are parents, *family members, and job holders. While some with disabilities suffer from physical and emotional pain, the disability community no longer thinks of those who are disabled as being uniquely singled out to suffer but believes that all persons, disabled and nondisabled alike, suffer during their lives.

People with disabilities now view themselves as contributors both to their houses of worship and to society, and they are entering the workforce of both religious denominations and society. Often their efforts to enter the workplace or participate in their religious communities are hindered by such obstacles as inaccessible buildings and discrimination. People with disabilities also have encountered and still face prejudice when they work with feminists. This form of *handicapism occurs in areas ranging from inaccessible buildings (such as *abortion clinics and *battered women's shelters) to patronizing attitudes (such as the feeling that disabled women should not have children).

Most people of *faith with disabilities now view disability as a social *justice issue rather than a health issue and see themselves (as feminists define themselves) as developers of their own theologies rather than as objects of theological inquiry or *ministry by others. Despite the problems disabled people encounter when they work with feminists, the theologies of *liberation that people with disabilities are now developing run parallel to the liberation *theologies of women, African Americans, and other oppressed groups. These disability theologies use the same methods of interpretation as the liberation theologies of the other groups.

Eisland [1994]; Fine/Asch [1988]; Shaw, ed. [1994]; Silvers, *Hypatia* [1995]

KATHI WOLFE

Discipleship of Equals The theological notion of "discipleship of equals" has been developed in the work of Elisabeth Schüssler Fiorenza as a radical democratic feminist concept that is rooted in biblical language. The word *disciple* translates the Greek for "learner" and designates someone whose allegiance is to the vision and commitment of a teacher or a movement. In the Bible this name is given to followers of Moses, Israelite prophets, the Pharisees, and also to Jesus. Discipleship means allegiance to not only the message, vision, and commitment but also "the way of life" of the intra-Jewish *basileia* movements. Throughout the centuries, Divine Wisdom has sent a succession of *prophets and messengers who have realized the open-ended, inclusive vision of the "discipleship of equals."

Qualifying discipleship with the word *equals* does not signify the sameness of the disciples but underscores their *equality in diversity. All of them have equal standing, worth, dignity, and access to the gifts of Divine Sophia-Spirit, although they bring different experiences, vocations, and talents to such a discipleship *community. Discipleship of equals announces a radical democratic vision and alternative reality to the "*patri-kyriarchal*," hierarchical systems of *domination. This vision and reality is embodied historically again and again in the emancipatory struggles to change patri-kyriarchal relations of domination, exploitation, and *marginalization. Hence the radical democratic concept "discipleship of equals" is another name for the *ekklēsia of wo/men* (women and men).

The tension between the democratic-egalitarian and the kyriarchal-hierarchical visions still comes to the fore in the linguistic notion of the word *church*. The Greek word *ekklēsia* is usually translated with "church," although the English word *church* derives from the Greek word *kyriakē*, i.e., "belonging to the Lord/Master." Hence, the original meaning of *ekklēsia* would be best rendered as "democratic assembly/congress of full citizens." The *translation process which transformed *ekklēsia* (democratic assembly) into *kyriakē* (church) indicates a historical development that has privileged the kyriarchal-hierarchical form of church. Thus the same word, *church*, in English entails two contradictory meanings. One derives from the patri-kyriarchal household in antiquity, which was governed by the lord/master/father of the house to whom freeborn women, freeborn dependents, clients, workers, and slaves, both women and men, were subordinated. The other meaning of *church* understands the equality of its members in terms of citizenship and *friendship. This meaning of *church* derives from the radical notion of democracy in antiquity that promised *freedom and equality to all its citizens, although in reality it restricted these to elite males.

The historical traces of radical democratic structures and visions that surface as "dangerous memory" in a critical reading of cultural and religious texts also surface in a well-known definition of feminism as "the radical notion that women are people." This definition positions feminism within emancipatory discourses and movements that assert the *power of the people. Its *contextualization evokes centuries of radical democratic struggles for the *liberation, emancipation, and equal citizenship of wo/men in society and church who fought for dignity, respect, well-being, and self-determination. These emancipatory movements have emerged again and again throughout the centuries because of the disparity between the radical democratic vision and its actual sociopolitical and cultural-religious realizations. Finally, such a radical democratic feminist notion which holds that all wo/men without exception, are both equal citizens in society and "equal disciples" in religion seeks to connect global emancipatory movements for freedom and equality with women's struggles in Christianity and biblical religions. Hence, the exploitation of the poorest and most despised women on earth exhibits the full death-dealing powers of structural sin and kyriarchal *evil. Their struggles for *survival and self-determination in turn realize again and again the vision of the discipleship of equals in the horizon of the *basileia,* G*d's intended world of well-being for all wo/men without exception. The change and transformation brought about by the ongoing emancipatory struggles of wo/men at the bottom of the kyriarchal pyramid express the fullest experience of Divine Wisdom's life-giving power in our midst.

Aquino [1993]; Russell [1993]; Schüssler Fiorenza [1993]; Schüssler Fiorenza [1983/1994]; Williams [1993a]

ELISABETH SCHÜSSLER FIORENZA

Doctrine The term *doctrine* derives from the Latin word *docere* (to teach). In contemporary usage, it can refer to the general teaching of a religious *tradition (Christian doctrine) or of a particular communion within that *tradition (Lutheran doctrine) or to a specific tenet of *faith (the doctrine of salvation). In Christianity, doctrine is understood to derive from established patterns of biblical interpretation and church tradition that identify the *community and guide its life and faith.

Though the all-male magisterium, as the official teaching body of the church, is unique to Roman Catholicism, over the centuries the articulation and development of doctrine in all Christian communions have been carried out overwhelmingly by privileged men. The historical contexts and *ideological biases of these men have had a pervasive effect on Christian doctrine, though this has been obscured by the recurrent tendency to identify church doctrine with immutable divine truth.

Feminist theologians affirm that all religious doctrine is a finite *social construct, intimately related to communal religious practices and power structures. There is a basic divergence within feminism between theologians who reject the doctrine of their tradition as irredeemably patriarchal and those who seek to reform it. Reformist feminists are active in Jewish, Christian, and Muslim traditions.

Reforming doctrine involves several steps. It requires *critique* of the *patriarchal bias in doctrines about God, humanity, and religious practice; the *recovery* of neglected strands of tradition that challenge these dominant doctrines; and the *reinterpretation* of sacred texts and doctrines so as to include the perspectives and experiences of women. Most significant, Christian, Jewish, and Muslim feminists have begun the task of *reconstructing* the basic doctrines of their faiths anew, as testimony to both their rootedness in their particular tradition and their hopes for its future transformation.

Carr [1988]; Cooey/Eakin/McDaniel [1991]; Ruether, *Scottish Journal of Theology* [1990]

AMY PLANTINGA PAUW

Domination Domination refers to a social system in which sociobiological *difference implies the superiority of one part of *creation over another. A system of domination encompasses all aspects of life: social, economic, political, symbolic, and discursive. Most societies, with a few exceptions, since ancient times have been systems of domination. Humans have dominated other humans (as in slave, tributary, and feudal systems), nations have dominated other nations (through war, colonialism, and economic imperialism), men have dominated women (*patriarchy), and humans have dominated other parts of the ecosystem (industrialism).

For feminist theorists, the system of patriarchy, in which men have dominated women, is thought to be among the earliest and longest-lasting systems of domination and a model for many other kinds. It is also closely linked, symbolically and possibly historically, to human domination of other parts of creation.

Systems of domination make those in the dominant rank the measure of all aesthetic beauty, moral rectitude, intelligence, and technical skill, while stunting or destroying the human potential of the subordinate group. Dominator systems encourage those in the higher rank to direct, control, subjugate, use, abuse, and sometimes even kill with impunity those in the lower ranks. The relationship is one of subject to object. Denied their subjectivity and *agency, those in the lower rank are forced into dependence on the dominator group and are often punished if they step out of their subordinate role. Systems of domination generally have dichotomous epistemologies, hierarchical and authoritarian social structures, and nonparticipatory decision making. They exhibit a high degree of social *violence and fetishize the values of competition and regeneration through violence and death.

One of the characteristics of a system of domination is the inculcation in both the dominators and dominated of a widespread belief in the system's inevitability and rightness. Religious institutions have played a major role in legitimating this belief. Thus, for centuries, emperors and kings ruled by divine right, women were made by God to be subordinate to men, black people were ordained by Noah's curse to be "hewers of wood and haulers of water" (Josh. 9:21ff.), and humans were created by God to "rule over" and subjugate plant, animal, and insect life. Since the Enlightenment, science has often served a similar, legitimating function.

In feminist theory, however, systems of domination are neither the product of natural evolution nor ordained by God. They are historically contingent *social constructs that can be changed through human will and agency. Feminist and liberation *theologians, however, go farther than many secular theorists in suggesting that domination has an inner, or spiritual, dimension. Domination has been linked to the concept of "principalities and powers," the demonic forces of biblical and classic *mythology. In this view, principalities and powers are the "inner or spiritual essence or gestalt of an institution or state or social system" (Wink, 1984).

Feminist theory contrasts dominator systems with what has been variously called the *partnership model, egalitarian systems, or complementary systems. Such systems, though historically few and far between, are based on epistemologies that involved linking, or connecting. They have nonhierarchical structures and voluntaristic or consensual decision making. They are nurturing of *community, growth, and life. They value diversity, flexibility, cooperation, and the nonviolent resolution of *conflict. Such systems represent the goal toward which feminist theologies and theological *praxis point.

Collins [1974]; Eisler [1987]; Ruether [1992]; Wink [1984]; Wink [1986]

SHEILA D. COLLINS

Dowry (India) The practice of a woman giving a "dowry" or gift to a man at *marriage is said to have had its origins in the system of *streedhan* (woman's share of parental wealth given to her at the time of her marriage). As a woman had no right to inherit a share of the ancestral property, *streedhan* was seen as a way by which the family ensured that she had access to some of its wealth. There is no clear proof as to when this practice was first started in India.

What began as gifts of land to a woman

as her inheritance in an essentially agricultural economy today has degenerated into gifts of gold, clothes, consumer durables, and large sums of cash, which has sometimes entailed the impoverishment and heavy indebtedness of poor families. The dowry is often used by the receiving family for business purposes, family members' education, or the dowry to be given for the husband's sisters. The transaction of dowry often does not end with the actual wedding ceremony, as the family is expected to continue to give gifts.

It was only in the middle of the 1970s that the women's movement and other human rights groups exposed the perniciousness of the system in India, when it was realized that there were an increased number of "accidental kitchen deaths" of young married women. The first reports to the police were often registered as suicides or accidents. The available statistics of dowry death are chilling and disturbing.

Initially, women's groups protested individual cases of dowry deaths. A national campaign focused on humiliating and socially boycotting the families in these cases. The campaign also demanded that mysterious deaths be presumed to be murders until investigated and proved otherwise by the police. The demand for special cells of women police officers to head investigations of dowry murders led to an amendment of the outdated Dowry Prohibition Act of 1961, which was later further amended so that all *streedhan* gifts (both movable and immovable) had to be registered in the wife's name at the time of the marriage.

Unfortunately, in India basic attitudes to female life have remained unchanged, and the dowry is seen as a bribe to the son-in-law to keep the daughter, who after a certain age is totally unwanted in her parental home. Families often know that they are virtually signing a death warrant when they give their daughter in marriage, and yet, they do so.

Fabella/Oduyoye [1988]; Gnanadason [1986]; Gnanadason [1993]; Kumari [1989]

ARUNA GNANADASON

Doxology The word *doxology,* derived from the Greek word *doxa,* or "glory," has traditionally been defined as "expressions of praise or thanks to God." These expressions typically have been understood to be characteristic of liturgical celebrations, where, traditionally, the inherent mystery of God's glory was considered to be made manifest. God's glory has, indeed, designated God's distance from humanity.

Feminist theologians, especially Elizabeth Johnson in *She Who Is: The Mystery of God in Feminist Theological Discourse,* are instead articulating a deep connection between the glory of God and human flourishing, or human *freedom to be fully alive. Johnson calls on the axiom of Irenaeus "Gloria Dei vivens homo: the glory of God is *homo,* the human being, the whole human race, every individual person, fully alive" (14). She makes visible the invisible of the Latin *homo* as she declares, "Gloria Dei vivens mulier: the glory of God is woman, all women, every woman everywhere, fully alive" (15). Johnson then makes clear the deep connection, not the distance, inherent to the glory of God: "Wherever women are violated, diminished, have their life drained away, God's glory is dimmed. . . . Conversely, fragmentary experiences of women's flourishing anticipate that new *heaven and new earth where the glory of God will be unfathomably justified" (15).

The significance of this definition of doxology as deep connection not distance is the insistence that what is at stake in women's theological work is at once a just, peaceful, sustainable human *community and the holy mystery of God's glory. God's glory and human, especially women's, flourishing are both tangible and tangled in human history. The creation of new and life-giving forms of human community and the life-giving capacity of the Christian *tradition are together in the balance.

Johnson [1992]; McFague [1993]

MELANIE A. MAY

Dualism "Dualism" describes a view of the world and of *relationships that divides reality into opposite categories and mutually opposed principles. Although *metaphysical dualism was rejected by the Hebrew Bible and by Christianity, the dualistic tendencies of Hellenistic *philosophy have had a significant impact on Christian theology. Such dualism can be seen in the dominant view of the self as defined over against the other and in the view of God as the divine being over against the world.

Western philosophy and Christianity have emphasized such dualisms as male–female, mind–*body, *culture–nature, spirit–matter, supernatural–natural, *soul–body, **agapē/*eros*. Dualisms of this kind are hierarchical, with one of the poles being viewed as superior to the other. Gender dualism associates males with the "higher" poles of the dualisms, such as *reason, mind, spirit, and women with the opposite and "lower" poles of bodiliness, passion, and matter. The lower poles are extended beyond females to various groups in society that are seen as "other" (peoples of color, homosexuals). *Ecofeminists have shown that the model of male–female hierarchical dualism is also imposed on the relationship of humans to nature.

The gender dualisms of Hellenistic philosophy were carried over into Christian *anthropology. The *doctrine that males and females are made in the *image of God *(imago Dei)* has been afflicted by these dualisms throughout the history of Christianity. The image of God has been unevenly divided. Men have been depicted as the primary image of superior qualities, while women have been relegated to secondary status in nature and *grace and have even been projected as the symbol of *evil. Thomas Aquinas (1225–74), for example, held that the male was the norm for humanity and the female was a defective form of human being. From this came a vision of woman's nature as distinct from men's nature, which formed, de facto, a two-nature anthropology. This bipolar view of the sexes projects different possibilities for men (to be active, rational, autonomous) and for women (to be passive, intuitive, emotional). The notion of the complementarity of sexes has not overcome the inequality but holds it in place by *stereotypes of masculine and feminine qualities and social roles that are predetermined by sex.

Feminist theology has sought to affirm that all persons possess a full and equivalent human nature and personhood, as male and female. At first the feminist response was to downplay sexual *difference as such and stress a single-nature anthropology that tended to hold out a single human ideal. This approach was criticized for devaluing bodiliness and human variety. Now feminists are developing a multipolar view that highlights the diverse ways of being human, which include more than sexual diversity: "one human nature celebrated in an *interdependence of multiple differences" (Johnson, 155). Hence other aspects of historical existence besides sex are seen as constitutive of identity: age, *race, social location, bodily handicap, historical time period. Highlighting the differences enables us to see diversity as normal and connection as possible. Identity need not be achieved through opposition or uniformity.

In place of the dualisms of opposition represented in male–female, self–other, God–world, and humans–nature, feminist theology argues for relations of mutuality. Such relations are based not on *hierarchy, dominance, or superiority but on an analogy with *friendship, a *metaphor signifying all caring relationships of reciprocity with independence. If the underlying opposition is let go, then it is possible to conceive of a new and rich synthesis of the dichotomous elements previously held as either-or.

Johnson [1992]; O'Neill, in LaCugna [1993]; Ruether [1983/1993]

MARIE J. GIBLIN

Ecclesiology Ecclesiology means literally, "thinking about the church." In this theological reflection, the church rethinks the meaning of its self-understanding as a community of Jesus Christ in every changing circumstance. The word *church*, or *ekklēsia*, in the Greek testament was not the only word used to describe the early Christians. An earlier term seems to have been *people of the Way*, and the word *koinōnia* (*community or *partnership) was often used to refer to the gathering of Christians in each place (Acts 24:14; 2:42).

The word *ekklēsia* is found only three times in the Gospels (Matt. 16:18; 18:15, 17). Paul and others working with the Gentiles seem to emphasize the idea that the Christian communities were like the other Greek political assemblies but were theopolitical assemblies of the people of God (Acts 18:32, 39–40). Within a few years it seems that the local churches were described as *ekklēsia tou theou* (church of God), gathered in the name of Christ (1 Thess. 2:14).

The usage of the word *ekklēsia* reflects its functional character. It is used as a description of the totality of Christians living in any one place (a city or a house; 1 Cor. 1:2; 16:19). It is also used to describe the church universal, to which all believers belong as part of the eschatological people of God (1 Cor. 12:28). These communities were defined simply by the presence of Christ in their midst. "Where two or three are gathered in my name, I am there among them" (Matt. 18:20). They viewed their task as proclamation of the *gospel (Matt. 28:18–20).

The church is a sign of the coming fulfillment of God's promise for *new creation. As a sign, it is always provisional and is in constant need of renewal in order to make an authentic witness to God's love and *justice in changing historical, political, economic, and social contexts. Indeed, it sometimes is in need of revolution, of building a new house of *freedom where people's hopes for human dignity are incorporated in both social structures and expressions of *faith and service. It is my contention, and that of many other feminists, that we live in such a time. One of the many serious *liberation challenges to the churches that are being raised from different parts of the world is the challenge of the women's movement to the patriarchal interpretation of ecclesiology.

Just as continued work on feminist interpretation of the Bible is needed, so, too, historical and constructive work on feminist interpretation of the church is needed to express the meaning of feminist advocacy in terms of the nature and *mission of the church. The need for a feminist ecclesiology or interpretation of the church has been recognized by Christian feminists for some time. Whenever one's paradigm or perspective on reality shifts, everything has to be thought through from this new perspective. Using a prism of feminist advocacy of the full humanity of *all* women together with men leads to critique, reconstruction, and reinterpretation of all the Christian traditions.

Much work has been done in the areas of critique and reconstruction related to the church. Earlier publications in this area include *Women-Church* by Rosemary Radford Ruether and *Bread Not Stone* by Elisabeth Schüssler Fiorenza. Most books on feminist theology include at least some sections on *doctrines related to the church, with a particular focus of feminist contributions to ecclesiology on *ordination of women and on *inclusive language and *liturgy. And many of the women who refuse to move out of their faith communities are at work to transform church traditions through the creation of women-churches or feminist Christian communities.

A traditional way of describing what it means to be the church is to talk about the *marks or signs of the church. These defining characteristics of the church are usually drawn from the addition made to the Nicene Creed by the Council of Constantinople in 381: "and in one holy catholic and apostolic church." Discussion of the signs begins here with a creed recognized by Orthodox, Roman Catholic, and Protestant traditions, but it moves to other signs as well, and it becomes controversial as one confessional body considers the marks of another invalid.

During and after the Reformation of the sixteenth century, there was a long period of controversial theology in which the Protestant Reformers and their descendants argued against the Roman Catholic reformers and their descendants about what made the church "truly church." The Protestants claimed that the true church was recognized not only by the visible signs (*signa*) of oneness, holiness, catholicity, and apostolicity but also by what they called the marks (*nota*) or distinguishing characteristics of the church. These marks were claimed to be what obviously constituted it as true church, namely, "where the word is truly preached and the *sacraments rightly administered."

The Reformers did not deny the importance of the Nicene formula, but they wanted to build their reformation on the scriptures. For this reason, they tried to discern in the biblical *tradition how the church might be faithful in its *preaching and sacramental life. Today, it is generally recognized by both Roman Catholics and Protestants that the witness of the scriptures to Jesus *Christ is the basis of the life of the church. From a feminist liberation perspective, however, faithfulness would require the marks or signs to include the dimension of God's justice and welcome to all those who are excluded, including those of different faiths.

One way of describing a feminist interpretation of the church is to say that the church is *a community of Christ, bought with a price, where everyone is welcome.* It is a "community of Christ" because Christ's presence, through the power of the Spirit, constitutes people as a community gathered in Christ's name (1 Cor. 12:4–6; Matt. 18:20). This community is "bought with a price" because the struggle of Jesus to overcome the structures of *sin and death constitutes both the source of new life in the community and its own mandate to continue the same struggle for life on behalf of others (1 Cor. 6:20; Phil. 2:1–11). It is a community "where everyone is welcome" because it gathers around the table of God's hospitality. Its welcome table is a sign of the coming feast of God's mended *creation, with a "guest list" that sounds very much like the announcements of the jubilee year in ancient Israel (Luke 4:12–14).

Ruether [1985]; Russell [1990]; Russell [1993]; Schüssler Fiorenza [1994]; Suchocki [1982/1989]

LETTY M. RUSSELL

Ecofeminism The connection between the words *ecology* and *feminism* is the basis of the word *ecofeminism.* This positive word is born of two negative situations: the destruction of the natural world and the oppression of women. *Ecofeminism* is a recent word created by women as a reaction against the destruction of life carried out by *patriarchal systems. It is a clear position that makes connections between the struggle for the dignity of women and respect for the different processes of life.

Ecofeminism is a *philosophy, theology, and wisdom and works with a unified understanding of life wherein each being and each vital process Is absolutely interdependent. In this sense, it proposes to go beyond the notion of *conflict between the genders that is promoted by patriarchal and *hierarchical systems. We need to consider, on the one side, women's special struggle for their *freedom, *equality, and self-determination in every *culture; on the other, "the feminine" as an oppressed reality of all human life and all biological systems, which are both masculine and feminine. These two aspects are absolutely linked in the ecofeminist perspective.

Ecofeminism advocates an inclusive philosophical position that has been observed and learned from all natural processes. Ecofeminist actions are aimed at the preservation of the life of present and future generations, both male and female, in a human perspective and in a wide biological and cosmic perspective.

Ecofeminism emphasizes the idea that we (all *creation) are one sacred Body. Patriarchal systems, in contrast, divide our social body into different parts, each one living by *domination of one over the other. This negative behavior, domination, is present among persons; among different groups; among nations, cultures, ethnic groups, sexes; and in human control over nature. For patriarchal systems, life is understood as a hierarchical process wherein each one can destroy the other in order to save the individual. The same competition present in the big trade markets is present in the relations of humans among themselves and with nature.

Ecofeminism also denounces the new forms of division resulting from the economic system, especially from multinational corporations that have succeeded in destroying natural resources and manipulating different cultures and environments in order to produce and sell more goods. These corporations are the new empires, able to go beyond nations, cultures, and differences. For them, the world is a mechanical body where the strongest parts and the strongest species are able to survive. They do not perceive the connectedness and *interdependence of everything, and they continue to be hostile to women, poor people, and nature, considering everything as an object to conquer.

Ecofeminism as a philosophy, theology, and wisdom of life is impacting various aspects of human knowledge. Ecofeminist groups denounce dangerous aspects of biotechnology, sociobiology, and other sciences and technologies as new ways to select and eliminate living beings. They argue that sexist and racist implications are always present in science's manipulation and ability to eliminate what it considers weak or undesirable, and that the integrity of nature, human beings, and, especially, women is being destroyed.

In patriarchal times, and even today when we should know better, women have been and are still objectified. Some new technologies make women objects of experimentation and control by scientific experts. Sometimes it is difficult to perceive the "variations" of the same old destructive process because all scientific studies are presented as serving the welfare, happiness, comfort, and security of humanity. This kind of destruction is always presented as scientific and "neutral" behavior. It appears "so clean" because scientists are working in clean, sterile laboratories; so "scientific" because they are working with such precise instruments; so "rational" because it seems clear that scientists want to preserve the human species. What ecofeminism perceives and denounces is that we are living in yet another kind of terrible "eugenic" society in which occurs a new, subtle domination of women.

Ecofeminism also invites us to rethink our Christian *tradition, as well as all religious traditions, to recover in them the values that can help all life in the present time. To rethink theological constructs in a "cosmogenesis perspective" means that all of us are revelations of the one and only Body in an evolutionary and creative process. Creative evolution allows human beings to intervene in different processes, and it is our *responsibility to stop the destruction and to initiate new behavior.

Patriarchal, *monotheistic religions have been structural accomplices of destruction in spite of their discourses about love and their good actions. Their complicity is a product of the hierarchical system and a support of all this enterprise of conquest. Ecofeminist theology is an effort for some to rethink Christian tradition in order to recover values, experiences, and commitments in an understanding of the way human beings are connected to the ecosystem. This new understanding invites us to welcome the Mystery that is everywhere and in everyone without reducing it to a masculine entity. Christianity is only one of the beautiful revelations of this Mystery, and all the other revelations are needed to preserve the beauty and the diversity of the unfolding dynamic of life.

Multiplicity and unity are present in all processes of life. There is no unity without diversity, and no diversity without unity as a force of convergence that links everything. To try to understand Christian experience in this perspective is to be able to announce that a universal, pluralistic, and concrete love is possible and is at work in us. This new understanding changes biblical interpretation, dogmas, and all traditional theological constructs.

Ecofeminist movements are flourishing in different parts of the globe with a new hope and a new constructive agenda.

Gebara [1994a]; Gebara, *RIBLA* [1994b]; Mies/Shiva [1993]; Shiva [1988]; Swimme/Berry [1993]

IVONE GEBARA

Economics of Class "Economics of class" is a category foundational to Marxist social theory. Karl Marx argued that the economic structure of any society shapes all aspects of social life and that the relationship of persons to this structure determines their class, a group with a common relation to the mode of production. Further, in all epochs of history the relationship between classes was antagonistic, marked by class struggle. Capitalism structures a fundamental opposition between the bourgeois and proletariat classes by which bourgeois exploitation occurs: accumulation of the surplus values of workers' labor, the commodification of social life, the division between mental and manual labor, etc. Marx's concept stands in sharp contrast to more dominant sociological discussions of class that lose the Marxist idea of class-based exploitation by defining class as a stratum marked by lifestyles, educational achievements, and income.

While Marxist, *socialist, and liberationist feminists have all drawn on Marx's work, they have pointed out that because the category of class is based on relationship to the mode of production, it cannot describe women's role in reproduction (childbearing and childrearing; general domestic labor). Nor, in fact, can it explain why women earn less and have lower-status jobs than men of their class. These feminists have offered proposals revising the economics of class which range from stating that women are their own class (however, postulating women as one class negates the differences among women emphasized by racial-ethnic, poor, working-class women) to analyzing the complex relations of capitalism and *patriarchy. Further work has been done to integrate *race and *imperialism into an evolving multidimensional analysis, which is essential for any feminist theological method that seeks to clarify relations of *domination and *oppression as part of a constructive project of social change.

Davis [1981]; Harrison, in Hough/Wheeler [1988]; Sargent [1981]; Wright [1985]

ELIZABETH M. BOUNDS

Ecumenism *Ecumenism (oikoumenē)* is a term that derives from the Greek word *oikos*, or "household." *Oikoumenē* is most often translated "the whole inhabited earth." Traditionally, however, this *translation has had as its referent the ancient Roman Empire or the Christian West, rather than the six diverse continents and the vast oceanic regions that are indeed the whole inhabited earth.

Shifting from a spatial to a temporal definition, during the twentieth century, "ecumenism" has referred to a movement toward cooperation among and between Christian churches—Eastern and Oriental Orthodox, Protestant, and, since Vatican II, Roman Catholic—on matters of witness and service and the search for *justice and peace. The ecumenical movement also seeks to go beyond cooperation to full and visible church unity, defined by mutual recognition of *baptism, *Eucharist, and *ministries, and, accordingly, by mutual recognition of one another as church. Inasmuch as the ecumenical movement has characterized unity in terms of *doctrines and church orders, it has been dominated by the men who have traditionally been the theologians and decision makers and clergy.

But by the beginning of the twentieth century, women participating in movements such as the Young Women's Christian Association (YWCA), the Women's World Day of Prayer, women's missionary and mutual aid societies, temperance unions, etc., were also pioneers of interchurch ecumenism. Indeed, already at the 1910 World Missionary Conference, often said to mark the emergence of the twentieth-century ecumenical movement, women's work was on the agenda.

Through their own ecumenical network, women were conducting research into the role of women in churches worldwide by the time the World Council of Churches was formed in 1948. After the assembly, a permanent commission on the life and work of women in the church was established.

Until the 1970s, the watchword of women's participation in the ecumenical movement was cooperation. Then, at an all-women's consultation sponsored by the World Council of Churches in Berlin in 1974, the word **sexism* became part of the ecumenical vocabulary. This consultation led to the Community of Women and Men in the Church study, which undertook theological and *biblical studies involving more local groups than any previous World Council study.

The community study in turn led to the inauguration of the Ecumenical Decade of the Churches in *Solidarity with Women (1988–98). The decade is a call to churches to examine their structures, their theology, their practices, toward a sharing of power among women and men in all aspects of common life. A mid-decade evaluation in 1993 concluded that the decade has so far been a women's decade more than a decade of the churches. Accordingly, among women worldwide three concerns came to the forefront at mid-decade: the global economic system and the *poverty of women; *racism and xenophobia; and *violence against women and children.

Crawford/Kinnamon [1983]; May [1989]; Oduyoye [1990]; Parvey [1983]

MELANIE A. MAY

Education Education is an organized form of learning that stimulates critical interpretations of meaning. Both of education's major components, the transmission of knowledges and the formation of persons in cultural contexts, are essential for the continuation of human societies. Feminist theory conceives education as a "practice of freedom" (Chopp, 86) that releases learners from the blinders of primary socialization in a *patriarchal system in order to build more just structures across gender, ethnic, economic, and political divisions.

Received Practices. In Western societies, education has been equated with language literacy and schooling. Educators have assumed that objective knowledge about the natural and humanly formed worlds is possible; that the one truth can be deciphered by philosophical, theological, or scientific methods; and that the normative human being is European, male, heterosexual, able-bodied, literate, and middle- to upper-middle-class. Schooling has been designed to build national identity and loyalty, to produce adequately skilled workers and managers, and to reproduce the social and economic relationships that form the *hegemonic international order.

Feminist Praxis. Feminist pedagogy is explicitly counterhegemonic. It promotes the analysis, *deconstruction, and reconstruction of all socially defined categories, including distinctions between the natural and human worlds. Feminist education is characterized by (1) grounding in one's own social location within a *community of accountability; (2) a commitment to alliance building between communities and cultures that emphasizes lived experience and the importance of individual and communal life; and (3) a political commitment to changing the position of women in every racial, social, economic, and sexual-identity group and, therefore, to changing society (Weiler, 58–59; Mud Flower Collective, 23–27).

The most recent wave of feminist education in the United States began among middle-class white women in the late 1960s in nonschool environments, primarily consciousness-raising groups. Women's studies programs and departments in universities developed during the 1970s and 1980s. Still dominated by white women in the 1990s, these programs have developed more adequate tools of analysis that include *race, class, economic injustice, and *heterosexism. As bell hooks reminds white feminists such as myself, our minds have been "colonized" and we must constantly widen our oppositional worldview to acknowledge our privileged positions and develop constructive alliances for *justice (hooks 1989).

Feminist Theological Education. Feminist theological education is both an outgrowth of and a parallel development to the field of critical pedagogy, which examines the cultural and social production and reproduction of knowledge, *ideologies, and class, race, and gender identities. Both fields share the fundamental premise that knowledge and, indeed, all of human reality are socially constructed.

Significant analysis of theological education was done by the Cornwall Collective and the Mud Flower Collective in the 1980s. In both works the writers argue that theological education must be primarily about justice and that feminist analysis must include *racism, economic injustice, community formation, and alliance building across cultural, racial, and economic barriers. Rebecca Chopp, Katie Cannon, Nancy Richardson, and Letty Russell, among others, continue to offer proposals for the feminist reconception of education within theological and religious circles.

In the United States, feminist theory has developed more fully in the fields of theology and *ethics than in the biblical, historical, or pastoral disciplines (with the possible exception of *liturgics), while feminist pedagogical process is more likely to be found within the pastoral fields. Book-length treatments of fundamental theological and ethical issues have been produced from *mujerista*, feminist, womanist, and Asian-American perspectives; we still await similar feminist treatment of, for example, Hebrew scripture studies as a whole or *pastoral care as a field, or a major revision of *church history written not with special attention to issues affecting women but from an inherently feminist stance.

Chopp, in Cheeler/Farley [1991]; hooks [1989]; Luke/Gore [1992]; Malson et al. [1989]; Minnich [1990]; Mud Flower Collective [1985]; Weiler [1988]

SUSAN E. DAVIES

Election

The verb *elect* comes from the Greek word *eklegomai*, meaning to choose or select, which is a translation of the Hebrew root *bḥr*, meaning to choose. In human terms, to elect, choose, or select means to separate out something of more value. When we read about God's election, we often think of a doctrinal concept of salvation where some are chosen, separated, or redeemed. Traditional theories of election assume that if there are winners, there must be losers, those who are "nonelect," or "not chosen." Because women often experience themselves to be among the "not chosen," a feminist reading of the term election questions whether God's *election* necessarily means there has to be a group of "losers" in order for the "winners" to feel chosen.

Election is a human problem, one of defining God's choices by human standards. It can be likened to sibling rivalry, as the children of God grapple for the most attention, blessing, and love. God's children do not trust the biblical promises of abundance for all, such as the mercy shown the Assyrians in Jonah, the feeding of thousands with manna (Exodus 16) and with a few loaves and fishes (Matt. 15:32–38; Mark 8:1–9), and the pouring out of the Spirit (Acts 2). Instead, different peoples and religions use their claim of being "elect" to justify the forced *domination of nations, the persecution of other ethnic groups, holy wars, inquisitions, and crusades. The *hierarchy of election is used to subordinate certain members within the community as well. Very often, females are considered less valuable and not as close to God as males. Thus we see degrees of election itself in this hierarchical model.

Feminists question the hierarchical model of election and challenge us to replace the concept of "chosenness" with the concept of "distinctness," thus honoring the unique gifts each part of *creation has to offer the whole community of God. Judith Plaskow suggests that, instead of thinking in terms of differentiation, we think in terms of part and whole. Biblically, being chosen is not a privilege or something merited but a gift of God's *grace, and it involves *responsibility to the whole world (Gen. 12:1–3; Isa. 42:1–4; 49:6).

Biblical *tradition shows us that God often lifts up the most unlikely, those whom the prevailing *culture deems unworthy because of birth order, gender, or ethnicity. Jacob, the younger brother, prevailed over Esau. Young David was anointed king instead of his older brothers. A band of unknown people was called Israel and was elected as God's *servant among the more powerful nations. Women were counted among Jesus' first disciples. Paradoxically, as soon as people claim to be elect, they are no longer the underdogs whom God traditionally uplifts! God, the loving parent, lifts up the lowly and despised and brings down the high and mighty, not as reward and punishment but as a way of sharing the blessing equally among all creation, so that all may experience God's election.

Corrington [1992]; Cott, *Journal of Ecumenical Studies* [1984]; Plaskow, in Cooey/Eakin/McDaniel [1991]; Tamez, *IRM* [1993a]

MARIANNE BLICKENSTAFF MOSIMAN

Emancipatory Historiography Emancipatory historiography is a method of investigation that involves a critical, socioethical analysis of the past, undertaken by examining who has been silenced, *marginalized, and excluded in specific historical records in order to achieve a more profound understanding of the structural interactions among varying dynamics of our forebears.

In our effort to reconstruct an accurate *memory of human activities, we employ four significant layers of analysis: (1) *theoretical analysis* identifies tools of inquiry that would be meaningful to the actors assessing the logic of *oppression as benchmarks in the *politics of resistance; (2) *systemic analysis* refers to the organizations and institutions (laws, customs, *education, and economic, political, and religious systems) of society lived by actual people in real social formation; (3) *cultural disposition* is a study of the cognitive descriptions that map the terrain of shared consciousness which people use in defining themselves and their actions in relation to other groups of people in everyday life; and (4) *collective action* lifts up the shared motivational constructs that enable groups of people in different places and times to pool resources in order to break open the past, in its full complexity, toward the common end of *liberation from *domination.

According to Beverly Wildung Harrison, this is the overall significance of doing emancipatory historiography: "The relevance of historical data must be judged by the need to understand how past collective action, as privilege and resistance to privilege, has led to our present situation" (249).

Harrison [1985]; Hines [1986]; Katznelson/Zolberg [1986]; Schüssler Fiorenza [1992]

KATIE GENEVA CANNON

Embodiment Embodiment is a theme that has been part of feminist theology from the earliest days. Starting from our body experience as women, feminist theologians have sought to reclaim the goodness of bodies, of femaleness, of *sexuality, of the earth itself. They have challenged the *patriarchal dualistic systems of thought that pit male against female, light against dark, *heaven against earth, and *soul against *body.

Even though the Hebrew Bible focuses on the goodness of *creation and the New Testament emphasizes God's *incarnation in the human Jesus, much of Christian theology has expressed deep ambivalence about the human body and has stressed a division between the human body and the soul. The body has been seen as merely a vehicle for the soul, at times even a trap, and has been treated disdainfully. The veneration of physical *suffering has further deepened the gulf between the despised body and the celestial spirit.

Feminist work on embodiment begins with the premise that our *experience is embodied.* It has involved a reclaiming of the body ranging from the celebration of menstruation, childbirth, and menopause to the connection of the body and human sexuality with the divine. *Lesbian feminist theologians and gay theologians in particular have underlined the connection between embodiment and sexuality. In the late 1970s, ethicist James Nelson began the work of undoing the negative Christian *tradition on body. He examined what it means for us as body-selves to take part in the reality of God, how the Word continues to become flesh, and how our bodies become words about the Word.

Carter Heyward's work focuses on the incarnation of God in the human Jesus as proof that the body is godly, the body is holy (137–47). In addition to the dominant patriarchal disdain for all things connected with the body, she notes that late monopoly capitalism has declared that female bodies (along with sex, passion, and the earth) must be controlled so that profit is maximized. Women are thus not very experienced at claiming and loving our own body-selves.

Christine Gudorf reminds us that the body is synonymous with the self. The mind is not over and against the body but rather is part of it, as are the *emotions. Both Gudorf and Heyward stress the importance of coming to terms with the goodness of our bodies and of human sexuality. Only in this way can the damage to women, children, and the earth begin to be undone.

*Ecofeminist theologians see the theme of embodiment as essential because those same patriarchal traditions that have deemed the body unworthy have sanctified the rape of both women and the earth. Carol Adams notes that the connection between nature and the body is a sacred source of divine *revelation. Ecological theologian Sallie McFague claims that embodiment is what we have in common with everything else on the planet and provides a web of relation with our environment in which we come to know "ourselves as bodies with other bodies."

Additional issues facing feminist theologians are the romanticization of embodiment and the notion of *difference. Because our female bodies have been exploited and many suffer physical and sexual abuse, embodiment is not always easy or pleasurable. The process of coming to value our embodied selves is, therefore, often difficult. Furthermore, embodiment must take into account the sociopolitical, cultural, and economic construction of the body, since varying degrees of privilege and *marginalization affect what it means to be embodied for different women. In other words, our *race, class, gender, sexuality, and physical and mental capacities influence how we experience our body-selves.

In conclusion, for feminist theologies, embodiment signals the overturning of *dualisms and raises questions about the nature of the relationship between human beings and God, human beings and one another, and human beings and the environment.

Adams [1993]; Bettenhausen, in Daly [1994]; Gudorf [1994]; Heyward [1984]; McFague [1993]; Nelson [1979]

ANNE BATHURST GILSON

Emotion The full spectrum of feelings, including not only joy but also sorrow, *anger, and fear, is seen as integral to human wholeness within feminist theologies. In contrast, patriarchal theologies are highly suspicious of "emotionalism" in general and condemn the "negative" emotions in particular. Apart from a few notable exceptions within spiritual theologies and eighteenth-century revivalism, most traditional theologies have denigrated the affections and advocated the Stoic ideal of emotional detachment. They commended the restraint, if not elimination, of the disturbing power of the affections. Though intense feelings were commonly associated with women, white *androcentric theologians held them to be simply not "ladylike" according to their tenets of "true womanhood."

The importance of the affections has been grossly underestimated within such theologies. Their suppression is part of a wider *dualistic pattern of loathing for the *body typical of *patriarchy. Yet people do not merely have feelings. We are affective. Emotions are an integral part of what it means to be *embodied. Feelings are gracious, life-enhancing sources of interconnection with others, the world, and God. Human emotions fuel all our *relationships; therefore, affectivity should be received with gratitude and nurtured. The struggle for emotional control recommended by most conventional theologians will inexorably necessitate the repression of the very passions that enable and dispose us to be in the world.

Within feminist theologies, feelings per se are not dangerous. It is their disintegration from the rest of the incarnate self (not their "unleashing") that is problematic. This shattering of our embodied integrity is a consequence and expression of *sin. It leaves us internally wounded, enslaved as well as empowered by emotions. People can be immobilized and overwhelmed by feelings. But redemption consists not in escape from feelings but in the transfiguration and fulfillment of them that comes from their integration with other emotions and *reason.

Emerson, *JFSR* [1989]; Goldenberg, *JFSR* [1986]; Harrison, in Loades [1990]; Milhaven [1989]

PATRICIA BEATTIE JUNG

Empowerment The term *empowerment* is used not only in feminist theology but also in the social sciences. It means the process by which individuals, families, groups, and communities increase their personal, interpersonal, socioeconomic, and political strength and influence in order to improve their well-being. Empowerment is not granted from an external source but emerges from within as persons and communities acknowledge and appreciate their gifts and their responsibilities.

In patriarchal *relationships, *power is often seen as a commodity to be used to establish control over others. Power in this sense is "power over," power as *domination, a zero-sum situation in which one person's (or group's) gain in power must result in the other's loss of power. A "power-over" version of divine power manifests itself in church and society in *hierarchies of relations of command and obedience.

In contrast, feminist views of power are more akin to the notion of "power to, that is, power seen as creative, transformative efficacy and *agency achieved through collaboration rather than domination. Rita Nakashima Brock, for example, envisions power as the power of interrelatedness that arises from our connection with one another and our ability to be co-creators in the world, linked in *partnership and collaboration with God.

In writing of power and empowerment, some feminist and womanist theologians have drawn on African-American poet Audre Lorde's essay "Uses of the Erotic: The Erotic as Power" in *Sister Outsider,* which portrays *eros as empowering, creative energy. This power or energy (far more diffuse than sexual pleasure) springs from our *embodied selves: our physical, emotional, mental, and spiritual depths. Erotic power is both nurturing and combative against *oppression. Rather than having a zero-sum quality, this power is increased as it is shared. Hence empowerment is a transforming process that enhances the moral agency of women and other oppressed groups and enables them to act toward *justice and right relations.

Brock [1988]; Friedman/Irwin, *CC* [1990]; Hinze, *Annual of the Society of Christian Ethics* [1992]

MARIE J. GIBLIN

Epistemological Privilege "Epistemological privilege" refers to the claim that, under the historical conditions of *patriarchy, women occupy the particular perspective from which divine *revelation may most fruitfully and accurately be interpreted. This commitment to the perspective of women is expressed in the methodological claim that "women's experience" should serve as the central norm used to critique traditional theological teachings as well as to construct new or revised *doctrines.

Feminist theologians differ in the extent to which they believe the perspective of women ought to be privileged in theological inquiry. In general, the preference given to women's experience by an individual thinker depends on the role she assigns to sources of religious truth, such as scriptural texts, that are traditionally viewed as transcending historical boundaries. Some feminists view women's experience in history, particularly women's struggle to free themselves from patriarchy, as the primary locus of all divine revelation. For these thinkers, the perspective of women can serve as the sole norm for theological inquiry. Other feminists hold that the criteria of women's experience must be balanced with more traditional sources that are also taken as normative for theological judgments.

Three main criticisms have been made against the claim for the epistemological privilege of women. Some critics have argued that in privileging a particular historical perspective, feminist theologians reduce the universal and timeless character of divinely revealed truth. Other critics accept that a theology written from the perspective of the oppressed will yield the deepest religious understanding but disagree with the feminist claim that gender ought to serve as the prototype for all forms of *oppression. Finally, critics influenced by *postmodern *philosophy have asserted that claims emerging from any particular sociohistorical location, even that of the *marginalized, inevitably silence perceptions of ultimate reality that might be offered from other social positions. As a result, it cannot be claimed that a theology written from the perspective of women offers enhanced knowledge of the Divine.

Daly [1973]; Davaney, in Cooey/Farmer/Ross [1987]; Schüssler Fiorenza [1984/1995]

SUSAN M. ST. VILLE

Equality "Equality" refers to the idea that all human beings have intrinsic worth. This idea is understood theologically as deriving from being created in the *image of God and philosophically from respect owed each person as a rational agent. In traditional thought, this idea of equality is affirmed when we transcend our empirical differences and recognize some "essential" quality of our common humanity.

In feminist and womanist thought, the emphasis on transcending empirical differences and positing some essence that makes us equal is critiqued. Although there is not an absolute distinction between the feminist and womanist critiques, each does tend to have different points of emphasis. Feminists tend to stress *embodiment as a corrective to the *essentialist position, and womanists insist that empirical differences (such as *race, gender, and class) are morally relevant. We are created in the image of God in particularity and *difference, and we affirm that image in others by respecting (not denying) difference.

Also, like liberation *theologies, feminist and womanist *theologies utilize various types of social analyses to debunk myths about groups of people, such as women, that are used to denigrate the humanity of those groups and exclude them from understandings of common humanity and moral *community; to expose *relationships of *domination (*power) that create *oppression and deny the humanity of these groups in order to limit their full participation in society; and to offer alternative sociopolitical and socioeconomic visions for creating just societies where equality can be actualized as sociohistoric *liberation.

Finally, equality in feminist and womanist thought is a relational concept, and the term is replaced by concepts such as *partnership, mutuality, and *solidarity. Equality thus refers to relationships that empower groups of people who have been considered unequal on the basis of differences, such as race, gender, and class.

Eugene et al., in Daly [1994]; Riggs [1994]; Russell [1981]

MARCIA Y. RIGGS

Eros In Western Christianity, *erōs* (Greek, "love") has signified romantic or sexual love, as distinct from *philia* (brotherhood, friendship) and *agapē (God's love for us and ours for God). In Christian theology these distinctions traditionally have been clear, especially between eros and the other, "higher," forms of love. In some modern theology (e.g., process *theology), these differences have been relativized to reflect both a more fully *incarnational deity and a higher regard for human *agency in general, human sexual choices in particular. Until the emergence of feminist theologies (Christian, Jewish, and others), eros was not understood among Christians as an intrinsically good power: the love of God.

African-American poet and *lesbian feminist theorist Audre Lorde's essay "Uses of the Erotic: The Erotic as Power" (1984) has been foundational for feminist and womanist theological discourses about eros. According to Lorde, eros is "an assertion of the life-force of women; of that creative energy empowered, the knowledge and use of which we are now reclaiming in our language, our history, our dancing, our loving, our work, our lives" (55). Lorde associates eros with wisdom, "the nurturer or nursemaid of all our deepest knowledge" (56), and with creativity: "There is, for me, no difference between writing a good poem and moving into the sunlight against the body of a woman I love" (58).

Drawing on Lorde in their reconstructive efforts to make connections between women's lives and sacred *power, a number of Christian feminists, rejecting the traditional distinctions among the forms of love, have equated eros with the love of God (Brock, Heyward, Gilson). In Carter Heyward's words, "The erotic is our most fully embodied experience of the love of God . . . , the source of our capacity for *transcendence . . . , the divine Spirit's yearning, through our bodyselves, toward mutually empowering relation. . . . This love is agapic, philial, and erotic. It is God's love and, insofar as we embody and express it, it is ours" (99). According to Gilson, "Eros is a yearning for embodied connection with one another, a movement toward embodied *justice" (115). Brock calls eros the "power of our primal interrelatedness" (25), and for Jewish feminist theologian Judith Plaskow, eros is "our fundamental life energy" (201).

Feminist theological treatments of eros and erotic power belong to the larger feminist commitment to reconstruct the divine–human relation in nondualistic, more fully embodied, and (among Christians) radically incarnational ways. There is no consensus, however, among feminists about the significance of eros as a constructive theological theme. An interesting tension in this area of theological divergence simmers between those who understand eros to be a creative energy in the struggle for women's *liberation from *race, class, gender, sexual, religious, and other oppressions and those who view it either as a distraction from serious liberation efforts or, worse, as a co-optation by *patriarchal interests into a preoccupation with women's *sexuality. There is general agreement among feminists that theological work on eros, even the most potentially liberating, runs the risk of being appropriated by dominant theo-ethical and political forces that exploit women as erotic objects.

In the grass-roots cultivation of Christian and Jewish theologies, the liveliest work on eros is emerging simultaneously in the work of womanist and other women theologians of color. Examples are Korean theologian Chung Hyun Kyung and Renee Hill, an African-American, lesbian, womanist Episcopal priest and theologian. In gay, lesbian, and bisexual religious communities, one of the most engaging instances of the creativity of eros is the lesbian evangelical *mission of Presbyterian minister Jane A. Spahr. Her mission throughout the United States takes her from coast to coast, *preaching the love of God as a liberating and powerfully erotic Spirit.

Brock [1988]; Gilson [1995]; Heyward [1989a]; Lorde [1984]; Plaskow [1990]

CARTER HEYWARD

Eschatology *Eschatology* means "last word": the logos of the last, of the edge of time, the end of the world; talk of the ultimate. The nineteenth-century neologism *eschatology* was designed to tidy up "the department of theological science concerned with 'the four last things: death, judgement, *heaven and *hell'" (*OED*, 1971). Yet the biblical base of those "last things" lacks such primly scientific finality, for eschatology refers, first of all, to the object of biblical hope.

Mainstream exegesis distinguishes between prophetic and apocalyptic eschatology. The *prophetic* expectation of a "day of Yahweh," when *justice is meted out and the social and natural world renewed, is not so much a final divine intervention as a historical transformation, when right relations reign once more, labor is not exploited, and people ripen like their grapevines. Afterlife, heaven and hell, hardly enters this picture, and death, as the natural end of a full life, does not sting. By Third Isaiah and Daniel, disappointment with history has reached such a pitch that eschatology goes *apocalyptic:* Yahweh will turn the tables of history, indeed, finally end history itself. This otherworldly eschaton culminates in John's Revelation, scripted as predetermined, earth-destroying tribulations, the second coming, a millennium of earthly justice, the final battle of good and *evil, and the new Jerusalem "coming down" from heaven.

More recent scholarship would insist on the continuity as well as the difference between prophetic and apocalyptic eschatology. If the *new creation of prophetic eschatology renews the order of genesis through a kind of cosmic exodus, the *new creation of apocalypticism, also socially emancipatory in its context, puts an end to the first *creation. The Gospels evince elements of both: Jesus seems to grow from the apocalypticism of John the Baptist to the subtler and earthier eschatology of the parables of the "kingdom of God."

Mainstream Christian eschatology repressed the anti-imperialism of both biblical models, reinforcing supernaturalism with a Hellenistic eternalism. Hence the historical edge was rubbed off of eschatology, leading to preoccupation with the salvation or damnation of individual souls. Yet outbreaks of revolutionary apocalypticism began to erupt a thousand years ago, announcing an egalitarian "millennium." In this century, the social *gospel and then liberation *theology picked up the biblical emphasis on social justice as the key to the "kingdom."

Is there feminist eschatology at all? If so, what kind of eschatology does feminism nurture? Or inversely, what kind of eschatology has nurtured feminism? Often feminism rejects any eschatology as dualistic, deterministic, and otherworldly. Certainly, feminist theory privileges history over eternity, social justice over supernatural deferral, and *responsibility over salvation. Its hope is oriented to life, not afterlife. In this sense, feminist theology stands outside of orthodox eschatology. Yet, in so doing, it willy-nilly stands within the *tradition of dissident millennialism. Indeed, whether or not they use the term *eschatological,* feminist theologians return persistently to the prophetic themes of collective hope for the disenfranchised, for bodily, social, and cosmic renewal.

What of the apocalyptic turn? Feminist theologians seek to counter the deterministic polarization of good versus evil as itself productive of the historic evil done in the name of God, Christ, and the church. Moreover, the play of gender *stereotypes in the construction of end-time imagery identifies women and evil: evil is symbolized as the "great whore" and good as the macho warrior-messiah on the white horse joining his "virgin bride," the new Jerusalem. Yet it has been precisely the rhetoric of apocalypse in Revelation, the only justice-centered book of the NT (Schüssler Fiorenza), that has stimulated all Western revolutionary and progressive movements. Feminism in this sense cannot deny its own apocalyptic roots: the U.S. women's movement emerged from the millennialist optimism of nineteenth-century America. As for feminist theology, think of Mary Daly's (1973, 95–97) early declaration of "the Second Coming of Women." Inverting the archaic *dualism, she declared "woman" herself the Antichrist for *patriarchal Christians. Similarly, Rosemary Ruether at once criticizes the destructive animus of apocalypse and affirms "ecological apocalyptic."

These apocalyptic associations may be as disturbing as they are undeniable. Feminist eschatology may constitute a fresh form of the denial of the tragic dimension of history (Sands). Along with the poststructuralist *deconstruction of some of the binary oppositions and utopian overgeneralizations of feminist history, we also note how our own proclivity to apocalyptic dualisms of "good feminists" versus "evil patriarchs" has alienated many women of color. Womanist theologians operate with a "multidimensional and bifocal" analysis (Douglas, 97), at once self-critical and pluralist, that renders the eschatology of political dualism impossible. At the same time, Audre Lorde exhibits the prophetic-apocalyptic tendency, facing possible disaster and calling for hope in *Sister Outsider* (1984, 123).

Apocalypse provides a bizarrely realistic lens for addressing the global scale of ecological destruction and socioeconomic injustice facing us in the next millennium. Perhaps a "methodological ambivalence" regarding this (and other) *doctrines serves us best. Feminism grows by resisting its own apocalypticism, i.e., by deliteralizing its own utopias, returning the future possibility to present *community. At the same time, resistance to injustice and insistence on the renewal of the creation will always draw fuel from the image of the new creation. Such a dialectic may not be unrelated to the ambiguity of the Synoptic parables. Perhaps Ada María Isasi-Díaz's *translation of Jesus' eschatological *metaphor of the "kingdom" into the "kindom" best characterizes the growing "edge" of feminist theology: a space-time of edgy hope, of present possibility already actualizing itself in relations of mutuality that prefigure a global *solidarity which is not yet.

Daly [1973]; Douglas [1994]; Isasi-Díaz, in Thistlethwaite/Engel [1990]; Keller, in Chopp/Taylor [1994]; Keller [forthcoming]; McFague [1993]; Primavesi [1991]; Ruether [1983/1993; 1992]; Ruether, in Thistlethwaite/Engel [1990]; Sands [1994]; Schüssler Fiorenza [1985]

CATHERINE KELLER

Essentialism "Essentialism" names a position that makes universal claims for its description of an entity (woman, for example). The "problem of essentialism" is one of the central issues in contemporary feminist theory, *philosophy, and theology. It seems self-evident that feminism needs to ground itself in some notion of female subjectivity (or what "woman" is). However, a number of problems appear to afflict that aim. Is there an essence of woman that all women share, regardless of social or historical location? If so, what is it, and where is it located?

Feminists have long been wary of "biological essentialism," that is, of locating a fundamental *difference between men and women at the biological level. *Patriarchy's traditional arguments for keeping women in subordinate positions have rested on claims about women's biological differences (their childbearing capacity, for example). Claims for an essence of woman at any level (biological, ontological, or otherwise) have been criticized for other reasons as well. Historians have argued that what it means to be a woman varies with historical context. *Lesbians and women of color have argued that the woman assumed to be the subject of feminism only purports to be universal. They have pointed out a number of ways in which *race privilege, heterosexual privilege, and class bias have shaped feminism's "woman" in such a way that she fails to reflect their experiences. For all of these reasons, feminists have come to prefer understanding the concept of woman as socially constructed. This allows feminism to continue to claim a distinctive constituency and still make room for the diversity within that constituency.

Armour, in Kim/St. Ville/Simonaitis [1993]; Schor/Weed [1994]; Spelman [1988]; Williams, *Journal of Religious Thought* [1986].

ELLEN T. ARMOUR

Ethics and Moral Theologies** Moral theology as a distinct discipline is particular to the Christian *tradition, though many of its questions are addressed in other religious traditions as well. Within Christian studies, moral theology is usually traced to the sixteenth century, when Roman Catholic ethical analysis emphasized casuistic and individualistic approaches to questions of the Decalogue and ecclesiastical law. This countered the Protestant Reformation's opposition to "good works" except as the "fruits of *faith," a perspective that emphasized both *gospel and law but worked against the development of moral theology as a separate discipline.

Moral theology and *Christian ethics* have been distinguished in a number of ways. For example, the former is usually identified with the Roman Catholic and Anglican traditions and the latter with modern Protestantism. Sometimes, however, the two terms are differentiated by their primary sources, with moral theology appealing more to theological and ecclesiastical tradition and Christian ethics more to scripture combined with philosophical resources. In neither of these ways is the distinction readily sustainable at this time, however.

The terms are often used interchangeably, which represents the radical shifts in Roman Catholic ethical methodology since Vatican II and an equally radical new interest in questions of Christian *virtue and applied ethics (such as biomedical ethics) in Protestant thought. In all of the Christian traditions ethics has seen both a return to the earlier great themes of *creation and *redemption, faith and *reason, law and gospel, *grace and historical human capacities, and a new focus on questions of moral practice and policy in spheres of medicine, law, business, the environment, economics, *politics, and military action.

As a contemporary theological discipline, general Christian ethics divides its concerns into questions of human *agency (free choice, *conscience, character, the complex structure of the human self), human *relationships (in the public and private spheres), and human actions (measured as good or *evil, just or unjust, responsible, truthful, etc.). Part of its work is descriptive, but much of it is normative. It accommodates a variety of ethical theories (such as *natural law, biblically based theories of neighbor love, human rights theories) and patterns of ethical reasoning (such as consequentialist and deontological). It includes ethical assessments not only of individual actions but of social structures. Its subspecialties range widely into areas of medical ethics, sexual ethics, ecological ethics, and so forth.

Feminist Christian ethics is theological in that it develops, works with, even grounds itself in understandings of God, creation, the human person, *freedom, grace, *liberation, and all the other major themes of Christian theology that are relevant to the discernment of what Christians should do and be in the world. Feminist Christian ethics is feminist because it is opposed to the subordination of women to men on the basis of gender and because it incorporates a central methodological focus on the experience of women. These two commitments reflect its origin in and continuing relation to a movement; however various the contemporary forms of feminist movements are they share *core assumptions* about the injustice of gender inequality and the significance of respecting women's concrete experience.

In addressing questions of human agency, structures of human relationships, and norms for human action, feminists have critiqued the canonical theological and philosophical sources for Christian ethics. The need for this has been nowhere more obvious than in the almost exceptionless historical views of the inferiority of women to men. Feminist challenges to the gendered doctrines of the *imago Dei,* the symbolic connection of women with evil, the assumed appropriateness of men for leadership roles, the privileging of the public over the private, have yielded clear critiques and alternatives to ethical rules governing respect for persons, differentiation of roles, rights of free choice, responsibilities for future generations, demarcation of the secular and the sacred.

What feminists soon realized, however, was that the ethical problem for Christians and others is not simply to extend the pool of the fully human to include women. To challenge gender inequality is inevitably to *disrupt the given order of things* (whether political, economic, ecclesiastical, familial). Systems that depended on a gendered differentiation of roles were therefore threatened, and alternatives have had to be imagined and argued. Actions and practices heretofore taken for granted needed critique, and actions and practices neglected in the past needed introduction. Thus feminist Christian ethicists, along with Jewish and other religious thinkers and feminist philosophical and political theorists, moved into the various spheres of what has been traditionally referred to as "applied ethics." Reproductive *rights, care of the elderly, *poverty, war and revolution, media *stereotypes, racial bias, domestic *violence, labor relations, child care, ecological dangers, pornography—all became issues for which a feminist perspective was significant. All were and are issues in which the subordination of women to men has been involved, and all were and are issues on which women's experience was not previously taken into account.

Two major reasons, then, have pressed feminist ethics to expand its agenda beyond only opposing the subordination of women to men and to nuance its commitment to women's experience as the initial significant source for ethical analysis. First, it became eminently clear that the issue of the subordination of women to men is inextricable from issues of *racism, poverty, militarism, colonialism, *heterosexism, and environmental *survival. Second, a commitment to the well-being of all women, and therefore to taking seriously the experience of all women, required acknowledgment of the diversity of women's contexts and experiences. Feminist ethics had to become not only Western European or North American ethics but world ethics; feminist Christian ethics had to challenge not only the Western *canon but, for example, Latin American male-biased liberation *theology and ethics; feminist religious ethics had to include the work of Jewish feminists and to be open to feminists from all religious traditions. Hence feminist Christian ethics came to respect and to need alignment with womanist ethics, *mujerista* ethics, and the ethical reflections and arguments of many other women whose particular experience both challenged and enriched the whole enterprise of theological ethics.

Key questions for feminist Christian ethics in all of its forms include traditional questions of moral agency. Yet these questions look different when they become questions of the moral agency of women. Not only does women's experience belie traditional notions of female diminished agency and women's inferior sense of *justice; it offers ways of understanding the connection between *free self-determination* and *emotional response.* Feminist ethics has engaged in revisionist interpretations of *desire and love (including Christian **agapē*), of passion and *anger and *pride. It has offered new understandings of human and religious virtues, vulnerabilities to evil and capacities for good, love that is both self-sacrificial and yet aims at mutuality. It incorporates alternative models of moral development that emphasize dispositions for caring that complement, if not supplant, dispositions only for justice. Feminist ethics has also addressed issues such as *addiction, questioning theories of biological determinism but also theories of the sheer power of the will.

Feminist concerns for *autonomy and freedom are almost always juxtaposed to concerns for *relationality.* As a feature of the human personality, relationality is addressed not as an abstract essentialist notion but as a concrete possibility and need, realized in concrete contexts of relationship. Whether in the form of *friendship, *family, *community, church, city, nation, or world society, the significant questions are ones of criteria for right relationships, dispositions for sustaining relationships, balanced requirements for love of the other and love of the self. Feminist ethics, therefore, has attempted to address the experience of "otherness," patterns of *power, the importance of sympathy, the meaning of *solidarity, the criteria and moral imperatives for inclusion in communities where exclusion has been the order of the day.

There is no univocal feminist Christian ethical theory. It reflects the *pluralism of feminist theory in general. Beyond the now questionable categories of liberal, Marxist, socialist, and radical forms of feminism, the disagreements within feminist ethics tend to occur along the fault lines of contexts versus principles, particularity versus universality, and justice versus *care. These are not unrelated theoretically, though they are distinguishable. Some feminist ethicists, for example, have been critical of the effectiveness of abstract principles to provide guidance in concrete situations. In contrast, some feminists remain strongly convinced of the importance of general principles such as truth telling, reproductive freedom, nonmaleficence, and *equality.

The *particularity and diversity* of women's own experience argues against too much reliance on abstract principles. But it also risks an unmitigated *relativism, something that a feminist ethics committed to gender (and racial, religious, etc.) equality cannot accept. Hence feminists struggle to work out a theory that will take account of particularity but not altogether rule out universal norms.

Women's experience also contributes to feminist disagreements on the importance of *justice* and the importance of *caring.* The influence of the work of Carol Gilligan and others on the moral development of women has called into question previous interpretations of moral experience in general. No feminist doubts that women's moral experience must be respected, but there is strong disagreement about its interpretation. Is there a specifiably feminine moral sensibility? Ought feminists to prefer attitudes of caring to principles of justice? Are there principles of caring that can and should incorporate norms of justice?

These questions shape the agenda for feminist ethics, along with significant disagreements about actions and policies. Among the latter are specific questions about affirmative action, pornography, sexual practices, reproductive technology, family structure, and environmental protection. Debates such as these provide urgency to the task of identifying feminist perspectives on all spheres of human life and feminist approaches to religious and moral pluralism.

Andolsen/Gudorf/Pellauer [1985]; Cannon [1988]; Card [1991]; Daly [1994]; Harrison [1985]; Isasi-Díaz [1993]; Plaskow [1990]

MARGARET A. FARLEY

Ethics, Womanist Womanist ethics has its roots in the work of Katie Geneva Cannon. Her essay "The Emergence of Black Feminist Consciousness" for the anthology *Feminist Interpretation of the Bible* (Russell, ed., 1985a) and her book *Black Womanist Ethics* (1988) laid the foundation for womanist ethics. Cannon makes an important distinction between dominant *ethics and ethics from communities of the dispossessed. Dominant or traditional ethics assumes *freedom and a wide range of choices for the moral agent. Dominant ethics makes a *virtue of qualities that lead to economic success: self-reliance, frugality, and industry. It assumes that the moral agent is free and self-directing, and it can make *suffering a desirable norm. In Cannon's view, this understanding of moral *agency is not true for African Americans. Such freedom is not available to white women, women and men of color, poor people, and representatives of marginal groups in U.S. society. White supremacy and male superiority force black folks to live in a different range of freedom. In situations of *oppression, freedom is not a choice; nor is self-reliance. Frugality is enforced and suffering is present, but neither is chosen. Therefore, womanist ethics explores black ethical values, obligations, and duties from the conscious perspective of *marginalization.

Many African-American women in the theological disciplines have gravitated to the use of Alice Walker's term *womanist* as both a challenge to and a confessional statement for their own work. Walker's four-part definition that contains the elements of *tradition, *community, self, and critique of white feminist thought provides a fertile ground for religious reflection and practical application (1983, xi–xii). Womanist ethics is an interstructured analysis that begins with *race, gender, and class. Such an analysis is not only descriptive but prescriptive as well. Womanist ethical reflection provides descriptive foundations that lead to analytical constructs for the eradication of oppression in the lives of African Americans and, by extension, the rest of humanity and *creation.

The confessional element of *womanist* means that it cannot be imposed but must be claimed by the womanist ethicist who is engaged in the eradication of oppression. The use of the term *womanist* to describe an ethicist's work is one of avowal rather than denotation. This confessional stance is crucial, as the ethicist engaged in womanist reflection is also holding in tension her own identity as a black woman with the various *methodologies of ethical reflection. This is an organic method involving constant self-reflection in the context of the "doing" of one's vocation and avocation.

There is no one voice in womanist ethical reflection. There is rich *dialogue about whether one should hold all of Walker's definitions within the womanist frame or pick and choose the elements one finds helpful in her work. Some womanist ethicists challenge Walker's inclusion of homosexuality as a desirable norm in the African-American community in the second part of the definition. Others resonate with the themes of the mother–daughter dialogue in the first definition and see this as pivotal for their work. Still others are drawn to explore the dimensions of self-care and self-love and affirmation in the third part of Walker's definition. Some focus on the need for a piercing critique of white feminism (academic and practical) implied in Walker's fourth part. Finally, there are those who believe all four of the parts of Walker's definition must determine one's theoretical and analytical framework.

Womanist ethics is interdisciplinary. Theology, *pastoral care, *biblical studies, pastoral theology, *church history, *liturgics, Christian religious *education, sociology, *anthropology, *psychology, history, biology, the physical sciences, and the arts are methodological conversation partners for womanist ethics. The concern is for ongoing reflection within a dynamic theoretical and practical tension.

Baker-Fletcher [1994]; Cannon [1988]; Cannon, in Russell [1985a]; Riggs [1994]; Townes [1993b]; Townes, ed. [1993a]

EMILIE M. TOWNES

Ethnography, Liberationist Ethnography has become a popular research tool of feminists and other researchers interested in the *liberation of people. This research strategy is used in the study of society and culture. An ethnography is a description of people and their actions or behavior. It describes the everyday, routine production of *culture. The people most likely to produce ethnographies are "social constructionists," who theoretically understand the world as a social product—a product you and I work hard everyday in tiny countless ways to shape, repair, and rebuild.

The classical goals of ethnography are to understand culture from the participants' perspective and to report or tell this cultural *story in such a way that the participants agree the researcher has understood their lives correctly. To achieve these goals, ethnographers take great care in locating sources or informants who are experts in their field and who are able and willing to communicate what they know across cultural barriers.

Some researchers go on to place their ethnography in a larger theoretical context that assists the reader in interpreting the story. The naming of the intentional location of a people's story in a theoretical context that might not have been constructed by the people observed is an important contemporary correction to earlier ethnographies that "read" stories through unnamed "lenses." For instance, we now have feminist, Marxist, feminist-Marxist, womanist, and *mujerista* ethnographies that clearly define the interpretive process used in analyzing cultural descriptions.

The goal of liberationist ethnography is to be in the service of humankind. Ethnography in the service of humankind uses what one learns about people to advance their well-being. In much the same way that James Spradley's early ethnographic work on urban alcoholics changed the way the United States regulated health care benefits, feminist ethnography is frequently socially "activist" in that it seeks to make women's lives better.

By clearly delineating the power structures in society, ethnographers reshape society's practical knowledge of itself. Ethnographers in service of humankind face the contradictions of writing about a people who can also write about themselves. Some feminists are encouraging their communities to produce their own ethnographies. These highly specific and localized stories are beginning to take shape in the form of narratives, plays, poems, *liturgies, and songs, and they are beginning to form the base of constructive feminist, womanist, and *mujerista* *ethics and *theology.

Fonow/Cook [1991]; Isasi-Díaz/Tarango [1988/1993]; Smith [1987]; Wolf [1992]

VICTORIA ERICKSON

Eucharist *Eucharist* describes a ritual meal that embodies *memory, imagination, *power, encounter, *freedom, *relationships, presence, blessing. It is an action in which the *community celebrates its *covenant connection with God. The word *Eucharist* derives from the Greek *eucharistia*, "to give thanks."

The Christian community since the second century has used the word *Eucharist* to describe its worship, a ritual meal in which, through word, bread, and wine, it remembers what God has done and imagines what God will do. God is blessed, thanked, and proclaimed in and with Christ through the power of the Spirit. By the end of the Middle Ages, when only the priest regularly ate and drank, the Eucharist was perceived less as a meal and more as an action the priest did while the people watched. The bread, now a host, was worshiped from afar rather than eaten. The people, whether present or absent at the Eucharist, appropriated the benefits of Christ's sacrifice. Reformers of the sixteenth century challenged these aberrations and revived original interpretations of the action, though frequent eating and drinking was still uncommon. In the twentieth century the early practice of eating and drinking together as a church gathered to tell its story in memory of Jesus has been revived.

The eucharistic action expresses the essence of the church, its identity with Jesus' life, death, and rising. At the same time it embodies its *mission, to receive and share the gifts of God, to praise and offer thanks for them in and with Christ, empowered by the Spirit. Feminism begins its critique at these junctures. The abundance inherent in the symbols is contradicted by the actual experience of the Eucharist. The performance defies the freedom the Eucharist promises. An embodied knowing of God is limited, an identity with Christ is partial, the experience of the Spirit is restricted when language, leadership, sacred stories, gestures, sounds are exclusive. The experience cannot express the ultimate gift of God's freedom and lavished love. In addition, the language of *sacrifice, where Jesus' death, in *atonement for our sins, is required in the redemptive plan of God, affirms the sacredness of victimization, a reality that has claimed too many women's lives.

Some feminist theologies consider the Eucharist unredeemable in its present forms. The traditions of people, texts, and action are too inextricably intertwined with patriarchal patterns. The sacrificial language, so deeply embedded in the heart of the action, cannot empower women. Others insist on reconstruction that includes rewriting texts, changing models of leadership, examining gestures and actions, and, in general, an opening of the experience to much more varied interpretations. Such a reconstruction implies a reorganization of power and a sharing of authority. It requires breaking down barriers and crossing the boundaries of gender, class, *race, age, physical abilities. Reconstructed celebrations will not only recall what has been missing in traditional retellings of the covenant story but also correct what has been oppressive. The witness of women and the stories of all those whose voices have been silenced will be incorporated. These Eucharists will be both festive and mournful, so connected are they with what has been done and left undone in this world. The intent is to empower each person, to affirm and evoke each one's story, as necessary components in the continuing identification with the life, death, and rising of Christ in our midst. *Justice in all its dimensions is a primary concern. To give thanks, *eucharistia,* is an expression of confidence in the persistent stirrings of the Spirit not confined by *patriarchal patterns, an acknowledgment of embodied relational power that can be received and given through bread, wine, Word.

Elkins [1994]; Procter-Smith [1990]

JANET R. WALTON

Evil

Traditions. In many traditions, evil is the opposite of good, the absence of good, or the inseparable but clear mixing of good with its opposite or with its absence. Sometimes evil is a divine power, equal to the divine good or subordinate to the divine good and controlled by it. Evil is the uncontrolled life-destroying in "nature," or evil is the life-negating result of human actions (society), or *evil* is a solely moral term, referring only to human intention(s) and result(s).

Evil is historically attributed to persons or objects who are mysterious, dominated, or unknown. Men have thus often located evil in women and their needs. Also, evil can be located in preferred male actions, though it is rationalized as being the fault of other agents, e.g., women "cause" rape; war against another belief system "that is false."

Feminist Options. For some, evil is the *treatment of other people as objects*, as inferior, as less intelligent. This treatment includes privileging physical *power over mental, emotional power. Evil is reducing a person or a community to one of its parts and ignoring the rest. Thus evil treats only women's wombs and ignores their brains. Evil is respecting only the spirit and demonizing the *body.

Evil is a system; not "*sin," which is individual action. Questions arise about the treatment of a single person, however. Is torture of one person "evil," or buying of *one* slave? Can evil be produced when human, personal agents are not so clear but the pattern of destroying persons by rejecting their basic human needs is? Both the agent and the effect are necessary in defining evil. Are any humans so powerless that they can never be agents of evil, whatever the tradition's definition of evil?

Evil is *proportionate to power*. It can describe a greatly advantaged privilege that gives huge capital to a few and asks hard work from multitudes (e.g., international corporations selling T-shirts and women sewing). It can describe a "traditional" mode of behavior, one that is seen as usual but is also dependent on an adult agent's belief and a child's lesser power (e.g., incest).

Ideals. Evil's definition depends on a vision or teaching of what could be or should be, on some ideal or at least preference. For some, reversing traditional visions of good and evil defines both in a new way: now women are good, men evil; now people of color are good, whites evil. But actions are interconnected and so not morally or in any other way perfectly good. The many ideals are historically, humanly created, and so, related.

If the ideal (*Goddess, *eros, relation, God) is omnipotent and benevolent, evil is what systemically or persistently violates this belief. But such evil is excluded from the nature of the divine. The ideal or divine thus is not really all-powerful. Attention to power and evil can be selectively chosen, so that being subject to the evil of *sexism (a systemic violation of an ideal) does not itself cover one's *responsibility for persecuting old women and men. A white woman subject to *disability prejudice should not be exempt from responsibility for perpetuating *racism.

Evil is here a possibility for all humans as agents. People's ability to perpetrate evil is proportionate to their power, including systemic organizing and acting in favor of what the agents define as good and what effectively reduces others' chance for basic daily living or life itself. Global, diverse meaning systems define evil in conflicting or similar ways. Women can describe the good of the specific, daily needs of humans as a living, interdependent species on the planet. Such *naming creates a possibility of action against actual evil even in the midst of religious *relativism.

Maxwell, *Zygon* [1992]; Sands [1994]; Smith [1992]; Townes, ed. [1993]

ELIZABETH BETTENHAUSEN

Exorcism The practice of expelling demons and evil spirits from objects and persons by means of *prayer was common among ancient Greeks, Romans, and Jews (and is also practiced by shamans and witch doctors in Asian, African, and Native American religions).

It was incorporated into Christianity following the examples of Christ himself. The Roman Catholic Church has distinguished between two types of exorcism, routine and real. Routine (virtual) exorcism does not presuppose the presence of demons. Part of the rites of *baptism and blessing, its goal is to purify persons, objects, and animals. Real exorcism is performed on individuals who are possessed by demons or evil spirits.

Demonic possession is exhibited by involuntary movements and seizures and the ability to speak in tongues and unveil secrets. In Western Christianity it has been a sign of religious transgression by either the possessed or the community at large. The exorcist's role was to diagnose the behavior as possession, identify its causes, and heal the possessed. During the Reformation, Luther ridiculed real exorcism, but it was nevertheless practiced by Lutherans, Anglicans, and Puritans. Calvin rejected both routine and real exorcism as papal magic. Catholics reaffirmed their belief in exorcism and used it to manifest Catholicism's power over demons. Still included in the Catholic rite, real exorcism is rarely used today.

In most societies, women are more likely than men to exhibit the signs of demonic possession. Traditional psychological explanations dismissed the possessed as hysterical, but recent explanations suggest that women's overrepresentation may have to do with their status deprivation and lack of access to other forms of public speech on religious matters. Other theories equate spirit possession with mediumship and argue, based on the cross-cultural belief that women are better mediums than men, that as possessed, women are enabled to convey religious messages to their communities. These messages usually reveal that sins have been committed, and the recovery of the possessed demands expiation of these sins.

Boddy [1989]; J. Forget, "Exorcisme," in Loth/Michel [1951–77, 3:1762–80]; Lewis [1971]

MOSHE SLUHOVSKY

Experiences Women's experiences are the locus and source of women's liberation theologies. Intrinsic to these theologies is a repudiation of universalist and transhistorical *reason, hitherto elaborated and maintained as revelatory and normative by males and *patriarchal structures. Instead, the daily experiences of women struggling for *liberation have become the core of women's liberation theologies' critical norms. Women's experiences, like all experiences, are social processes and as such include not only given actions but also the evaluations, ethical value judgments, tendencies, and perspectives of the subject-agent. Women's daily experiences, however, are not only particular reflective actions but also involve the social, economic, political, and cultural factors that frame such actions. This indicates that there is a communal aspect to experiences, that they are socially located and connected to *power and "value-defined and interest-laden" (Davaney, 46).

Multiple discourses on women's experiences are not seen as providing objective historical facts but rather as revealing and validating comprehensive ways of self-interpretation, of seeing and understanding the world, of constructing self and society from an ever "expanding range of contexts and social locations" (Welch, 174). Women's discourses on their experiences do not assume or refer to some sort of universal women's experience with a *metaphysical claim, nor do they endorse the possibility that the experiences of any given woman or group of women offer exclusive access to the truth. Rather, women's discourses on their experiences are to make clear that no "human perspective has a privileged access to ontological reality" (Davaney, 43–44). These discourses, which show commonalities as well as particularities among women's experiences, are pivotal for the development of nonoppressive structures and inclusive strategies. At the same time, they raise the issue of *whose experiences are to be considered* in the elaboration of norms and how the truth of one person's experiences is affirmed in the face of another person's experiences.

The attention and importance given to women's daily experiences leads to recognition and valuing of differences, as well as to the need to determine how to deal with *differences and the grounds for determining whose experiences to privilege at any given moment. Because ultimately feminist theologies are about the liberation of all women, it is precisely liberation understood in a holistic sense—that is, liberation at the structural as well as at the personal level, at the *ideological level (which includes religious or theological perspectives) as well as at the historical level—that offers the basis for determining whose experiences to privilege: those of women who benefit least in a material, psychological, or religious sense. These experiences, with their particularities and specificities, are the ones to be privileged by feminist theologies.

The appeal, then, is to the experiences of particular women whose very existence is constantly thwarted and endangered. These women, conscious of their oppression and committed to liberation, have the most to contribute to the elaboration of strategies for radical social change. Their experiences are privileged at the theoretical as well as at the practical level, in the elaboration of liberative discourses and of effective political action, precisely because they are better able to envision a future radically different from the oppressive present from which they benefit the least, if at all.

Privileging the experiences of others means that *differences have to be understood, valued, and embraced* in such a way as to lead to engagement and interaction. They are to be valued and not ignored, merely acknowledged, or simply attended to only as they resemble one's own experiences. For differences to be seen as a positive factor, those who are different must feel free to be themselves, instead of being required to act or present themselves first and foremost in a way intelligible to those who determine or profit from what is normative. Thus honesty about the limits of one's own experiences, as well as the willingness to enter into the world of others, is an essential requirement (Lugones, 43). For differences to generate lasting and effective engagement and interaction among women, the role of power in feminism and in feminist theology has to be analyzed.

Analysis of experiences in women's liberation theologies does not posit universals but points to particularities and specificities. It also teaches us that differences are to be valued and embraced as an intrinsic element, while taking into consideration whatever power relationships are inherent in them.

Davaney, in Atkinson/Buchanan/Miles [1987]; Lorde [1984]; Lugones, in Card [1991]; Russell et al. [1988]; Welch, in Kim/St. Ville/Simonaitis [1993]

ADA MARÍA ISASI-DÍAZ

Faith Faith is a life orientation of the whole person in *partnership with God. It is not reducible to beliefs alone, nor solely to acts, but involves a mutually informing process of action and reflection. Faith is the *praxis of God's love and *justice in the context of particular communities of struggle and hope. Traditionally, Western theologies have defined faith as a gift from God involving knowledge (*notitia*), trust (*fiducia*), and action (*assensus*). Feminists affirm the multiplicity in such perspectives while critiquing what they overlook. Feminist re-visions correctively assert (1) the significance of human experience in knowing God, (2) the primacy of action, and (3) the importance of *community.

Feminists critique perspectives treating faith as a passive-receptive phenomenon. Faith involves active partnership with God, a relational opening of persons both to God and to the world made possible by the divine–human partnership in Jesus Christ. By emphasizing human participation, feminists affirm human experience, and therefore the ordinary lives of women, as places where God becomes known.

Faith involves engagement in the world. Defining faith "from the underside" stresses action in the praxis of faith. Such faith entails living out an ethic of God's love and justice. Some male-oriented theologies use obedience to describe this aspect of faith. Feminists, suspicious of the differential application of concepts such as obedience to women and other oppressed peoples by dominant groups, instead favor action, or praxis.

Faith happens through the work of the Spirit in communities of shared struggle and hope. In the face of Western theologies' individualistic concern with personal salvation, feminist theologies locate faith in communities. Currently, North American feminists are asking about the eclipse of faith's poetic dimensions in male-oriented theologies, the place of (*patriarchal) scripture in faith communities, and the adequacy of traditional *christological formulations (such as the *doctrine of Christ's *atonement) as *metaphors for depicting God's partnership with humanity.

Brock [1988]; Carr [1988]; Chopp [1989]; Russell [1993]

JOYCE ANN MERCER

Fall Many religions articulate a notion of the Fall, a moment when the human situation changes from a more ideal state to a lesser one. In Manicheism and *Gnosticism, for example, the spirit "falls" into the body, becoming entrapped there, where it cannot rise and return to God. In the Christian *tradition, Genesis 3 comprises the narrative of the Fall: the serpent persuaded Eve, the first woman, who lived in paradise, to take some of the fruit from the tree of the knowledge of good and *evil and eat it; she then shared that fruit with her husband, Adam; "then the eyes of both were opened and they knew that they were naked" (Gen. 3:7). When God questioned their self-consciousness of their nakedness, Adam gave the narrative that would dominate Christian perceptions of women: "The woman whom you gave to be with me, she gave me fruit from the tree, and I ate" (Gen. 3:12). God first punished the serpent, then turned to Eve: "I will greatly increase your pangs in childbearing; in pain you shall bring forth children, yet your desire shall be for your husband, and he shall rule over you" (Gen. 3:16).

In the Middle Ages and early modern period, this narrative was the foundation for the church's teaching on women, their place within *marriage, and their *sexuality. In particular, the church stipulated that women's relationship to their husbands was to be one of subject, not partner. First the church fathers, then medieval theologians anchored their discussions of women's sexuality in this text and in those *Pauline texts that referred to it: women's sexuality was perceived increasingly as irrational, easily led by the "serpents" of *desire, longing, "lust," and as active, even reaching out in its hunger. Theologians as disparate as Thomas Aquinas and Martin Luther would cite the necessity of constraining female sexual activity in their justification of marriage.

The narrative of the Fall was most important in Christians' construction of the story of human *redemption. It was seen as the necessary antecedent to the life of Christ, God's act of supreme mercy. Christ was the "new Adam," the Adam unpolluted by *sin, unself-conscious. In the Middle Ages the Virgin Mary increasingly was accorded a parallel role to Christ: Mary became the counterpoint to Eve because her innocent childbearing helped to compensate for the sin of the first woman. So, too, the Fall was understood as the moment of origin for human sexual desires: Eve was seduced by her desire to know; the most immediate consequence of the first couple's disobedience was their unease with nakedness. In the Middle Ages, Christ's celibacy and Mary's virginity were more than a sign of their holiness; their sexual *asceticism was essential to the story of human redemption. Hundreds of visual images as well spoke of the singular role Eve played in the story of human frailty and divine mercy.

When European missionaries traveled to the Americas, Africa, and Asia, beginning in the sixteenth century, they carried with them the images and *metaphors in which Eve's story had become embedded, imprinting it and all the associations it had developed on women throughout the globe. To this day, missionaries still carry the story of the Fall, and Eve's particular role in the fall of all humankind, with them to every continent. This scapegoating of women as the cause of disobedience and sin continues to be taught as people interpret and reinterpret the third chapter of Genesis.

Miles [1989]; Pagels [1988]; Suchocki [1994]; Trible [1978]

LEE PALMER WANDEL

Family The *Oxford English Dictionary* (1971) defines family as descendants of a common ancestor or as a people descended from a common stock. It also considers a group of people living as one household or bound together as a unit to be a family. Feminists point to the diversity and inclusiveness implicit in such dictionary definitions of family. Families come in all shapes and sizes and are constantly changing in their cultural definition. Families' definition and welfare are key concerns for feminists, who have written extensively examining family roles and responsibilities because the issues of commitment and *justice are so entwined.

Conservative political rhetoric has portrayed feminist thought as hostile and destructive to family life. In fact, the opposite is true: feminists are concerned because they wish to contribute to helping families grow stronger and better. Feminists and social scientists have reexamined the understanding of commitment and accountability in *relationships such as *marriage partners and parents and children. Ethicist Margaret Farley has contributed significantly to redefining the *ethics of personal commitments (1986). Letty Russell has written extensively proposing new models of *partnership in society (1979).

Feminist thought has centered on the issue of mutuality in partnerships, and this has revealed the many oppressive and *hierarchical dimensions of marriage as a social institution. Many feminists propose new concepts of partnership and family that strive for *equality for women and are inclusive of homosexual and *lesbian relationships.

Within the fields of *psychology and pastoral counseling, perhaps the greatest recent shift is the growing research in family systems theory. Study of family systems and communications patterns within families is of widespread interest to social scientists and counselors. Feminist theologians and pastors are actively working to probe and address the changing concepts of relationship in family and society. Work to reassert an ethic of mutuality and accountability is vital.

New concepts and forms of family have emerged in the last thirty years. These appear to be related to several factors. Certainly, the availability of more reliable birth control has been a major influence in family life. Women have been more able to exercise control of reproductive functioning. They have sought employment, and the majority of families now depend on a dual income. Both of these changes have contributed to significant shifts in the role of women in families. Social scientists record a major increase in the number of single-parent families. A large percentage of divorced fathers refuse to pay child support, thus leaving the economic support of children solely to the mother.

Specific problems signal the stress on families today. Family *violence is currently seen as a major public health problem in the United States, and it is a critical issue affecting women and children in families throughout the world. Preventing family violence and sexual violence has been a central topic for Christian feminists. Marie Fortune has written several excellent books and developed several films that discuss sexual and family violence.

Couture [1991]; Fortune [1983]; Glaz/Moessner [1991]; McGoldrick/Anderson/Walsh [1989]

LEE MCGEE

Feminist Hermeneutics Feminist hermeneutics (from Greek *hermeneuō,* "to interpret") is best defined as theory, art, and *praxis of interpretation in the interest of wo/men (women and men). While wo/men of *faith always have interpreted the scriptures, feminist hermeneutics is a newcomer in theology. Only in the context of the wo/men's movements of the nineteenth and twentieth centuries have feminists begun to explore the implications and possibilities of a critical hermeneutics that takes the institutional silencing of wo/men in biblical religions into account. Hence feminist biblical hermeneutics aims to empower wo/men for becoming subjects of interpretation and for engaging in the critical construction of religious meanings. By reclaiming the authority of wo/men as religious and theological subjects of interpretation, feminist hermeneutics attempts to reconceptualize the act of interpretation as a moment in the struggle for wo/men's *liberation.

Feminist biblical hermeneutics engages two seemingly contradictory insights. On the one hand, the Bible is written in kyriocentric (centered on the lord/master) language, has its origin in the patri-kyriarchal (lord/master/father rule) cultures of antiquity, and has functioned throughout its history to inculcate misogynist mindsets and oppressive values. On the other hand, the Bible has functioned in the past and still functions today to inspire and authorize wo/men in their struggles against dehumanizing *oppression. What has been said about the scientific research of Marie Curie seems equally to apply to wo/men's biblical interpretation: it simultaneously serves as a resource for wo/men's religious *empowerment and for their continuing victimization.

Consequently, a critical feminist hermeneutics does not begin by placing the Bible at the center of its attention but instead focuses on the struggles of wo/men at the bottom of the patri-kyriarchal pyramid of *domination and exploitation, because their struggles reveal the fulcrum of oppression and dehumanization threatening all wo/men. Such an experientially based systemic analysis provides a hermeneutical perspective that is conscious of its social, political, and religious location, an advocacy stance that is shared by all critical liberationist forms of hermeneutics, be they womanist, *mujerista,* Asian, African, Latin American, European, or North American.

Popular and academic biblical interpretations by women, the reading of the Bible as *a woman,* and its interpretation in terms of *gender* are not simply identical with a critical *feminist* biblical hermeneutics, insofar as they do not problematize their own kyriocentric cultural hermeneutical lenses. In contrast to both academic women's studies and gender studies, a critical feminist hermeneutics focuses on the systemic analysis of wo/men struggling to change patri-kyriarchal structures of oppression.

This crucial methodological difference between women's and gender studies' hermeneutics using only woman or gender as their lenses is overlooked when one argues that feminist theologians must respect conservative women's readings of the Bible because such readings give meaning to their lives. Yet such a critical feminist hermeneutics insists that conservative interpretations are not feminist simply because they are readings of women. Insofar as such conservative, biblicist readings do not employ a critical feminist analysis of wo/men's sociopolitical and ecclesial-religious subordination and second-class citizenship, they tend to construe respect and dignity for women in terms of the internalized *ideological frameworks of cultural femininity and true womanhood. Consequently, such conservative readings cannot but sustain the ideological structures of wo/men's oppression. By insisting that such readings are not feminist or liberationist, one does however not deny *agency and respect to individual women.

Equally, a critical feminist hermeneutics does not subscribe to the kind of subjectless play of meaning, apolitical nihilism, or agnostic *relativism that is advocated by some forms of poststructuralist gender studies. A critical feminist interpretation for liberation operates not only within a different theoretical framework from that of poststructuralist theories. It also employs a different understanding of texts, insofar as it focuses on the rhetorical dimensions and elements that are generated by the materiality of texts, the historicality of readers, and the politics of communication in past and present sociohistorical hermeneutical contexts. Hence feminist hermeneutics is a practice of sociopolitical rhetorical inquiry that aims at the formation of a critical historical and religious consciousness. Whereas hermeneutical theory seeks to understand and appreciate the *meaning* of texts, rhetorical inquiry pays close attention to the kinds of effects biblical discourses produce, how they produce them, and for whom they are produced. It moves beyond "mere hermeneutics" to a complex model for a critical process of feminist interpretation and evaluation. It seeks to overcome the hermeneutical binaries between sense and meaning, explanation and understanding, critique and consent, distancing and empathy, reading "behind" and "in front of" the text, the present and the past, interpretation and application, realism and imagination.

Such a critical feminist hermeneutical process entails four rhetorical strategies of analysis: suspicion, reconstruction, evaluation, and imagination. These strategies are not simply successive independent steps of inquiry or methodological rules. Rather, they are interpretive practices that interact with one another in a feminist interpretation of a biblical or any other cultural text. These four strategies, however, have a doubled reference point: the language systems, ideological frameworks, and sociopolitical and socioreligious locations of contemporary interpreters, on the one hand, and the linguistic systems and sociohistorical locations of biblical texts, social contexts, and their effective histories of interpretation, on the other.

A critical feminist hermeneutic of liberation that understands biblical interpretation as a cultural-religious practice of resistance and transformation utilizes not only historical-, literary-, and ideology-critical evaluative methods that focus on the rhetoric of the biblical text in its diverse historical contexts. It also employs methods of storytelling, bibliodrama, poetry, painting, dance, music, and ritual for creating a "different" religious imagination. Its critical hermeneutical-rhetorical processes are not limited to *canonical biblical texts. They can be equally applied to extracanonical sources and other classics of *religion and *culture. They also can be and have been used successfully in work with illiterate women, highly trained theologians, and feminist Bible study groups around the world.

Demers [1992]; Felder [1991]; Kwok [1995]; Russell [1985a]; Schüssler Fiorenza [1984/1995]; Schüssler Fiorenza, ed. [1993; 1994].

ELISABETH SCHÜSSLER FIORENZA

Feminist Theologies, Asian Asia, the home for over half of the world's population, is the birthplace of major historical religions of humankind. Divided into seven major linguistic groups, Asian people have lived for centuries in a multiracial, multicultural, and multireligious world. Christianity is a relative latecomer in these ancient civilizations. *Marginalized in their mainstream *patriarchal religious traditions, Asian women play some significant symbolic and ritualistic roles in shamanism and some popular *Taoist and Buddhist traditions.

For centuries, the majority of the Asian people have suffered under the yoke of European, American, and Japanese colonial powers. Asian women were systematically exploited and sexually abused under colonialism and the military control of Asia. Asian countries regained political *autonomy after the Second World War, but the situation of women has not been much improved. Today, three-quarters of the world's illiterate population live in Asia, the majority of them women. Although economic development in some Asian countries creates new job opportunities for women, many are exploited because of sexual discrimination in the workplace and exploitation of multinational corporations. Asian women also suffer as a result of sex tourism, the spread of *AIDS, militarism, neocolonialism, and political instability.

Asian feminist theologies emerged as a response of Christian women to these multiple forms of *oppression. It began as a grass-roots movement when Christian women gathered to read the Bible and raised questions based on their life *experiences. Different *ecumenical networks, including the Women's Desk of the Christian Conference of Asia, the Women's Commission of the Ecumenical Association of Third World Theologians, and the Asian Women's Resource Centre for Culture and Theology, have nurtured the women's theological movements in Asia (cf. *In God's Image*). Asian women theologians have found that white, male, and middle-class theologies have often been used to legitimate cultural *imperialism and exploitation of the earth. Furthermore, neither Asian male theologies nor Western feminist theologies provide adequate help to address the situations of Asian women. They have to find new sources, symbols, images, and stories from their own contexts to articulate their own understanding of the Divine.

The relationship between *gospel and *culture is a crucial issue for Asian feminist theologies. Christianity emerged from the multicultural context of Judaism and Greco-Roman religions. Both the Western and the Orthodox churches historically have incorporated into their teachings and practices many elements from their cultural environments. But when Asian women theologians begin to use their indigenous symbols, legends, and rituals in their theologies, they are criticized as "syncretistic" and "pagan." Asian women theologians insist that Western culture does not have a monopoly over Christianity, which must interact with diverse cultures, including the different women's cultures of the world.

Because Christians make up less than 3 percent of the Asian population, religious *pluralism is another challenge for Asian feminist theologies. Many Asian women theologians have found that Asian religious traditions are less institutionalized than Christianity in the West, and the boundaries between different religions are more fluid. In their struggle for *survival, poor and oppressed Asian women often transgress religious boundaries and assimilate many elements from different traditions. Living in a multireligious world, Asian women theologians have argued that they embody the diverse traditions of shamanism, *Buddhism, *Hinduism, *Confucianism, and Christianity simultaneously. With multiple identities and heritages, they challenge us to move beyond doctrinal *purity and artificial segregation of spiritual traditions of humankind. They insist that we must move beyond interreligious *dialogue to religious *solidarity, working for *justice across religious traditions.

Most of Asian women's theological reflections focus on reinterpretation of the Bible. Some women theologians have used the myths, legends, and cultural resources from Asia to reappropriate biblical stories. Through the process of dialogical imagination, they bring the biblical story and the Asian stories into interaction with one another. Others borrow insights from cultural *anthropology and show that a social structure defined by honor and *shame can be found in both the New Testament world and some Asian societies today. Asian Christian women emphasize that women in the Bible are divided by *race, class, and *religion, just as women are today. The Bible is a product of complex interaction among many cultures. Discovering the cultural dynamics shaping the biblical narrative helps us understand how the Bible functions cross-culturally. Through dramatization, storytelling, and creative performances, Asian Christian women develop an oral hermeneutics to reclaim the gospel message for their own *empowerment.

Asian women live in an enchanting world of gods and goddesses, with colorful religious festivals and rituals and alternative forms of spirituality. Some Asian women theologians have begun to speak about God from a more inclusive viewpoint, taking into consideration the religious sensibility and cosmological awareness of Asians. For some of them, the maleness of Jesus is a problem only if one is assuming a Chalcedonian, substantive understanding of *Christ. Western *doctrine has turned a "historical accident" into an ontological necessity. Asian women theologians find Jesus liberating not as a male but as a person who led a particular way of life. The presence of many gods and goddesses in Asian religions also makes it easier for Asian women to relativize the significance of the gender of God. Jesus exemplifies a way of relating to God and to the world that is significant for Christians. Emerging images of Jesus in Asian women's writings include liberator, political martyr, mother, shaman, worker, and grain. Salvation brought forth by Christ applies not only to human beings but to the whole groaning and mourning *creation.

Asian women theologians have also redeemed Mary from a docile, sanctified, and gentle mother to a self-defining woman, bringing forth transformation and wholeness. She is imaged as a model for a fully liberated human being and for true discipleship. She accepts the challenge of the *Holy Spirit and acts as coredeemer for human salvation. For Asian women, Mary symbolizes a woman who yearns for *liberation of the oppressed people and nurtures the hope of new humanity through perseverance and *suffering.

Asian women theologians challenge the patriarchal church *hierarchy, which is reinforced by an *androcentric interpretation of Christianity and patriarchal Asian social structures. They point to the need for continued *conscientization of women in the church and call for a new, inclusive, egalitarian pattern of relationship, team *ministry, ecumenical dialogue, and equipping of all people of God to work for God's reign.

The twenty-first century has been hailed as the Pacific century because of the rapid increase of business transaction and capital flow across the Pacific. Mindful of the plight of indigenous people, the untouchables (*dalits*), minorities, and refugees, Asian women theologians condemn the structural *sin brought by the globalization of the market economy and the so-called new world order. Searching for alternative orderings of the world that value women's labor, *sexuality, and dignity, they call for an eco-spiritual vision based on care of the earth and of all marginalized and displaced people. Through music, poetry, dance, drama, and storytelling, they give expression to a spirituality that is life-affirming, creative, and energizing. Rediscovering the power of subversive protest in popular Asian religions, as in shamanism, Asian women theologians delve deeper into the rich Asian traditions and learn to speak the language of poor women to articulate their theology and spirituality.

Abraham et al. [1989]; Chung [1990]; Fabella/Park [1989]; Gnanadason [1993]; Katoppo [1980]; Kwok [1995]; Lee-Park, *IGI*

KWOK PUI-LAN

Feminist Theologies, European

The catalysts for the development of the diverse European feminist theologies were the Second Vatican Council [1962–65], the work of the World Council of Churches, the influence of the secular feminist movement, and the rise of multidisciplinary women's studies, together with the stimulus of the writings of American feminist theologians. The development of feminist theology in Europe can be seen in three phases. Different women were and are prominent in each phase, stimulating content and focus.

The First Phase, 1960–75. Several women played a significant part in raising awareness of the position of women in the church and in Christian *tradition in this initial stage. Gertrude Heinzelman wrote *We Are Silent No Longer: Women Express Themselves about the Second Vatican Council* (Zurich: Inter-feminas Verlag, 1964). Her focus, which was developed in later publications, continued as part of the struggle for change in church law and in the university structures, as well as with sexual morality and human values. At about the same time, Mary Daly was studying in Fribourg, Switzerland, and wrote her first book, *The Church and the Second Sex* (1968). Unlike in her later, post-Christian writings, Daly was critical of the church's attitude to "the second sex" yet hopeful of renewal. In the Netherlands, Catharina Halkes had been deeply involved with the Second Vatican Council and published her first book, *Storm na de stilte* (Storm after Quiet) (Utrecht: Ambo, 1964). It described the position of women in the church for council members.

The first scholarly study of the position of women in Christian tradition, traced through the thought of Augustine and Thomas Aquinas, was that of the Norwegian theologian Kari Børresen, *Subordination and Equivalence* (Oslo: Oslo University Press, 1968). In Belgium, Maria de Leebeeck's book *Being Woman: Fate or Choice?* (The Hague: Lanno, Tielt, 1967) was intended for a wider public and translated into German and Italian. In Germany the writings of Elisabeth Gössmann were prolific and influential, ranging from her first book, *Woman and Her Mission* (Freiburg: Herder, 1961), to a later work, *The Contentious Sisters—What Does Feminist Theology Want?* (Freiburg: Herder, 1981). Elisabeth Schüssler Fiorenza's first work, written in Germany, belongs to this period: *The Forgotten Partner—Foundations, Facts and Possibilities as to the Professional Participation of Women in the Salvific Work of the Church* (Düsseldorf: Patmos-Verlag, 1964). The question of the *ordination of women was brought specifically to the fore in a groundbreaking doctoral thesis by Ida Raming ("Der Ausschluss der Frau vom priesterlichen Amt: Gottgewollte Tradition oder Diskriminierung?" Cologne, 1973).

At the same time, the activities of the World Council of Churches (WCC) stimulated much attention to the position of women in church and society. From its conception there had been a gender awareness. In 1953 the committee "On the Life and Work of Women in the Church" (founded in 1949) was reorganized to become the Department of the Man–Woman Relations in Church and Society. Many studies, consultations, and publications resulted. Among the most significant was *The Community of Women and Men in the Church*, whose immediate catalyst was the 1975 WCC assembly in Nairobi, at which, for the first time, women held their own program. The WCC is also responsible for two important developments: the inauguration of the process entitled "Justice, Peace and the Integrity of Creation," which has had a great impact on the lives of women; and the Ecumenical Decade "Churches in Solidarity with Women."

The Second Phase, 1975–85. This phase saw many key structural developments. The International Year of the Woman gave it a good start, and in June 1975 the first European Symposium on Women's Studies was held. It was initiated by a Swedish scholar but organized by Catharina Halkes, whose career is crucial to the development of feminist theologies in Europe. Her involvement in the Second Vatican Council, the World Council of Churches, and many pastoral networks both in the Netherlands and in Europe as a whole resulted in the creation of a chair in Feminism and Christianity in the theology department at the Catholic University of the Netherlands. (Her successor from 1989 to 1993 was Mary Grey; the present holder is the Jewish scholar Athalya Brenner.)

The Belgian/French group Femmes et Hommes dans L'Eglise was founded in 1970. This decade also saw the founding of the European Society of Women in Theological Research. Called together initially by Bärbel von Wartenberg and Joann Nash Eakin from the WCC subunit on Women in Church and Society, a small group of women (including Catharina Halkes, Luise Schottroff, Elisabeth Moltmann-Wendel, Dagny Kaul, the late Fokkelien Van Dijk-Hemmes, Ellen Juhl Christiansen, and Joann Nash Eakin) met at Boldern, Switzerland, in 1985. The society holds a biennial conference and aims specifically to stimulate and support research in feminist theology.

In 1982 another organization, the European Ecumenical Forum of Christian Women, was founded. With an office in Brussels and three presidents from different parts of Europe, the forum's strength is its ability to work on many levels, including a spirituality group and a Commission on Theology, Ecology and *Bioethics. Its presidents have been tireless in highlighting the position of women in the newly "liberated" countries of Eastern Europe.

The Third Phase, 1985 to the Present. The current phase of the development of European feminist theologies has brought many changes. First, a new generation of women scholars finds itself much less closely bound to the church and Christianity (even though Christian feminism is still developing as an academic discipline, a grass-roots *liberation movement within the churches, and a *culture critique in society). This phase is in much closer *dialogue with the many disciplines of women's studies in the universities. The fall of communism in Eastern Europe, the *postmodern climate in *philosophy, the regrouping of the European countries after 1992, and the war in Bosnia have had many consequences for feminist theologies in Europe.

The need for a new *pluralism is deeply felt, with a consequent need for a decrease in the dominance of Christian feminist theology and an emphasis on dialogue with Jewish and Muslim women scholars, as well as others of the great world faiths. Thus the dialogue that feminist theological scholarship holds with tradition has been expanded to include the traditions of women in the *world religions. The need to become more familiar with the theology and the struggles of women in Eastern Europe is deeply felt. At the same time, European women theologians are taking seriously the legacy of European *imperialism and of *racism within Europe itself. They are attempting to enter into dialogue with women theologians from the Southern Hemisphere with the intention of being in *solidarity in the struggle against the many *oppressions. Thus there is now a sense that the connections and solidarity among women at a global level, a solidarity that affirms and respects *difference, sets the agenda for the future of feminist theology in Europe.

Bekkenkamp/Droes/Korte [1986]; Brotherton [1992]; Esser/Schottroff [1993]; Gill et al. [1994]; Gössmann et al. [1991]; Halkes, in Esser/Schottroff [1993]; King [1991]; Parvey [1983]; Schaumberger/Maassen [1986]

MARY C. GREY

Feminist Theologies, Jewish Partly because theology as a whole is marginal to the Jewish religious enterprise, there is relatively little formal Jewish feminist theology. Jewish feminism, like much Jewish religious expression, is *praxis-oriented. Its goal is the transformation of Jewish history and law, religious practice, and communal institutions in the direction of the full inclusion of women. Thus feminist theological reflection is generally embedded in ritual and *liturgy, novels and historical research, and textual interpretation and *midrash. This said, however, it is possible to identify theological themes in Jewish feminist work as they appear both in theology proper and in other types of writing.

Jewish feminist thought emerged in the early 1970s as an attempt to describe and protest the subordination of women within the Jewish *tradition. The first feminist works generally agreed on the contours of women's subordination, but different Jewish feminists understood the causes of women's *marginalization in different ways. While some saw women's disabilities as sociological in origin, others saw women's subordination as rooted in the central categories of Jewish *religious life. The latter position underlies most feminist theological writing.

Transforming the Categories of Tradition. Torah, both as the five books of Moses and as the history of oral interpretation, is at once the central symbol and complex content of Jewish religious reflection. While no Jewish feminist simply turns her back on Jewish sources, non-Orthodox feminists often characterize Torah as partial and incomplete. Only a portion of the record of the Jewish encounter with God has been passed down through the generations. Before Jewish feminists can transform and transmit Jewish teachings, they must first hear women's voices within the tradition and discover the contours of women's religious experiences.

This task of discovery takes place on many levels simultaneously. While partly a historiographical project, it also assumes a process of continuing revelation through which women, in interaction with both traditional sources and one another, "receive" new understandings of themselves and of Jewish stories, practices, and concepts. What is important theologically is that Jewish feminists are defining and accepting the insights emerging from diverse avenues of exploration as Torah. Torah in its traditional sense is decentered and placed in a context in which the experience of the *whole* Jewish people becomes a basis for legal decision making and spiritual and theological reflection.

Within the larger category of Torah, Jewish law poses particularly complex issues for feminists. While women's legal disabilities were the first object of Jewish feminist attention and remain central for Orthodox feminists, some feminists have begun to examine the presuppositions of the *Halakhic system.* Rachel Adler has suggested that Jewish religious life rests on the continuing interpretation of a received body of knowledge that excludes the perceptions and concerns of women. Large numbers of questions women might raise about how to function as *autonomous religious agents lie completely outside the realm and imagination of normative Jewish sources. This problem cannot be resolved through a more sensitive application of the rules of Halakhah; it requires a new moment of "jurisgenesis," a transformation of "the normative universe Jews inhabit." Moreover, as Judith Plaskow has argued, since Halakhic interpretation as a mode of religious discourse and experience has rested solely in the hands of a male elite, it is not clear whether, given the choice, women would turn to Halakhah has a dominant form of religious expression or the mode through which they would redress issues of women's subordination.

Jewish feminists, like their Christian counterparts, have been sharply critical of hierarchical dualisms, particularly the association of groups of human beings with oppositional categories such as spiritual–material or sacred–profane. Dvorah Setel has argued that the central conflict between Judaism and feminism revolves around not the legal and historical treatment of women but the Jewish understanding of holiness as separation, as opposed to the feminist value of relationship. The Hebrew word for "holy," *kadosh,* means "separate" or "set apart," with separateness often being understood in oppositional and *hierarchical terms. Jewish feminist thought, in seeking to reconcile Jewish and feminist worldviews, looks for ways to speak about the distinctiveness of Jewish identity, belief, and practice that are not invidious or hierarchical. Thus, in terms of Jewish practice, the Havdalah ceremony's "paradigmatic statement of hierarchical dualism" has been rewritten by feminists to affirm both distinction and connection. In terms of Jewish theology, Judith Plaskow has tried to rethink the central concept of chosenness, using a part–whole rather than a hierarchical model.

The paradigm of hierarchical *dualism within Judaism is the traditional concept of God. In seeking to transform traditional imagery, feminist experiments with God-language have both altered the gender of God and reconceptualized God's nature and power in far-reaching terms. Calling for the freeing of our symbolic imaginations, feminists have offered a plethora of new images for God, from the female (Shekhinah, mother, queen) to the conceptual (flow of life), to the natural and gender-neutral (lover, friend, fountain, unseen spark). They have emphasized *immanence over *transcendence and God as empowerer rather than as majestic and distant power.

Underlying this explosion of new images and concepts is a new understanding of *monotheism. As long as the dominant Jewish conception of God identifies God's oneness with the worship of a single image of God, thinking of God as female seems to threaten monotheism. But feminists have offered an alternative conception, arguing, in Marcia Falk's words, that an "authentic" monotheism is not "a singularity of image but an embracing *unity* of a *multiplicity of images.*" Monotheism is not the worship of a finite being projected as infinite but the capacity to find the One in and through the changing forms of the many.

New Directions. At present, Jewish feminists are exploring new theological themes in a number of directions. Topics such as the problem of *evil and the *Holocaust, neglected in the first spate of feminist writing, are receiving new attention. Feminists are using literary analyses of Jewish texts as vehicles for explicitly theological reflection. Feminists influenced by *postmodernism are addressing the multiplicity of Jewish feminist identities and trying to refine the categories of feminist analysis. Such explorations, Lori Lefkovitz suggests, may lead to abandonment of patriarchal categories such as Torah and Halakhah in favor of more anarchic and female classifications such as "fluids" and "voices."

Adler, *Conservative Judaism* [1993]; Falk, *JFSR* [1987]; Greenberg [1981]; L. H. Lefkovitz, in Rudavsky [1995]; Plaskow [1990]; Setel, *JFSR* [1986]; Umansky, in Plaskow/Christ [1989]

JUDITH PLASKOW

Feminist Theologies, North American The term *North American feminist theologies* refers to a body of theological perspectives and ways of working that are as distinctive and diverse (culturally, ethnically, racially, religiously, sexually, socioeconomically, and as to abilities and ages) as are the women writing them. Just as there is no one "traditional" (European-American, middle-class, men's) theology, neither is there one feminist theological position or method. Moreover, the term is inclusive of critical and creative study of what have traditionally been discrete theological disciplines (scripture; *church history; doctrinal and systematic theology; *ethics, sociology, and psychology of religion; pastoral counseling; etc.). Feminist theologies are further distinguished from traditional theologies by their regard and respect for the personhood of all women and by advocacy on behalf of women's personal and corporate well-being.

Although the term *North American feminist theologies* is contemporary in cast, women have done theology critically and creatively in North American contexts since the nineteenth century, at least. Retrieving what she calls a hitherto unrecognized *tradition of feminist theology, Mary Pellauer (1991), for example, explores the thought of Elizabeth Cady Stanton (*The Woman's Bible,* 1895), Susan Brownell Anthony, and Anna Howard Shaw. Anna Julia Cooper and Matilda Joslyn Gage (*Woman, Church and State,* Persephone Press, 1980) are among the many other nineteenth-century foremothers of contemporary feminist theologians in North America.

Two insights have been catalytic of the composition of the contemporary body of North American feminist theologies, beginning in the 1960s. The first insight is that what has been named "human" experience and taken to be human understanding has been men's experience—not women's—and men's understanding—not women's—of themselves, the world, and God. Theologians Valerie Saiving and Judith Plaskow, for example, in the 1960s and the 1970s, respectively, argued that "traditional" understandings of *sin as *pride or egocentricity reflect the experience of men and ignore the experience of women, whose temptations derive from tending to dissolve self through devoted service to others.

A second catalytic insight follows from this. Not only do traditional theologies reflect men's experience and understanding; they reinforce—indeed, sacralize—social behaviors, attitudes, and structures that privilege men while violating women or relegating women to a secondary and derivative status. Mary Daly, in her 1973 classic, *Beyond God the Father,* put this point precisely when she saw and said that if God is male, then male is God.

Common to these two catalytic insights is the question of *theological language.* Believing in the world-making power of words, i.e., affirming that language shapes the ways we see and act in the world in which we live, feminists have asked why both male images and language have predominated traditionally. They have recovered female images, both human and divine, forgotten in scripture and in Christian and Jewish traditions. Some feminists also attempt to retrieve images of the *Goddess to nurture women's unique experience and spirituality.

The distinctiveness of women's experience has been and is, then, a creative source for North American feminist theologies, as well as a lens through which traditional theologies have been and are viewed critically. Its distinctiveness, however, also poses a number of problems to word definition. First and foremost, the term *women's experience* is increasingly problematic for women doing theology in North American contexts. Through the 1970s and 1980s, the women's experience claimed as source and substance was, more often than not, white, European-American, middle-class, heterosexual women's experience. The *classism, *heterosexism, *racism, etc., of white women's theologies have been exposed as African-American women, Native American women, working-class women of various ethnic identities, Latina women, *lesbians in diverse racial and class locations, Asian-American women, women living with unique physical and mental abilities, etc., have begun to speak up and speak out of their own unique experiences.

This outpouring of theologies among women in North American contexts poses other problematic elements as well. One is found in the word *feminist* itself. Many African-American women doing theology—for example, Delores Williams—have claimed the term *womanist,* coined by Alice Walker in her introduction to *In Search of Our Mothers' Gardens* (1983), to name themselves and their theologies as distinct from African-American men and white feminists and their theologies. Accordingly, Latina theologians such as Ada María Isasi-Díaz have named themselves *mujeristas.* Recognizing that women's right to and *responsibility for self-naming is integral to the theological task, it is unclear whether or in what way the term *feminist* can or will refer to women who are not white, European-American, and middle-class.

Another problematic word definition relates to the word *theology.* Almost all women doing theology in North American contexts refer to "women's experience" as a source and authority for their work. However, one woman working theologically, like one man working theologically, may draw from some sources more than others or may consider certain sources more authoritative than others, according to the religious tradition with which she is in *dialogue: Jewish, Christian, Goddess, or other traditions.

For example, Rosemary Ruether (1983, 23–24) and Letty Russell (1993, 199–201) find within scripture a "prophetic-messianic message" or a "liberating tradition," respectively, that serves both as a self-critique of scripture and as a critique of Christian tradition and of all structures of *oppression. Yet the primary source for other women's theological work is reflection on ritual gatherings of women who celebrate *liturgies created of symbols both inside and outside Jewish and Christian traditions. Some women take *prostitution, the global sex trade, and sexual abuse as the source for their theological work, thereby affirming God's presence in these places and authorizing the stories of *healing as well as crucifixion they hear therein, while other women are reinterpreting Christian *doctrines such as the *atonement and *Christology with regard to women's experience. Seeking to reconnect spirit and *body (the human body, the body of Christ, and the earth's body) some women are exploring *ecclesiology, while others enunciate the theological implications of environmental concerns.

North American and *feminist* and *theologies* are, in short, words that refer to the body of women's theological writings in North America. They are also words whose definitions point to problematic points within this diverse body. North American feminist theologies compose a contested as well as a creative body. A final problematic issue arises here concerning whether women writing North American feminist theologies can authentically say the word *we*. As more and more women work theologically out of their own experiences, the interconnectedness of forms of oppression (cultural, ethnic, racial, sexual, physical, class, etc.), in North American contexts as around the world, becomes more and more clear. This clarity calls women who are working theologically to acknowledge conflictual alliances and concrete controversies among and between women and women's theologies, rather than assume and affirm a "sisterhood" that has no real referent.

Daly [1973]; Isasi-Díaz [1993]; Pellauer [1991]; Plaskow [1980]; Ruether [1983/1993]; Russell [1993]; Saiving, in Christ/Plaskow [1979]; Williams [1993a].

MELANIE A. MAY

Feminist Theologies, Pacific Island Pacific Island feminist theologies are part of an emerging movement for change of structures that hinder better opportunities and *equality for women. These theologies appeal to the scriptural affirmation that both male and female are created in God's *image and believe in the liberating acts of God that bring forth *justice, transformation of life, and the full humanity and participation of women.

The Pacific Islands are populated by three distinctive groups of people: Micronesians, Polynesians, and Melanesians. The population is traditionally rural but currently becoming cosmopolitan in nature. The term *Pacific Islands* is geographically interpreted as a numerous variety of large, medium, and small islands scattered around and about the vicinity of the equator and inhabited by indigenous people. Epeli Hau'ofa, a Pacific anthropologist, used the name Oceania to refer to this region, connoting small areas of land surfaces sitting on top of submerged reefs or seamounts, along with their inhabitants. He referred to the world of Oceania, where ancestors made their homes and bred their generations of seafarers, and where they moved and mingled unhindered by boundaries (1993, 8). The invasions of colonial powers, modern migration, and the enormous influences of technology have had marked impact on the people.

Feminism is a belief that women should have the same rights and opportunities (legal, political, social, economic, etc.) as men. Any definition of feminism has to be viewed in the light of the social structures and the cultures of the people. The structures of Pacific Island societies are relatively *patriarchal, and this has been encouraged and strengthened through Christianity. Women are regarded as second-class citizens and are almost passive listeners to any decision of the community. Thus, as Shamima Ali of the Women's Crisis Centre, Suva, Fiji, told Lisa Meo in 1992, Pacific Island feminism can be defined as an effort to raise awareness in the *community so that women may be recognized and encouraged to participate fully in all the community's decision making.

Women are beginning to take action to bring forth *conscientization. This involves the full realization of the denial of women's rights, the organizing of women's groups, the *education of men and women, and the opposition of all forms of *oppression that enhance the suppression of women. This action demands a total commitment, *solidarity, and the determination of those who are sympathetic to women's situations in order to take effective action. A feminist recognizes oppression, exploitation, and discrimination against women and is committed to take liberative actions for a better life that leads to full recognition and participation of women. A feminist is an activist who commits her- or himself to take risks and advocate justice for women who are unjustly treated because of their gender. Feminist militant or aggressive approaches, however, have negative connotations in the Pacific communities because they appear contrary to the Pacific way of dialogue.

Theology is a study about God and God's nature and the foundation of religious belief. It is a human effort to gain knowledge about God that generates a reciprocal relation. One can say that theology is an acknowledgment of the sustaining power and nature of God's presence in our midst. Feminist theologies are "women's God-talk" which recognizes that both male and female knowledge and discussion about God are important.

Theology in the Pacific Islands reflects a multireligious context. Our ancestors have their own traditional beliefs about gods prior to Christianity. Pacific Island ministers and laity were asked the question: "What was the heart of the traditional beliefs of the Pacific Island people?" A senior minister responded that the true meaning was the search for *power. The people wanted power to catch fish, power over other people, and power to get well when they were sick. They sought this power in the spirits and through magic. When Christianity came, the people saw it as a new source of power (Mavor, 17).

For Pacific Island people, theologies are an integration of traditional and Christian beliefs of the nature of God and gods, and a craving for God's power. God's power brings blessings, *mana*, and to be without God's power means a curse, or *sau*. One can interpret feminist theologies as an acknowledgment of God's power that will bring forth *empowerment for the powerless, especially, in this case, women. Once women are empowered, they will discover their own identity as creatures created into God's own image. Theologies are concerned with God's relation to human beings and with human beings' response in acknowledging God, the creator and sustainer of their life. A Christian feminist clings to her or his reciprocal relation with God because it is sustaining and affirming.

Feminist theology is a form of liberation *theology and shares in the latter's focus on freeing or liberating people who are oppressed. The oppressed include various sexual, racial, ethnic, and economic groups. Jesus' teaching about good news for the oppressed is welcomed by those who are *suffering from injustices. Feminist liberation theology focuses on the status of women who are oppressed because of the patriarchal *culture, those who are economically poor and politically marginalized, and those with second-class status within the religious institutions of the world, including Christianity.

Pacific Island feminist theologies focus on oppressed women within the Island communities. The Pacific Island feminist theologian takes the message of Jesus to heart and applies it, through advocacy and empowerment, to rid women of all forms of oppression. In this way, the women will take their equal place alongside men and fully participate in decision making by utilizing their long-buried talents.

Feiloaiga, *Pacific Journal of Theology* [1992]; Forman [1982]; Griffen [1989]; Kanongata'a, *Pacific Journal of Theology* [1992]; Mavor [1977]; *Weaving* [1994–]

LISA MEO

Feminist Theologies, South Asian

While there have been sporadic theological contributions by women in South Asia for some years, the challenge to search for a specific Asian feminist hermeneutic came from the Ecumenical Association of Third World Theologians (EATWOT). Through their Women's Commission, EATWOT worked from 1984 to 1986 to gather the voices of women and initiate consultations on theology of *liberation from the perspective of women in the *third world (Fabella).

It was in this context that national-level meetings were held during that time in India and in Sri Lanka. Since then, a few women in other South Asian countries have also become more articulate. The national-level meeting in India was a pathbreaking event. Protestant and Roman Catholic women came together (formally for the first time) to discuss a "theology of humanhood from women's perspectives." The conference began with "The Story of Indian Women." Group work focused on specific struggles of women as exposed by the secular women's movement (rape, *dowry deaths, and the *violence of some Indian myths and proverbs were named). The women affirmed the need "to base all theological perceptions in the context of Indian women's lived *experiences, and the realities of women's oppression" (Gnanadason 1989).

Some characteristics of the emerging feminist theology in South Asia are the following:

Starting from the Experiential Base. Women in South Asia live in societies that reflect some of the worst violence in the world. Amy Gonsalvez from Bangladesh writes, "The structure in traditional Bangladesh society was and still is dominated by the chauvinist male. It is a society where women are seen as second class citizens; used and handled as the personal property of men, exploited and oppressed, retaining no real identity of their own. The Bangladeshi woman is still a slave in the home, one of the many playthings for a man to enjoy. A woman seems to be always burning with pain" (1994, 70).

While affirming the great contributions made by South Asian religions and spirituality, women point to the *patriarchal roots in all religions and cultures as the major force that legitimizes and sustains the violence they experience. As Sri Lankan women describe it, "[Nevertheless] patriarchal *ideology has invaded all religions and is deep seated and strong and cannot be easily dislodged. All religions have the concept of the feminine as *evil and all attack female *sexuality. She is seen as a temptress. She is impure and unclean and must be submissive to man" (Hensman/Silva/Perera 1992, 143–44).

It is out of such a context that Indian women once asked, "Given this fact that an Indian woman belongs to society that considers women to be almost valueless, how can she contribute to the theological enterprise? How can she do theology if she does not exist? What resources has she to do theology if she does not have enough to eat? How can she speak prophetically if she has no voice? What practical possibility is there for her to do theology if her only place is in the home? Can she even recognize God as existing and caring for her and her sisters?" ("Report from India," 144).

This valueless status of South Asian women has become central to the articulation of theology of liberation for Asian women. There is a clear movement toward a specifically South Asian women's theology. This became evident as women prepared for the first Asian regional meeting of women in theology (held in 1990). As the Sri Lankan women described it in their document, "[But] for us in Asia, the perspective in which women's hermeneutics is carried on includes not only what is good and universal in the struggle for democracy, against clericalism and so on. . . . It takes into account also of our colonial experience and struggles for independence . . . and also of peoples' movements in country side and cities to get beyond feudal and sexist distortions in the interpretation of religious texts. . . . It leads towards the rediscovery of our indigenous traditions of economy and spirituality which are resources for the future" (Hensman/Silva/Perera, 1992, 143).

Affirming the Rainbow Colors of God's *Creation. Another characteristic of the emerging feminist paradigm in South Asia is the affirmation of the "rainbow colors of God's creation, respecting the values and aspirations of particularly those on the periphery. It has drawn together women of all faiths, all classes, all castes and of various ideological persuasions. The common struggle for *survival and human dignity has encouraged women to find a common platform for their struggle without undermining the plurality of experience and of cultural and traditional diversities that India is composed of" ("Breaking the Silence," 3).

Gabriele Dietrich writes, "There have been attempts within the Indian women's movement to re-look at the role of religion without blindly rejecting it as anti-women. This has been done either by reinterpreting the social environment and by tapping the unexpressed 'protest potential' in religious traditions. The concepts of shakthi and Kali have become symbols of women's inherent strength" (1988, 189–90). Therefore, the "theologizing activity" within the women's movement has to be done without "religious" labels, respecting the liberation strands of all faiths and encouraging the search for protest elements in all faiths. This is the most vital contribution that South Asian women in theology are making to the global feminist theological movement: offering a new paradigm that respects the integrity and value of all the great living faiths.

Going to the Roots—An Eco-Centered Spirituality. South Asian women have engaged in recent years in a search into the "women-centered" popular religions of Asia and the prepatriarchal fertility cults that are based, among other things, on the images of the mother-goddess and the female power principle. These women would affirm that it is women in their societies who have been able best to articulate a new value system that is a life-centered and eco-centered spirituality, which is at the heart of most of Asian religious belief and practice. "As Asian women participate in this process of struggle, they give birth to a spirituality that is particularly women's and particularly Asian. The Great Mother breaks out of all that has bound her and frees, creates anew, and liberates all creation 'which has been groaning as a woman in travail.' Shakthi emerges triumphant. . . . The rebirth of Shakthi has led Asian women to have a *'hermeneutics of suspicion' of traditional spiritualities, of traditional interpretations of scriptures. . . . It has made women conscious of their *responsibility to all of humanity—particularly the most oppressed—and all of creation. It is in this re-emergence of Shakthi, or spiritual energy, that Asian women find God" (Gnanadason 1989, 15–18).

Motherhood has been an important

concept for South Asian women, and there is a constant reference in South Asian feminist theologies to the fact that it is within the context of the *community that any theologizing activity can take place. The Bible continues to play a central role and is not rejected for its patriarchal roots. Rather, the search is for the liberative strands in the *faith *tradition.

The attempt to draw on South Asian religious and spiritual traditions for inspiration is still in its nascent stage. Part of the problem lies in the fact that liberation theologians in South Asia have, by and large, been in *dialogue with the metacosmic religions that worship powers beyond those of the natural world, and had not taken seriously the fact that these religions have all systematically legitimized the *oppression of women. Now an effort is being made to go to the cosmic religiousness of people, turning, by and large, to the prepatriarchal, woman-centered cults that worship the invisible powers of nature.

"Breaking the Silence" [1990]; Dietrich [1988]; Fabella [1993]; Gnanadason [1986]; Gnanadason, in Lee-Park, *IGI* [1989]; Gonsalvez, *Voices* [1994]; Hensman/Silva/Perera, *Voices* [1992]; Pathil [1987]; "Report from India," *Voices* [1994]

ARUNA GNANADASON

Feminist Theology, African Africa is the land mass from the Nile Delta to the Cape of Storms. That this contribution on African feminist theology has no input from some parts of Africa reflects the author's limitation and not the extent of the geographical entity that constitutes Africa. That the perspective is limited to Christian women is a deliberate choice and makes no statement about the nature of feminism in Africa. This description reflects the theological articulation of women who consciously theologize out of their own and other women's *experiences. In recent times, this Circle of Concerned African Women Theologians has opted to work together toward a liberative theology in the African context (cf. Oduyoye/Kanyoro). Many of them are teachers and others are pastors. They are supported by church women who, but for the many other demands on their time, would have written "feminist" accounts of life and church and God.

The context of spiraling *poverty, the legacy of colonialism and neocolonialism, shapes women's theology. The diversity of communities raises identity questions for all Africans. The challenge of *inculturation of Christianity in this multiple religious context raises questions about *Christology and urges all who do theology to review their theology of religions. For many, the latter centers on the resilience of African religion, which undergirds their *culture. African feminist theology is being crafted in the context of other African theologies, some liberating, others domesticating. It is being crafted in an atmosphere of risk, for its architects may be muzzled and the theology snuffed out for being dangerous to womanhood as defined by *tradition.

There is an inevitable prophetic dimension to this theology, which is what risks bringing us into conflict with both the African and the Christian communities to which we belong. In addition, African feminist theology is developing in the context of global women's liberative and critical theologies and therefore runs the risk of being judged by the parameters of feminists elsewhere. A *deconstruction of the African context to eschew mystification is itself a colossal risk and task. Hence, while we communicate with women in other contexts and share common ground, we focus on our own specific challenges. Like other *liberation theologians, we join in the analysis, deconstruction, construction, and advocacy that will bring *healing and transformation to our communities. To do this, we seek to tap the latent power of our *faith communities, and we attempt to draw sustenance from the resources of Christianity's faith convictions.

The theological reflections so far undertaken may be described by five themes and characterized as a theology for transition and transformation. We do not know what we may become, but we are convinced of the vision encouraging us to make more apparent the *image of God in African womanhood and our affirmation of the reign of God in Africa. Meanwhile, we want to name ourselves and say our own word.

Resources for the theology are found in traditional sources for Christian studies, but in addition, African women theologians delve into African cultural history, *religion, and the sources of spirituality available to Africans. Scriptures are not limited to Christian sources and include the language of oracles, prayers, symbols, and rites of Africa's combined religion and culture. While we reread the Bible, we do not overlook the need to review the traditional interpretations of Africa's own spiritual sources.

Cultural similarities between contemporary Africa and biblical times make **biblical studies* most crucial for crafting a liberating theology in Africa. Reading the Bible from Africa, we have seen a development of the understanding of God in human history that has a more familiar ring. The interpretation of culture as influenced by divine promptings and of *community as a gift of God to be treasured become hermeneutical principles for reading the Bible. In dealing with "divine promptings," the question we examine is: "Who is interpreting and translating the intentions, will, and guidance of God?"

A traditional theme that captures our attention is *Christology*. The question, however, is posed differently from traditional theology's concern for the "inner being" of the *Christ as the second person of the triune God. Our question has been: "Who is Jesus Christ for Africa, for African women, and for persons and communities among the many socially disadvantaged in Africa?" For African women, the Jesus of the *gospel comes through as the friend, healer, advocate, and source of transformation of which we are critically in need. Further, Jesus "the boundary breaker" is a source of hope for women bound on all sides by religions and cultures of Africa. This is the Christology that stimulates women's "protest theology." Empowered by the *Holy Spirit, we risk announcing the good news of God's *jubilee.

Arising out of women's experience, our theology is keenly contextual, taking into account religion, culture, and socioeconomic and political developments in Africa. Living has no boundaries, but in doing theology we have called attention to *religion and culture* as facets of life making the most impact on women in Africa. They also enable us to see life whole, as Africa's economic, political, and societal developments are all imbued with religion and infused with religious beliefs and practices. It is this context that prompts African women theologians to research and write on African culture from various cultural perspectives. We call attention to culture in religion and religion in culture in the designation *religio-culture*. This cultural hermeneutic is an important shift from the Western theology in which most of us have been nourished.

Who are we that God so cares about us as to come to the world through and for us? This is the question that women ask of Christian *anthropology, an aspect of Christian affirmation that fails to become reality where women are concerned. Made in the image of God (as is the case for men), we find ourselves struggling for the meaning of such a momentous affirmation in view of the realities we live as women. What does it mean to be human and woman? Key to this discussion is the issue of human **sexuality*, its links with *marriage, procreation, and the eternal generation and regeneration of humanity. What word is needed in the context of the quest for eternal life through progeny?

The unease about human sexuality stimulated by religions comes in for much analysis and reflection. The myths that make sexual activities the source of pollution and that require women to see themselves as inferior and men to treat them as such are being challenged and exposed in African women's theology. The racist myths of African promiscuity are being challenged from research into marriage patterns and celibate life in traditional African religio-culture. Elements in the fear of sexuality that result in the repudiation of *matriarchy and in *violence against women form part of African women's theological challenge. Links between biological sex and social roles are being severed, as there is no direct link between brain and brawn. Rather than a source of pollution and disruption, sexuality is admitted as an integral part of our humanity, to be honored, nurtured, and celebrated.

Women theologians see the church as continuing the *healing *mission* that Jesus the Christ brings to all creatures. In their reflections they celebrate their own and others' healing. When we join in the analysis, advocacy, and reconstruction that is aimed at bringing healing, we draw on the latent powers of our faith convictions, both Christian and specifically African. Where *racism has wounded communities, *ecclesiology is studied with a view to determining the church's role in the mission of God and women's participation in this mission. The spirituality that keeps women Christian and in the church is revealed in the *power to struggle in hope, to risk voicing the unmentionable and doing truth and *justice with *compassion. Mission is seen in terms not of condemnation but of making apparent God's love to all humanity and all *creation. God does not play favorites; all people are chosen by God, since God chose to create humanity in the divine image.

African women's theology is yet to achieve bold *naming and denunciation of injustice in church and society. The cardinal need to uphold community *solidarity at times gets in the way of announcing and working for the liberation and fullness we stand for. Yet we all would say that being feminist is refusing to keep silent about issues of life, especially if they are oppressive to women.

The need to make connections with other feminist groups in Africa is pressing. We need to work together on what our different religious traditions mean for women. Apart from the overtly theological approach, there are women's rights and well-being organizations among professionals, lawyers, doctors, and medical personnel, that we need to work with on what would make for transformation in Africa. Finally, in spite of the charges of imitation, we cannot isolate ourselves from the global movement to guard and promote the humanity of women. We remain open to share concerns with all, including African men, as we work for the well-being of our communities.

Fabella/Oduyoye [1988]; Oduyoye [1986; 1995]; Oduyoye/Kanyoro [1992]

MERCY AMBA ODUYOYE

Feminist Theology, Latin American Latin American feminist theology understands itself as critical reflection on women's experience of God within our socioecclesial and intellectual practices, which seek to create a new civilization based on *justice, human integrity, ecological equilibrium, and the well-being of the whole creation. The purpose of this theology is to encourage and accompany the various commitments of women to the transformation of structures and theories that negate, limit, or impede the fullness and integrity of women in anthropological, political, social, and religious terms.

This purpose is based on the Christian vision of common human dignity, egalitarian participation in the power of the Spirit, and the vocation to fullness in God for each person and every people. Supported by theoretical models of feminist criticism, Latin American feminist theology poses a rigorous critique to the present models of civilization, social organization, and the church because those models are based on principles of exclusion, *hierarchy, and antagonism. This theology offers also a critique of the *androcentric conceptual frameworks with which the dominant theological discourse operates, including Latin American liberation *theology. This critique extends to the traditional sources of *faith and to the church's practice, discourse, and institutions.

At the same time, Latin American feminist theology seeks to rethink systematically the content of divine *revelation from the context of present *experiences of struggle for *liberation. Already this theology has occasioned three important developments. First, it allows androcentric theologies to be delegitimized as universal and normative. Second, it reconstructs and rehabilitates the emancipatory contribution of women who have preceded us in history. Third, it recovers the emancipatory force of Jewish and Christian traditions, along with those of Latin America and the Caribbean. For these reasons it can be said that Latin American feminist theology acquires the status of a fundamental theology.

The immediate audience of this theology consists of women interested in eliminating *oppression and *violence against women. Therefore, we interpret the experience of faith from the point of view of impoverished and marginalized women. From here we establish a *dialogue with other women in theology, be it in theological conferences or through their writings, and with male theologians and other social groups of women and men who also work on behalf of alternative models of social relations.

History and Development. It has as a background the activities, the critique, and the vision of women concerning the principles and values that regulate *relationships in the human community. It results from a long process in which women, by their own initiative and often inspired by religious values, have sought to change the social and ecclesial situations that impede their incorporation into the experience of human integrity. As social actors, even from the time prior to the great European *colonization, Latin American women have sought to influence the direction of socioreligious institutions and conceptual frameworks. The indigenous cultures take into account the involvement of women in all arenas of social life.

Our history includes numerous movements of women against the aggressive European expansion during the sixteenth century, and also women's resistance and rebellions during the colonial period in the seventeenth and eighteenth centuries. The extensive work of Sor Juana Inés de la Cruz (1651–95) reflects well this attitude. During the nineteenth century and the first half of the twentieth, Latin American women reclaimed political and intellectual rights, including emancipation from slavery. In the second half of the twentieth century, the organizations of women whose purpose is to advance feminist objectives of social justice and fundamental human rights have multiplied. The systematic development of feminist theology has been accomplished in several important events sponsored by the Ecumenical Association of Third World Theologians (EATWOT) and its Women's Commission, beginning in 1979. This dynamic history of women *in movement* is what justifies the existence of Latin American feminist theology in its own right.

Characteristics. Latin American feminist liberation theologies are emerging from different contexts, but they still share some common characteristics. They acknowledge the interconnection that exists between intellectual activity and the corporal, sexual, racial, social, and cultural configuration of those who perform it. The experience of indigenous, black, mestiza, and white women is expressed in the knowledge of the faith and in the values that govern our reflection. For that reason, this theology reclaims intellectual *autonomy as a right, in order to interpret with legitimacy and *authority our own experience.

For this theology there exists a structural unity of knowledge and practice. According to the biblical *tradition, the truth of words is verified in deeds. Therefore women's practice on behalf of justice, more than any ethical criterion, has come to occupy an epistemological status of its own. Rather than merely explaining the experience of faith lived out by women, this theology seeks to translate such faith experience into commitments on behalf of greater human integrity and egalitarian forms of social relations. In keeping with all liberation theologies that have incorporated critico-practical reason, this feminist liberation theology emphasizes the transforming function of theology.

This reflection on the experience of faith attempts to establish the relationship between the message of the *gospel and the reality lived by women. Therefore it incorporates reality, as it presents itself in its unity and diversity. It is concerned with the real world, which is both personal and social, local and global, and it seeks to articulate a response of hope in order to anticipate greater well-being for the human community, especially for the victims of injustice. This theology understands that the predatory logic of the present social model is not directed toward greater levels of justice, ecological equilibrium, or recognition of basic rights for women. Therefore it proposes to change the existing model formed by the combination of socioecclesial *patriarchy, neoliberal capitalism, and the neocolonialism of the dominant Eurocentric cultures.

Different Expressions of Latin American Feminist Theology. *Indigenous theology* done by women seeks to establish the connection between the participative and egalitarian springs at the source of the stream of indigenous socioreligious traditions and the liberating root of the Christian message. While Western theologies have shown themselves to be colonizing and antagonistic, this theology is strongly marked by the understanding of the relatedness of women, men, the earth, and God.

Black feminist theology understands itself as a critical reflection on the experience of faith lived by black women throughout their history and in their daily lives. In 1994, at the EATWOT International Dialogue of Women Theologians held in Costa Rica, the Brazilian black feminist theologian Silvia Regina Lima said that this theology allows the rethinking of the revelation of God in the cultures and religions that have emerged from the motherland of Africa, in the history of *survival and victories against slavery, and in the present struggles of the black people to advance justice. This theological current emphasizes the encounter of cultures and traditions, especially Christian and Afro–Latin American. However, that encounter occurs through a critical reading that seeks to unmask the *ideological factors used by theology to legitimize *racism and *sexism.

Holistic, ecofeminist theology offers an interpretation of the human experience that seeks to be integral and interconnected. It understands that women and men are part of a large, living organism called the *cosmos, and it recognizes itself within the critical tradition of modernity. From here it critiques *dualistic theologies and supplies a reinterpretation of Christian traditions and symbols.

In summary, Latin American feminist theology finds itself in a vital process of self-construction, oriented more by what we seek than by what we know. The self-awareness that we Latin American women are bearers of divinity strengthens the value of our own identity and places us in an attitude of dialogue with other religious expressions. For that reason, this theology affirms its ecumenical dimension.

Aquino [1988; 1993; 1994]; Bingemer/Gebara [1989]; Gebara [1989; 1990]; Tamez [1987; 1993b]; Tamez, ed. [1989]; Tepedino [1990]

MARÍA PILAR AQUINO
(TRANS. SHARON H. RINGE)

Feminist Theories** Feminist theories arise out of intellectual movements found partly within the academy and partly within women's social and political efforts to end oppression—and often within both at the same time. These theories provide a critical analysis of the forces that subordinate women to men. They have had a profound impact on the field of religion, both by direct influence on the thinking of feminists in religion and by indirectly shaping the intellectual community in which feminist scholars participate. Because of their roots in political and social work for the emancipation of women and in women's *experiences of *oppression, rather than in traditional academic schools of thought, feminist theories tend to be interdisciplinary and to employ various methods of inquiry and analysis. In addition, an inherent instability, which could be described as an absence of a reigning school of thought, is characteristic of feminist theories and intrinsic to their various attempts to address the complex experiences of women around the world, in many social locations.

While interdisciplinary, inclusive, and relatively fluid, various feminist theories do, however, often employ a dominant academic field for their primary investigative approach, for example, a psychological, sociological, philosophical, anthropological, literary, legal, biological, or historical approach, all of which are also utilized in theological work. Through these various approaches, feminist theories interrogate structures of male dominance and of *patriarchy, and their accompanying systems of gender. In examining patriarchy, feminist theories expose the structures, such as class, *race, region, *religion, *sexuality, and nationality, that subordinate and oppress women. The result of such examinations has been the generation of knowledge on subjects such as female bodies, *violence against women, patriarchal states, the socialization of consciousness, *heterosexism, and male-dominant cultures. This is *new* knowledge of women's *reality that has been virtually invisible or highly distorted by *androcentrism. It has been created by women and pro-feminist men from a variety of social locations, religious and racial groups, nationalities, and sexual orientations.

A Beginning of Feminist Theories in the 1950s. Women's experience is vast, and women's social movements are diverse and many. Until recently, however, the academic aspect of feminist theories has been dominated by the perspective of white, middle-class, urban, well-educated women and men, who belong to the group that maintains *hegemony within the academy. These feminist thinkers and researchers have scrutinized virtually every intellectual form of thinking and research and utilized a wide range of issues and subjects. Pivotal concepts that dominated feminist theories at the beginning of the current feminist movement (from 1950 to 1980) were formulated by Simone de Beauvoir (1971) in her discussions of "woman" as a *social construct and the androcentric basis by which woman is made "other," inessential in relation to "man," who is deemed essential.

Theorists such as Shulamith Firestone (1970), Kate Millett (1970), and Mary Daly (1968) identified the oppression of women, called *sexism. They described it as the fundamental, primary category of oppression, under which other forms of oppression fell, and called for the elimination of sexism in order to overcome every other form of oppression. Such analyses of patriarchy identified its complex, hydra-headed dimensions, which permeate every corner of life from *marriage, childrearing, and religion to international law, economics, and *politics. These analyses created the starting assumptions of many feminist theorists who followed. "Woman" in these theories referred generally to middle-class, white women, so that women were discussed as a group separate from slaves, blacks, Hispanics, Jews, Asians, etc. Betty Friedan (1963) described the dissatisfaction of middle-class, white women with the roles assigned to them in the 1950s and inspired a movement for women's right to *work outside the home. She reinforced de Beauvoir's assertion that women must have *equality with men and economic independence if they are to gain the same freedoms as male citizens.

Zillah Eisenstein, a *socialist, and other radical feminists such as Barbara Deming, Marilyn Frye, Susan Miller Okin, and Alison Jaggar challenged the middle-class assumptions of humanistic, liberal feminism by arguing that the oppression of women was so embedded in the structures of middle-class, heterosexist society that women's equality would seriously disrupt it. They argued that women should strive for a restructuring of society at its roots rather than for equality on its current, androcentric terms. Critiques of androcentrism include maintaining suspicions about the transformative potential of socialist theory for women if it does not have an explicitly feminist dimension (e.g., the work of socialist feminists Heidi Hartmann and Michele Barrett). Along with a critique of society at its roots, feminist theorists criticized the assumptions about objective knowing (Sandra Harding), scientific inquiry (Evelyn Fox Keller), and disciplinary boundaries that dominate academe (virtually every theorist crosses disciplinary boundaries). In the social arena, Susan Brownmiller's groundbreaking 1975 treatise on rape was early in a subsequent flood of work on *misogyny in such forms as domestic violence (Susan Schechter, Richard Gelles, Claire Pedrick Cornell), incest and child molestation (Florence Rush, Judith Hermann), pornography (Andrea Dworkin, Susan Griffin), and sexual harassment (Catherine MacKinnon). Adrienne Rich, Audre Lorde, and Susan Griffin, poets and essayists, addressed a wide range of issues from *racism, motherhood, pornography, war, science and medicine, to sexuality, heterosexism, and *lesbian existence. Language itself—linguistic structures, etymologies, and literary theory—was analyzed by such writers as Robin Lakoff, Sandra Gilbert and Susan Gubar, Julia Penelope, Deborah Tannen, Deborah Cameron, and Geneva Smitherman.

In addition to analyses of patriarchal societies and women's oppression, feminist scholars such as Maria Gimbutas and Gerda Lemer searched the past for matrilineal *goddess traditions and discussed the development of patriarchy. Carolyn Walker Bynum and Joan Kelly found alternative readings of androcentric history and new material about women's lives. Feminist researchers such as Margaret Mead, Peggy Reeves Sanday, Marla Powers, Michelle Zimbalist Rosaldo, and Sherry Ortner examined cross-cultural evidence for male dominance, as well as for egalitarian societies of gender equality. In feminist theories, gender may or may not be related to investigations of biological sex, but the two are differentiated. Biology has been soundly rejected as destiny. Cross-cultural studies of gender have heightened this distinction by demonstrating the variety of ways human societies organize roles, status, and behavior according to assumptions about gender.

The Divergence of Feminist Theories. In the 1980s, American feminist theories diverged in two directions. Some white, middle-class feminists turned to French deconstructionist philosophers and feminists such as Michael Foucault, Jacques Derrida, Jacques Lacan, Hélène Cixous, Catherine Clément, Monique Wittig, Luce Irigaray, and Julia Kristeva. These deconstructionists, drawing from European continental traditions in phenomenology, existentialism, and psychoanalysis, influenced such thinkers as Judith Butler, Shoshana Felman, Barbara Johnson, Jacqueline Rose, and Juliet Mitchell in examining patriarchal hegemony, language, the quest for power, and personal identity and truth as social constructions.

In another direction, women of color such as bell hooks, Angela Davis, Barbara Smith, Cheri Moraga, Audre Lorde, Mitsuye Yamada, Nellie Wong, Gloria Anzaldúa, Trinh Minh Ha, Maria Lugones, Paula Gunn Allen, Rosario Morales, Patricia Bell Scott, and Gayatri Chakravorty Spivak raised criticisms about the feminist tendency to separate race and colonial oppression from gender, noting that "white" is a racial identity. They began to speak about issues raised by the cross-cultural, multiply held identities of women of color. Issues such as the dominance of white *culture and language through colonialism, genocide, *imperialism, and intellectual hegemony; European norms of rationality, *education, and religion; and the exploitation of some women by other women have been raised to correct the overgeneralizing tendencies of many white feminist theories, including the tendency to focus on the experience of elite, educated, urban women. In this arena, *deconstruction has been used especially by postcolonial feminists. Many postcolonial feminists, feminists of color, *mujeristas,* and womanists have used the constructive strategy of establishing separate cultural, social, and religious discursive traditions to give voice to marginalized women made "other" by middle-class, Euro-American feminisms, including women from indigenous, shaman-based cultures such as Korea (Chung Hyung Kyung), Mexico (Gloria Anzaldúa), the Caribbean (Luisah Teish), and Africa (Mercy Amba Oduyoye).

In addition to their contributions to feminist, womanist, *mujerista,* and postcolonial feminist theories, lesbian theorists have brought lesbian issues into the discussion of the social construction of gender, heterosexism, and the meaning of the term *woman.* For example, Monique Wittig rejects the word *woman* because its social, normative construction does not include lesbians. Hence to choose the term *lesbian* identifies a female less oppressed by sexual identity. Adrienne Rich (1979; 1986) defined the nature of white heterosexist culture and positive lesbian alternatives, and Barbara Smith and Audre Lorde (1984) challenged the connection between racism and homophobia. Also, Smith proposed a black feminist aesthetic, and Lorde constructed an alternative view of love based in black lesbian experiences. Hence the status of lesbians and lesbianism as an anomaly within patriarchal, heterosexist cultures further challenges the norms of thinking that subordinate and oppress most women. Other important lesbian theorists include Eve Kosofsky Sedgwick, Judith Butler, Susan Griffin, Gloria Anzaldúa, Paula Gunn Allen, Merle Woo, Mary Daly, and Marilyn Frye.

Out of research on patriarchies and their alternatives and out of reflection on the personal experiences of women oppressed by male dominance, feminist theorists also examined the contributions to society made by women, as judged not only by androcentric standards but also by new standards based on women's experiences. This investigation is what Peggy McIntosh (1988) has called "women-centered research," which explores the worlds, behaviors, and roles traditionally associated with women, such as mothering, creating and maintaining complex *relationships, and organizing associations. Patricia Bell Scott, Jacqueline Jones, Adrienne Rich, and Sara Ruddick have examined the role of *mothers and the values that can be learned from the social constructions that surround mothering in the lives of African-American and white women. Nancy Chodorow's psychoanalytic work on white, middle-class mothering, which resonated with Dorothy Dinnerstein's earlier work, had an impact on a number of fields. Feminist scholars extensively applied her insight that men use separation for identity and women seek connection and relationships. Carol Gilligan and Nel Noddings extended this idea into the area of moral development, Nancy Hartsock and Sandra Harding into standpoint theory (that we see according to our own social location), and Evelyn Fox Keller into gender perspectives in science.

Traditional androcentric connections between women and nature have been transmuted by *ecofeminist theorists such as Karen Warren, Carol Adams, Susan Griffin, Carolyn Merchant, Starhawk, and Charlene Spretnak into work that addresses questions of ethically sustainable life. While ecofeminists do not write exclusively about environmental issues, their concerns pivot around the early, groundbreaking work of Rachel Carson. In addition, Native American women such as Paula Gunn Allen have noted the connections between environmental destruction and the genocide of people of color. The *power of the constructive work generated out of a focus on the positive value of women's *survival and creativity has undergirded the constructive aspects of feminist, womanist, and *mujerista* theologies.

As feminist theories have become more complex and inclusive of increasingly diverse perspectives, the nature and value of *difference has grown as an area of investigation. In addition, more attention has been paid to the ways women oppress each other by race. For example, Peggy McIntosh and Marilyn Frye have addressed white privilege by class, sexual orientation, age, and physical ability. In addition, pro-feminist men such as John Stoltenberg and Michael Kimmel have examined the social construction of masculinity as experienced by men, which has affected the work of a number of pro-feminist theologians.

In addition to discussing theories addressing colonialism, racism, heterosexism, etc., feminist theorists such as Dale Spender and Peggy McIntosh have analyzed the role of feminist theories in the academy. Both discuss the revolutionary potential of integrating feminist theories into traditional curricula. McIntosh also examines the necessity of transforming women's studies as part of academia's commitment to address the lives of women not included by the dominant culture of America. With more than twenty years' influence on the academic curriculum and with the phenomenal growth and rates of publishing successes, feminist theories have become an established element of academic life at many institutions, whether or not those institutions have women's studies programs. Current discussions center on concerns that feminist theories, as a part of the intellectual mainstream, will simply become another part of the hegemony of academe and have little impact on the social movements worldwide that struggle for *justice for women. However, if we examine the relationship of feminist, womanist, and *mujerista* theologies and religious reflection to social movements in religion, at the grass-roots level in the United States and at the level of religious leadership, we can see a profound impact facilitated by the cutting-edge work of these theorists from a wide range of fields.

Chopp [1989]; Collins [1991]; Donovan [1988]; Frye [1983]; hooks [1984]; Jones [forthcoming]; Nicholson [1990]; Tong [1989]

RITA NAKASHIMA BROCK

Feminization of Poverty The phase "the feminization of poverty" was first used in 1978 by Diana Pearce, a research analyst at the Catholic University of America, to refer to the increasing *poverty of women and children among urban African Americans. As significant numbers of men in the African-American community were incarcerated or murdered during adolescence and young adulthood, women bore economic and child-care responsibilities alone. *Violence, coupled with high male and female unemployment, left women few opportunities to marry or become self-supporting. Even without *marriage, women continued to mother so that, increasingly, poor, urban, African-American households were female-headed.

In 1985, Lenore Weitzman extended the meaning of the phrase to include middle- and upper-class women who became impoverished due to inadequate no-fault divorce settlements. Weitzman also highlighted the problem of inadequate and unpaid child support. No-fault divorce law was intended to base the ethic of the law on distributive rather than retributive *justice. Too often, however, early no-fault settlements reflected a principle of strict *equality that did not adequately account for the way homemakers' contributions to the *family left them with substantially less economic power than their husbands had.

Together, the two analyses hold three points in common: (1) women are generally economically disadvantaged, due to their inferior economic position; (2) *mothers with dependent children are additionally at risk; and (3) women of color who live in historically poor communities where social institutions have deteriorated are especially likely to be poor. When the phrase became popularly associated with divorcing women rather than women in poor communities, however, women of color charged that the concern for spells of poverty among middle-class women obscured the plight of women who had historically borne the brunt of poverty in the United States. Given this ambiguity, the use of the phrase "the feminization of poverty" in theology is discouraged.

Couture [1991]; Pearce, *Urban and Social Change Review* [1978]; Pearce, *Society* [1983]; Weitzman [1985]

PAMELA D. COUTURE

Free Will Are human beings free to choose ideal life (e.g., God's commandments or political utopia), bound to choose less, or without ability for real choosing? Free will has been understood as the opposite of determinism. External causes would contradict or limit this *freedom. Free will is autonomous and not self-contradictory.

Today, new meanings are given to free will:

1. "Free will" is a phrase describing a complex relationship of knowing, desiring, and acting. A person is a process of interacting conditions, not a division of isolated skills. Knowing, desiring, and acting for a particular sense of the good or ideal is the function of free will and human *agency.
2. Free will is *not* *autonomous but rather operative in multiple systems of meaning, which provide different choices.
3. Free will is a characteristic of both individuals and groups. Reciprocity between a social system on the one hand and individual knowing and felt behavior on the other is one element of free will. If the individual has little power in a system, free will may be more social than individual. This reciprocity also is active between groups.
4. Free will is expressed in relation to basic human needs and limited by available resources. Willing food is essential and free but might be limited by political powers or personal psychological conditions. Free does not mean "without limits." However, basic human needs are not the only things willed.
5. "Free" does not mean "undetermined"; rather, free means neither solely coerced by another nor solely internal to the individual (without external effect).
6. Social context is crucial in specific descriptions of free will. Women who are deemed contrary to a system's ideals are usually called a threat to freedom. If free will were an unchanging, essential human characteristic, this opposition could not be changed. The willing of freedom for women is a feminist exercise of free will.

Daly [1994]; Douglass [1985]; Smith, in Andolsen/Gudorf/Pellauer [1985]

ELIZABETH BETTENHAUSEN

Freedom Freedom from a womanist perspective means "wholeness." It derives from that part of Alice Walker's definition for *womanist* in which she says a womanist "is committed to survival and wholeness of entire people, male *and* female" (xi). In this regard, the meaning of freedom/wholeness has several dimensions. First, freedom/wholeness refers to the elimination of the interlocking system of *oppression (i.e., *racism, *sexism, *classism, and *heterosexism), which is especially hostile to African-American life and freedom. Second, it implies that the African-American *community is not divided against itself but united in its struggle for "life and wholeness." Third, freedom/wholeness means that individual women and men have confronted the ways in which complex societal oppression has left them less than whole persons (spiritually, psychologically, emotionally, and so forth). Fourth, freedom/wholeness points to a world where all women, indeed, all humanity, live together in relationships of respect and mutuality. It is grounded in the dictum that "no woman is free if all [that is, men and women] are not free." Finally, while freedom/wholeness points to a particular vision of reality, as specified in this definition, it also implies a *liberation process of struggle toward that vision.

Collins [1991]; Walker [1983]

KELLY BROWN DOUGLAS

French Feminism As it is used in the American academic context, French feminism refers to a sector of feminist theorists in France whose writings have revolved around the questions of human subjectivity and gendered identity. The two figures most often associated with French feminist thought are Luce Irigaray and Julia Kristeva. In their approach to the issue of subjectivity, the French feminists are influenced by poststructuralist trends in *philosophy. They take an "anti-essentialist" stance, claiming that there exists no given human identity that is meaningful in itself and that can be isolated from the multiple external influences acting on a person. Rather, the French feminists tend to accept that a person attains full subjectivity only by forming *relationships with others. It follows that the attainment of subjectivity entails the negotiation of the social norms defining the interactions that are acceptable in a *culture. These norms are understood to be carried in and perpetuated by the common language.

To understand the cultural discourse that reigns in the West and the possibilities for subjectivity it provides, French feminists often draw on the work of the psychoanalyst Jacques Lacan. Influenced by Freud's theory of Oedipal relations, Lacan argued that in order to enter the social or "symbolic" realm and so to form a coherent identity, a child must abandon his pre-social attachment to the mother and establish a relationship with the father. Most French feminists find Lacan's depiction of the symbolic useful because it articulates clearly that the relationships privileged by *patriarchy are those between men, specifically fathers and sons. As a result, the opportunities for women to attain subjectivity under patriarchy are severely limited. While Lacan's analysis has descriptive value, none of the French feminists accept his view as indicative of a necessary state of affairs.

In her own theory of subjectivity and language, Irigaray explicitly emphasizes the differences between the genders. She envisions an alternative to patriarchy, calling for a socio-symbolic order where not only relationships between men but also relationships between women are valued. An order structured around this variety of interrelationships would provide women with multiple opportunities for identity formation. The specific question of gender differences has been less central to Kristeva's discussion of subjectivity. She has argued that the socio-symbolic order reigning in Western culture is less rigidly structured than it appears on an initial observation, and she has sought to highlight the possibilities for revision that are latent in this order. On her view, as the symbolic system as a whole is renewed, the possibilities it provides for subjectivity will also expand.

Feminist theologians have found in French feminist thought useful tools for examining their own methodological assumptions. Some thinkers, for example, have drawn on the work of the French to argue that the category of "women's experience of the Divine," which has traditionally served as the base for feminist theological inquiry, assumes an *essentialist understanding of the self. These critics argue that no given experience of women exists that can be located apart from multiple cultural determinants, and they question whether "women's experience" can serve as a foundation for theological claims.

In addition, under the influence of the French thinkers, feminist theologians have begun to view religious language and practices as cultural discourses. They have questioned the opportunities for subjectivity that the dominant religious discourses provide for women and have attempted to revise the existing discourses or to construct alternatives that might better serve women. While French feminists themselves have been sharply critical of religious language, they have identified some linguistic constructs, such as the mystical writing of women, that may serve to expand options for subject formation.

Crownfield [1992]; Kim/St. Ville/Simonaitis [1993]

SUSAN M. ST. VILLE

Friendship Friendship is a freely chosen relationship in which one intends the well-being of the other. Indeed, *friend* and *free* come from the same Indo-European and Sanskrit roots, meaning "to be fond of" or "to hold dear." That is what friends do.

Friendship is a relatively rare topic in patriarchal Christian theology, having long taken a backseat to *marriage as the normative adult human relationship. This led to the *hegemony of heterosexual marriage as the standard by which all other relationships were measured and, de facto, found wanting. But taking friendship seriously is a way to level the ethical playing field and make a range of relational options possible and good, depending on their generativity and not their gender.

From my European-American, Christian, feminist perspective, friendship is increasingly accepted as the most inclusive way to describe *a variety of voluntary *relationships* (including women with women, men with men, women with men, adults with children, humans with animals, persons with the Divine, humans with the earth) that ground the common good. It is an antidote to the patriarchal proscriptions, a way to lift up and celebrate the variety of love in creation.

Friends attempt to live out *equality and mutuality, love and *justice, as qualities of their relationships. They do not always succeed, but they endeavor to pay attention to one another in a focused way, which distinguishes friendship from other efforts at human relating. Friendship is an equal opportunity relationship, with virtually everyone having at least the potential to form such connection. It is versatile, offering various options for intimacy throughout a lifetime. Freed from the either-or of *patriarchy, friendship as a norm invites rich, diverse relational possibilities.

In all friendships there are dynamics that include love and *power, physical *embodiment or *sexuality, as well as spirituality, which is, broadly speaking, a way of making choices about the quality of common life. Friends note rather than pass over these dynamics and, in paying attention, seek to enhance their own and their friends' possibilities. The loss of friends is always painful.

As friendships deepen, there is an effort to change social and economic structures that divide people, to build relationships of integrity that ground justice work. In this way, a feminist theology of friendship is deeply political. This feminist view contrasts sharply with the patriarchal model of friendship, based on Aristotelian *hierarchical categories, that is used as the foundation of virtually every nonfeminist theological treatment of friendship. The patriarchal model is based on men's experiences of having fewer and fewer friends as one ascends the ladder of intimacy. Ironically, at the pinnacle there are only men, whose wives are even excluded from the possibility of true friendship with their husbands.

Women's experiences, both contemporary and historical, are quite different. Women befriend and are befriended in multiples, beginning with oneself, then with others, and extending to the planet and the divine. From this feminist perspective, "friends" almost don't exist in the singular because friendship is always a self-involved relationship, automatically plural. Relatives can be friends, as with *mothers and daughters. Friendships can supersede even the most rigid expectations in surprising ways. The power of friends to generate social change, to motivate people to build communities of justice seekers, is part of what makes it so appealing. The call to "go and make friends in all nations" resounds among women throughout the world. Those friendships hold the promise of global community.

Daly [1984]; Hunt [1991]; Lugones, in Kramarae/Spender [1992]; Raymond [1986]

MARY E. HUNT

Gaia *Gaia* is the Greek term for Earth in the personified form of a *goddess of all living things on the earth. The Homeric Hymn to Gaia the Mother of All expresses this understanding of personified Earth as a goddess with the words "I will sing of well-founded Earth, mother of all, eldest of all beings. She feeds all creatures that are in the world, all that go upon the goodly land, and all that are in the paths of the seas and all that fly: all these are fed of her store" (Homer, 456).

The term *Gaia* and the "Gaia hypothesis" have been adopted by a group of contemporary planetary biologists to express the view that the whole earth is a living organism. In the thought of scientists such as James Lovelock and Lynn Margulis, the earth is not a dead rock whose conditions allow living plants and animals to live on its surface, but the planet Earth as a whole, including the seas, soils, and atmosphere, operates as an organic biofeedback system. Animals and planets cogenerate the atmosphere, and the forests act as lungs that draw clouds and create rain. To understand the evolution of the earth and its present ecological sustainability, one has to understand this total system of Earth as a living, organic whole in self-balancing interaction with itself.

While these scientists are not interested in seeing the earth as a goddess or an object of religious worship, their view of the earth as a living biosphere has lent itself to a revival of views of the earth as a sacred being. In the view of those who cultivate such "Gaia spirituality," the Bible particularly has lent itself to a Western secularized view of nature as a mere dead object that can be used at will by powerful humans. To regain a life-sustaining relation between humans and the earth, they believe that humans must resacralize the earth and regain a sense of reverence for the whole earth community of life as a whole.

Homer [1914]; Lovelock [1988]; Ruether [1992]; Thompson [1987]

ROSEMARY RADFORD RUETHER

Gender Construction Simone de Beauvoir's classic statement that "woman is made, not born" remains a fair summary of the claims that gender is socially constructed, not biologically determined. Malestream Christian theology classically viewed gender and roles assigned to gender as part of God's created order and therefore universal and eternal. *Natural law theory, as well as other construals of the *doctrine of *creation, based large segments of Christian sexual *ethics on the foundation of obedience to the created order, understood as biologically determined, socially relevant, and theologically inscribed.

Analysis of the social construction of gender, as distinct from the biological fact of sex, has been a foundational feature of feminism in general and Christian feminism in particular. Early in this wave of feminist scholarship, de Beauvoir used the term *Other* to designate her claims that "woman" was a construct defined entirely by her relationship with men, having no independent ontological status apart from that relationship. Women were not subjects in the same way that men were; "woman" was a derivative concept and existed only as object of men's attention.

De Beauvoir's analysis was reflective of the experience and life pattern of middle-class, white Frenchwomen in much the same way that Betty Friedan's *The Feminine Mystique* described the reality of "women" in light of a small group of middle-class Euro-Americans. Subsequent feminist analysis, especially that conversation which includes voices from diverse social locations, expands beyond a focus on individual women and ceases making universal claims on the basis of the experience of a few. Without repudiating the fact that gender is socially constructed rather than biologically determined, feminist analysis of gender has become much more sophisticated and complex with the recognition that gender is but one among a variety of socially constructed realities, e.g., *race, class, economic location, and that all of these factors interact and are interdependent parts of a vastly complex process of social construction of persons and societies. In addition, scrutiny of gender construction by Christian feminists is in useful *dialogue with work being done in gay and *lesbian studies on gender as imitation and performance. Contemporary Christian feminist analysis acknowledges complex and subtle interactions between sex and gender without thereby repudiating the importance of the discussion of the social construction of gender.

Feminist analysis of gender construction has important ethical dimensions. If the biological reality of males and females is detached from the social construction of gender, with its roles and expectations, then those roles and expectations are also rendered free from gender, and gender is not a relevant factor in their assignment. Furthermore, if gender, with its attendant social and theological meanings, is a human construct and not a divine creation, then persons and cultures are both freer and more responsible to construct gender according to theological ethical commitments such as *justice, mercy, *compassion. Exposing the gendered and oppressive nature of theological constructs themselves, including the nature of God, has been important work in feminist theology. Finally, feminist analysis of the social construction of gender is part of the project of social and political theorists who study institutions, including religious ones, and who note and document the gendered and inequitable character of such constructs as rights and welfare and language itself, both verbal and nonverbal, which both create and carry *culture.

Though widely adopted in feminist theology and ethics, an understanding of gender as socially constructed is not universally accepted. There are still many people who hold some version of natural law theory in which sex and gender are identified. There are feminists, as well, who argue for something "essentially feminine," often including an implicit or explicit argument that there is an inherent superiority in the feminine over the masculine and sometimes including a separatist agenda. Finally, feminists influenced by Freudian theory, including contemporary French feminists, propose a complex mix of *essentialism and social constructionism that cannot quite be characterized simply as one or the other.

Butler [1990]; hooks [1990]; MacKinnon [1987]; Morrison [1992]

SALLY B. PURVIS

Gendered Institutions Gender as a *social construct is a major component of the power structure and *ideology of many societal systems, including the economy, the polity, the *family, the elite professions, and religious institutions. The degree to which an institution is "gendered" is reflected in the extent to which it is led mainly by one gender, the group who also define and assess movement toward systemic goals in line with their particular, gender-related value perspectives.

Dominant (white) male past and present leadership of most U.S. institutions means typically that men hold the top positions, evaluate achievement in terms of male-defined values, and, whether consciously or not, subordinate women both structurally and culturally within the institution. Women may be revered in *patriarchal institutions for exemplifying "feminine virtues" of reproduction and nurture but are not considered as capable of production or exercising leadership. Religious institutions most gendered toward male dominance include the historic religions as well as some of the newer authoritarian religious movements and cults.

The more female-gendered an occupation, the more it is likely to have lower social prestige and lower salary for both women *and* men practitioners. Because *ministry is less prestigious and pays less than many secular professions at present, there are fewer well-qualified clergymen for low-paying church positions than there are clergywomen. Eventually there may be more women in pulpits than men. Feminists debate what consequences may ensue from the potential reversal in the gendering of the ordained ministry from male majority to female majority.

Most feminists would agree that ignoring the role of gender in institutional dynamics strengthens rather than mitigates its impact. An ongoing challenge for feminists, therefore, is to uncover sexist bias often obscured in overtly *objective practices and value-neutral statements made by institutional leaders as well as by scholars.

Acker, *Contemporary Sociology* [1992]; England et al., *Social Forces* [1994]; Kaufman [1989]; Russell [1993]

ADAIR T. LUMMIS

Gendered Representation The term *gendered representation* reflects a new awareness, particularly among contemporary feminist thinkers who have been very influenced by psychoanalytical theory, of how symbols shape our consciousness. The concept implicitly acknowledges that we live in a post-theological world but nevertheless challenges social theories and philosophies that rely exclusively on physical phenomena, especially those influenced by *materialist *philosophy. These are replaced by a sophisticated analysis of how men and women experience their psychic development, their being in a male or female *body, and how these experiences construct the social world so that men are dominant.

This analysis can help us understand how this construction is reflected in the symbol system or theological worldview. For instance, analysis of gendered representation shows that the absence of an *empowering female symbol system both reflects and effects the subordination of women. This very lack shapes and deforms the way we think and how our bodies respond to certain stimuli, and the social system established is inherently detrimental to the interests of women.

The concept *representation* is broader than that of *theological worldview* for two reasons. On the one hand, it includes post-theological systems of *mythology, symbols, and beliefs, especially those generated through the arts and the media, whose influence now often supersedes that of formal religion. On the other hand, by the inclusion of factors of *power, physical phenomena, and psychic phenomena, it enables the critique of *patriarchy to be taken to new dimensions. The perspective allows us to look again at issues such as the resistance to female *ordination as being derived from the need to maintain "the sacrificial social contract," the roots of which lie in our early struggle to separate from our primary caretakers and the effects of which shape the social order and exist beyond a religious worldview. Postmodernist feminist thinkers, however, differ on the question of whether this is an inevitable rather than an incidental outcome of early psychic processes and on the relative merits of privileging specifically feminist religious practices and philosophies.

Grosz [1994]; Irigaray [1987]; Jay [1992]; Kristeva [1984]; Sanday [1981]

MARY T. CONDREN

Gnosticism From the Greek *gnōsis* (knowledge), Gnosticism is the umbrella under which is found a complex religious movement that interacted with and affected developing Christianity, especially in the second century. Many of the ideas and tendencies that came to be called Gnostic were, by the time of their interaction with Christian ideas and stories, already rather old. Many historians acknowledge that what came to be seen as orthodox Christianity was identified at least partly in contrast to various Gnostic groups. The significance of Gnosticism for feminist theologies occurred in three areas: (1) Gnostic use of feminine names for the divine; (2) the social role of women in Gnostic groups; (3) the Gnostic identification of the locus of religious authority. There is no unanimity on how these issues factor into feminist theologies.

Gnostic Use of Feminine Names for the Divine. Making generalizations about Gnostic groups gives rise to considerable problems. Historians do better to make specific claims about particular groups, many of whose leaders or founders and writings we can identify today (especially through the Nag Hammadi texts, first discovered in 1946). We can say, for example, that the Valentinian Gnostics spoke of the divine creative activity in terms of a male engendering and a female birthing. They viewed the heavenly realm as populated with male and female pairs of beings, or, better stated, divine being in male and female aspects.

Another Gnostic text, the *Apocryphon of John*, like many others, makes heavy use of Sophia-language for the divine figure who creates. In this text, *Sophia seeks to reproduce herself by herself, that is, apart from the activity of a mate. In so doing, she produces what seems most exactly translated as "an *abortion," a shapeless mass of gloom, evil because it was conceived "unnaturally." In an effort to hide her mistake, Sophia enfolds herself over the birth, (unintentionally?) giving it power and creating the first Archon, from which comes the demiurge who will eventually rule over the material world. Thus, in this example of Gnostic ideas, a feminine image is employed for divine power, but it is not necessarily a flattering or *empowering use of the image.

A further problem lies with the sheer difficulties of translating the Nag Hammadi texts from Coptic, especially in sorting out to what extent a linguistically gendered term necessarily implies *sexuality. In any case, second-century Christianity is often described as marked by a struggle for identity, and the winning Orthodox theological position shows a pronounced lack of female metaphors for God.

Social Roles for Women in Gnostic Groups. We have available a number of Gnostic texts and quite a few hostile descriptions of Gnostic ideas and practices from opposing Christian writers such as Irenaeus (late second century) and Hippolytus (early third century), but almost nothing sympathetic or firsthand that indicates how women fared in the social world of Gnosticism. Irenaeus complains (*Adversus haereses* 1–13.1–6) that "silly women" who were seduced to join Valentinian groups by claims that they too could prophesy were later drawn into sexual immorality. Irenaeus also reports that Valentinian initiated a claim that, having received the gift of the *Holy Spirit, the women would be freed from the power of the demiurge. Thus when they gathered for worship (including a kind of eucharistic ceremony), all the initiates present, even women, drew lots to determine who would preside.

This practice was in sharp contrast to emerging catholic Christianity, whose views are found in the slogans "One God, one bishop" and "Where the bishop is, there is the Spirit." Did second-century Christian women find the Gnostic versions more appealing than the orthodox versions because of more active female roles? Some scholars have made this case. Others are skeptical of such conclusions and begin by noting that much of Gnosticism encouraged a serious *asceticism, eschewing sexual relations as belonging to the lower realms. Second-century cultural patterns of thinking identified women as more bodily and men as more spiritual. Were Gnostic groups able effectively to rise above these cultural limitations? Historians confronted with Gnostic texts that employ feminine images as metaphors for spiritual realities and stories about women as leaders in worship come to conflicting conclusions about the value of Gnosticism and Gnostic ideas for women's lives.

Locus of Religious Authority. Second-century makers of Christian *orthodoxy often emphasized an external, "objective" character to their authority—a book (the emerging *canon), a statement (early versions of the *Creed), a centralized figure (the bishop). Some of the Gnostic opponents to the emerging church system seem to have suggested that the solution to the human problem lay not in obedience to external authorities but rather in greater self-understanding, a more profound *gnōsis,* usually a knowledge of the *cosmos and one's own place in it. Women (but not only women) have long been instructed to turn to someone or something else for justification of themselves or confirmation of a truth claim.

While the particular second-century Gnostic answers to the questions of human existence are not likely to satisfy persons today, many contemporary feminist theological approaches include some element of turning inward, including some aspect of greater self-knowledge as a part of understanding divine reality. Easy conclusions about second-century Gnosticism and its value to women's spirituality are hard to defend with historical claims, but Gnostic ideas and texts continue to be attractive to many persons today and worth serious study.

King [1988]; *Nag Hammadi Library in English* [1988]; Pagels [1979]

NADIA M. LAHUTSKY

God The term *God* has traditionally been used to signify the supreme or ultimate reality, perfect in wisdom, goodness, and power, whom people worship as creator, sustainer, redeemer, and goal of all creatures. In Christian theology, as in every religious *tradition, God is the central and integrating symbol of the whole religious system, representing what the community considers to be the highest good, the profoundest truth, the most appealing beauty, and, conversely, powerfully shaping personal and communal identity and *praxis.

Traditionally cast in male images, the symbol of divine mystery is most often modeled in monarchical terms, so that God is a transcendent ruler who has dominion over the world. Modern academic theology since the Enlightenment placed emphasis on the idea of God arrived at through philosophical inference from "his" created effects, rather than through biblical testimony or religious experience. As a result, divine attributes were described in stark contrast to creaturely limits. In standard theology, God is the supreme being who is absolutely simple, spiritual, eternal, omnipotent, omniscient, impassible, and, most critical of all, fundamentally unrelated to the world (for relationship would set up a dependency unfitting for the infinite One).

Critique. Feminist theologies mount a multifaceted critique of this traditional theology of God. First, exclusive use of images and concepts of the ruling male leads to these being taken literally rather than metaphorically, so that God really is thought, however subliminally, to be a masculine ruler rather than incomprehensible mystery beyond all imagining. In a word, divine mystery becomes distorted into an idol. Furthermore, this usage forges an ontological connection between human maleness and divinity that has practical effects on human affairs. It sets up divine legitimation for the rule of men in spheres both religious and civil, public and private, thus abetting structures that are politically oppressive to women. Finally, traditional theology of God has a harmful effect on women's spiritual identity and religious journey. By excluding from the realm of the sacred anything related to femaleness, whether imagery or correlative ideas, it blocks women from full ownership of their own holiness and identity as created in the *image of God.

Strategies. In the face of this dominant tradition, feminist theologians employ different strategies to articulate the divine. Judging Judaism and Christianity to be irredeemably male-dominated religions, some embark on an exodus from these religions to circles that connect with female deities or the *Goddess. Here the term *God* is no longer used to express experience of the sacred but only to signify the supreme dominating being of the tradition that has been rejected (e.g., Mary Daly, Naomi Goldenberg, Carol Christ). Classifying *God* as a male, generic term inadequate to express an inclusive theology, others nevertheless find usable elements in traditional Jewish and Christian understandings, such as the prophetic and liberating God of the exodus and the story of Jesus. In this group, Rosemary Ruether suggests the unpronounceable term *God/ess* be used to point to the as yet unnameable understanding of the divine that would transcend *patriarchal limitations. Drawing on the possibilities of the wisdom tradition, Elisabeth Schüssler Fiorenza devises other strategies to mark the inadequacy of traditional thinking about divine mystery, writing at first of Sophia-God, then using the form *G-d,* and now, listening to criticism from Jewish feminists, writing *G*d*. Still others opt to keep the term *God* but destabilize its patriarchal connotations by combining it with female metaphors or grammatically feminine pronouns: thus "God as Mother" or "God . . . She" (Sallie McFague, Elizabeth Johnson). The search for a viable term for divine mystery, redemptive for women as well as men, remains one of the ongoing tasks of feminist theology.

Resources. To reimagine symbols and rethink concepts of the sacred, feminist theologians draw on a variety of sources, chief among them women's *experience in *dialogue with some aspect of still-existing or lost tradition. Women's experience may include bodily, cultural, political, economic, social, intellectual, religious, historical, or contemporary feminist experiences that traditionally were excluded from the realm of the sacred but now are interpreted as worthy *metaphors for the divine. At the deepest level, this source becomes available as women possess themselves as acting subjects of their own history, with the full dignity of a human person created in the image of the divine: "i found god in myself and i loved her, i loved her fiercely" (Ntozake Shange 1977, 63).

From this stance, other sources are tapped to yield imagery or ideas that can serve feminist transformation of the sacred. Biblical tradition yields critically prophetic and liberating principles, as well as fragments of female images of the divine: mother, female spirit, midwife, coin seeker, and the great divine personification *Sophia, who is creator, liberator, *justice teacher, and friend of her people. In ancient paganism, as well as in countercultural movements in Christian history such as *Gnosticism or Shakerism, feminist theologians find glimpses of alternatives suppressed by Western patriarchal religion: female deity or women's messianic *equality. While these elements have their own dark sides, the dialectic between them and the major tradition allows a new wholeness to be envisioned. Finally, traditional theology itself can also be a resource. It emphasizes the utter incomprehensibility of divine mystery, not able to be captured in any image or set of *doctrines, and insists that all language about God is analogical, metaphorical, symbolic, referring to the Holy One indirectly rather than directly. Thus its own tenets contain an inbuilt dynamism toward *deconstructing an absolute idol.

Transformations. Feminist theological work on the images of divine mystery has produced usable and influential results: God as Mother, Lover, and Friend of the world, which is God's body; Holy Wisdom, Sophia-God; Holy One; She Who Is; Matrix who surrounds the world with the power of life. In Christian theology some have gone further, seeking to retrieve the symbol of the Trinity not as a trio of male figures generating and spirating each other but as a symbol of the divine as ultimately relational, a communion of equal persons in mutual relation. If mutual and equal communion is the very nature of divine mystery, then this sets the norm for a pattern of *relationships among persons.

Scholars who speak from social locations of *suffering due to *racism and *poverty make further distinctive contributions. Many womanist theologians bring the experience of *friendship with Jesus Christ to bear when interpreting divine intentions for the world. *Mujerista* theologians analyze how, in Hispanic *culture, the divine is refracted through the figure of Mary. Women theologians of the *third world consistently approach the divine as life-giving Spirit, the divine presence walking with people in their struggle for justice.

The concepts that arise from feminist imagery transform traditional divine attributes by stressing the Holy One's relationship with the world, all-embracing *immanence, ability to suffer with, willingness to be changed, power that empowers toward resistance, and absolute *compassion and inclusivity. No ally of oppressive structures, her purpose is intent on life and *liberation. Nor is this a matter of imagery and concepts alone. The image of God functions in open-ended ways. All feminist theologies seek symbols of the divine that function to endorse women, build just and equal relations in the community of women and men, and, increasingly, create harmony between humanity and the living earth itself.

Daly [1973a]; E. A. Johnson [1992]; LaCugna, in LaCugna, ed. [1993]; McFague [1987]; Ruether [1992]; Trible [1978]; Williams [1993a]

ELIZABETH A. JOHNSON

Goddess That feminists have become interested in exploring feminine images of God was, at least in hindsight, predictable; what is perhaps more surprising is the enormous multiplicity of images produced, imagined, and recovered, and the variety of ways in which religious feminists have related to these Images.

Goddess entered the feminist vocabulary early in the feminist theological enterprise. Goddesses were, of course, known prior to this but were usually regarded in the West as the preserve of *pagan, occult, ancient, tribal, or "other" religions (such as *Hinduism, *Shinto, or *Buddhism). Early Western feminists experimented with these religions (in large part owing to the gender of their deities), but it was not until Jewish and Christian theologians began questioning the gender of the monotheistic *God of their traditions that Goddess became the rich and diverse symbol that it is today in feminist theology. This questioning of gender was often a two-step process. First, male images and masculine language for God were critiqued for both reflecting and constructing a male-dominated society, and gender-neutral conceptions of divinity were advocated. Then, concerned that gender neutrality did not go far enough toward removing the male associations of the Western God, gender reversal was proposed, and the Goddess was born.

Though Goddess is a fairly recent aspect of feminist theology (one often stemming from nothing more sophisticated than irritation with a male God), she has quickly become a fully formed deity. The **thealogy* constructed on her behalf goes well beyond gender reversal to address many issues of concern to feminist theologians, including the *immanence of divinity, the proper human relationship to the natural world, the *empowerment of women, and the sacralizing of the women's movement.

There is a broad, nearly universal consensus among feminists who use the term *Goddess* that she should fulfill the basic functions of empowering women and fostering ethical and harmonious *relationships among different peoples and between humans, animals, and the natural world. The consensus goes no further. Indeed, there is not only variety but also controversy involved in Goddess thealogy; for if it was the work of Jewish and Christian feminists that set the Goddess movement rolling in the West, the trend was quickly adopted by feminists not (or no longer) affiliated with the mainstream, monotheistic traditions. These women generally took a freer hand in developing Goddess thealogy. In addition, women from cultures that had a much stronger historical claim to Goddess worship (East Asian, South Asian, African, and Native American cultures, for example, and practitioners of neopaganism) had their own ideas about how the Goddess or goddesses could be adapted for feminist use.

The main cleavages in Goddess thealogy today are between Goddess as *metaphor and Goddess as deity; feminine exclusivity and gender inclusivity in the Godhead; and *monotheism and polytheism (and various meldings of the two).

Jewish and Christian feminists have tended to use Goddess as metaphor or image: as one (but only one) means of talking about, imagining, or relating to the divine. In a popular phrase, these feminists are recovering "the feminine face of God" from scriptural and historical sources, or they are inventing it outright as a way of more fully conceiving the mystery of the sacred. Jewish feminists especially, as part of a radically monotheistic *tradition, have typically worked with Goddess as image or language rather than deity. Christian feminists, who are comfortable with a trinitarian formulation for deity, have taken greater latitude in conceiving of Goddess as one identity in the Godhead. Feminine exclusivity in Jewish and Christian Goddess thealogy is virtually unheard of; the divine may be called "she" for the particular spiritual experiences and political meanings this evokes, but is finally no more "she" than "he" or "it." Gender in the divine is *chosen,* may be *evoked,* but is not ontological.

In polytheistic faiths, in contrast, the goddesses are importantly and unchangeably female. Feminists who are Hindu, Buddhist, Native American, or practitioners of African traditional religions have sought out the female divinities within these religions and interpreted the art, lore, and theology surrounding them in a uniquely feminist way. These goddesses are rarely (and then only ultimately) understood as image or metaphor for a genderless divinity; they are instead deities with distinct individual features. They are suprahuman personages or symbols with whom the worshiper interacts, and their femaleness is integral to who they are and what they are able to do for those who seek out their presence. (Some Christian feminists, particularly Catholic feminists, work in a similar way to rehabilitate female saints [especially the Virgin Mary] for feminist ends, treating these figures as expressions of divinity or as semidivine rather than as individual deities. Jungian feminists and others interested in myth have also at times practiced a functional Goddess polytheism, though they regard the goddesses as mythic symbols or psychic realities rather than as deities.) Feminist theologians in polytheistic traditions usually recognize the existence of male deities as well (and may regard them as variously uninteresting, helpful, or hostile), but there is rarely any effort to excise them from the tradition.

Many feminists in the West who are not born to polytheistic traditions have adopted them or, more commonly, adopted their female deities into a syncretistic spiritual feminism. It is only here (and in a few neopagan traditions) that one finds something approaching Goddess monotheism. The one Goddess may be expressed in a variety of symbols, approached in many ways, present in many different aspects (sometimes including male ones); but she is finally one, and she is female. This femaleness is frequently construed in reproductive biological terms. For example, it is she who gave birth to the world and she who nurtures us with her body. This type of Goddess worship is not a tactical exercise of imagining femaleness into the Godhead or the pantheon but a recognition that the sacred mystery is actually, and importantly, female.

This belief is often strengthened by a companion belief that the human race from the time of its origins worshiped the divine as female. Worship of a superior male God or gods is said to be fairly recent (dating from 8000 B.C.E. to 1700 C.E., depending on the theorist and/or the area of the world in question) and consistently linked to *patriarchal social relations. Adherents of this theory feel that the Goddess worship they practice and advocate is a recovery of the form of religion that has characterized human society for the vast proportion of its existence. Thus many of the images they offer for Goddess are from prehistoric art and sculpture or ancient myth. This theory and these images have also played a role (though a somewhat different one) in other types of Goddess thealogy, including Jewish and Christian feminism.

As yet, there is no single thealogy evolving out of this plethora of Goddess lore and worship, but exploration of female divinity is sure to be an enduring aspect of feminist theology.

Carson [1992]; Daly [1978]; Eller [1993]; Gadon [1989]; Plaskow/Christ [1989]

CYNTHIA ELLER

Gospel *Gospel* means "good news." The term has three referents in Christian theology that stem from the New Testament. First, Jesus' proclamation of the reign of God is identified as gospel (Matt. 4:23; 9:35; Mark 1:15; Luke 4:43; 8:1). Second, Paul uses the word *gospel* about fifty times to refer to the message he proclaims about Jesus *Christ and especially about Christ's death and *resurrection. Third, the word refers to literary accounts of Jesus' *ministry, teaching, death, and resurrection, in particular the Gospels of Matthew, Mark, Luke, and John found in the NT.

The opening verse of the Gospel of Mark is the earliest example of the use of the noun *gospel* at least in part to designate a narrative about Jesus. In addition to the four canonical Gospels, manuscripts of other Gospels have been found, for example, the Gospels of Thomas, Peter, Mary, the Ebionites, and the Hebrews. Some tell only of Jesus' birth and childhood. Others, like the *Gospel of Thomas,* present only a catalogue of teachings, with little reference to Jesus' ministry, death, or resurrection. Some clearly differ from the picture of Jesus found in those Gospels that were accepted into the *canon, or they present *doctrines that the church judged unacceptable. Others simply may not have been well enough known among the early Christian communities to have won support for inclusion in the canon.

Even the four canonical Gospels differ in their portraits of Jesus. Neither Mark nor John, for example, refers to Jesus' birth or childhood, and the best manuscripts of Mark have no stories of appearances of the risen Christ to the disciples. All four trace Jesus' ministry from his connection to John the Baptist through a time of teaching and other activities (including a ministry of *healing) to a final drama including a time with the disciples, arrest, administrative hearings before religious and political authorities, condemnation to death, crucifixion, and the discovery by some women of the empty tomb. Despite this general similarity, the four do not agree in the content or order of events and teachings they relate.

Such differences would be distressing if the Gospels were biographies of Jesus. Instead of providing data about Jesus as an important figure of the past, however, each Gospel proclaims Jesus' significance for the ongoing life of the Gospel writer's own community. All four of the New Testament Gospels were written in the final third of the first century, several decades after Jesus' death. They came from communities of varied ethnic composition (Matthew and John, for example, predominantly Jewish, and Mark and Luke with a larger proportion of Gentiles), living in various cities of the Hellenistic world (or, in the case of Mark, perhaps in rural Galilee or southern Lebanon). The writers drew on collections of teachings attributed to Jesus and stories about him that had been circulating in oral or written form among the early Christian communities, and later writers may have incorporated Gospels written earlier. In that process of *memory, interpretation, and transmission, traces of the ministry of Jesus in rural Palestine early in the first century were altered in accordance with social realities and theological beliefs of churches shaped by the Roman–Jewish War of 66–70 C.E. That process of formation of the Gospels makes it difficult to discern women's roles in the ministry of Jesus and among his earliest followers, for the portrait of women in each Gospel incorporates perspectives on women that derive from social and ecclesiastical contexts which postdate Jesus' ministry. Since the NT epistles portray a steady reduction of women's *freedom and of openness to women's leadership during the later decades of the New Testament period, women may have been more prominent in the early movement than the Gospels suggest.

Brock [1988]; D'Angelo, *JBL* [1990a]; Kinukawa [1994]; Newsom/Ringe [1992]; Schüssler Fiorenza [1983/1994]

SHARON H. RINGE

Grace Traditionally, grace is fundamentally understood as God's mercy and power, apart from humans, whereby God recovers individual persons from *sin while granting forgiveness and new life. A related traditional understanding is grace as God's power in persons, freeing them to choose or enabling them to do just acts. A more contemporary understanding of grace is God's loving power that provides security throughout human history.

Feminist theologies present plural conceptions of grace. Generally, these distinguish the function of grace in improving or affirming life for persons. One conception identifies grace as moments of self-acceptance in *community that provide strength for ongoing self-realization. Another conception presents grace as conferral of dignity on persons who experience inhuman humiliation in *poverty. Here grace issues from divinely engendered interactions that motivate persons to oppose injustice and untruth. A third conception expresses grace as intense love for others that disposes and empowers persons to work for *justice. While the first two conceptions contradict the traditional idea of grace originating solely in God, the third perspective challenges the existence of grace apart from human-to-human *relationships.

In spite of plurality, conceptions of grace in feminist theologies share several emphases. Perhaps most significant is the overall assertion that *grace occurs in connections between persons.* This differs from conventional understandings of grace as functioning only for individuals and transforms the notion of grace as solely divine power, asserting instead that grace emerges as fragility and dependence. Definitions of grace in feminist theologies also imply *ethics, generally pointing to communal action with sociopolitical consequences. Affirming creativity and human initiative, this contests traditional ideas that the natural disposition in all persons is toward egocentric self-assertion. Significantly, discussions in feminist theologies all challenge the traditional tendency to define grace universally.

Brock [1988]; Plaskow [1980]; Tamez [1993b]; Welch [1990]

ROSETTA E. ROSS

Guilt Classical theology understands guilt as consequent on the original *sin of the *Fall of Adam and Eve in the Garden of Eden. According to Augustine, no human being is free from this inherited guilt, which is transmitted by sexual intercourse. The problem for feminist theology is that, according to the dominant interpretation of the Fall in Christian exegesis, women have frequently been scapegoated for this original transgression. The consequence of this attribution of guilt is that society continues to blame women for sin, particularly sexual sin; to denigrate female *sexuality; and to hold women inordinately responsible for the "moral fiber" of society.

This has made it extremely difficult to hold society accountable for violent crimes against women as, according to popular myth, women "ask for it." This all-pervasive belief has caused women to internalize the guilt and frequently to believe that they have been attacked through some fault of their own. Another problem is that many male clergy increase this internalized guilt of women by assuming not only that women have indeed provoked an attack but that their obligation is to forgive, to reconcile, to restore domestic peace at all costs.

The feminist theological task is fourfold: first, to highlight the links between guilt and *power and to reject the interpretations that attribute the fault of the Fall to Eve alone; second, to continue to reflect on and identify what is genuinely sinful for women as women, in the diverse contexts and levels of *freedom that women have for *autonomous action; third, to replace the *patriarchal, *dualistic understanding of sexuality that causes a derogatory understanding of the *body and its functions to be projected onto women; and finally, to move from the internalizing of guilt toward a healthy understanding and acceptance of what *responsibility women have for good and *evil in their particular contexts.

Daly [1973a]; Grey [1989]; Pagels [1988]; Schaumberger/Schottroff [1988]

MARY C. GREY

Han *Han* is a Korean word expressing a deep feeling that rises out of the unjust experiences of the people. *Han* is difficult to translate into English because it is more than *suffering; it is the cluster of suffering experiences and the suppressed experience of *oppression. It is often said that *han* is the underlying feeling of Korean people who have suffered from numerous invasions from surrounding powerful nations and have continually suffered the tyranny of their rulers. So *han* designates the psychological phenomenon of people's suffering and is a feeling of the hopelessness of the oppressed, a feeling of just indignation, or a feeling of unresolved resentment against unjustifiable suffering. *Han* is sometimes compared to "the blues" in the black experience in the United States. It is not a one-time psychological response to an unjust situation or treatment but an accumulation of such feelings in response to numerous unjust, oppressive experiences.

Korean shamanism, which is mostly practiced by the deprived, is often called the religion of *han*. *Han* has been a central concept of shamanistic ritual. It is usually acknowledged in the personal dimension as a resentment that is believed to bring misfortunes such as sickness and *poverty. The shaman, who is usually female, tries to resolve the *han*- ridden mind or spirit and to bring back the person's hope, strength, and health. In this sense, the shaman is called the priest of *han*.

A Korean poet named Kim Chi-ha developed *han* as a collective concept and theme of Christian theology. He summed up the experience of **minjung* as *han*. *Minjung* is a Korean word that indicates those who are economically, politically, and socially deprived. Kim first expressed the belief that *han* can be sublimated in dynamic form as the energy for revolution. While Korean shamans read and treat *han* as personal, Kim understands *han* in a collective sense.

It was Korean *minjung* theology, emerging in the 1970s, that responded to the *han* of the *minjung*, which was a central motif in Kim's writings. *Minjung* theology is strongly influenced by the social biography of the *minjung*, in which the most important political consciousness of the *minjung* appears as *han*. In *minjung* theology, *han* is not just an individual experience of repression but a collective experience of the oppressed. The feeling of *han* has both negative and positive elements. In a negative sense, it is a dominant feeling of defeat, a submission to fate, so it does not change anything in reality. *Minjung* theologians often see, however, a transforming element in *han* and argue that it can be used as the energy for a revolution.

It is often said that the core experiences of Korean women in history have been *han* and that Korean women thus are the *minjung* of the *minjung*, because they have been oppressed first as women and then as persons who are economically, socially, and politically deprived. Even though *minjung* theology and feminist theologies share the common vision of *liberation from oppression, it should be noted that in *minjung* theology *patriarchy has not been criticized in a full sense and that the categories of feminist theology are broader than those of *minjung* theology. It should be also noted that while the *han* of the *minjung* rises out of sociopolitico-economic oppression, the *han* of Korean women mainly rises out of a rigid sexual discrimination against women and out of their not fulfilling the patriarchal expectations, such as being born as a girl or being unable to bear a son. Unless the root causes of *han* are carefully examined from a feminist perspective, the *han* of women cannot be used as the energy for transformation in a concrete reality.

Commission on Theological Concerns of the CCA [1981]; Lee [1988]; Suh [1988; 1991]

KANG NAM-SOON

Handicapism Handicapism is also known as "ableism" and "disabiliphobia." It means discrimination, both subtle and overt, against people with disabilities. Handicapism has existed since the beginning of history and is still the predominant attitude worldwide toward people with disabilities. Under its auspices, employment, housing, parenting, *marriage and other loving *relationships, access to facilities and information, and, in some cases, life itself, have been and continue to be denied to disabled people.

Today, however, disabled people are fighting back against handicapism through legal action, awareness campaigns, grass-roots activism, and civil disobedience. They are insisting that *disability, rather than being a "fate worse than death," is a natural part of life. Only a few feminists understand or participate in the disability civil rights movement. Most still believe that people with disabilities are frail, passive objects of charity who need healing.

The disability civil rights movement runs parallel to feminists' struggle against *sexism. Because anyone can become disabled, the movement must struggle with its own *racism, sexism, and other forms of prejudice. Disabled women and feminists share some goals: they want the discrimination against them to cease; they want to be seen as active participants in life rather than as passive objects or victims; and they want to make choices concerning their bodies, health, and reproductive *freedom.

Disabled women frequently are in conflict with feminists over such issues as *abortion and reproductive freedom. Too often, pro-choice feminists advocate that all pregnant women should have abortions when tests show that their babies would be born with disabilities. Far too many feminists use the threat of bearing a disabled child as the reason for having legalized abortion. This position is offensive to disabled people: it sends the message that the world would be better off without children with disabilities; that, indeed, disability is a "fate worse than death." While many disabled women oppose abortion, many others are pro-choice. Those who are pro-choice support the right of women to have abortions (including aborting fetuses with disabilities) but believe that women should make choices informed by knowledge and experience of disability and disabled people.

Tensions between disabled women also arise over inaccessible facilities (such as *battered women's shelters) and whether or not women with disabilities should have children. Though some progress has been made, most feminists still don't work with disabled women to address these issues.

Disability Rag/Resource [September/October 1993]; Eisland [1994]; Fine/Asch [1988]; *Mainstream Magazine* [1994–]; Shaw, ed. [1994]

KATHI WOLFE

Harlot "Harlot" is one of several expressions, including "whore" and "prostitute," used to translate the Hebrew *zōnāh* and Greek *pornē* in English Bibles. In both Hebrew and Greek the primary term for prostitute is related to a verb describing general sexual promiscuity, often extended to designate immorality in general. A unique *metaphorical usage of the Hebrew Bible characterizes Israel's relations with other gods and nations as "harlotry." Apostate Israel, portrayed as an unfaithful wife, is said to "play the harlot" or "whore after" other lovers, behaving like a brazen prostitute (Hos. 1:2; 2:4–5; Lev. 20:5, 6; Judg. 8:27, 33).

This figurative usage is commonly derived from the practice of "sacred *prostitution," widely held to characterize Canaanite religion. Recent scholarship has cast doubt on this interpretation, however, finding no clear evidence for the institution and no association of prostitution with cultic office or sacred ritual in ancient Near Eastern texts. The Hebrew term generally translated "sacred prostitute," *qedeshāh,* means simply "consecrated (person)," from the same root as *qadosh,* "holy." Identification of this cultic functionary as a type of prostitute appears to rest on three OT passages in which *qedeshāh* is paralleled to *zōnāh,* "prostitute" (Genesis 38; Deut. 23:17–18; Hos. 4:14). Through this juxtaposition Israelite authors polemically represent the *qedeshāh* as "simply" a kind of prostitute.

Prostitution, in its ancient and modern forms, has as its defining characteristic the granting of sexual access for payment. Although widespread, it is not universal. Rather, it is a distinctive feature of *patriarchal societies, permitting males to enjoy sexual relations outside of *marriage while maintaining exclusive control over their spouses' *sexuality. Thus the prostitute is normally female; and it is she, rather than her male partner, who bears the major burden of *shame that everywhere attaches to the institution—however varied the degree and expression. Male prostitutes (weakly attested in the ancient Near East, more common in the Greco-Roman world) serve only to extend the range of available partners and do not represent a complementary institution serving female needs.

The Hebrew term for prostitute (*zōnāh*) is a feminine participle with no masculine counterpart. It derives from a verb that normally describes the promiscuous sexual activity of an unmarried woman, a crime punishable by death (Gen. 38:24; Lev. 21:9; Deut. 22:20–21). What is tolerated for the prostitute, as a class set apart, is strictly proscribed for all other women.

Both testaments disparage prostitution, though in varying manner and degree. In the OT the prostitute is tolerated and may even appear in the role of heroine (Josh. 2:1–21; cf. 1 Kings 3:16–26). But narrative praise of character or action does not change her social status; she remains an outcast (Gen. 34:31; 1 Kings 22:38). Wisdom admonitions warn men against the wiles and waste of prostitutes (Prov. 7:10; 23:27; 29:3; cf. Luke 15:30), and Deuteronomic legislation prohibits payment of vows with wages from prostitution (Deut. 23:18 [19 Heb.]). Priests are forbidden to marry a prostitute (Lev. 21:7) or force a daughter into prostitution (Lev. 19:29). The figure of the prostitute appears as an antitype of the virgin in metaphorical representations of cities and nations (Nahum 3:4; Isa. 23:16–18; cf. Isa. 47:1; Amos 5:2).

In the New Testament prostitutes (*pornē*, f. sg.) are grouped with tax collectors to represent the lowest class, viewed in moral terms (Matt. 21:31–32; cf. Luke 15:30). The masculine noun *pornos* (a male prostitute in classical Greek) is used in the NT only in the general sense of "fornicator" or "one who practices sexual immorality" (Eph. 5:5; 1 Tim. 1:10; Rev. 21:8). It often occurs, along with the noun *porneia* "fornication," as a collective or lead term in catalogues of vices (Mark 7:21; 1 Cor. 5:9, 11; Gal. 5:19) and is often associated with Gentile practice, especially *idol worship (Acts 15:20, 29; 21:25). Revelation continues the figurative usage of the OT, describing Babylon as the "great whore" and its offenses as "fornication" (Rev. 17:1–2; 18:3; cf. Isa. 1:21).

Bird, *Semeia* [1989]; Bird, in Day [1989]; Goodfriend, *ABD* [1992]; Van der Toorn, *ABD* [1992]; Westenholz, *HTR* [1989]

PHYLLIS A. BIRD

Healing Within the Christian *tradition, many women have followed the example of Jesus, who during his earthly *ministry healed people of various physical and mental maladies. Twentieth-century healers include Maria Woodworth-Etter, Aimee Semple McPherson, and Kathryn Kuhlman. However, in feminist theology the word *healing* is most often used in a theological, psychological, or ecological sense. In theological terms, healing is found in the overcoming of *duality and dichotomy, which Virginia Ramey Mollenkott in her book *Godding* identifies as both delusion and *sin. The most basic duality is simply "us" and "them," played out in terms of gender, *race, social class, denomination, *religion, sexual orientation, etc. Healing is defined in terms of inclusivity and recognition of and respect for *pluralism, tolerance, and understanding.

While physical threats remain in such diseases as breast cancer and *AIDS, women also seek psychological healing and wholeness, healing from physical, sexual, and emotional abuse in their childhoods and in their adult *relationships. Healing is spoken of in terms of *liberation from *patriarchal expectations and roles, abusive relationships, constricting *stereotypes, and growth-stifling situations. Wholeness is defined in terms of self-esteem, *freedom of choice, creative and mutually fulfilling relationships, spiritual nurture, and growth. For example, in *Touching Our Strength*, Carter Heyward speaks of healing not only our wounded selves but also our broken bonds. She finds healing in the acknowledgment and celebration of the physical, the erotic, the power of right and mutual relation.

Women also speak of healing the planet by fighting pollution, conserving energy, saving threatened species. Unless we heal our planet, our mother earth will be endangered and the human race will be threatened with extinction. Thus in feminist theology healing is a very comprehensive term. Healing is not only personal but also interpersonal and global.

Adams [1993]; Heyward [1989a]; Mollenkott [1987]

NANCY A. HARDESTY

Heaven Classical Christian *doctrine regarded heaven as a state of blessedness in which believers dwelt eternally in God's presence. Heaven has been a doctrine in which gender and *sexuality have figured prominently. For most of Christian history, believers posited heaven as a realm in which isolated, asexual individuals contemplated the divine. Since the eighteenth and nineteenth centuries, however, Christians have envisioned heaven as a realm in which families, particularly married couples, were reunited, so that the sexuality expressed in *marriage continued in heaven as a *sacrament of God's love.

Both traditional views present difficulties for feminist theologies. The asexual view is problematic in that the early church which conceived it was particularly skeptical of the goodness of woman's sexuality. Only celibate, ascetic women, who in sublimating their sexual urges became "like men," were understood to escape the sinful nature into which Eve was presumed to have condemned women. The later view, by envisioning life in heaven as a continuation of traditional earthly marriage, has obvious heterosexist overtones.

Feminist theologies generally demythologize heaven. Aware that oppressors often justify their privileged status by urging the oppressed to set aside their longings for equity and to wait for redress in the life to come, feminist theologies stress the importance of realizing *justice and establishing mutuality in the here and now. Biblical texts of relevance offer images of consummation, such as the establishment of a new heaven and a new earth (Isa. 65:17; 66:22) in which pain and *oppression have passed away or the proclamation of *jubilee, the acceptable year of God, wherein *suffering is abolished (Luke 4:18–19). Other relevant texts point to communal experiences of mutuality, such as the new Jerusalem (Rev. 21:2–4) where human beings and God dwell together in joy and unity of purpose.

Baldwin, *Journal of Religious Thought* [1984]; Clark [1983]; Lang, *Religion* [1987]; Pellauer, *C/C* [1987]

VALARIE H. ZIEGLER

Hegemony The basic definition of hegemony is political rule or *domination, particularly in relations between states. The work of the political theorist and leader of the Italian Communist Party Antonio Gramsci extended it to include the relationship between social classes. From these twin roots, the feminist conception of hegemony captures the interstructuring of cultural, economic, political, and social forces that coalesce to ensure the domination of the ruling elite. It marks a pervasive cultural and social formation that extends to all of lived experience.

Culture is seen as a social process where humans define and shape their lives through *tradition and practice. This process encompasses history and *memory and the ways in which we order our lives and act out of that order. *Ideology becomes the formal system of meanings, ideas, beliefs, and values of the ruling elite.

The distribution of *power and the reality of domination and subordination in the social and religious order are key considerations. The social process is a compilation of dominant meanings and values that saturate our practices and perceptions. Key is the realization that this is a *lived* system of meanings and values which shapes our sense of reality. This circular relationship ensures both the domination of the ruling elite and the subordination of the masses along *race, gender, and class lines. The narrative of the ruling elite becomes the reality of society, despite counter- or metanarratives that challenge the assumptions of the ordering of society and the subjective nature of meaning and values. Therefore, hegemonic processes function in such a way as to keep the ruling elite in power by ensuring that others see the world the way those in power see it.

As a lived process, hegemony functions as a complex of experiences, *relationships, and activities that maintains the status quo. It is continually being renewed, re-created, defended, and reformed by the ruling elite and resisted, altered, challenged, and transformed by communities of resistance.

Gramsci [1971]; hooks [1990; 1992]; Knoppers, in Van Leeuwen [1993]

EMILIE M. TOWNES

Hell Classical Christian *doctrine regarded hell as a state of torment in which damned souls eternally dwelt after death. A counterview *(apokatastasis* or universalism), advocated by Origen in the early church and more recently by Karl Barth, contended that, ultimately, all persons find salvation in Christ.

Feminist theologies challenge the doctrine of hell on several grounds. Because the doctrine typically posits either the damnation of those who fail to profess faith in the one savior or the eventual acknowledgment from all souls of the lordship of Christ, it represents a paradigm of the *hierarchical model of truth that feminist theologies reject. Moreover, warnings regarding the horrors of hell have on numerous occasions been self-serving. From Dante's *Inferno* (which consigned the lowest levels of hell to the author's political enemies) to plantation evangelists who warned African-American slaves that those who disobeyed their masters were bound for hell, the doctrine has frequently served to legitimate the social status of those who preached it.

Finally, because classical theology has depicted Jesus' death as the event that persuaded God the Father not to damn those who professed faith in God's Son, the doctrine of hell typically posits God as a divine child abuser. Some Calvinist readings, moreover, have encouraged believers to welcome their own damnation as an object lesson to other sinners or as a way of glorifying God.

Feminist theologies renounce understandings that depict the divine as abusive or that elevate self-annihilation to a theological *virtue. They also tend to demythologize hell, decrying torment in the here and now rather than focusing on some mythic hereafter. Feminist theologies call persons, in the face of present alienation from God and from one another, to unite together with God in seeking *healing, *community, and love. Those who resist God's call, choosing to side with the structures of *oppression and estrangement rather than with the community of God, are understood already to experience divine *judgment (John 3:19).

Baldwin, *Journal of Religious Thought* [1984]; Brown/Parker, in Brown/Bohn [1989]; McFague, in Loades [1990]; Ruether, in Thistlethwaite/Engel [1990]

VALARIE H. ZIEGLER

Heresy The term *heresy* is derived from the Greek *hairesis,* meaning "*doctrine" or "received opinion." In Acts it has a neutral value in reference to Pharisees, Sadducees, Stoics, Pythagoreans, and Christians (cf. Acts 5:17; 24:5; 26:5; 28:22). However, in the *Pauline and *pastoral epistles it takes on negative and suspicious overtones, implying "sect" or "erroneous teaching" (cf. 1 Cor. 11:19; Gal. 5:20; 2 Peter 2:1). By the third century C.E., heresy had acquired its common Christian meaning: a willfully erroneous doctrinal position.

Heresy and **orthodoxy* are reciprocal terms that developed in the search for valid, salvific *faith. Doctrinal standards in the patristic period were molded by Roman legal apprehensions of truth as an exclusionary rather than inclusionary principle. When the Reformation broke the monolithic power of the Western church, much greater doctrinal variance was encompassed by orthodoxy, although the exclusionary principle remained in effect.

In the late twentieth century, the global crisis of meaning and *authority is shaking the foundations of the white, male philosophical and theological *hegemony. In the United States, reactionary groups within many mainline denominations are forming "confessing" movements built on claims of loyalty to the demonstrably false assertion that orthodoxy upholds "that which was held always, everywhere, by everyone" (Oden, 57).

Throughout Western history, heresy charges have been used to control or destroy women who challenge patriarchal definitions, as was the case with the "witches" murdered in Europe and the United States. When Chung Hyun Kyung drew on the **minjung* traditions of Korea for her World Council of Churches presentation in 1991, she was accused of syncretism and heresy. Women at the 1993 Re-Imagining Conference in the United States, part of the Ecumenical Decade in Solidarity with Women, were called heretics and blasphemers for their use of the *Sophia traditions. Accusations of heresy have always been used to defend existing social or ecclesiastical *power.

Chung [1990]; Joy, in Joy/Magee [1994]; Oden [1983]; Williams [1993a]

SUSAN E. DAVIES

Hermeneutics of Suspicion A process of interpretation, hermeneutics suggests that understanding arises in the encounter between text and reader. In this meeting the reader's presuppositions, familiarity with other materials, *experiences, competence, community, expectations, desires, etc., influence either consciously or subconsciously the construction of the meaning. Problems arise, however, when the reader finds contradictions or inconsistencies within the text itself or when what the reader judges to be factual, liberating, aesthetically valuable, or even of interrogative interest is apparently ignored, undercut, or denied by the text.

This recognition of the gap between text and perception is neither new nor unique to feminist observation, nor is it limited to analyses of scriptural and theological works. It finds its antecedents in the modes of interpretation proposed by Friedrich Schleiermacher, Friedrich Wilhelm Nietzsche, William Dilthey, Martin Heidegger, Hans-Georg Gadamer, and others. These philosophers recognized problems in the use of language (e.g., what one says and means may not be what the other hears and interprets); with historical and ethnic distance (e.g., shifts in cultural codes and understandings of human nature); with authoritative texts (e.g., the privileging of the perceived authorial intent over the reader, the import of the canon); and so forth.

Jürgen Habermas moved the discussion to *ideological critique by insisting that the possibilities of *domination within any interpretive move be acknowledged—that interpretation is not innocent but interested. Paul Ricoeur speaks of "interpretation as exercise of suspicion" in reference to Marx, Nietzsche, and Freud, the "masters of suspicion" who "look upon the whole of consciousness primarily as 'false consciousness' " (Ricoeur, 32–33).

Elisabeth Schüssler Fiorenza advanced the term *feminist hermeneutics of suspicion* in developing such interpretive observations for explicitly feminist historical reconstruction and theology (1984, 15–17). Along with other hermeneutical modes (proclamation, imagination, remembrance, creative actualization, etc.), she set forth both theoretical and practical means of redressing oppressive, reductive, and/or inaccurate histories and theologies.

Schüssler Fiorenza (1992a, 53, 57–62) proposes two critical moments leading to a hermeneutics of suspicion: consciousness-raising and systemic analysis. Both arise from *conscientization (a term adopted from Paulo Freire), "learning to recognize sociopolitical, economic, cultural, and religious contradictions," and from *cognitive dissonance, recognizing the gap between experience and personal values on the one hand and texts and interpretations that deviate from or occlude lived experience on the other. Examples of such disjunctures are manifold, for example, the absence of references to women in various canonical works, translations, and exegesis. Feminist readers recognize from historical studies, textual analysis, and their own experiences that such absences indicate not *objective reality but subjective, ideological presentations, if not intentional omissions. Feminist readers problematize the insistence that generic male terms (*man, he,* etc.) are universal, and they similarly question the construction of the ideal "self" as male, rich, heterosexual, etc., in contradistinction to other subject positions and life situations. Similarly, readers sensitive to Judaism question the accuracy of the Gospels' portrait of the Pharisees or the claims of some Christian feminists that Jesus needed to liberate women from a monolithic, repressive, patriarchal Judaism. Required, then, is "the *deconstruction of the historical 'master' paradigm of Christian-Western society and *culture . . . attentive to the traditional patterns of domination and subjugation in society, church, and academy" (Schüssler Fiorenza 1992a, 178).

Since all texts, both ancient narrative and modern commentary, presuppose *and* reinforce cultural codes and ideological structures, the hermeneutics of suspicion is not limited to reading canonical texts. It recognizes as well the potential for interpretations to gain *hegemonic status, since interpretations are invested with the power to influence one's understanding of not just the past but also the present and future, as well as self and society. Practitioners of this reading strategy recognize the constructed and hence provisional nature of interpretations and therefore seek to deconstruct their meaning. Finally, they insist that both ancient text and modern exegesis be evaluated, as Schüssler Fiorenza (1984, 136) puts it, "in terms of a critical theology of *liberation."

Applied, the hermeneutics of suspicion challenges even readings that may initially appear helpful. For example, it asks whether a liberating interpretation comes at another's expense. It asks if an interpretation uplifting for one particular culture or circumstance (e.g., the relationship between Ruth and Naomi read as commending intergenerational alliances) might be oppressive to another (e.g., the application of this interpretation in situations where daughters-in-law are required to submit to their mothers-in-law). It asks if the text at hand presents the whole *story, and it frequently appeals to countervoices and countertexts: to the restriction of Christian women in the *pastoral epistles, it evokes the *Acts of Thecla;* to the claim that Israelite women were valued only for childbearing, it evokes Deborah, the wise women of the Deuteronomic history, and Huldah. To various representations of women preserved in texts, it both reconstructs the agenda of the author and seeks the social roles of real women behind those texts; to translations that speak of brothers and sons, it inquires about sisters and daughters; to readings that privilege a particular model or *gender construct, it highlights the reductionist and ahistorical dangers of *stereotyping and *essentialism.

A deconstructive reading strategy, feminist hermeneutics of suspicion locates the means by which a text signals underlying ideological stances by seeking contradictions, gaps, projections, and silences. It then moves beyond such identification to more complete historical reconstructions and more inclusive modern appropriations. Neither ahistorical nor paranoid, neither redemptory nor dismissive of the object of its investigation, feminist hermeneutics of suspicion investigates the process of textual production, with all the liberationist and oppressive potentials that process entails.

Foucault [1980]; Ricoeur [1970]; Schüssler Fiorenza [1984/1995; 1992a]; Schüssler Fiorenza, *ABD* [1992b]

AMY-JILL LEVINE

Heterosexism in Biblical Interpretation Heterosexism is the privileging and absolutizing of heterosexuality (and, by implication, male–female *power relations of *domination and submission) in all aspects of relational life. This systemic *oppression and *marginalization of a person or group due to their real or perceived same-sex orientation, preference, or identity has yet to be addressed in biblical interpretation. Seemingly still "acceptable," oppressive realities in the United States and Western Europe, including the use of the Bible to "justify" gay bashing and other heterosexist and homophobic *violence, are not being widely countered by academic discourse on the topic. This silence indicates a lack of safety, in both public and private contexts, to speak openly on the issues.

Heterosexism in the text (Bible) and heterosexism in the reader (translator, interpreter) are distinguishable yet reinforce each other. Bible verses often cited allegedly to legitimate heterosexist behavior include prohibitions in Lev. 18:22; 20:13 and Rom. 1:26–27, as well as stories such as Gen. 19:1–11 and Judg. 19:22–30. They have become "texts of terror" for lesbians, gay men, bisexual and transgendered people, and their friends. References to additional texts (Gen. 2:22–24; Mark 10:5–12; 1 Cor. 6:9–10) are frequently invoked to cement "heteroreality." Yet study of the biblical texts and their sociohistorical contexts has shown that understandings of *sexuality and human intimate *relationships at the time of the Holiness Code in ancient Israel or the *Pauline letters in the first-century C.E. Greco-Roman world have nothing in common with contemporary concepts of *lesbian, bisexual, gay, and transgendered existence, nor with concepts of heterosexual relationships in a time of contraceptives. Rather, these often-cited texts concern issues of hospitality, ritual *purity, procreation, or the securing of *hierarchies in the Roman Empire. Nevertheless, the history of interpretation of these biblical texts has been fateful and sometimes fatal to lesbian, gay, bisexual, and transgendered people and their supporters.

Feminist liberation *theology and feminist biblical interpretation address this painful legacy, remembering and mourning the victims of these "texts of terror," correcting traditional interpretations through research in sociohistorical, political, cultural contexts; and searching for other biblical voices with liberating potential. Positive texts mention, for example, paired women such as Mary and Martha (Luke 10:38–42), Tryphaena and Tryphosa (Rom. 16:12), Euodia and Syntyche (Phil. 4:2), and often Ruth and Naomi (Ruth 1:16–17). Offering instances for identification with possible "protolesbians," these texts have enabled and empowered women's relationships in Western cultures. In Japan and Korea, however, the Ruth story functions differently in upholding mother-in-law hierarchies over daughters-in-law. Similarly, biblical traditions of neighborly love (Lev. 19:18; Matt. 19:19; 22:37–39 par.), of *creation in the divine *image (Gen. 1:27), of the call to free the oppressed (Luke 4:18), and the *metaphor of the rainbow (Gen. 9:8–17) are supportive voices for the lesbian, gay, bisexual, and transgendered liberation movement.

Liberative potential lies also in Bible translations that allow for ambiguity (e.g., "woman" instead of "wife" for the Hebrew *'iššâ*, or "women friends" instead of "neighbors" for the Hebrew *re'ût*). They allow for greater variety in identifications. Likewise, the practice of *midrash invites the telling and retelling of biblical stories in light of contemporary women's *experiences and feminist perspectives, subverting traditional "authority" without making any claim to historical accuracy in biblical times. Most important, feminists need to challenge direct analogies between contemporary understandings of relationships and the understandings reflected in the Bible in order to indict and overcome heterosexism in biblical interpretation.

Alpert, in Balka/Rose [1989]; Brooten [1996]; Brooten, in Atkinson et al. [1985]; Comstock [1991]; Countryman [1988]; D'Angelo, *JFSR* [1990b]

ANGELA BAUER

Hierarchy In its etymological origins, *hierarchy* means "holy dominion"; the word has been used by Christians to denote those holding sacred authority within the institutional church. More broadly, hierarchy refers to the ordered structuring of persons, concepts, values, virtues, etc., that accords more value to the items on the top of the hierarchy than to those on the bottom. Such hierarchical relationships are an intrinsic feature of *patriarchy, which depends on gradations of privilege. Instead of recognizing and acknowledging *difference, patriarchy reads superiority and inferiority into differences.

Feminist and womanist theologies have focused critical attention on the hierarchies of gender, *race, class, and sexual orientation, social arrangements that value male over female, white people over peoples of color, the wealthy over the impoverished, and heterosexuals over homosexuals. In contrast, feminist theologians point to the biblical vision of God's realm as one of *justice and mutuality, rather than a realm of hierarchies of *domination and subordination. Instead of transforming differences into hierarchical gradations, feminist theologians propose respect for differences and the fostering of more egalitarian communities.

Rosemary Radford Ruether highlights the figure of Jesus and his criticism of the religious and social hierarchies of his times. She argues that Jesus' *ministry broke down the barriers between rich and poor, clean and unclean, healthy and sick, sinner and righteous. Women of *marginalized groups (Samaritans, Syro-Phoenicians, *prostitutes, the ritually unclean, *widows) play roles in the iconoclastic, messianic vision of Jesus. "This reversal of social order doesn't just turn hierarchy upside down, it aims at a new reality in which hierarchy and dominance are overcome as principles of social relations" (Ruether, 136). Rita Nakashima Brock emphasizes that it was not just Jesus but the community that gathered around him which supported the demystification of social hierarchies.

Brock [1988]; Fulkerson [1994]; Ruether [1983/1993]

MARIE J. GIBLIN

Hinduism Hinduism is one of the oldest religions in the world. It consists of so many different strands that it is difficult to make universally valid statements about it. This applies equally to women in Hinduism, who, in different periods of history, have held very different positions. Hinduism is strongly *patriarchal. Much of it is the creation of the male Brahman caste, which has always enjoyed the highest status in Indian society. By contrast, women as a group have enjoyed a much lower status; normative Hinduism does not consider them as equal to men, not even to men of their own caste. Yet "woman" is given such high symbolic value that Hinduism has perhaps more female figures associated with the Divine than any other *world religion.

During the early, Vedic period of Indian history, over three thousand years ago, women enjoyed a higher status than in subsequent centuries. Women were able to wear the sacred thread, the distinguishing mark of the higher castes; they could learn the sacred language, Sanskrit, and take part in religious rites. The early Upanishads mention several women who, similar to men, pursued the quest for sacred knowledge and wisdom, the path of *jnana,* but this was later forbidden.

The Traditional Image of Woman. In the foundational texts of the *Dharmashastras,* women are ranked with the lowest castes. Like them, women are not allowed to recite the Vedas or even to listen to Sanskrit recitations. Woman is exclusively defined by her social function as wife and mother and kept in lifelong dependency. She is always subordinate to a male: in childhood, to her father; in adult life, to her husband; in old age, to her sons. For a married woman, her husband is her god; she acquires religious merit primarily through him but also shares with him certain religious responsibilities.

A woman's specific duties, her *stridharma,* are closely related to the *family. Women have important functions in the daily household ritual, around which much of Hinduism revolves, and also in the celebration of festivals. There exist many religious practices that belong specifically to women, but these are mainly for the benefit of the husband and children. Women scholars are now discovering the richness and variety of these rituals among women of different castes and regions.

Traditional Hindu texts proscribe women's access to the path of renunciation. Women could not take *sannyasa* (renunciation) or follow *jnana yoga,* so that unlike *Buddhism and Christianity, traditional Hinduism does not have separate women's religious communities. However, in some strands of Hinduism, such as *yoga,* individual women ascetics are known, although they never enjoy the same status as male ascetics. Women were categorically excluded from the highly prestigious Vedanta movement. Only through the reforms of the twentieth century has it become possible for women to take *sannyasa.* The Ramakrishna Order (founded in 1897) has had a branch of women religious since 1954, named Sarada Devi Math after Ramakrishna's wife. Other gurus, too, have founded women's communities and encouraged women to learn Sanskrit, participate in Vedic rites, and take *sannyasa.* But the number of Hindu women ascetics and religious is very small when compared with male ascetics or the large number of Roman Catholic women religious in India.

As women were excluded from *asceticism, the only religious path to *liberation (*moksha*) open to them was that of *bhakti,* intense devotion and surrender to a personal god, the path most highly praised by the Bhagavad Gita and most closely connected with the *popular religiosity of the majority of Hindus. The *bhakti* strand of Hinduism is represented by a large number of devotional movements which claim that members of all castes and both sexes have equal access to their chosen deity and can find final liberation through their devotion. Over the centuries, numerous women saints and *mystics arose who, through their example, poetry, and song, made a great contribution to the spiritual heritage of Hinduism.

The traditional Hindu image of woman is characterized by a strong tension between the high value assigned to woman as mother (an evaluation largely dependent on a son) and the complete subordination of women to the authority of males. Modern Indian women complain that traditional Hinduism does not possess suitable role models for women in contemporary society. The image of the ideal woman is Sita, the heroine of the epic *Ramayana,* an ideal of sacrificial love, silent *suffering, and steadfast faithfulness to her husband, even under the most difficult circumstances. It is an ideal that Hindu women find just as difficult, if not impossible, to follow as Christian women do the figure of Mary.

The Goddess. Perhaps there is no other country in the world where the worship of goddesses is more alive and widely practiced today than India. The universal devotion to the great Indian Goddess, the Devi, expresses itself in many forms, from the countless Indian village goddesses to the all-encompassing metaphysical principle, the great One, the root of the universe, who expresses herself in ever so many different female forms.

The Indian model of God comprises within itself the experience of sexual polarity; thus all divine manifestations on earth find expression in both male and female forms. The Divine is active in the world through creative energy (*shakti*), which is always considered female and takes physical form in the goddesses. Here exists another tension, however, for the *goddess can either be a "spouse goddess" attached to a male god, subordinate to her consort, or an independent mother-goddess whose power is equal to, or even higher than, that of a male god. The polarity and synthesis of god and goddess are iconographically depicted in androgynous forms of the Divine.

In the *Devimahatmya* (sixth century C.E.), the great Indian Goddess is celebrated as the absolute ground of all reality but also as a woman of absolute beauty, power, and strength. Many individual goddess figures possess great ambivalence, especially Kali or Durga. Yet Hindu female deities provide powerful resources for contemporary feminists because of their rich symbolism and representation of many cultural activities. But at present, only a few Western feminists have discovered the wealth of female symbols in the religious world of Hinduism.

Hindu Women in the Modern Period. The modern Indian women's movement has achieved a great deal on behalf of women's place in contemporary society. The struggle against colonialism and the rise of the Indian independence movement were much influenced by the so-called Hindu Renaissance, which included a strong belief in the power of the Mother-Goddess as helping in the struggle to make India free from political *oppression. Women made important contributions to the independence movement, and their support for Mahatma Gandhi much enhanced the esteem in which Indian women are held today.

Many past and present female religious figures provide inspiring examples for women's *empowerment; so can the rich goddess heritage in Indian literature and art. This heritage expresses deep insights about women's creativity, independence, strength, and courage. The rich symbolism of the goddess assigns a positive value to female *sexuality in quite a different way from that in the religious traditions of the West. Yet contemporary India still knows many appalling examples of women's oppression, and numerous women's groups are working for greater *equality, *justice, and liberation for women today.

Altekar [1959/1983]; Falk [1994]; Gross, *JAAR* [1978]; Joshi [1988]; Kinsley [1986]; Leslie [1991]; "Women Bhakta Poets," *Manushi* [1989]

URSULA KING

Holocaust The term *Holocaust* refers to the systematic discrimination against and expropriation, deportation, and annihilation of European Jews by Nazi Germany between 1933 and 1945. This legally sanctioned, bureaucratically administered, and industrially organized mass murder of approximately six million women, men, and children affects feminist theology in several ways.

The Nazis encountered little resistance from the churches. This was because of longstanding theological beliefs that the Jews were cursed for their opposition to and murder of Jesus Christ. Jewish *oppression was accepted as just punishment for their "blind and stubborn" refusal to acknowledge Jesus as the Messiah. God was believed to have rejected the Jews and elected the Gentiles instead. The leadership of the churches tolerated and ignored the "Final Solution of the Jewish Question." Rescue efforts by courageous individual Christians were often directed toward "non-Aryan" Christians, members of the church who were defined as Jews because of ancestry. Feminist *solidarity was likewise hampered by cultural, religious, and *racist forms of *anti-Judaism. Recent Christian feminist theology has responded to Jewish feminist calls to critically assess remnants of the "teaching of contempt" and to disassociate from the heritage of Christian Jew-hating.

Feminist theories of *patriarchy must include anti-Semitism in the analysis of women's experience. Jewish women suffered from the combined forces of anti-Semitism and *sexism. Anti-Semitic laws regulated and constricted Jewish places of residence, freedom of movement, work, food, and assembly and affected men, women, and children equally. In addition, women were victimized because of their gender: as *mothers, women were gassed together with young children on arrival in extermination camps. They became targets of sterilization campaigns, forced *abortions, and medical experiments; women were raped, forced into *prostitution, and sexually abused by Gentile and sometimes by Jewish men. Histories of the Holocaust and feminist theory of patriarchy must address this dual victimization of Jewish women as Jews and as women.

Survivors' haunting despair has resonated with feminist theologians. The magnitude of the senseless *suffering of the innocent questions traditional *doctrines of *redemption and divine *justice, mercy, and omnipotence. In *Night,* Elie Wiesel questions God's omnipotence and affirms God as co-sufferer with the Jewish victims. This echoes feminist discontent with traditional theology that asserts God as the patriarchal ruler of the universe who acts in history by testing, punishing, and redeeming his servants. After Auschwitz, the power and goodness of God are experienced as fragile and precarious, dependent on human efforts to create "right relation" (Carter Heyward, 1982).

Heinemann [1986]; Kaplan, in Bridenthal/Grossmann/Kaplan [1984]; Ringelheim, in Rittner/Roth [1993]; von Kellenbach [1994]

KATHARINA VON KELLENBACH

Holy Spirit *Holy Spirit* is a highly contested term in Western Christianity, as is epitomized by the *filioque* clause in the text from the Council of Constantinople (381 C.E.): "And we believe in the Holy Spirit, the Lord and Giver of life, who proceeds from the Father [and the Son; *filioque*]." At issue is a broad versus a narrow understanding of divine Spirit: the life-giving breath (Heb *rûaḥ*) that animates all things versus the re-creation of life available only through Christ. The Christian *tradition has tended to stress the latter at the expense of the former: *redemption versus *creation; a "second birth" versus the first, common birth; an exclusive focus on Jesus as the one way to God versus the universal and immanent *empowerment of all life.

The Hebrew scriptures, some pneumatological Christian sects, and many contemporary feminist theologies (Native American, womanist, goddess, Christian "Sophian," Korean, *ecofeminist) are "holy spirit" theologies in the first sense. The capitalized term *Holy Spirit* usually refers to those Christian perspectives that limit the sacred Spirit to Christ and his followers. Thus, while the Holy Spirit as the third member of the Christian *Trinity is theoretically equal to the "Father" ("fully God"), its power is, in effect, limited to those who accept the "Son," Jesus Christ.

Some Western male theologians have attempted to "accommodate" feminist criticisms of the all-male Trinity by suggesting that the Holy Spirit is the feminine dimension of God, the dimension concerned with giving and nurturing life, with relationality and mutuality. But most feminists have insisted that God should be imaged not as basically masculine with a feminine side but in *both* female and male images. This is seen, for instance, in the *image of God as Sophia-Spirit, who is the source of both creative and transformative energy among all creatures, including non-human ones (cf. Johnson). Some feminists and womanists understand "holy spirit" as neither male nor female but as "it." Here "spirit" is the way to speak of divine energy as permeating each and every entity in creation in ways unknown and unknowable in human, personal categories. "God ain't a he or a she, but a It. . . . It ain't something you can look at apart from anything else, including yourself. I believe God is everything. . . . Everything that is or ever was or ever will be" (Walker 1982, 177–78).

A striking example of a feminist theology of the Holy Spirit that incorporates some principal notes found in many other feminist theologies is Korean theologian Chung Hyun Kyung's address to the 1991 World Council of Churches assembly at Canberra, Australia. The theme of the assembly was "Come Holy Spirit—Renew the Whole Creation," which Chung interpreted in a way that underscored divine empowerment for life and liberty in both the natural and human worlds. She invoked the Holy Spirit through the spirits of the oppressed, from the murdered "spirit of the Amazon rainforest" to the spirits of exploited women and indigenous peoples, victims of the *Holocaust and of Hiroshima, as well as Hagar, Jephthah's daughter, Malcolm X, Archbishop Oscar Romero, and all other life-forms, human and nonhuman, that like "the Liberator, our brother Jesus," have been tortured and killed for greed and through hate. The closing words sum up this stunning hymn to the Holy Spirit that moves through and empowers all life: "Dear sisters and brothers, with the energy of the Holy Spirit let us tear apart all walls of division and the culture of death which separates us. And let us participate in the Holy Spirit's economy of life, fighting for our life on this earth in *solidarity with all living beings and building communities for *justice, peace, and the integrity of creation. Wild wind of the Holy Spirit blow to us. Let us welcome her, letting ourselves go in her wild rhythm of life. Come Holy Spirit, renew the whole creation. Amen!" (123).

Three distinctive notes of feminist understanding of the Holy Spirit stand out in Chung's address: its *immanence, its transforming and liberating power, and its scope, which encompasses both the natural and the human worlds. First, the emphasis here and in other feminist theologies on the immanent, earthly presence of God is in sharp contrast to the Western transcendent "sky-god" tradition. While the Holy Spirit has often been seen as the immanent side of God, feminists see God as basically and radically immanent and the Holy Spirit as a central, if not the primary, "name" for God. Criticism of the external, *transcendent, *hierarchical, *imperialistic, *patriarchal deity, a notion that supports *dualistic thinking, deprecating women and nature, is a hallmark of feminist theologies. Second, a relational, immanentist understanding of God (the one in whom we live and move and have our being) is that of the God of love and empowerment, of life and liberty, for people and for the natural world. The holy spirit's work is creation and re-creation, first and second birth, the "political economy of life" in all its dimensions and for all beings. The holy spirit's work is not the forgiveness of sins for those who accept the atoning death of Jesus Christ but identification with the spirits of the oppressed, from "the spirit of Amazon rainforests" to the spirits of exploited women. Third, the Holy Spirit moves in *all* things, not just Christians and not just human beings. As "spirit" it encompasses the vitality, grit, and determination of people banding together to fight *oppression, as well as a spirited horse or the spirit of a grove of trees. As "holy" it means the divine is moving in and under all spirits in the human and natural worlds, to liberate them when possible and to suffer with them when tragedy overcomes them.

In summary, it is interesting to note that an aspect of the divine which used to be considered the most abstract and otherworldly (as in the term *Holy Ghost* for holy spirit) has, in the hands of feminists, come to mean the most intimate, powerful, and creative presence of God. It means the gift of physical life, the spirit that gives breath to our bodies, as well as the sacred power that renews our tired bodies and flagging spirits in the fight against all forms of oppression.

Chung, *C/C* [1991]; Diamond/Orenstein [1990]; E. A. Johnson [1992]; McFague [1993]; Plaskow/Christ [1989]

SALLIE MCFAGUE

Ideology The meanings of ideology important to feminist theologies derive from Marxist and post-Marxist traditions. Because of the dichotomy between ideology and science in Marxist determinism, this genealogy has produced some ambiguities. According to the science of historical *materialism, the true understanding of reality is based on material relations of production. The failure to grasp the material basis of knowledge results in ideology. Ideology thus reflects a false consciousness, the lack of awareness of material forces. Given contemporary criticism of the ideology–science split, the meaning of ideology as a description of systems of thought and discourse frequently slips between a pejorative sense, implying systematic distortions, and a neutral sense, describing the conditions of human existence within language.

Feminists have criticized determinist understandings of ideology, arguing that, in conjunction with material structures, ideology is a site of *power relations and thus ideology critique is an important site of *praxis. For example, womanist Marcia Y. Riggs criticizes race and class ideologies as part of the "roots of the dilemma" facing contemporary black *liberation. Jewish feminist Susan Shapiro suggests that ideology critique is crucial in religious studies, given its focus on interpretation of texts and *traditions, and can be accomplished through refiguration which moves rhetorical practice away from its traditional figuration as dishonest because feminine. Christian feminist Rebecca Chopp also argues that women can be empowered through speaking practices which reinterpret rhetoric in order to emphasize the transformation of *community. Thus, for feminist theologies, ideology critique is intertwined with alternative and resistant knowledge production. For example, second-wave European-American feminist movements undertook this type of knowledge production through "consciousness-raising," or in Nelle Morton's terms, women "hearing each other to speech." *Mujerista* Ada María Isasi-Díaz intertwines reflection and action by defining praxis as critically reflective action, locating Hispanic women as theologians who produce both knowledge and moral *agency.

Chopp [1989]; Gunew [1990]; Isasi-Díaz [1993]; Morton [1985]; Riggs [1994]; Shapiro, *JAAR* [1994]; Williams [1983]

JANET R. JAKOBSEN

Idolatry Idolatry is the worship of anything that is not God, treating it as though it were divine. Therefore, to identify something as an idol, it is necessary first to know what God is. From a feminist perspective, the obvious question is who decides what is or is not divine and by what criteria.

The Hebrew Bible retains traces of worship of female divinities (e.g., Jer. 7:17–18), which was ruthlessly suppressed as idolatry in the name of the Father-God. Similarly, early European Christianity grappled with the nature goddesses, particularly among the Celts, until masculinist *monotheism triumphed and all these traces were condemned as idolatry and *witchcraft. In the colonial period, missionaries were sent from European countries (and later also from North America) to "heathen lands" to convert "*pagans" from their worship of "idols" to the worship of God—and to economic and cultural compliance with the conquering nations.

"Idolatry" is always a name assigned by an outsider, as opposed to what is seen to be happening by the worshiping group: no one would say of herself, "I am worshiping an idol." Accusations of idolatry have often been based on crude (and culpable) misunderstandings, such as supposing that a "heathen" group was really worshiping a material object rather than the divine being which that object was taken to symbolize. However, there is within Christianity also an idea of "spiritual" idolatry, that is, giving to something other than God, such as money, *power, or knowledge, the central place in one's life; constructing these things in the place of God. Many feminists might argue that masculinity itself has been taken as an *image of God and has become idolatrous.

Condren [1989]; Long [1992]

GRACE M. JANTZEN

Image of God This phrase is traditionally used in theological *anthropology to signify the dignity and *responsibility of human beings, who are created in the image and likeness of God: "Then God said, 'Let us make humankind in our image, according to our likeness; . . .' So God created humankind in his image, in the image of God he created them; male and female he created them" (Gen. 1:26–27). The character of humanity as *imago dei* is a gift of *creation. Although marred by *sin, this image is restored by the *grace of Christ and will come to its fulfillment in the glory of *heaven.

Interpretations of the precise content of the image of God differed over time. In Genesis it is located in human stewardship of the earth and its creatures. Early Christian writers defined it in a more essential way, as the human race's innate bond with divine reality. While medieval thinkers placed the image of God in the human *soul, with its powers of rationality, the Reformers found it in the conformity of the human will with divine will. More recent interpretations have linked the image of God with human creativity, human *community, or human bodiliness and sexual differentiation as male and female. Some stress the incomplete character of the *imago dei,* since it is the eschatological destiny for which human beings are intended.

Critique. Feminist theologies bring to light a powerful ambiguity of the image-of-God *tradition regarding women. On the one hand, women's full and equal inclusion in this religious bedrock of human dignity is deeply rooted in biblical and theological insight. On the other hand, traditional Christian theology accepted gender *dualism in its strong Greek form, identifying men with the spiritual, rational principle of the world and women with the physical and sexual, irrational, and emotional principle. Consequently, women were projected as the lower part of human nature, and it became difficult to see how they could enjoy being fully in the image of God, as God is understood in traditional theology. Instead, fullness of humanity was identified with maleness, while women were relegated to subordinate, peripheral status, considered deficiently *imago dei,* and included in this dignity only when taken together with men, who were their head. It was a small step from this to the perception of women as lacking the image of God altogether. Some strains of traditional theology do see women as temptresses, the very symbol and embodiment of *evil.

Transformations. Converted to their own human dignity, women are claiming themselves as acting subjects of their own history, free to be human in all their *difference. Rejecting dualistic and subordinationist interpretations, feminist theologies craft varieties of egalitarian anthropologies, retrieving the fullness of the image of God for women in all their dimensions, including their creative, intellectual capacity and sexual powers. The dignity of the full humanity of women as image of God even functions as criterion of feminist theology, so that whatever promotes it reflects the authentic message of *redemption and whatever denigrates it is untrue (Ruether). Womanist, *mujerista,* and women theologians of the *third world likewise stress the inclusion of women oppressed by the injustices of *racism and *classism in the circle of those who image God. The cutting edge of discussion concerns how mutual, respectful relations enable women to affirm and celebrate differences rather than set up a new tyranny of the ideal image. All seek a continually expanding definition of inclusive community, wherein the fullness of redeemed humanity as image of God, while still ahead, is glimpsed even now as a bedrock of women's authentic humanity and *equality before God.

Carr [1988]; King [1994]; Ruether [1974]; Schmidt [1989]

ELIZABETH A. JOHNSON

Immanence Derived from the Latin verb *manere,* "to remain," immanence refers to a theology of God dwelling within *creation. This is contrasted with *transcendence, in which God is "beyond" or "above." A transcendent God may be viewed as a God in and beyond history; an immanent God is one of continuing *revelation within creation. Immanence at its most radical becomes *pantheism or animism. Many theologies hold these ideas of transcendence and immanence in dialectical tension.

Biblical accounts of God's presence contain both themes. In the Exodus story of God's revelation to Moses (Ex. 3:14), God uses the Hebrew verb of being, "I AM WHO I AM," implying active presence yet transcendence. The Johannine Jesus reassures his disciples that he will make his home with those who love him and keep his word (John. 14:23). In the book of Acts, Pentecost is described as the day on which the *apostles were "filled with the Holy Spirit" (Acts 2:1–4).

Absolute immanence, lacking the complementarity of transcendence, proclaims a self-sufficiency that denies the supernatural. Polarities in the divine nature are present in many religions and may be more vividly expressed in artistic form, e.g., *Hindu devotional poems (Carman, 157–87). Christmas carols comfortably contrast "majesty and humble condescension." The personal relationship of *mystics with an immanent God becomes the basis of meditation and *prayer (e.g., Mahadeviyakka, the twelfth-century Indian disciple of Shiva, and Teresa of Avila, the sixteenth-century Spanish Carmelite nun).

Simone de Beauvoir used the term negatively in *The Second Sex,* viewing the male of our totemic ancestors as the "incarnation of transcendence" while the woman was "doomed to immanence" in the restrictive aspects of role (73–74). Women's *anger with the absent and unapproachable transcendent God of *patriarchal institutions has led to renewed interest in this evolving term. In an ecological, nuclear age, Sallie McFague envisions God's transcendence as "worldly" and God's immanence as "universal," leading to a greater reverence for the body of God, the world (1987, 185).

Carman [1994]; de Beauvoir [1971]; Hirshfield [1994]; McFague [1987; 1993]

VICTORIA R. SIROTA

Imperialism This term developed in the nineteenth century to refer to the economic and political relationship among advanced capitalist countries and to the impact of international monopoly capitalism. The word *imperialism* has become synonymous with the *oppression and exploitation of weak, impoverished countries by powerful ones. In feminist discourse, imperialism refers to totalizing prescriptions applied to other women and thus includes cultural and religious as well as political and economic forms of imperialism.

Modern Western empires set out to conquer the world, justifying economic and political *domination by treating newly conquered territories as inferior. For imperialist purposes, the native was cast as an "Other." Christianity especially has been an essential part of such imperial ordering, morally legitimating the mechanisms of controlling markets and raw materials to exploit the colonies and their populations.

Exploitation of human and natural resources continues under neocolonialism, which imposes rapacious financial mechanisms and world trade patterns that perpetuate Western cultural imperialism. Imperial logic underlies the global situation where the vast majority (those on the underside of history) live in a state of underdevelopment and unjust dependence, and where women form the underside of the underside.

In feminist theological terms, imperialism is a structure of *evil. Some feminist theological work engages in anti-imperialist *deconstruction, for example, to understand how imperial and colonial relations have shaped the experience of two-thirds-world women and in ways that have benefited many women in the Northern Hemisphere. Imperialism is also used in reference to *culture and *religion, for example, Christian over Jewish, Anglo over Hispanic, and white over black. Complicity in a history of imperialism is evident where such imposed relations exist, while struggles against multiple colonizations generate postcolonial, anti-imperialist discourses in feminist theology.

Aquino [1993]; Mohanty, in Mohanty/Russo/Torres [1991]; Oduyoye [1986]; Soelle [1977]

MARILYN J. LEGGE

Incarnation Throughout history, the crux of the debate regarding the *doctrine of incarnation has been how much of which nature (human or divine) was part of the incarnation of God in Jesus of Nazareth. The fifth-century christological debate, culminating in the Chalcedonian Definition of Jesus Christ in 451 C.E., was based on the conjunction of two natures: godhead and humanity united in Christ. This definition has held sway for centuries and has consisted of the view that the divine became flesh once, and only once, in the person of Jesus of Nazareth. As a result, divinity has been emphasized over humanity, as has spirit over flesh.

Nevertheless, the subject of incarnation has played an important role in the development of feminist theologies, as it has been closely connected with a feminist emphasis on **embodiment*. Many feminist theologians no longer view the incarnation as being limited to Jesus of Nazareth. God becoming incarnate in human flesh has been reinterpreted to mean that humanity, *bodies, females, *sexuality, and the earth are good.

Patricia Wilson-Kastner describes the incarnation as God becoming manifest in the life of Jesus, complete with all of the human limitations of such a life. Incarnation, she maintains, brings human beings to a deeper relationship with God. Indeed, the incarnation brings the diversity of *creation into divine life, and unity is found through centering oneself in God, who is revealed in Christ. Wilson-Kastner posits that through focusing on the *revelation of divine love in incarnation, theological *tradition can be critically evaluated in terms of the influence of *sexism (89–119).

Rita Nakashima Brock urges readers to go beyond critiquing the doctrine of incarnation solely through the lens of sexism by focusing on the concrete particulars of *race, class, gender, *culture, and sexuality that are embodied in human beings. When our concrete particularities are affirmed as part of our connection to others, we "continue to become the fullest incarnation of erotic power" (63). Womanist theologian Jacquelyn Grant has written about the importance of Jesus for black women. Jesus, she declares, *is* a black woman.

Carter Heyward's work has focused on relational theology as an incarnational liberation *theology. She focuses on reimaging Jesus because she sees in his life the human ability to make God incarnate in the world, an ability as much ours as his. God, for Heyward, is "incarnate" in relation. She claims that our God is so actually *in-carnate*—in flesh, in humanity, in the world—that "we are never without the option of choosing to befriend God in the creation, *liberation, and blessing of the world." Such an incarnational/relational theology is liberative; it is about incarnating God in the connections between us, and it values our humanity, our body-selves (1984, 94–99).

Ecological theologian Sallie McFague maintains that we come to know God both "through divine incarnation in nature" and through Jesus of Nazareth. Experiencing creation in all of its raw beauty joins together *transcendence and *immanence. An incarnational theology thus means that we should cultivate a nature spirituality and "assures us . . . that we are not alone in loving the bodies of our planet" (194). Other feminist liberation theologians have developed the concept of incarnation as a way of explicitly bestowing God's blessing on human sexuality. Incarnation thus becomes an ongoing movement between humanity and God, in which we actively incarnate God in *all* aspects of our *relationships.

Further issues facing feminist theologians include how the notion of the *differences between us affects the reimagining of incarnation, Jesus, and embodiment. Questions concerning the nature of relationships between our embodied selves, God, and creation, as well as the *healing of alienation caused by centuries of pitting divine against human, spirit against bodies, and *heaven against earth, remain to be explored in more detail.

Brock [1988]; Gilson [1995]; Grant [1989/1992]; Heyward [1984; 1989b]; McFague [1993]; Wilson-Kastner [1983]

ANNE BATHURST GILSON

Inclusive Language Inclusive language pictures humanity and the divine in such a way as to include, honor, and do *justice to diverse human *experiences. The concern for inclusive language began to reemerge in U.S. churches in the early 1970s, after exploration by nineteenth-century feminists, in relation to the way gendered terms are used, especially in worship. The work of theologians Rosemary Ruether, Marcia Falk, Letty Russell, Judith Plaskow, and Mary Daly, as well as the growth in numbers of women clergy, contributed to this emerging concern. The "generic" use of male images and pronouns to include women was criticized for treating males as normative and rendering females invisible. Christian and Jewish feminists also questioned constant *liturgical use of male images and pronouns for God and the absence of corresponding female images and pronouns. Given general theological agreement that God has no sex, unbalanced male language creates serious ethical problems: it makes males seem more godlike than females and lends support to male *domination and abuse of women. The imbalance also creates a problem for evangelism: identifying God with one side of a human domination–subordination relationship makes it harder for some people to experience God's love.

This new sensitivity led to further questions about the ethical and evangelical impact of liturgical language. Given the context of *racism in U.S. society, is it not problematic always to use "dark" and "black" as negative images and "white" and "light" as positive images? What about images concerning physical disabilities? Why are "blindness" and "deafness" so often used as *metaphors for spiritual insensitivity? Does the language of worship honor childhood, youth, middle adulthood, and later years? And are some people, such as single and gay and *lesbian people, rendered invisible in the language of worship services? These questions were often more poignant because scripture frequently uses male language, negative imagery about people with disabilities, and imagery that becomes problematic in a cultural context of racism against darker-skinned people.

Three strategies address these issues. The first *avoids* terms referring to gender, color, or *disability. Thus "people" replaces "brothers," Parent replaces Father as a name for God, and all references to color or physical abilities are avoided. The second approach *balances* male and female terms and seeks positive images of darkness. Such worship language adds "sisters" to "brothers," names God Mother as well as Father, and explores the darkness of the womb or soil nurturing life as positive images. The third strategy, which Marjorie Procter-Smith calls *emancipatory* (111–15), takes a deeper look at language, going beyond numerical balance to consider how language functions to free or oppress. Thus one questions whether Mother suffices as the only female name for God, since such usage implies that women are like God only when they bear and nurture children. The much-debated use of Wisdom/Sophia as an image for God grows out of the search for alternative biblical female images for God. An emancipatory approach also asks whether worship portrays God as taking the part of the poor and the oppressed, that justice may be done. It emphasizes cultural diversity and draws connections between racism, *sexism, and other forms of injustice, rather than focusing mainly on gender issues. Thus the emancipatory approach draws on the work of womanist, *mujerista,* and *liberation *theologians more than do the other strategies.

Beginning with the publication of the *Lutheran Book of Worship* in 1978, committees editing worship books and hymnals for major religious groups have sought inclusive language with diverse strategies and to varying degrees. At one end of the spectrum, books such as the Southern Baptist hymnal of 1991 and the Reformed Church in America hymnal of 1985 avoided generic language about humanity but not about God. At the other end, the United Church of Christ has sought in its most recent hymnal and worship book, with few exceptions, to avoid or balance gender language for God and humanity and to avoid negative use of images about darkness and disabilities. A sprinkling of hymns and prayers that could be called emancipatory appear in most current books. The hymn "Lift Every Voice and Sing," by James Weldon Johnson and J. Rosamond Johnson, often called the black national anthem, is a notable example; it speaks of God's presence in the African-American people's struggle for *liberation. The *United Methodist Hymnal* of 1989, in which hymns appeared from different global traditions in varied languages, marked a turn toward more serious commitment to cultural diversity.

Various unofficial supplements and collections of prayers and hymns by single authors have ventured farther than official books. The Hebrew *prayer book has been complemented by several worship resources published in English in the Reform Jewish *tradition. Roman Catholic author and hymn writer Miriam Therese Winter has explored female and emancipatory language for God, as have Anglican Janet Morley, British Reformed hymn writer Brian Wren, and many others. Issues raised by feminist theologies about the nature of divine power, Christian *atonement theories, the affirmation of the human *body, and expressions of *sexuality find their way into these pioneering resources.

These issues have quite naturally provoked much debate in religious communities, because they raise challenging theological and ethical issues. At the same time, they have inspired much creativity, enriching the language of worship.

Duck [1991]; Elkins [1994]; Morley [1988]; Procter-Smith [1990]; Procter-Smith/Walton [1993]; Ruether [1985]; Winter [1991]

RUTH C. DUCK

Inculturation Created out of **culture,* inculturation has a specific meaning in the context of missiology. It arises out of the experience of the Western church's response to the so-called Great Commission of Matthew 28. Western Christian churches (Roman Catholic, Protestant) constituted themselves into "sending churches." In fact, the Western missions were begun by individual Christian missionaries rather than churches.

Roman Catholic missions to North Africa, China, Japan, and India, facing the challenge of Oriental religions and cultures, sought the path of accommodation. In other parts of Africa, however, neither Protestant nor Catholic missions in the nineteenth century considered the path of accommodation, as they had prejudged the African scene as being devoid of religion and used the model of planting Christianity. In Africa the scheme was only a partial success. The resilience of the religio-culture of Africa called for a modification of the missionary policy of assimilation of Africans into European religion and culture.

The earliest challenge came in the form of translating the Christian Bible into the vernacular. The search for dynamic equivalents for the language of Christianity demanded a better acquaintance with Africa's religio-culture. Rites, rituals, music, structure of prayers, and other liturgical forms and elements of African religion became subjects of investigation. In practice, church music, musical instruments, and rites of passage underwent adaptation to respond to the resilience of Africa. A more intensive study was needed to determine the criteria for this adaptation. The search produced different approaches described as "acculturation" or "inculturation," all aimed at the *incarnation paradigm of *mission that was to replace the agricultural model.

The acculturation approach turned attention to the deepening of the adaptation attempts by theologizing the effort to reach what might be called a culturally identifiable church. Such churches already existed: Russian Orthodox chants and Lutheran Church hymns are culturally identifiable; Russians and Germans were and are at home in their respective forms. Africans, and Asians too, felt the need for a Christianity in which they would be at home. They proceeded to craft hymnody and *liturgies in which they would feel at home. Acculturation raised issues concerning the cultural content of mission Christianity, both its theology and its biblical exegesis. Questions arose on the essentials of Christianity and of Christian living. Central to all this was the need to study the interaction of the Christian *gospel and the cultures into which it had been inserted. Does or should the interpretation of the meaning of the Christ event change in the process of this interaction?

Inculturation as the preferred terminology for this *paradigm shift in mission policy emphasizes the total transformation that the Christ event is believed to bring to the whole of human history and to all human cultures. Inculturation indicates a recognition of how the gospel message has been adapted to different situations throughout history. Exegesis and theology have reflected various epochs of history and the situation of the community that is attempting to live in Christ and have Christ reflected in the specific challenges and opportunities presented to the church.

Accommodation, assimilation, acculturation, and inculturation are all attempts of Christians to live the incarnational principle in response to the context in which the church finds itself. However, it is inculturation—and the even more recent term **contextualization*—that holds the most promise from a feminist *liberation point of view. Rather than importing additional *patriarchal criteria about women's roles, it asks about ways women can live out the gospel in each place and culture.

Oduyoye [1986]; Oduyoye/Kanyoro [1992]; Pobee [1994]

MERCY AMBA ODUYOYE

Interdependence Interdependence captures feminism's identification of human beings as persons embedded in a web of *relationships. At the interpersonal level, feminists have been critical of notions of the human person that exaggerate independence and individualism while losing sight of human connection. In accounts of the moral life, for example, feminist theory has focused on the tendency of women to emphasize relationships with others. Such accounts of morality contrast with theories that characterize persons as radically independent in the *autonomy of their choices. Interdependence encompasses and requires both autonomy and relationality.

In feminist theologies, interdependence is global as well as interpersonal. Feminists seek to understand and to communicate the experience of women. That experience reaches across class, *race, *religion, and nation. A first step in global interdependence is for feminists to listen to the voices of women whose cultural experience is different from their own. Feminist theologians from different cultures and nations have identified the *solidarity among women in their common experience of *oppression, *suffering, and struggle.

Feminist interdependence is also ecological. Traditional accounts of *creation emphasize man's dominance over nature and the subordination of all living things to human beings. Feminist theologies of creation accentuate the relationship of humanity to all other living creatures, to the environment, and to the universe. They mandate a respect for nature as well as a respect for persons.

At all three levels, feminist accounts of interdependence value the importance and the dignity of the individual experience. Autonomy remains central to interpersonal relationships. Global commonalities do not eradicate individual *traditions and *cultures. Ecological interdependence respects the intrinsic value of all created beings. The individual does not live in an isolated independence but is instead always located in a web of interrelationship.

Farley, in Outka/Reeder [1993]; Gilligan [1982]; King [1994]; McFague [1993]

LESLIE GRIFFIN

Islam Islam, the religion preached by the prophet Muhammad of west-central Arabia (570–632), is followed by almost one-fifth of the world's population. It consciously situates itself within the *tradition begun by Judaism and Christianity; its major *doctrines include beliefs in one God; angels; prophets, who include many biblical figures such as Abraham, Moses, David, and Jesus; divinely revealed scriptures, including the Torah, Psalms, *Gospel, and the Qur'an (Koran), the book revealed to Muhammad; a last day in which the dead will be raised and individuals judged according to their deeds; and an afterlife in paradise or hellfire.

The Qur'an was revealed piecemeal during the twenty-three years of Muhammad's prophethood, and it often responds directly to events in Muhammad's life. Muhammad had a relationship of great mutual respect with his first wife, Khadija, but after Khadija's death Muhammad acquired as many as thirteen wives. According to tradition, one of Muhammad's wives complained that the Qur'an appeared only to address men. Subsequently, the Qur'an addressed believers in both masculine and feminine forms, with the assurance that women will receive the same spiritual rewards as men for the performance of the same spiritual duties. In the Qur'anic story of Adam's creation, temptation, and expulsion from the garden, his (unnamed) wife is neither created from his body nor blamed for his *sin, nor is any curse attached to his disobedience.

In the Qur'an, women's secondary status appears not in the primordial myth but in the context of social law. Men are given the right of *polygamy (4:3) and *marriage to non-Muslims, but women are not. Men are allowed to "change one wife for another" with ease, although the Qur'an encourages men to treat their wives justly and fairly. Hadith (the body of traditions relating to Muhammad) records Muhammad's statement that of all permitted things, divorce is the most hateful to God; Islamic law as developed in the eighth and ninth centuries placed no restrictions on a man's ability to divorce his wife by simple verbal pronouncement. Women are urged by the Qur'an to seek reconciliation (4:128) and can obtain a divorce only if their husbands agree and if they return the dowry they were given at marriage.

Qur'an commentators specify that physical punishment should be used on wives only as a last resort and should not cause bleeding or injury. However, men's authority and permission to beat their wives is inscribed in the Qur'an itself (4:34). Furthermore, Qur'an commentators interpreted the "superiority" or "favor" that God has given to men to include physical, intellectual, and spiritual superiority. This is also true of the "rank" men enjoy over women in verse 2:228, which says, "Women shall with justice have rights similar to those exercised among them, although men have a status [or rank] above them."

The Qur'an assigns the same legal punishments to men and women for similar offenses and assumes women are able both to take moral *responsibility and to own and manage property. Loan contracts, however, require two male witnesses, or if two men cannot be found, one man and two women, "so that if one of them forgets, the other will remind her" (2:282). The implication that women are more forgetful than men was not lost on medieval Muslim men, and in Islamic law a woman's witness is always worth only half that of a man's and sometimes is disallowed altogether.

Hadith literature purports to be narratives of what Muhammad said and did. Committed to writing only in the mid-ninth century, these tales reflect the mentality of the eighth and ninth centuries more than Muhammad's own. Although Hadith affirms women's right to go to the mosque and urges men to be kind to their wives, it also develops a definite perspective on the moral and intellectual inferiority of women. It laid the foundation for an extensive misogynist literature and popular notions on female inferiority.

Medieval Muslims believed that women's moral inferiority made it the responsibility of men to keep them secluded from all possibilities of transgression. The Qur'an enjoined modesty for women, but Hadith specified that this meant covering the entire *body except for the face and hands. The entire body of a woman was said to be *'awra*—literally, "pudendum"—and in need of covering, just like the pudenda of a man. Even her voice was *'awra* and should not be heard. The story of Eve's creation from Adam's rib and her culpability in Adam's *fall were introduced into Qur'anic commentaries through tales collected from Jewish informants to fill out the scanty details of the Qur'anic story. The *misogyny implicit in the traditional Judeo-Christian interpretation of the *creation myth was fully embraced and developed in Islam. Women's innate "crookedness" (since woman was created from a rib) implied, according to popular belief, that educating them would merely make them more able to engage in treachery.

Islam's mystical tradition, Sufism, encouraged the renunciation of all fleshly *desires and the union of the spirit with God. This allowed the possibility that truly spiritual men and women could interact in a gender-free manner. Although Muslims eventually came to see marriage as mandated by Islam, early Sufis often embraced celibacy along with strict fasting, which not only freed women from the responsibilities of marriage but also suppressed the menstrual cycle, which is a legal impediment to *prayer. Many women became distinguished Sufis, the most famous being Rabi'a al-'Adawiyya (d. 801). In contrast with common Muslim perspectives on sex as a purely physical and functional act, the great mystic Ibn 'Arabi (d. 1240) wrote that man can realize the greatest spiritual insights only in relation to woman and particularly in intercourse.

In the modern period, many Muslims have come to question the authenticity of Hadith literature and the misogynist views it contains. Muhammad 'Abduh (d. 1905) of Egypt argued that men and women are equal in humanity and moral capacity. His associate, Qasim Amin (d. 1908), wrote *The Liberation of Women*, arguing that the seclusion and veiling of women had distorted women's nature, which is essentially the same as men's. He advocated educating girls, allowing women to *work in public, the abolition of polygamy, and divorce through the courts, made equally available to men and women. His book touched off a heated debate in the Muslim world that has not abated to this day.

Although Europeans have attacked Islam as a whole for its treatment of women (linking the status of women with the status of Islam itself), hardly any Islamic serial publication fails to publish frequent articles on the rights and dignity of women in Islam. Most Muslims insist that women are equal in humanity with men but different from men in their basic natures, more subject to emotions that make them fit to be *mothers but unfit for work in the public sphere. Women's education is universally acknowledged as important, however, and economic exigencies are forcing women into the public sphere more than ever. Muslim fundamentalists strongly insist on the importance of sexual segregation and the danger of women's public appearance, but they also promote female militancy and activism on behalf of Islam, appealing to the model of early Muslim women militants and warriors.

Feminists wishing to improve the status of Muslim women cannot avoid seeking justifications within Islam itself, both by reinterpreting the Qur'an and by the models from early Islamic tradition. Two contemporary women, Riffat Hassan of Pakistan and Amina Wadud-Muhsin of the United States, have turned to analysis of the Qur'an in an effort to overturn medieval misogynist interpretations. Hassan has focused on exposing the incompatibility of the traditional Eve myth with the Qur'an, while Wadud-Muhsin follows the hermeneutic of the Pakistani scholar Fazlur Rahman (d. 1988), which insists that the social laws of the Qur'an need to be seen in terms of their general moral thrust and the limitations of seventh-century Arabian society, in order to apply Qur'anic morality in fresh and more appropriate ways to modern society. Wadud-Muhsin has also examined key words in the Qur'an that have been used to justify the subordination of women and has shown that their original meaning and context defy such interpretations.

Ahmed [1992]; Hassan, *Al-Mushir* [1985]; Hoffman-Ladd, *International Journal of Middle East Studies* [1987]; Hoffman-Ladd, *Mystics Quarterly* [1992]; Rahman, in Nashat [1983]; Stowasser [1994]; Wadud-Muhsin [1992]

VALERIE J. HOFFMAN

Jubilee According to Leviticus 25, a "jubilee year" occurs at the end of seven cycles of Sabbath years, and liberty is proclaimed "throughout the *land to all its inhabitants." That liberty has four dimensions: land under cultivation is allowed to lie fallow; debts are canceled; persons imprisoned because of their accumulation of debts are released; and family lands sold to get needed cash are returned to their original owners. The provisions of this law reflect ancient Sabbath year laws (Ex. 21:2–6; 23:10–11; Deut. 15:1–18) and royal edicts from Israel's neighbors, but the provision for a jubilee year as a "super–Sabbath year" dates only from the postexilic period.

No evidence has been found that a jubilee year has ever actually been declared. The same language of "release" and the proclamation of good news for poor people, however, characterize the beginning of God's reign of *justice and peace according to such texts as Isa. 61:1–2. These same themes found their way into Jesus' proclamation of the reign of God as represented in the Synoptic Gospels (Luke 4:16–30; Matt. 11:26 // Luke 7:18–23; Matt. 6:9–13 // Luke 11:2–4; Mark 11:25–26 and other places).

Despite the theme of *liberation, the jubilee laws are of ambiguous significance for feminist theologies. First, the joyous proclamation of "release" applies only to the people of Israel and not to any other peoples living in the *land. The indebtedness and imprisonment to which marginal economic status might condemn other peoples would be permanent. Second, the provision for the return of land to its original owners, in principle, would maintain the just distribution of land by God when Israel first entered Canaan. No consideration is given, however, to the implication of expropriating those lands from other residents. In contrast, the restoration of land would allow the newly pardoned debtors to earn a living and not just begin anew the cycle of indebtedness and imprisonment.

Lebacqz [1987]; Ringe [1985]; Sloan [1977]

SHARON H. RINGE

Judgment In Christian *eschatology the concept of judgment usually refers specifically to the last judgment, when God will decide on the saved and the damned. The names of the saved are in God's book (Rev. 20:12). The reward for the righteous is eternal dwelling with God in paradise, or *heaven, after the resurrection; the wicked will dwell far away from God in *hell. Visions of heaven and hell predominate in Christian eschatological thought. Conservative Christian theology describes heaven and hell in much detail and affords great *power and influence to *evil in human form, the devil, or Satan. More mainstream Christian eschatology stresses God's saving power and *grace reaching out to fallen humanity. Emphasis in both is often on the moral imperatives to be included among the saved. There are clear divisions on insiders and outsiders.

Such exclusivistic, often violent visions of *justice are questioned by feminist and womanist theologians. The focus of the womanist definition of judgment is on social witness. This witness means working for justice in the face of multiple (interstructured) *oppressions. The emphasis is not on visions of physical heaven and hell; rather, the vision is one of hope, glory, and social transformation. A recent theme in feminist eschatology is ecological *responsibility in the face of possible ecological apocalypse. Feminist and womanist visions of judgment are more universalistic and focus on the here and now, on the worth and value of all peoples of the earth. The emphasis is not on a judgment of destruction but on a *new creation.

McFague [1993]; Ruether [1983/1993]; Townes [1995]

TINA PIPPIN

Justice Feminist theologians define justice broadly: *right relationship*, with self, others, *creation, God. Discussions of *power, *oppression, *liberation, abuse, *agency, interdependency, and other dimensions of life are often understood to be implicit discussions of justice.

For feminists, questions of power and oppression are central to justice. Right relationship precludes oppression or exploitation and requires that both individuals and groups are empowered as moral agents. Feminists attend to injustices in personal *relationships such as *marriage, in social structures such as economic institutions, and in cultural forms such as language, myth, and narrative. Liberal feminists stress rights and liberties; socialists focus on economic concerns; radical feminists take sex and gender as central to oppression; womanist and *mujerista* ethicists stress the centrality of *race. Some advocate a "network" or "web" approach to the complexities of *sexism, *racism, and *classism, while still others adopt a *postmodern view, cautioning against cross-cultural judgments or ethical absolutes.

Justice for feminists is not simply "giving to each what is due" or "treating equal cases equally." The scope of justice is broader than the distributive paradigm of liberal *philosophy. In particular, justice requires attention to groups and an option for the poor and oppressed. Social structures are judged by how they impact on the life prospects of the *marginalized, particularly of women. Further, justice includes an *epistemological privilege of the poor and oppressed: social arrangements must be judged from their perspective. Attention is therefore given to lifting up silenced voices. Justice happens when there is *solidarity among people struggling for liberation from oppression.

Justice is therefore *power-in-relation.* For feminist theologians, justice and liberation cannot be separated from love and reconciliation. Theological feminists may not separate "caring" and "justice" as feminist philosophers have sometimes done.

Some feminist theologians have argued that justice is rooted in rectification of injustice. Attention to concrete injustices of women's lives, use of narrative and *story to lift up aspects of the struggle, and a sense that justice making is an ongoing journey characterize feminist theological approaches to justice.

Chung [1990]; Harrison, in Rasmussen [1983]; Harrison [1985]; Heyward [1982; 1984]; Lebacqz [1987]; Townes [1993a]; Young [1990]

KAREN LEBACQZ

Justice and Social Change ** The centrality of women's experience to the theological enterprises of women's *liberation is nowhere more evident than in dealing with justice and social change. (The word *feminist* is used here to refer to the variety of women's liberation struggles and theologies that have sprung up around the world. Some of these struggles and theologies have coined their own names: *mujerista* refers to Latina women in the United States; *womanist,* to African-American women. Others use their ethnic, geographical, or racial realities to specify their theologies: Latin American *feminist theology, Asian-American feminist theology, African women's theologies. "Feminist," then, does not indicate that the *experiences and understandings of white women of the dominant groups from so-called first-world countries are considered normative or are privileged in any way.) It is precisely the *oppression all women suffer, the daily experience of the vast majority of women, that gives rise to theological-ethical understandings of *justice.

A thorough analysis of oppression, of its multiple causes and expressions, is therefore the starting point for radical social change, whose goal is to establish justice for all women. This goal is not possible without establishing justice for all peoples. Feminist accounts of justice do not aim to establish an overall theory of justice that applies a few general premises about human beings (or women in particular) and societies to all. Instead, feminist accounts of justice deal with establishing justice in concrete *relationships, situations, and places. Justice, then, in women's liberation *theologies is more than an understanding. It is a theological-ethical *praxis-reflective action geared to radical change at both the personal and the societal level—levels that feminist theory insists cannot be separated.

Because of the all-pervasive nature of the oppression women suffer, feminist theologies initially have concentrated on uncovering, understanding, and rejecting oppression. To do this, women first have had to recognize the privileges and benefits that often come hand in hand with certain forms of oppression. Second, women have come to understand that oppression inhibits the ability of the oppressed to develop and exercise their capacities and to express their needs, thoughts, and feelings. Oppression refers to "systemic constraints that are embedded in unquestioned norms, habits, and symbols, in the assumptions underlying institutional rules and the collective consequences of following those rules." Oppression includes "the vast and deep injustices some groups suffer as a consequence of often unconscious assumptions and reactions of well-meaning people in ordinary interactions, media and cultural *stereotypes, and structural features of bureaucratic hierarchies and market mechanisms—in short, the normal processes of everyday life" (Young, 40–41).

It is impossible to give a single definition of oppression because there are different reasons, or combinations of reasons, for the oppression women suffer, as well as different modes of oppression. Certainly, there is no moral primacy among the causes or factors or elements of oppression: there is no one oppression that is worse than another, no one mode of oppression that is more oppressive than another. Differentiating the modes of oppression, however, is important for the elaboration of effective strategies for social change.

Exploitation, one common mode of oppression, has to do with transferring the results of the labor of some to the benefit of others. Exploitation is concerned with what *work is, who does what for whom, how work is compensated, and how and by whom the results of work are appropriated.

A second mode of oppression, **marginalization,* is perhaps the most dangerous form of oppression. The marginalized are seen as not contributing to society and, as such, are subjected to severe material deprivation and even extermination. The marginalized are seen as surplus people, who, because they are considered by others to be useless, often come to understand themselves that way as well. Marginalization "involves the deprivation of cultural, practical, and institutionalized conditions for exercising capacities in a context of recognition and interaction" (Young, 55), which leads to lack of self-respect, identity crisis, and lack of self-worth: a lethal combination indeed.

Powerlessness is a third mode of oppression. The powerless lack authority; they have little or no opportunity to be self-defining or to assert their interests and visions of what they believe to be good for themselves and their communities. Powerless persons lack status, are not considered respectable, are not trusted.

*Cultural *imperialism,* a fourth mode of oppression, is the basis for ethnic prejudice and *racism. To experience cultural imperialism is to experience how the dominant meanings of a society render other perspectives invisible. Those who live and operate according to their own nondominant views are stereo-typed as "other," as "outsider," because the experience and *culture of dominant groups establish the norm in society. Those of the dominant group "project their own experience as representative of humanity as such." All other experience is construed largely as deviant and inferior. "The culturally imperialized are stamped with an essence. The stereotypes confine them to a nature which is often attached in some way to their bodies, and which thus cannot easily be denied. These stereotypes so permeate the society that they are not noticed as contestable" (Young, 59). The most destructive aspect of cultural imperialism is what it makes the oppressed do to themselves. The oppressed internalize the judgments of the dominant culture and find themselves acting according to the very image society has of them. Little by little, the culture and self-understandings of the oppressed become as invisible to them as they are to the dominant culture. And that invisibility finds expression in a rejection of their own cultural customs and values, and of themselves; all the more insidious because of its imperceptibility even to the oppressed (Lugones, 35–44; Young, 60).

The fifth face of oppression is *systemic *violence,* which causes the oppressed to live with the fear of random, unprovoked attacks on their persons or property. These attacks aim to damage, humiliate, or destroy. What makes systemic violence a mode of oppression is not particular senseless acts, no matter how horrible they are, but the fact that there is a societal context which makes such actions possible and acceptable. What makes violence such a destructive mode of oppression is that the *suffering violence inflicts, physically and psychologically, is so devastating and all-encompassing that the possibility of such violence becomes an ever-present threat which coerces the oppressed constantly. The insidiousness of violence, then, is that, as an ever-present threat, it makes the oppressed do what they do not choose to do—and this without the oppressor actually having to do anything (Wartenberg, 91–104).

Using the oppression of women as their source and locus, feminist accounts of justice are discourses specific enough to force options and concrete enough to play a central role in devising strategies to bringing about radical social change. Feminist accounts of justice articulate concrete historical projects in which women have a protagonist role, through which women contribute to what is normative for society. In other words, because of their liberationist perspective, feminist accounts of justice are not only about women's rights but also about women's responsibilities; they are about women as moral subjects and agents as well as about the social consequences of personal behaviors and institutional policies.

There are three elements in all Christian feminist theological-ethical accounts of justice. The first one is the use of Judeo-Christian *scripture* and Christian *histories and traditional theologies.* These sources provide motivation for many women who struggle for justice. As such they are important. But there is no prevailing view of the role biblical elements and those from traditional theologies have or should have in the elaboration of feminist accounts of justice. Most seem to agree that, given the variety of women's experiences of oppression (stemming from different ethnic, racial, social, cultural, political, and economic realities), it is useful to look at references from the scriptures of other religions, women's religious experiences and practices that have not been codified, as well as histories of women's struggles for justice hitherto hidden or ignored. The use of such a plurality of resources is seen not as an option but as a necessity if feminist visions of justice are not to be at the expense of others or of the earth and the animals with whom humans share this world.

This means that a second element of all feminist theological-ethical accounts of justice has to be a radically disparate *understanding of *difference* from the one regularly used. True plurality rejects an essentialist meaning of difference that places groups and persons in categorical opposition, in mutual exclusion. Difference does not have to imply that groups lie apart from one another. Difference does not mean that there are not overlapping experiences or that there is nothing in common. Difference among groups and persons does not exclude some similarities and the potential sharing of some attributes, experiences, and goals (Young, 168–73).

Differences have to be embraced so they can be understood as "ambiguous, relational, shifting, without clear borders that keep people straight—as entailing neither amorphous unity nor pure individuality" (Young, 171). Embracing differences does not in any way mean an acceptance of total *relativism or of an individualistic ideology. Embracing differences is only possible as part of an ideology of *solidarity, an ongoing search for justice, and a solid commitment to "fullness of life" for all, usually referred to as "the common good" (Boff, 11–15). Embracing differences requires interaction, which cannot happen without honest *dialogue, which in turn requires equalization of *power among those in dialogue. Thus a third element in feminist theological-ethical accounts of justice has to do with *understandings and use of power.* Power has to be understood as both a personal and a structural process that can be used for either oppression or liberation. Oppressive power uses force, coercion, and/or influence to control and limit self-determination and decision making in individual persons or groups of persons. When liberative, power transforms oppressive situations, no matter what mode of oppression is involved (Wartenberg, 184).

The historicity of all feminist accounts

of justice, their *contextualization and concreteness, makes them an evolving reality. Insofar as they point to concrete, historical realities, feminist accounts of justice can be considered *ideologies, programmatic visions fully able to be implemented in our world. If these accounts of justice are considered as pointing to unfolding concrete, historical realities that, given the limitedness of humanity, cannot be fully realized in this world, they also point to religious or theological understandings related to the unfolding and full realization of the "kin-dom" of God, a nonclassist, nonsexist term that links the biblical understanding of "fullness of life," "abundance of life," to *family, a construct that is very much part of women's daily experience.

Boff, *Pasos* [1994]; Isasi-Díaz [forthcoming]; Lebacqz [1987]; Lugones, in Card [1991]; Wartenberg [1990]; Young [1990]

ADA MARÍA ISASI-DÍAZ

Justification by Faith A reading of justification by faith from the perspective of women cannot be understood as an abstraction, such as forgiveness for a sinner or being freed from *guilt, without exploring several historical considerations. First, women as a group have been condemned by society. It has not been their works of injustice (Gk *adikia*) that have been the basis of their condemnation by the *patriarchal, *androcentric world, but rather the simple fact that they are women. Therefore, it is not possible to speak of forgiveness or *liberation from guilt without further elaboration: Are women guilty for being women? Is it a crime to be a woman? Of what are they forgiven?

It is a fact that many women feel guilty when they do not entirely fulfill the roles assigned to them by the patriarchal society. Frequently they feel dirty for belonging to the female sex and for being used as sexual objects. Psychologically, they have to be freed from guilt in order to feel themselves to be persons of worth. This fact demonstrates the great injustice of society in making an innocent person into a guilty one. And the injustice is made worse when a reading of justification by faith does not take into account the particular faces of the subjects, instead declaring the real guilty person—the one guilty of the *oppression of women—to be free and forgiven, by *grace. Justification is liberation and forgiveness for all insofar as those who are justified make visible their new life in Christ: that is to say, live as persons of worth and practice *justice.

Sin has to do with sociocultural reality, and justification must be understood against that same horizon. Justification by faith is closely related to the justice of God, independent of the justice of the law. The systematic *violence against women is the *sin of a patriarchal structure that creates victims and victimizers. The logic that governs that structure is the logic of the law. Every type of law (institutional, cultural, or judicial) is fulfilled in order to ensure that the existing structure continues to function. It is in this sense that the fulfillment of the law leads to the knowledge of sin (Rom. 3:20).

Women are the principal victims of this patriarchal structural sin, in which all human beings, women and men alike, are accomplices and to which they are slaves. A feminist reading understands the event of justification by faith as a liberation from that sin. To be justified by faith and not by the works of the law is a gift that challenges every woman and every man to live *as persons of worth before God* and before society, without requiring their own merits; for at issue is a gift given by grace. That gift likewise invites one to follow a logic different from that of patriarchal law, sin, and death. The good news for those who are justified, who receive faith as a new way of living, is the awareness of being subjects of their own lives and of the possibility of transforming the society ruled by the sin manifest through the patriarchal structure. When one is justified, one has the power of *faith to believe that God raises to life the innocent crucified victim, as God did with Jesus.

Tamez [1990; 1993b]

ELSA TAMEZ
(TRANS. SHARON H. RINGE)

Kenōsis A Greek term for "emptying," *kenōsis* first appears theologically in a Pauline christological formulation found in Phil. 2:5–11. The text refers to Jesus as having emptied himself of his divinity when he assumed or grasped full humanity. Paul focuses on *kenōsis* as a deliberate humbling, exemplified by Jesus' perfect obedience to God and by his self-sacrifice "to the point of death—even death on a cross" (2:8). From Paul's perspective, *kenōsis* warrants God's exaltation of Jesus as Lord. In the church, Paul teaches that Jesus' *kenōsis* is a model for Christians' behavior, especially of how the "strong" within the church community ought to relate to the "weak" (Phil. 2:3–5; 1 Cor. 9:12, 19; 10:24, 33; 12:23). Later theological appropriations have emphasized obedience and self-sacrifice as exemplary Christian *virtues for all humanity.

Feminist theologians have pointed out the dangers of absolutizing obedience and self-sacrifice as virtues, particularly for disempowered people of both genders. Feminists have preferred to interpret *kenōsis* as a rejection of patriarchal *power. They have reconceptualized *kenōsis* with respect to *doctrines of God, as well as with reference to *Christology. For example, in *Sexism and God-Talk,* Rosemary Ruether interprets the same Pauline passage as God's abandonment of patriarchal power (120–21), speaking of "Kenosis of the Father" in her introductory midrash (1–11).

Rita Nakashima Brock in *Journeys by Heart,* by contrast, interprets *kenōsis* as Jesus' own release from bondage to patriarchal power without specific reference to God. From her perspective, this release occurs in the *gospel account of the woman with a discharge who touches the hem of Jesus' garment and is healed (Mark 5:25–34). Brock emphasizes the moment of the woman's touch, when Jesus perceives "that power had gone forth from him" (5:30), as a "*kenōsis* of patriarchy" (84). That a woman initiates this release, thus overcoming a taboo against females touching males, redefines power as power shared by all life, in contrast to patriarchal power of *domination. Rather than stressing obedience and self-sacrifice, Brock valorizes mutuality, for the woman's act releases Jesus from bondage to *patriarchy even as she is healed.

Brock [1988]; Knox [1967]; Ruether [1983/1993]

PAULA M. COOEY

Kerygma *Kerygma* transliterates the Greek word for "preaching." It occurs infrequently in the New Testament (e.g., Rom. 16:25), but the reality it designates is central to the New Testament message. The term carries several connotations. First, kerygma points less to the act of *preaching than to its content, namely, the "good news" (*gospel) that Jesus of Nazareth, crucified and risen, is the Christ, the *Son of God, the savior of all who believe. Second, it emphasizes the proclamatory rather than expository mode of the preaching. Third, kerygmatic preaching of the gospel is not a self-assumed task but an officially commissioned one (e.g., Jesus commissions the Eleven [Matt. 28:16–20], Mary Magdalene [20:17], Paul [Gal. 1:11–17]). Finally, preaching is not primarily the communication of information about the past but a summons to salvation in the present through acceptance of the Word of God.

In this century, especially under the influence of Rudolf Bultmann, a rich existentialist theology of kerygma was developed. While the Protestant development of this theology tended to emphasize the event of proclamation as summons to existential commitment, the Catholic development insisted also on its content, including the teaching and paschal mystery of Jesus and the unfolding of this mystery in the life of the church. In post–Vatican II theology, kerygma was joined to *koinōnia* (community) and **diakonia* (ministry) to speak about the identity and *mission of the church as herald, sign, and instrument of the reign of God.

Although women (e.g., Mary Magdalene) were commissioned by Jesus to preach the gospel, their participation in the kerygmatic *ministry of the early church was soon suppressed. The preacher is not only the agent of salvific proclamation but also its medium, since it is through God's call that one encounters and incarnates the mystery one proclaims (cf. Gal. 2:1–10). Consequently, the absence, for most of the church's history, of women's official and public witness to the fact and meaning of salvation has seriously impoverished and even distorted the church's preaching of the gospel.

Craghan, in Komonchak/Collins/Lane [1987]; Schillebeeckx, in Foley [1983]; Schneiders, in Foley [1983]; Schüssler Fiorenza, in Burke [1983]

SANDRA M. SCHNEIDERS

Land "Land" as treated here designates the planet Earth and all its nonhuman inhabitants, as well as the immediate gaseous environment of this planet; i.e., all parts of *creation that constitute the material ground for human life and are in turn affected by human actions. The principles of feminist theology are fully compatible with the perspective of the contemporary "deep ecology" movement, which asserts that the health of all living things depends on the recognition that land and its components are not primarily "real estate" or "natural resources," whose chief value lies in their utility to human beings. Rather, land is fundamentally a *community, in which *homo sapiens* participates not as conqueror but as "plain member and citizen" (Aldo Leopold, 240). In this biotic community, as in all subcommunities, "life in abundance" (John 10:10) must be characterized by diversity, interconnectedness, and self-regulation, i.e., observance of limits so that the basic needs of all members may be met.

The biblical injunction to the first humans to "serve and keep" the garden (Gen. 2:15, Heb.) suggests that the distinctly human role in the biotic community is to work with conscious respect for the land and its limits and, further, to complement nature's spontaneous praise of God with our own verbal praise (Psalms 19, 96, 98, 148, et al.). "Land," *'eretz,* is a primary theological category in the Hebrew scriptures, where the land consistently functions as the index of the health of the relationship between God and humanity (Gen. 3:18–19) or the people Israel in particular (Deut. 29:21ff). The land of Israel and Jerusalem are often represented as a woman: espoused by God (Isa. 62:4), widowed and without comfort (Lamentations 1), enlarging the tent to make room for her returning children (Isaiah 54). Arguably, the Song of Songs is the most extended metaphorical evocation of the passionate attachment between God and the land of Israel.

Devall/Sessions [1985]; Leopold [1966]; Meyers [1988]; Wright [1980]

ELLEN F. DAVIS

Lectionary "Lectionary" refers both to a system of reading scripture in public worship and to the book of texts chosen for such a system. Readings for a lectionary may be chosen to suit the liturgical season *(lectio electa),* or they may be read directly from the biblical text in course *(lectio continua).* Mainline Christian churches in North America generally use a combination of these two systems. Roman Catholics follow the Roman Sunday lectionary (1969), a three year system of readings that combines *lectio electa* during the seasons of Advent–Christmas–Epiphany and Lent–Easter–Pentecost with modified *lectio continua* during the remainder of the year. Mainline Protestant churches have adopted versions of the Roman lectionary: the

Lutheran Book of Worship lectionary (1978); the Episcopal *Book of Common Prayer* lectionary (1979); and the *Revised Common Lectionary* (1992), adopted by the United Methodist Church and the Presbyterian Church (U.S.A.). Other churches use local systems of choosing readings for Sunday worship, often leaving the selection to the minister. All existing lectionary systems fail to benefit from the work of feminist biblical scholarship in recognizing the presence of *androcentrism and *misogyny of the biblical texts.

Published lectionary systems minimize and marginalize the presence of women in the biblical record by omission, by combination of texts, and by use of oppressive texts. The *Revised Common Lectionary* and the *Inclusive Language Lectionary* have attempted to correct some of these problems; nevertheless, any lectionary system that selects central actors and events from the androcentric biblical text can only intensify its androcentrism. However, because a lectionary (or any public reading of scripture) relocates the text in a contemporary *liturgical-ritual context, possibilities exist for an approach that would incorporate insights of feminist biblical scholarship. A feminist lectionary would challenge the androcentrism of the biblical texts, relocate *revelation and *redemption away from the central male biblical actors, and focus on the marginal, the silenced, and the forgotten voices hidden in the texts.

Campbell [1990]; Procter-Smith, in Schüssler Fiorenza/Collins [1986]; Procter-Smith, *Studia Liturgica* [1992a]; Uhr, *St. Mark Review* [1988]

MARJORIE PROCTER-SMITH

Legal Theory Legal theory undergirds the law, a system of norms and rules that regulates society. Western legal theory is linked to theological and philosophical conceptions of women and men. Feminist legal theorists share with feminists in other disciplines a commitment to understand how their societies have viewed the role of women and to interpret the experience of women.

In the law, this emphasis on the experience of women has led to the recognition that law is a patriarchal institution. Feminist legal theorists examine how the law maintains and perpetuates *patriarchy. They have challenged this patriarchy by insisting that legal institutions must take account of the perspectives of all women.

In some traditional accounts of jurisprudence, legal theory is an abstract and speculative enterprise. For this reason, some feminists forsake legal theorizing and advocate instead concrete reforms in the law that will respond to specific problems encountered by women. Other feminists propose alternative legal theories in the belief that all practical legal reform has some theoretical basis and that theory is necessary to challenge the current legal order.

Feminist legal theory has been consistent in its commitment to the joining of theory and reform and has rejected abstract versions of legal theory that do not affect women's lives. Feminist legal theorists seek to use the law to improve women's economic, social, and political circumstances. Many writers have offered theoretical critiques of the relationship between law and gender. They have then applied this feminist analysis to specific areas of the law, including *family and employment law.

In the United States, feminist legal theory began with the demand for *equality between women and men. In the early stages of legal reform, equality with men is interpreted as "sameness." In a legal system that excludes women from the legal profession and regulates women's working conditions under different rules from men's, sameness is an improvement. Men and women should be treated the same way in the workplace. Some commentators describe the failed Equal Rights Amendment as a legal reform based on the legal theory of *equality as sameness*.

Questions of reproduction, in particular the treatment of pregnancy in the law, challenge the adequacy of equality as sameness. Instead, attention turns to the concept of *equality in *difference.* The concern is that "sameness" law cannot take account of the biological and cultural circumstances of women. In the law, sameness theory might achieve for men the things that women had attained (e.g., a place in nursing school) and yet fail to improve women's lives.

Lawyers thus have turned to protect the differences between men and women by reforms in the law. Yet difference theory also faces criticism. Lawyers ask whether difference can justify disparate legal treatment of women in the military draft and in the law of statutory rape. Moreover, once feminists engage in the enterprise of identifying the different nature of woman, they face the charge of *essentialism. In the quest to define the different nature of women, the many different voices of women, with their range of backgrounds and *experiences, are at times excluded.

The sameness and difference theories are also criticized, most notably by Catharine MacKinnon, for their failure to take account of the subordination of women to men. MacKinnon questions both the sameness and difference accounts and looks at legal theory through a lens of *dominance and subordination.* As with all feminist legal theory, this approach is then applied to concrete areas of the law, such as rape, pornography, and sexual harassment.

Legal theory and legal practice remain intertwined as feminists seek to incorporate these different notions of *equality into the written law.

Bartlett/Kennedy [1991]; MacKinnon [1987]; Rhode [1989]; Smith [1993]

LESLIE GRIFFIN

Lesbian A lesbian is a female homosexual, so named because of the women beloved by the poet Sappho (sixth century B.C.E.) on the Greek island of Lesbos. Women may recognize their sexual orientation as lesbian (or bisexual or heterosexual) by paying attention to their feelings of attraction. The challenge is to be honest with oneself about equal or predominant same-sex attractions, because society is generally so unaccepting of such feelings. Lesbian women come in all shapes and sizes, races and colors, ages, and degrees of masculinity and femininity. Some are ballerinas, stewardesses, or secretaries; others are research scientists, truck drivers, or attorneys. Many are *mothers. Some refer to themselves as "dykes" or as "queer"; others find these words offensive. During the 1950s and 1960s, some lesbians assumed "butch" (masculine) and "femme" (feminine) roles in their dress, demeanor, and sexual behavior, but such role-playing has now become relatively rare. A number of studies have suggested that lesbian couples are more frequently monogamous than heterosexual couples.

*Patriarchal society requires heterosexuality (or at least the appearance of it) in return for as much first-class citizenship as is accorded to women. Therefore it is difficult to say what percentage of the population is lesbian. Although lesbians are prominent among religious writers, seminary professors, and ordained and lay congregational leaders, the *heterosexism of Christianity and Judaism forces many of them into a costly silence concerning their *sexuality and hence their very lives.

Among feminists, lesbians have been variously defined as women who are erotically attracted to other women; as women who draw the majority of their emotional support from other women; or as women who bond with other women in political opposition to male supremacy, refusing with their lives to collaborate in their own betrayal. Whatever the definition, cutting-edge religious issues for lesbian theologians have included reimagining Judaism and Christianity in ways that empower women; seeking *ordination for qualified, openly lesbian or gay candidates for the *ministry or priesthood; developing *liturgical blessings and rituals for same-sex unions; and articulating a theology of relationship in which the mutual supportiveness of *friendship becomes normative for all domestic partners, heterosexual or homosexual.

In society as a whole, lesbian theologians, like other feminist theologians, pursue *justice for people of all races, color gradations, classes, creeds, ages, sizes, nationalities, abilities, gender differences, and sexual orientations. Justice issues particular to lesbians must include the fact that lesbianism carries an economic penalty: according to a nationwide survey, from 1989 through 1991 the average annual income of lesbian women in full-time employment was only $15,068, as opposed to $18,341 for heterosexual women, $26,321 for gay men, and $28,312 for heterosexual men (*New York Times*, city edition, December 4, 1994).

Because of the economic discrepancy and because most lesbians experience *oppression as females before they experience heterosexist or homophobic oppression, the lesbian subculture differs drastically from the gay male subculture. Yet the *AIDS crisis has caused a new cohesion in the lesbian, gay, bisexual, and transgendered community, and lesbian women are currently hoping that gay men will reciprocate their support with regard to AIDS by becoming equally supportive concerning breast cancer, osteoporosis, and other women's health issues. Whether or not such reciprocity materializes, however, lesbians share many concerns with gay men, among them struggling to gain domestic *partnership benefits equivalent to those of legal *marriage, such as estate and income tax exemptions and deductions, Social Security survivors' benefits, and next-of-kin rights in case of catastrophic illness or accident; winning legal protection against discrimination in jobs, schools, housing, and the military; and reducing *violence against lesbian and gay people, including name-calling, beatings, and murder.

A major challenge facing lesbian and feminist scholars is the retrieval of lesbian lives in history. If women's achievements have often been forgotten, lesbian achievements have often been deliberately blotted out through altering pronouns, deleting or doctoring letters and papers, and biographers' discounting of intense expressions of love between their subject and other women. The Lesbian Herstory Archives in New York City seek to counteract this conspiracy of erasure. But their work is made more difficult by the heterosexism of even some feminist writers and editors. For instance, in their 1985 *Norton Anthology of Literature by Women*, during their four-page introduction to the works of poet-theologian Emily Dickinson, Sandra Gilbert and Susan Gubar fail to mention that anyone has ever noticed the passion with which Dickinson addresses Sue Gilbert in letters bowdlerized by Dickinson's niece but restored by Thomas Johnson in 1958. Nor do they indicate that any scholar has ever recognized Dickinson's passion as lesbian (for a list of such scholars, see Martha Nell Smith in *Women's Studies Quarterly* 19 [fall–winter 1991]). By calling lesbians such as Alice B. Toklas, Edith Lewis, and Ada Russell the "companions" of, respectively, Gertrude Stein, Willa Cather, and Amy Lowell, lesbian history is caused to vanish.

Heterosexism has been fueled by the claims of the religious Right that the Bible condemns same-sex love. But among the Bible's 31,173 verses, only eleven have been construed to refer to homosexual acts and only one to sex between women. Hence it must be acknowledged that the modern obsession with "the Bible and homosexuality" reflects our era's hang-ups, not biblical priorities. In fact, the biblical authors knew nothing about sexual orientation or same-sex lovemaking as an adult consensual form of intimacy, so consulting the Bible about lesbianism is anachronistic. It is, however, possible to extrapolate from the Bible certain relational principles, such as fidelity to *covenant or sexual intimacy as conferring "one-fleshedness" or the importance of mutuality, in order to apply these principles even-handedly to same-sex and heterosexual unions.

Christian lesbians have recently formed a national organization called CLOUT (Christian Lesbians Out Together).

CLOUT, P.O. Box 10062, Columbus, OH 43201; Cruikshank [1982]; Faderman [1981]; Hunt [1990]; Jay/Glasgow [1990]; Kitzinger [1993]; Marcus [1993]; Scanzoni/Mollenkott [1994]

VIRGINIA RAMEY MOLLENKOTT

Liberation Liberation is the struggle for *freedom from *oppression as subjugated people become conscious of their situation and work to transform the conditions of their existence. Such transformation includes personal and social change. Theologies of liberation emphasize the biblical theme of God's action on behalf of enslaved, poor, and outcast persons as a central paradigm for *faith. Feminist liberation *theologies stand in *solidarity with Latin American and other liberation theologies, by affirming (1) the importance of grass-roots communities engaged in critical reflection on the *gospel and acting together toward liberation in their particular context; (2) that God as liberator acts through human history; and (3) that God's "*preferential option for the poor" is a call to solidarity with *suffering persons, including those oppressed by unjust *power relations structured around gender.

Liberation relates to the Reformation emphasis on Christian freedom, historically conceived as freedom from the law and *sin. While dominant-culture theologies may include some notion of liberation, they generally understand liberation in terms of interior consciousness, the freedom from personal *guilt and sin. In contrast to such individualism, feminists expand sin to include its expressions in historically constituted structures of oppression (such as *family roles requiring the subordination of women), emphasizing a more just society in which all people may fully participate. Feminists thus stress the need for liberation from material conditions of *poverty, *sexism, *racism, *classism, *heterosexism, colonialism, and other forms of cultural *domination. Womanist theologians and feminists of color internationally (from the two-thirds world) rightly critique the tendency of white North American feminists to dilute their concrete struggles for *survival in the face of the interstructured oppressions of *race and class with gender. Current white feminist work on liberation includes an emancipatory ethic for a white, middle-class U.S. context; *postmodern theories addressing women's subordination as the product of binary opposition between male and female; and *pastoral care's shift toward a more social understanding of personhood.

Couture [1991]; Kim/St.Ville/Simonaitis [1993]; Russell [1974]; Welch [1990]; Young [1990]

JOYCE ANN MERCER

Liturgy The term *liturgy* is from the Greek *leitourgia,* meaning "public work." In Greco-Roman civil discourse, it referred to public service of any kind. In Christian and Jewish religious discourse, it was a way of referring to worship and avoiding cultic references used in *pagan religions of the time. Recent Christian usage has preferred the etymological interpretation "the people's work," emphasizing the communal nature of worship. Feminist critique has pointed out the male-dominated nature of traditional worship. Denial of women's access to liturgical leadership is central to this fact, but the implications go far beyond questions of women's *ordination. Language and symbols for God and for the Christian community, stories remembered and forgotten, have reflected the male *domination of the church. Liturgy has not been "people's work" so much as "men's work." For liturgy to live up to its name, it must also become "women's work."

While mainline Christian churches in North America have reformed their worship in accord with the male-dominated, Eurocentric liturgical movement, women's groups all over North America and elsewhere have worked on their own to create liturgy that is women's work. Central to this "feminist liturgical movement" have been women claiming liturgical authority. Some of the gatherings are explicitly Christian in identity, others include Christians and non-Christians, while still others leave Christian *tradition behind to create new forms of feminist spirituality. Many women's liturgy groups move rather freely among these options. Although it is difficult to generalize about diverse and intentionally independent groups, the following characteristics seem common:

1. Feminist liturgy is nonhierarchical and egalitarian in leadership and planning. Leadership as exercised in feminist liturgies is intended to be catalytic rather than dominant. Verbal and nonverbal elements strive for reciprocity and mutuality.
2. The particularities of women's experiences are honored, resulting in a high degree of flexibility in *naming of *experiences and in ritual ways of reflecting those experiences. There is also openness to other religions and traditions, texts, myths, and symbols.
3. In contrast to traditional liturgies, which honor men's *relationships with one another and God and women's relationships with men, feminist liturgies honor women's connections with one another and with women of the past. This forms the context in which the deity is named and worshiped as female.
4. Feminist liturgies value women's bodies and bodily functions, in all their diversity, as reflections of the holy and loci of divine *revelation. Feminist liturgies generally include the use of the whole *body and the senses.
5. The presence of the holy in the everyday and extraordinary experiences of women is affirmed. Because *violence, pain, and *suffering are so often part of women's lives, expressions of lament, rage, and grief are often included.
6. Feminist liturgies reject *patriarchal dichotomies, affirming the nonhierarchical interconnectedness of all life as a model of the divine life. This interconnection is understood to include nature.
7. Feminist liturgies are rarely repeated the same way, and rarely written down. Although some feminist liturgies are now published, they tend to be oral, particular to the occasion and the group, inclusive of spontaneity and group participation. There is a refusal to mystify the origins of any ritual or symbol or to fossilize them into an "official" form. Freedom, creativity, and imagination are valued.
8. Feminist liturgies intend to articulate an alternative moral vision of the world and our relationships within it. This often entails naming of *evil and rituals of *exorcism, as well as enactment of *freedom.
9. Feminist liturgies generally question traditional forms of *authority, both human and divine. Traditional texts, symbols, and ritual practices are evaluated as to their potential for contributing to the well-being of women and other oppressed people, rather than in reference to some intrinsic authority.

Elkins [1994]; Northup [1993]; Procter-Smith [1990; 1992b]; Procter-Smith/Walton [1993]

MARJORIE PROCTER-SMITH

Marginalization *Marginalization* means "action to marginalize," from the Latin *margo* (margin), which refers to what is accessory as opposed to what is central. In the general sense, as is shown by the French language usage from the 1960s and 1970s, this concept refers to the category describing destitute and disadvantaged people in a wealthy environment, isolated or excluded because of their moral and societal nonconformism or from their environment's *politics. Thus it refers to a categorization, often discrimination, that may be social (social classes), cultural, economic, racial, physical, sexual, or religious.

In the feminist theology literature, marginalization is the expression of the effects of the dialectic relationship between the sexes. Women's lives and actions were not a part of the historical reality considered important by the *patriarchal societies that created biblical texts and Christian *tradition. As a consequence, only men's experiences constituted the norm of theological productions and religious symbols. Women were no more than a "peripheral category" of Christian *anthropology. One will note few references to women in the history of public life. They are often mentioned for some activity characterized by spiritual actions that would fit the compartmentalization in the private domain, the inner world, as opposed to the public domain. Their systematic exclusion from priesthood and religious structures was due to their gender.

There have been efforts underway for the past few decades in the theological domain for an intellectual recreation of the first Christian times in order to render the past intelligible and to break with the androcentered historiography; to give back to women the *power of which they have been deprived (Schüssler Fiorenza 1983, xix–xx). Feminists' commitment to oppose this legacy of subordination imposed in the church, society, and culture is supported by their new understanding of the past; that is to say, with Judy Chicago, woman's power can come from their historical legacy.

hooks [1984]; Schüssler Fiorenza [1983/1994]

VUADI VIBILA
(TRANS. CECILE PERRAUD)

Mariology Mariology is the theological reflection of the Christian church on the significance of Mary, the mother of Jesus, for life and *faith. The basis of this *doctrine about Mary is an elaboration of the texts from Matthew 1 and Luke 1—2 about the birth of Jesus to an unmarried woman, who came to be called a "virgin" in church dogma. The development of Marian piety began in the early church and has been elaborated over the centuries in the Roman Catholic Church. A key point of Mariology is the Marian image of a new Eve who is obedient to God's word, in contrast to the first Eve.

Over the centuries, the church elaborated the doctrines about Mary. She was declared the Mother of God, perpetual virgin, immaculate in conception, assumed into *heaven at her death, mother of the church, and Mother of the Redeemer. Since the Second Vatican Council, emphasis has been placed on Mary as a participant in the history of salvation and as the first believer and archetype of the church. The doctrines of Mary and the piety attached to her veneration provide some of the missing female imagery for God that was lost in the male, *monotheistic traditions. When the Protestant Reformers rejected worship related to Mary as unbiblical, they provided an important critique but also eliminated this source of female imagery in worship.

Since the late 1970s, there has been a great transformation of Mariology through the work of feminist theologians. They have criticized traditional Mariology as an *ideology of *sexism. The concept of perpetual virginity is seen as *misogyny and disdain for women's *sexuality. Mary's words of assent, "Let it be with me according to your word" (Luke 1:38), and her image as the new Eve have been criticized as tools for the *patriarchal order of the church. The *dualism represented by Mary, the sinless virgin, in contrast with Eve, the sinner, is rejected by women who understand this to be a false *stereotype of women as either saint or sinner.

At the same time, some feminist theologians have sought out the positive aspects of Mariology and worked to transform the traditional doctrines. For instance, Mary's virginity is seen as a symbol of *autonomy, as she is not dependent on any man and could carry out God's liberating action directly through her own life. Mary's obedience and servanthood is reinterpreted to emphasize her active response of faith to God's call. As Chung Hyun Kyung has put it, Mary becomes "a model for full womanhood and of the fully liberated human being" (77). She no longer is understood as a model of *oppression of women but as a model of their *liberation.

A new understanding of Mariology is emerging from the *third world. Mary is identified with the oppressed and their liberation. In Latin America and Asia, Mary is an indigenous Madonna (e.g., the Black Madonna of the Philippines; Our Lady of Guadalupe of Mexico; the Black Aparecida of Brazil; Purisima of Nicaragua). The white, Euro-American Madonna is rejected as a symbol of the oppressors. Feminists of the third world emphasize the Magnificat from Luke 1:46–55 as the main text for feminist Mariology. Mary is seen as the representative of the oppressed people. She represents God's *preferential option for the poor. Her prophetic words are understood as the basis of a spirituality of revolution, a call for liberation of women and of all victims of *poverty and injustice.

Some Asian feminists think that the *virgin birth is a symbol of God's judgment against the patriarchal order because a man had no part in the birth. Positively, it is a sign of the birth of a new order through *suffering and struggle. That Mary gave birth to Jesus means that she took part in the messianic revolution; therefore Mary is a common savior with Jesus. For Asian women, Mary is present in their daily *experiences and becomes a model of *sisterhood in the struggle for liberation. So Mary is no longer an idol or object to be worshiped on a pedestal and removed from women's *reality. On the contrary, Mary is identified with the *mothers today who suffer as their children are being massacred and who are taken as political prisoners for their actions on behalf of *justice and love.

Bingemer/Gebara [1989]; Chung [1990]; Katoppo [1980]; Ruether [1983/1993]

HAN KUK YOM

Marks of the Church Christianity began as a spirit-filled messianic sect within Judaism. The earliest disciples functioned as a renewal movement, believing that in Jesus Christ they had been "called out" for special service. The first mark of the church is that it is "a called people," literally, *ekklēsia*.

Second, early Christians believed that old patterns which subordinated women and slaves had been transcended by the message of the *gospel. In the church, created for a messianic age, people no longer needed to be bound by traditional hierarchies. The second mark of the church is that it is a *community where women participate in the *covenant as equals with men.

Unfortunately, the cultural habits of *hierarchy and *patriarchy are very strong, and before long the church developed organizational structures patterned after the Roman Empire. In spite of these developments, however, the church continued to insist that discipleship occurs in community. Theologians such as Cyprian, Luther, and Calvin insisted that outside the church there was no salvation. Another mark of the church is its identity as a community mediating God's saving *grace in a sinful world.

The marks of the church, therefore, are theological, historical, and practical. It is one (unified), it is holy (somehow connected to God), and it is apostolic (linked by *tradition and loyalty to the earliest followers of Jesus). Sixteenth-century Protestant Reformers believed that the church could be found wherever the word of God was purely preached and the *sacraments rightly administered.

Contemporary feminists have approached the marks of the church in three ways: they have denounced many of the criteria used by the male tradition to define the church (thereby becoming *post-Christian); they have tried to (re)discover alternatives to existing understandings of church (living within a creative theological tension); and they have sought to create alternative visions for the church.

Women-Church, as one of these alternative visions, is a community of *liberation from patriarchy. As such, its existence moves toward the transformation of society. Participants in *Women-Church may substitute it in place of conventional church life or become involved to supplement or survive the traditional church. According to Rosemary Radford Ruether, the marks of Women-Church are four: (1) it is a community of study, wrestling with biblical materials out of the context of life; (2) it is an autonomous base for women's theologizing and worship, seeking to overcome linguistic deprivation and eucharistic famine; (3) it is a center of social involvement where belief and conviction find expression through engagement with the world, moving out beyond the needs of its own members; and (4) it is a center of collective life and sharing, whereby members pool resources and apportion obligations to benefit the larger group.

Furthermore, within feminism the marks of the church reclaim the inclusive vision, inviting women and men to create formal and informal communities that will nurture their journey into wholeness. They retrieve the heritage of the early church. They explore metaphors that emphasize cooperative, integrative, and egalitarian structures rather than the pyramidal, hierarchical, and authoritarian power found in the male-dominated heritage of the church.

Ruether [1985]; Russell [1993]; Thistlethwaite [1983]

BARBARA BROWN ZIKMUND

Marriage Traditional marriage is an interpersonal, sexual, domestic, economic, and social *partnership of heterosexual persons. Procreation of children is not necessary to constitute marriage, but marriage typically has been undertaken to produce and nurture children and to transmit property within kinship structures, including spouses' families of origin as well as spouses' own progeny and descendants. Marriage has virtually everywhere been *hierarchical and *patriarchal, institutionalizing men's exchange of women's sexual, reproductive, childrearing, and other domestic services for material or political goods.

The practice and social ramifications of marriage have varied significantly worldwide, however. Some central points of difference are whether marriage is *polygamous or monogamous; whether any degree of consent is required of a bride; the customs and laws that define the initiation of marriage; the relationships among the multiple wives and their children in a polygamous marriage; what relationship a married woman retains to her natal *family; to whom the children of spouses belong; the meanings of marital sex beyond reproduction; the extramarital sexual *freedom of men and women; whether, how, and by whom a marriage can be ended; what happens to a woman in the event of divorce; and the social role of a *widow.

In ancient Israel and in the Hebrew Scriptures, women were given in marriage by men and found their fulfillment in bearing sons who would carry on both the family line and its religious beliefs and practices. To be barren was a curse and a reason for the husband's marriage of a second wife or for his begetting of children with a concubine (Gen. 16:1–4). Divorce was the prerogative of men. Monogamy and permanency in marriage were ideals, however, and sex was celebrated for its intrinsic goodness and pleasure, not only for its procreative potential (Song of Songs). Women, some married, could gain acclaim in their own right for accomplishments in religious and political affairs, as well as in domestic ones (Miriam, Sarah, Rachel, Deborah, Ruth, Judith).

In the Greco-Roman setting of early

Christianity, women passed in their early teens from the household and the control of their fathers to a husband twice their age or more. Women's education was limited; they were to bear and raise children and manage households for their husbands. A good wife served her husband, accepted his sexual infidelities, and rarely left the boundaries of their domicile. A right to inherit property from her natal family gave her some independence, but she could be divorced at the will of her husband or even her father, in which event the husband retained custody of their children. At a spouse's death, a woman ideally renounced remarriage and passed into the *authority of her sons.

The Christian *tradition has to some extent counteracted the pervasive cross-cultural subordination of women to men in marriage, even as it has enshrined women's maternal, nurturing, and self-sacrificial roles and encouraged women to be submissive to men in the name of Christ. The Jesus of the Gospels approaches women directly as disciples, so that their religious identity does not depend on that of fathers and husbands or on being married and bearing children. The prohibitions of divorce attributed to Jesus may have functioned to protect women from male abandonment or manipulation (Matt. 5:31–32; 19:9; 1 Cor. 7:10–11). Paul declares women and men equal in Christ (Gal. 3:28), speaks of the marital relation as mutual (1 Cor. 7:3–4), and encourages the leadership of women in his churches (Prisca, Chloe, Phoebe). There is a sacramentalizing tendency in early Christianity: marriage is seen as a mediating experience of the Divine and as a realm of sanctification for both spouses, even apart from childbearing. At the same time, and inconsistently, some *Pauline letters adapt the Hellenistic "household codes" for Christian use, thus reinforcing male *hegemony in marriage (Eph. 5:21–33).

In Western Christianity an ambivalence toward marriage and toward women's role in it is rooted in *dualistic attitudes toward the *body, sex, and procreation. A prototypical and influential example is Augustine, who, in *On the Goods of Marriage*, sees sex for pleasure alone as sinful yet defends children, sexual fidelity, and the indissoluble bond, or "sacrament," in marriage. Roman Catholicism has defined marriage as a sacrament mediating God's presence in the church and forbids divorce with remarriage, which both Orthodox and Protestant churches permit. The Reformers saw marriage as a natural estate, not an ecclesiastically regulated sacrament. Marriage was a covenantal and social relation, although procreation remained sex's primary purpose.

Since the Enlightenment, modern Western cultural values of individuality, freedom, and *equality have contributed to greater gender parity in marriage, caused love and affection to supersede procreation, and contributed to a view of sexual pleasure as good in itself and conducive to union. Individual fulfillment, personal and sexual, is today valued more than the economic, political, or familial functions of marriage, at least in the industrialized nations.

Christian feminism likewise seeks to transform marriage toward greater equality and reciprocity of partners; it has challenged the *domination of sexual meaning by procreation, upheld sexual intimacy and pleasure, and disputed the assumption that marriage entails maternal and domestic roles for women. Intercultural *dialogue challenges feminists to integrate women's *autonomy and rights with the values of *community, family, and motherhood. Christian feminists are reenvisioning marriage as a committed and equal partnership, possibly including same-sex unions; open to, though not requiring, parenthood and nurture of children; responsible to the common good; and embodying Christian ideals such as respect, fidelity, and *compassion.

Achtemeier [1976]; Brundage [1987]; Cahill [forthcoming]; Gudorf [1994]; Mackin [1982]; Roberts [1987]; Scott/Warren [1983]

LISA SOWLE CAHILL

Martyr Originally derived from the Greek word for "witness" (*martys*) and used in a Christian context to designate persons who had experienced directly the living or the resurrected Christ, the term *martyr* acquired by the end of the second century a more technical meaning of "blood witness," referring to those who had died during periods of persecution rather than renounce Christian identity. "Do you see this vase here . . .?" responds the North African martyr Perpetua (d. 203) when harshly confronted in prison by her angry father. "Could it be called by any other name that what it is? Well, so too I cannot be called anything other than what I am, a Christian" (Musurillo 1972, 106–31).

One of our earliest textual references to Christians in the Roman Empire (ca. 111) comes from the correspondence of Pliny the Younger with the Roman emperor Trajan. A brief series of letters outlines the processes of legal examination and compulsion that produced martyrs and highlights the role of women both as leaders and as martyrs in the early church. Here Pliny, acting as a provincial commissioner, reports that to gain more information about Christian belief and practice, he ordered two women, called ministers or deaconesses (*duabus ancillis, quae ministrae dicebantur; Letters of Pliny* 10.96), to be tortured. Pliny's expectation (ultimately thwarted) that women would yield most readily under torture offers *pagan corroboration of what became a recurrent motif in early Christian and medieval literature, that of the "virile woman," or the woman who in her endurance, humility, or both shames and outdoes men in matters of faith. The Christian adaptation in martyrdom accounts of this originally Stoic ideal of the virile woman indicates a social field in which "virility," while bearing more elevated connotations than "femininity," was a state earned by virtue and not conferred by biology.

Theologically, Christians of early and medieval churches understood martyrdom as a *grace for which an individual was selected by God. A martyr's death paralleled and partook of the passion of Christ, whose reciprocal participation in the martyr's death galvanized her or his body against pain and reflexive recoil. This emphasis is particularly vivid in the *Passion of Perpetua,* which has the additional distinction of incorporating the martyr's prison diary. Like the passion of Christ, passions of martyrs were frequently represented as battles or contests with the devil. Furthermore, the martyr-to-be, regardless of gender, assumed within the Christian communities the highest status and spiritual *authority, including the normally episcopal power to forgive sins and reconcile penitents to the church. A confessor, or one who confessed rather than denied her or his *faith in the face of torture or death, joined the rank of presbyters without benefit of *ordination.

Even if we set aside legendary St. Ursula and her eleven thousand martyred companions, women comprise a high percentage of traditionally celebrated martyrs. From the end of the second century, local communities commemorated the anniversary of a martyr's death at his or her tomb. Soon churches were built on sites where martyrs died or were buried. The supernatural *power animating a martyr's remains and intimately related to her powerful role as intercessor between the human and divine spheres resulted in frequent attempts throughout the Middle Ages to acquire and enshrine martyrs' relics. From the fourth century, anniversary celebrations included the preaching of a panegyric on the life of the martyr, a practice that soon expanded into increasingly elaborate and codified *liturgical compositions and performances. In this way many female martyrs became a regular part of the liturgical, architectural, literary, and imaginative fabric of medieval culture. Catherine of Alexandria (patroness of teamed women and educators), Cecilia (associated with music and learning), Geneviève (patron saint of Paris), Margaret (protector of women in labor), and Faith of Conques (object of veneration at a major pilgrimage site in southern France) are just a few of the most well known martyr-saints. In the tenth century the nun Hrothsvitha, a dramatist and the most outstanding literary figure of her time, adopted martyr accounts as plots for her plays. Her *Dulcitius* takes place during Diocletian's persecution (284–305) and dramatizes the fantastic and somewhat inconclusive martyrdoms of three clever and determined women whose Greek names mean love, snow, and peace. In Hrothsvitha's *Sapientia,* the learned matron Sapientia endures the martyrdom of her three daughters Fides, Spes, and Caritas (faith, hope, and love) by order of Emperor Hadrian.

Although cultic veneration of martyrs was rejected in the sixteenth century by the new Protestant churches, Protestants retained a keen sense of the martyr as a religious ideal, as testified by John Foxe's Calvinist martyrology *Acts and Monuments* (1563, expanded English version), usually referred to as *Foxe's Book of Martyrs,* and by *The Bloody Theater,* or the *Martyrs' Mirror,* published by the seventeenth-century Dutch Protestant Thieleman van Braght. *The Bloody Theater,* a collection of Anabaptist martyrdoms, contains a remarkable prison letter addressed by a religious radical named Elizabeth to her infant daughter. This letter, written soon after giving birth and just before Elizabeth's execution, is comparable in themes and power to the prison diary of Perpetua (also a nursing mother) and the plays of Hrothsvitha. Catholic piety in the sixteenth and seventeenth centuries, fueled by newly revived ideals of heroic sanctity and by the deaths of missionaries in Asia and the Americas, continued to sustain a high status for martyrs. The recognition of the importance of women in the *conversion of non-Christian peoples, particularly women and children, ensured that female missionaries would number significantly among the present Catholic martyrs.

Aspergen [1990]; Droge/Tabor [1989]; Dronke [1984]; Ferguson [1990]; Musurillo [1972]; Strayer [1987]; van Braght [1951]; Wilson [1988]

KATHERINE GILL

Marxism The social theory of Marxism is important to feminist liberation *theology and economic *ethics because Marxism's ongoing critical theory of capitalism illuminates the potential for better social arrangements and a more just economy. Marxism yields important insights about those areas of political economy where the struggle for economic *justice should focus.

Marxism is not a unified theory but possesses great breadth and diversity, as it has continued to evolve since the nineteenth century. Many theorists within it critique the *materialist reductionism, economic determinism, rationalistic scientism, and monistic approach to social theory of much traditional Marxian theory, especially that of the (white male) political parties.

Marxism contributes to the struggle for social justice with its economic (class) analysis, which Marx hoped would transform the consciousness of workers to enable their revolutionary *praxis. Marx wished to distinguish analytically the capitalist class process from all other processes so as to uncover the precise dimensions of economic injustice in ways he believed other social critics had missed. Marx believed that creative social change was jeopardized if social theory failed to grasp the actual character of capitalist dynamics and economic relations.

Among the insights of neo-Marxist theory that are useful to religious economic ethicists are the following: a dialectical method or epistemology that promotes thinking systemically and historically, since all reality is interrelated over time; a materialist outlook that views capitalism as creating an economic environment that reproduces nonmutual relations at all levels of society; a belief that humans are creatures of praxis who are not only shaped by their society but capable of transforming it through freely determined and courageous collective action. In addition, some feminist economic ethicists claim that neo-Marxian social theory meets important theoethical criteria, such as attending to *poverty and *oppression, that are not met by neoclassical economic theory.

In the late 1960s, Marxist scholars who wished to work on theory that would guide the *liberation of women asked a question central to feminist theology and ethics: What is the relationship of women's specific oppression to class exploitation and the evolution of the struggle for justice? Some Marxist feminists have developed a theory of women's oppression within Marxism that has asserted the primacy of private property and class to account for the multiple sources of oppression impacting on women. However, *socialist feminists, while supporting the Marxist claim that women's oppression has material roots, wish to give equal weight to other sources of oppression such as *racism, male dominance, authoritarianism, and cultural dynamics. These are viewed as having relatively autonomous origins that have become intertwined in capitalism. For example, some women are oppressed by men and by whites, not just by capitalists.

As racism and *sexism cannot be finally reduced to economic relations, so materialist theories are not sufficient to account for subjective experience, psychological dynamics, and *culture. Domination and subordination are about more than control of labor power, and the transformation of society is immensely complicated by the variety of different psychic investments groups have in the status quo, regardless of people's objective material conditions.

Socialist feminists also acknowledge that while it is essential to do a multiple analysis, there are serious problems with simplistically paralleling sex, *race, and class as comparable sources of oppression. This can deny the distinct character of each oppression, the fact that some groups of women are more harmed by one or multiple forms of oppression than others, and the fact that some women benefit from forms of oppression.

In short, given the particularities of women's lives, whether there is a common "women's oppression" is debated. Developing theory both for the anatomy of each mode of oppression and for the interconnections between them is paramount for socialist feminist theory and feminist liberation theology and ethics as Marxism continues to develop.

Albert/Hahnel [1978]; Brubaker, in Zweig [1991]; Harrison [1985]; Sargent [1981]

MARY E. HOBGOOD

Materialism Broadly speaking, materialism is a philosophical concept according to which matter is the element that explains human reality in its entirety. Materialist ideas, which originated in ancient Greece, were banned by Christianity during the Middle Ages but returned forcefully in the Renaissance as the foundations of scientific theory.

In the modern era, *Marxism is the main school of thought based on materialism. The Marxist view of history, *historical materialism,* states that production of the goods necessary for the survival of human beings is the fundamental historical fact. The core of Marxist *philosophy, *dialectical materialism,* is summed up in Marx's *Theses on Feuerbach:* "The philosophers have only interpreted the world in various ways; the point, however, is to change it" (1964, thesis 11, p. 72). This marks a break with ancient philosophy and idealism, proposing *praxis as the criterion of truth. Philosophy must relate to the world as the object of its action.

Theologians who use Marxist concepts in their writings, particularly those linked to liberation *theology in Latin America, see no logical implication of atheism in the materialist conception of history. A materialist or atheistic *metaphysics does not necessarily follow from a materialist position in epistemology (the primacy of being, of reality). Similarly, an idealist position in epistemology does not, of necessity, entail a deistic attitude in philosophy.

One of the most forceful feminist criticisms of Marxism focuses on the limits of its materialist basis, which excludes childbirth and childrearing from the concept of production. Thus activities performed in the home are regarded as naturally rather than historically defined, and historical changes in their organization are seen as an effect of changes in production relations. Reduction of the economic sphere to production of objects in a modern factory entails a failure to take into account the impact on markets of factors such as gender, ethnicity, *religion, *culture, and *politics. The current concept of *work does not cover tasks traditionally performed by women, such as childrearing and housework.

Albert et al. [1986]; Harrison [1985]; Rowbotham [1994]

MARIA JOSÉ F. ROSADO NUNES

Matriarchy The term *matriarchy* has had a mixed reception among feminist theologians as a descriptor of an ideal society or vision toward which we as feminists might orient ourselves. Some find the term unhelpful, reasoning that the female dominance implied by matriarchy can in no way be morally preferable to the male dominance of *patriarchy, as dominance of either gender over the other is problematic. Others feel free to envision and work toward matriarchy because they believe that if women were socially dominant, they would create not a mirror image of patriarchy but something qualitatively different. The rule of women, they suggest, would involve not *violence, *hierarchy, or the *oppression of men but a nurturing environment for all. Finally, there are those who do not view matriarchy as the social dominance of women but as the social dominance of certain values historically (or perhaps biologically) associated with women, such as cyclicality, nurturance, connection to nature, and so forth. However, many of these thinkers substitute other terms for matriarchy (e.g., *matrifocal, gynocentric*), fearing that matriarchy's obvious assonance with patriarchy will create only misunderstanding.

Matriarchy is also significant in feminist theologies as a descriptor of prehistoric societies worldwide. Drawing from a variety of *anthropological, *archaeological, and *mythological sources, many feminists argue that prior to "the patriarchal revolution" (dated to approximately 3000 B.C.E. in the Middle East and southern Europe), all societies were in some way woman-centered. These thinkers differ as to whether women held all religious and political *power, controlled access to this power but dispensed it to men, or were venerated religiously while sharing political power equally with men. The archaeological evidence is inconclusive, but ideas of a prehistoric matriarchy continue to appeal to feminist theologians as both myth and putative history.

Gimbutas [1991]; Gottner-Abendroth [1987]; Lerner [1986]

CYNTHIA ELLER

Meek The Homeric period commends women for quiet *virtues such as meekness and qualities such as beauty, skill in weaving and housekeeping, chastity, and faithfulness. Men's qualities appear in contexts of public excellence and competition. Greek poetry and *philosophy value justice and self-control.

Aristotle (384–322 B.C.E.) commends several virtues, including meekness (*Rhetoric* 1366b). Thus the quiet virtues of slaves and women came to replace the competitive ones of male heroes, probably because of their social benefits. Traces of these quiet virtues persist in Sirach 36:28 and in 1 Peter 3:4—"[Wives] . . . let your adornment be the inner self with the lasting beauty of a meek [NRSV: gentle] and quiet spirit, which is very precious in God's sight"—and in Plutarch

(46–120 C.E.), *Consolation to His Wife* 608d: "She [their deceased daughter] has by nature a wonderful contentedness and meekness."

Paul and subsequent authors commend meekness as enhancing common life (Gal. 6:1; Eph. 4:1–2; Col. 3:5–12; Titus 3:2). The Matthean and the Qumran communities, following psalm language, understand themselves to be "the meek." Male emperors, commanders, rulers, *apostles, and bishops, as well as Jesus himself (*Gospel of Thomas* 90; 2 Cor. 10:1), practice *authority by showing graciousness or *meekness* to those less powerful.

Sometimes the notion of exercising meekness through subduing or taming is also present, not just ideologically, as an expression of a *patriarchal society. Nations, humans, and useful domestic animals such as horses also need discipline. In Plutarch's discussion on the control of *anger, men as leaders exercise *compassion while women, like other less powerful creatures, display only rage. Plutarch argues that while the training of leaders can induce meekness, other factors such as sex, social status, and one's nature promote its appearance. Along with other disenfranchised groups such as older men and slaves, women's lack of *power prevents them from controlling anger and thus showing compassion or *meekness*.

Gutzwiller/Michelini, in Hartman/Messer-Davidow [1991]; Spicq, *Revue biblique* [1947]

DEIRDRE J. GOOD

Memory Memory is necessary for identity, both personal and historical. In feminist theology it refers both to women's awareness of themselves and their pasts and to the corporate nature and history of the religious community. Memory is often expressed dynamically as *re-membering,* which expresses *metaphorically the idea of incorporation into a *community or *tradition.

Feminist theologians view memory both as problem and as resource. It emerges as an issue in considerations of women's experience, history, and tradition and in Christian theological topics, especially *God, Jesus *Christ and salvation, church, and *liturgy. As a problem, feminist theology points to the lack, erasure, or distortion of women's memories: i.e., women's experiences have not been fully included in official practices, theologies, and traditions. Indeed, women have themselves not been fully aware of their *experiences and their histories. As a result, women have been harmed and oppressed and religious traditions have been incomplete and inadequate. As a resource, memory includes the process of reclaiming women's experiences and the histories of women as important correctives and as sources for theological and historical reconstruction. Memories of women's *suffering, struggle and *agency, participation, and leadership in all their forms are recalled.

Feminist theologians define memory as both existential/ontological and historical. Mary Daly's ontological approach urges women to remember their real beings by rejecting *patriarchal existence and its memories as false. Elisabeth Schüssler Fiorenza's and Judith Plaskow's historical approaches argue for redefining tradition as a changing process of remembering in order to incorporate women's participation more fully. Schüssler Fiorenza, adopting and adapting Johann Baptist Metz's idea of "dangerous memory," offers a multifaceted hermeneutics of historical recovery and communal formation. Such memories might stir persons to resistance and to action for *liberation of persons and transformation of social and religious structures.

Daly [1984]; Plaskow [1990]; Schüssler Fiorenza [1983/1994]; Welch [1990]

FLORA A. KESHGEGIAN

Metaphor Traditionally, metaphor has been defined as figurative language of transference in which something unknown or imperfectly known is clarified, defined, or described in terms of a known.

For instance, if we are "born of God," then God (the imperfectly known) is being described in terms of a known, the human mothers we all were "born of." In metaphor, each term preserves its distinctness: God is not literally a birthing mother. Yet in the momentary coincidence or confrontation between *God* and *birthing mothers,* as implied by the metaphor "born of God," each term is modified. The interaction between "God" and "birthing mother" is like nuclear fission: a truth explodes into meaning through the collision of the imperfectly known and the known. Factor A, the imperfectly known concept "God," and Factor B, the known concept "birthing mother," retain their conceptual independence but at the same time merge into the unity of Factor X, the metaphoric point of resemblance: we are "born of God."

It must be emphasized that metaphor involves duality but not *dualism. Although some literary critics have used words like *unification* or *identity* to express the complete metaphorical relation, clearly it would be a distortion to imagine that the metaphor "born of God" implies literal identity between God and birthing mothers. To the contrary, it is the energy of tension or bipolarity between "God" and "birthing mother" that causes the singular point of resemblance to strike our minds with resonance and power. So God both is and is not our mother when we are "born of" her. The terms are dual and remain dual, but they are struck into a flame of momentary identity through their metaphorical juxtaposition, so they are not incorrigibly dualistic either. Like two people entering into *partnership, the terms remain themselves, radically different, even as they merge into the third factor of a relationship or resemblance that may be complex, instantaneous, or even nonlogical.

Metaphor is essential to all theological language. As Aristotle said, it is "from metaphor that we can best get hold of something fresh [i.e., new]" (*Rhetoric* 1410b), and "a good metaphor implies an intuitive perception of the similarity in dissimilars" (*Poetics* 1458b). But metaphor becomes dead when the user forgets or does not know that a metaphorical relation was formerly implied or is still capable of being implied. And it is at this point that the current importance of metaphor to Christian feminist theologies comes into focus. The fact is that, for many Christians, the fatherhood of God has become a dead metaphor. The identity between "God" and "father" seems to the users absolutely literal, so that any other *naming of God (especially any gynocentric naming) seems blasphemous or antibiblical.

To repudiate feminist use of gynocentric names and pronouns concerning God, or even the lifting up of biblical imagery of God as female, opponents of inclusive God-language have claimed that female terms for God are used in the Bible only in similes, which supposedly are mere comparisons, and never in metaphors, which supposedly predicate or name. But the function of both similes and metaphors is to compare, similes explicitly (with "like" or "as") and metaphors implicitly. And in fact, the Bible uses both similes and metaphors concerning God's "femaleness."

Elizabeth Achtemeier's article on metaphor in *The Oxford Companion to the Bible* (Metzger/Coogan, eds., 1993) provides feminist theologians with the rationale for their opponents' distortion of the definitions of similes and metaphors in order to maintain exclusively *androcentric and controlling metaphors concerning God's relationship to humankind: "If they [female terms for God] are interpreted as metaphors, the deity is then connected with the images of birth and suckling, and they erroneously result in the view of a *goddess giving birth to all things and persons, who then participate in the divine being. The distinction that the Bible insists on between creator and creature is then lost."

Totally submerged in this statement is any awareness of the duality of metaphor: the "is not" as well as the "is" of all language about God, whether the metaphors are gynocentric, ecological, or androcentric. Perhaps, if we all were to remember how metaphors function, it would become evident that although the Bible sometimes depicts God as one who "is" and "is not" a *transcendent king, judge, husband, father, lord, or master, it just as certainly depicts God as one who "is" and "is not" an *immanent mother, friend, female lover/beloved, woman in grief, tripersonal mystery of love-in-relationship, midwife, liberator, female homeowner, physician, nurse, baker-woman, rock, wind, or water. The point is that by allowing such metaphors to clash in all their magnificent duality, we are reminded that, for all our knowing, God is still imperfectly known, still beyond us as well as within and through us, still worthy of our reverence and awe as well as our familiar love and even identification.

C. S. Lewis (in McFague 1982, 203 n. 27) provides an illustration of the fact that the only way to avoid fossilizing metaphors is to use many metaphors that jostle against one another. If a woman had never seen ships on the ocean, from metaphors like "sea-stallions," "wave-riders," and "ocean-trains" she could get an imperfect but useful concept of ships at sea—as long as she kept all these metaphors together in her mind. But if she were to decide that only the metaphor "ocean-trains" were acceptable and then proceeded to use exclusively that one metaphor, she might eventually wind up insisting on ocean-trains as literal entities about which there could be no further discussion. It is precisely in that kind of irrational bog that Christianity has bemired itself through exclusively androcentric and controlling God-language.

Jeffrey [1992]; E. A. Johnson [1992]; Lewis [1962]; McFague [1982; 1987]; Newsom/Ringe [1992]; Preminger [1974]; Soskice [1985]

VIRGINIA RAMEY MOLLENKOTT

Metaphysics Contemporary metaphysics is the attempt to answer the question, "What must be the case for the world to be structured as we experience it?" In an earlier age, the question would have been phrased, "What must be the case for the world to be as it is?" The physical sciences developed to describe the way the world is, and metaphysics was the attempt to answer just why such physical structures described the world. "Metaphysics" literally went "beyond physics."

The shift in the contemporary way of phrasing the question reflects shifts in epistemology, or the study of how it is we know what we know. A *"postmodern" world no longer has great confidence that we can give accurate descriptions of the world that correspond exactly with the way the world is in itself. Rather, how we know is conditioned by our physiology and by our sociocultural location. What we call knowledge is an interpretation of experience. This replaces the "correspondence" theory of truth that long held sway in Western thought.

Given these shifts in knowledge, to attempt to reason about the ultimate structure of the universe and why the universe is so structured is considered philosophically tenuous. Feminists have been particularly wary of metaphysical theories, since too often they have been projections of sociological male privilege into theories of the ultimate structure of the universe.

Nonetheless, the contemporary reframing of the question of metaphysics is of value. It calls attention to the human experience that is at the heart of the metaphysical question. Also, the question draws us into consideration of existence beyond our human selves, even while entry into the question must be acknowledged to be located precisely in and through our histories. The generality of metaphysics calls attention to the particularity of the perspectives within which the metaphysical questions arise. Finally, the logical rigor required in metaphysics is balanced by the requirement that its theories be adequate and applicable to experience. Such a methodology facilitates cogency and coherence in the more particular tasks such as *ethics, social theory, and gender analysis that are important in feminist thought.

Daly [1984]; Davaney [1981]; Frankenberry [1987]; McFague [1993]

MARJORIE HEWITT SUCHOCKI

Methodologies Methodologies are the principles through which theology is crafted. As tools for construction, methodologies provide both a framework of understanding and a way to provide internal coherence for the credibility of theology. The history of theologies is composed of widely variant methodologies, with genuine disagreement and conflict around how scripture is to be interpreted, what counts as *tradition, how experience is conceived, and how theology itself interprets, guides, or governs Christian life.

Common Basepoints. Feminist theological methodologies can be said to share five common basepoints. First, the general method of feminist theologies might be termed a *pragmatic critical theory.* A critical theory is a theory that is historically and socially contextual. It does not attempt to make universal arguments or constructs that will hold for all times and places. A critical theory arises in a specific situation and, using the symbols, images, and concepts involved in that situation, attempts to move against distortion and dysfunction to shape new forms of flourishing. Second, the material norm of theology is around emancipatory transformation: *freedom from *suffering and into flourishing. This norm might be called "saving work," the saving of all the earth from various forms of *sin and destruction and for human and planetary flourishing.

Third, feminist methodologies share strategies of *ideology critique, *deconstruction, and hermeneutics of suspicion to uncover distortions in the relations of knowledge, interest, and *power. A distinct contribution of feminist methodologies has been the use of gender analysis to demonstrate the oppositional construction of man and woman and the use of such oppositional thinking to distort natural, personal, and social relations. This gender critique has been applied to scripture and its interpretation, to theological texts, to institutional structures, and to cultural representations. Fourth, feminist methodologies are prospective; they seek imaginatively to envision new possibilities to speak of God, human life, the earth, etc. Methodologies that self-consciously claim the reconstructive aspect of Christian theology are used to anticipate future possibilities of flourishing.

Fifth, feminist methodologies combine *ethics and epistemology, insisting that the good and the true must be connected. Against modern methodologies that have separated ethics from epistemology, feminist methodologies bring ethics into the center of feminist theology. Interpretation of scripture, reconstruction of *doctrine, and theological attention to cultural concerns place ethical questions at the very heart of knowing God and world.

Important Debates. Though feminist methodologies share some common basepoints, there are also important debates about certain topics in methodologies. One topic of debate is around the theme of *difference. Can simple gender analysis represent all difference? Is *sexism the foundation of all other forms of *oppression? Or do we have to develop sophisticated methodologies that reveal the interstructuring of oppressions of *race, sex, class, and sexual orientation? The "depth" and "radicality" of difference are topics of debate in feminist methodologies.

A second topic of contestation in feminist methodologies has to do with the possibility of making normative claims in theologies. On one side of the debate are "idealists," who argue that there is and must be one true form of Christianity from which one can make normative claims. On the other side of the debate are the "social constructionists," who argue that the very definition of Christianity is whatever persons say it is and that norms occur only because persons give them *authority. As in any such debate, many feminists prefer to try to develop a mediating position that seeks some kind of contextual normativity.

Feminist methodologies have made a substantial contribution to theological reflection in terms of the emphasis on contextuality, the importance of gender analysis, and the possibility for creative transformation of Christian symbols.

Chopp [1989]; Fulkerson [1994]

REBECCA S. CHOPP

Midrash In its classical sense, *Midrash,* which has as its root the Hebrew word *darash,* meaning "to seek out," refers to a body of rabbinic literature made up of anthologies of biblical exegesis and homilies dating from the tannaitic period (70–200 C.E.) through to the Middle Ages. The most well known anthology of midrashim is *Midrash Rabbah,* which provides a running midrashic commentary to the five books of the Torah, as well as to the "five scrolls" (Esther, Ruth, Lamentations, Ecclesiastes, and Song of Songs).

Midrash uses allegory and additional narrative to fill in the gaps left by an often terse biblical text. Midrash is creative and imaginative. It can take the form of artwork, dance, music, as well as poetry and prose. Midrash is subversive as it winds its way between and around stern, stark, seemingly stagnant texts. As Judith Plaskow has stated, "Jews have traditionally used midrash to broaden or alter the meaning of texts" (in Davidman/Tenenbaum, 80). Midrash assumes that the black letters of scripture as well as the white spaces between them are holy; that the explicitly stated as well as that which can be inferred from the Bible can be manifestations of God's word. Midrash is a kind of scriptural archaeology, bidding us not to stop at surface appearances but to dig down deeply into the text to uncover hidden riches. Therefore midrash is a valuable tool for feminists, because it allows for, indeed calls for, the exploration of the ignored, buried, forgotten aspects of the Bible—which, of course, are the very places where women's *experiences, women's perspectives, women's voices can be found.

A midrash can be written in response to glaring omissions in the biblical text. For example: how did Lot's daughters feel when their father offered them to the mob of men that surrounded their house? Where was Sarah while Abraham was taking Isaac to the top of Mount Moriah to sacrifice him? What did Jephthah's daughter do during those two months before she had to return home to be sacrificed at her father's hand? These white spaces provide the canvas on which to paint midrashim. To attempt to answer these kinds of questions is to create a midrash. It is important to remember that within the realm of midrash there is no single truth; the text and life itself are seen as a prism of truths, many different colors converging in those white spaces.

Midrashim can also be based on subtleties in the text: a strange use of a word or phrase, a misspelling, a grammatical inconsistency, a pun, a language pattern discerned. For example, Delores Williams, in reading the story of Hagar and Sarah through the lens of womanist theology, points out that the verb used to describe Sarai's treatment of Hagar is the same verb (*'nh*) used to describe how the Egyptians treated the Israelites when they were enslaved (19). What does this mean? What is the text telling us about *oppression, about being an oppressor? These are the kinds of insights and questions on which midrash draws.

Finally, because midrash frees us from the constraints of logic and linear time, it can take a total flight of fancy. It can take us on a journey through uncharted ground by considering, for example, how a female deity would have tested Abraham, or by imagining, as Judith Plaskow did, what a conversation between Eve and Lilith would be like (in

Ruether, 341). The possibilities are endless.

The creation of modern midrashim is a way to engage, protest, and wrestle with problematic texts through the presentation of alternative readings. Midrash is tied to the text by a thread from which a new tapestry can be woven. It is fluid. It reminds us that the Bible is, in fact, not "written in stone."

Cohen [1995]; Corre [1975]; *Encyclopaedia Judaica*, 1971, 11:1507–23; Plaskow, in Ruether [1974]; Plaskow, in Davidman/Tenenbaum [1994]; Trible [1978; 1984]; Williams [1993a]

DONNA BERMAN

Ministry A theology of feminist ministry distinguishes itself in many ways through opposition to patriarchal *ordination. Whereas traditional ministry has been described in terms of authoritative leadership and action done for or on behalf of the community, feminist ministry takes a less hierarchical viewpoint. Traditionally, the minister is charged to administer the church, preach the word, pray, offer sacrifice, administer *sacraments, visit the sick and shut-ins, and visit from house to house. In "high church settings" the minister is called by God to act as God's special representative on earth. The clergy are set apart and given higher standards to live by, often leading to expectations of perfection and a voluntary giving up of worldly pleasures so as to be good role models for the laity.

Feminist Ministry. In the broadest sense, ministry is service (Gk **diakonia*). Service can be translated into a feminist understanding of giving: giving of oneself, one's gifts, money, talents, and service. Ministry is not limited by age; young children can minister through smiles and hugs, the very old through forms of touch and wisdom. Feminist *diakonia* is preferably given from abundance rather than scarcity. It neither requires **kenōsis* nor particularly values *martyrdom in the patriarchal sense of being tortured or killed for one's beliefs. It does invite one to "stand firm in the *faith" in the sense of giving radical witness to persons and voices previously made invisible or unheard: to speak on behalf of women and children, the poor and marginalized, through work against *racism, *sexism, heterosexist privilege, *classism, *ageism, or the cult of the able-bodied.

Feminism knows and honors the fact that those called to the fullest forms of witnessing opposition to *patriarchy, who must resolutely stand against the "malestream," whether male or female, may undergo deep *suffering. Many such women and men have been silenced for their viewpoints in North America. In other countries, feminists and other liberation *theologians face death, because traditionally patriarchy kills those it fears will upset the structures of the status quo.

Ministerial Support. Feminists' ministry has a great concern for those who are overgiving, those who become "burned out." Many clergywomen leave parish ministry after serving a number of years. They find themselves overused or abused through sexist practices wherein no amount of giving is enough and there is no opportunity for refreshment or replenishment, or because they are geographically isolated from like-minded persons. They may quit the professional ministry altogether, though more often they may get specialized training to work in other settings (i.e., hospitals, nursing homes, hospice ministry, college chaplaincies, pastoral counseling centers) where patriarchal structures have less *power to control. This may be because those most in need of *care are least likely to impose sexist requirements on the caregiver.

Various Forms of Ministries. Pastoral ministry has been described as *healing, reconciling, sustaining, and guiding persons through the faith. Feminist ministry goes beyond these actions to include also a variety of forms of *ecumenical work, *justice work, coalitions, as well as working in *battered women's shelters, in *AIDS ministries, in building houses with Habitat for Humanity, etc. A minister is one who serves on behalf of the *community (which may be church, synagogue, or another religious faith community, such as Women-Church, or a subgroup such as Dignity, the Reconciling Church Movement, More Light Churches, etc.). She or he serves in the name of all that is life-giving and sacred. Traditional ministers more often see themselves as *called by God to represent God and God's teachings to the community. Women scholars of religion find themselves called to be scribes for the community of the marginalized, helping them through the cycles of experience, action, and reflection in order to relate their theologies to the academy in terms and categories understood by academicians. In general, feminist theologies have said that certain individuals may be called to be set apart for full-time or professional ministry on behalf of the community in the name of the sacred, at the same time honoring the *priesthood of all believers in whatever forms of service that may take.

The Household of Faith. Ministry is best done in *partnership or community rather than in isolation because of the desperate needs of people and the earth. Everywhere one turns there is reconciliation to be made, bodily and emotional wounds to be healed, *relationships to be righted, wrongs to be amended, and simple acknowledgment to be made. Ministry is impure or untrue if done to garner personal gain or even numerical advances in terms of growth of one's community of faith. If others chose to join in service because of the minister's or community's modeling, then this is a blessing but it is never a purpose. No one religious group, denomination, *religion, or sect is deemed more necessary for the work of the Spirit than any other.

Ministry is *preaching, educating, healing, sustaining, reconciling, justice work. It is most honored by the feminist community when it challenges the status quo and helps bring about ancient and new visions of *equality, mutuality, and a shared, resourceful world. Strife is soothed through mediation, bodies are protected, and the poor are fed and uplifted. All varieties of feminist theologies, especially womanist, *mujerista,* Asian, native and indigenous, and lesbian theologies and their critiques of dominant white women's theology, must be mainstreamed. Hands-on training, case studies, Clinical Pastoral Education–like adaptations, internships, along with current growing globalization and local ministry concerns must be primary in focus. No longer can the *hierarchy of systematic over practical theology continue, since most women and men who obtain a patriarchal seminary education complain that they are not equipped for a ministry of *survival, much less of vision.

Ackermann, *Journal of Theology for Southern Africa* [1985]; Finson [1985]; Mud Flower Collective [1985]; Russell, *Ministerial Formation* [1991]; Swidler/Conn [1985]

GAIL LYNN UNTERBERGER

Minjung *Minjung* is a Korean word. It is a combination of two Chinese characters, *min,* translated as "people," and *jung,* "the mass." These two letters, *minjung,* can be translated as "the mass of people." Social scientists define *minjung* as economically exploited people, but *minjung* theology uses the term more broadly. *Minjung* theology developed a sociopolitical biography of Korean Christians in the midst of the Korean people's struggle for their just and basic rights during the 1970s. In *minjung* theology, theologians seek to preserve the subjecthood of the *minjung* through their own definition of themselves, which is a relational definition, particularly in terms of *power. Therefore the *minjung* perceive themselves as powerless and oppressed for various reasons: class, status, *race, *culture, *religion, etc.

Korean feminist theologians call Korean oppressed women the *minjung* of *minjung*. There are two categories of oppressed women in Korea. In the first category are "*minjung* women," those doubly oppressed as *minjung* and women under poor political, economic, and social conditions. In the other category are "women *minjung*," those discriminated against under the power of male *domination because they are women. Both *minjung* women and women *minjung* live in the full feeling of **han*, which is a collective experience of *oppression among the *minjung* of Korea. As Suh Nam-Dong observes, "Under *Confucianism's strict imposition of discrimination against women, the existence of women was han itself" (CCA, 58). However, throughout history Korean women have untangled their complex webs of *han* through their *survival wisdom, named *han-pu-ri*, expressed through songs, dances, and rituals (Chung, in Fabella/Park).

Chung [1990]; Commission on Theological Concerns of the CCA [1981]; Fabella/Park [1989]; Suh [1991]

SOOK JA CHUNG and SUN AI LEE PARK

Misogyny The literal meaning of *misogyny* is the hatred of women. It further denotes the belief that women are not only morally and intellectually inferior to men but also the source of the *evil in the world. Interestingly, there is no parallel term for the hatred of men. Misogyny has roots not only in the oldest Western traditions but in the oldest Eastern traditions. For example, *Confucianism has a strong *tradition of misogyny, regarding woman as promoters of evil, the cause of disorder, and inferior to man by nature. In the Confucian view of women, to be a woman means to submit. Due to this misogyny, women have been excluded from learning and producing knowledge in Confucian *culture.

By the dictum that a woman is a misbegotten male, Aristotle has played a major role in developing misogyny in Western thought, regarding males as normative human beings. Theologians of the Christian tradition have also been guilty of misogyny. For instance, Thomas Aquinas regarded woman as a defective male, following Aristotle's biology. His views have influenced the Roman Catholic Church's exclusion of women from the priesthood.

Feminist theologies have criticized the anti-body *dualism of dominant Christianity and further claimed that this false dualism has sustained misogyny. Male–female and spirit–body dualisms are predicated on the view that maleness is superior, with the rejection of the *body. In this sense, hatred of *sexuality and hatred of women are identified. Misogyny often takes on mystified forms, such as the praise of the virginal woman, romanticization of the unassertive woman, or indirect manipulation of women's actions. Misogyny runs through the Christian tradition and society, in which woman's degradation and subordination are made a necessity. Only a feminist analysis can clarify misogyny of various forms in religion and society. When misogyny disappears, gender *justice will be realized.

Clark/Richardson [1977]; Harrison [1985]; Park [1994]; Ruether [1975]

KANG NAM-SOON

Mission Mission is carrying out God's work among people who are struggling to live with dignity and wholeness and in harmony with nature. It has been understood as the sending of missionaries to make disciples according to the so-called Great Commission (Matt. 28:16–20). A church-centered understanding of mission as planting churches and saving souls has been criticized as reinforcing the cultural supremacy of the West and is closely intertwined with colonial expansion. In twentieth-century ecumenical theology there has been a shift to understand mission as an attribute and activity of a Trinitarian God. Participation in God's saving activity, or *missio Dei*, is understood as witness to God's love toward all people and work for the promise of God's reign.

A feminist understanding of the mission of God debunks the triumphant and Eurocentric understanding of Christianity, challenges the male bureaucratic organization of mission agencies, and demystifies the conservative agenda of right-wing televangelists. Mission is to proclaim the good news that God affirms life over death and that God acts among the poor, the majority of whom are women who are victimized in the globalization of the market economy and left out in decision-making processes. Mission is forming *partnership, building bridges and coalitions, and strengthening grassroots movements to struggle for life and work for *justice for all people.

The mission of God challenges the churches to be contextualized in theological thinking, ways of worship, and *community life. To equip the whole people of God for mission, male-dominated religious structures must be challenged and women must be *empowered through leadership training. In our multiracial and multireligious world, people of other faiths must not be treated as missiological objects but as partners in understanding the fullness of God and building *solidarity across different *faith *traditions, for the welfare of the whole of humanity and the planet.

Hill [1984]; Hoekendijk, *IRM* [1952]; Kwok [1992]; Larsson [1991]

KWOK PUI-LAN

Monotheism Monotheism is that about the western theological tradition to which feminist critique at its most profound has directed attention. This is true of many schools of feminist religious thought: post-structuralist, process, *"Goddess," *post-Christian, and indeed Christian feminist.

"God" in Christian tradition (as Hebraic gospel met Greek thought) has been conceptualized as transcendent, omnipotent and, for example most interestingly, as having "aseity" (completion within "himself"). This appears to be a masculinist projection; though not necessarily one which magnifies man, who may rather designate God in terms of his ideals while denigrating himself, as the great atheists of the modern era, Feuerbach, Marx, Nietzsche (following Hegel) and Freud adduced. Monotheism has its social import, so feminists working in biblical studies and in theology have contended, as man has in turn understood himself as "god," construing woman as "other" to himself, within what is a dipolar and oppositional ordering of reality. Feminist thinkers thus point to monotheism as the ideological legitimation of a hierarchical and masculinist society.

By contrast feminist thought has stood for heterogeneity. Feminists promote horizontal (not vertical) relations of equality. Some feminist thinkers look to an envisaging of the divine as female; though this may be to deny the existence of a discrete entity, "God," rather than having a similar, now female, divinity. For others, God is to be understood as spirit and non-gendered. Spirituality becomes a process of self-realization, in which that which is God is found within relations of mutual interchange. This presupposes a different social ordering.

It is a matter for debate as to whether women must necessarily have a female transcendental if women are to come to themselves; or whether humanity as a whole may move beyond a legitimization of *patriarchy through a masculinist projection of the divine.

Gross, *JFSR* [1986]; Hampson [1995]; Irigaray, in Whitford [1991]; Kristeva [1977]; Plaskow [1990]; Plaskow/Christ [1989]

DAPHNE HAMPSON

Mothers/Motherhood The prevailing cultural ethos in the United States romanticizes motherhood at the same time that it devalues it. Feminist analysis has consistently evaluated social, economic, religious, and political systems by the effects they have on women, including mothers. Critics of feminism, however, claim that feminist thought itself devalues motherhood by urging women to forsake *family in exchange for careers. While early feminist theory was vulnerable to this charge, feminist and womanist theologians have recently identified the experience of motherhood as a significant source for theological reflection. Because feminist theology draws from women's *experience, it rightly focuses on the common, albeit not universal, experience of motherhood. Alongside celebrating women's ability to give birth, nurture, and care for children, feminist theology is critical of many myths of motherhood.

The Romanticization of Motherhood. Feminism understands that women's ability to give birth, nurture, and take care of children *can* be used as a means to oppress women. Although motherhood is not in itself oppressive, its romanticization diminishes the value of women's vocation beyond motherhood and devalues women who are not mothers. Furthermore, the devaluation of motherhood itself often accompanies its romanticization. Those who hail motherhood as the highest calling for women often promote structures for the family, workplace, and legal system that are detrimental to mothers and children.

In the 1950s the romanticization of motherhood was reflected in popular television shows such as *Father Knows Best* and *The Donna Reed Show*. Here, in the "ideal" family, fathers had careers while mothers were full-time homemakers, an ideal that sharply divided private home life from public work life. The recent political and religious call to return to "family values" supports this separation of private and public spheres and the relegation of women's vocation to the home. The romanticized ideal of mother as full-time homemaker, however, applies only to women with economic security. While upper-middle-class mothers are criticized for pursuing careers, "welfare mothers" are criticized for not seeking employment. Arguing against any single ideal imposed on women, feminist and womanist visions of motherhood support mothers from all economic, cultural, and social settings, addressing the needs of single and married mothers, poor mothers, and mothers with careers.

The Consignment of All Women to Motherhood. Feminism celebrates women's ability to conceive, bear, and nurture children without making it a requirement for achieving true "womanhood." Women without children have their own valid calling and are not required to choose motherhood to fulfill their vocation as women. Women's vocation is not defined biologically (because we can conceive, bear, and nurture children, we *must* become mothers). Furthermore, because God calls each woman to tasks that fit her gifts, there are a variety of ways to fulfill one's vocation as mother: adoption provides an equally valid way to become a mother to giving birth; lesbians are as capable of becoming good mothers as heterosexuals; single mothers can provide a loving home as well as married mothers; and so forth.

Mothers at Home. The *doctrine of vocation, interpreted from a feminist perspective, eliminates the tension between mothers who choose to be full-time homemakers and mothers who have careers. The expectation that mothers must abandon their careers and the expectation that mothers must have careers are equally oppressive. Whether mothers choose careers or full-time homemaking, feminist theory promotes the well-being of women and children at home by advocating peaceful means of childrearing, curtailing domestic *violence, and addressing the effects of *poverty on families.

Mothers in the Workplace. The workplace has long been structured for workers without children or for workers whose wives are full-time homemakers. The forty-hour-per-week, fifty-weeks-per-year work schedule fails to address the needs of most families. Home life, in contrast, is so highly privatized that domestic responsibilities, including child care, remain the sole *responsibility of parents, especially mothers. Mothers, in fact, often labor under a "double workday," managing one day's labor at work and another day's labor at home. Feminists contend that when motherhood and children are valued, child care becomes society's responsibility, not in place of parents but in support of them. Maternity leave, paternity leave, on-site day care, job sharing, and flexible hours stand among those benefits that support mothers in the workplace.

Best Interest of Children. In the legal system the rights of adults often take priority over the best interest of children. Some children are removed from loving foster or adoptive homes and returned to biological parents they have never known or who have previously abused them. Feminists challenge the *patriarchal idea that children are property and fight against the physical, psychological, and sexual abuse of children worldwide.

Motherhood of God. In addition to focusing on women's experience of motherhood, feminist theology finds biblical and theological warrant for addressing God as "Mother." The Old Testament describes God as being in labor (Isa. 42:14), giving birth (Deut. 32:18), and offering motherly care (Isa. 63:13; Jer. 31:20). The New Testament likens Jesus to a mother hen (Matt. 23:37; Luke 13:34) and describes God parabolically as a woman looking for a lost coin (Luke 15:8–10). Feminists know that the mystery of God cannot be captured by any one image such as "father." Even traditional theologies argue that reducing God to a human understanding of fatherhood is idolatrous. Feminist theologians avoid such *idolatry by using multiple images for God, including the image of God as mother.

Atkinson [1991]; Carr/Schüssler Fiorenza [1989]; Collins [1991]; Miller-McLemore [1994]; Rich [1986]; Williams [1993a]

NANCY J. DUFF

Mystics/Interior Journeys

The word *mystic,* used to mean a person who has experienced a union with God, was first defined in the seventeenth century in the context of Christian debates about rational and affective forms of religiosity. In the modern period, the term has been progressively refined and redefined, especially by scholars who have thrust the definition far back into previous historical periods and undertaken revisionist historical studies. Twentieth-century scholars of "mysticism," notably Evelyn Underhill at the beginning of the century and Bernard McGinn at the end, have focused on a systematic, structured definition of mysticism and have, in the process, come up with an overwhelmingly male list of Christian *mystics. Women, even such important figures as Teresa of Avila, appear in Underhill's study almost as an exception. Obviously, Underhill was not much interested in women's experience.

In contrast, McGinn has benefited from recent study of medieval women, the work of scholars who have unearthed, edited, translated, and analyzed little-known or even unknown religious texts by women. But McGinn also admits the exclusion of some prominent female figures such as Elisabeth of Schönau and has qualms about other, even more famous ones, such as Hildegard of Bingen, because their experience seems more "visionary" than strictly "mystical" according to his definition. Even though McGinn, unlike Underhill, is largely sympathetic to women's potential for mystical union and allows for cultural differences between the *experiences of women and men, he once again creates a set of categories according to which women's experiences are at a disadvantage.

This *tradition of scholarly definition tends to underestimate the complexity of women's *relationships with a *patriarchal deity. In fact, especially in the Christian tradition, women who might be characterized as mystics most often called themselves by other terms. Hildegard of Bingen called herself a "prophet,"

Catherine of Siena was known to her contemporaries as an "apostle," Joan of Arc was a "messenger." Most often, though, women who have experienced special closeness to the Divine were thought of, by themselves and others, as "illuminated ones" or visionaries.

What these women share is the experience of an interior journey that leads to God. The first steps of this journey often begin from the outside, with a *call or a divine interruption of normal life, rather than from an inward and progressive spiritual discipline. Often this journey is expressed in love language, ending in a passionate embrace; this was characteristic of Beguine love mysticism in northern Europe in the Middle Ages. Nor was such an interior journey always private and exclusive: as Phyllis Mack has shown, Quaker women of early modern England were leaders in a prophetic movement of interiority that was allied to sweeping exterior social and political changes.

Feminist scholarship has been crucial in forging new understandings of women's experiences of union with the Divine in two ways: by abandoning restrictive definitions that tend to exclude women, and by taking women's lives seriously. Caroline Walker Bynum has called attention to such everyday realities as the socially constructed role of food in women's spiritual experiences. Ulrike Wiethaus has suggested that women's mystical experiences make up distinct maps of flesh and light, which we are just beginning to read. Ongoing feminist scholarship by historians, literary scholars, philosophers, and students of religion continue to reevaluate the history of women mystics. This work is related to currents in contemporary women's spirituality. The goal is a better reading of the maps with which women have undertaken the interior journey to, in a paraphrase of Ntozake Shange, find god in ourselves and love her fiercely.

Bynum [1987]; Mack [1992]; McGinn [1991]; Wiethaus [1993]

E. ANN MATTER

Mystics, Medieval A mystic is a person who, through divine *grace, directly experiences God, often in ecstatic states. The European Middle Ages (ca. 500–1500) was endowed with many such unusual individuals, whose piety culminated in the direct transcendent knowledge of God. Formerly, scholars of medieval mysticism tended to classify types of mystical experience, which resulted in valorizing great male intellectuals such as Augustine, Bernard of Clairvaux, and Meister Eckhart while denigrating female mystics' highly emotional experience as neurotic and hysterical. This, for example, was Margery Kempe's fate until Clarissa W. Atkinson reclaimed her from the margins in *Mystic and Pilgrim: The Book and the World of Margery Kempe* (1983).

Intensive feminist scholarship since the late 1970s has validated medieval women's mystical experience by accepting its striking physicality. Caroline Walker Bynum launched the revision with studies of thirteenth-century German nuns whose mysticism differs from yet complements the lives of male clerics. Her seminal work on religious women and food practices, *Holy Feast and Holy Fast: The Religious Significance of Food to Medieval Women* (1987), argues that holy women sought positive meaning in their lives by fusing themselves with Christ through fasting. A different interpretation by Rudolph Bell in *Holy Anorexia* (1985) posits that medieval female *asceticism was an often tragic struggle for *autonomy against a repressive society. Feminist scholarship today tends to divide over this positive or negative assessment of female mystical experience, although John Coakley, in his introduction to *Creative Women in Medieval and Early Modern Italy: A Religious and Artistic Renaissance* (1994), retains both, suggesting that the contrasting perspectives are useful for viewing religious women within their society.

Feminist scholarship has revealed a high proportion and rich variety of women mystics in the later Middle Ages.

Mystical women included professed and lay, married and single, young and old, rich and poor. Among their number was the internationally famous German Benedictine abbess Hildegard of Bingen. Until her death in 1179, she presided over two well-endowed convents in the Rhineland and passed God's message to the world through learned theological treatises, musical compositions, illuminated manuscripts, and poetry. Born two years before Hildegard, in the Low Countries, Marie d'Oignies was married at fourteen but talked her husband into living a chaste and simple life nursing lepers; she later entered a Beguine community seeking greater austerity. Her vita describes severe penances, self-inflicted wounds, but also visions of extraordinary sweetness, such as cradling the infant Jesus to her breast. Catherine of Siena was born a dyer's daughter in mid-fourteenth-century Italy. Against her family's wishes she became a Dominican tertiary, living a life of austerity coupled with social action that made her a public and controversial figure. Her mystical experience was crowned with the gift of the stigmata. In contrast, a late-fourteenth-century English mystic, Julian of Norwich, lived quietly in great simplicity as an anchoress, responding to a single life-changing vision. Such women have been discovered, reanimated, and reinterpreted by feminist scholars through source translations and fresh examination.

Among important unresolved issues are how (or, indeed, if) gender differentiates mystical experience; how to disentangle women's voices from those of their male biographers; and why the climate for religious women became chilly at the close of the Middle Ages.

Atkinson [1983]; Bell [1985]; Bynum [1991]; Matter/Coakley [1994]; Nichols/Shank [1984–87]; Petroff [1986; 1994]

PENELOPE D. JOHNSON

Mythologies Built out of myths, mythologies are collections of stories that explain the origin and meaning of the world of human *experience. In modern usage, a "myth" can mean a "lie"; a mythology would be a collection of fictitious stories. A deeper understanding looks beyond a level of rationality to the eternal truths that myths express. It may be correct to say that both the Greek myth of Pandora's box and the Jewish and Christian myth of the *Fall of Adam and Eve are "mere myths," that is, that they never really happened. But these myths admit a reality that modern *culture refuses to see: that human life is a painful, and terminal, condition. The power of myth lies in insight into the human condition rather than in verifiable fact.

Mythologies, then, express the beliefs by which a people live. Among the mythologies of the modern Western world are stories about the knowledge of medical science, the cleansing and redeeming power of *violence, the innate superiority of some racial groups (and one gender) over others. These are *patriarchal myths on which much of modern life is built.

In contrast, some mythologies contain stories that explain the world through the experience of women or through the *power of the feminine. Many of these myths are as ancient as the first recorded human civilizations in Mesopotamia and Egypt; others are modern stories, retold or invented by modern women. Not all woman-based mythologies have a feminist consciousness: Robert Graves's famous study of the "White Goddess" has the ultimate purpose of reaffirming a male-dominant power structure. But feminists have made it a point to reclaim the power of women's mythic truth. Charlene Spretnak has articulated a feminist vision of ancient Greek mythology, while Anne Cameron has shared the powerful women-centered *creation stories of the native peoples of Vancouver Island. These visions are powerful for many women who have found traditional patriarchal mythologies hopelessly alienating and destructive and who long for mythology in the key of our own songs.

Cameron [1981]; Graves [1948/1966]; Spretnak [1992]; Wolkstein/Kramer [1983]

E. ANN MATTER

Naming Naming is the *power of giving identification labels to someone or to something. In many cultures, children are given names by their *mothers. The naming ceremony in the African cultures, described in *The Will to Arise*, is a ritual of community joy and celebration (Oduyoye/Kanyoro, 40–53). Yet even in such celebration there is a transparent distinction between the naming of male children and that of female children.

In the Hebrew Bible, naming is understood as a means of power over another person or object. In the *creation stories it is said that God gave Adam the task to name the living creatures and the woman. The indication that Adam named Eve in the Bible has been used to argue that men have superiority over women, thus underscoring the issue of the power of naming. The dilemma of women reading the Bible is often made louder by the numerous nameless women appearing in the text. Women scholars are attempting to reinterpret naming texts and to retrieve some of the names of women. For instance, Phyllis Trible (95, 133) claims that *domination in naming is reflected only in Gen. 3:20 and not in 2:23; and Elisabeth Schüssler Fiorenza has retrieved the name Justa for the Canaanite woman in Matt. 15:21–29 (103–4).

In society, women have not usually had the possibility of participation in naming the issues of the world; hence the obnoxious invisibility of women in historical records, written or even oral. In recent history, women have used the term *naming* to refer to the necessity to identify those areas that need women's worldview and the designing of ways for women to become part and parcel of the shaping of the world agenda.

In this process, feminist historians are at work researching women's history, publishing biographies of women, republishing books and articles by women that have not been allowed to have an impact on the world. Women theologians are giving new interpretations to old issues through their lenses as women. The whole process is part of women's participation in renaming themselves and the reality of the world.

Metzger/Coogan [1993]; Oduyoye/Kanyoro [1992]; Schüssler Fiorenza [1984/1995]; Trible [1978]

MUSIMBI R. A. KANYORO

Nationalism Among many meanings, nationalism refers to national sentiment, to the historical process of nation building, and to the *ideology of the nation-state. Individuals who regard themselves as belonging to a nation identify with a political system and state apparatus. An objective basis for this identity may include a common origin, language, and history and shared values, such as religion and cultural *traditions. National identities are also constructed in opposition to what is defined as "foreign." In this case, pursuing the national interest above all else often means internal intolerance of ethnic minorities or rejection of international political and religious movements.

As a historical process, nationalism is a modern phenomenon linked to the construction of nation-states in Europe in the eighteenth and nineteenth centuries and closely related to colonialism. The constitution of a nation-state involves the concept of citizenship. Critical feminist theories discuss whether it is a viable proposition to demand female citizenship in acknowledgment of the historical process that excluded women (besides the poor and nonwhites) from that status. Separate categories exist de facto: all citizens are said to be equal, but men and women do not effectively enjoy the same rights.

As the ideology of the nation-state, nationalism can be considered a secular religion. The good of the nation, elevated above all else, requires sacrifices just as the gods do. Like them, the nation offers protection and happiness in exchange. A national *mythology is created, with public rituals, commemorations, and symbols.

Historically, nationalist ideology has often gone hand in hand with the expression of religious belief. When the struggle for independence commingles with the defense of religious *freedom, expansionism tends to take the form of a "crusade." However, the appeal to ethnic or national allegiance has had ambiguous historical effects. Nationalism that underpins *imperialism, war, *racism, and intolerance can also be an engine of revolt against foreign *domination and pursuit of self-determination.

Comblin [1979]; Ruether/Ruether [1989]; Turner/Ferguson [1994]

MARIA JOSÉ F. ROSADO NUNES

Natural Law As a method of ethics, natural law can be used metaethically to provide a base for moral discernment or normatively to prescribe duties. As a political theory it can be used either to challenge or to justify *oppression. These variable functions of natural law depend on operative discourses about human nature and law.

Thomas Aquinas understood humans to be inherently social, embodied, dynamic, intelligent, and attracted to their true good. Law referred to dynamic movement toward an end. In his hands natural law provided metaethical judgments about the goods necessary for human flourishing. It could be used to condemn social arrangements that failed to promote human well-being. In contrast, physicalist versions of natural law equate nature with biology and understand law as obligation. It then proscribes actions deemed unnatural and legitimizes the status quo.

Feminists have sought to redefine nature in ways that do not dichotomize biology and reason from history and that avoid reifying historical particularities into ontological truths. This effort leads poststructuralist feminists to deny any reality to human nature and to regard any version of natural law as inevitably oppressive. *Socialist and *Marxist feminists also reject the idea that humans have a nature, yet many smuggle in claims about humans in order to identify and condemn what inhibits their flourishing. Radical feminists think maleness and femaleness reside in nature but lack the means to prevent ascribing conditioned habits to inherent nature.

Feminists and womanists offer correctives to natural law as a method of *ethics. While engaged in struggles to free themselves and others from external and internal bondage, they have generated hypotheses about what harms humans and what is necessary for their well-being. These working hypotheses are tested in *praxis by how well they explain the oppressed's collusion with and resistance to oppression, avoid regarding people as inherent victims or oppressors, help people distinguish internalized oppression from more human ways of being, expose false universalizing and denial of *difference, and promote universal solidarity. By using these hypotheses to inform their praxis, women are discovering if in fact they provide an adequate account of what is good for humans.

Liberatory praxis in communities of resistance and *solidarity, by preceding the formation of ontological claims and then being used to test those claims, can generate a feminist version of natural law capable of futhering human emancipation.

Chopp, *Journal of Religion* [1987]; Kay, *Hypatia* [1994]; Parsons, *Modern Theology* [1988]; Traina [1992]

JUDITH WEBB KAY

New Creation The expression "new creation" derives especially from 2 Cor. 5:17, in which Paul declares, "So if anyone is in Christ, there is a new *creation:

everything old has passed away; see, everything has become new!" (cf. Gal. 6:15). Elsewhere Paul uses other *metaphors to describe the transformation of the one who confesses *faith in Jesus and is baptized. For example, in Romans 6, Paul argues that in *baptism believers "died with Christ" and so ended their enslavement to *sin; they are now enslaved not to sin but to God, or to *righteousness, and they walk "in newness of life" (Romans 6:8). As a second example, in Galatians 3, Paul claims that those baptized into Christ have clothed themselves with Christ: "There is no longer Jew or Greek, there is no longer slave or free, there is no longer male and female; for all of you are one in Christ Jesus" (3:28). These varied metaphors make a single claim: because of Christ's death and *resurrection, the old categories that structured the world have broken down, and God is implementing a radically new order.

In making such a claim, Paul stands in continuity with other biblical authors who asserted that God's work of *redemption is a work of *remaking* or *recreating* the person and/or the world. For example, in Jer. 31:33–34, God declares that the new *covenant with the people will be "written on their hearts." Jeremiah's prophecy of a new covenant that will be different from the covenant at the time of the exodus (31:32) is directly analogous to Paul's language about a new creation, for the exodus was itself viewed by the ancient Israelites as an act of creation—the creation of a people. (Other biblical authors explicitly combined exodus language and creation language in prophesies of God's future acts of redemption; see, for example, Ps. 74:12–14; Isa. 51:9–11; cf. Ps. 89:8–13.) In the exodus, as at creation—and as in God's acts to implement a new creation—God orders and controls the forces that separate persons from God and from one another, or that in other ways oppress and destroy (cf. Rom. 8:18–23; Eph. 2:15–16; Revelation 21).

For women, such ways of envisioning God's ongoing work of redemption are to be critiqued insofar as they identify the old, rejected structures with female ways of thinking and being, so that women must effectively deny their own identities as female in order to participate in the new order. For example, Paul's expression that "there is neither male nor female" is problematic if one assumes that it is the "female" components of the self (i.e., irrationality, enslavement to the passions) which must be erased. (Such a view was probably taken for granted by some early Christians, perhaps even by Paul himself.) On the other hand, the new creation and related images can be interpreted as positive and powerful symbols, offering *liberation from social, anthropological, and cosmic structures that bind persons and prevent them from realizing God's purpose for their lives. Paul's expression that "there is neither male nor female" may legitimately be construed as the promise of a new order, in which gender and other categories are no longer used to subordinate some and elevate others.

Levenson [1988]; Minear [1994]; Ruether [1983/1993]; Russell [1981]

SUSAN R. GARRETT

Objectivity The term *objectivity* implies a relation between a knowing subject, an object known, and an idea or proposition by which the subject formulates or communicates a perception of the object. Objectivity refers to the adequacy or conformity of the subject's formulation to the object that it describes. An idea or argument is said to be not merely "subjective" but "objective" in the truth of its content.

The ideal of objective knowledge was transmitted into the modern period under the influence of Enlightenment ideals of rationality and scientific method. The ideal reflects a confidence that *philosophical and moral truths can be discerned clearly by the human intellect and given logical and universally intelligible expression. This ideal has come under attack by *Marxist and *postmodern epistemologies, which discount the ability of *reason to transcend its historical and cultural settings. They also suggest that claims about "reality" and "the nature of things" usually serve the interests and *power of particular social groups, making objectivity elusive if not impossible.

The problem of objectivity is important for feminism because feminists want both to criticize lack of objectivity in *patriarchal ideas about women and to claim in turn that just and unjust treatment of women can be "really" and "truly" recognized. Many feminist theologians refer to "women's experience" or "the full humanity of women" as touchstones for an objective, not merely subjective or relativist, interpretation of women's situation and needs. For example, rape, domestic *violence, and employment discrimination are said to be wrong in all cases. Especially with the advent of intercultural conversation and critique, feminists do recognize and affirm real *differences in women's *experiences and perspectives. Most feminist theologians, while rejecting *relativism, assume that a historically qualified objectivity is both possible and necessary for effective social criticism and transformation.

Benhabib [1992]; Bernstein [1983]; Grimshaw [1986]; Nussbaum, in Nussbaum/Sen [1993]

LISA SOWLE CAHILL

Oppression Oppression is not a traditional analytical category in theology. Yet the biblical meaning of the word has been emphasized by *liberation and feminist theologians to describe the social dimension of *sin. Oppression is understood as a social system that denies persons room to breathe and live as human beings (Isa. 49:19–20; Russell). The biblical understanding of oppression as a denial of God's *justice is underlined in such texts as Isa. 61:1–2a and Luke 4:18–19. In contemporary theologies oppression is named as *classism, *racism, *sexism, *heterosexism, etc.

Oppression is also not a traditional analytical category in sociology. However, the sociological concepts of *domination and exploitation both relate meaningfully to the notion of oppression. In *Economy and Society*, Max Weber analyzes domination as a form of power, defined as the possibility of imposing one's will on the conduct of others (Roth/Wittich 1968 ed.). His typology of domination (traditional, legal/rational, and charismatic) is based on the origins of the *power wielded by those who rule. Patriarchs, bureaucracies, and charismatic leaders exercise domination in different ways, but all invoke power, respect, and prestige to secure obedience.

Weber distinguishes sheer *violence and force from domination. As a social relation, domination assumes interaction between the individuals or groups who hold power and those who obey. All types of rule entail the pursuit of legitimacy. No domination endures without a minimum of legitimation, but the relationship between domination and force is not so simple. There is a complex dialectic between the threats made by the rulers against those who refuse to be ruled and the consent granted by the dominated group. Abusive power is violent and oppressive even when subtly exercised and camouflaged. Feminist critique of the theory of consent points out that the dominated group has little power to resist consent, as in situations of domestic violence or racism.

The concept of oppression as exploitation is central to *Marxism and has a precise meaning. It refers to surplus-value production and class struggle in capitalist societies. In classical Marxist thought, it is exploitation of labor by capital that, in the last analysis, explains the functioning of social institutions and social reality in its entirety. Social relations are thus hierarchalized, with production relations determining all others. Gender and *race relations are subordinated to class relations.

Feminist critics note the narrowness of the classical Marxist concept of exploitation and the difficulties posed for a thorough understanding of the political domination and economic exploitation undergone by women and nonwhites. They also highlight the limitations of these propositions for an analysis of women's role as political actors and agents of social change.

A discussion of women's social situation in terms of oppression indicates that the logic of women's domination and exploitation is a logic of production and reproduction of their social inferiority. It also points to the historical nature of the forms of this oppression and the possibilities of changing it. Exposing this logic entails a critique of "naturalism." The analysis of gender relations as social relations involves refutation of the idea that anatomical differences create the gender *hierarchy and sexual division of labor. Only social practice can transform into a category of thought a physical fact that, like all physical facts, has no intrinsic significance. Feminists propose a similar analysis of racism. The basis for the inferior social status of nonwhites is not skin color, they argue, but how this phenomenon is treated socially. Logically speaking, therefore, *differences between the sexes, like those between "races," do not preexist the social relationship that creates them.

Women's Oppression and Religion. Feminist historical studies show how certain religions have used their moral authority to legitimate situations of domination and exploitation based on class, gender, and ethnicity. Moreover, religions create their own forms of oppression. The official rhetoric of most religious institutions conceals and reinforces the social logic of women's oppression, attributing it to the eternal order of nature and God's will. The religious principle of female inferiority has been sustained in the face of social change. By devaluing women's bodies and exalting motherhood as a "natural calling" that defines women's very identity, religious discourse and practice help organize and legitimate women's relegation to the home and become violent instruments for controlling women's *sexuality.

In contrast, concrete analysis of the way in which *religion functions in different societies at different times shows that, under specific historical circumstances, religion can act as a catalyst to raise women's consciousness of their social and religious exclusion. Because modern society has relegated religion to the private sphere, it has tended to become a "women's issue." Thus a sphere of female sociability may arise, in which women are able to express themselves with relative *freedom. Christian religious discourse is contradictory when it affirms that all human beings have equal rights to the goods of salvation but excludes women from the production, administration, and control of those goods. Such contradictions sometimes lead to the dissemination of feminist ideas about the affirmation of women's *autonomy and function in certain cases as a channel for social protest by the female population.

Bartky [1990]; Russell [1981]; Townes, ed. [1993]; Welch [1985]

MARIA JOSÉ F. ROSADO NUNES

Order of Creation This term is used in modern Protestant (especially Dutch and German) theology to designate a number of social *relationships, such as *marriage and *family, *race, and state. These orders of creation *(Schöpfungsordnungen)* are God-given, unchangeable, and binding for everybody, Christians as well as non-Christians. Thus the term comes close to what the Catholic *tradition understands by *natural law, except that orders of creation point explicitly to God the creator as the ultimate reason for the obligatory character of such orders. Some of the most influential "theologians of order" are Emil Brunner, Paul Althaus, and Helmut Thielicke. This theological line of thought has had serious political implications in the twentieth century, especially in Nazi Germany of the 1930s (anti-Semitism) and in South

Africa (apartheid). Karl Barth is known for his opposition to Nazism, but his sexual *ethics is explicitly based on orders of creation.

In the theology of order, different races, sexes, and nations have different tasks and responsibilities. Plurality of *creation is translated into *differences at the level of society and family. Departing from this rule is considered unnatural and sinful. Obedience is thus the only correct way to relate to the orders of creation.

The concept of order itself is one of the most influential in Western *philosophy. It never has been ethically neutral. Latin American *liberation theologians maintain that from the dominant position, what lacks order lacks goodness. Feminist critique of order and order of creation has questioned not only the consequences that theologies based on these concepts have in society but the very hierarchical structure of them. Obedience, a concept widely used mostly in modern Protestant moral theology, in this system is especially destructive for women and other groups with lower status in the *hierarchy.

The different liberation theologies agree with one another that all the forms of *oppression, whether based on class, race, gender, or sexual orientation, are contrary to creation. Feminist theologies, in their emphasis on the goodness of the bodily and sexual character of creation, more than any other liberation *theology represent an anthropological optimism.

Harrison [1985]; Soelle [1990]; Thistlethwaite/Engel [1990]

ELINA VUOLA

Ordination In human history, it is common for certain persons to be recognized as religious leaders and designated to officiate at religious ceremonies on behalf of *family or the wider community. Sometimes such holy leaders are born to their responsibilities, at other times they are chosen. In all cases they are ritually blessed and entrusted by the community to keep sacred teachings and practices.

Christians of diverse traditions call such a process *ordination,* believing that through *prayer and laying on of hands, God sets apart certain persons for leadership as priests, pastors, teachers, and servants. In some *traditions, *authority for priestly *ministry is passed through individuals (bishops) as a direct inheritance stretching back to the first *apostles and to Jesus Christ (apostolic succession). In other communities, authority for ministry is seen as a spontaneous gift of the *Holy Spirit, repeatedly reclaimed and recognized by each gathered church.

Within the early church, women and men functioned as equals. Women served as key leaders in the biblical period, and some women were ordained priests. Gradually, however, ordination was reserved for male leaders, and still later in Western Roman Catholicism, only for celibate men.

The sixteenth-century Protestant Reformation challenged patterns of hierarchical priesthood and rejected distinctions between clergy and laity. Protestants argued that although clergy were set apart, their separation was only so that they might perform a duty that any Christian was entitled to fulfill. Protestants rejected the celibate priestly ministry and encouraged clergy to marry. At the same time, Protestants continued to hold a "high" view of the ministerial office. Ordination remained a special calling (for men), in spite of the fact that the whole Christian community was called to exercise great power over the ministry. Furthermore, the sacramental efficacy of ordained persons remained grounded in God and not dependent on the personal character or private *purity of individual clergy.

This evolution of attitudes and understandings about ordination eventually led to the question of women's ordination. If the entire community is a royal priesthood, if all persons are called to ministry by their *baptism, and if there is neither Jew nor Greek, male nor female, in Christ Jesus (Gal 3:28), why can't women be ordained?

Institutional concern about the ordination of women began shortly after the American Revolution. The colonists had won their independence from England, and after the war, many Christians broke formal ties with European ecclesiastical structures to establish American churches. Female religious leaders often provided hospitality or financial support for the newly independent churches. Women also functioned as itinerant evangelists, "witnessing" and "sharing" their *faith while "planting" new churches. Widows kept local congregations together after the deaths of their pastor-husbands. Sectarian religious groups such as the Shakers and the Quakers provided new opportunities for female religious leadership.

The first woman formally ordained to the Christian ministry in an established denomination was Antoinette Brown. After receiving her theological education at Oberlin College, Antoinette Brown was called to a small Congregational church in South Butler, New York, in 1853. Her ordination took place without controversy because the free church polity of Congregationalism allows each congregation to ordain its own pastor. By the end of the century, many of those denominations that call and ordain pastors without wider church authorization (Congregationalists, Universalists, Unitarians, Northern Baptists, and Disciples) were ordaining women.

Women's ordination in more ordered denominations was more difficult. By the late nineteenth century, Methodists, Presbyterians, and various Holiness denominations began to debate the theological question of women's ordination. Sometimes the arguments were biblical and theological, but increasingly they became practical. Lutherans, Anglicans, and Roman Catholics confronted the issue in the early twentieth century. Within Pentecostalism, women were active leaders but lost status when the movement sought to "order" its clergy.

By the mid-1970s, women were ordained in most mainline Protestant denominations. Approval for Methodists and Northern Presbyterians came in the 1950s, for Southern Presbyterians in the 1960s, for Lutherans and Anglicans in the 1970s. The Roman Catholic Church firmly rejected the idea, insisting that women are not in the "image of Christ, who is male," and therefore cannot be ordained. Southern Baptists and many biblically conservative denominations continued to deny ordination to women because scripture prohibits women from exercising authority over men.

The numbers of ordained women have increased dramatically in the last quarter of the twentieth century. The 1990 U.S. Census shows approximately 11 percent of all clergy are female. In some mainline denominations, women are now 20 percent of the clergy, and at some ecumenical seminaries, women constitute 80 percent of enrollments. Even as more women seek ordination, because they believe that if men can be ordained it is unjust to deny it to women or because they believe that women will eventually transform understandings of ordained ministry, other women question the very concept of ordination and refuse to buy into its hierarchical presuppositions. They suggest that the truly egalitarian church of the future will not need ordained leadership.

Douglass [1985]; Parvey, in B. Stendahl [1985]; Torjesen [1993]; Zikmund, in Ruether/Keller [1995]

BARBARA BROWN ZIKMUND

Orthodoxy *Orthodoxy* derives from the Greek words *orthos* (right, correct) and *doxa* (opinion) and means the right belief. It is usually associated with the holding of correct religious belief, as opposed to *heresy or heterodoxy. In the history of Christianity, the term has been used in three distinct ways: (1) indicating acceptance of a creed, most commonly the Apostles' Creed and the Nicene Creed (creeds are believed to embody the revealed truth content of Christianity and are therefore of normative character); (2) to refer to those Christian churches of the East, holding onto the Byzantine *liturgical *tradition, that followed the church of Constantinople into schism from Rome in the eleventh century; (3) to refer to Protestant Orthodoxy, a movement of the late sixteenth through the early eighteenth centuries within the Lutheran and Reformed churches, where the Bible was viewed as a verbally inspired and inerrant deposit of objective information and religious truths.

Contemporary theology, especially different *liberation theologies, have questioned the use of traditional Christian truth claims for social, political, economic, racial, and *sexual oppression. Latin American liberation *theology gives great emphasis to *orthopraxis,* not as opposed to orthodoxy but as its essential component. The "epistemological break" in liberation theologies refers to the NT emphasis that doing the will of God is the condition for knowing the truth. Knowing and doing are dialectically related, and theology is seen as the second step in relation to the primacy of (ortho)praxis. According to Gustavo Gutiérrez, theology is the critical reflection on historical *praxis in the light of the Word of God.

The critique of dogmatic truth claims and creeds for their inherent *sexism makes feminist theologies critical of much of contemporary theology. Feminist theologies challenge the *tradition (e.g., in such central questions as the fatherhood of God, the virginity of Mary, and the doctrinal implications of the masculinity of Jesus Christ). Much of the orthopraxis of contemporary liberation theologies has left out women's praxis and experience. Black women have challenged the sexism in black theology, and Latin American women want to become visible in the category of "the poor." The womanist and *mujerista* critique of white feminist theology has made it clear how easily one orthopraxis (particularity) can become a new orthodoxy (universality). To avoid the danger of a feminist orthodoxy, a plurality of perspectives is built into the very structure of feminist critique of religion. Hence the term *feminist theologies* instead of a/the *feminist theology.*

Although it is maintained that terms like *orthodoxy* and *heresy* are products of a dualistic, *androcentric, and intellectualistic tradition that in itself is opposed to a more holistic, inclusive understanding of reality, they are being elaborated also in feminist discourse. The feminist critique of traditional Christian teaching has meant that much of the tradition is, in fact, seen as heresy from women's point of view. Among the feminist theological movement, the *post-Christians maintain that feminism and Christianity are not compatible at all.

A constructive feminist understanding of orthodoxy underlines the need for plurality, particularity or concrete universalism, and a holistic worldview, as opposed to holding one truth over all others, false or abstract universalism, and *dualism. A feminist orthopraxis brings the plurality of women's *experiences into the contemporary liberation theological construction of orthopraxis. That means that women are the poor of the poor, oppressed not only by their gender but also by their *race and class.

In *ethics, feminist theologies are claiming the importance of *care and relationality, (women's) bodily integrity and *sexuality (heterosexual as well as *lesbian), and *emotions. A feminist ethical orthopraxis wants to show the interconnection of mutuality, sexuality, power in relationship, and justice making.

Gutiérrez [1990]; Hampson [1990]; Ruether [1983/1993]; Sobrino [1978]

ELINA VUOLA

Pagan The Latin word *paganus,* referring to the countryside and what pertains to the rural, agricultural communities, has become in the English language the pejorative word *pagan.* It has absorbed the Greek attitude of labeling all who do not use their language "barbarian," "people of inferior *culture," "uncouth," and "uncultured." Originally, being pagan was neither being without religion nor living a lifestyle that was technologically primitive. On the contrary, being pagan was living close to nature and valuing it as spirit-filled and of divine origin. It had nothing to do with primitive ideas about deity, for the Roman pantheon existed for all, not just for the people of the countryside. When Origen called Celsus "pagan," he was distinguishing the new religion, Christianity, from the existing Greco-Roman religions. It was only as the powerful emperors Constantine the Great and Theodosius began their deliberate Christianization of the Roman world that the word *paganus* began to take on a religious meaning that was negative.

Being pagan cannot be equated with being superstitious. Superstition is the other person's spirituality and accompanies all religions. Nor can it be dismissed as adhering to a primitive polytheistic religion that needs to grow to maturity. This developmental approach to humanity's spiritual journey does not satisfy all the evidence of the human quest for religion. The so-called great *monotheistic religions of the world are at pains to reconcile the beliefs they articulate about the one God and the world of experience that is a challenge to this concept. The notions of religious superiority generated in the Christian world, followed by the scientific and philosophical development in western Europe, produced a cultural history replete with notions of superiority and inferiority.

The atrocities committed by the nonpagans—that is, those who had adopted Christianity—in the name of "depaganizing" the world are unspeakable. The mandate for this depaganization was said to derive from Gen. 1:27–31. Human beings have moved from their status as "earth beings," an integral part of *creation, to a position of exploiters of all that exists for the development of human culture. In this process the sectors of humanity that remained close to nature were included in what is to be conquered, converted, or destroyed. Indigenous peoples, human communities that have remained outside these dominant and dominating cultures, have been put together with other species in the ecosystem and labeled "endangered species." They, like the biblical Canaanites, were deemed disposable.

It is not religion but science that is reconverting humanity to pagan ideals of the integrity of the ecosystem and the stewardship status of humans within it. Science calls attention to the danger facing planet Earth. It has generated a renewed consciousness of ecology and human *responsibility within it. Neopagans, people who value and want to care for nature and to relate to the natural with respect, are developing fresh rituals for sustainable living styles. Traditional rituals of clearing waterways and recycling what we take from the earth have their scientific equivalents. As a result, human beings are awakened to the integrity of creation, their own createdness, and the challenge of sustainability. The life embodied in vegetation and especially in trees and waters is once again recognized and honored.

Paganism in the sense of a belief in a world that is living and therefore dependent on the inbreathing of the divine and the *care of humanity may yet pull us back from the brink of disaster. Contemporary paganism and neopaganism call for a shift from an anthropocentric to an interdependent vision of life and being.

Adler [1986]; Ariarajah [1985]; Fabella/Oduyoye [1988]; McFague [1993]; Oduyoye [1986]

MERCY AMBA ODUYOYE

Pantheism *Pantheism*, a term derived from the Greek words *pan* (all) and *theos* (god), is traditionally opposed as a Christian theological position on the grounds that it obliterates the distinction between creator and creature, between *transcendence and *immanence.

This negative reaction is found among feminist theologians also, who, like

Dorothee Soelle, resist the pantheist challenge as a dissolution of logical categories such as transcendence and immanence. These, however, convey meaning only when relations of opposition between them are assumed. For instance, immanence functions as transcendence in a description of the Trinity as both economic and immanent.

A creatively fluid use of these categories lies behind Marjorie Suchocki's theology of *sin as a violation of the world's well-being, which also necessarily violates God's well-being. The *suffering of the world entails the suffering of God. Sallie McFague, aiming at integrating scientific views with theology, offers a *panentheist* model of God, in which God is in all finite creatures yet not identical with the universe (149). She rejects pantheism on the grounds that pantheism says that God is embodied, necessarily and totally. But the notion of *embodiment, as Michael Levine shows, is absent from the most typical type of pantheism, which denies that God is a person, let alone embodied.

Pantheism offers feminist theologies a valuable critique of traditional God-concepts; of accepted notions of *agency and *freedom, divine and human; of canonized teachings about how and where God is revealed and to whom. A pantheist ontology offers a *metaphysical basis for an ecological ethic, connecting what is morally right and wrong with our own natures, the nature of other things, and the nature of God.

Grace Jantzen sums up for and against pantheism: if the element of asymmetry between God and world is not ignored, and if pantheism is understood as an affirmation that all reality is God's reality, then it is not an alternative to Christian theology but an ingredient in it.

Jantzen [1984]; Levine [1994]; McFague [1993]; Suchocki [1994]

ANNE PRIMAVESI

Paradigm Shift The Greek-derived word *paradigm* means an example, pattern, model, or typical instance. At its most general, a paradigm refers to a particular worldview underlying the theories of science. More specifically, a paradigm relates to universally recognized scientific achievements that, for a time, provide model problems and solutions to a community of practitioners (Kuhn). A paradigm shift therefore indicates a process whereby established scientific ideas are changed and replaced by new ones.

The idea of a paradigm shift has been transferred from the sciences to other areas of society and *culture. By radically critiquing and overturning established, *patriarchal ways of thinking, contemporary feminist theories have produced a major paradigm shift, creating new models, methods, generalizations, and modes of inquiry. The foundational category of gender, with its pervasive ramifications for self, society, *politics, culture, and *religion, has also produced an important paradigm shift in theology and religious studies. This shift is transforming religion both as practiced and as studied. It changes our knowledge and the way we come to know, seen as rooted in *experience and action as much as in analysis and reflection. The shift is from an *androcentric, exclusively male-oriented perspective to one that gives full recognition to women's own experience and is inclusive of both genders. The shift is also from a *hierarchical ordering of social and personal reality to an egalitarian, participatory one. This has a radically transforming effect on our models of God and all other constructs of Ultimate Reality.

The paradigm shift involves making women's own voices heard; overcoming their *marginalization in all cultural institutions, including those of religion; empowering women and making them everywhere as visible as men. Women scholars of religion are studying women's religious experience across different religious *traditions, thus constructing new theologies and providing new interpretations of all traditional aspects of religious *doctrine and practice.

Christ, in Farnham [1987]; King [1995]; Kuhn [1970]; Plaskow, *Women's Studies Quarterly* [1993]; Warne, *Religious Studies and Theology* [1989]

URSULA KING

Parasitic Reference *Parasitic reference* is the term used in linguistics for a word whose meaning has overtaken that of another word. Most often parasitic references occur when a product name or brand name becomes so popular that the noun to which it refers begins to be called by the brand name. Examples might be *Kleenex* for *tissue* or *Xerox* for *photocopy*. In religious language, one might say that *Father* has overshadowed the word *God*. Just as people say, "Hand me a Kleenex," when they want a tissue, they also invoke the term *Father* when they are referring to God.

The use of the term *Father* as a synonym for *God* in the Hebrew scriptures is very rare, occurring only about a dozen times. In the Gospels, the incidence of *Father* increases relative to the date of the writing of the text. Mark, the earliest Gospel, uses the term only four times to refer to God. In Luke the usage increases to seventeen, with thirty-two instances in Matthew and ninety-four in John. In the secular world, trade names overtake generic terms; in the theological world, metaphorical imagery becomes one with its referent, thus collapsing the *metaphor into a one-to-one relationship with its noun.

Beardsley, *Philosophical Forum* [1973–74]; Clarkson [1989]

J. SHANNON CLARKSON

Partnership Partnership or *community in the church and in society is not by any means a new invention. The biblical message of God's intervention in human history is a message of God reaching out to partner women and men so that, in turn, they can learn how to live as partners with one another. Jesus' own ministry was one of reaching out to the marginal and misfits of Israel. By overturning the tables of the religious systems of his time, Jesus sought to include the outcasts at God's table and to teach us all how to come as one family to the feast (Matt. 21:1–17).

In the New Testament, the word most frequently used for sharing with someone in a common bond with Jesus Christ is *koinōnia* (partnership, participation, communion, community). Paul's writings stress *koinōnia* as the participation of the believer in Christ, in the blessings of Christ, and in the Christian community (1 Cor. 10:16–17). Partnership may be understood theologically as a new focus of relationship in the common history of Jesus Christ that sets us free for others. In this relationship there is continuing commitment and common struggle, in interaction with a wider community context.

In advocating patterns of shared *authority and partnership, feminist theologians are well aware of the structures of *oppression that deform attempts to create more egalitarian communities.This awareness is crucial in order to guard against a rhetoric of "cheap partnership" that avoids the difficult *conversion process of rejecting the old superior and subordinate roles. For instance, white, affluent U.S. feminists have often continued the practice of *domination of women of color and poor women while talking about shared authority. Partnership is not a substitute for *liberation. It is a gift of God that most often comes *after* the shared struggle for liberation has made it possible to relate to one another beyond roles of domination and subordination.

hooks [1984]; Russell [1979; 1987]; Schüssler Fiorenza [1984/1995]

LETTY M. RUSSELL

Pastoral Care

The Imagery of the Shepherd and His Flock. Traditionally, the leading image in pastoral care is "the good shepherd" of

Jesus' parables, a sweet and gentle man leading his flock to green pastures and clear waters. His main concern is to feed his flock and keep it together: the sheep that goes its own way is wrong; it has to be brought back into the flock. The whole flock has to reach the safe stable when evening comes. Feminist theologians have criticized this image, its blatant absence of mutuality, and the emphasis on obedience as the highest *virtue.

As we are stuck with the name *pastoral care* (care as of a shepherd), it may help to go further into the biblical image of the shepherd. Jesus could use this image because his audience understood its meaning. Which bells rang in the heads of the people around Jesus? Probably verses from the prophets came up; verses from Ezekiel 34, perhaps. There we find no sweet and gentle shepherd for whom the flock is just a mass of sheep. God presents himself as the true shepherd, looking for green pastures and clear water for the flock, leading them to a place of life abundant. Not less important, however, is the anger of the shepherd: "I will judge between the fat sheep and the lean sheep" (vv. 17 and 20). Sternly the shepherd condemns the strong rams and goats spoiling grass and water. In the text we meet the blazing anger of a shepherd whose aim is *justice. This shepherd is partial: the sheep that are driven away (v. 16) because they are thrust aside by the strong animals have his special attention.

This shepherd image still lacks mutuality, but it can inspire pastors to do more than dress wounds and bring the stray back into the flock. It brings forth critical pastors, who give attention to the *causes* of *suffering, to what drove a sheep away. Often these "sheep" are "being thrust aside by strong ones," an experience many women have. Pastoral care from a feminist perspective is care in the context of justice. People suffering because they lack what they need to stay fully alive—actual food, emotional nurture, spiritual nourishment—need pastoral attention and *care. But a true pastor does more: she or he gives attention to the power structures, in society and church, that cause actual, emotional, and spiritual starvation. Many women, measured implicitly or explicitly by the norm "woman" as the image of the counterpart and desire of the patriarchal man, feel starved in multiple ways. In a patriarchal society and church, the truth about women is too threatening, because the truth is that women are different from the projections of *patriarchy. They are full neighbors of men; fully human in their own right. Not to be controlled, they believe that they are called to explore their own *experiences and *responsibilities from their own point of view. Feminist pastoral care is partial like the good shepherd, carefully taking women's own experiences at heart.

Jesus embodied the good shepherd of the Hebrew Scriptures. Theologically speaking, the congregation embodies Jesus, acknowledged as Christ. If so, not the minister as pastor but the congregation represents and embodies the true shepherd. Nobody can live and believe all by her- or himself. We need one another to broaden our perspective, to open our eyes and ears, and to embody God's just care. We need this care not only in the crises of our lives, but as well in the dreariness, the boredom, the hectic business of our days. If "the pastoral congregation," rather than the pastor, becomes the starting point for our reflection on pastoral care, true mutuality becomes possible. All are called to give this care and justice to one another.

The Goal of Pastoral Care. The goal of feminist pastoral care is not adjustment to the flock; its highest virtue is not obedience. The aim of feminist pastoral care is life abundant for everybody. But this can be obtained only if injustice becomes explicit and clear. Injustice must be *named. Who is "thrust aside" by whom? Who is silenced by whom? Who feels she cannot raise her voice, for fear of being laughed at or put down? The aftermath of the Re-Imagining Conference in

1993 makes it clear that the voices of many women are silenced, voices that say new things about *God/ess, about her/his relationship with this world, and about the way s/he longs to obtain an open relationship with this world: by pure *grace, perhaps without even needing the *cross as substitutive punishment or *sacrifice. Very threatening voices! Feminist pastoral care and justice listens to voices that are easily thrust aside.

Pastoral Care as Being an Ally. Jesus, imaging the true shepherd, took the sheep, driven away, to heart. The cause of the driven-away sheep became his cause. To look at another person, take her seriously, and listen "care-fully" to her can be called "pastoral" if we, just like the True Pastor, take her cause to heart.

Pastoral care and justice is never cheap or easy. To know about somebody else's hunger or pain is to become involved. Listening to her is not enough. She has to come to her own senses and be encouraged to use them. Maybe she is hurt because she was "woman" in somebody's eyes: beaten by her husband, sexually abused, or just ignored. If so, pastoral care has to dress her wounds but also to become her ally, fighting for her cause. The structures of society and many aspects of the theology in the churches that made her suffer by "thrusting her aside" have to be analyzed, criticized, and, finally, altered.

Feminist pastoral care dresses wounds, it nurtures, but it also fights injustices fiercely. Its leading image could be: a community of Amazons.

Bons-Storm [1996]; Glaz/Moessner [1991]; Graham/Halsey [1993]

RIET BONS-STORM

Pastoral Epistles In 1753 a German named Paul Anton called the three short letters attributed to Paul and addressed to Timothy and Titus "pastoral epistles," because they appeared to reflect an older pastor writing to give advice to a younger pastor. Because their vocabulary, style, and theology are un-Pauline, scholarly consensus assumes they are pseudonymous (written by someone else and attributed to Paul). Their author apparently knew the Acts of the Apostles; therefore they were probably written after 95 C.E., perhaps as late as 135 to 150, although 110–115 C.E. seems likely since Polycarp knew them but they do not reflect the situation of Ignatius of Antioch.

The Pastorals depict the emerging institutional church. They represent the second crisis of a founded religion. The first occurs when the founder dies, and results in written literature; the second, at the death of the founder's associates, results in institutionalization. The Pastorals show Christianity evolving from original simplicity toward defined patterns of structure, *authority, and *doctrine. Pseudonymity is theologically important because the claim of apostolic authorship supports the letters' authority.

The epistles reflect their churches' practical problems, chief among them church order, "*heresy," and social acceptability. The problem of church order is reflected in attention paid to offices of *ministry (1 Tim. 3:1–15; 5:3–22; Titus 1:5–9). Heresy is reflected in polemics, as the writer excoriates those holding alternative positions (2 Tim. 2:14–19; 3:1–9; 4:3–5; Titus 3:1–11). The problem of social acceptability is reflected in the writer's advice, calculated to make the church appear positively to outsiders (1 Tim. 2:1–2; 5:14; 6:1–2; Titus 2:1–10). A minority group and members of an illegal religion, Christians were vulnerable to social ostracism and political disfavor. Good repute was necessary to the church's *survival.

The pastoral epistles are full of material on women (1 Tim. 2:9–15; 3:8–13; 5:3–16; 2 Tim. 1:5; 4:19–21; Titus 2:3–6). Unfortunately, uncritical quotation, especially of 1 Tim. 2:11–15; 5:11–15 and 2 Tim. 3:6–7 has undermined women. Studies by feminist scholars correct such misreadings.

David C. Verner's book *The House-*

hold of God: The Social World of the Pastoral Epistles (Chico, Calif.: Scholars Press, 1983) broke ground for sociological examination of the letters. Verner demonstrated that the patriarchal household was the basic unit of Greco-Roman society, associated on a symbolic level with its stability. Those who challenged patriarchal household order challenged society. Christianity's message of *equality (cf. Gal. 3:28) was a perceived threat. To preserve itself, the church moved from its original espousal of equality of men and women in Christ to more "socially acceptable" positions. The Pastorals contribute evidence for such a shift.

Jouette Bassler asserts that this shift toward *patriarchy led women to form communities preserving the original spirit. In "The Widows' Tale: A Fresh Look at 1 Tim. 5:3–16" (*JBL* 103, 1 [1984]: 23–41), Bassler argued that Christianity began as an egalitarian movement attractive to women and slaves. The church developed and adapted to Greco-Roman society and became increasingly *hierarchical and patriarchal. Hence the *widows embraced a celibate lifestyle intended to recover the church's original equality.

Feminist scholars note that the Pastorals provide evidence of the leadership and influence of women. Restrictions placed on women reflect the writer's discomfort with their influence and power. Subordination to male authority is made a test of appropriate Christian behavior. Feminist scholarship also gives guidelines for interpretation of the Pastorals. It asserts that the texts are not descriptive but prescriptive; they attempt to change, not describe, existing situations. Rhetorically their polemic reflects standard modes of attack on opponents, not the positions actually held by opponents. That so much space is devoted to behavior appropriate to women shows that women were, in fact, prominent in Christian communities. (Offices for women clearly existed; cf. 1 Tim. 3:11; 5:3–16.) The Pastoral writer limits their activity precisely because it was important and influential.

Dewey, in Newsom/Ringe [1992]; MacDonald [1983]; Maloney, in Schüssler Fiorenza, ed. [1994]; Thurston [1989]

BONNIE THURSTON

Pastoral Misconduct *Pastoral misconduct* is a general term describing unethical behavior committed by a person in a position of pastoral leadership. While most reported cases involve sexual abuse by the pastor or pastoral counselor, pastoral misconduct may also include embezzlement, breaches of confidentiality, and so forth.

It is unethical for a minister (clergy or lay) to engage in sexual contact or sexualized behavior with a congregant, client, employee, student, etc. (adult, teen, or child) within the pastoral, professional relationship. Crossing the sexual boundary is a violation of the pastoral role, a misuse of the *power and *authority of the role, a violation of the vulnerability of the congregant, client, etc., and lacks authentic consent (due to the other's vulnerability in the relationship). As such, it is a breach of fiduciary duty, i.e., the obligation that a helping professional has to act only in the best interests of the congregant or client rather than in one's own personal interests.

Pastoral misconduct involving sexual abuse is a long-standing problem in religious organizations. Narratives describe the misconduct of significant historical figures, such as the Reverend Henry Ward Beecher, and fictional accounts, such as Nathaniel Hawthorne's *Scarlet Letter*, portray the painful consequences of clergy misusing their roles. But the contemporary manifestation of the problem began to be disclosed only in the mid-1980s, as individuals who had been victimized by their ministers began to come forward.

This abuse is not unusual, and it involves the abuse of adult congregants as well as the molestation of children by religious leaders. Religious institutions, initially ill prepared to respond to these disclosures, began in the early 1990s to establish policy and procedures with which to respond. They were often motivated by legal actions brought by survivors demanding a just response and accountability for the pastoral abusers.

Fortune [1989]; Lebacqz/Barton [1991]; Ormerod/Ormerod [1995]

MARIE M. FORTUNE

Patriarchy *Patriarchy* means the "rule of the father." Patriarchy refers to systems of legal, social, economic, and political relations that validate and enforce the sovereignty of male heads of families over dependent persons in the household. In classical patriarchal systems, such as were found in Hebrew, Greek, and Roman societies, dependent persons included wives, unmarried daughters, dependent sons, and slaves, male and female. In Roman law, the term *familia* referred to all persons and things ruled by the *paterfamilias,* including animals and *land.

Although male slaves and dependent sons were also ruled by the patriarch, women were subjugated in a more total way. Sons grew up and male slaves could be emancipated to become independent householders. Women, as daughters, wives, and *widows, were defined generically as dependent persons under the male head of the household in which they lived. The female slave, combining the subjugated status of female and slave, was even more vulnerable, having no protection from physical or sexual abuse.

Patriarchy as a social system was found in classical societies around the world. Some anthropologists have believed that the patriarchal family was the aboriginal order of human society and hence is "natural" and inevitable. Others, especially feminist anthropologists, have challenged this assumption. They have argued that patriarchal systems arose at a particular time in human history with the change from food gathering and gardening to plow agriculture, private landholding, urbanization, and class stratification. In the ancient Near East this happened sometime between the seventh and fourth millennia B.C.E. Thus the classical societies and religious cultures of the Hebrews, Greeks, and Romans that lie behind Christian society and theology were shaped by patriarchal *ideological and social patterns.

The status of women in patriarchal societies has many nuances, depending on such factors as how women's physical protection and the property deriving from their own families of origin are related to their status within their husband's family. Economic and legal liberalization and the spread of women's *education also modified women's subjugation in classical times, particularly during the Hellenistic and the later Roman periods. However, in classical antiquity women never gained the status of citizenship with an independent, legal political status, the right to vote or hold office.

Although one cannot define a single system that would be true of all patriarchal societies at all times, one can generalize about the characteristics usually found in patriarchal societies. The general characteristic of the status of women under patriarchy is one of subjugation without legal status in their own right. Other aspects of this subjugated status include the following: (1) the lineage of children is passed down through the father; (2) male children are preferred to female children; (3) as wives, women's bodies, *sexuality, and reproductive capacity belong to their husbands; (4) the sovereignty of the husband over his wife includes the right to beat her and to confine her physically, sometimes even to sell her into bondage; (5) because women do not have public roles in *politics and *culture, their education is usually limited to household skills and sometimes minimal literacy; (6) their right to inherit property as daughters or widows is restricted, and what property they do inherit is usually administered by a male relative or guardian.

The exclusion of women from public political and cultural offices and from the higher education that prepared men for such offices accounts for the almost exclusively male elite formation of public culture under patriarchy and the definition of women from this male point of view. Women typically have had great difficulty gaining visibility and credibility as creators of culture, even when they manage to gain education and skills and produce cultural creations of comparable quality to those of ranking males. Because the cultural creations of women have not been incorporated into the public heritage that is taught to the next generation of students, such cultural accomplishments as women did achieve have been continually lost, erased from public *memory, or else have survived by accident, often by being attributed to a male.

These patterns of patriarchy were reconfirmed in early modern European law codes and continued to define women in Europe and North America until the feminist movement of the nineteenth and early twentieth centuries. This movement succeeded in winning for women the legal status of citizens, with the right to vote and hold political office as well as to make property transactions in their own name and have access to higher education and professional employment. Similar changes in women's social status have taken place in other parts of the world in the twentieth century through liberal democratic or *socialist revolutions.

However, many remnants of patriarchal ordering of society still remain in "modern" societies. Women are seen as the primary houseworkers and child raisers, and their capacity to compete economically with men is thereby limited. Cultural patterns and legal restrictions continue to limit women's economic, political, and social *equality and to ratify the view that women are subordinate to men as a gender group, a subordination that is interstructured with class and racial subordination.

The major *world religions have been deeply shaped by the patriarchal ordering of society as the contexts in which they developed. Christianity inherited patriarchal religious and cultural patterns both from Greek and Roman *philosophy and law and from the Hebrew world. Patriarchy rooted in these ancestral sources shaped a Christian worldview that took for granted the male hierarchical ordering of society and the church as the "*order of creation" and the "will of God."

God is typically imaged as a patriarchal father and lord. The patriarchal *hierarchies of male over female, father over children, and master over slave are reduplicated symbolically in the relation of God and Christ to the church, as father to sons, lord to servants, and bridegroom to bride. The image of Christ as head of the church which is his body reduplicates the legal view in which the wife lacks her own "head" (self-direction) and belongs as body to her husband.

For some church fathers, such as Augustine, this concept of male headship led to the conclusion that women lack the *image of God in themselves and are included in the image of God only under their husbands as their "head." Women are seen as naturally subjugated and inferior by nature, more prone to *sin, lacking *reason and self-control, and defined by their *body and sexuality. As such, women cannot represent Christ in the ordained *ministry. These views have flowed from patriarchal patterns taken into Christian theology and church polity.

Feminist theology arises by challenging this patriarchal distortion of Christian theology. Feminist theology dismantles the legitimization of patriarchy as God's will and the "natural order" and redefines it as sinful distortion of good human relations and as an apostasy from God's true mandate for *creation. Feminist theology builds on the partial *liberation of women in modern societies and calls for a completion of that liberation in society and in the church and its theology.

Ehrenberg [1989]; Herlihy [1985]; Lerner [1986]; Pomeroy [1975/1995]; Ruether [1975/1995]; Sanday [1981]

ROSEMARY RADFORD RUETHER

Pauline Texts "Pauline texts" refers to letters written by Paul to early Christian churches between 49–59 C.E. (Romans, 1 and 2 Corinthians, Galatians, Philippians, 1 Thessalonians, and Philemon, the undisputed Pauline letters); letters written in Paul's name somewhere in the period between 70 and 95 C.E. by followers of Paul, who modified Pauline language and ideas (Colossians, Ephesians, and 2 Thessalonians, the "deutero-Pauline" letters); and letters that speak to matters of church *ministry in the early second century and claim the *authority of Paul for their positions (1 and 2 Timothy and Titus, the *pastoral epistles). Sometime in the second century, these diverse writings were collected under the name of the apostle Paul and included in the New Testament *canon. The prominence given to Paul's letters in the canonical New Testament is reflected and amplified in the theological *tradition, which considers Paul to be the authoritative interpreter of the Christian *gospel in the early church. As scripture, Paul's letters have been a foundation for Christian theology.

Feminist Interpretation. Feminist interpreters have attended especially to those passages within the Pauline texts that address the proper behavior for women in church and the relationship between wives and husbands, because these passages have been used to support the exclusion of women from leadership in Christian churches and the submission of women to men. Feminists have also explored the implications of Paul's mode of expression, including his use of the metaphors of slavery and *marriage and his use of flesh–spirit *dualism, for society in his own time and in succeeding centuries of interpretation (Martin, Castelli).

The authority that Paul's name came to have in the formation of the Christian canon offers the central challenge for feminist interpreters of the Pauline texts. When the New Testament canon is used as the interpretive context for the letters, Paul's earlier letters are read through the lens of the later letters, which sharply curtail women's leadership and limit the role of women to accepting their subordinate position in the Greco-Roman *patriarchal household. Following the directions of the authors who wrote in Paul's name, the traditional view sees Colossians and Ephesians and the pastoral epistles as the natural development of the Pauline legacy.

By employing the methods of historical criticism and considering Paul's different letters as situational letters written in particular social and historical contexts, feminist scholars have recast the picture of the development of the Pauline tradition with respect to women. Paul's undisputed letters reveal a fundamental ambivalence about the relationship between male and female. In Rom. 16:1–16, Paul greets Christians by name. Among these are female coworkers and colleagues in ministry, whom he refers to as "deacon," "benefactor," and "apostle." In Gal. 3:28, Paul cites a tradition in which *baptism is described as invalidating the divisions between Greek and Jew, slave and free, male and female. When he addresses sexual relations within marriage, Paul commends reciprocity of obligation between wives and husbands (1 Cor. 7:2–5). However, also within the undisputed letters, Paul subordinates wife to husband, as in the discussion of head coverings in 1 Cor. 11:2–16. In 1 Cor. 14:33–36, Paul commands that women be silent in the churches and that they be subordinate.

The authors of Colossians and Ephesians resolve Paul's ambivalence by introducing the household codes (Col. 3:18–4:1, Eph. 5:21–6:9), which explicitly prescribe submission of wives to husbands. The author of the pastoral epistles erases any ambiguity about Paul's view of the position of women when, in the name of Paul, he enjoins women to keep silent and forbids them to teach or have authority over a man (1 Tim. 2:11–12). Thus the developing Pauline tradition represented in the canon shows a marked restriction of the activity and *autonomy of women in the churches.

Methods of Interpretation. A major feminist approach to the Pauline texts has been *historical reconstruction* of the history of early Christianity (Schüssler Fiorenza). Feminist historians resist reading the letters as the canon directs and see the evidence of the Pauline letters not as a natural development of *orthodoxy but as a struggle between the egalitarian impulses of early Christianity and those forces that would organize the church along the lines of the traditional patriarchal household. Historical reconstruction seeks not to reiterate men's views about women but to discover evidence for women's participation in the early church. Work on the history of Jewish women has further complicated and enriched the context in which to understand Christian women (Brooten).

Another feminist approach selects *theological principles* within Paul's thinking that may be applied to the human situation to critique the subordination of women. For example, in the theme of the impartiality of God in Romans, in which God judges and redeems each human being without regard to special privilege, women may find a way to evaluate society's conventions that elevate men over women (Gaventa). With this approach, Christian feminists preserve the authority of Paul's thought while placing his thinking in the service of *liberation.

A related approach also gives authority to the Paul represented in the canon but distinguishes between Paul's own letters, in which glimpses of *equality are seen, and the later letters in the Pauline tradition. Paul's views in the undisputed letters are enlisted in the struggle for liberation and represent the standard against which departures from Paul's theology are judged. Study of the social setting of Colossians and Ephesians may provide historical reasons for the retreat from the initial *freedom promised in Paul's preaching. The household codes may have been a means of maintaining the church's public image in the face of friction caused by Paul's preaching in an earlier generation (E. Elizabeth Johnson).

A third approach to feminist interpretation of the Pauline texts uses the method of **rhetorical criticism* to reconstruct and recover other theological positions within early Christianity that differ from the positions Paul asserts. This approach resists the claims of the canon, which ranks Paul's voice as the ultimate authority. It reads critically the rhetoric of Paul's letters themselves, in which Paul portrays members of his audience as opponents and himself as the final arbiter of disputes. Instead of picturing divergent interpretations of the gospel as *"heretical," this approach reads the New Testament for evidence of alternative positions *within* early Christianity. For example, Paul's rhetoric in 1 Corinthians has been used to reconstruct the position of women *prophets in Corinth who interpreted their baptism as giving them the Spirit, cancelling social privilege, and allowing them to experience new life with Christ as a present reality (Wire).

The position of the women prophets, read along with such early Christian traditions as the baptismal formula in Gal. 3:28, is seen as a legitimate Christian position that can be compared with and evaluated with Paul's. The noncanonical *Acts of Thecla* is evidence of a Christian tradition that interpreted Paul's teaching as advocating celibacy and authorizing women to teach and to baptize, in direct contrast with the prescriptions in the pastoral epistles. This approach places authority not in Paul the apostle or in the canon but in the early Christian community as a whole, and in today's communities of interpreters who identify, compare, and theologically evaluate diverse articulations within early Christianity.

The feminist approaches of historical reconstruction, theological critique, and rhetorical criticism all face *androcentric texts that, because of their authority in both religious and cultural contexts, have had an enormous impact on *marginalized persons. The variety of feminist approaches results from multiple responses to the problems of canon and authority.

Brooten, in Nickelsburg/MacRae [1986]; Castelli, in Schüssler Fiorenza, ed. [1994]; Gaventa, in Newsom/Ringe [1992]; Martin, in Felder [1991]; Schüssler Fiorenza [1983/1994]; Wire [1990]

CYNTHIA BRIGGS KITTREDGE

Philosophy The word *philosophy* derives from two Greek words, *phileō* (I love) and *sophia* (wisdom), and literally means "the love of wisdom." In the West, philosophy has its roots in Greek thought, with Plato and Aristotle still considered to be two of the greatest philosophers of all time. According to Plato, the seeker after wisdom is characterized as the one who tries as much as possible to be detached from bodily concerns, since wisdom or knowledge is held to be of the mind, not of the *body. Similarly, death is to be welcomed, because death is the release of the mind from the prison house of the body. Since women were conceptually linked with the body, the earth, and reproduction and men with the mind, rationality, and God, philosophy was from ancient times designated a male activity. Though there were a few female philosophers, such as Hypatia, they were considered to be honorary males, somehow having a male mind in a female body.

In Hellenistic times philosophy was not thought of as one branch of human knowledge among others but rather as human knowledge in its fullness, with all its many branches. Aristotle began some of the major divisions still found in Western philosophy. Logic, *ethics (or moral philosophy), and *metaphysics are conceived today along much the same lines as they were by Aristotle, but "natural philosophy" has become natural science in all its many branches.

From its early years, Christianity had an ambivalent relationship with philosophy. There were those like Tertullian who rejected philosophy, asking, "What has Athens to do with Jerusalem?" Others, such as Justin Martyr and Augustine, were deeply influenced by Platonism and held that Christianity was the summit of all truth and philosophical truth was included within it. Augustine went so far as to suggest that Plato might have made a visit to the prophet Jeremiah, and therefore Platonic philosophy was at least in part divine *revelation. Thomas Aquinas, in his massively influential *Summa Theologiae* in the thirteenth century, saw theology as the "queen of the sciences" and philosophy as her (highly honored) handmaiden. What Christianity did not question was the exclusion of women from philosophy. Aristotle had characterized the female as a misbegotten male, intellectually and morally defective; and this evaluation was repeated many times by medieval Christian writers.

With Descartes in the seventeenth century, two major shifts occurred in the understanding of philosophy. In the first place, rather than seeing philosophy primarily in terms of truths to be known, attention shifted to the knower, the subject of knowledge. Second, philosophy ceased to assume the existence of God. The combination of these two features meant that philosophy in modernity has been endlessly preoccupied with epistemology, the problem of how a human mind can be certain of anything at all. The two major strands of modern philosophy are rationalism and empiricism, the former arguing that minds can know certain truths independent of any experience, the latter holding that some experience is essential for any knowledge to be possible.

Feminists have pointed out that the assumptions on which modern philosophy rests are inimical to feminist thought. The ideal of the disembodied knower, objective knowledge as a "view from nowhere," detachment as proper *methodology, and isolated individualism as the underlying *anthropology have all been challenged by feminist philosophers, who argue for an embodied and contextualized knowing.

Some of the alternatives suggested by feminist philosophers are also promoted by what is labeled "postmodern philosophy," which has highlighted the social construction of knowledge and the arrogance of ignoring the unconscious and the working of *ideologies in the constitution of subjects of knowledge. Feminists are deeply divided about the value of *postmodern philosophy. Some argue that the decentering of the subject and the recognition of social *contextualization are essential to *deconstruction of the oppressive ideologies of gender; others, however, are worried that too great an emphasis on social construction can result only in *relativism, wherein central feminist concerns of truth and *justice are lost.

Bar On [1994a; 1994b]; Garry/Pearsall [1989]; Nicholson [1990]

GRACE M. JANTZEN

Pluralism, Religious Pluralism refers to the presence of three or more distinct meaning systems or *ideologies setting normative values for an area of social life. Among the most important types of pluralism are moral pluralism, in the form of quite different views of appropriate moral conduct; political pluralism, represented by several political parties; and religious pluralism, indicated by the presence of a number of faiths in a society.

Religious pluralism is often predictive of moral and political pluralism. In societies with only one *religion, the moral, political, and spiritual values tend to merge into one more or less comprehensive and totalitarian civil religion, while *dualistic societies, with two major competing religions, tend to be conflicted because the lines of political, social, and religious cleavage likely converge in two opposing groups.

In contrast, societies that tolerate multiple, coexisting religions also tend to be pluralistic morally and politically and to value highly individual *autonomy. But this very *freedom of choice in the presence of diverse normative values may impede a society's working in common cause when needed. Further, a high degree of societal pluralism in times of rapid change can lead confused youth particularly to join religious groups where they have little autonomy of choice in belief or action. For these reasons, pluralistic societies have both many religions that maintain cordial relations with one another and numerous pockets of cultlike groups that are internally authoritarian and avoid much contact with outsiders.

Internationally, religious pluralism can negatively evoke bigotry against a whole people whose leaders are at odds with another's. To promote understanding, attempts are made by one country's religious leaders to share beliefs with leaders of different faiths and nations. This cross-cultural communication can be *dialogue either for the purpose of increasing tolerance and cooperation or for evangelism in converting the other to one's own *faith perspectives. Communication between actual leaders of different traditions may involve dialogue and evangelism, as parties try to listen but also to convince each other of the value of their unique beliefs.

On an ideological level, however, there is a division between those who believe it is important to seek common truths among *world religions (*ecumenical religious pluralism) and those who believe this is foolhardy at best, either because religious concepts are so culturally embedded that they are intrinsically different from one another, despite surface similarities (postmodern religious pluralism), or because any attempts to show commonalities across religions and ethnic groups can result only in distortion of what persons in other religions really believe (radical religious pluralism).

Religious feminists, too, may hope to find common values and cause among women of many *faith traditions but also tend to be aware that this may not be fully realizable, given the plurality of women's *experiences across their myriad ethnic, national, economic, and familial contexts. Sometimes the dilemma of whether to tolerate or to change religious practices is very difficult. Feminists are often ambivalent or divided on how to address pluralism in morality, *politics, and religion. Much in feminist theologies would lead proponents to criticize patriarchal concepts of God and the diminution of women's role in religious bodies. But the very pluralism of this society may contribute to a dilemma for feminists of deciding when to exit patriarchal religions and join or create more desirable communities of faith and when to stay and fight for desired changes.

ADAIR T. LUMMIS

Pluralism: Theological Responses

Religious pluralism refers to the variety of religious traditions practiced around the world. The diversity of traditions, with their differing and sometimes opposing claims to truth, generates conflict among religions and peoples. Christian theological responses to the existence of multiple religious traditions have varied historically according to whatever specific *tradition Christian theologians have encountered in any given historical period. By and large, male Christian theologians have responded in three ways. Some have responded to an encounter with other *faiths by asserting Christian superiority. For example, Karl Barth in *Church Dogmatics,* while claiming that all religion (including Christianity) is *idolatrous, nevertheless asserts that Christianity is a vehicle of God's *grace. It is the only true religion because God definitively and solely reveals God's self in Jesus the Christ (280–361). This response is consistent with Christian evangelism and is formulated as official *doctrine for Reformed Protestants in the Barmen Declaration. A second, universalist response has been to assert that all religious people, insofar as their ethical teachings and practices are in keeping with those of Christianity, are, by default, Christians. This position maintains the centrality of Christianity by universalizing its claims to truth. In contrast to both exclusionist and universalist positions, pluralists have argued for a multiplicity of religious truths and the necessity for *dialogue, without the intention to evangelize, for the purpose of mutual understanding.

Feminist theologians have, for the most part, affirmed pluralism and dialogue with a further intention in mind. They have sought to build coalitions with women across traditions based on global concerns with *oppression according to gender, ethnicity, *race, and class, as well on reconstructing the various traditions themselves. For example, women who practice *Buddhism, Christianity, *Hinduism, Judaism, *Islam, Native American religions, and Feminist Free-thinking traditions have joined together to analyze critically the *patriarchy of their traditions (cf. Cooey/Eakin/McDaniel). In some cases, feminists reconstruct their respective traditions; in other cases, feminists establish new, nontraditional ways to reflect a more egalitarian vision that is nevertheless pluralist. Their work is thus grounded implicitly, if not always explicitly, in a shared concern for women around the world who themselves differ vastly from one another, rather than in a shared substantive vision of a single religious truth.

Attempts to sustain a genuine pluralism notwithstanding, Christian feminist theologians in particular still have a way to go. For example, Judith Plaskow has pointed out in "Feminist *Anti-Judaism and the Christian God" that Christian feminists have often uncritically appropriated anti-Judaic and supercessionist rhetoric, rooted in Christian scriptures, into their theologies. In addition, some feminist Christians have used antipagan rhetoric. Anglo feminist Christians have furthermore been vulnerable to ignoring the religious pluralism within their own tradition by assuming Anglo-European

Christianity as normative for all Christians and by appropriating the works of womanists, Asian and Asian-American women, and *mujeristas* without addressing racial, ethnic, and class differences. These difficulties have roots in Christianity itself, as a tradition that emerged by simultaneously identifying itself with and negatively distinguishing itself from Judaism. Christianity has further competed for converts aggressively with its own successor, Islam, and has occasionally sought to maintain internally its own doctrinal *purity through violent purges, some of which, notably the Spanish Inquisition and subsequent Puritan witch trials, were directed specifically against women.

Barth I/2 [1956]; Cooey/Eakin/McDaniel [1991]; Plaskow, *JFSR* [1991]

PAULA M. COOEY

Politics Politics is at the heart of feminist theologies, as it is for all *liberation theologies. The relationship of theology and politics is not a question of politicization, as many critics claim, but a reassertion of the political dimension of *religion that challenges simultaneously the truncated definitions of both politics and religion dominant in modern Western societies. Politics is not merely a matter of interest groups competing for *power within the state but the negotiation of all aspects of organizations, public activities, and social and cultural practices. Because power is inherent in all of these activities and institutions, all are open to the possibility of political critique and action.

There are two main streams influencing current feminist theological conceptions of politics. One is the foundational political engagement of all forms of liberation *theology, which understands theology as *praxis, an integral act of theological reflection and transformation of oppressive social structures. The other is the radical reenvisioning of the scope of politics emerging with Western feminist movements, which argue that "the personal is political." Challenging the liberal distinction between the public sphere (the world of politics) and the private sphere (the world of apolitical personal life), feminist activity has revealed the political nature of *sexuality, domestic *violence, rape, pornography, etc. Feminist theology has showed how such topics as the exclusion and subordination of women in scripture, the all-male *ministry, and the exclusive use of male images of God are all political questions.

Previously, feminist politics in the Euro-American world has existed in four main categories: (1) liberal feminism, which calls for the reform of existing political institutions to offer equal merit-based opportunity to individual women; (2) radical or cultural feminism, which seeks to develop a women's *culture in opposition to the fundamental patriarchal control of women's bodies; (3) *Marxist feminism, which links women's emancipation to class struggle against capitalism; and (4) *socialist feminism, which analyzes women's position at the juncture of capitalism and *patriarchy and evaluates change in light of the interconnections of *race, class, and gender *oppression.

In more recent years, these categories have been broken up by some other distinctive developments that may be broadly characterized as *"postmodern": (1) a new visibility of political projects of women of color and indigenous women (in both the first and two-thirds Worlds), who may participate in any of the other categories discussed here but insist on the political distinctiveness of struggles based in racial and ethnic experiences; (2) the further definition of *lesbian and bisexual cultural or identity politics; and (3) the emergence of poststructuralist/*deconstructionist feminism, which describes subjects as constructed by coercive discourses of power and knowledge and seeks to deconstruct all notions of "women" subjects in favor of the free play of a plurality of *difference. These trends in very different ways lead to a concern with a *politics of identity*, where identity is both a starting point and a subject of political activity. The influence of these developments on feminist theology is evident in the growing presence of womanist, *mujerista,* Asian-American, indigenous, lesbian, and deconstructive theologies by women in the Euro-American context and also in African, Asian and Pacific, and Latin American feminist work. In all of this varied work, women seek to name the sacred present in the specificity of their particular struggles. The challenge is to situate these ongoing explorations of identity in their social contexts in ways that foster the connections and coalitions essential for political transformation.

Fulkerson [1994]; Harrison [1985]; Jaggar [1983]; Townes [1995]

ELIZABETH M. BOUNDS

Polygamy Technically, polygamy means the marrying of many wives or husbands simultaneously. The practice of one woman marrying many husbands, a form of polygamy known as "polyandry," is uncommon today. Therefore the term *polygamy* has shifted in meaning and replaced the term *polygyny,* which is a matrimonial relationship in which one or more women are married to one man. "Consecutive polygamy" refers to a series of marriages in which there is only one spouse at a time.

Until recently, the subject of polygamy has appeared in Christian debates mainly as a moral issue relating to *marriage. Convinced that the scriptures advocate monogamy through texts such as the *creation of Adam and Eve (Gen. 2:23–25), the Christian church had taken pains to condemn those *cultures in which polygamy is a form of accepted matrimony. Considering polygamy immoral and all those involved sinners, the church then refused to accept men, women, and children in polygamous families as church members. Often men were asked to choose one wife and to leave the others in order to be accepted in church. The church also found fault with *Islam for legally stipulating a maximum of four wives to a man.

Recent studies by women in books such as *The Will to Arise* (Oduyoye/Kanyoro) look at polygamy as an institution oppressive to women. Polygamy thrives in *patriarchal cultures, which believe in the superiority of male persons. Men may own not only property but women and their productive powers as well. Polygamy has tended to exploit women and children's labor because the practice is justified as a means of enhancing the productivity of the man's property. Polygamy also depicts women as weak and needing constant protection of men. It reduces women's ability to cope with circumstances of their *body, such as barrenness. Both in the Bible and in many cultures, women who do not give birth or who give birth to only girl children are diminished and find themselves perpetuating polygamy.

The church finds evidence in the scriptures that seems to advocate monogamy, yet there is no direct condemnation of polygamy in the Bible. African feminists argue that the case for monogamy should be based on the dignity of women rather than on moral judgments or the justification of one form of marriage over another. Failure to teach true *equality between the two sexes is failure to instill in society that the superiority of man over woman is contrary to God's intention for human beings.

Bahemuka [1993]; Hastings [1973]; Kanyoro, in Pobee [1994]; Maimela [1994]; Oduyoye/Kanyoro [1992]

MUSIMBI R. A. KANYORO

Popular Religiosity Popular religiosity contrasts with the form of religion or *faith practiced by the elite classes within any given religious *tradition. Popular religiosity or faith characteristically depends on oral transmission. Its practices focus on ordinary concerns and experiences, such as *healing the sick, finding lost objects, establishing desired *relationships with other humans or other animals, getting the crops to grow, safely delivering healthy babies, and properly preparing the dead for their departure from the earth (concerns that are historically rooted in the domestic realm or rural society, associated with physicality, and often feminized). In addition, popular religiosity may reflect a synthesis of indigenous traditions with later, invading traditions, as, for example, in the case of Mexican practices surrounding the Day of the Dead, celebrated on November 2, which combine Aztec with Roman Catholic motifs.

Because of historical restrictions placed on *education according to gender, class, and *race, in conjunction with elitist privileging of texts over oral transmission, popular religiosity has been the domain of the poor and people of color of both genders, as well as women of all classes and races. Until recently, scholars of religion have tended to identify popular piety with magic and superstition and to devalue it in relation to elite religion. Likewise, elite Protestant theologians have tended to view popular piety as deviant; potentially, if not actually, *heretical; and therefore in need of policing. Provided that assimilated practices remain subordinated to elite practices and do not threaten institutional authority, Roman Catholic theologians have, by contrast, been more sympathetic to popular religiosity and have consciously sought assimilation.

Feminist theologians have criticized the privileging of sacred and theological texts over all other forms of symbolism, experience, and practice. They have done so by seeking to transvalue, or reevaluate critically, the ordinary. This transvaluation has gone in different, sometimes conflicting directions. Some feminists have sought to elevate the status of popular religiosity. Feminists who argue for the sacralizing of women's experience fall into this category. Penelope Washbourn's *Becoming Woman* represents a classic example of this kind of effort. More recently, some feminists have cautioned against the impulse to sacralize women's experience on the grounds that the very act depends on establishing an elite group by distinguishing what is sacred from what is profane. Such acts thus duplicate and perpetuate elitism rather than overcome it. Victoria Lee Erickson's *Where Silence Speaks* represents this point of view.

Feminists who have sought simultaneously to value positively the religious experiences and practices of dispossessed people and challenge elitist theologies within their specific traditions represent a third direction. Judith Plaskow argues in *Standing Again at Sinai,* for example, that Jewish women's *experiences be formally recognized as authoritative within the *covenant between God and the Jewish people and be valued positively in their difference from male elite practices. For Plaskow, this transvaluation requires that Jews relinquish the claim of *election, or chosenness, in favor of a distinctness that rejects exclusion on the basis of gender elitism or religious elitism.

From a Christian perspective, Paula Cooey argues in *Religious Imagination and the Body* that both religious experience and *religion are artifacts of human *culture that reciprocate in the making of human culture and identity. As such, they enjoy no special status except insofar as they may serve to foster a more just society; they most effectively serve this purpose when they detour all impulses to sacralize. The differences among these three alternatives are significant; nevertheless, they share a common concern to value positively what counts as popular religiosity as a means of overcoming the popular–elite dichotomy.

Cooey [1994]; Erickson [1993]; Plaskow [1990]; Washbourn [1977]

PAULA M. COOEY

Pornography Pornography is the visual or oral "degrading and demeaning portrayal of the role and status of the human female," according to a governmental commission (*Report of the Commission on Obscenity and Pornography,* 1979). Feminists and womanists have found this definition to be less than adequate, because it does not address the social and political impact of pornography or the violence-prone, sexually exploitative industry that produces pornography. Taking account of the social and political costs, Susan Brownmiller, in her groundbreaking work *Against Our Will: Men, Women and Rape,* defined pornography as "the undiluted essence of anti-female propaganda" (443).

The *patriarchal objection to pornography, as represented by the 1954 American Law Institute's *Model Penal Code* (251.4) is that it appeals to "prurient interests" or a "morbid" interest in nudity and sexuality. From the perspective of feminist theology, the denigration of sexual stimulation or pleasure as "prurient" is one of the roots of patriarchal culture's denigration of and *violence toward the material world and women as symbols of the physical, especially the sexual. This patriarchal sexual ethic subordinates sex to heterosexual, marital procreation and condemns as illicit all other forms of sexual stimulation. It also has too narrow a focus on the genital aspects of human sexuality, ignoring or repudiating an attitude of pleasure toward the world.

The claiming of the *erotic* as one of the goods of human life has been a key theme in womanist and feminist writing. The erotic is the "fundamental power of life, born into us, [which] heals, makes whole, empowers and liberates" (Brock, 25). Therefore, a display of pleasurable, mutual sexual expression that does not demean or degrade is not pornographic; it is a depiction of several of the goods of life. By contrast, Audre Lorde's "Uses of the Erotic: The Erotic as Power" declares, "But pornography is a direct denial of the power of the erotic, for it represents the suppression of true feeling. Pornography emphasizes sensation without feeling" (54).

Pornography, from the perspective of feminist and womanist theology, is that which depicts a contempt for human sexuality and thus for human life. This is most often portrayed as the degradation and violent treatment of women and children. Pornographic content is also indicated by the *male gaze,* a term describing the orientation of text, film, or audio toward the consumer, inviting him or her to identify with the dominator and experience a feeling of sadism. In this sense, pornography degrades the dignity of not only the victim as portrayed but the victimizer in the form of the consumer as well.

Feminist activists against the pornography industry, such as Women Against Violence in Pornography and Media, have documented that those who produce pornography are engaged in explicit practices of sexual exploitation, rape, and child molestation. The so-called kiddie porn industry has grown exponentially around the world, and many children "employed" in this industry are runaways or "throwaways," street children from both the first and the third world, who are exploited by this industry (Rush, in Lederer, 71–85). Racism also constructs the pornography industry. African-American women such as Luisah Teish have worked hard to make clear that slavery continues "in the exploitation of women's bodies through prostitution and pornography and denial of reproductive rights" (in Lederer, 115).

In the United States, feminists, particularly in the decade of the 1970s and in the early 1800s, have disagreed on legal approaches to pornography. From a liberal feminist perspective, civil rights and *freedom of expression demand a "free speech" approach to pornography. Activists in the movement to end violence against women have argued that obscenity, i.e., "hard core" pornography, is not and should not be covered by the First Amendment. Those in this industry who kidnap, molest, restrain, and rape primarily women and children should be prosecuted under laws appropriate to those offenses. In general, most activists favor an "antidefamation" approach through education, consciousness-raising, and community-based actions (Kaminer, in Lederer, 241].

Brock [1988]; Brownmiller [1975]; Griffin [1981]; Lederer [1980]; Lorde [1984]; *Report of the Commission on Obscenity and Pornography* [1979]

SUSAN BROOKS THISTLETHWAITE

Post-Christian The term post-Christian is widely used within feminist circles involved in issues of theology and spirituality in Britain, following my use of it in my book, *Theology and Feminism,* and elsewhere. It designates someone standing within the western theological tradition who is not a Christian. (Thus one will find "Christian feminist" and "post-Christian" given as two possible positions; "Goddess" is almost non-existent.) The term might well refer equally to a man who holds this position and is used by men of themselves. But it is mostly women, who are feminists, who have left Christianity behind them at least in part on account of a feminist critique who so employ it.

That this term has come to be adopted may well be seen to be a consequence of the different cultural atmosphere prevailing in Britain and in the British theological scene than is the case in North America. The term "Christian" still means something. There has been public debate (notably following the publication of *The Myth of God Incarnate,* ed. Hick, 1977) and with the current controversy over "non-realism" following Don Cupitt's advocacy of such a stance) as to the truth and limits of Christianity. In the United States in particular, by contrast, it seems that "Christian" is a much wider cultural term (used to describe those who are not Jews or atheists). The difference may also be a consequence of the fact that in Britain only 10 percent of the population attend church, and thus designate themselves clearly as "Christian," this meaning something in what is otherwise a secular society.

I myself argue, within such a context, that the legitimate boundary as to what is Christian is belief in the uniqueness of Jesus as the Christ; this uniqueness having been variously expressed during different periods. Such a designation leaves space for people to say that they are theist (not atheist), but that they cannot believe the "myth" of Christianity to be true or that there can have been a human who had a second and divine nature—or any other expression of that uniqueness. The term is good in that it expresses that one has come out of the Christian (and not any other) tradition and that one may have taken much with one; while also acknowledging that one no longer adheres to Christian faith. It is problematic if it becomes confused with the term post-Christian (as in post-Christian society) meaning simply secular.

The term was earlier used by Mary Daly (in an article of which I was unaware); and then, modified as "postchristian" *(sic),* in widely disseminated work (as in the Introduction to the second edition of *The Church and the Second Sex,* the book having the subtitle *With New Feminist Postchristian Introduction by the Author),* after she had left the church. Daly may thus claim to have invented this term having this usage. (She later abandoned it, post-1975, presumably as conveying a reaction to, and thus dependence upon, Christianity.) I do not believe that Daly's use of the term, though I was not unaware of it, was instrumental in my choice of post-Christian; rather was it its precision which commended it to me. My different spelling is thus of significance. The issue of disengaging the Christian myth from the crediting that humans have experienced a dimension of reality which we may name God (and which, it is argued, should now be differently conceptualized) has not been to the fore in Daly's work. Post-Christian has had, in the British context, this double connotation in relation to the western religious tradition.

Daly [1973a; 1973b]; Hampson [1990; 1995]

DAPHNE HAMPSON

Postmodernism The term *postmodernism* is so diffuse that *postmodernisms* would be more correct. Its open-endedness and fluidity make it an attractive epistemological model, but these same characteristics make postmodernism difficult to define. This diverse philosophical and political movement can be viewed through three "moments."

The Three Moments. The first moment is the postmodern *critique of modernity,* which consists in unmasking modernity's contradictory impulses and results. Modernity promised *freedom, *equality, and unlimited progress. What modernity produced instead was genocide, ecological disaster, and multiple forms of *oppression, particularly of indigenous populations and women. Its rampant capitalism produced extreme *poverty and class inequality. Modernity seeks to create the self as ahistorical and universal. This autonomous individual found itself imprisoned and disempowered by bureaucracy and meaninglessness.

The second moment in postmodernism concerns this autonomous self, for postmodernism seeks the *"disappearance" of the subject.* The autonomous self of the Enlightenment centered meaning in itself and its belief in its unlimited *power and freedom. Since this power and freedom have proven illusory, the shift has been away from the subject to communal forms of meaning. For feminists, this undoing of subjectivity is important, as it provides the basis for the questioning of feminine, masculine, and sexual identities. The meaning of "woman" is no longer sure. It allows the interrogation of patriarchally produced sexual meanings and enables the formation of less reified sexual identities and expressions.

The third moment of postmodernism concerns the *end to universal and *hegemonic definitions,* discourses, and worldviews. It calls into question the meaning of individual words, construing them as open with multiple meanings. The prevalent discourses of groups in power are overturned. Universal worldviews, whether they are *Marxist, Christian, Stalinist, or other, are considered no more superior than the worldviews of magic, occult, and superstition. Even science, seen as the site of ecological destruction, is no longer considered "objective"; it takes its place as one among many belief systems. The term *"objective"* itself is no longer operative. The playing field of opposing worldviews becomes level, even tipped toward local and alternative epistemologies. Foundations are considered mythical, uncertainty becomes a *virtue, and the fragmentary is elevated.

Promise to Feminist Theologies. By calling into question the Enlightenment project, postmodernism enables feminist theologians to interrogate the male bias of even so-called liberal theologies. Liberal theologies, which, on the surface, seem to uphold the equality of women and minorities, can be shown to mask the hegemonic power arrangements that constitute modernity. A theology deeply rooted in the failed modern paradigm, with its unfounded optimism, cannot take seriously women's oppression and need for *liberation.

Feminist theology can benefit from the attenuation of the subject. A more open subjectivity can free women from oppressive identities and the definitional constraints of what a woman is and "should" be. By decentering the subject, the importance of communal *solidarity, of women joining with other women to achieve liberation, becomes primary. Women are freed from an isolation that can lead to their continued control by *patriarchal structures. Women can now create their own meaning together.

The end of universal definitions and meanings can free feminist theology from operating under male terms. *God, Word, Scripture,* and other theological terms are now open signs that can receive new meaning, using feminist values and images. New words can be created. Definitions are no longer fixed but operate under the concept of "play." Rigid moral systems become relativized, allowing women's values and virtues to come into the game. Opening up the concept of "woman" breaks feminism free from its own bondage to the white middle class, enabling women of color and other classes to define themselves.

Drawbacks for Feminist Theologies. While the Enlightenment and its bourgeois values had their oppressive component, their liberatory component with its emphasis on human rights cannot simply be discarded. It was the Enlightenment that began the movement away from the *domination and superstition of medieval times (with its witch burnings and "gynocide") toward an emancipatory ideal, even though it was originally restricted to white property-owning males. While feminist theology might not want to be rooted in Enlightenment rationality, discarding it completely seems unnecessary. An extreme decentering of the subject could lead to a utilitarian consideration of the group or the project over the dignity and value of the person.

In the same way, a kind of total *relativism about local meanings could lead to groups being able to oppress women, claiming the protection of their local knowledge. This could be true of Christian groups who practice a kind of confessionalism that allows discrimination against women as one of its components. Unless women's emancipation remains a universal value, postmodernism itself could become oppressive. However, if it is used by feminist theology not in an absolutist fashion but in the open manner its own characteristics imply, then postmodernism can be an important theoretical tool in the feminist theological project.

Chopp [1989]; Rosenau [1992]; Welch [1985]

SUSAN DOLAN-HENDERSON

Poverty Currently, the word *poverty* denotes a lack of material possessions. In some religious traditions we speak about "spiritual poverty," which can be interpreted as a positive feeling of acceptance of our human poverty before the wealth of God's reality. Also, some accept material poverty as a way of welcoming the mysterious will of God. These ideas of poverty are linked to a concept of retribution in the life after death. This reinforces a *dualistic point of view about human history.

It seems very important to recognize that the idea of accepting poverty is a *social construct which comes from *patriarchal societies. This acceptance concerns not only economic issues but also gender issues. Women are poorer than men. Women are more powerless than men. This is considered part of the "natural order" that a patriarchal understanding of human life has developed in a very special way. In this sense we can speak about "anthropological poverty." This means that in the deepest understanding of human beings, men are considered more important and richer than women. There are different historical, social, and religious consequences connected to this understanding of human beings, all having negative effects in women's lives. We call this anthropological poverty because it is present at the root of the understanding of human beings and is the support for economic and social poverties. This anthropological poverty becomes a kind of *"metaphysical" reality that allows all kinds of social and religious poverty to exist and even to be encouraged.

Class struggle is a fight within a divided society where an elite has all the rights and the means of production and exploits the masses to its own benefit. In the traditional interpretation of class struggle, anthropological poverty is not taken into consideration as an *ideology that undermines the social system. When theorists spoke about mankind's sufferings, they were thinking especially about the life of men, in spite of some inclusion of women's and children's *suffering. From this perspective, in the same patriarchal system, the poor needed to struggle only to have civil, social, and political rights. The viewpoint that supports various social and religious injustices was not acknowledged, neither in its origins nor in its historical development in human behavior.

Feminists are beginning to perceive this anthropological reality and to denounce it as a way of continuing injustice and *violence against women, children, nature, and poor populations. Feminists are beginning to denounce this same anthropology in Christian theology and Christian *tradition. Rebelling against patriarchal "anthropological poverty," women denounce the presence of *sexism as an ideological part of this understanding of human beings. Women all over the world are the most important workforce, but they never earn just compensation. Women throughout the world have primary *responsibility for the care of children, old people, victims of war, the sick, etc., and yet women are still considered as a class inferior to and weaker than men.

Rebelling against anthropological poverty as a basic premise of anthropology in a *hierarchical system is not claiming a position of honor for women in this patriarchal society. It is to claim a process of transforming our own understanding of human beings, as well as transforming the patriarchal and hierarchical society in which we live. This also means the ability to recognize that we are linked to the ecosystem, to the various processes of life. If we exploit and kill the ecosystem, we are also killing human beings, and especially the powerless among them.

Women's poverty is linked to social economic processes and to the destruction of nature. These processes derive from political and economic decisions taken by powerful elites in every country and by corporations all over the world. The powerful work in a transnational perspective, with special regard for making profit and not for the lives of millions of people and of other, nonhuman beings. The patriarchal system not only dominates women and nature but also exploits them, until the final result is destruction and death. This process of destruction and death is linked to the anthropological understanding present also in the Western Christian tradition: that man is called to dominate all the earth and subject it to himself, and that this human work of conquering Mother Nature includes *sacrifice as a natural consequence. But only the powerless, women, and nature are objects of sacrifice, and only male conquerors are glorified. All these behaviors are rooted in a kind of *discontinuity* between God and earth and humans, between men and women and nature. From this perspective we are considered as separated beings directed by the separated, independent Big Being. We are considered as opposed to one another.

This destructive reality challenges us to rethink poverty in the largest and most inclusive sense. Today, the option for the poor means an option for all life. Without the life of all lives, there is no living planet, there are no human beings. We are also invited to rethink human traditions, and especially the Christian tradition. Our tradition needs to be understood as a way to help the human and natural ecosystems to be alive together, as a single body. All is connected with all, and each suffering, each poverty, affects all of humanity and the whole universe. New feminist perspectives are working to build a worldwide struggle and a new hope to go beyond all violent and unjust poverties.

Couture [1991]; Gutiérrez [1983]; Thomas [1994]

IVONE GEBARA

Power In writing a feminist theology of liberating *praxis in the South African context, it is crucial to consider issues surrounding the nature and exercise of power. A conventional understanding of power is the ability or means to accomplish ends. Ideally, power is reciprocal, collaborative energy that engages us personally and communally with God, with one another, and with all of *creation in such a way that power becomes synonymous with the vitality of living fully and freely. Grappling with the concept of power, feminist theologians have, however, encountered three persistent problems: definition of power, the relationship between power and *difference (understood as particularity), and the theological meaning of power.

Problems of Definition. The very act of defining power is problematic because understandings of the nature of power differ profoundly, and the exercise of power is so implicitly part of life that it defies tidy definition and identification. A common definition of power simply sees it pejoratively as "exploitative *domination." This view denies the complexity of power and the manifold mechanisms employed in the exercise of power. If power is domination, it is ultimately destructive. Such a notion conflicts with the understanding of a powerful God who supports and redeems all of creation.

A further description of power restricts it to two modes: "power over" (bad power) and "power to" (power for good). Such a dichotomy cannot be sustained, as it does not take cognizance of the realities of life. For instance, a parent making decisions for a child exercises power over that child, and such power may not necessarily be bad. A further problem with this view of power is that it can become trapped into the *dualistic identification of "power over" as masculine or patriarchal power and "power to" as feminine or relational power. Linking power to gender in an *essentialist manner does not accord with reality. Women also have "power over." For instance, apartheid gave white women power as exploitative domination over black women and men.

Definitions of power need to take into account the fact that power is evidenced in diverse and interrelated ways: as power over, power to, power for, power with; as related to knowledge, love, difference, *violence, resistance, and *embodiment. Power is present in the very fabric of our lives, in political, social, economic, and religious structures and it has both internal and external aspects.

Power, Difference, and Women's Lives. The asymmetry of power between women and men has informed feminist analyses and conceptions of history, uncovering gender as a powerful and pervasive force in the organizing of society. Feminists seeking to unmask discriminatory and oppressive views and practices with regard to women use the concept of *patriarchy, understood as the systematic exercise of male power in all spheres of life, to seek the transformation of society from historically entrenched, unequal relations to a redistribution of power. A critique of this analysis is that it can lead to a dichotomous view of the individual vis-à-vis society, as well as of powerful men vis-à-vis powerless women. Women then become an undifferentiated category to whom passivity is imputed.

Differences in terms of *race and class among women show that power cannot be reduced to the simple categories of oppressed and oppressor. A more multiple and diffuse understanding of power helps locate the differences among women in particular social and historical settings. Women in third-world contexts do not have identical *experiences of race, gender, and class; neither are their experiences the same as those of women in first-world contexts, whose experiences in turn also differ among themselves. As Chandra T. Mohanty points out, when the category "powerful–powerless" is applied to minorities or to women in the third world, the struggle for equity and *freedom is reduced to one of binary structures and oppositions. Third-world women are categorized as powerless and, as such, are seen as being helpless, without social, moral, or political *agency. This allows first-world women to assume positions of power in the social, moral, and political spheres, which, in turn, seriously damages the forging of alliances among women. An integrated understanding of the relationship between power and difference is needed if relationality and mutuality, values central to feminist theologies, are to prevail.

Feminist Theologies and Power. Feminist theological understandings of power begin with analyses that acknowledge the diversity of women's experiences. Such analyses recognize the multiple faces of power in the interrelated spheres of the personal and social. Power is understood as a process or an event that is inherently dynamic and embodied. One of the shadowy sides of power is found in violence toward women. Analyses of women's experience of power should uncover both women's collusion with the forces that sustain power as domination over them and their participation in domination over others. Analysis is the first step in assessing the ethical context of the concrete exercise of power. It can also validate strategic resistance to existing power relations. The aim is not to overturn one system of dominance for another but rather to deconstruct power relations analytically in order to transform or reconstruct social values and institutions.

The setting of a feminist theological agenda is often primarily a question of power. Women doing theology in third-world contexts struggle for access to resources that first-world women take for granted. First-world feminist theologians need constantly to acknowledge and challenge the power dynamics of race and class in their own communities and their complicity in the exercise of "power over" women of the third world.

Foucault [1980]; Harrison [1985]; hooks [1984]; Mohanty/Russo/Torres [1991]

DENISE M. ACKERMAN

Praxis The term *praxis* signifies intentional social activity. In feminist theologies, praxis refers to the social activity of emancipation in Christian feminism. Praxis brings together a stress on the interconnectedness of historical existence and normative concerns of *freedom, on the one hand, and *responsibility to change oppressive conditions into possibilities for human and planetary flourishing, on the other. As a central interpretive lens of feminism, praxis focuses on the very nature of Christianity, the shape of theology in feminism, and the ongoing construction of Christian doctrines and symbols.

The concern for praxis goes back to Greek *philosophy and is related to the question "How do we live a good life?" For Aristotle, praxis refers to the life of the *polis* and has to do with the determination of that which can be other. The ability to make the necessary judgments for life in the polis is called *phronēsis,* or practical reasoning. As a particular type of knowledge, *phronēsis* has to do with character, judgment, insight, and practical wisdom. The history of Christian theology in the classical Western *tradition has shied away from identifying Christian life with praxis and *phronēsis,* preferring to locate religious activity in the personal or in the otherworldly and thus to relate theology to theoretical or existential knowledge. In modern Western philosophy, renewed attention to praxis and practical reason stressed the importance of freedom and normative action, as in Kant's stress on *ethics and Marx's stress on the necessity of philosophy not merely to interpret history but to change it.

Though praxis has often been neglected as a formulation of Christian life and as a form of theological knowledge, at least in the classical Western tradition, contemporary theologies of various types stress the importance of some type of reflection on praxis. The necessity to understand the historical nature of knowledge, to analyze the social character of existence, and to take seriously the responsibility of freedom in times of historical change is increasingly important for all types of

Christian theology. Feminist theologies, like other forms of liberation *theology, not only reflect on praxis but seek actively to be a form of praxis: to shape Christian activity around the norms and visions of emancipation and transformation.

Praxis as the Nature of Christianity. Feminist theologies name Christianity as itself a praxis: an activity of freedom in the world. Womanist theologians such as Jacquelyn Grant and Delores Williams suggest that Christianity is an activity for *survival and *liberation, enabling black women to survive in a world that denies them necessary resources. Rosemary Radford Ruether has suggested that Christianity become a prophetic movement for freedom in the world. Christian praxis means the work of God and Christians in alleviating *oppression, in forming communities of survival and hope, and in providing new ways of flourishing. Because of this central reshaping of Christianity through historical possibilities for emancipation, human *agency takes on a new importance. Ethics, including "new" ethical concerns regarding sexual *violence, ecological destruction, and *sexuality, have emerged as leading concerns in Christianity for feminist theologies. A spirituality of connectedness, *embodiment, and openness as shaped through Christian praxis is another vital concern for feminists who seek both to retrieve forgotten or neglected women in history and to explore new resources for spirituality in the present.

Praxis as the Shape of Theology. Perhaps one of the most important contributions of feminist theology has been to create a form of theological knowledge that is itself a praxis, an activity of freedom in the world. Feminist theology is contextual; it works within specific situations to name experiences, to identify sufferings, and to articulate possibilities of transformation. As a type of critical theory, feminist theology is a form of knowledge that is self-reflexive, aimed at emancipation and enlightenment. It seeks to uncover distorted relations between knowledge, power, and interest, including those relations that reinforce the false *ideology of a universal "woman" as opposite and inferior to man. Feminist theology demonstrates the pervasiveness of *dualism and binary opposition in knowledge and in social organization. Such binary opposition, with its attendant *hierarchical ordering, characterizes earth, women, and those who are not elite, Western white males as weak, irrational, something to be feared and controlled. But feminist theology is itself a praxis, not only through its critical uncovering of distorted thought and social organization but also through its creative envisioning of new possibilities. Ethics and epistemology are joined in feminist theology because the knowledge of God involves transformation of self, others, and world.

Praxis and the Transformation of Doctrines and Symbols. The imaginative work of feminist theologies can be easily seen in the tremendous amount of work feminists have done to reconstruct Christian symbols and doctrines to guide Christian praxis. Sallie McFague has constructed models of God as mother, lover, and friend. Rita Nakashima Brock has suggested that Jesus Christ be understood as the Christa/Community of erotic power that heals the woundedness of women and men. Elisabeth Schüssler Fiorenza speaks of the *ekklēsia,* the community of democratic participation. Rebecca Chopp has reinterpreted the *doctrine of *sin to cover the lamentations of *suffering, the critical analysis of systems of destruction, and the depth ordering of phallocentrism as a self-perpetuating *idolatry. Such symbolic reconstruction allows Christianity personal and social power to guide human action and to produce new images and possibilities for flourishing.

Chopp [1995]; Ruether [1983/1993]; Schüssler Fiorenza [1992a]; Williams [1993a]

REBECCA S. CHOPP

Prayer Prayer is a critical subject in academic circles, congregations, and grassroots communities. Intense debates transpire concerning the nature, form, action, and content of prayers of a feminist nature. A corpus of knowledge is proliferating, coming from women's subcultures around the world: through feminist rituals groups, women clergy, laity gatherings, Women-Church, Wicca, and *pastoral care settings. Because religious groups from every period of history and all cultures have invented or re-created their own prayers to represent their own *anthropology and cosmology, the women's movement also has called forth new challenges for authentic women's liberating *liturgies and prayers commensurate with fresh interpretations, new symbols, and our hearts' more courageous spoken yearnings.

Language, *Naming, and the Nature and Function of Prayer. Insofar as prayer utilizes language, feminist theological principles call for an end to the exclusive use of masculinist names, attributes, and images not only for humanity but also for the Divine in our prayer life. Women have chosen alternative ways of describing the sacred, from God/She to *Goddess, Mother, Parent, *Sophia, Shekhinah, Light, Holy One, Bakerwoman God, and countless others. Generally preferred are appellations that are not militaristic, triumphalistic, narcissistic in the holy attributes or domineering or "juvenilizing" of women. Also important is concern for animals, the biosphere, and the *cosmos.

Traditional theologies have stressed the importance of prayer in spiritual life and struggled with how God might "answer our prayers." Many feminists find it helpful to affirm that prayer often changes the one who prays rather than persuades an omniscient God. Feminist process theologians, who have been most involved in thinking about the mechanics of such change, have posited that because of the intricate interactive relationship between God and humanity, both are transformed through prayer.

Contributions from Our Diversities That Broaden and Enrich Prayer. White feminist, womanist, *mujerista,* Asian theologies all call for a decentering of *patriarchal and Euro–North American thought. Prayer is truly enriched through the sharing of prayer styles, content, meanings, and theologies of all cultures. Jewish women have worked to find and redeem the prayers of women through the ages, searching for authentic language of prayer and changing the whole of Judaism. Christians are sharing the importance of Sophia, or Wisdom, and her role in reimaging Christianity beyond solely patriarchal religion. Women of color, at least dually oppressed, may find solace in praying to a God who suffers with us, while black Christian women remember how Sojourner Truth said, "I cried out and none but Jesus heard" (Foner, 103). Womanist theologians distrust the *metaphors of slavery and servanthood for discipleship and teach us all that social witness is strongly yoked with spirituality.

Latinas may have a relationship with Mary, our Lady of Heaven, while women with disabilities pray to a God who receives, not hears, their prayers. Abused women, not satisfied with a God/ess who weeps, need one who rages against *violence and screams out for *justice to prevail with regard to not only abusers but also the religious structures of *evil undergirding such death-dealing ways. Asian women teach us how haughty any theological stance is that proclaims *heaven exists for only the peoples of one *faith or creed. *Lesbians remind us of our *heterosexist and homophobic themes in prayer and suggest that a friend/sister/lover god may represent our most personal experience of intimacy. Reverence for the earth by native peoples teaches a consumer society that is rapidly hurtling toward destruction and leads us toward a *pantheistic theology. These examples name only a few ways in which social class and racial and ethnic location particularize prayer and enrich our theologies of prayer.

Toward a Feminist *Thealogy/Theology of Prayer. Although women's spirituality has all too often been deemed trite on the one hand and dangerous on the other, recently our reimaging of symbols and traditions has again shaken the foundations of patriarchal religions. Redefining prayer (including reimaging the receptor of our appeal) and celebrating prayer in all of its diverse forms are just the beginning. *Heresy is not of consequence to women searching for new ways to name themselves and to reconnect with the sacred and ignite *relationships within divine reality.

In summary, women's affinity for mystery, warmth, the earthy and concrete, the particular, listening, humor, storytelling, candor, availability, and paradox will provide a new prayer life from the point of view of women struggling to be free, bringing along their children, *families, the earth, and the cosmos. No doubt basic theological categories such as modeling of God, God's relationship to human beings, divine and human will, and struggle and evil will be radically changed as women's theologies of prayer become published. Indeed, they have already emerged whenever women gather together to center on our experience in the light of that which we hold most dear in our lives.

Anderson [1991]; King, in Procter-Smith/Walton [1993]; LeFevre, *CTS* [1982]; Spiegel/Kremsdorf [1987]; Tamez, ed. [1989]; Wylie-Kellerman, *Witness* [1993]; Zangano [1993]

GAIL LYNN UNTERBERGER

Preaching Preaching as an act of *ministry brings together the world of texts, the world of religious traditions, the world of individual psychological and spiritual needs, and the world of the larger social context in which people live. As religious proclamation it interprets and constructs personal, social, and ecclesiastical reality; it is a public act of theological *naming. Traditional white, Western, male Christian preaching most often has taken the biblical text and the community of *faith as the two primary starting places and points of focus for proclamation. For many preachers of social, economic, and cultural privilege, unquestioned *authority is still given to scripture and *tradition in the preaching act. Individual nurture and inspiration are often the goal of such preaching.

Women who preach from various feminist perspectives and men who embrace similar convictions and analysis share a belief that many dimensions of the Christian tradition contribute to injustice and stand in need of radical transformation. With this in mind, at least two primary tasks face preachers who preach from feminist perspectives: (1) to reflect critically on every aspect of one's own theology in order to discern the ways it perpetuates and undergirds the *oppression of women, and (2) to probe the connections between women's oppression and all other forms of oppression in our day.

Preaching from a feminist perspective relies on feminist theology because creating theological, social, and ecclesiastical transformation is feminist theology's primary agenda. Feminist theology begins its work with critical reflection on women's *experience of oppression and *marginality. The feminist theologian then draws on those experiences to transform and reshape theological categories, ethical paradigms, biblical hermeneutics, the reconstruction of *church history, and the practice of ministry. Similar commitments and work face those who embrace preaching from a feminist perspective. In an effort to proclaim and create transformation, preachers place the traditional discipline and craft of homiletics in constant *dialogue with the critique and vision of feminist, womanist, *mujerista,* Asian women's, and First Nation women's theological work. Feminist religious preaching is the integration of women's critical and constructive theological thought and homiletical practice.

Preachers who preach from feminist

perspectives commit themselves to the task of rethinking every dimension of preaching in relation to all the forms of oppression and injustice that violate women's lives. God-language, biblical interpretation, *christological *doctrine, and all theological categories put forth in the act of proclamation need to reflect an awareness of women's distinctive experiences and oppression.

This is only the first step in a transformational preaching agenda. Feminist preaching assumes a very broad agenda for its work. In addition to the explicit theological task of preaching and its focus on women's lives, feminist preaching is committed to making connections between women's oppression and all other forms of systemic injustice. The proclamations of preachers influenced by feminist perspectives will reflect an awareness that *sexism is fundamentally connected to *classism, North American *imperialism, *ageism, "ableism," white *racism, militarism, and *heterosexism. Feminist preaching understands the absolute necessity of thorough *social analysis for all preaching. It is preaching that proclaims a religious and ecclesiastical vision which assumes the sacred quality of all *creation. It seeks theological, pastoral, biblical, and ethical language that will reflect the diversity of all human experience. Feminist preaching is transformational by its very definition and nature. It commits individual preachers to the critical and constructive task of examining every aspect of the pastoral, hermeneutical, theological, and social ramifications of their religious proclamations.

Farmer/Hunter [1990]; González/González [1994]; Smith [1989/1992]

CHRISTINE M. SMITH

Predestination *Predestination* is a technical term for that voluntary act of the divine will to set in advance the course of each human life and its final destiny. Many religions have grappled with the relationship between human *free will and divine omnipotence, particularly as that relationship pertains to the causes of human *redemption. In the Christian *tradition, predestination is also inseparable from questions of divine mercy and *grace and human *sin. There are many scriptural allusions to some sort of preordaining of each human life, particularly to the idea of *election or divine choice.

A number of Greek church fathers took up related questions—divine *freedom and foreknowledge, for example—but Augustine (354–430 C.E.) was the first to take up the question of predestination directly. His formulation allowed for human free will even as it accorded God complete *power over the course of each human life, integrating efficacious grace, vocation, and the true *agency of each will: God knew beforehand the effect of grace in each human being, even as each person chose good or *evil.

In the Reformation, election emerged as the issue that separated the range of Protestant positions (Luther's, Zwingli's, Calvin's, and others') from the Catholic tradition, formulated most fully at the Council of Trent (1545–63). Many Catholic and Protestant theologians followed Augustine in distinguishing between divine prescience and human knowledge: the destiny of each human being was invisible to all but God. But Protestants insisted upon grace as the precondition for salvation. Grace was not earned through human effort but was a condition granted by God. Calvin drew the radical implications of God's perfectly free will: God grants grace to whom God wills, and therefore, one is predestined to salvation or damnation, irrespective of merit.

In subsequent history, many theologians and philosophers have tried to deal with the contradictions inherent in the idea of a God who loves the world and a God who chooses only some for salvation. Among modern theologians, Karl Barth has been most helpful in affirming the grace of God as the source of salvation, but emphasizing that God's election is focused not on a particular people but on the One who represents the chosen people. In Christ, God has created and chosen all humankind and taken the part of those who are elected and those who were supposedly rejected (1957, II/2, 351–53).

Feminists have not developed an extended critique or transformation of predestination, but they clearly want to question this *hierarchical model of privilege that sets some persons outside of God's hospitality. Letty Russell has pointed out the dangers of deformation of this *doctrine when free gift becomes a form of privilege and an excuse for *domination, *oppression, and exclusion (168–72). Judith Plaskow has worked on the Jewish understanding of election in *Standing Again at Sinai,* emphasizing the importance of "distinctiveness that opens itself to *difference" rather than "chosenness that cuts off" (107).

Plaskow [1990]; Russell [1993]; Tanner [1992]

LETTY M. RUSSELL
and LEE PALMER WANDEL

Preferential Option This term is rooted in the Latin American Roman Catholic bishops' declarations of Medellín (1968) and Puebla (1979), which called the church to opt for the poor: to work preferentially, not exclusively, with the poor and on their behalf. More important, the documents state that the perspective of the church, following that of Jesus, should always be the perspective of the poor.

In feminist theologies the preferential option refers to working with oppressed women and on their behalf. Such theologies always use the *liberation of all women as a hermeneutical lens, and not mere *equality with men within oppressive structures. In feminist theologies, women struggling for liberation constitute a world of interlocutors. This means not that women are passive subjects of a preferential option but rather that women struggling for liberation are moral agents and subjects of their own histories. Women's liberation from *sexism, *heterosexism, ethnic prejudice and *racism, economic exploitation, and other forms of *oppression is the central paradigm of feminist theologies, shaping their theories, questions, methods, and procedures. Preferential option for women's liberation is not a mere theoretical category of theological and ethical reflection but also a way of life for women's liberation theologians and for all others making this option.

The preferential option for women's liberation is not based on some understanding that women are better persons, more innocent, or purer in their motivations. It is based on a conviction that privileges freeze the oppressors' view of *reality and distort it. Women who do not benefit from present structures and who struggle for liberation are able to conceive an alternative reality; they can see and understand what oppressors cannot. The multifaceted oppression women suffer and their hope for liberation make it feasible for them to hope for radical social change and to provide the impetus to make such a change a reality for all peoples (Bonino, 22).

Antoncich, in Ellacuría/Sobrino [1993]; Bonino [1987]; Rejón, in Ellacuría/Sobrino [1993]

ADA MARÍA ISASI-DÍAZ

Pride The word *pride* has a double meaning. Sometimes it is understood as the satisfaction a person feels because of things of personal significance he or she considers valuable or because of qualities she or he deems to have merit. This is its positive sense, and it corresponds to self-esteem. At other times pride is perceived as a feeling of superiority over other persons, toward whom one adopts an attitude of contempt and with whom one tries to avoid all dealings. This is its negative sense, and it corresponds to arrogance and boastful vanity. Pride as a feeling of superiority has many manifestations in Euro-American *culture: of the white *race over others, of the dominant class over the impoverished ones, of one's own religion over those of other people, of the masculine over the feminine gender. The pride that emanates from *sexism considers the male as the point of reference, the norm and criterion of what it means to be human.

Some of the biblical writers are harshly critical of the attitude that some persons adopted who considered themselves superior to others or that *election is a form of privilege. Superiority comes not from *power or wealth but from faithfulness, duty, and *justice. In Jer. 9:23ff., the prophet argues that anyone in Israel who boasts of bodily circumcision should beware he might be uncircumcised in his heart. Paul makes use of the *tradition to oppose every act of human boastfulness: "No one might boast in the presence of God. . . . 'Let the one who boasts, boast in the Lord'" (1 Cor. 1:29–31). And in another letter Paul affirms, "For it is not those who commend themselves that are approved, but those whom the Lord commends" (2 Cor. 10:18). These are the ideas that sustain the Pauline theology of *justification.

Faced with the overestimation of miracles by the Jews and of wisdom by the Greeks, Paul focuses his attention on the *cross of Christ, which is deemed a scandal by the first and foolishness by the second. And Paul does so not only through his preaching but also in his own life. When he arrives in Corinth, a city of wisdom and eloquence, he boasts of neither. He prides himself only in knowing Jesus crucified, who shows the power of God. The cross, which the world sees as weakness and foolishness, constitutes the privileged arena of God's self-revelation. Whoever believes in Jesus can feel proud only of her or his own weakness, because in it the liberating power of God is made evident.

With reference to women, pride has a positive meaning that corresponds to self-esteem and which should be encouraged to the point where it achieves the full recognition of their rights as persons and as women. After centuries of externally imposed *marginalization and of self-negation, self-esteem entails accepting ourselves as women and freeing ourselves from the false images that the *patriarchal society has projected on us in its own self-interest. Self-esteem also constitutes a critical response to the pride of the male who believes himself to be master and lord of all, including of women.

Pride in being a woman should not be considered a feeling of arrogance or conceit born of appearances or external appraisals. It is rooted in interior riches, in the profundity of woman's being, which contrasts with the widespread idea of frivolity and fickleness that continues to be attributed to the feminine gender. Pride in women is not understood as self-satisfaction. It must be characterized by self-critical judgment and by the tension between what is and what ought to be, overcoming the dichotomy between superior and inferior and finding one's own personal unity.

Plaskow [1980]; Rodriguez [1994]; Saussy [1991]; Valcárel [1991]

MARGARITA PINTOS
(TRANS. SHARON H. RINGE)

Priesthood of All Believers

The "priesthood of all believers" asserts the full spirituality and humanity of all women, as it maintains that *any* person can be a priest (Ammerman, 58). That message of *equality is proclaimed in such biblical passages as 1 Peter 2:5–9 and Rev. 1:6. This subversive phrase, which derives from the New Testament, postulates that God calls all of us to be priests and "posits that all believers are priests to each other because of the priesthood of Jesus Christ" (Stewart, 180). Church authorities have sometimes ignored or misused this egalitarian concept and have instead created hierarchies or hierocracies of *power and exclusivity where men have traditionally dominated.

The pivotal word *priest*, or *hiereus* (Gk), is never used in the Bible for ministers, pastors, rabbis, or clergy. The high priest was one who entered a sacred space, the

Holy of Holies, to offer a *sacrifice and to intercede on behalf of others in God's presence once a year. Christ came to fulfill this priesthood even as he abolished and transcended the *patriarchal arrangement; Christ became both sacrifice and high priest. What became revolutionary in this new configuration was the finality of Christ's sacrifice and the inauguration of direct access to the Holy of Holies. The term *priesthood of all believers* therefore stands in direct opposition to the dominance in patriarchal, hierocratic structures. Ironically, the very word for priest, *hiereus*, stems from the same root word as created *hierarchy and hierocracy. Yet the word as used in priesthood of all believers establishes an egalitarian base to the church universal.

Feminists in the Christian *tradition agree on this egalitarian basis of the church. Some feminists would critique the role of Christ in this *doctrine because he is both male and mediator. Varieties of interpretation also emerge as the conversation turns to distinctions of gifts and functions within the church. Does the priesthood of all believers exclude all forms of hierarchy? Is there a place for ordained ministers, clergy, priests, rabbis? These debates are not new and reached a fervor in the Reformation and Counter-Reformation. Some extremes in the controversies are manifested by the Society of Friends, who have no ordained ministers at all, and by traditional Roman Catholics, who use the word *priest* only in the context of clergy. Feminists have used the doctrine of the priesthood of all believers as an aperture for women's *ordination and as an affirmation of our need to be priests to each other in *community.

Ammerman, in Shurden [1993]; Bass, *CTS* [1985]; Sehested, *Review and Expositor* [1986]; Stewart, in Pero/Moro [1988]

JEANNE STEVENSON-MOESSNER

Prophecy, Church Women's Prophecy may be defined as the *call to nurture, proclaim, and develop an alternative consciousness that is different from the dominant *patriarchal *culture and religion that surround us. It proclaims abundant life for the *marginalized and excluded in the context of our own experience and in the light of our *faith, by being open to the Spirit who calls us to discern the times, to denounce all that destroys life, and to proclaim God's *new creation for women and men.

Although a dominant conservative understanding is that *prophets tell of the future, prophets are also messengers of God in times of crisis. From a feminist perspective, it is important to note that the prophets spoke in the midst of the concrete history of a people struggling for *liberation and life. The *mission of the biblical prophets was to keep the memory of God's purpose alive in the people's minds.

The prophets of the Old Testament, both men and women, fought for the cause of *justice. But while male prophets frequently condemned, threatened, or promised punishment, women prophets more often proclaimed, encouraged, and challenged people to work for justice through practical action in defense of the nation's life.

Women prophets play a very important role in Pentecostal churches. They draw on divine power for *healing, *counseling, and challenging the community. Like the *Machi* in the Chilean indigenous community, they make it possible that the human and the Divine can be harmoniously connected for the sake of the people. María, my grandmother, was one of these prophets. Her *authority as a prophet came from her deep spirituality and her engagement in the community.

Irma, my mother, was also a prophet who felt that she had to do something for her people, who were persecuted by the military regime in Chile. She set about doing so with wisdom and devotion. Her prophecy was given from inside the community as she spoke out against abuses, entering into the pain and *suffering of the people and encouraging signs of life and *solidarity. Her work and that of other women opened up new paths of prophetic witness for our church.

Throughout human history, women prophets have identified with the whole people, resisting destruction and despair in the silence of daily life. They generally have no part in political or religious *power structures. When traditional leaders are absent or do not fulfill their duty, the women spontaneously come forward as prophets from among the people. The women who engaged in prophetic activity among the people of Israel challenged the established powers by affirming the law of life. Today, women are also left by the wayside: the *mothers, the *widows, the orphans; the mothers of disappeared children, victims of a patriarchal society that marginalizes and oppresses them. Women in such situations have answered the call to speak out, to proclaim hope, to summon people to action: Rigoberta Menchu and Rosalina Tujuc, indigenous women from Guatemala; the Mothers of the Plaza de Mayo from Argentina; Madelaine Barrot, a prophet from France during and after the Second World War; and many others. In the highly individualistic, exclusive, and marginalizing cultures that predominate around us, the principal challenge for prophecy is not simply to denounce and criticize but to nurture an alternative consciousness.

MARTA PALMA

Prophets, Biblical Women A prophet is a person called and inspired by God to speak God's word. A prophet discerns the *sin and apathy, anger, pain, and despair of the people and speaks the word of God in ways that make the community of *faith take notice and make changes. A prophet won't let us give up in the face of overwhelming *evil but speaks words of challenge and hope that encourage us at the same time as they cajole us into action. Believing that we can experience the love and *justice of God in our own lives, here and now, a prophet envisions the consequences of maintaining the status quo and exhorts us to work toward a future where God's love and justice are more fully realized. Many who are not specifically called prophets in the biblical text nevertheless fulfill prophetic functions.

In the Hebrew Scriptures, the first woman to be called *naviah* (feminine Hebrew for "prophet") is Miriam, who led the women in singing and dancing beside the sea after the escape from slavery in Egypt (Ex. 15:19–21). Though remembered in Micah 6:4 as an equal partner to Moses and Aaron, Miriam was silenced in later Hebrew *tradition (Numbers 12; see Trible). We do not hear of her again until her death, when Miriam (whose name sounds like the Hebrew word for "sea") becomes a symbol in death of the lack of water for the community in the desert (Num. 20:1–2). When Miriam died there was, symbolically, no life-giving water.

Deborah was a prophet and judge during the time of the Judges. She is remembered as a "mother of Israel" (Judg. 5:7) who had the wisdom and integrity to settle disputes among the people. She led a successful military campaign against Canaanite oppressors, a victory won by two women, Deborah and Jael. Her song of victory is a call to action and justice (Judg. 4:1–22; 5:1–31), chiding the apathetic tribes who did not join her efforts.

In the book of Proverbs, "Wisdom" (*Sophia) is personified as a woman who cries out in the marketplace and at the city gates where important business is done, in the manner of a prophet (Prov. 1:20–33; 8; 9). Other women prophets include the woman of Tekoa (2 Sam. 14:1–24), Huldah (2 Kings 22:11–20; 2 Chron. 34:22–28), Noadiah (Neh. 6:10–14), and the wife of Isaiah (Isa. 8:1–4).

In the New Testament, Anna (Luke 2:36–38) and the four daughters of Philip (Acts 21:8–14) are said to receive the gift of prophecy. It is also likely that women were present in the group of disciples gathered in the house when the *Holy Spirit filled them with prophetic speech, when the prophet Joel is quoted: "Your sons and your daughters shall prophesy" (Acts 2:1–21).

Women remembered as coworkers and missionaries by Paul may also have served the role of prophet. Phoebe was called *diakonos,* the same title given to charismatic preachers in Corinth (though she is not Paul's opponent, as they were). Phoebe was a preacher and leader in Cenchreae, whom Paul introduced with affection and gratitude in Rom. 16:1–2 along with many other women whose roles are not defined (Schüssler Fiorenza). Paul took for granted that women did prophesy in the early church, insisting only that their heads be veiled (alternative *translation: "that their hair be bound") when they did so (1 Cor. 11:2–16).

Farmer [1991]; Kraemer [1992]; Scanzoni/Hardesty [1992]; Schüssler Fiorenza, in Loades [1990]; Trible [1989]; Wire [1990]

MARIANNE BLICKENSTAFF MOSIMAN

Prostitution *Prostitution* is a term used to designate the selling of sexual favors. Historically and generally, women are the objects of this activity, although there are men prostitutes and definitely a growing number of prostituted boys. *Patriarchal society has justified prostitution of women throughout the ages as a necessary outlet for men's libido that cannot be contained within the confines of a monogamous *marriage. This is especially true for military men and other men whose work brings them away from home for some length of time.

Factors Contributing to Prostitution. Although there are some women, mostly from first-world countries, who claim it is their right to work as prostitutes, many prostituted women, mostly in underdeveloped countries, consider themselves victims of economic necessity. Poverty can be considered the one decisive factor that impels women to enter into prostitution. However there are contributing factors.

Side by side with economic need is the decision of countries with chronic economic crises to make tourism a pillar of their economy. In the Philippines this policy was adopted in the 1970s, and because about 70 percent of tourists were unaccompanied males, there was an unprecedented rise of prostitution, which became an institutionalized vice involving travel agencies, law enforcement agencies, hotels, and so forth.

Underlying the phenomenon are the *stereotyped values that have been internalized by both men and women in society. Women are considered "derived beings," whose significance comes from their relationship, usually that of service, to males. Many women have internalized the value of virginity before marriage, and they feel an irreparable sense of worthlessness with its loss. Interviews with prostituted women reveal that many of them point to the loss of virginity as the immediate occasion for them to accept work as a prostitute. On the side of males, there is the subconscious sense of proprietorship over women, their right to women's *bodies, their "need" for sexual gratification.

Types of Prostitution. There are prostitutes who cater to local customers, and these are usually poorly paid. There are women who acquire "sugar daddies," who support their schooling. Around military bases prostitution usually springs up. In the Philippines, two prostitution cities, Olongapo and Angeles, grew around the U.S. military bases, which were used as rest and recreation centers for U.S. soldiers especially during the Vietnam War.

Prostitution connected with tourism is the most institutionalized and the most lucrative. In the 1970s, Japanese package-deal sex tours were conducted in the Philippines, Bangkok, and Taiwan. These were incentives given by employers to workers, and the package included hotel, golf facilities, and sexual services of women, all prepaid in Japan. Militant action by feminist groups reduced this type of prostitution. There is a special, high-class prostitution catering to visiting businessmen; it is a part of the standard operating procedure of local subsidiaries to include this in their hosting obligations. They usually choose women from middle-class families, especially students in elite colleges.

Although child prostitution is not new in some Asian countries, as in the case of the temple prostitutes *(devadasis)* in India and Nepal, child prostitution as a commercial enterprise is relatively new in underdeveloped countries. Girls and boys from ages seven to fourteen are now recruited to cater to pedophiles.

Women entertainers in Japan coming from the Philippines, Taiwan, Bangkok, etc., are recruited as singers and dancers in bars but usually end up working as prostitutes. They are called *Japayukis.* Mail-order brides *(hanayomis* in Japan) are those who get married to foreigners through the commercial transaction of agencies. When marriages break up and the women find no work in the countries of their husbands, they often end up working in brothels.

Consequences of Prostitution. Prostituted women usually develop low self-esteem and reap social ostracism, which may lead to deep depression and in some cases to suicide. They are vulnerable to physical *violence from sadistic clients. When made pregnant, they resort to hole-in-the-wall *abortions that can result in sterility, infection, or even death. They are exposed to sexually transmitted diseases such as *AIDS and other venereal diseases. Child prostitutes are likely to become drug addicts and, eventually, drug pushers, and can end up in criminal activities. Prostitutes around military bases are left with children of foreign soldiers who have moved on, and are saddled with the support of these children as single *mothers.

Feminist Theology and Prostitution. Feminist theologians view prostitution not from a moralistic point of view but from a holistic perspective, taking into consideration the socioeconomic aspects of the problem. They see prostitution of women as the culmination of a country's prostituted economy. They analyze and denounce the patriarchal values that justify and perpetuate it. They point to the role of the church and church teachings in perpetuating the *sexist and stereotyped images and roles internalized by both women and men.

Feminist theologians advocate the use of the resources of the church for services to and organization of prostituted women and eventually for the rehabilitation of those who have decided to change jobs. Above all, and going beyond welfare services, is the emphasis on consciousness-raising, theological reconstruction, and economic restructuring that could lead to a fundamental solution to the problem of prostitution.

Magno, in Mananzan [1987/1991]; Mananzan [1987/1991]; Miralao/Carlos/Santos [1990]

MARY JOHN MANANZAN

Psychology of Women. Psychology is a diverse discipline of many theoretical and clinical perspectives, concerned with cognitive, intellectual, and emotional development; issues of identity and consciousness; and the diagnosis and treatment of psychopathology. Feminist perspectives have sought to expose gender bias and *androcentrism in psychology and to generate theoretical foundations for new patterns of woman-centered theory and practice in areas as diverse such as psychotherapy, *ethics, gender identity, and spirituality. There are three areas of particular significance for feminist theologies: ethics, *pastoral care, and spirituality.

Ethics. Carol Gilligan's studies in developmental psychology of the differential moral sensibilities of boys and girls concluded that girls derive a distinctive moral "voice" from principles of connectedness, relationality, and *interdependence. Similarly, the influence of feminist object-relations psychoanalysis, as in the work of Nancy Chodorow and Dorothy Dinnerstein, is seen as providing an account of the formation of women's gender identity in which women's propensity to intimacy and nurturance is rooted in the mother–daughter relationship. Such work is regarded as providing the grounds for a distinctively feminist or woman-centered ethic.

Pastoral Care. Feminist psychological perspectives on the pastoral needs of women are also beginning to inform the practice of Christian *ministry. The psychological dynamics of sexual *violence, mental illness, and eating disorders among women offer important resources for exposing and alleviating such problems, although they should not obscure the social and economic causes of women's lack of status and low self-esteem.

Spirituality. Feminist Lacanian psychoanalysis is providing a radical new vocabulary for understanding women's "subjectivity" (consciousness or identity). Francophone philosophers such as Julia Kristeva and Luce Irigaray argue that authentic feminine/feminist identity exists in a literally unspeakable and unnameable realm, akin to the repressed unconscious, beyond the pale of *patriarchal discourse. The search for such a distinctive psychic energy in this marginal world of "madness, holiness, and poetry" is leading such writers into an exploration of women's mysticism and spirituality as examples of transgressive, woman-centered expression. Such work represents a creative and novel synthesis between feminist theology, *philosophy, and psychology.

Bem [1993]; Berry, in Berry/Wernick [1992]; Brown/Gilligan [1992]; Gilligan [1982]; Glaz/Moessner [1991]; Miller [1976]

ELAINE L. GRAHAM

Purity–Impurity The concept of purity–impurity was very basic for identifying the boundary of God's people in the biblical world. The Hebrew community was to be *holy* (set apart) for God. Especially after the exile, the integrity of the community was preserved through rules for religious purity and impurity. Impurity was quite often connected with physical symptoms seen in ailments or in normal activities of the human body (Lev. 11–15, 20). The chapters in Leviticus render women impure because of their menstruation and childbirth and restrict their behavior at home as well as in the social and religious spheres of life. Thus biologically healthy functions of women were lopsidedly treated as unclean and defiling to men (12:6–8; 15:29–30).

By the time of the NT this *dualistic concept included minute rules of daily life on how to keep oneself religiously clean through choosing appropriate food (Col. 2:16; Acts 10:14; Rom. 14:14), dealing with daily utensils very carefully (Mark 7:3–4), observing certain occasions (Gal. 4:10), wearing certain clothes (1 Cor. 11:5–16), and so forth. Infringement of the purity laws meant being excluded and becoming "the Other" or a "nonperson."

It is not easy to define how much these restrictions were actually at work and how this stigma of impurity influenced the women of Jesus' time and the early Christian era. Levitical laws probably are more prescriptive than descriptive, but it is also true that laws, when orally spread by people and distorted in transmission, generally exert a superstitious, binding *power over ordinary people.

The physical impurity of women and men with *evil spirits, leprosy, or fever resulted in social and religious discrimination. Bleeding symbolized death for a woman because it identified her as taboo to her society (Mark 5:25–34). Jesus' radical actions of acceptance and *healing broke through the distinction of pure and impure and declared that all are welcome in God's reign. We can also detect in the *gospel texts that women took initiative to cross over the religious impurity laws and create a stage for Jesus to become truly a boundary breaker.

Douglas [1966]; Kinukawa [1994]; Malina [1981/1993]; Selvidge [1990]

HISAKO KINUKAWA

Race Some concept of race or way of understanding *differences has probably been around since the first people who saw themselves as "a people" (more likely, *the* people) encountered other people who understood themselves as *the* people but looked different, saw things differently, and came from a different place. As a contemporary concept, however, race is a classification of a group of people who share certain inherited physical characteristics. When European society originated this concept, it was an attempt to design a scientific classification system of the human differences they were encountering in their explorations of the earth. Over the three centuries of attempting to perfect such a system, however, social and biological science has discovered that such "perfection" is impossible. Most reputable scientists agree that human beings are not so neatly distinguishable from one another. As this has become clearer and as other peoples have entered the dialogue on definition, race on a material (concrete) level has often been extended to include other shared characteristics of history, geography, and *culture to get more accurate categories or classifications of human differences.

As we have come to experience it in the United States, *race is more political than descriptive.* It is basically the discourse between people of European descent, who see themselves as "white people," and those who would influence them about who people of European descent are in relation to other human beings and to the earth. In *Playing in the Dark,* Toni Morrison writes, "Race has become metaphorical—a way of referring to and disguising forces, events, classes and expressions of social decay and economic division far more threatening to the body politic than biological 'race' ever was" (63).

This metaphorical discourse, Morrison points out, takes place on all levels of meaning: economics, *anthropology, *politics, biology, theology, and any subject that talks about human beings in relationship to themselves and their world. Thus shared characteristics or traits in the U.S. discourse on "race" become a way of comparing white people (who are generally people of European descent) to other "races" and of determining *responsibility and relationship, or lack of it, to those being compared. As the world gets smaller and the population gets larger, this discourse becomes more obviously about who has a right to exist and what right or claim people have to the *land of their ancestors and the resources of that land.

Because the discourse is about how white people see themselves in relation to the rest of humanity, it is more obscure as to how other "races" of people think about and image race, and it is more difficult to trace the history of thought about this. Most theories by other peoples are dismissed as "unscientific" or "superficial" or "politically correct" because the people promoting them do not have the context of a *hegemonic thought system and political structure to support them. (E.g., how do Navajos think of "race," or where does Frances Cress Welsing's theory of race and *racism fit into the general understandings of race held by U.S. citizens of African descent and in the history of the relationship of peoples of African descent to other peoples?)

This does not mean that there is not a full system and history of thought held by other "races" (systems that make meaning of the amazing differences that exist between groups of human beings). It simply means that the majority of peoples does not have equal exposure to or appreciation of those thought systems as it does to the "white" understanding of reality. Such systems of thought and understanding can be found but are in no way central to the understanding of race that dominates most people's perceptions. The understandings of race that are dominant are grounded in European history, and particularly its history of expansion in which Europeans spilled over into and claimed the right to own other people's or races' land, resources, and, in some cases, the people themselves.

Land or the earth and our relationship and right to it are at the foundation of the concept of race, much as they are in some white feminists' interpretation of their relationship as women to white men (e.g., Susan Griffin's *Made from This Earth*). There are innumerable factors that affect and drive theories of race, but at the root is the relationship of people to the earth (the concepts of homeland, origins). Race as we experience it today is the politicization of the human relationship, not only to one another but to the earth and any other territory (space, sea) humans may learn to inhabit.

Griffin [1982]; hooks [1992]; Morrison [1992]; Morrison, ed. [1992]; Welsing [1970]

DONNA BIVENS

Racism Racism has shaped the face and soul of the United States since its inception. From the genocide of native peoples and the enslavement of African peoples to contemporary policies that disproportionately exclude people of color from jobs, health care, adequate housing, and quality education, racism has persisted in every aspect of our public life. The changing political landscape has given rise to various justifications for the maintenance of white supremacy. Defining native peoples as "savages" and peoples of African descent as "beasts" in the formative years of the United States laid the groundwork for incarcerating Japanese Americans as wartime "enemies" in the 1940s and for contemporary anti-immigration laws that deny immigrants of color access to basic health and education by targeting them as "illegal aliens." The old images have thus been reinscribed into new images that need to be analyzed and understood for the effect they have in maintaining and perpetuating racism in contemporary life.

Despite the persistence of racism, the understanding of it has remained muddled, with it generally being defined in such a way as to suggest that differences across race occur on a "level playing field" and that remedy of historical inequities can be accomplished by changing attitudes or eliminating the most egregious methods of racial discrimination. Such a view, however, belies the depth and complexity of racism. Racism is a systemic problem in which one race maintains supremacy over another race through a set of attitudes, behaviors, social structures, and *ideologies.

In the United States, racism is best understood as a *system of white supremacy* that is maintained by social and political institutions. Understanding racism, then, requires more than understanding individual and interpersonal attitudes regarding race. It requires understanding the complex dynamics of *power that shape the social and political institutions of the society. The policies and practices of those institutions are rooted in and given legitimacy by the norms and values of the dominant white *culture. The resources needed to maintain and perpetuate those institutions are controlled by white people. The decisions regarding essential institutional policies and procedures, despite some inclusion of people of color in some settings in recent years, are made and enforced by white people. In short, "reality" is defined in these institutions and, through these institutions, in the society at large by a dominant white elite.

White feminist theology, like white feminist theory more generally, has not escaped this racism. Too often white feminists have analyzed their own situation of *oppression and generalized from that to speak of "women's oppression" rooted in "*patriarchy," failing to recognize the racial oppression suffered by women of color and obscuring their own complicity in the racism affecting women, men, and children of color. Moreover, the dynamics of sex and class as they intersect with racism have often obscured white women's ability to see and understand racism.

Women of color have challenged these tendencies in white feminist theology and theory and have developed womanist, *mujerista*, Asian, and Asian-American theologies that reflect their perspectives. Womanist theologian Delores Williams, for example, affirms the principle of "the full humanity of women," as articulated by Rosemary Radford Ruether and other white feminist theologians, but at the same time insists that her affirmation of this principle is also grounded in a history of black resistance to white supremacy.

An analysis of women's *experience as a basis for identifying the requirements for the full humanity of women is a cornerstone of feminist theologies. An adequate use of this resource as a basis for constructive theology demands recognition and analysis of the profound and *different* effects racism has had on the shaping of women's lives. Failure at this level of analysis results in a denial of white women's complicity in a history of racism and a distortion of feminist efforts to ensure the dignity and well-being of women in contemporary society.

Addressing racism is, then, critical to feminist theology, for the normative principles on which it is based require attention to the effects of social and political dynamics on the lived experience of all women. Feminist theologies attentive to racism ask whose experience and what definition of "well-being" are included at every point of analysis. The struggle necessary to find adequate answers across the barriers of race is a legacy of racism. Acts of *solidarity, despite the legacy, are essential to developing feminist projects.

Andolsen [1986]; Brock [1988/1992]; Harrison [1985]; Russell et al. [1988]; Spelman [1988]; Townes, ed. [1993]; Williams [1993a]

NANCY D. RICHARDSON

Reality, Women's Traditionally, the quality of "being real," reality, has been defined by the powerful in society. In Western cultures, elite white men have named Western "reality." This male-ordered reality often is characterized as hierarchically structured, governed by a *dualism that pits men against women, mind against *body, white against black. The initial step of feminist scholarship was to show that this reality was not "real" for everyone. Feminists labeled this reality "patriarchal," arguing that it reflected the experiences of privileged men. In a world where the term *man* sufficiently defines all persons, "woman" becomes derivative.

Feminist scholars have turned to women, perceiving their unique ways of knowing and interpreting the world. Essentially, they unveiled women's reality as a concept that acknowledges and names the real *experiences of women within *patriarchy. The experiences of women are neither swallowed up into the experiences of "man" nor erased; instead, women themselves are allowed to define their own perceptions of the world. Articulating a women's reality also entails a commitment to transform what counts as true and valuable in society. While men's reality locks women out, women's reality validates their different voices and ways of being.

Although feminist scholars have advocated inclusion of *all* women's experience in women's reality, they have risked taking one group of women's experiences and using it falsely to define all women's experiences. In practice, this has meant that women's reality actually translates into "white, middle-class women's reality." However, not all women share a common vision of women's reality. Feminists are coming to realize that gender, *race, class, and nationality are woven together in complex ways, creating many different identities. The pressing question facing feminism is: "Can we still talk of women's reality without erasing the *differences distinguishing women from one another?" Clearly there is a multiplicity of realities in which women live.

Collins [1991]; Frye [1983]; Schaef [1981]; Spelman [1988]

DEANNA A. THOMPSON

Reason/Passion Traditionally, the terms *reason* and *passion* have been defined in opposition to each other, and their definitions have been neither value-free nor gender-neutral: reason has been valued and identified with men, while passion has been devalued and identified with women. Feminist scholars have focused their critique on how traditional definitions have reflected and perpetuated the patriarchal ordering of society.

The dichotomy between reason and passion has its roots in classical Greek thought, which defined the terms within a dualistic and *hierarchical worldview that opposed mind and matter, *soul and *body, male and female, reason and passion and reflected the ancient belief that women were biologically inferior to men and inherently more irrational. The Greek ideal was the proper ordering of the soul, defined as the dominance of reason over the passions. This rhetoric of order and dominance mirrored and justified a society in which males dominated females and masters dominated slaves. The widespread belief that *evil resulted from lack of control over the passions was developed by Paul's Jewish contemporary Philo, who wrote an allegorical interpretation of the *Fall in which the mind (represented by Adam) was tempted by pleasure (the serpent) through the senses (Eve). Adam's *sin was that he permitted his senses to overwhelm his self-control; Philo's solution to the Fall was the proper taming of the passions by reason, expressed in the submission of women to men in *marriage.

Beginning in the Enlightenment, reason was defined as the capacity for dispassionate "reasoning," and the ancient dichotomy between reason and passion was transformed into a *dualism between culture and nature. Females continued to be seen as inherently more passionate and therefore as unable to attain the Enlightenment ideal of the rational, free, self-controlled moral agent. The goal of human knowledge was articulated as the dominion of culture (ordered, male) over nature (chaotic, female). Although nature and passion were valued more highly in the romantic reaction against the Enlightenment, they were most often seen as necessary stages in the arrival of a "higher" or "universal" reason, which again excluded women.

The construction of woman as more passionate and therefore incapable of reason has shaped Western understandings of what it means to be human, influenced biblical texts regarding the proper place of women in society and the church (e.g., 1 Tim 5:11), and been used to justify the exclusion of women from theology and other cognitive tasks. Challenging the traditional dichotomy between reason and passion by analyzing its historical development and by offering alternative constructions of the self that are not rooted in *patriarchy will continue to be central to feminist reconstructions of theology.

Carson, in Halperin/Winkler/Zeitlin [1990]; Harvey/Okruhlik, eds. [1992]; Lloyd [1984]; Sly [1990]

WENDY SUE BORING

Redemption/Salvation Redemption means to free, and this is a basic element in the *doctrine of salvation (the technical name is *soteriology*). The Christian *tradition has its own expressions of the process of salvation, emphasizing the unique role of Jesus. He is savior by his *incarnation, for being both God and human he is able to bridge the separation between God and humans. Jesus is savior in his public *ministry by his acts of *compassion and *liberation. Finally, he is savior in his sacrificial death and *resurrection, which effect deliverance from *evil and reveal God's merciful act of love and reunion.

The Christian church has never officially sanctioned a particular understanding of the saving work of Jesus Christ. Rather, several different interpretive themes of *Christology and *atonement have had *power or find preferential usage in the diverse thought and worship life of the church. Most of these motifs find a basis among the many titles and terms of the New Testament that suggest, but do not develop, interpretations of the saving work of Jesus Christ. Other motifs that explain the salvific work of Jesus Christ come under the rubrics of pastoral-theological paradigms, drawn from Christian communities to which these texts speak today.

The *ransom theory* takes its name from the *gospel saying that Jesus Christ came to give his life as "a ransom for many" (Matt. 20:28; Mark 10:45). The problem is that human beings are enslaved to *sin and therefore to Satan, and only divine intervention can free them to live in joyful obedience to God. Only God, who judges sin, can ransom them. Jesus is the ransom. The second-century theologian Irenaeus is linked to this view. A second interpretation is the *satisfaction theory*. Jesus is the vicarious *sacrifice (like the lamb slain for the Passover or those sacrifices regularly made at the Temple) as a propitiation to effect atonement for sin. He gave his life freely and obediently as a way by which God and humanity could be reconciled. This interpretation is linked to the eleventh-century theologian Anselm of Canterbury. A third interpretation is the *moral influence theory*, linked to the twelfth-century monk and scholar Abelard. For him, the life, death, and resurrection of Jesus move hearers to repentance, through which they find forgiveness and restoration from God (salvation) and the power to live the new life in Christ.

Because these basic theologies involve an "exchange" between a sinful humanity, which deserves God's condemnation, and the sinless Christ, who enacts God's love, it seems to introduce a division, or at least a tension, into God. Salvation, or atonement, to be sure, is initiated by God in order to accomplish God's initial purposes for *creation; but it is presented as resolving a problem "within God," as though the second person of the Trinity must satisfy the conditions of divine *justice or even propitiate the Creator's wrath in order that sinners be forgiven or justified.

All theories of this type, furthermore, view *suffering and even punishment as salvific—an assumption that has been questioned on moral and psychological grounds, most recently by liberation, womanist, *mujerista*, and feminist theologians who see it as a reinforcement of *domination and abuse. And yet, in contemporary theology, the *cross is often linked with a wider divine suffering and identification with those who suffer in order to overcome evil. Which kind of suffering must be rejected, and which can be accepted?

Groups have often used definitions of salvation to exclude those who are different, classifying as "unsaved" those who do not exhibit similar cultures, creeds, or common experiences. Over the ages, churches have struggled to determine the true church, the *elect. Feminists, womanists, and *mujeristas* are particularly sensitive to this history of exclusion of the "different." For them, the gospel message, and God's vision for humanity and all creation, is not only that the different are accepted but that their *differences provide crucial insight into the salvation story and into the possibility of *new creation itself.

A contemporary expression in diverse liberation *theologies locates the problem in the structures of human society that crush or dehumanize people. The solution is the liberation of the oppressed, a sign of the reign of God, and the strategy is the practical struggle to overcome injustice. Jesus suffers in the suffering of God's people, and his resurrection promises the power to overcome evil. Salvation, the lived experience of being saved, should not be understood just as salvation of the *soul but in the biblical sense of total human salvation and wholeness, under the rubric of pastoral theology. It cannot be limited to the liberation from personal sin but must be understood to mean also liberation from social and political *oppression. Conversely, oppressive and destructive biblical traditions cannot be acknowledged as divine *revelation.

For example, feminist, womanist, and *mujerista* theologies have pointed out that women are oppressed and exploited by *patriarchal and *sexist structures and institutions. Therefore, according to a pastoral-theological criterion, biblical revelation and truth can today be found only in those texts and traditions that transcend and criticize the patriarchal *culture and religion of their times. A critical scrutiny and evaluation of biblical texts according to whether or not they contribute to the salvation, well-being, and *freedom of women should not be understood in terms of the doctrinal-essence and historical-relativity models of Irenaeus, Anselm, Abelard, and others, as if it were possible to separate culturally conditioned, patriarchal expression from a timeless, nonsexist essence of revelation. It should not be understood in terms of the pristine-deterioration model of salvation, as though nonpatriarchal traditions are limited to the earliest traditions of the New Testament. Such a critical criterion of evaluation must be applied to all biblical texts to determine how much they contribute to the salvation or oppression of women.

For womanists, feminists, and *mujeristas*, the meaning of salvation is glimpsed in Jesus' explanation to his disciples that they are no longer servants but friends (John 15:15); in the promise that Jesus' friends will do still greater things than he has done (John 14:2); in Jesus' association with the lowly and outcasts (Luke 7:34); and in the promise of new being and new creation (2 Cor. 5:15). These texts, so interpreted from a broadly feminist perspective, suggest that Jesus did not come to redeem humans by showing them God's love manifested in the death of God's innocent child on a cross erected by cruel, *imperialistic, patriarchal power. Rather, the texts suggest that the Spirit of God in Jesus came to show humans life.

Redemption/salvation in this hermeneutic provides thematics for a soteriology of righting relations between *body, mind, and spirit through an ethical ministry of words (such as the Beatitudes, the parables, the moral directions and reprimands); through a *healing ministry of touch and being touched (for example, healing the leper through touch, being touched by the woman with an issue of blood); through a militant ministry of expelling evil forces (such as exorcising the demoniacs, whipping the money changers out of the Temple); through a ministry grounded in the power of *faith; through a ministry of *prayer; through a ministry of compassion and love.

Brock [1988]; Rhodes [1987]; Schüssler Fiorenza [1984/1995]; Williams [1993a]

TOINETTE M. EUGENE

Relationships There may be no more central concept and concern in feminist theological *ethics than relationship. It has appeared in one form or another at the heart of feminist theory in general as well as in feminist theology, *psychology, sociology, political theory. Relationships are important to women; relationships have all too often been distorted or diminished by inadequate ways of understanding them; relationships are appropriate or inappropriate, helpful or harmful, according to criteria that are significant to feminists.

The importance of relationships to women hardly needs documentation. Yet the nature of their importance is still being explored. For example, a variety of feminist theories of moral development place the sustaining of human relationships at the center of women's *experience. Debate, however, rages over whether this makes women essentially different from men, whether gender determines the priority given to relationality over *autonomy, or whether the well-being of all human persons requires respect for individual *freedom as well as for a capacity for relationship.

The importance that feminists give to relationships is evident in the growing literature on sexual *partnership, parenting, relationships in the workplace, *friendship, models for professional relationships, etc. Attention is paid not only to relationships between individuals or within small groups but to human relationships across groups. In all of these explorations, relationships among women are particularly interesting to many feminist thinkers, though clearly the agenda is not limited only to these.

Feminism, in a sense, begins with a critique of relationships--not of relationship as such but of historical forms in which it has been realized. Feminism is, after all, against the subordination of women to men on the basis of gender. Most of human history tells of gendered relationships in which women are considered inferior to men. Hence roles are differentiated, unequally open to women and men, giving priority and privilege to the roles that men fill. Inequality of *power, little expectation of mutuality, and unfair patterns of economic sharing have thus characterized sexual relations, parental responsibilities, and political systems. These same patterns have marked relations between racial groups, classes, and religions. A feminist critique of these models of relationship often begins with an analysis of "otherness," frequently the code for the treatment of those who are different as less worthy of respect. The feminist critique, however, does not remain at this level of abstraction but is turned on, for example, positions of privilege in the church, colonization of peoples, sexual harassment in professional settings, inequitable domestic responsibilities, *violence between partners and nations, and so forth.

The critical function of feminist theology and ethics assumes a positive understanding of relationships and criteria by which relationships can be measured. Thus, while there are significant differences in kinds of relationships (for example, between parent–child relations and business partnerships), the paradigm of human relationships is marked by *equality of power, mutuality of freedom and *responsibility, love that is other-centered yet neither neglectful nor destructive of the self, and fidelity. Revisionist theological paradigms have included the triune God, *covenant, and a *discipleship of equals. For many feminists, not surprisingly, the model and the goal of human relationships is therefore friendship. It is a model that, as a goal, can extend to *solidarity with all.

Hunt [1991]; Russell [1979]; Welch [1990]

MARGARET A. FARLEY

Relativism Set in opposition to the view that human beings have access to a singular truth, "relativism" names the position which acknowledges that there may be many different claims to truth, all of which may be legitimate. Feminist scholars have been some of the loudest and most forceful critics of "objectivism" (one truth), pointing to how our contexts and our values influence the ways in which we experience truth and make sense of the world. This critique has led to the accusation that feminist scholarship lapses into "relativism" (many truths). This label is meant to be derogatory, implying that in rejecting the idea of one truth, feminism necessarily supports the validity of *all* positions and thus the position that "anything goes."

In response to this accusation, feminists protest the *dualistic presentation of objectivism versus relativism and argue for a third alternative. Steering a course between objectivism and relativism, feminists advocate a view of truth which asserts that all truths are contextual and yet acknowledges that notions of normative truth are necessary for the formation of communities of *faith and *justice. They recognize that radical relativism is dangerous because it prevents feminists from critiquing positions that perpetuate *oppression and thus allows unjust relationships to be given as much credence as just ones. Anyone who experiences the destructive effects of *sexism, *racism, *classism, or homophobia knows that an "anything goes" approach belies the truth of oppression. Feminists thus recognize that they must continue to hold onto notions of justice and truth, but they add that such truths are always socially constructed. For feminists, truths that are normative should be constructed by communities struggling for justice and against the oppression of women. In this manner, they avoid the objectivism–relativism dichotomy by searching for "truth" in the context of liberating *praxis.

Code [1991]; Collins [1991]; Harding [1991]; Hartman/Messer-Davidow [1991]

DEANNA A. THOMPSON

Religion There is no one satisfactory definition of *religion,* but it is usually understood to refer to a wide variety of human beliefs and practices relating to the divine. Religion and religions are studied in many disciplines, including *psychology, sociology, history, and *philosophy. Viewing religion theologically (as opposed to, say, sociologically or psychologically) and from a Judeo-Christian perspective, one might say that religion is made manifest in two basic ways: *recognition* and *response.*

For centuries in the West, religion was associated with recognition, as it was largely equated with belief in a supreme and *transcendent deity; only relatively recently has the response side of religion been emphasized. Religious response has been variously characterized as, for example, awareness of the holy (Rudolf Otto), feeling of dependence (Friedrich Schleiermacher), humility before the wholly other (Karl Barth). Today, we can claim that both manifestations are important and interrelated. To be religious is to assent to certain truths but also to organize life around them. Religion is awareness of the transcendent actualized in practice, *tradition, ritual. Also, recognition and response are communal as well as individual.

Feminists have transformed both recognition and response by taking women's *reality seriously. Belief changes as doctrines are reformulated and texts reinterpreted in light of women's *experience. Feminists have been particularly attentive to religious language, insisting that the way things are named facilitates or hinders recognition. Feminists have also reclaimed ancient ideas and practices, seeing old things anew. At other times, feminists have had to force recognition of the silences and gaps within religion. Response, for feminists, often means assuming the position of the *marginalized.

For many feminists, the central dilemma religion poses is how to reject only its *patriarchal elements and not the whole. They examine many religions, asking in what way they are or are not liberating to women. Some seek out new forms of religious experience, while others reform from within.

Cooey/Eakin/McDaniel [1991]; Jay [1992]; King in Eliade, vol. 12 [1987]

BARBARA J. BLODGETT

Religious Life In the Roman Catholic Church, religious life is a canonical form of consecrated lay life wherein religious orders or congregations of women profess solemn vows (nuns) or simple vows (sisters) of poverty, chastity, and obedience (known as evangelical counsels) and live according to an approved rule or constitution characterized by the distinct charism of their founder.

From the fourth century, nuns called to a contemplative life of *prayer, *asceticism, and manual labor lived apart from the world in self-governing monasteries, which evolved to include schools and other services within the enclosure (cloister). From the seventeenth century, sisters with an apostolic vocation to do good works in the world lived semicloistered, semicontemplative lives in hundreds of new congregations dedicated to serving the poor, alleviating *suffering, and educating children. Prior to Vatican II, the Sister Formation Conference in the U.S.A. launched a successful national movement to educate sisters and nuns to a level of professional competency in all fields in which they were actively involved. Subsequently, new theological understandings and a reevaluation of *mission in light of the signs of the times led to radical changes in lifestyle and governance and revised constitutions.

Now fully engaged in the midst of the world, today's women religious worldwide link contemplation and action through works of mercy and advocacy rooted in *gospel values. Despite diminishing numbers, energies, and resources, sisters and nuns carry on practical and prophetic ministries oriented toward the transformation of religion and society. Social and systemic *justice works include *community development, *conscientization, leadership training of oppressed peoples, and *empowerment of the poor. In *solidarity with other women in a global *sisterhood, radical feminist, womanist, *mujerista*, and Asian sisters and nuns are in the forefront of the newly developing feminist theologies, *liturgies, and spirituality currently challenging the institutional church.

Donovan [1989]; Leddy [1990]; Neal [1990]; Wittberg [1994]

MIRIAM THERESE WINTER

Responsibility Responsibility refers both to the nature of moral action and to the character of the moral agent; that is, both actions and persons are said to be responsible. A modern notion, it has ties to older concepts of duty and obligation, as well as to correlative concepts of *autonomy, *freedom, deliberation, and character.

Philosophical *ethics has typically cast responsibility as response in the sense of an answer to or accountability for actions. A person is responsible for her actions if two conditions are met: the action is *free* and *intentional*. Aristotle introduced the idea of a distinction between voluntary and involuntary actions; Kant developed the notion that if we are to impute moral action to an agent, she must be capable of it (later dubbed "ought implies can"). In other words, responsible actions cannot be coerced or otherwise determined actions. Furthermore, to be responsible, actions must be deliberate; agents must have some motive or intent in doing them and must be aware of their consequences. Debates about whether moral agents are ever truly free and whether their intent can ever be surely ascertained have complicated both theoretical and practical determinations of responsibility.

Theological ethics has, in the last century, framed responsibility as response to God and to others, displayed in behavior that is socially construed and contextually fitting. Key figures in this development are Martin Buber, Dietrich Bonhoeffer, H. Richard Niebuhr, and James Gustafson. "Responsibility ethics"—envisioned as an alternative to both deontological ethics (based on moral obligation or duty) and teleological ethics (based on consequences or ends)—views agents as relational, not isolated, and calls them to fit their actions to their interpretation of reality and context and to their continuity with the community of other agents and with life before God.

Feminists have built on these insights in their own distinctive ways. Particular attention has been focused on caring as a distinctly female mode of fitting response. The work of Carol Gilligan and others suggests that caring is a characteristically female activity and, moreover, represents a distinct style of moral reasoning. An ethic of *care has been proposed as an alternative to a characteristically male ethic of *justice. Instead of attending to rules and principles, caring involves attending to the web of *relationships in which the agent is located and finding solutions to moral problems that will maintain these relationships. Indeed, moral problems arise more from conflicting roles or responsibilities than from competing rights claims. Solutions are practical and flexible rather than abstract and absolute.

Other feminists question whether caring represents a genuine alternative moral system and an advance or merely an accommodation to *oppression. Perhaps women's subordinate social location requires that they act in ways to sustain relation. Additionally, some feminists fear depicting women as unprincipled thinkers and are reluctant to jettison the concept of rights, by which many feminist gains have been won. Recently, some feminists have joined *postmodern theorists in challenging the notion of an autonomous self. A new twist on the old freedom–determinism debate, this challenge asks whether *social construction leaves us any self to generate or fashion in responsible ways.

Finally, because of its recognition that women constitute a group, feminism adds the concept of collective responsibility to the concept of individual responsibility. Men, for example, can be held collectively responsible for perpetuating the *sin of *sexism (and perhaps women for accepting it). The church and other institutions may be held responsible for perpetuating the discrimination, harassment, and *marginalization of women and other oppressed groups. Responsibility ultimately becomes advocacy and action toward change.

Gilligan [1982]; Harrison [1985]; Kittay/Meyers [1987]; Ruddick [1989]

BARBARA J. BLODGETT

Resurrection Resurrection is a central theme in Christian *faith. Biblical language about resurrection is framed within the context of Jewish and Christian apocalyptic discourse. This forces it to retain a strong *metaphoric element and to resist unidimensional or narrowly conceptual forms of interpretation. Resurrection refers first of all to the Easter event proclaimed in the New Testament: Jesus' rising from death to life and his appearances to the disciples. Second, resurrection is understood as interpretation of the Easter event, found both within the New Testament itself and in subsequent Christian reflection. Finally, and in the context of eschatological hope, resurrection refers to the Christian belief that the Easter event was the "first fruits" of the transformation of our humanity and our world. It is this eschatological dimension which forces us to remember that the language of resurrection is the language of *transcendence and must retain a metaphoric and mythic dimension and an openness to the future.

In the first place, feminist attention is directed to the *role of women in the resurrection narratives.* According to these, Mary Magdalene and the group of women who were present at Jesus' crucifixion were also the first to encounter and to recognize him as risen Lord and the first to receive the mandate to proclaim the good news of the resurrection. These women represent the continuity between the crucifixion of Jesus and the appearance of the risen Christ. This primacy of encounter and *mission has encouraged feminist commentators to claim the title of "*apostle" for Mary Magdalene and her companions, in the sense outlined by Paul and implied by the author of Luke-Acts, for whom an apostle was a disciple of Jesus who had seen the risen Lord and proclaimed the news of his resurrection (1 Cor. 15:1–11; Luke 24:45–48; Acts 1:1–8).

In the second place, with regard to the interpretation of the resurrection narratives, feminist reflection asks about *the nature of the victory accomplished* by Christ's death and resurrection. Much feminist theology rejects an interpretation of Jesus' death as repayment for *sin. Rather, Jesus' whole life is seen as representing the saving power of God. In Jesus this saving power is made present through a *praxis marked by mutuality rather than submission, by life-evoking love rather than abusive control. Jesus resisted all forms of dominating *relationships. His *solidarity with the *marginalized and *suffering evoked fear and rage on the part of the authorities, and they moved to obliterate his life and praxis. Jesus' resurrection therefore represents the victory of his graciousness and love. God's raising up of Jesus represents the victory of mutuality and love over *domination. The power of God's Spirit is at work in the world, and its final victory is assured. That victory will not be won through *violence and *oppression but through the power of solidarity and compassionate love.

According to the language of Paul in 1 Corinthians, those who are joined to Jesus as his disciples participate in his dying and rising, becoming "members of one body in Christ." Feminist theological reflection looks with suspicion at the way this language quickly loses *its eschatological dimension,* to function oppressively in the lives of women. The maleness of Jesus is thus invoked, restricting the religious imagination to exclusively masculine symbols of God and authorizing forms of power equated with domination. Christian eschatological hope is marked by the demand that we remain open to the transcendent future of God. In the light of this demand, Christian theology must also remain open to the Spirit of the risen Christ and willing to undergo consequent transformation of its interpretations.

Johnson [1990; 1992]; Perkins [1984]; Purvis [1993]

MARGARET M. CAMPBELL

Revelation Revelation in Christian theology is traditionally understood as the disclosure of the divine purpose for the human race and of such truths about God's nature as are deemed fit for human understanding. These truths were expressed in the form of propositions or *doctrines, and the extent to which they are subject to change and reformulation in the light of changed contexts is much disputed. The problems of the traditional view are twofold: that women have had no part in the formulation and transmission process of these "truths of revelation," and that the nature of revealed truth is permeated by a *patriarchal and *dualistic understanding of God and God's relationship with *creation. The dominant interpretations have diminished rather than enabled the full humanity of women.

Contemporary theologies of revelation attempt to move beyond the God who is remote from the world and to be inclusive of human experience but have not been successful as long as women's *experience has been ignored. Particularly problematic for women are the symbolizing of God predominantly as male and the maleness of Jesus, which is understood as normative for humanity. In addition, Adam's *sin of *pride did not match the life experience of powerless women, and the *cross of Jesus was often interpreted as legitimizing the *suffering and victimization of women. Resurrection was frequently seen as undervaluing embodied life on earth.

In response, there have been two distinct phases in feminist theologies of revelation. In the first, feminist attempts were *reformist* or *radical.* The reformist approach took the traditional categories of Christian revelation—God, Christ, Spirit, Trinity, church, salvation, sin, eschatology—and attempted to reformulate them in a way inclusive of the full humanity of women. The radical approach rejected revelation as beyond redemption, moved beyond traditional categories, and tried to create a "woman-identified" experience of the sacred. The second phase is *pluralist, contextual,* and *conscious* of the constructed nature of all knowledge of God and the interpreted texture of all human experience. It is also conscious that Euro-American feminist discourse does not escape the very *hegemonic character it seeks to replace. Thus womanist theology has a distinctive *Christology and understanding of sin and *grace, deriving from the history and experience of slavery in the United States.

Asian, African, and Latin American women are developing understandings of revelation that reflect both experiences of *oppression and their powerful sense of hope and celebration of life. Many women scholars work in an interreligious manner, both because Christianity is a minority religion in their cultures and because *colonization eradicated much of the indigenous *theology and spirituality. Recovering the lost myths and symbols is recovering the specificity of God's history among their people. Similarly, the Jewish scholar Judith Plaskow has redrawn the Jewish experience of the *covenant with God, but this time, women are placed as central within this relationship.

Another strand of this newer phase takes a metaphorical approach: Sallie McFague sees God's revelation through the lens of the world as the body of God, to inspire a different attitude to nature and to break the God–world dualistic separation. For the same reason, Mary Grey uses the *metaphor of interconnectedness as the language of God's communication for our times. Elizabeth Johnson synthesizes many of these strands in her interpretation of God as *Sophia moving through history, revealed as compassionate and suffering, close to the experiences of women and all oppressed peoples, specific to the context, yet ultimately, profoundly mysterious.

Chung [1991]; Grant [1989/1992]; Grey [1993]; Johnson [1992]; McFague [1993]; Plaskow [1991]; Russell [1979]

MARY C. GREY

Rhetorical Criticism Rhetorical criticism is an exegetical discipline used in the study of the Bible. The discipline owes its identity to James Muilenburg, a professor at Union Theological Seminary in New York City from 1945 to 1963. He sought to supplement the analysis of genres (types of literature) by attending to the particularities of texts. His guiding rubric holds that appropriate articulation of the form-content of an individual literary unit yields appropriate articulation of its meaning. Components in the background of rhetorical criticism include classical rhetoric, literary-critical theories of the Western world, the long history of the literary interpretation of the Bible among Jewish and Christian commentators, and the discipline of form criticism.

Since the pivotal work of Muilenburg, rhetorical criticism has developed according to two overlapping understandings of rhetoric: the art of composition and the art of persuasion. The former explores the structure, substance, and style of discourse. The latter explores the ways a speaker or writer shapes discourse to affect an audience. Both understandings have contributed to feminist interpretation of the Bible, as samples of exegesis from the First Testament, the *Apocrypha, and the Second Testament demonstrate.

In the First Testament, rhetorical criticism has produced an alternative to the traditional reading of Genesis 2—3. The alternative shows, for example, that the first creature formed by Yhwh/God (Gen. 2:7) is not man the male but rather "the human [*hā'ādām*] from humus [*hā-'ădāmâ*]," a sexually undifferentiated character out of whom Yhwh/God makes the two sexes (Gen. 2:21–24). Rather than being subordinate to the man, the woman is his equal. The Hebrew word *'ēzer*, often translated "helper" and then applied to her, usually signifies superiority (e.g., Ex. 18:4; Deut. 33:7, 26, 29; Ps. 33:20; 121:2), but the qualifying phrase "fit for" or "corresponding to" tempers that meaning to suggest mutuality between the sexes (Gen. 2:18–20). The statement that the man rules over the woman (Gen. 3:16), occurs only after their shared act of eating the forbidden fruit. These words describe, rather than prescribe, life lived in disobedience. They do not legitimate male *domination and female subordination. In addition, the absence of the word *curse* in reference to the woman (Gen. 3:16) counters prevailing ideas about her. Close reading of this text seeks to persuade readers of an understanding of *creation, male and female, that is different from the patriarchal version.

Compositional analysis of the apocryphal book Judith offers another instance of rhetorical method joined to a feminist perspective. The twofold structure of the story sets up a contrast between opposing leaders, one male and one female. In chapters 1—7, Nebuchadnezzar, king of Assyria, dominates. He threatens to destroy the people and the God of Israel. In chapters 8—16, the Israelite widow Judith prevails. She decapitates the Assyrian general Holofernes, thereby making possible victory for Israel and its God. A chiastic arrangement keeps the focus on her. At the beginning, Judith is introduced (A, 8:1–18); Judith plans to save Israel (B, 8:9–10:9a); Judith and her maid leave the city Bethulia (C, 10:9b–10). At the center comes the critical episode in which Judith outwits and kills Holofernes (D, 10:11–13:10a). At the end, Judith and her maid return to Bethulia (C, 13:1b–11); Judith plans the destruction of Israel's enemy (B^1, 13:1–16:20); Judith's story is concluded (A^1, 16:21–25). Articulation of structure and content highlights the female orientation of this story.

In exegesis of the Second Testament, rhetoric as the art of persuasion has aided feminist interpretation. This approach fits, for example, the task of reconstructing the theology and role of women *prophets in the church of first-century Corinth. Writing to this community, Paul seeks to persuade it of his point of view. By analyzing his arguments, the reader can tease out of the text the views of those with whom he differs, most especially the women who have shifted interest from bearing children to activities within the community of *faith. They do not adhere to Paul's argument for the separation of public from private life, with the concomitant subordination of women to the traditional household system. Abstaining from sexual relations, these women are no longer subject to male authorities (1 Cor. 7:1–4). In the house church, they prophesy and pray with their heads uncovered, a mode of dress that Paul finds unacceptable (1 Cor. 11:13–16). His demand that the women be silent attests to their prominence.

The theological arguments of Paul unveil further the contrasting views of the Corinthian women (and some of the men). Whereas Paul sees the power of the resurrected Christ mediated through past witnesses and the future dead (1 Cor. 15:1–11, 23–28, 51–54), they stress direct access (1 Cor. 4:8; 14:36). Whereas Paul privileges the male, identifying him with God's *image and glory (1 Cor. 11:8–16) and identifying the female only as man's glory, they hold that life in Christ abolishes this privilege to bring about a *new creation in which no human being has *authority over another. Whereas Paul would restrict the Spirit to those he deems wise (1 Cor. 8:9–13; 10:14–22; 11:23, 29), they rejoice in its outpouring on all who believe (1 Cor. 1:26; 2:6–16; 4:10; 10:3). Accordingly, women have central roles in the communal experiences of prophesying and praying. Rhetorical analysis recovers diversity within the early church, a diversity that expands the horizons of the Christian *gospel.

Both as the art of composition and as the art of persuasion, rhetoric is a tool available to various hermeneutical endeavors. Biblical authors and editors availed themselves of this tool as they told stories, composed poetry, formulated laws, pronounced oracles, and wrote letters. Studying their rhetoric constitutes the discipline of rhetorical criticism. When joined to a feminist perspective, it helps to illuminate issues of gender. It recovers lost voices and views that counter *patriarchal biases, exposes *misogynist dimensions embedded in the text, and exploits ambiguities and ambivalences in constructing biblical theology. Overall, rhetorical criticism has contributed substantively to feminist hermeneutics.

Craven [1983]; Trible [1978; 1984; 1994]; Wire [1990]

PHYLLIS TRIBLE

Righteousness To be righteous is to be in right relationship by acting right (common in the Hebrew Bible, Jewish *tradition, and the Gospels) or by the other party saying, "It's all right" (common in Pauline writings and Christian theology; justification). To demystify words in this family, cross out the "eous": *righteous* means "right." Note that not everyone agrees on the specifics of what is right.

Biblical writers present God as the standard setter and model for righteousness. Some texts accent God's opposition to wrong; others emphasize God's desire and action for blessing. The Bible speaks of righteousness in natural as well as human contexts. Like *justice (a closely linked concept in both Hebrew and Greek scripture), right(eous)ness may go beyond or against law. Judah declares Tamar "more righteous" than he (Gen. 38:26) because her bold action restores fractured family relationships.

Western Christendom has focused largely on individual righteousness with God. Theologians and *mystics tend to speak of righteousness through divine forgiveness. In this view, God's action frees the human to act rightly in grateful response. In practice, many congregations promote works as the path to righteousness with God. Some define right action in ways that counter *oppression. Others mandate submission to abuse. Jewish tradition strongly associates righteousness with charity.

Feminist theologies tend to shun legalistic interpretations of righteousness. Instead they emphasize righteousness as the establishment and maintenance of fruitful, healthy relationships, not only religious (human–God) but social (human–human) and ecological (human–all creatures) as well.

Lebacqz [1987]; Schmid, in Anderson [1984]; Tamez [1993b]

MARTI STEUSSY

Rights, Animal *Animal rights* denotes a specific philosophical argument: that animals have inherent value as individuals. It is also the general term for the movement to end the exploitation of (other) animals by people. The animal rights movement targets the predominant forms of animal exploitation (eating, wearing, exhibiting, and experimenting on animals) and is composed predominantly of women.

Western feminism inevitably confronts the status of animals, because historically, the *ideological justification for women's alleged inferiority was made by appropriating them to animals: women were seen to be closer to animals than to men. The dilemma feminists then confront is whether to say, "We are not animals, we are humans, like men" (the liberal feminist response), or "Why are humans afraid to acknowledge our kinship with other animals and the rest of nature?" (the radical feminist, cultural feminist, and *ecofeminist response). Specific feminist challenges to the exploitation of animals offer visions of *liberation that include other life-forms besides human beings. This transformative feminism perceives all *oppressions as interconnected, arguing that no one creature will be free until all are free.

Theological issues raised by feminist animal advocacy include (1) whether animals' exploitation is sacralized in biblical passages; (2) the problematic role of animal *sacrifice in religious ceremonies; (3) whether the resistance to examining the treatment of animals is a way of avoiding a recognition of our own animality; (4) the need for a "theology of relinquishment," not only for men in relationship to women but for people in relationship to animals; (5) the recognition that male-centered theology can accommodate neither women nor animals; (6) that an anthropomorphized God excludes animals from the godhead.

As feminism transforms theology, the space for acknowledging animals is created. The more theology moves from being androcentric, the less anthropocentric it will be.

Adams [1994a]; Adams/Donovan [1995]; Donovan/Adams [1996]; Gaard [1993]

CAROL J. ADAMS

Rights, Children's The issue of children's rights arose as a secular concept within late twentieth-century liberalism, largely as a consequence of the feminist-inspired rethinking of patriarchically defined *family roles. Patriarchy had assumed that the welfare of children was assured by parents, motivated by both parental love for the child and parental self-interest in securing their progeny. Western religion generally reflected this patriarchal approach, as in, for example, Catholic social teaching from Leo XIII through John Paul II.

Within the West, the piecemeal dismantling of traditional *patriarchy involves legal (national) intervention in the family and in economic, social, and political institutions in the name of individual rights. The rights of racial minorities, women, and children have all been asserted and defended in this way. The case of children stands out, however, in that there has been little or no effort at empowering children, at making children subjects rather than objects, in keeping with liberal precepts on human *freedom, rationality, and *autonomy. The continued understanding of children as naturally and necessarily dependent has served to make the state, rather than the parent, the final guarantor of the welfare of children. For this reason, most contemporary use of the phrase "the rights of children" by states, courts, the United Nations, and churches is followed by a list of things that children should have provided for them either by parents or by the state as surrogate parent, including safe housing, food, basic medical care, *education, and familial affection.

As feminist theological reflection on the family deepens, it is beginning to question the great divide in modern thinking between children, understood as dependent, and adults, understood as rational and autonomous, and to recast understandings of both children and adults in terms of a theological *anthropology focused on human relationality and aimed at mutuality. Within such reflection, the basic right of children appears as the right to participate in all decision making that affects their lives. This participation in decision making should be implemented in the family, in education, in law, and in health care; the degree of children's participation in decision making should increase throughout children's maturation process.

Gudorf, in Andolsen/Gudorf/Pellauer [1985]; John Paul II [1983]; Keller [1986]; Miller [1981]

CHRISTINE GUDORF

Rights, Human In the 1990s a global women's movement for the human rights of women is growing, after a long history of neglect. In the seventeenth century, European propertied males claimed that they were born with civil and political rights. Such rights protected the individual from government coercion. Individual reason and *culture created by males were found superior to feudal governing offices, which were now seen as changeable, not essential or divinely created.

For other people, gaining civil and political rights has been a long, bloody struggle. In the United States, indigenous people were given no active human rights but were often slaughtered instead by human rights holders. African men, in the Constitution of the United States, were given only three-fifths of human status. Enslaved or immigrant women were given none under the new government. After decades of struggle, women in the United States gained the right to vote in 1920. Selective human rights developed in many countries.

At the forming of the United Nations in 1948, economic, social, and cultural rights were becoming as important as political and civil rights. Women were insistent that they be explicitly included in the original documents, including the Charter of the United Nations and the Universal Declaration of Human Rights, and they achieved their goal. Many states have since been more guided by traditional attitudes toward women than by the international human rights agreements. But the 1993 World Conference on Human Rights produced the Vienna Declaration and Programme of Action. Women's experiences have a crucial place, thanks to the global women's movement for human rights.

Key issues are both ancient and current, and urgent. First, the universal basis of human rights and the specificity of each group live in tension. If being born is what gives every person human rights, what *differences among people still affect human rights? Applying human rights to public life (freedom of speech, *freedom from torture, e.g.) but not to private life leaves women regularly violated. *Violence against women is global and gender-specific. In the Vienna Declaration, governments recognize this somewhat. They say that sexual abuse of women in armed conflicts violates international human rights. Violence against women in private life, however, still raises the question of state *responsibility. In human rights, states and organizations have been bound as public realities. What happens in the home has been understood in human rights activities as private, not subject to state oversight. Women's human rights are violated by *battering, rape, sexual slavery, etc. Bringing domestic and international human rights laws to acknowledge this actively is part of the current movement.

Second, human rights for women involve bodily, including genital, integrity: no battering, no rape, no coerced pregnancy, no conflict between genital integrity and community membership, no submissive starving or self-burning, no working to death. Data on women's *body situations in all countries are increasingly available and necessary to the responsibility of states to ensure human rights. Literacy and *education of women are also essential to assembling data on human rights; indeed, they are themselves human rights. Rejecting the traditional separation of body and mind is crucial to a new human rights view created by women.

Third, focusing on economic, cultural, and social rights as much as on civil and political rights is urgent to women's human rights. Traditional teaching in many cultures, religions, and states places women in economic and religious subordination. Defining basic human needs such as health, shelter, and chosen work as human rights, and honoring them, is lifesaving for women. Women are insisting that states and nongovernmental organizations focus equally on economic, social, and cultural rights. Religious and cultural rights that violate women's human rights can be changed or rejected.

Cook, *Human Rights Quarterly* [1993]; Peters/Wolper [1995]; Sullivan, *American Journal of International Law* [1994]

ELIZABETH BETTENHAUSEN

Rights, Reproductive Reproductive technologies include a variety of methods to enhance the possibility of conception, to evaluate the health status of the fetus in utero, and to monitor and control childbirth. This entry will not discuss technologies for performing elective *abortions.

Prior to feminist debate, most religious ethicists focused on *marriage as the morally essential context for responsible reproduction. They discussed the moral status of the human embryo throughout its developmental process, the harms that the prospective child might suffer from technology, and the moral obligations and rights associated with genetic ties. Some thinkers decried the commercialization of human reproduction and warned about unethical *domination of the child, viewed as a technical product. Many theologians promoted a view of procreation as an unambiguous gift from God, who created new life through sexual unions.

Most feminists are suspicious of increased control of women's reproductive power by a male-dominated medical establishment. As medical research provides more techniques to intervene in pregnancy on behalf of the child in utero, some doctors view pregnant women as potential obstacles to fetal welfare. The tendency to separate the interests of the fetus from the needs and desires of the pregnant woman is exacerbated by technologies that allow scientists easily to view the fetus in the womb (Petchesky). Advances in technical knowledge have led to a greater range of technological interventions before conception and during pregnancy and childbirth. Examples include maternal serum alpha-fetoprotein screening, chorionic villi sampling, and fetal monitoring during labor. These technologies could become tools for increased medical and social control over fertile and pregnant women. Women might be pressured or even compelled by law to submit to technological interventions because, in the opinion of medical experts, they are necessary for the health of the child to be born. Prenatal screening techniques, in particular, raise profound issues about the social identification of mental and physical "defects" and about the provision of social resources for persons with *disabilities.

Women make reproductive choices against the backdrop of particular cultural constructions of motherhood. The advent of new infertility treatments raises fresh ethical questions about the place of pregnancy, childbirth, and childrearing as aspects of human fulfillment for women. If psychological and social experiences of mothering contribute in a unique way to female flourishing, then many reproductive technologies represent a morally positive service for infertile women. If women accept risky, burdensome infertility treatments in response to pro-motherhood cultural pressures and undue pressure to satisfy male desires for genetic offspring, then the moral *agency of such women has been compromised.

Feminists are united in their insistence that the moral agency of women seeking to shape their procreative lives must be accorded respect. Some feminist philosophers and lawyers have insisted that reproductive technologies expand the procreative choices available to women. These feminists emphasize procreative liberty, a woman's right to complete control over her own body, and the personal fulfillment afforded infertile women who achieve maternal happiness through technology. Other feminist philosophers and theologians warn that reproductive technologies may be used in ways that exploit women, particularly women from socially disadvantaged groups. They emphasize that women make moral choices within specific social circumstances. For example, in a *racist, capitalist society, in vitro fertilization coupled with embryo transfer could enable persons who have class and *race privilege to hire poor, racial/ethnic women as surrogate *mothers.

There are important ethical questions concerning just access to reproductive technologies. Infertility rates are highest among poor women, but they rarely have access to expensive, high-technology infertility treatments. Certain reproductive technologies allow *lesbian women to conceive children apart from heterosexual intercourse. Yet some conservatives would deny lesbians access to reproductive technology because they and their children are not part of "normal," i.e., *patriarchal, families.

Feminist ethicists have not paid enough attention to the public policy aspects of reproductive technology, with the exception of the role of the state in regulating surrogacy arrangements. Feminist social ethicists should advocate public policies, such as vigorous enforcement of occupational safety regulations, that preserve fertility for those women and men who wish to have children. Rationing of reproductive technologies is now happening based on ability to pay. An ethical debate is needed about alternative ways to determine which reproductive health services offer the greatest benefit at affordable costs and then to guarantee all women and men access to, and choices concerning, the most beneficial modes of reproductive health care.

Ethicist Beverly Harrison has criticized theologians who romanticize each human conception as a gift from God. She declares that all human choices about reproduction involve an interplay of human *freedom and human finitude. Hard reproductive choices must be made by women (and men) who understand the difficult work involved in bringing a child into being and nurturing its capacity for genuine personal existence. Therefore, human beings have a grave *responsibility as co-creators with God to shape their procreative power in a fashion that enhances positive relationality, promotes the public good, and safeguards the well-being of the earth.

Andolsen, in Richardson [1987]; Andrews, *Logos* [1988]; Harrison [1983]; Overall [1987]; Petchesky, in Stanworth [1987]; Ryan, *Hastings Center Report* [1990]

BARBARA HILKERT ANDOLSEN

Rituals, African A ritual is a prescribed, formal, and symbolic act. Even though the word is often used in a religious context, it is not necessarily limited to the sphere of religion. There are nonreligious rituals, such as a prescribed manner of greetings between categories of people in certain social and cultural contexts. For example, the youth in some African societies ritually bow or prostrate themselves before their elders in accord with custom. Similarly, in certain societies it is the ritual to receive guests by first seating them and offering some form of drink as a gesture of welcome.

In contrast to these nonreligious rituals we may give an example of religious rituals in some communities. A typical example from the Christian *tradition is the celebration of the Eucharist in the church. We can also refer to the ritual of ablution as another example of a religious ritual. From the African religious heritage, a typical example would be the pouring of libation to gods, goddesses, and ancestors at certain periodic ceremonies associated with birth, puberty, marriage, and death. Comparable systems of rituals may be found in many *cultures and religious traditions across the world.

The important element of rituals is that they are meant to symbolize some important beliefs, values, or practices that are cherished in the particular societies in which they occur. Further, rituals are performed to maintain good relations among the human beings themselves, on one hand, and between the human beings and the objects they worship, on the other. They are also performed to bring certain benefits to the individuals and community as a whole. The ultimate aim of all rituals, then, is to sustain life in general for all who perform them.

In practice, however, in the actual performance of these rituals, many instances of contradictions occur among these stated elements. For example, in the performance of some rituals, disputes arise that may defeat the goal of unity of purpose and welfare as ideally stated. In the same way, certain cherished human *rights are visibly violated or incautiously set aside in performances of these rituals. It is not unusual to find that in the context of ritual performances, actual physical *violence occurs; and in some cases, human lives are lost. Illustrations of these points could easily be cited from various types of rituals such as female circumcision and widowhood and puberty rituals, which still persist in many African and other cultures. Often it is women who suffer because they are entirely excluded or *marginalized, or they suffer immensely in the performance of the rituals.

Clearly, rituals are an important part of the cultural and religious traditions of various societies. They are seen to have some functions, but they can also be seen to be dysfunctional in certain cases. Important as they are, rituals should be modified or eliminated if they negate the human dignity, self-esteem, and ultimate *survival of persons.

Eboussi-Boulaga [1984]; Girard [1981]; Oduyoye/Kanyoro [1992]

ELIZABETH AMOAH

Rituals, Women's Rituals are agreed-upon patterns of symbolic action that spring from, evoke, and develop complex and often deep layers of feeling and thought. As such, they carry the values and intentions of communities. How do rituals work? They objectify a community's shared, subjective experience. Through symbolic acts, the deepest-held feelings and beliefs of a group are made objects that exist in time and space. These objects have a shape: they begin at a point in time, move toward another point, and then end. What occurs within the frame of "Here we begin . . ." and "Well, that's that!" has the power to transform the life of the *community that acts.

Women's rituals often embody certain characteristics: (1) they unite *emotion and intellect; (2) they work with the *body and images of the natural world; and (3) they take place in circles where *hierarchy of leadership is either modified or abolished altogether.

Traditionally, scholars claimed that rituals were discovered rather than created; that is, they arose out of the depth of the collective psyche of a *culture, out of centuries of practice. Such an understanding of rituals has been used to denigrate the ritualizing being done by women who gather, create them, and, in many instances, then discard them. However, the ephemeral quality of these rituals underscores the particularity of women's *experience. The ritual one group of women might do lacks meaning to another, or even to that same group a year later.

Women's rituals are essential to the continued vitality of the various contemporary movements to establish the worth of all people, because they manifest in space and time women's experience in all its variety. In many institutions in our society, critical decisions that affect the lives of humankind are made in an atmosphere in which the distortions of *patriarchy remain the only *reality. Other realities need to exist alongside patriarchal perspectives to point out these distortions and limitations and to help people dismantle or change them.

Clark/Ronan/Walker [1978]; Dillard [1982]; Marshall [1984]; Starhawk, in Plaskow/Christ [1989]

LINDA J. CLARK

Sacraments Sacraments are central constitutive rites in Christianity. The term comes from a Latin word, *sacramentum,* meaning "oath of allegiance," and is not found in the New Testament. By the third century, the word was being used to describe *baptism and the *eucharist as sacred actions of Christian worship. By the thirteenth century, the Roman Catholic Church numbered seven sacraments: baptism, confirmation, penance, eucharist, holy orders, matrimony, and extreme unction. Most Protestant churches, following Reformation preferences for the "gospel sacraments," acknowledge the sacraments of baptism and eucharist (Matt. 28:19; Acts 2:38; Matt. 26:26–29), although some refer to these rites as ordinances.

Traditional historical development of sacramental theology and practice has emphasized *patriarchal protection of the correct form and matter, as well as *hierarchical and clerical control of the distribution of and access to sacraments. Reservation of sacramental actions to the ordained is found in most Protestant as well as all Catholic and Eastern Orthodox churches. Today there is considerable *ecumenical agreement in defining "church" as a baptismal and eucharistic *community. Contemporary Christian theology tends to describe sacraments generally as encounters between God and the believer.

Rethinking and reconstructing sacraments are part of feminist critique of patriarchal theological practices as well as language. Feminist assessments note the complexity of interlocking *oppressions in traditional sacramental theology that work to deny *power to women, protect male privilege, and render the laity largely passive (Procter-Smith). Feminists have described Christian history as "sacramental sex discrimination" and eucharistic ritual (in some churches) as symbolizing "the structural *evil of *sexism." Rosemary Ruether attributes the theological root of alienated, clericalized sacraments to "a quasi-Manichean Augustinianism that divorces nature and *grace, *creation and *redemption" (77). Similarly, Susan Ross, among others, points to ways sacramental theology is used today, as in official Roman Catholicism's opposition to women's *ordination, to denote women's bodies and natures as ontologically inferior to men's. Ross instead points to the intrinsic sacrality of the *body and nature, reclaiming (as Elisabeth Schüssler Fiorenza asserts) women's bodies as the body and image of Christ.

This entry on sacraments largely excludes *goddess feminists and other *pagans, who nevertheless continue to influence construction of women's rites in general through creation of new sacramental actions and rituals. Instead it emphasizes those feminists who are concerned with dismantling clericalism and sexism while reforming and restoring sacramental power to women. This is an important task because women in sacramental churches, in particular, experience painful alienation and exclusion from full sacramental life and leadership. Roman Catholic theologian Ann Carr (along with Catherine Mowry LaCugna, among others) calls for a new understanding of the church as sacrament with men and women participating in all *ministries, adding that only then would the sacramental church embody full participation.

Feminist principles for sacramental renewal include placing emphasis on women's diverse *experiences, memories, and imagination; advocating women's involvement in shaping their own symbolic universe; overcoming false *dualisms of spirit over matter, mind over body, and male over female; contextualizing the development of ritual; and depending on mutual and/or rotating *responsibility for leadership. Ruether's depictions of *Women-Church involve gathered, emancipatory communities, each with the right to interpret and reform its own sacramental life. The result is not fewer but proliferating *liturgies and rites, as women, more than ever before, celebrate what is holy in new ways (Procter-Smith/Walton).

Christian feminist sacramental reform has tended to focus on the central rites of baptism and eucharist. There are divergent emphases on baptism. Some point to the central baptismal declaration of Gal. 3:28, affirming baptism as the sacrament of the *discipleship of equals; they want to make sure all (including children) are welcomed. Others acknowledge the persistent courage and spirituality of those generations of nurses and midwives who have (often without official sanction) baptized infants, although these critics warn against narrow understandings of baptism as removing the stain of original *sin, which often prompts these baptisms. Still other feminists advise radically restructuring this rite of initiation to avoid the danger of making a commitment on behalf of another. They focus on adult *conversion as a rite of passage moving from alienation toward commitment to the *new creation. These feminists also advise adding some sort of "naming celebration" for a new child, a rite that points toward adult baptism.

Feminist revisions of eucharistic practices have offered strong criticism of the concept of *sacrifice in eucharistic liturgies, stressed inclusion and hospitality, and envisioned true eucharistic celebration as a feast of *liberation and a paradigm for just relations. In particular, feminist sacramentality, underscoring that the divine is not separate from daily material existence, emphasizes connection over separation and honors the sacred character of women's leadership, lives, and bodies.

Carr [1988]; Duck [1991]; Procter-Smith [1990]; Procter-Smith/Walton [1993]; Ross, *Horizons* [1989]; Ruether [1985]; Russell [1993]

FREDRICA HARRIS THOMPSETT

Sacrifice, the Bible, and Christ In the Christian West, sacrifice has been the major way of interpreting Christ's significance. The interpretation of Jesus' death as sacrifice for the forgiveness of sins makes sacrifice a central value. Yet it is a value detrimental to the well-being of nondominant groups, particularly women. Furthermore, sacrifice is not the primary way of understanding Jesus' death in the NT.

Sacrifice is the ritual killing of animals or humans in the belief that it pleases some god. It was culturally very widespread but not universal. The sacrificial slaughter of animals was carried out daily by Jewish priests in the Temple in Jerusalem. Sacrifices to various gods and goddesses occurred at temples throughout the Mediterranean world. It was the standard religious practice of the world in which Christianity was born.

There are problems with valuing sacrifice. It exalts deliberate killing and thereby sanctions and encourages a culture of *violence. It functions to help maintain and legitimate *imperial and *patriarchal *power. Those without power in a culture are admonished to subordinate or sacrifice themselves to those with power over them as their religious duty. Sacrificial systems value men over women: the blood of deliberate killing is understood to bring protection, establish *covenant, and make *atonement, while women's blood of menstruation and childbirth is viewed as defiling. Blood connected with death is valued while blood connected with birthing is rejected. Furthermore, priests who sacrifice are almost always male; women are excluded.

Sacrifice is an integral part of the Hebrew Bible. There are early traditions of human sacrifice—the near sacrifice of Isaac (Genesis 22) and the actual sacrifice of Jephthah's daughter (Judges 11). There are sacrifices establishing the covenant with God (Exodus 24). Much of the Torah is concerned with sacrificial legislation: types of sacrifices, animals to be sacrificed, and *purity regulations for priests. Animal sacrifice at the Temple of Jerusalem was understood to maintain the divine–human relationship. There are prophetic passages, however, that reject sacrifice (e.g., Isa. 1:11–13; Micah 6:6–8). Actual sacrifice ended with the Roman destruction of the Temple in 70 C.E.; the Jews gradually formalized other ways of worship.

Sacrifice is less central in the NT. Given the ubiquity of sacrifice in the Mediterranean world, it plays an astonishingly small role. Sometimes Christian life is described in sacrificial metaphors (e.g., "a living sacrifice," Rom. 12:1). A few (generally late) NT writings use sacrificial terminology for Jesus' death (e.g., 1 John 1:7; 2:2; 1 Peter 1:2, 18; 2:24). Paul sometimes uses cultic terminology among other *metaphors for Christ's death (Rom. 3:25). Only in Hebrews, an atypical NT text, is sacrifice central: Christ is portrayed as both the priest and the victim whose sacrifice ends all sacrifice. Since the NT has no concern about who can celebrate the *Eucharist, we can conclude the Eucharist was not understood sacrificially.

More fundamental to NT understandings of Christ's death, underlying both Paul and the Synoptic Gospels, was the notion of political *martyrdom. One was executed by the state for threatening its control; one's execution was an example for others, helping them to remain steadfast in face of political persecution. Such an understanding corresponds to Jesus' crucifixion, which was a political, not a religious, death. It also connects Jesus' death with his life, during which Jesus already forgave sins (e.g., Mark 2:1–12 // Matt. 9:2–8 // Luke 5:17–26; Luke 7:47–50). There is no need for a sacrificial death to enable forgiveness. Western Christian emphasis on Christ's death as sacrifice for *sin seems due more to the conventional thinking of the ancient world than it does to the beliefs of early Christians as found in the NT.

Brown, in Brown/Bohn [1989]; Jay [1992]; Levenson [1993]

JOANNA DEWEY

Sacrifice / Self-negation Sacrifice involves giving up or forgoing something for another that is held to be important. Another element involved in this concept is that one gives away space, life, interest, and, indeed, oneself for others to grow, nurture, advance, develop, and live fully. In different cultural situations, such as my African context, women are, more often than not, expected to give up and forgo many opportunities in the interest of children, husbands, partners, and the *family in general. For example, where a great premium is placed on formal *education, it is not unusual to have a situation where female children are sidestepped in favor of the male children. The idea underlying this is clearly in line with what we have observed, that females should give space, surrender opportunities, in favor of males; that is, sacrifice themselves and their interests in the general context of male-biased social systems.

Thus the concept of sacrifice so far has been construed in terms of self-negation. The intention is not to suggest that this element of self-negation is always gender-linked. The general idea that one gives up something in the interest of a higher good or a higher value is crucial. If we consider contemporary political and socioeconomic structures in many of the developing countries, a consistent plea for this type of sacrifice is evident. In such situations, the call for sacrifice is directed to all, irrespective of gender. But it is also conceivable that, given a male-biased society, women would bear the brunt in such adjustment schemes.

The basic idea underlying any form of sacrifice is that individuals give up something valuable for a better spiritual and material growth and development. Definitely, the idea of self-negation should not be the sole center of the concept of sacrifice. There must be an element of benefit for the offerer as well as the receiver. Therefore, in sacrifices, one should not give away everything to one's own doom. Sacrifice should be interpreted to mean a balanced giving of something valuable to another, in the expectation of advancing the spiritual and the material welfare of both giver and receiver.

Brown/Bohn [1989]; Fabella/Oduyoye [1988]; Jay [1992]; Oduyoye/Kanyoro [1992]

ELIZABETH AMOAH

Seeing Seeing is a disciplined task, not confined to the physical, biological function of sight. Ocular vision is not a necessity or even the point of departure for the discipline of seeing. Rather, seeing is the critical discipline of delving beneath surface, affective, and customary appearances; delving into the very constitutive, constructed layers of re-presented *reality and theology.

A feminist theological discipline of seeing begins with the methodological assumption that God and reality, as we know them, are political, cultural, and theological constructions. We construct understandings of *God, *race, class, *sexuality, and gender, as well as any "normative" customs and categories, on principles and/or theologies for the establishment of a particular theocultural order. For example, elaborate theological constructions have "justified" the establishment of slavery and*racism, as well as the prohibition of women from the priesthood. A critical seeing unveils these constructions, however, as principally based on an economic and *patriarchal order, rather than on any divinely sanctioned ordering of humanity. A feminist theological framework requires a critical investigation, i.e., "seeing," of theological and social constructs, especially if these are being employed to perpetuate oppressive institutions and *relationships. On the visual plane, these constructs are re-presented and immortalized in the visual images of *culture and religion. For example, many mass media images "define" the cultural roles for women (subordinate to men), whereas some churches eternalize Christ as ethnically European through religious art. On the social plane, these constructs are embodied in the cultural ordering of human relationships and endorsed through institutional structures (e.g., a husband rules the *family, *marriage is a divine absolute, priesthood is defined by the manhood of Jesus).

Seeing, therefore, calls the viewer to a critical consciousness informed by a *hermeneutic of suspicion and committed to *liberation: the viewer seeks to see from the margins, from the perspectives of those who are silent or silenced within the dominating culture. A feminist theological discipline of seeing requires the viewer to see with "eyes" scanning for the seemingly invisible cultural prejudices that distort and hide inequity, for the experience and perspective of people cloaked or misrepresented by cultural *stereotypes and *mythologies. Seeing faithfully disobeys any reigning cultural (mis)constructs, unveiling the lived reality of marginalized humanity and the institutions perpetuating their *marginalization.

Furthermore, a feminist theological discipline of seeing invalidates any ultimate *authority in a "pure," objective viewing of reality, for all seeing is intrinsically interactive with viewers' social and theological locations. Seeing requires viewers to confess their cultural, theological, and personal contexts, which render all viewing and inquiry of God and reality as multifactorial and inherently interpretative.

The discipline of seeing, however, is a participatory event, also making known and converting the viewer: "The discipline of seeing involves the total engagement of the viewer, and the viewer in turn is transformed" (Apostolos-Cappadona/Adams, 5). In the NT, Paul confirms this intrinsic relationship between seeing, knowing, and becoming known (1 Cor. 13:12). In classic literary parallelism, Paul writes, "For now we *see* in a mirror, dimly, but then we will *see* face to face. Now I *know* only in part; then I will *know* fully, even as I have been fully *known*" (emphasis added).

Paul proclaims a spiritual encounter of knowing and being known as essential to the discipline of seeing. That we now see "dimly" testifies to seeing as an eschatological act, neither static nor stationary but participatory in a forthcoming *revelation and promise of liberation. This eschatological dimension of seeing summons the viewer to delve into reality with eyes always yearning (and prepared) to see in greater fullness.

Apostolos-Cappadona/Adams, in Adams/Apostolos-Cappadona [1985]; Berger [1972]; Hunter, *JSFR* [1992]; Yamane/Polzer [1994]

JANN CATHER WEAVER

Servant / Slave "Servant" and "slave" are both possible renderings of the Hebrew *'ebed* and the Greek *doulos*, as well as the gender-specific Hebrew *šipḥāh* and *'āmāh* and Greek *doulē* (female slave/maidservant) and, less frequently, *paidiskē* (female slave) and the more differentiated *oiketēs* and *oiketikos* (house slave). The choice of *translation is debated among biblical translators whenever there is any ambiguity as to the sociopolitical context(s) of the word field. Lack of attention to or knowledge of the sociopolitical contexts of the respective biblical texts and/or their translators' and interpreters' attitudes toward servanthood, servitude, and slavery contributes to difficult and often painful discussions, with deeply rooted theological views at stake. Thus the issues arise in two major categories: the contexts of the biblical texts and the context(s) of the contemporary reader(s)/audience.

The Contexts of the Biblical Texts. The words *'ebed* and *doulos* for "slave" or "servant" are used more than one thousand times throughout the Bible. Slave labor, the institution whereby a person or group of people becomes the property of someone else for the service of the owner, appears in the biblical texts as the Hebrew people's slavery in Egypt, which precipitates the exodus event (Exodus; Leviticus; Deuteronomy); in reference to the slaves or servants of the patriarchs (Genesis); as forced labor during the monarchy (1 and 2 Samuel); as the working conditions during the Israelites' captivity during the Babylonian exile (Isaiah; Jeremiah; 2 Chronicles); and as slavery in the Roman Empire (Pauline epistles; Synoptic Gospels). While the conditions of these contexts varied as to the kind of service, the treatment of the slaves, the length of service, and the regulations for manumission, slaves, once they were slaves, had no choice over rendering service. Considered a basic form of movable property, like livestock, and/or part of the extended *patriarchal household (e.g., Gen. 12:16; 20:14; 24:35; Ex. 20:17; Acts 16:15–34; 1 Cor. 1:16; 16:15; Eph 5:21–6:9; Col. 3:18–4:1), slaves in biblical times were sold into slavery (debt slavery) or captured as prisoners of war. The length of their slavery was legally regulated with a sabbath and/or *jubilee year promising manumission (cf., e.g., Ex. 21:2–11; Lev. 25:39–55; Deut. 15:12–18; 20:10–14; Jer. 34:8–17). While slavery as an institution is not criticized in the New Testament, the prophet Amos explicitly condemns debt slavery (cf. Amos 2:6).

Another use of *'ebed* and *doulos* language in the Bible is figurative or *metaphorical. Patriarchs, *prophets, and kings are called *'ebed* of YHWH (e.g., Ex. 32:13; Lev. 25:55; 1 Sam. 3:9; Ezra 9:9), and so is the central figure in the so-called Servant Songs in Deutero-Isaiah (cf. Isa. 42:1–9; 49:1–6; 50:4–11; 52:13–53:12); elsewhere, others call themselves or are called "slave(s)/servant(s) of God" or "slave(s)/servant(s) of Jesus/Christ" (e.g., Luke 1:48; 2:29; Acts 2:18; Rom. 1:1; 1 Cor. 7:22; Gal. 1:10; Phil. 1:1). In these biblical texts, servant/slave language designates a special, honored, and cared-for relationship to the Divine. Throughout history, these metaphorical passages in the Bible have been utilized to romanticize the realities of slave labor and to suggest euphemistic language of servitude, thus supporting so-called biblical justifications of slave *ideology, for example, bolstering the institution of American chattel slavery.

The Context(s) of the Contemporary Reader(s)/Audience. Translation is the task of the contemporary interpreter and reader, who makes choices between "servant" and "slave" as possible renderings of *'ebed* and *doulos* language in the Bible. The sociopolitical contexts of the respective biblical texts guide that decision. Yet, while the institution of slavery in biblical times is not identical with the chattel slavery in the eighteenth- and nineteenth-century United States, it is this history of slavery in the United States that provides the context for contemporary readers in the West. Race and class shape the ways *'ebed* and *doulos* language in the Bible is heard today. As communities of faith(s) have identified with various groups of people in the biblical texts, the stories of the exodus have become a paradigm for *liberation in black theologies and in black churches, while womanist theology has shown Hagar as a prototype of African-American women's lives.

Feminist liberation *theology needs to ally with people of color in translating *'ebed* and *doulos* language in the Bible as "slave" whenever possible. Actually, even *servant* functioned as euphemism for *slave* in colonial America. And after emancipation, it has been people of color and poor white folk that have labored as "servants" of property owners. Further, glorification of servitude, especially as found in hymnody, needs to be critically analyzed and the underlying theology questioned, asking for whom, if anyone, it is liberating. The challenge for feminist biblical interpreters in dealing with servant/ slave language in the Bible is to join womanist scholars in producing antiracist advocacy translations, sensitive to women's issues, that do not veil but name the realities of *race and class then and now.

Cannon, *Semeia* [1989]; Martin, *JFSR* [1990]; Martin, in Felder [1991]; Meyers, in Newsom/Ringe [1992]; Pomeroy [1975/1995]; Schottroff [1995]; Williams [1993a]

ANGELA BAUER

Sexism Sexism refers to gender stereotyping of men and women as hierarchically ordered (men over women) and also as confined to limited cultural identities and roles as "masculine" and "feminine." "Masculinity" is identified with *reason, action, capacity to rule and use force against others, while "femininity" is tied to gentleness, passivity, and an auxiliary relation to men. These *differences are assumed to be biologically based and necessary for good social order, rather than unjust *social constructions that limit the full humanity of women and also men.

Sexist stereotyping is used to keep both men and women in their place by attacking women who aspire to larger roles as "unfeminine" and males who are sensitive and artistic as "effeminate" or "sissies" (sisters). Attacks on male homosexuals typically employ such hostile comparisons of these men to women; thus homophobia is related to sexism (see *Heterosexism).

Sexism is expressed on many levels. Sexism is expressed in stereotypic images of women and men in all aspects of public *culture, such as literature, advertising, and religious symbols. Sexism is reproduced from generation to generation through the socialization of both women and men, in families, schools, churches, and other institutions, to accept these *stereotypes and act out of them. It is reenforced in the form of verbal and physical assaults on women as sexual objects, often accentuated when a woman is perceived as "getting out of her place" as a woman, as well as assaults on males who appear "effeminate." It is expressed in the exclusion of women from certain types of employment or leadership roles that are assumed to be the prerogatives of males, and in the confinement of women to unpaid domestic work and lower pay for the same paid employment, keeping women in economic dependency.

Sexism is thus expressed in personal, interpersonal, cultural, economic, legal, and political terms. It is part of a total social and cultural system with a long history (see *Patriarchy). Patriarchy is a broader concept than sexism, referring to systems through which the patriarchs or male heads of families exercise collective sovereignty over wives, children, and slaves of both sexes and over nonhuman property. It includes *racism when class *hierarchy and slavery are based on the *domination of one racial-ethnic group over another. Sexism, then, refers to the component of patriarchy that enforces gender hierarchy through cultural, psychological, physical, economic, and legal means.

Although those legal aspects of patriarchy that excluded women from citizenship, property holding in their own name, higher *education, and professions have been largely modified in modern democratic societies, sexism continues as a pervasive patterning of psychological and cultural conditioning that continues to enforce gender stereotyping in personal and social relations, even though women are theoretically "equal" before the law. Thus sexism can be regarded as the continued assertion of the cultural *hegemony of males over females, masculinity over femininity, and its enforcement through various forms of social pressure.

Feminism, then, can be defined as an effort by women and men critical of sexism to dismantle this cultural hegemony of males over females, as well as masculinity over femininity in both male and female identities. Feminism seeks to assert an alternative culture, not only of female *equality in personal and social relations but of a different value system based on mutuality and holistic development for women and men rather than on the dominance of male over female. The dismantling of sexist cultural and social relations must then address all the above aspects of masculinist hegemony, including those found in religious *ideology in the church.

Decrow [1974]; Hartsock [1983]; Ruether [1983/1993]

ROSEMARY RADFORD RUETHER

Sexuality Definitional perspectives on sexuality in Christian theology are linked to different proposals about *con-*

trol of sexuality. In Hebrew scriptures, sexuality is a source of defilement to be controlled with *purity laws, and it is a source of (male) gratification and of heirs, to be controlled by property laws. For early church writers and Reformation theologians, sexuality is the source of passion that tends toward chaos unless it is controlled within the *family, for the purposes of procreation and where children can be cared for.

There are multiple challenges to the view that sexuality is primarily instrumental and should be controlled by priests or patriarchs. The NT writers rejected physical purity as the ground of their ethic, replacing it with purity of intention or of the heart. But they did not reject the principle of respect for sexual property. Rather, Jesus is depicted as seeing sexual access in itself as a fundamental good of the created order. Because sexual access is an important possession, he forbade his followers to rob others of it by divorcing a woman who did not have a parallel right to divorce. In making the wife equal to her husband, Jesus implied that she was no longer merely an instrument of his natal family in their quest for heirs or an instrument of the husband for his sexual gratification and household labor (Matt. 19:3–9; see Countryman, 255).

Although procreationism is still a mark of contemporary Western *culture (Gudorf, 29–32), theologians have developed an appreciation for the inherent worth of sexuality, seeing its appropriate control to be lodged in moral agents. James B. Nelson has encouraged seeing sex as the language of *body meanings. Like all languages, sexuality involves a symbol system that is socially and historically relative. Beverly Harrison views sexuality as foundational to human beings. The capacity to feel sensually is the basis of any moral sensitivity to what is happening in the world. Sexuality, when self-directed, unmediated by dominance relations, and an expression of bodily integrity, is the tender sensuality of mutual pleasuring (105–7).

Christine Gudorf expands on the meaning of sexuality to personality. It affects the structure of our brains, the way we relate to persons, the way we understand our world and attempt to structure our lives, occupations, choices around sexual activity, and social status. Most of all, in sexual activity is pleasure (54, 94). Mary Pellauer adds that when reflecting on aspects of "good sex," it becomes possible to ground the movement against sexual abuses, as hostility and *domination do not mix with the elements of ecstatic sexual pleasure (161–82).

It is contested territory to affirm the inherent worth of sexuality. Patricia Hill Collins contends that the history of slavery in the United States is the backdrop to efforts to control black women's sexuality, and such control is the heart of black women's oppression. Carol Robb (147–60) concurs that women's sexuality is still a medium of *oppression and that childbirth and childrearing, domestic *violence, sexual harassment, and *lesbian identity are examples of arenas in which what is owed to women because of what we create of social value is denied us because our sexuality is not ours but public (i.e., male) property. Sexuality, as the language of the body and as oriented toward pleasure, has provided the basis for articulating an alternative to external control, though a material basis in the economy is needed to substantiate this vision.

Collins [1991]; Countryman [1988]; Gudorf [1994]; Harrison [1983]; Nelson [1979]; Pellauer, *JFSR* [1993]; Robb, *JFSR* [1993]

CAROL S. ROBB

Shalom / Peace Shalom (*šālôm*) is the word used in the Hebrew Bible for a concept of comprehensive peace with *justice. The noun (and forms of the basic verbal root *šlm*) share a core meaning of "wholeness, completeness, well-being." Peace in the sense of shalom thus is much more than "simply" an absence of war. It is a physical, economic, sociopolitical, and spiritual reality.

In the Hebrew Bible, shalom includes individual health in a peaceful life (e.g., Josh. 10:21; 1 Kings 22:17; Isa. 38:17; Ps. 55:18) as well as communal well-being in political security, prosperity, and peace (e.g., 2 Kings 20:19; Isa. 32:18; 54:13; 66:12; Ps. 37:11; 147:14). Shalom is also often connected with the language and theology of *covenant, where it participates in a reality of relationship between God and people (e.g., Num. 25:12; Isa. 44:10; Ezek. 34:25; 37:26). The association of shalom with covenant introduces further covenant language and concepts such as justice (*mišpāṭ*, e.g., Zech. 8:16; cf. Jer. 6:6; 8:11, 15), truth (*'ĕmet*, e.g., Zech. 8:16, 19), and *righteousness (*ṣĕdāqâ*, e.g., Isa. 32:17; 48:18; Ps. 72:7; 85:10) as parts of shalom-wellness. Like covenant, shalom is understood as a gift from God, a blessing when present (e.g., Gen. 41:16; Isa. 52:7; 55:12; Ps. 29:11) and a vision for eschatological times (e.g., Isa. 9:5; 11:1–5; 11:9; 60:17; 66:12). The understanding of peace (*eirēnē*) in the New Testament is influenced by the Hebrew concept of shalom, well-being in comprehensive peace with justice.

Beyond offering a wonderful biblical vision, shalom has been an important concept for women in several ways—for women working in peace movements around the globe and for women engaged in doing feminist theologies. Women have been prominent in pacifist movements in the nineteenth and early twentieth centuries: for example, in Western Europe and the United States, Rosa Luxemburg, Anna White, Mary Woodbridge, Bertha von Suttner (Nobel Peace Prize, 1905), Jane Addams (founder of the Women's Peace Party, 1915), and Dorothy Day. Women have also been the leaders of peace movements in the 1970s, 1980s, and 1990s all over the world, from the Mothers of the Plaza de Mayo to the women at Greenham Common in England, from the women in the East and West German peace movement(s) of the 1980s to the women working for Witness for Peace in Nicaragua, from the Women's Peace Encampment at Seneca Falls, New York, to the Women in Black in Israel.

In doing feminist liberation *theologies, shalom as wholeness, as comprehensive peace with justice, offers a vision and a challenge. As a yearning of many women in various contexts, shalom necessitates the work of making the connections between the factors that hinder its realization: all the interrelated forms of *oppression that women face in their particular contexts (sexism, *racism, *classism, *heterosexism, anti-Semitism, "ableism," etc.). The vision and legacy of shalom challenge feminist *liberation theologies to analyze particularities of women's well-being and to articulate what shalom means: for whom, when, and where. As a physical, economic, sociopolitical, and spiritual reality, shalom addresses issues of ecology as well as women's well-being in worship. Shalom thus stands as a reminder and a goal to commit oneself to work for right relations that foster justice, peace, and the integrity of *creation.

Duchrow/Liedke [1989]; McAllister [1982]; McFague [1987]; Soelle [1990]

ANGELA BAUER

Shame Shame is the feeling of "inadequacy" or "failure" to live up to societal ideals about what people should be able to do, be, know, or feel. People's healthy sense of *pride and honor is based on living up to these ideals. Shame arises in the loss of pride and honor that occurs as the "real" does not live up to the cultural "ideal." Feelings of shame correspond to a diminished self-esteem and produce feelings of inferiority, incompetence, and weakness. To experience shame is to feel psychologically naked, exposed, and needing to hide or cover the self. Thus shame reflects the limitation of the self, while pride and honor reflect the potential of the self. Without awareness of both the potential and the limitation of the self, authentic self-realization is impossible. And the fear that shame stimulates is that of *community rejection, alienation, abandonment, or loss of social position.

Shame relies heavily on "group pressure," and consequently, it is found most prominently in group-oriented societies, where a person's main source of identity comes from belonging to the strongly bonded group. Because identity stems from the group, the group is capable of exerting great pressure on a person's behavior. In this type of society, shame functions not only as a means of social control but also as a way of dominating or manipulating social status.

In group-oriented societies such as ancient Israel, children represented both *survival and salvation, and women were valued as producers of children. Their role as *mothers may have led to more equal sharing of shame with men, although those who were barren bore great shame (1 Sam. 1:9–11). During the shift away from group orientation and toward individual orientation in the Greco-Roman period, the value and status of women often declined, leading to an increase in the bearing of shame by women. This change may be reflected in the development of the "*sin and *Fall" interpretation of Genesis 2—3 with its emphasis on both shame and *guilt, which has its origins in the Greco-Roman period and is never mentioned in the Old Testament.

Bechtel, *JSOT* [1991]; Bechtel, in Hopfe [1994]; Malina [1993]; Nathanson [1992]

LYN M. BECHTEL

Shintoism Shintoism (the Way of God) is a traditional ethnic religion that came into existence spontaneously from among the indigenous people of Japan (*Jinja Shinto:* Shrine Shinto, whose activities center around rituals and festivals at its shrine for the people in a village or a town). It has no particular *doctrine or founder. It began in the latter half of the fourth century C.E. It has four basic characteristics: it is ritualistic, this-worldly, particular, and patriarchal. Worship is directed at *kami* (native deities, including deified emperors and heroes, spirits of nature, and mythical subjects). Jinsha Shinto has long found its place in the rituals of guardian deities in communities. Therefore, it does not proclaim doctrine but puts value in its *liturgical or festive practices, which are either communal or familial.

As *Buddhism, *Confucianism, *Taoism, and Christianity came into the land, Shintoism sought a way to coexist with them by formulating its systematic doctrine of beliefs (*Gakuha Shinto:* Doctrinal Shinto). But its practices of *rituals and festivals supported by blood *relationships or shared territorial bonds have not been much influenced by any other religion. It is not unusual to find a Buddhist temple and a Shinto shrine in the same complex.

From 1868 to 1945, a new form of Shintoism, *Kokka Shinto* (State Shinto), initiated by the Meiji government, played a central role in religious legitimation of the emperor system as the national regime. To legitimize the *power of emperors as the center of the nation, it accepted the emperor as head priest and living god. This state religion, a combination of Jinja Shinto and *Koshitu Shinto* (Imperial Shinto), was formed on the basis of imperial rituals and shrine festivals.

Thus, under State Shinto, the emperor held the highest power in the political sphere and the highest *authority in the religious sphere, as a living god. The emperor was the father of the big *family of Japan, and thus *patriarchy was literally enacted. Not only making him the father of the state, the system played a central role in creating the concept of ethnicity at the cost of the concept of individuality, yielding a group-oriented mentality. It also yielded a racial exclusivism, promoting the ethnic purity of blood under the living god: ultranationalism. Patriarchy penetrated into family life as a small model of the emperor system. In every household the father was to be the authority, and the rest of the members, including his wife, were subjugated. Wives and girls were segregated in every sense of life.

In Shintoism, a woman is not considered polluted as a person, but menstruation and childbirth have been considered unclean. For certain periods, a woman was secluded so that she might not defile others, and only after she was purified might she resume her ordinary life. It is not difficult to find places where this custom was practiced until recently, especially in rural areas. It has been said that women invoke the wrath of the gods if they pass under *torii* (divine gates in front of Shinto shrines) during their periods. Even those women who did not practice such cultic customs were taught, or thought themselves, that their bleeding was abhorred by society as unclean. Thus in Japan, just as in first-century Palestine, religious *purity codes have contributed to the establishment of cultural identity and to the support of the power structure and various kinds of segregation.

Japan was forced to abolish State Shinto, including the emperor system, in 1947 as a result of its defeat in the Second World War. However, the *androcentrism that both the religion and the system had held as their central idea is still strongly reflected in many spheres of society. For example, emperors must be succeeded by their male offspring. Women cannot become priests but only maidens to serve in shrines under male priests. Women cannot step up on the sumo ring, which is supposed to be a divine precinct.

Hardacre [1989]; Murakami [1991]; Namihira [1986]; Reid [1991]

HISAKO KINUKAWA

Sin Within the Western Christian *tradition, sin has been understood first in terms of "original sin," or the condition into which all persons are born, and second as the actions that follow as a result of one's sinful nature. The first intends to describe the existential condition of all human beings, and the second describes the communal and personal effects of this condition throughout history.

For most of Christian history original sin was based on a historical interpretation of the Genesis story of Eve and Adam. Augustine gave the definitive account, arguing that in the unfallen state the *body was subject to the *soul (or intellect), even as the person was subject to God. However, through *pride, the first human beings turned away from dependence on God to themselves. This turning of their wills corrupted their created nature by disrupting the rightful ordering of mind over body, resulting in lust: a disordered love that taints the intellect, the will, and the body. This condition and its *guilt are transmitted to each generation.

Of particular interest is the role attributed to woman in this classical understanding of the *Fall. Eve was considered less intellectual than Adam and therefore closer to nature than to rationality. As such, she was more vulnerable than Adam. Hence it was she whom the devil tempted, and she who then tempted Adam through sexual wiles. With this model, "woman" is perceived as the seductress who lures man into sin. Since lust is the result of sin, and lust is most evident in the way that sexual *desires can override the intellect, *sexuality is also associated with sin and women. Through this Christian interpretation of the Genesis story, woman was identified with weakness, nature, sin, and sexuality. Even when the story lost its historical currency in the Enlightenment, its denigration of women continued to pervade Christian *culture.

It is no accident, then, that the contemporary wave of feminist theology began with the 1960 publication of Valerie Saiving's article "The Human Situation," suggesting that theologians reconsider the issue of women and sin. Saiving suggested that sin as pride may apply to men, but given the social conditions mitigating against women's strong exercise of selfhood, the besetting sin for women is triviality rather than pride. Two decades later, Judith Plaskow in *Sex, Sin, and Grace* (1980) and Susan Nelson Dunfee in

"The Sin of Hiding" (1982), respectively, extended Saiving's work by examining the cultural circumstances that influence women's fear of exercising *freedom and becoming a self. If the task for humanity is for each person to become a self, failure in this regard is sin.

Since this early work, feminists have given sustained attention to the social and cultural factors of *oppression insofar as they manifest the sins of oppressors and foster sins of victims. Rather than confining sin to the personal sphere, feminists look to social structures and their effects on the human psyche and on human behavior. Womanists such as Delores S. Williams have played a prominent part in this redevelopment, analyzing the double oppressions of *racism and *sexism under which women of color suffer. Sin becomes the disparagement of women and sexuality and the internalization of the effects of such disparagement in women's feelings of unworthiness.

Whereas the traditional understanding of sin located sin within individuals who collectively and individually rebelled against God, womanists and feminists focus more strongly on the social context of sin as oppression, which is the violation of any aspect of earth and its inhabitants. Sins are ecological as well as social and personal. The pervasiveness of sin follows from the competitiveness of finite life and the dynamic this creates to protect and perpetuate one's own kind over against those who are perceived as different. This, combined with negative symbolism, leads to an objectification and exploitation of those who are "other" to the dominant group, resulting in the diminution of the "other's" well-being. Thus the objectification, exploitation, and diminution of women suggested through the peculiar Christian interpretation of Genesis is itself sinful.

The feminist reshaping of sin totally undercuts the classical association of sin with sexuality, for the essential problem is not that the body does not obey the mind but that the notion of "well-being" is confined to too small a circle. In an interdependent world, well-being must extend ecologically and communally throughout the earth. To the extent that individuals and communities violate well-being, they are involved in sin.

Dunfee, *Soundings* [1982]; Engel, in Thistlethwaite/Engel [1990]; Saiving/Goldstein, in Christ/Plaskow [1979]; McFague [1993]; Plaskow [1980]; Suchocki [1994]; Williams, in Townes, ed. [1993]

MARJORIE HEWITT SUCHOCKI

Sisterhood "Sisterhood is powerful" has been the rallying cry in the emerging second wave of feminism in the North American context since the late 1960s. Similar to the first wave of feminism beginning in the mid-nineteenth century, "sisterhood" has connoted the assumption that women, as a class or group, "are the oldest oppressed group on the face of the planet," and that this oppression is *the* unifying bond for women's *liberation (Morgan). However, in a variety of contexts, *sisterhood* generally signifies the complementary yet contrasting, *patriarchally constructed term *brotherhood.* As such, it has been less valued as a concept indicative of the experiences of women and representing humanity as a whole.

Within the development of multiple feminist theories and *praxis, *sisterhood* is a contestable term. Through concrete social, economic, and political struggle against interstructured forms of *oppression in everyday life, different socially located groups of women are analyzing the nature, meaning, and demands of sisterhood through such social relations as *racism, *classism, neocolonialism, *ageism, and physical and mental capacity. In doing so, the meaning and usage of sisterhood is challenged for its elevation as a universal, descriptive category deduced from *essentialist notions of female oppression, without regard to historical, cultural, and economic *differences between and among women (Mohanty).

Feminist, native, womanist, *mujerista,* Jewish, and Asian and Asian-American women's theologies and *ethics are producing a critical discussion of sisterhood (its desirability and reality) through exploring the notions and norms of reciprocity and *appropriation in our theoretical work and praxis. Integral to our understanding are analyses of *power issues and differences between and among us and in relation to our communities of accountability. Any notion of sisterhood or *solidarity must emerge from engagement with the differences and power issues and from *empowerment, rather than from *transcendence of these and mere well-meaning intentionality.

Daly/Levine [1994]; Mohanty, in Barrett/Phillips [1992]; Morgan [1970]; Mud Flower Collective [1985]

JOAN M. MARTIN

Social Analysis To engage in feminist theologizing requires submitting one's own *experience to a critical examination in trying to discern the direction toward which God's *justice is pointing, and then situating that experience within the larger social and symbolic frameworks of which it is a part. Social analysis is the second step in that process. It describes the process through which those wishing to engage in the humane transformation of systems of *oppression learn how these systems function. It requires an analysis of the ways in which systems of *domination are erected, legitimized, reinforced, and transformed over time.

Social analysis of modern society requires systemic thinking. It involves an examination of how at least five different, complexly interstructured forms of oppression or domination (*racism, *sexism, *heterosexism, *classism, militarism) operate along six dimensions: the cultural, symbolic, and religious sphere (including language); the interpersonal and kinship sphere; the sphere of *community; the economic system; the political system; and the ecosystem. Social analysis requires an analysis not only of the interconnections between the five systems of oppression but also of the interconnections between the six spheres or dimensions.

The development of social analysis as it has been used by feminist theologians was a gradual process. The consciousness-raising groups that were the impetus for the first wave of the second women's movement at the end of the late 1960s and early 1970s were an early example of social analysis. Such consciousness-raising was first developed by women participants in the U.S. civil rights movement of the 1960s. As a result of their involvement in this struggle for *liberation, dignity, and *equality, they discovered their own oppression as women or as *lesbians. Such women sought to discover the roots of and the mechanisms that legitimated and reinforced their subordination to men.

Feminist theologians learned still more from the tools of Marxian analysis that were adapted by Latin American and other third-world theologians and shared through writings, conferences, and participation in *solidarity movements. These tools were especially helpful in analyzing the capitalist economic system and its manifestation in political systems. The development of environmentalism has added yet another dimension to our understanding of the way in which systems of domination work.

Albert et al.[1986]; Merchant [1992]

SHEILA D. COLLINS

Social Construct A social construct refers to a product created through human interaction. For example, "gender" is a social construct, produced by societies to establish and regulate masculine and feminine behaviors. The *social construction of reality* means that all reality is produced through human interaction, through a particular relationship between the mind and the world. Many social constructionists hold that we have no objective base from which to know the world. We know as we create everyday life.

Feminist social constructionists examine the ways women know the world through speech and material conditions. All *experiences are shared; women's lives are constructed out of their interactions with other women and with men. A *malconstruction* refers to a construct that limits interaction or behavior in negative ways. Many social constructionists use *ethnography to document the taken-for-granted practices that produce social constructs such as gender. For example, when babies are born and assigned blue or pink blankets based on their genitalia, the process of teaching these newborns how to construct gendered lives has begun. For many people the giving of blue and pink gifts is seen as "natural" or as "what one does." The teaching, shaping, directing practices of everyday life are buried in the actions themselves.

Feminist theology and spiritual practice recognize that sacred texts and *patriarchy are themselves produced from webs of social interactions that have shaped women's religious lives. However, women, too, shape their lives together though kitchen theologies and the spiritual practice of women's gatherings. Feminist theology focuses on women's reconstructions of religious and spiritual life.

Beginning with the radical Karl Marx, the liberal Max Weber, and the conservative Emile Durkheim, Western social constructionists hold that religious notions of the sacred and the profane are socially created. Feminists point out that the sacred and profane are also gendered constructions that order women's lives in significant ways. Across socioeconomic and political differences, they evaluate social constructs and seek to establish building blocks for social interaction. Through socially constructed expectations, actors are held accountable to society for the reproduction of the social order. Feminists then seek to reconstruct and redefine social *relationships and accountabilities.

Erickson [1993]; Lorber/Farrell [1991]

VICTORIA ERICKSON

Socialism–Capitalism Feminist theological, ethical, and pastoral work requires a historically grounded and nuanced awareness of political-economic discourses as well as religio-cultural concepts. Yet clarity about the meaning of terms central to the more than a century-old debate about political-economic systems has never been more difficult. Defining terms such as *capitalism* and *socialism* has always exposed one's political commitments. This is because proponents and critics of both capitalism and socialism use their own, not their opponents', assumptions to define the other. They use favorable characteristics to define their own positions but stress negative realities in naming the others.

For example, the vast majority of socialists define socialism as economic democracy or as a political-economic system in which economic decisions are shaped by a society's broader political democracy, processes open to all—not merely to the rich. Capitalism, from a socialist perspective, is a specific historical arrangement in which those who have economic power demand and set limits on political options for the sake of perpetuating existing economic patterns. According to socialists, wealth, not people's democratically determined preferences, has the last say in setting priorities in capitalist societies. Conversely, capitalists define capitalism as a system that maximizes "free-market" economic activity and delimits political activity to specified "spheres." Political policies must, in particular, be prevented from unduly discouraging the presumed enhancement of economic wealth. Socialism is usually defined by capitalists as state-centered interference in so-called spontaneous economic activity or so-called free markets. Economies, it is argued, prosper only when relatively unfettered. Politics should broker only those matters not central to economic growth. Conversely, socialists deny that capitalism is, in fact, characterized by free-market exchange. For them, monopoly and refusal to give needs a place, even if ventures are not profitable, are capitalism's central tendencies. Capitalists deny that socialism is democratic precisely because economic liberty is constrained by political decisions.

In discussions of political economy prior to the 1980s, all European-based progressives acknowledged that a national political economy required some political checks on the owners or controllers of wealth. Western European nations that used greater degrees of state economic planning to shape some sectors of their economy came to be known as "mixed economies" tending toward socialism. These societies developed multiparty political systems in which "workers parties" or "labor parties" achieved some *power and a considerable success in translating certain economic provisions into political "rights."

By contrast, in those nations that were more completely identified with capitalist *ideology, especially the United States, efforts to build a labor-based political movement floundered for complex historical reasons and a "mixed economy" was rejected adamantly. The powerful antilabor polemic of business and Christian churches was more effectual in the United States than in Europe, in part because of the deeply grounded belief of immigrants that the "New World" held out the promise of divinely sanctioned economic prosperity. To challenge capitalism in the United States always appeared in popular ideology to be an assault on opportunity or the American dream.

The definition of political economy is also more difficult today because of the current historical situation, which is also read differently by socialists and capitalists. In all the so-called developed countries, ideological control of public discussion has increased so that a socialist interpretation is rarely presented by competent interpreters. The current capitalist line is that socialist "second-world" political economies have utterly failed. Some capitalist ideologists have even declared the "historically untranscendable" character of capitalist political economy. In their view, we should give up the search for alternatives to capitalism, which, it is presumed, has completely triumphed. Both the demise of the Soviet Union and the Chinese political economy's accommodation to global capitalist economic relations are construed by these ideologists as a sure sign of "the death of socialism." The new polemic against socialism is harsh and sows confusion in feminism, whose history, except in the twentieth century in the United States among white feminists, was closely intertwined with socialist movements and *politics.

Socialist theorists, including most socialist feminists, perceive the recent dissolution of several major postcapitalist political economies to be the result of a twofold dynamic. The first is the ever more obvious global crisis of late-twentieth-century capitalism itself. To socialists, a capitalist "crisis" is a reduction in an economy's ability to accumulate wealth. (What is called "failing profitability" or "inefficiency" by capitalists is called "labor exploitation" by socialists.) In such a crisis, existing economic forces dictate a politics aimed at unfettering economic power, i.e., capitalism moves to conservative ideology and policy. Earlier gains of working peoples' struggles get lost. Socialists call this *fascism.* From a socialist perspective, the so-called second world appears to be simply one part of a global capitalist market system and, because resistant to capitalist patterns, the most vulnerable area of that system. All global sectors ("south," or the so-called third world; "second," or postcapitalist; and "first," or capitalist) have to accommodate, because the refusal of any nation to do so means that nation cannot buy and sell goods and services in "the world market." The "wrath" of the newly created "real" power centers of the changing capitalist world system—the World Bank, the International Monetary Fund, and GATT (Global Agreement on Tariffs and Trade)—will be directed toward any policies except capitalist ones. Currently, there are no political ways to impact on these new power centers that determine everyone's fate.

In this historical scenario, socialism, or policies that move toward economic democracy, is understood to be in its very earliest phase of historical development. The collapsed second-world economies were internal to a global capitalist system and therefore were not well suited to resist and survive so inclusive and catastrophic a "crisis" as global capitalism is now undergoing. However, socialists, especially feminist socialists, also insist that the large, state-centered "command economies" that were generated by communist movements were in critical respects a betrayal of the historical vocation of socialism itself.

Feminists insist that one-party political systems, even if justified in moments of revolutionary historical chaos, quickly betray the socialist goal of extending democracy to include democratic participation in setting economic priorities. This defeats socialism from within. In light of recent experience, most contemporary socialists also believe that this greater political openness must develop simultaneously with new modes of decentralizing economic activity. Centralization and bureaucratic rigidity make ecological destruction, which must be curtailed, harder to stop.

As noted, these controversies strongly affected the first movements of feminism, at least in Europe. Most European feminists were socialists. Most remain so, even though, beginning in the 1970s, the *postmodernist controversies and what is known as *French feminism disconnected feminist work from socialist or radical theories of political economy. French feminism connected instead to a socially constructed, gendered version of Freudian *psychology and a nonsocial conception of *embodiment and *materialism.

U.S. feminists, particularly white feminists, often suspicious of a radical political economy because of their cultural contexts, have nevertheless carried on extended discussions of how feminism and radical social theory relate. Perhaps the central challenge to feminist liberation *theology and *ethics in the twenty-first century will be to formulate more holistic theories, ones that neglect neither genuine political-economic change that increases democracy at every level nor the versions of sacredness generated by religio-moral-cultural communities. We must learn not to deny or minimize concrete physical or material need, while celebrating the spirituality of all our longings for connectedness in and through sacred power.

Amott/Matthaei [1991]; Luntley [1990]; Marable [1983]; Rowbotham [1994]; Thomas/Visick [1991]; Zweig [1991]

BEVERLY WILDUNG HARRISON

Solidarity Solidarity has to do with the action of those not directly *suffering from a situation of *oppression in concert with those who are. It is both an attitude and a practice. Solidarity is an ethical principle, a direction human life should follow, operating both as a *virtue (a character trait) and as a norm (a guide to human behavior). Solidarity refers to the community of feelings, interests, and purposes that arises from a shared sense of *responsibilities; it leads to action and social cohesion. Thus solidarity moves away from the false notion of disinterest and altruism and demands a love of neighbor that is intrinsic to a love of self.

Solidarity as an ethical norm is a *praxis of mutuality: an intentional, reflective action aimed at the building of *community of those who struggle against oppression and for *justice. The movement toward mutuality between oppressed and oppressors starts with the cries of the oppressed, with their denunciation of injustice. These cries and denunciations impose themselves as a kind of categorical imperative on oppressors, whether they are directly connected with establishing and maintaining the injustice being denounced or benefit from it directly or indirectly. The cries of the oppressed and their denunciations of injustice are what move oppressors to respond by listening and allowing themselves to be questioned by the oppressed. They, in turn, question and judge the oppressive structures that they support and from which they benefit. Solidarity as a praxis of mutuality, however, is not simply a matter of mutual understanding and support. It requires effective political action, a liberative praxis that has as its goal radical structural change, on the part of those who stand in solidarity with the oppressed (as well as on the part of the oppressed themselves).

In the struggle for *liberation and justice, solidarity operates both as a theory and as a strategy. As a theory, solidarity starts with the oppression suffered by those who are exploited, *marginalized, powerless, those who suffer cultural *imperialism and systemic *violence. The theory of solidarity insists on the connection of all forms of oppression. It is the basis for a commonality of principles among the oppressed and between the oppressed and those who stand in solidarity with them. Mutuality is a central element of solidarity. It shapes a new order of *relationships that opposes any and all forms of *domination.

As a strategy, solidarity is about specific actions that have as their goal the radical structural change of present oppressive structures, not merely opening participation in those structures to those who are at present excluded. Strategies of solidarity are elaborated so as not to sacrifice any one group of oppressed people for the sake of another group. It is a highly effective political strategy in the struggle against oppression.

Isasi-Díaz, in Thistlethwaite/Engel [1990]; Scannone [1976]; Welch [1985]

ADA MARÍA ISASI-DÍAZ

Son of God The term *son of God* refers to an individual, a group, or a thing God regards highly. Psalm 2:7 and 2 Sam. 7:14 record the words of God to Israel's anointed ruler: "I will be a father to him, and he shall be a son to me." Israel (Ex. 4:22) and the angels of the divine court (Job 1:6–12) are son(s) of God. A righteous individual (Wisd. Sol. 2:13) and charismatic rabbis (*m. Ta'anit* 3:8) extend the identification into Greek and rabbinic worlds. Mark and Matthew frame their narrative "good news" about Jesus by referring to him as "Son of God" (Mark 1:1; 14:39; Matt. 1:23; 27:40, 54).

In all these cases, knowledge of God sets the individual or group apart. As individual, the person no longer is one of the group; as group, they are distinct among surrounding nations. If distinctiveness is seen as positive, the individual or group may hold office or be highly regarded. If not, harassment and persecution may be their lot, even to death. Knowledge of God means that the individual or group has a particular claim on God. Insight means they have information about God to share. In a context of afterlife, an individual's claim on God as "child of God" may extend even beyond death.

Matthew's Gospel in particular (probably following the Wisdom of Solomon) explores the meaning of the term to include the context of Jesus' birth, *ministry, death, and raising by God. While the Son of God is male, the insight that the meaning of the particular relationship between the heavenly father and the human son will evolve in a *community context from birth to life after death, and that only that full narrative will disclose God's presence, is surely not gender-specific.

"Child of God," in *AILL*, 245 [1986]

DEIRDRE J. GOOD

Son of Man The term *Son of man* belongs to a Semitic language world. In Hebrew and Aramaic, the term has both an exclusive ("son") and an inclusive ("man" = "human being"; Heb: *'adam*) reference. The biblical record uses the term to refer to a generic mortal (Job 25:4–6; Ps. 8:4) and an individual male (Ezekiel; cf. Rev. 1:13–16). The cognate phrase "daughters of humans" occurs only in Gen. 6:4 (NRSV). The exclusive sense, with probable messianic associations, appears at Qumran (4Q*246*). Some Jewish writers in the first century C.E. apparently understood the phrase to refer to a supernatural being (*1 Enoch* 71: 14–17; cf. Acts 7:56).

Traditional scholarship understands the phrase on Jesus' lips to refer to the present authoritative figure, the coming heavenly figure, or a figure who suffers and dies. Whatever Jesus may have meant, once the phrase becomes identified exclusively with him in a particular historical context and rendered as a title, it sheds any other associations it might possess. Scholars in the Jesus Seminar (a guild of scholars devoted to studying the historical Jesus) use "son of Adam" in order to interpret the second element inclusively to mean "any descendant of Adam and Eve." The NRSV distinguishes the Hebrew phrase from the Greek. The Hebrew phrase as it appears in Ps. 8:4b, "mortals," is made plural, while the direct address of God to Ezekiel is "Mortal!" Daniel 7:13 describes "one like a human being." Yet in its *translation of the Greek text, the NRSV has Jesus speak of "the Son of Man." This distinction in the NRSV (between human and divine) prevents the reader from making a connection between the testaments in the way ancients and Jesus himself might have done. Where capitalized, the term can be read only as a title.

Extracanonical material strives to realize the inclusive and celestial implications of the term. Christian *Gnostic literature transfers historical event to the mythological level by understanding not only that Jesus as Son of man is the same as *Son of God but also that the *gospel phrase "Son of man" is *androgynous (*Dialogue of the Savior,* NHC III 5; 44,13–35; *Sophia of Jesus Christ,* NHC III 4; 105,19–22). In one text, "Son of man" is both "Son of God" (male) and "Sophia" (female) (*Sophia of Jesus Christ,* 104,1–22). Yet the same text is unable to sustain inclusivity: Son of man subsequently consents with *Sophia, his consort. This is exactly what happens in *tradition: inclusive renderings of the phrase have not been sustained against the exclusively male reading of this phrase with respect to Jesus.

A way to redeem the phrase, if redemption is possible, is to sing a new song by reconceiving the biblical record to maintain the inclusive character of the generic reference. Stephen Mitchell (1993, 5) proposes for Ps. 8:4, "What is man that you love him, and woman, that you gladden her heart?" God could address Ezekiel as "Human!" and Job 25:4 could read, "How can a human be righteous before God? How can one born of woman be pure?" To destabilize the traditional *translation and to suggest rather than reify the historical element, Matt. 8:20 could read, "Foxes have holes, and birds of the air have nests; but the Child of humankind has nowhere to lay his head." The historical referent remains secondary to the celestial allusion when the third person singular masculine pronoun "his" recurs in apocalyptic contexts (Matt. 25:31; Rev. 1:13). But in Matt. 12:31–32, a Greek wordplay would allow us to read, "Therefore I tell you, every *sin and blasphemy will be forgiven to humankind. . . . Whoever speaks a word against the Child of humankind will be forgiven."

"The Human One (RSV the Son of Man)," *AILL,* Year A, 283–84 [1986]

DEIRDRE J. GOOD

Sophia / Wisdom *Sophia* is the Greek word for "wisdom" (Heb: *ḥokmâ*). Biblical scholars use the designation *wisdom literature* to refer to certain books in the Hebrew Bible and *Apocrypha because of this material's focus on the search for wisdom as part of the life of *faith (Proverbs, Ecclesiastes, Job, Sirach [Ecclesiasticus], and Wisdom of Solomon). The term is important for feminist thought because in Proverbs, Sirach, and the Wisdom of Solomon, the concept of "wisdom" is literarily personified as a woman who has significant *relationships to both humans and God. Recent feminist use of Sophia as a way of *naming God has occasioned a backlash of accusations of "*goddess worship," i.e., *heresy.

Wisdom in the Bible. In Proverbs, female-personified Wisdom appears in instructional poems in the book's nine introductory chapters, while a figure called the "capable wife" (so NRSV; literally, "woman of worth"), cast with language reminiscent of Woman Wisdom, is the subject of the book's concluding poem (31:10–31). This bracketing of the book's central collection of proverbs (chaps. 10—30) with female imagery already suggests its importance.

Woman Wisdom appears in several different roles. Like the capable wife, who provides her husband not only material gain but also wise counsel, good children, and public honor, Woman Wisdom sets a feast for those who seek her (9:1–6), exalts and honors the one who embraces her (4:8–9), and ensures her lovers enduring wealth and prosperity (8:17–18). The man's relationship both with his wife and with Wisdom is described in more intimate terms as well. He is to rejoice in the wife of his youth, be satisfied with her breasts, and be intoxicated with her love (5:18–19). Likewise, he should love Wisdom, embrace her, call her "sister" and "intimate friend" (4:6, 8; 7:4).

Alongside this wifely lover and provider stands the image of Wisdom as the prophet who appears in public places (1:20–21; 8:23), announcing doom to those who ignore her and security to those who listen (1:24–33). More than the typical prophet, though, Wisdom seems to identify her own words, actions, and gifts with God's (1:23, 25, 30; 8:6–9, 15, 35), and indeed, some of this imagery likely originated in the goddess traditions of Egypt and Canaan. Most dramatic is her statement in 8:22–31, where she claims to have been with Yahweh before *creation (Yahweh "acquired" or "conceived" her, depending on the *translation of a key verb in 8:22, but not "created," contra NRSV). Present during God's creative activity, Wisdom portrays herself as a mediator between the divine and human realms: "I was daily [Yahweh's] delight / rejoicing before him always / rejoicing in his inhabited world / and delighting in the human race" (8:30b-31).

Consideration of Proverbs' Woman Wisdom must also mention her counterpart, the strange or alien woman (not "loose woman" or "adulteress," contra NRSV: 2:16–19; 5:3-6, 20; 7:5–27), also called "the folly woman" (9:13–18). Love of Woman Wisdom guarantees protection from this stranger, whose identity, though uncertain, melds a variety of male Israelite fears (of foreigners, of sexually autonomous women, of cultic impurity) into an *embodiment of Otherness.

The book of Sirach walks a line between simple objectification of wisdom and true personification. Several poems use the term as the subject or object of active verbs, yet without distinctively human, much less female, attributes (1:1–10; 6:18–31). Elsewhere, human *metaphors of teacher, bride, and mother enhance the personification (4:11–19; 15:1–2). Throughout Sirach, wisdom is associated with following the Torah, most notably in chapter 24 where personified Wisdom "praises herself, / and tells of her glory in the midst of her people" (v.1). Reminiscent of Genesis 1 and 2, she says, "I came forth from the mouth of the Most High, / and covered the earth like a mist" (v. 3). She seeks a home, and God commands her to dwell in Israel. The poet concludes, "All this is the book of the *covenant of the Most High God, / the law that Moses commanded us / as an inheritance for the congregations of Jacob" (v. 23).

Over the course of almost six chapters (1:1–11; 6:12–11:1), the pseudonymous author of the Wisdom of Solomon exalts Woman Wisdom in a manner previously unsurpassed. She is not only his passionately desired beloved (8:2 and passim); she is also virtually identified with the

Deity by means of descriptions of her qualities (e.g., 7:22–8:1) and by retelling the stories of creation, the Genesis ancestors, and the exodus with Wisdom performing the actions usually ascribed to God (10:1–11:1). If she is not quite God ("she is a reflection of eternal light, / a spotless mirror of the working of God, / and an image of his goodness" [7:26]), neither is there any way for the reader to distinguish her from God.

"Sophia's presence in the New Testament is strong, but more convoluted" (Cady/Ronan/Taussig, 33), pushed partly, but not completely, aside by John's Logos theology (note the strong correspondence between his prologue and Prov. 8:22–31 and Sir. 24:8); by resistance to the *Gnostic version of Christianity, which had embraced her; and by rejection of female leadership in the church. In spite of these forces, Paul describes Jesus as "the *sophia* of God" who, by God's action, has become "our *sophia*" (1 Cor. 1:23–25; 2:6–8). Colossians 1:15–17 and Eph. 3:9–11 sound like hymns to the creative work of Sophia, now equated to the person of Jesus. Apparently referring to himself, Jesus says, "Wisdom is vindicated by her deeds" (or "by her children" [Matt. 11:19; cf. Luke 7:35]), and Matt. 11:16–30 shows Jesus in a variety of Wisdom's roles (cf. Sir. 1:6, 8; 6:24–28; 51:26; Wisd. Sol. 9:17–18).

Sophia in Contemporary Theology. Several recent scholars have devoted significant attention to Woman Wisdom. Building on her work in *In Memory of Her* [1983], Elisabeth Schüssler Fiorenza has now further elucidated the importance, to both the historical and the contemporary church, of understanding Jesus as the messenger of Divine Sophia (*Jesus: Miriam's Child, Sophia's Prophet*, 1994). Elizabeth Johnson's *She Who Is* (1992) develops a Sophia theology in *dialogue with traditional Trinitarian theology. In *Gender and Difference in Ancient Israel* (Day 1989), Carol Newsom's essay is a word of caution about the use of wisdom material in Proverbs 1—9 because such material is written from a *patriarchal view, speaking to the reader as father to son. Claudia Camp's book and several articles (1985; 1988; forthcoming) suggest that the feminist history and theology of Sophia also need to take account of the influence (both disturbing and creative) of Proverbs' "strange woman."

Conservative protest arose in mainline Protestant churches as theological reflection on Sophia moved from academic circles to contexts of worship. The furor centered first on *Wisdom's Feast* (1989), by Susan Cady, Marian Ronan, and Hal Taussig, which presented teaching tools and liturgies centered on the biblical material. Debate flared again in response to the Re-Imagining Conference (1993), celebrating the midpoint of the World Council of Churches' Ecumenical Decade of Churches in Solidarity with Women. This feminist theology conference included one *liturgy that both named God as Sophia and used fairly explicit, sensual language to image women.

This combination of sexual language for humans with female imagery for God strikes chords with two different strands of biblical *tradition. While the conference liturgists called on Woman Wisdom and the Song of Songs, protesters were reminded of the Bible's rhetoric that conjoins ritual sex and goddess worship. (It must be noted that this biblical rhetoric is just that: rhetoric, without any clear historical basis.) Clearly, the debate over Sophia has important implications not only for feminist thought about God and not only for women's right to claim our own *bodies and *experiences but also for our right to read and interpret the Bible.

Cady/Ronan/Taussig [1989]; Camp, [1985]; Camp, *Semeia* [1988]; Camp, in Bea/ Gunn [forthcoming]; Johnson [1992]; McKinley [1994]; Newsom, in Day [1989]; Schüssler Fiorenza [1994]

CLAUDIA V. CAMP

Soul In the Hebrew scriptures, the word *soul* represents almost exclusively the Hebrew word *nephesh,* meaning not immortal soul but "life principle" or the "living being." There is no such thing as a disembodied *nephesh*. In the New Testament, the Greek word *psychē* again means "vitality" or "life." Feminist theologies would welcome a return to the original holistic understanding, wherein *body and soul are not separated. But because of later dualistic notions, with the division of flesh and spirit, body and soul became divorced from each other, with soul being elevated and body being degraded.

Efforts to keep body and soul together are the primary focus of feminist energy around the word *soul*. Soul is of special importance to womanist *theology because its imagery had links to *freedom during U.S. slavery in the prayers and spirituals of the day, but the freedom meant corporeal as well as spiritual liberation. Because dualisms have so obscured the notion that the soul is affected by the abuses and pleasures of the body, the first step has been to reunite the two, so long divided. Where body had been detested as the flesh, the soul was to be regarded as "pure spirit." For feminists, the term *soul* is a deep, holistic reference to the web of body, mind, intellect, *emotions, longings, and that ephemeral human aspect which is able to self-transcend or penetrate deeply into human experience. For instance, Chung Hyun Kyung has pointed out that there is no place for *dualism between body and soul in Asian spirituality, because soul arises from women's everyday, bodily experience. The soul is fully imbued with all of human existence and not able to be easily divided out into dualisms such sacred and profane. It is the most particular, individual sense of the self: the combination of experience, hope, choice, and connection with every living thing and the earth.

Chung [1991]; Joseph/Lewis [1981]; Unterberger [1990]

GAIL LYNN UNTERBERGER

Spirituality, Aboriginal While the indigenous peoples of North America comprise many distinct cultures, *aboriginal* (or native) *spirituality* is the term generally used to describe the spiritual approach to life shared by indigenous peoples across tribal lines.

Generations of Christian missionaries were not successful in eradicating aboriginal religious beliefs and practices. During the years of intense religious persecution, sufficient numbers of practitioners kept their people's traditions alive, and the late twentieth century has witnessed a resurgence of native ways and values. Disillusioned with established forms of dominant Western religion, many nonaboriginal people also have been attracted to indigenous forms of spirituality.

Aboriginal spirituality views all of life as sacred, with sun, moon, and stars; every animal and plant; plus the elements of earth, wind, fire, and water created as gift, each with its integral role in the interconnected web of *creation. Humans are not viewed to be set apart from other creatures; rather, they have choices to make about living in harmony or discord with the rest of creation.

Spirit helpers (comparable to angels in Christianity) can be invoked through prayers and ceremonies, dreams and visions, songs and stories, to offer guidance on the path of life. Walking the aboriginal spiritual path is a challenge for those in a world where competition and material wealth are at odds with the key spiritual *ethics of cooperation and communal sharing. Appropriation also has become a problem, that is, the commercialization of native spirituality by nonindigenous people who have little appreciation of the collective identity of tribal peoples or commitment to the *justice these peoples continue to seek.

Aboriginal spirituality shares considerable common ground with forms of feminist spirituality: for example, a critique of *patriarchy and *domination and a valuing of *interdependence, mutuality, relationality, sharing; respect for *difference; and consensus as a preferred model of decision making.

Allen [1989]; DeMallie [1984]; Solomon [1990]; Wall/Arden [1990]

JANET SILMAN

Spirituality, Celtic Female The term *Celtic female spirituality* is used by those who wish to return to the beliefs and practices of the Celtic nations: Ireland, England, Scotland, Wales, Brittany, and the Isle of Man. However, the term *Celtic female spirituality* is something of a misnomer, for the following reason. The Celts were a *patriarchal people from northern Europe who largely colonized the pre-patriarchal Celtic nations. There is evidence in myth, *archaeology, history, and linguistics of the inroads made by the patriarchal Celts on the matricentered peoples. Female deities were ridiculed, raped, killed, and otherwise overthrown; the old archaeological sites featuring the goddesses were systematically dismantled; and the female symbolic system honoring the cycles of nature was gradually replaced by a triumphalist suppression of nature. All of this was assisted by the rise of a warrior-based patriarchal mythology and social organization. Insofar as it has any historical legitimacy, the term *Celtic female spirituality* refers, therefore, to those knowledges, rites, religious practices, *prayers, and beliefs that predated and survived this Celtic onslaught.

Goddess figures such as Brigit were highly ambivalent. Originally a European *goddess, Brigit effectively took over and replaced all the positive functions, *traditions, and characteristics of the old Irish goddesses in a far-reaching act of religious *imperialism. Her transmutation into Christian saint completed the process whereby she, "alone of all her sex," became the acceptable female religious image, surpassing initially the veneration of Mary. However, the deep undercurrents attending her image were never entirely suppressed.

The traditions of the old pre-patriarchal goddesses, their imagery and practices, and the veneration accorded to their sites both continued and constantly erupted through the oral traditions, to the present day. Their sites are now being revisited under the auspices of Celtic female spirituality. Sites such as Newgrange, Knowth, and Dowth, the womb and tomb of the old religions and where the Triple Goddess was venerated, are now recovering their significance. These, together with sites such as Emain Macha, Dun Ailinne, and Kildare in Ireland; Stonehenge and Glastonbury in England; as well as many other sites in Scotland and Wales, are now being revisited. The desire is to uncover the *reality and significance of a powerful female symbol that might challenge the patriarchal view of reality. For instance, for the pre-Celts there was an inseparable connection between *ethics, ecology, and *justice. If the rulers were brash, overbearing, or unjust, the crops would refuse to grow and blight would fall on the land. A sign of their righteous rule was that women should enjoy safe childbirth. The *mythologies of the time spoke of complementarity between the sexes before the onslaught of the warrior invasions.

The Celtic year was punctuated by the festivals of Imbolc (February 1st), Beltaine (May 1st), Lughnasa (August 1st), and Samhain (November 1st). Each of these festivals marked a significant shift in the ecological cycle, and they are now, together with other lunar and solar rhythms, being revived and celebrated as a means of reinstating the sacredness of the natural earth as our primary ground of being.

Condren [1989]; Jones [1994]; Ross [1967/1986]; Sjoestedt [1982]

MARY T. CONDREN

Spirituality Groups In the history of Christianity, the phenomenon of women gathering for *prayer and spiritual discernment is as ancient as the early church. In American religious history the phenomenon dates back to the meetings Anne Hutchinson held in her home in the 1630s in the Massachusetts Bay

Colony, until she was banished for voicing an independent point of view and threatening *community.

Historian Barbara Brown Zikmund identifies "prayer and women's support groups" as one of the five types of women's organizations in American Protestant church life (1993, 116–38). During the nineteenth century, the belief that women should not pray publicly in meetings of men and women together led to the forming of separate women's prayer and Bible study groups. These often strengthened a sense of denominational allegiance among women.

At the close of the twentieth century, a new type of women's spirituality group is emerging. While such groups sometimes are held in churches, more often they meet in homes and transcend denominational boundaries. When authors Sherry Ruth Anderson and Patricia Hopkins mentioned their "Tuesday-evening prayer group" in the best-selling *The Feminine Face of God: The Unfolding of the Sacred in Women* (1991), they spoke of one such group. Describing members as active and inactive Catholics, Protestants, Jews, and Buddhists, they wrote, "Despite these differences, we share one fundamental belief: that we all participate in a mystery that lies at the heart of our being, and one way we can come closer to that mystery in ourselves and each other is by praying together" (183).

An extensive, nationwide study of women's spirituality groups was conducted by three researchers affiliated with Hartford Seminary and published in 1994 as *Defecting in Place: Women Claiming Responsibility for Their Own Spiritual Lives* (Winter/Lummis/Stokes). Some 3,746 women (most of them Catholic or mainline Protestant, white, and highly educated) responded to a lengthy survey. Results yielded information about common characteristics of the new-type feminist groups. Most arise out of a felt need, are small and relatively stable, meet regularly, compensate for what is lacking in institutional religion, contribute to the raising of feminist consciousness, liberate individual women, are feminist with or without the label, deepen spiritual connections, and continue only for as long as the felt need exists.

In most feminist spirituality groups, members feel dissatisfied with or alienated from the institutional church and are seeking some aspect of change. But the majority do not withdraw from participation in congregations or denominations but instead "defect in place," or work from within to bring about change. Women say membership in the group empowers and emboldens them to be and do what they previously had not dared. Unlike traditional women's groups, feminist spirituality groups do not exist to support or foster institutional goals or to promote institutional loyalty but to offer critique and challenge (150–51).

Typically, group gatherings reflect flexible design and agenda, shared leadership, full participation, *freedom of expression, decision by consensus, personal sharing, mind-body- spirit integration, acceptance and affirmation, nurture and *empowerment, creativity and inventiveness, and alternative worship experiences. The controversial Re-Imagining Conference held in Minneapolis in November 1993 may be viewed as a large-scale occurrence of what is happening in living rooms in every state in the nation. The burgeoning phenomenon of women's spirituality groups means women no longer need to do theological work in isolation, to reinvent the wheel continually. Instead, with the support of sisters, they are discovering the feminine face of the divine and finding their voice.

Anderson/Hopkins [1991]; Lerner [1993]; Winter/Lummis/Stokes [1994]; Zikmund, in Carroll and Roof [1993]

ALLISON STOKES

Spirituality, Medieval Sources for medieval spirituality include the various strains of monasticism; liturgical practices, especially *preaching and *Eucharist; liturgical drama; the Crusades;

veneration of the saints; pilgrimages; the art and architecture of the cathedrals; *prayer forms and penitential practices; "heresies," such as the Cathars and Waldensians; the theology of the monasteries and the schools; Reformation spiritualities.

In standard histories of medieval spirituality, women are often grossly underrepresented due to the biases of male authors and the paucity of resources. Recent scholarship on medieval women is quickly correcting this lack. During this period, there was a proliferation of religious roles open to women; the number of women saints increased; and, as Caroline Walker Bynum notes, for the first time in Christian history we can identify a woman's movement (the Beguines) and speak of specifically female influences on wider spiritual developments.

The medieval period saw a burgeoning of women's religious enthusiasm. Women founded and joined monasteries, created new forms of semireligious life, went on religious pilgrimages, became recluses, engaged in care of the sick and poor. Visionary experiences and innovative religious structures enabled women to escape unwanted constraints of marriage and family, bypass ecclesial *authority, and condemn clerical abuses.

Medieval women's spirituality reflects a flowering of mystical experience characterized by an intimate, wide-ranging, affective encounter with the human/divine Christ. In some cases women engaged in extreme forms of penitential *asceticism, motivated by a desire to imitate the *suffering of Jesus. By the end of the Middle Ages, however, there was increased hostility to the forms of women's spiritualities. Women became more isolated and constricted and by the fifteenth century were subject to widespread accusations of *heresy and *witchcraft that often ended in torture and death.

In the twentieth century, the retrieval of information about medieval women and their spiritual paths has revealed the depth, wisdom, and continued relevance of their experience. They provide fresh insight and inspiration for today's spiritual quest.

Atkinson [1991]; Bynum [1982]; Nichols/Shank [1984–87]; Petroff [1986; 1994]

ELIZABETH A. DREYER

Spirituality, Women's** The spirituality of women has a long and venerable history in virtually every religion ever practiced by human beings. With the rare exception of the male-only religion, women have consistently found, been given, or carved out a space for themselves in even the most hostile religious environments. Sometimes these forms have coincided with male spirituality or been codified within a male-dominant religion as specifically female forms of spirituality; at other times, women have fended for themselves, creating female folk religious practices that embody their own seeking after spiritual knowledge and experience.

In recent years, however, feminists, detecting a pervasive *misogyny and a lack of appropriately woman-honoring spirituality within established religions, have begun creating new forms and resurrecting old ones to serve their spiritual needs. This process has occurred internationally and interreligiously, both within established religions and on their fringes. Most established religions have long had some separate spiritual space for women: women's religious orders in Christian *Orthodoxy, Catholicism, *Hinduism, and *Buddhism; ladies' *mission societies and *prayer breakfasts in Protestant denominations; Hadassah organizations (Jewish women's groups) and women's hours at the *mikvah* (ritual bath) in Judaism; etc. In addition, folk religious practices, the "little *tradition" of religious life, have long been a realm where women have had greater freedom to explore their spirituality, frequently connecting it to the domestic activities that have formed the bulk of their lives. But feminists have deemed these finally inadequate and sought either to redeem them through a greater emphasis on their feminist potential or to cast them off entirely as too much a part of irretrievably patriarchal religions.

Feminist spiritual movements inside and outside established religions share much in common, particularly on the North American scene. There are also notable similarities between white and nonwhite feminist spirituality in North America. Yet there remain sociological fault lines between many of these feminist spiritual expressions, with women effectively segregated by *race, ethnicity, religious tradition, and occasionally (though less often) by class, age, and sexual preference. Sometimes this segregation has been fruitful: for example, Jewish and Christian feminists have shared resources, spiritual techniques, and theological innovations with one another and then found ways to interpret them within the context of their own traditions. At other times, segregation has been a source of tension for women's spirituality, with nonwhite women complaining of tokenism or the white cooptation of their indigenous spiritual resources, and white women puzzled as to why other women are so reluctant to embrace a shared *sisterhood with them.

Within established religions, feminists have searched for spiritual resources in scripture and tradition. This has yielded, in the case of Judaism, for example, new rituals to mark female life-cycle events such as menarche, childbirth, and menopause; the recovery of female images from Torah, Talmud, and kabbalah and of women's prayers and poetry from the centuries of the Diaspora; and the reintroduction of traditional women's *rituals (where these have fallen into disuse or failed to include feminist elements), such as those for Rosh Chodesh (new moon), *bat mitzvah, the birth of a daughter, and so on. Similarly, in Christianity there has been renewed attention to the biblical and apocryphal figures of Mary and *Sophia, women-only rituals for female life-cycle events and Christian holidays, scholarly attention to women's spiritual communities in Christian history, etc. Efforts to find and reclaim resources for women's spirituality have occurred in like fashion in *Islam, Buddhism, Hinduism, and Native American and African religions. At times these efforts have led to the creation of what are essentially splinter groups within the larger religious organization: in Roman Catholicism, for example, the *Women-Church movement has, for some women, replaced traditional forms of Catholic religious practice and become a "church" in its own right.

Other women have chosen to abandon established religions (or at least the religion of their early identity and training) and create a spirituality for women from elements found in alternative religions (such as paganism, the occult, and New Age religions) and in religions to which they are not personally committed. In the case of white North Americans, this includes everything from Buddhism and Native American religions to voodoo and Santería. The only real exceptions, the places to which these women will not go for spiritual sustenance, are Christianity, Judaism, and Islam: the established religions of the West. Even here, occasional exceptions are made for such practices as the veneration of Our Lady of Guadalupe or the Shekhinah or Sufi dancing. The greatest openness to including Christian elements is found in African-American women's spirituality. Even when this spirituality is formally separated from any established church, Jesus may be included as one of many helpful manifestations of the divine. However, there remains a great difference between women who seek spirituality within a single tradition to which they retain a commitment and those who take individual elements from these same traditions and combine them freely with elements from other religions worldwide. The former are best described as Jewish spiritual feminists, Christian spiritual feminists, and so on, while the latter claim a variety of labels such as *pagan, witch, or, most simply, spiritual feminist.

In spite of this great diversity, there

are a number of theological themes that characterize recent feminist experimentation with spirituality. First, there is a central concern with *women's *empowerment.* Where some spiritual traditions consider the aspirant's weakness and detachment from worldly affairs to be a sign of the success of their spiritual ventures, women's spirituality insists that the individual be strengthened by her practice, that it have a positive impact on her sense of self and her ability to act for her own best interests and those of women everywhere. Although women occasionally seek to be merged with the divine, they typically walk away from the experience not with a sense of their puniness in relation to its grandeur but with a sense of shared *power and renewed ability to confront a resistant world.

Second, there is a strong emphasis on the *goodness and sacredness of nature.* In the feminist spirituality movement per se (that which exists outside established religions), this is an especially central feature. Many spiritual feminists insist that there is no divine outside of nature, that the divine exists within and throughout the natural world. This tendency toward *pantheism is given additional weight by a commitment to *ecofeminism. Ecofeminism has both secular and religious partisans, but they are united in saying that there is an important relationship between the exploitation of nature and the *oppression of women. Nature, seen as female, is treated as female: women, seen as more "natural" or connected to nature, are treated as nature is. The equation is said to work to the detriment of both in Western *patriarchy.

Within women's spirituality, this special connection between women and nature is rarely denied. Women (for reasons that range from the biologistic to the historical) are believed to be closer to nature, more in tune with its rhythms, more sensitive to its well-being. The ecofeminist aim is not to win women over to humanity, with men and against nature, but to win humanity, women and men both, over to nature. Women are seen to have a unique role in this, and for spiritual feminists, it is a religious role. Women's spontaneous spiritual experiences are often reported to be connected to nature: for example, to a sunset or the wind in a forest or the rising of the full moon. They are also sought in nature. Many contemporary women's rituals are practiced outdoors, to coincide with seasonal and planetary events (such as solstices and equinoxes). And even indoor rituals are frequently accompanied by symbols meant to evoke nature: seashells, burning sage, feathers, evergreen branches, and so forth.

This emphasis on nature is linked to an emphasis on the *body and *sexuality and to a theology that is at times radically immanent. In contrast to much of Western theological tradition, contemporary spiritualities of women deem the body and sexuality to be sources of knowledge about the divine and regard female bodily experiences (particularly childbirth and menstruation) as opportunities for spiritual learning and growth. Here the divine is found in and through the self; the emphasis on nature dictates that the divine is found in and through nature and our daily immersion in it; together these yield an immanent theology. The divine is rarely portrayed or experienced as a deity that stands above us or over against us, to whom we must appeal from our position as subordinates in a cosmic *hierarchy. Rather, the divine is portrayed as the web in which we live, in which we are secured and tied to one another.

A third aspect of women's spirituality is the *use of female images for the divine,* ranging from the use of female *metaphors for an allegedly genderless *god to the worship of goddesses or a single *goddess. Such use of female images relies on notions of what practitioners believe to be uniquely female, or to put it another way, on what has been missing in god when god has been named exclusively male. These qualities are many and diverse, but the most important image to surface in the spirituality of women is that of motherhood: god or goddess is like a mother or is the literal mother of humanity and nature. She is portrayed as nurturing, wishing her children's ultimate *equality with her in a nonhierarchical relationship, and as containing us, giving birth to us in a way that makes us never truly separate from her.

Fourth is a reliance on a *revisionary history of Western (or world) civilization and religion*. This is of greater or lesser importance, depending on which community of spiritual women is under discussion, with the feminist spirituality movement being most dependent on this history and women's spiritual movements in established religions regarding it with the most suspicion or lack of interest. It is the most comprehensive account available to spiritual women of how patriarchal societies and patriarchal religions came to be and why they need not be regarded as inevitable. It is thus attractive to a wide range of feminists, spiritual and otherwise. According to this myth, all of prehistory was characterized by goddess worship, peace among different peoples and tribes, and an enhanced or even superior status for women as compared to that of men. The downfall of these "matriarchal," "matristic," or "gynocentric" societies is believed to be roughly coincident with the period of recorded history, starting around 3000 B.C.E. in the Mediterranean region. Men took power, either through internal rebellion or external invasion, and established societies based on war, hierarchy, the oppression of women, the exploitation of nature, and the worship of a male god or gods who sanction all of this. This patriarchal civilization is thought to have reached its zenith in the West with the European witch persecutions of the Middle Ages, viewed by spiritual feminists as the unadorned persecution and murder of women. Today, spiritual feminists believe, there is an opportunity to return to the values of the earlier goddess-worshiping cultures, and it is this that gives feminist spirituality its political agenda.

In addition to these similarities in theological themes, contemporary women's spiritualities share similar ritual practices: worshiping in circles, building altars, following guided meditations, invoking spiritual powers and female images or deities, and utilizing ritual elements that appeal to the proximate senses of touch, taste, and, smell (such as dance, physical contact among worshipers, the use of incense and candles, and the sharing of food).

There are vast differences among women who are exploring explicitly feminist spiritualities, and sometimes deep and passionate disagreements on questions of religious tradition, theology/*thealogy, and the inclusion of men. Yet the similarities between them are perhaps even more profound, illustrating that these diverse expressions from many traditions, countries, and ethnic groups are all arguably part of a feminist revolution in women's spirituality.

Eller [1993]; Falk [1996]; King [1989]; Plaskow/Christ [1989]; Ruether [1985]; Starhawk [1989]

CYNTHIA ELLER

Stereotypes Stereotypes are standardized mental images, held by social groups, that are based on prejudiced attitudes or lack of critical judgment. This concept has been used in feminist theory to describe beliefs about women and men that are held to be natural but actually are *social constructions of gender (what it means to be male or female). An example of such beliefs would be stereotypes of women as weak, passive, irrational, and men as strong, active, and rational. Stereotypes such as these are used to support claims that women are inferior to men and thus legitimate relations of male *domination and female subordination.

Feminist theology deconstructs stereotypical assumptions about women and gender in Christian theological *tradition. For instance, Rosemary Radford Ruether has exposed the way stereotypical beliefs about women are embedded in the *hierarchical *dualism characteristic of much of Christian tradition, which equates and values mind, culture, male over *body, nature, female. Feminist theologies examine the ways stereotypes about masculinity and femininity have been imposed on God and explore the interrelation of gender stereotypes and gendered theological symbols. Elizabeth Johnson attempts to dismantle the dualistic framework. She reenvisions theological symbols and categories so that stereotyped oppositions of masculine and feminine are transformed into "a liberating, unified diversity." For example, she speaks *christologically of Jesus-Sophia.

Feminist theologies also examine stereotypical thinking about *race, ethnicity, class, nationality, and sexual orientation and the impact of this thinking on women's lives. Womanist theologian Delores Williams analyzes the "colorstruck" state of mind, whose devaluation of black and overvaluation of white contributes to racial oppression. She also explores how an understanding of what is "acceptably female" varies among *cultures. Feminist theologians continue to explore commonalities and *differences among women and debate what, if any, characteristics are "essential" to women's experience.

Johnson, E.A. [1992]; Ruether [1983/1993]; Wetherilt [1994]; Williams [1993a]

PAMELA K. BRUBAKER

Story Story is the articulation of one's experience in verbal narrative (talking circles, talking story with friends, consciousness-raising groups), in song, poetry, fiction, (auto)biography, *liturgy, and sacred texts. Though often understood in a folksy sense of telling tales, stories are the fabric of the chronicles of history and the essence of religious sacred writings: narratives of human experience that act in shaping reality.

The hearing, telling, *naming, and inclusion of women's stories is necessary to doing our theology; without our stories, there is no feminist theology. In all the current *liberation movements, finding one's voice and speaking/hearing the stories of those whose existence has been silenced, sidelined, and stereotyped are considered key to moral *agency, key to full participation in society and history.

"Women's stories have not been told. . . . It is important for women to name the great powers of being from their own perspective and to recognize their participation in them" (Christ 1, 10). The telling of our stories serves as a critique of *patriarchal theologies, which have been presented as universal when they are, in fact, partial truths and perspectives.

Womanist, *mujerista,* Pacific and Asian-American, Native American, and other diverse women's voices also render a critique of partiality to the predominantly white, middle-class stories that have shaped most of feminist theologizing. As more women tell their stories, witness is made to the intersections of *race, sexual orientation, class, *education, mental and physical ability, and religious identity in shaping story along with the experience of gender.

New metaphors, new relationships to the principalities and powers, new images of and relationship with the Divine emerge from women telling their stories, in being "heard to speech" (Morton). Equally important, in naming the *violence and abuse inherent to women's *oppression, formerly unspeakable truths are identified. Out of such naming and storytelling, the transformation of both individuals and society becomes possible. Placing the stories of our experience at its source makes feminist theologizing an act of *justice and *healing: a radical act of "going to the roots."

Broner [1993]; Christ [1980]; Grant [1989/1992]; Morton [1985]

MITZI N. EILTS

Suffering Suffering is a human experience that points to the need for *redemption, at the same time that it raises questions about the goodness of life and the effectiveness of redemption. Suffering refers to a condition of pain, sorrow, and/or anguish, which may be experienced physically, emotionally, or spiritually, personally or corporately. It may be the result of what is termed *natural *evil,* i.e., such things as earthquakes and disease, or the result of historical evil or human action, i.e., such things as war and injustice. Theologians have long raised the question of why suffering occurs. This area of inquiry is usually referred to as the question of evil or the issue of theodicy, i.e., the *justice of God: If God is all good and all powerful, why do people suffer?

Traditionally, Christianity has maintained that much suffering is a result of *sin, evil, ignorance, and death and is related to human disobedience or disregard for God's intended and good purposes in *creation, i.e., suffering is a result of the *Fall. The remedy for suffering is therefore found in the salvation offered through the life, death, and *resurrection of Jesus Christ. Especially in Western Christianity, the passion and *cross of Christ have been regarded as the locus of God's action for salvation. As a result, Christianity developed the notion of redemptive suffering: suffering as a good or necessary condition for salvation and as imitative of Jesus Christ's saving act.

Feminist theologies variously challenge both the understanding that suffering is a result of the Fall and the claim that suffering may be good or redemptive. These challenges are rooted in the recognition that women have been regarded as especially responsible for the Fall and have been expected to suffer obediently and meekly as a result. Feminist and other liberation *theologies also raise into critical awareness the suffering of those victimized by *oppression and abuse. Oppression is the result of political, social, economic, and *ideological systems that subjugate certain classes or groups of people. It is manifest through systems of *sexism, *racism, *classism, *heterosexism, etc. Abuse is an action of harm toward a less powerful person by a more powerful person. Systems of oppression allow for and encourage abusive actions that cause suffering.

A major contribution of feminist theological thinking about suffering has been to focus pastoral and theological attention on concrete and often hidden situations of abuse, especially those that affect women and children, such as domestic *violence, sexual harassment and abuse, rape, child abuse, and forced *prostitution. The suffering of abuse is not deserved and is not the result of sinful action on the part of the person harmed. Feminist theologies maintain, however, that the theological tradition which regards suffering as a result of sin and as redemptive and good may nurture and reinforce abuse and foster an attitude of compliance with suffering. This tradition thereby contributes to the suffering of the oppressed and powerless, who are so often women.

Feminist theologies seek to develop more complex approaches to suffering which would differentiate between suffering that seems intrinsic to the human condition, with its limitations and contingencies; suffering that one inflicts on others; and suffering that one experiences as the result of injustice, oppression, or abuse. None of these is deemed good or redemptive in itself. Yet another kind of suffering which ought to be considered is that which may result from choices made by a person who is trying to change or right a situation of abuse or oppression: e.g., the process of recovery from an abusive situation may entail a certain amount of pain; action against an oppressive government may result in torture or assassination; entering into *solidarity with those who suffer or are oppressed may entail painful challenges and changes in one's own life.

Feminist theologians differ among themselves about whether these types of suffering are to be considered good or redemptive. Though there is general agreement that suffering may be inevitable, some feminist theologians go further to assign a value to the suffering: either to consider it not good, though inevitable and therefore tragic or problematic, or to consider it good and effective for redemption. Many womanist, *mujerista,* Asian, Latin American, and African theologians argue for the importance of suffering in solidarity, though they add further nuances reflective of their particular situations.

A key locus and point of *difference is the way in which Jesus' suffering and death are to be understood. For example, in *Christianity, Patriarchy, and Abuse* (Brown/Bohn), Joanne Carlson Brown and Rebecca Parker survey the complicity of Christian theologies of the cross in the abuse of women in order to argue that Jesus' suffering ought not to be considered redemptive. Womanist theologian Delores Williams thinks it important to focus on African-American women's *survival rather than their suffering, and so she, too, wants to move away from the cross as the locus of Jesus' redeeming action. Other theologians see the cross in a new light as symbol of God's presence in solidarity and *compassion with those who suffer. The image of *Christa, a crucified woman, makes such presence concrete for some. Even those who argue for the redemptive value of the cross, however, are careful not to suggest that suffering is good in and of itself. Rather, suffering for the sake of justice and compassion, *healing and *liberation may be effective toward redemption. These differences call for further exploration and development.

Brock [1988]; Brown/Bohn [1989]; Farley [1990]; Pobee/Von Wartenberg-Potter [1986]; Soelle [1975]; Townes, [1993]; Williams [1993a]

FLORA A. KESHGEGIAN

Survival Survival is a major issue in some womanist theology. Womanist theologians who focus on this issue claim it to be at the center of African-American women's *experience in the United States. Inseparable from black women's struggle for a positive, productive quality of life for themselves and their families, survival as a hermeneutical strategy lives in tension with *liberation hermeneutics. This is especially true with theological interpretation of biblical traditions. Whereas many liberation *theologians point to the exodus event in the Old Testament and to Luke 4 in the New Testament to validate their liberation norms, some womanist theologians point to the Hagar references in the Old and New Testaments, to the *wilderness *traditions, and to the Babylonian captivity to validate their claims about God's activity in the African-American community's survival and quality-of-life struggle.

Womanist theology, emphasizing survival and quality of life as major heuristic devices, consults sources that have not before been reflected on by black liberation theologians. Along with black women's sources, works of the survivors of the Jewish *Holocaust in Germany and the works of Native Americans who survived genocide and the Trail of Tears in North America are important for womanist theology. All works that tell stories of a struggle for survival and the effort to achieve a positive quality of life amid the survival struggle are relevant to womanist theology.

Lorde [1984]; Townes [1993]; Williams [1993b]

DELORES S. WILLIAMS

Tao In the earliest Chinese texts, the term *tao* indicates a road or a pathway; it is not until the later Chou dynasty (770–256 B.C.E.) that tao takes on the meaning of the correct or natural "way" something is done. By continued extension, the term comes to mean "the way all things are done" or "the order/ law/ way of the *cosmos," i.e., ultimate reality. The term had wide currency among classical Chinese philosophers and religious thinkers; not only Taoists but *Confucians, Mohists (followers of Moh), and others discerned a tao, variously characterized, at work in the world.

The Taoists' tao is the formulation of a cosmic principle that is most familiar to those outside cultural China. As encountered in the *Tao te ching,* it is appreciated as a "natural" way of thought to be aligned with "feminine" traits and thus is often invoked as an alternative to Western masculinist visions of *transcendent *reality. The perceived association of the tao with the feminine, or the perception of the tao itself as feminine, is traceable to the text's frequent references to images of water, the valley, the ravine, and the gateway as receptive, dark, passive, and remote; mysterious and humble, they are celebrated for their perseverance and ultimate triumph over things aggressive and prominent. The Taoist sage is one who lives in harmony with the natural movements of the tao, submitting and adapting to the continuous process of phenomenal change.

The true tao, however, is metaphenomenal. The opening lines of the *Tao te ching* state clearly that the tao that can be "tao-ed," i.e., called "tao," is not the constant or ultimate tao. The ultimate tao is unconditioned and undifferentiated, beyond all that is fragmented and that therefore needs identifying names. Once humans discern *heaven as distinct from earth, or distinguish the forces of *yin and yang, that which we call "the tao" is already removed from its absolute origin, becoming instead the gendered mother of the "ten thousand things."

The nameable, generative tao, having "mothered," i.e., given birth to, the world, does not then nourish it; the sage may cling to "the tao" as a babe to its mother's breast, but the *Tao te ching* implies the tao's indifference to all things, as even heaven and earth see them as so many ephemeral "straw dogs" (chapter 5). Rather, it is the inherent capability or *power of the phenomenal tao, its *te,* or "virtue," that moves to carry all things along to completion. The *te* of tao, rather than the phenomenal tao itself, is the active force observable in processes of change. As the active force driving natural cycles and progressions of change, the gendered association for *te* in traditional cosmological speculation would then be "masculine." Like yin and yang, heaven and earth, tao and te are necessary complements but are secondary to considerations of ultimate reality.

The real, ultimate tao is not sexed, gendered, or in any way emblematic of an absolute or essential femininity. In truth, the *Tao te ching* was more political treatise than religious or philosophical work, addressing itself to the ruler who would preserve his state and his life. Composed during a period of intense interstate warfare, the text advocates humility and passivity for the ruler as a means of diverting attention from himself and his resources. Despite the efforts of some scholars, the text itself in no way valorizes "the mother" or women; nor does it value "the feminine" beyond its political utility. To be like the secondary, nameable tao—mysterious, passive, hidden away, "feminine"—is merely to survive.

Later Taoist sectarian traditions, despite the textual prominence of female imagery, the worship of *goddesses as well as gods, and an appreciation for female adepts (typically venerated by elite males and circumscribed by their social roles as daughters or wives), neither championed "the feminine" nor allowed women to hold significant leadership positions within worship communities.

Ames in Guisso/Johannessen [1981]; Chen, *International Philosophical Quarterly* [1969]; Chen, *History of Religions* [1974]

VIVIAN-LEE NYITRAY

Thealogy Thealogy is reflection on the divine in feminine and feminist terms. The word is used both as a positive alignment with *Goddess, goddesses, or God in female terms and as an iconoclastic term to create awareness of the *androcentrism of theology.

Canadian Jewish feminist Naomi Goldenberg coined the word, and it has been used by other authors, most notably in *Laughter of Aphrodite* (Christ) and *To Make and Make Again* (Caron). Goldenberg and Carol Christ use the term specifically in reference to the Goddess. Christ states that her thealogy grows out of her own *experience and the experience of other women, from the understanding that the earth is holy and our home, and from connection with ancient goddesses. *To Make and Make Again* asserts similarly that thealogy flows from women's experience of and insights about the divine but seeks understanding of a nonsexist deity, god/dess or otherwise.

The primary contribution of thealogy to feminist theological debate is its political agenda of legitimizing female *power. Thealogy lives in the active struggle toward eliminating *patriarchy and implementing a world where *justice and well-being for all women exist. Thealogy is concrete and contextual, grounded in life on this earth. It is life-affirming. Christ also notes "the primacy of *symbol* in thealogy in contrast to the primacy of the *explanation* in theology" (123). This means that the modes of engaging in thealogy are often artistic, employing *ritual, music, and literature. Experiencing the divine in concrete, human life is more significant in thealogy than are explanations of the nature of the divine or philosophical discussions about her being. Thealogy with its holistic approach enables new symbol systems and new terms for the divine to be integrated. It intends to create a new social, political, psychological, and spiritual culture.

Caron [1993]; Christ [1987]; Goldenberg, *Studies in Religion/Sciences religieuses* [1987]

CHARLOTTE CARON

Theological Education Theological *education has been defined as the task to motivate, equip, and enable the people of God to develop their gifts and give their lives in meaningful service. It has been affirmed as "theological" in the sense that it involves people in a commitment to *mission and *ministry, a commitment to the study of God in the sense of God's *revelation in the life of Jesus Christ and God's continuous working through the *Holy Spirit.

The privileged *dialogue partner in male-dominated theological education structures has been the academy. In this way, academicians try to construct a university-based theology. Nevertheless, today feminist theologians affirm that theological dialogue refers to what the people of God and their communities do.

Two significant issues in theological education are (1) who is and ought to be doing theology today, and (2) what is and ought to be the perspective for doing theology today. First, feminist theology affirms that those people who are *marginalized in the church, excluded from the church's theologizing—that is, the "nonclergy," blacks, aboriginals, young children, differently abled persons, *lesbians, male homosexuals, and women—should be recognized as capable of making and being equipped to make their contribution to theology. All God's people are recipients of God's promise that they will see visions and dreams (Joel 3:28). That is, they will be empowered to understand God's design for the world and will all be given theological visions that create the future that God wants for all humanity.

Second, it is affirmed that the perspective of doing theology today must take into account the experience of the vast majority of people in today's world for whom *poverty and impoverishment, injustice and the struggle for justice, indignity and aspirations toward human dignity and *freedom, *oppression and the longing for *liberation, emptiness and yearning for full life are the stark realities of daily life. Theological education, then, must be a personal, ecclesial, social transformation process for individuals and for society. God, in *solidarity with the poor and *suffering, challenges both our traditional style of theologizing and the way theological education has been conducted.

Women's contribution to theology is radicalizing the theological method. Their process includes a recognition of the suffering of those who are victims in their "own bodies" of the consequences of a "culture of violence" within society. Being active agents of change, women are trying to break down the ancestral weight of male-centered, *patriarchal church structures that exclude women from theological training and from a significant role in ministry. Some areas of their work are the following:

Seeing theological education in an ecumenical and pluralist perspective. Pluralism is meant in terms of sound *doctrine. It is a *pluralism in terms of *tradition, context, ethnic background, gender, etc. There is not one *hegemonic discourse unfairly claiming the privilege of being universal but rather the concept of all nations, praising God. Feminist theologians give various names to women's action and the fruit of their reflection as Christians (womanist, *mujerista,* women's liberation *theology, etc.).

Building a community-based ecclesial theory. Theological education cannot be a clergy-based education. It is offered to facilitate theological production and make the latter as relevant as possible, relevant to the community's *faith and relevant to the community's traditions and to the situation in which the community is living. "Establishing connections" is the key phrase for this ecclesial theory.

Questioning the epistemological foundations of theology. Rather than learning historical facts, this involves learning to analyze and reconstruct history; rather than learning doctrinal systems, learning a theological *methodology; rather than accepting biblical *revelation without suspicion, reexamining the Bible from the perspective and perception of women.

Reinforcing the theory–practice relationship. The elements of everyday life have entered into the way women do their theological discourse. Feminist theologians are using other modalities besides the reasoning ones, symbolic, liturgical, spiritual expressions that are fundamental to our teaching processes. The *experiences of the "excluded" teach us that we need to work for a permanent integration between theology and life. This involves true integration between theory and *praxis and between discourse and pastoral ministry.

Katsuno/Keay/Ortega [1994]; Mud Flower Collective [1985]; Ortega [1995]; Rhodes/Richardson [1986]

OFELIA ORTEGA

Theologies, Contemporary** Literally, theology means "God-talk"; more broadly, it can be taken to mean disciplined reasoned inquiry and reflection on ultimate meaning and value. Theology interprets scripture and *tradition in particular historical, social (i.e., political, economic, technological), and cultural situations for particular *faith communities. Theology takes its language, questions, and concerns from particular communities in particular situations; the answers it can provide are tentative, partial, provisional. Because theology is a matter not only of faith but also of *culture, significant or large-scale change in the cultural horizon often causes corresponding change in theology. To speak of "contemporary theologies" is to presume that these theologies are changes from the Protestant and Catholic theology of previous generations; to admit change in the horizon within which theology emerges.

Although culture is fluid and resists borders, most scholars agree that the culture shaped by classical Greek *ethics, aesthetics, and science has collapsed; however, they share little agreement about modernity and *postmodernity. Modernity's break with the classical horizon was clean: it was secular rather than religious, it injected progress as change into history, it prized *objectivity and intellectual independence rather than dependence on religious and philosophical authorities, it relinquished government to bureaucracy and technical rationality. Postmodernity's break with modernity resembles fracture: it disputes, reduces, and rejects all totalizing worldviews or systems, whether religious, philosophical, or political; it dissociates itself from modernity's failed project of progress, with its "cover stories" of emancipation and *liberation; and it affirms, even as it interrogates and problematizes, human persons in their concrete diversities, histories, and cultures. Contemporary culture rises in the fissures between modernity and postmodernity. Contemporary culture is global and globally eclectic; it pirates, concocts, and markets the goods, artifacts, and cultural forms of yellow, red, brown, and black peoples around the world; it reproduces and sells their joy, their vibrancy, their audacity, and their anger.

The historical, social, and cultural situation of the past fifty years has pressed theology to undergo several large-scale or *paradigm* changes. In other words, the ways in which theology understands its tasks, presuppositions, sources, and methods have shifted; moreover, the ways in which it arrives at metaphysical, logical, and existential judgments about truth have changed. Theology articulates its new self-understandings practically and theoretically in several forms, including, but not exhausting, the liberal, neo-orthodox, *transcendental, process, metaphorical, political, liberation, contextual, and queer.

Liberal, Neo-Orthodox, and Political Theologies. It is no longer controversial to assert that the Second World War was a moral stumbling block for theology. Nineteenth-century liberal theology attempted to bridge the distance between God and humanity, but its anointment of progress, uncritical approbation of individualism, and privatization of *religion muted *suffering in Protestant Christianity. Neo-orthodox theology in Germany reaffirmed human creatureliness and sinfulness before God. Moreover, its explicit and unequivocal confession of obedience to the word of God opposed Nazism. Neo-orthodox theology did what liberal theology failed to do, which was to distinguish sufficiently between Christianity and culture. But outside that historical situation, neo-orthodoxy was timid. It overlooked its own temptation to *ideology, grew apolitical and ahistorical, and tamed religion to culture. After Auschwitz, such a theology could only be bourgeois. As a critical, practical, and public corrective, German theologians Jürgen Moltmann, Johannes Baptist Metz, and Dorothee Soelle advocated political theology. The basic project of political theology was one of empathetic *memory and *solidarity with dead and past victims of injustice, ideology critique, and social *praxis in memory of the suffering, death, and *resurrection of Jesus Christ.

Political theology made a decisive break with liberal and neo-orthodox theologies, precisely because it was oriented toward social praxis. It engaged a *hermeneutics of suspicion, analyzing uncritical assumptions and values underlying the social order and the idealization of the bourgeois (middle-class) human subject. This last, in particular, was a reaction to the philosophical *anthropology of Roman Catholic transcendental theology, which treated the potentialities of the human subject rather than concrete realities.

Theologies of Liberation. Political theology addressed the displacement of religion within the secularized social and cultural context of post-Enlightenment Europe; theologies of liberation address the intentional social and cultural *marginalization of those whom Caribbean psychiatrist Frantz Fanon lovingly called "the wretched of the earth." Theologies of liberation developed in the midst of global armed and negotiated struggles for cultural and social *justice that were initiated and sustained by the poor, the colonized, the vanquished, the segregated, the marginalized, the disenfranchised; the invisible women, men, and children of the *third world. In North America and Africa this paradigm of theology resists protracted, institutionalized anti-black *racism and colonialism. In the Caribbean, this theology focuses on decolonization and critical contextual analysis for emancipation. In Latin America and Asia this theology focuses on the direct relation of overdevelopment in the first world to underdevelopment in the third world.

In their interpretation of scripture, theologies of liberation combine ideology critique, hermeneutics of suspicion, and *social analysis (a tool for understanding the history and underlying structures of social oppression) with commitment to social transformation. While these theologies concede *poverty as a *metaphor for understanding the depth of human reliance on God, they never omit its concrete massive effects. Thus, in reading and interpreting scripture, the poor possess, through no right whatsoever, a "hermeneutical privilege." Theologies of liberation also constitute what Gustavo Gutiérrez calls an "epistemological rupture" (1973/1988). This means that theologies of liberation differ from liberal and political theologies in their grasp of logical, metaphysical, and existential truth. These theologies do not reject logical thinking; rather, they expose undeclared assumptions and sources of logic from the perspective of the poor and insist that truth is never independent of cultural, social, or historical conditions.

(White) Feminist Theologies. "The Human Situation: A Feminine View" (1960), by Valerie Saiving, put forward an incipient feminist analysis. Saiving contended not only that a theologian's gender contributes to her or his perspective in doing theology but that, historically, theology had been based on male experience to the detriment of women. Saiving's criticism anticipated the notion of *social location,* i.e., acknowledgment of the effect of a theologian's gender, race, cultural-ethnic background, and social-class status on theological practice.

The Church and the Second Sex (1968), by Mary Daly, presaged what is now known as (white) feminist liberation *theology. Daly's second book, *Beyond God the Father: Toward a Philosophy of Women's Liberation* (1973), anticipated some of the premises of this paradigm: critical analysis of women's experience, the need for new terminology, critique of patriarchal ideology and the patriarchalization of God. About this time, Rosemary Radford Ruether prepared a collection of critical historical studies that disclosed the extent to which misogynist ideology permeated the religions, cultures, and consciousness of peoples of the West (1974; 1975). Elizabeth Clark and Herbert Richardson edited a sourcebook on *Women and Religion* (1977), and Carol Christ and Judith Plaskow edited the anthology *Womanspirit Rising* (1979); both became indispensable in teaching feminist theology. Letty Russell produced the first of several important works that elaborated human liberation from a feminist perspective (1974; 1979; 1981). Unlike Daly, Russell has not abandoned Christianity; her work advocates *partnership between women and men in church and in society. Phyllis Trible (1978; 1984) and Elisabeth Schüssler Fiorenza (1985/1995) offered critical interpretative studies of the sexist presuppositions of the Hebrew and Christian scriptures that called for transformation, not only in patriarchal understandings of God but also in historical-critical scholarship.

Sallie McFague delineated a metaphorical theology that limited the use and emphasis on the image of God the Father and promoted a variety of metaphors and models for speaking about God and the divine–human relationship (1982), but constructive discussion of the "maleness" of Jesus floundered. In *She Who Is: The Mystery of God in Feminist Theological Discourse* (1992), Elizabeth Johnson proposed the female figure of personified Wisdom as a foundational metaphor by which to speak about Jesus as the Christ, thus facilitating inclusive rather than exclusive interpretation.

Social ethicist Beverly Harrison incorporated social analysis in her work to discuss the relation between U.S. *imperialism abroad and class stratification at home, especially for women (1985). The most thoroughgoing historical and interpretative study of racism within the U.S. white feminist movement came from social ethicist Barbara Hilkert Andolsen (1986). Soelle (1977; Soelle/Cloyes 1984), Sharon Welch (1985) and Rebecca Chopp (1987) probed questions of *materialism, class conflict, and Christian identity. Carter Heyward introduced and correlated critiques of homophobia, racism, and *misogyny (1982; 1984), laying the ground for queer theology, which not only affirms the humanity and worth of gays and *lesbians and contests discrimination and oppression against them but claims Jesus as one who "acted up" (Goss 1993).

Theologies of liberation issued from the labor of white feminists and black, brown, red, and yellow male theologians who, but for notable exceptions, ignored the presence and condition of black, brown, red, and yellow women. White feminist analysis often disregarded the intraracial *difference of class: even if white women were proper subjects of theology, not all of them were upper- or middle-class or even extensively educated. Black, brown, red, and yellow male liberation theologians overlooked their collusion, albeit limited, in *patriarchy through internalizing and reproducing (sexist) practices and traditions that suppress and disvalue black, brown, red, and yellow women.

Theologies for the Liberation of Black, Yellow, Brown, and Red Women. Black, yellow, brown, and red women from around the globe have initiated the most recent *paradigm shift in theology: projecting into Christian theological reflection the voices and *experiences of women who have endured double or triple burdens. Moreover, the theologies of black, yellow, brown, and red women are committed to the liberation of *all* black, yellow, brown, and red women and men. Space allows only the most abbreviated presentation of their signal contributions in method, biblical hermeneutics, christological reflection, ethics, and spirituality, to the liberation of theology.

For these theologies, the "hermeneutical privilege" of the poor takes on a special character when the "option for the poor" is grasped as an option for poor women, for women among the **minjung*. Drawing from fiction, folktales, poems, slave narratives, case studies, interviews, shared conversations, these theologies tease forward women's own faith-filled understandings of their conditions. This method of doing theology is communal and gives active voice to poor and illiterate women whose "mother wit," raw courage, and defiant faith crush any insinuation of passivity or naïveté (Fabella and Oduyoye 1988; Fabella 1993; Gebara, in Tamez, ed., 1989; Bingemer/Gebara 1989; Isasi-Díaz 1993; Isasi-Díaz/Tarango 1988; Chung 1990).

Theologies aimed to liberate black, yellow, brown, and red women contribute to new approaches in biblical hermeneutics. These theologies interrogate the biblical text and various interpretations of it to expose possible misrepresentations, seek out and proclaim liberating values that have been obscured intentionally, comb the text for the feats of women, and engage in creative reinterpretation of the material so that *revelation addresses poor and marginalized women in their need, suffering, and resistance. Furthermore, these theologies are unafraid to recontextualize biblical demands and themes in nonbiblical and popular religious contexts (Tamez 1993a; Weems 1988; Kwok 1995).

The "maleness" of Jesus proved a sticking point for white feminist theology, but theologies aimed to liberate black, yellow, brown, and red women recognize, to paraphrase Mercy Amba Oduyoye, the need to rewrap *Christology in new leaves and to free Jesus of Nazareth from the Christ of the West (1986). Jacquelyn Grant, in *White Women's Christ and Black Women's Jesus: Feminist Christology and Womanist Response* (1989), posed a similar concern.

Rather than revive the "liberal quest for the historical Jesus," these works take Jesus' solidarity with women in the New Testament as a point of departure not only to rid the church and society of false and distorted images of women but to support oppressed and marginalized women in rejecting damaging ideologies of self-denial. These theologies underscore Jesus' identification with the "little people," his willingness to accompany them in their struggles, his affirmation of their humanity, and his active hope in and for their participation in the "reign of God." While these theologies bracket *metaphysical and ontological discussions about Jesus, they keenly perceive the concrete metaphysical and ontological implications of the *incarnation. However, Kelly Brown Douglas, in *The Black Christ* (1994), in particular resists the normativeness of Chalcedonian concerns.

From the outset, theologies aimed to liberate poor, oppressed, marginalized women united systematic or constructive theology with ethics. The historical objectification and pornographic eroticization of the bodies of black, yellow, brown, and red women demand this coherence. While sexual *violence renders all women "other," it denies black, brown, red, and yellow women the very right to exist as human, as women, as themselves. Marianne Katoppo identified the egregious spiritual and social consequences of the sexual violation and exploitation of Asian women (1980). Aruna Gnanadason uncovered this vicious dynamic in the *dowry deaths of Indian women (1986), and Katie Cannon founded *womanist* *ethics (1988) on historical and literary analysis of the sexual and physical abuse of black women. Delores Williams extended this analysis, drawing on the African-American *appropriation of the biblical Hagar. In *Sisters in the Wilderness: The Challenge of Womanist God-Talk* (1993a), Williams recontextualized the rape of black women in slavery as "coerced surrogacy" and interrogated black women's continuing oppression as "social-role surrogacy."

By explicitly correlating critical analyses of the social and historical context and of women's experience with the notion of spirituality as a way of living and a way of following Jesus, theologies aimed to liberate poor, oppressed, marginalized women resist the sterility of much academic theology. These theologies of liberation derive their spiritual virtues from the daily, ordinary, lived lives of poor women especially, what *mujerista* theologians term *cotidianidad* (dailiness). This spirituality does not romanticize suffering or strength or gratitude, for these virtues ought not to be confused with limitation or repression. Rather, poor, oppressed, marginalized women follow Jesus best by breaking with long-standing habits of passivity and silent acquiescence. They are called to conversion, to new personal and historical possibilities for the graced exercise of *freedom (Mananzan 1987/1991; Fabella/Park 1989; Consuelo del Prado, in Tamez, ed., 1989).

M. SHAWN COPELAND

Theologies, Evangelical Sometimes called "biblical feminism," evangelical theologies usually start from scripture, wrestling with the interpretation of biblical passages dealing with women's roles in the home, church, and society. Feminist notions first began to surface in evangelical periodicals in the late 1960s. From 1966 to 1973 a number of articles were published by Letha Dawson Scanzoni and Nancy Hardesty.

The first book-length treatments were Scanzoni and Hardesty's *All We're Meant to Be: Biblical Feminism for Today* (1974; 3d ed., 1992); Paul Jewett's *MAN as Male and Female* (1975); and Virginia Ramey Mollenkott's *Women, Men, and the Bible* (1977/1988). The biblical feminist newsletter *Daughters of Sarah* was founded in 1974, as was the Evangelical Women's Caucus (EWC; now the Evangelical and Ecumenical Women's Caucus). The first conference on the topic was titled "Evangelical Perspectives on Woman's Role and Status," held in 1973 at Conservative Baptist Seminary in Denver.

Evangelical feminist theologies begin by arguing that both Genesis 1 and 2 teach the unity and *equality of male and female. From the first *creation account they emphasize that both male and female are created simultaneously in God's image (1:27). In the second account they note that when God created a "helper fit" for Adam (2:18, KJV), it was "bone of my bones and flesh of my flesh" (2:23, NRSV), an equal, not a subordinate. They also note that while all *relationships were fractured in the *Fall in Genesis 3, God neither prescribed distinct gender roles nor instituted female subordination as a punishment, though *patriarchy can be seen as a result of original *sin.

In the New Testament these writers again find equality and mutuality between the sexes. In the life and teachings of Jesus they see no hint of women's subordination in the home or of men's elevation to particular spiritual or ecclesiastical roles. Scanzoni and Hardesty speak of "Woman's Best Friend: Jesus." Mollenkott sees Jesus' instruction to the disciples that "the highest among you must bear himself like the youngest, the chief of you like a *servant" (Luke 22:25–26, NEB), as a description of "the Christian way of relating."

Interpretation of the epistles is more difficult. The key text for these authors is Gal. 3:28: "There is no longer Jew or Greek, there is no longer slave or free, there is no longer male and female; for all of you are one in Christ Jesus." Concerning *marriage (discussed at length by Scanzoni and Hardesty and by Mollenkott), they argue that Paul's comments should be seen in the broader light of his teachings on equality and mutual submission among Christians. They note Paul's recurrent theme of the church as the body of Christ in which all members are valuable and his persistent instructions to "love one another with mutual affection" (Rom. 12:10), "bear with one another" (Col. 3:13), and "be subject to one another out of reverence for Christ" (Eph. 5:21). Mollenkott and Jewett suggest that Paul's comments on marriage, like those on slavery, represent concessions to his *culture in the light of what he saw as Christ's imminent second coming.

While not explicitly denying Pauline authorship of the pastorals or Ephesians, these writers attempt to highlight the obvious *ministries of women in Acts and the genuine Pauline letters. They point to Paul's discussions of spiritual gifts in Romans 12 and 1 Corinthians 12, the fact that women prophesied and prayed in the church (1 Cor. 11:5), that Phoebe was a deacon (Rom. 16:1; cf. 1 Tim. 3:11), and that a host of women are described by Paul as fellow laborers in the *gospel (e.g., Tryphaena and Tryphosa, Rom. 16:12; Euodia and Syntyche, Phil. 4:2–3). All favor the *ordination of women and find biblical support for it in the ministries of the Hebrew women *prophets and New Testament women disciples, prophets, and deacons. In 1980, Jewett published *The Ordination of Women* (Eerdmans, 1980). Hardesty's dissertation, published as *Your Daughters Shall Prophesy* (1990) and in revised form as *Women Called to Witness: Evangelical Feminism in the Nineteenth Century* (1984), rediscovered the roles of evangelical women in the nineteenth-century woman's rights struggles and their biblical arguments for women's rights, suffrage, and ordination. These themes have subsequently been developed by such works as Patricia Gundry's *Woman Be Free!* (Zondervan, 1977) and *Neither Slave nor Free* (Harper, 1987); Linda Mercadante's *From Hierarchy to Equality* (Vancouver: Regent College, 1978); Willard Swartley's *Slavery, Sabbath, War, and Women* (1983); Gilbert Bilezikian's *Beyond Sex Roles* (Baker, 1985); and Virginia Mollenkott's *Godding* (1987) and *Sensuous Spirituality* (1992).

Sexuality issues have proven divisive. Christians for Biblical Equality (CBE) emerged in 1986 after EWC adopted a resolution supporting *lesbian and gay civil rights. CBE affirms "the *family, celibate singleness, and heterosexual marriage as the patterns God designed for us." In 1987, evangelicals calling themselves the Council on Biblical Manhood and Womanhood (CBMW) responded with the Danvers Statement, declaring that "distinctions in masculine and feminine roles are ordained by God as part of the created order," that "Adam's headship in marriage was established by God before the Fall," and that in Christ, "husbands should forsake harsh or selfish leadership . . . ; wives should forsake resistance to their husbands' *authority and grow in willing, joyful submission to their husbands' leadership." CBMW also believes that "some governing and teaching roles within the church are restricted to men."

Hardesty [1984]; Mollenkott [1987; 1988; 1992]; Scanzoni/Hardesty [1992]

NANCY A. HARDESTY

Theologies, Liberation The term *liberation theology* arose simultaneously in North and South American Christianity in the late 1960s. By 1985, theologians around the world recognized a plurality of Christian and non-Christian liberation theologies, including U.S. feminist (and womanist and *mujerista*), black (U.S.), Latin American, South African (and other African), Korean **minjung*, *lesbian and gay, Jewish, the liberation theologies of *dalits* in India, and liberation theologies of indigenous peoples around the world.

Liberation theologies understand theology as reflection on the presence of the divine within the *liberation struggles of the *marginalized. It is therefore an activity for whole peoples and movements, not a completed body of knowledge to be inherited from previous communities. Because theology is reflection on the liberation struggle (on the activity of God within the struggle; on the strategies, failures, and achievements of the struggle; on the pain and *suffering endured; and on the *solidarity and new spiritual paths discovered within the struggle), the marginalized seize theology from academic, ecclesiastic, and social elites.

The liberation struggles on which liberation theologies reflect are concrete socioeconomic and political struggles specific to local circumstances; they thus give rise to different theologies. Most varieties of liberation theology have some feminist elements, but the feminist dimension was slow to develop, due to (1) identification of feminism with first world white, middle-class women; (2) fear of splitting popular movements along sex lines; and (3) acceptance of sex roles and discrimination as natural. Feminist liberationists around the globe struggle for the liberation of women both in separate women's organizations and within broad popular movements. They are distinguished from other feminists by their commitment to include other categories of sinful oppression, such as *race, class, and sexual orientation, in addition to sex and gender, in their reflection.

Cone [1975]; King [1994]; Peter-Raoul et al. [1990]; Pieris [1988]

CHRISTINE GUDORF

Theology, Historical** Christian theologians have long believed that the past holds important keys to understanding the present. The past, like a mother, gives birth to the life we call "today's *faith." Just as a mother, through hard labor, brings from her own flesh new and independent life, so, too, past generations of Christians have formed, through their struggles, the founding beliefs and practices that shape the new and changing communities of faith today. The term *historical theology* denotes study of this Christian past with special emphasis on the founding "doctrines" or "theological teachings" that previous generations have passed on to the present. The hope is that by studying the theology of previous generations, contemporary Christians might better understand their roots in the past and thus also the direction in which they should (or should not) grow in the future.

General Features of Historical Theology. Over the centuries, theologians have developed different methods for studying the past, such as John Henry Newman's "faith-centered" analysis of *doctrine in the eighteenth century and Adolf von Harnack's twentieth-century "scientific" history of theology. In recent years, feminist theologians have expanded the range of methods by asking new questions concerning the place of women in the history of Christian thought. They are particularly interested in exploring the complex interrelations between ideas about God and ideas about and from women's experience, as each has developed in different eras and cultures.

Like more traditional historical theologians, feminist historical theologians do this by analyzing *doctrines,* a term referring to thematic topics that regularly appear in the history of theology and play a normative role in shaping Christian faith. The most common doctrines in Western Christianity are the following: *God (*Trinity), *creation, humanity, *sin, *Christology, *incarnation, *redemption (*atonement), pneumatology (the *Holy Spirit), soteriology (salvation), *ecclesiology (the church), and *eschatology (the "last things"). When studying these doctrines, historical theologians conceptually analyze the ways doctrines are defined, organized, and developed in different times and places.

In addition to this conceptual analysis, feminist theologians, like more traditional historical theologians, explore the relationship between doctrines and the past communities that developed and used them. This interest in the links between *community and doctrine derives from a recognition that the historical meaning of doctrines cannot be ascertained apart from an analysis of the varied languages and cultural contexts within which doctrines arose and were used. To determine the meaning doctrines acquire in a given context, theologians examine not only the linguistic conventions of a community but also its broader beliefs, actions, attitudes, and values.

Thus historical theologians not only ask basic questions such as: What did the term *atonement* signify in a fourteenth-century northern Italian community? They also ask questions such as: What kinds of social and religious institutions were built by the Italians who believed in this doctrine? What kinds of moral values did these people hold? What kind of "worldview" accompanied this doctrine at the time? And what types of personal and communal dispositions or attitudes did it nurture or contest in its practitioners? Historical theologians assert that asking these questions is necessary for understanding how a specific community's language of faith functioned in its particular cultural context.

Issues in Feminist Historical Theology. The unique contribution of feminists to this critical interrogation of *culture and doctrine is their interest in the roles that women and gender constructions have played in the history of theology. There are several ways in which feminist theologians integrate this interest into their historical analysis and theological reflection.

1. *The search for women in history.* Since their early years, feminists have tried to expand the scope of the Christian *tradition by uncovering and analyzing the theological writings of women. While this task has proved quite difficult, given the widespread silencing of women's voices in history, it has neverless been fruitful in recent years, providing the feminist community with a new history of women's faith traditions and theological reflections. This new history has led, in turn, to a growing appreciation of how women's *experiences give them a different perspective on theology. In the years ahead, a continued recovery of these perspectives promises to expand our conceptions of the Christian tradition as a whole. Feminist scholars working in this area quite frequently make constructive use of the women's writings they

uncover, as is seen in present-day feminist reconstructions of such topics as the *Sophia traditions and the creation spirituality of medieval *mysticism.

2. *The *social construction of gender.* In addition to uncovering the lost voices of women, feminists further enrich their projects by exploring the varied ways in which different cultures construct and deploy categories such as "woman," "female and male," "*sexuality," "*family," and "*patriarchy." This analysis involves carefully discerning, for example, what constituted being a woman or being oppressed or being part of patriarchy in a given time and place. Through this type of careful analysis, feminist theologians have shown that the meaning of these terms is never static or ahistorical but varies significantly from one generation and place to the next.

This insight into the constitutive role culture plays in defining such terms as *woman* and *patriarchy* has important consequences for how feminists approach the task of analyzing doctrines. It suggests, for example, that "being a woman" in seventeenth-century Brazil signified something quite different from its meaning in twentieth-century Canada. Similarly, it suggests that patriarchy as it existed in the feudal world of tenth-century northern Europe is not the same as the patriarchy that typified French colonial rule in nineteenth-century North Africa. As both of these examples further suggest, feminist theologians must forgo simple definitions of such topics as "women's piety," "female faith experience," or "patriarchal God-talk." Instead, they must give multiple accounts of the varied cultures and contexts within which "women" and "gender" have meaning and take on theological significance.

3. *Reexamining sources.* In the process of analyzing how cultures construct doctrines and gender, feminist theologians inevitably confront the task of defining what qualifies as a theological resource for their reflection. Until recently, the principal subject matter of historical theology has been the writings of Western history's most influential theologians (e.g., Augustine, Aquinas, Luther) or collections of writings that represent theological schools of thought (e.g., nominalism, Oxford movement). However, when feminists take up the two tasks mentioned above (finding women's voices and analyzing gender and culture), their enterprise requires expanding the scope of significant sources to include media other than written texts.

The turn to additional media is important because women often leave traces in history that never appear in written form. These media (frequently referred to as "texts" as well) include material objects such as quilts, popular clothing, and domestic architecture, along with such resources as folk music, dance, and cooking. Similarly, feminists use as sources nonmaterial social practices such as domestic work patterns, juridical discourses on *marriage, and the rhetoric of familial roles. They look to these discourses for insights into the mechanisms by which a given culture constructs and perpetuates the economy of its gender relations. Interrogating the cultural logic of such discourses further provides feminist theologians with material for their reflections on the relation between the construction of gender and Christian doctrine.

4. *The other side of *authority.* When feminists attempt to reconceive the nature of theological sources, they immediately confront the question of authority. How does one determine which texts are normatively illustrative of a given tradition and which texts are marginal to the development of a historical theology? Until recently, the answer to this question was straightforward: one should evaluate as authoritative those texts and doctrines which clearly state, in affirmative theological terms, those beliefs that a given Christian community confessed as their theological measure and guide. Traditionally, these authoritative measures have taken the form of creeds, confessions, statements of faith, and catechisms. While feminists remain

interested in these most obvious forms of doctrinal authority, they add that one can learn much about a tradition by looking at the theological perspectives it rejected or ignored.

The logic of attending to such "outsider" perspectives rests on the assumption that a culture's beliefs are often defined negatively or oppositionally, with reference positions "beyond" or "outside" the normative boundaries of its central doctrine. If this is the case, it then follows that one might determine the dominant theological values of a community by examining its repressed or excluded theological voices. In many instances, feminist theologians have discovered that when one ventures beyond the normative boundaries of a tradition, one discovers among the outsiders, *heretics, and *pagans a number of women's voices that were *marginalized because they did not conform to the dominant culture's view of appropriate women's roles. And from this conversation on the margins, feminists have discovered new norms, alternative boundaries, and hence the critical roots of hitherto hidden doctrinal possibilities.

5. *Rereading the *canon.* In addition to exploring the "edges" of doctrine, feminists also devote their attention to the traditional "center" doctrines and examine doctrines and figures from the mainstream canon of Christian theology. They engage in this study because they recognize that, in both negative and positive ways, traditional figures and doctrines have enormous influence on the present. Because of this influence, studying the canons of the tradition can reveal to contemporary Christians much about who they are and what they confess.

The results of such study are often quite surprising. Not only have feminist theologians discovered that the Christian past is filled with innumerable doctrines that actively perpetuated the *oppression of women; they have also discovered that it holds potentially liberating theological treasures as well. These treasures consist of such findings as the "radically relational" Trinitarianism of the Cappadocians, the theological grounds in Aquinas for same-sex unions, and Calvin's defense of making the language of prayer inclusive.

6. *History and contemporary feminist theology.* As suggested by the issues outlined above, work undertaken in the field of feminist historical theology is never done in isolation from questions and concerns related to the oppression and *empowerment of women in today's world. Feminists recognize that their work on the past needs to further the ongoing struggle for the contemporary *liberation of women, and they work to accomplish this in a creative and engaged manner. They strive to learn from the past about different types of oppression, particularly as it is manifest in doctrines, in order to understand the shifting dynamics of oppression in theology today. They seek to learn as well about women's resistances, their theological insights, and their conceptions of a women-loving God, in order to gain perspective on the character of feminist faith in the present. They thus strive to use the past as a resource for changing the present, borrowing images and insights that are liberating, justice-loving, and caring while rejecting doctrines and traditions that are demeaning, exploitative, and destructive. In these ways, feminist historical theology accomplishes its most important function, that of creatively serving the emancipatory projects of womanist theology, feminist theology, *mujerista* theology, *lesbian theology, Asian women's theology, and many other constructive theologies of liberation.

Clark [1986]; Coakley [1994]; Douglass [1985]; Johnson [1992]; Jones [1995]; LaCugna [1991]; Miles [1992]

SERENE JONES

Theology, Indigenous Women's

Indigenous women's theology is being developed by indigenous women and is informed by their consciousness both of being women and of having an indigenous cultural heritage. Due to the repression of women and indigenous cultures throughout the history of Christian missions in the Americas, few indigenous women with feminist consciousness remain in the church. Given alienation of the original peoples of the *land from dominant Euro-American society, many Canadian aboriginal and Native American women are also reluctant to identify with "white" feminists.

Nevertheless, increasing numbers of indigenous women are exploring what it means to be aboriginal or Native American *and* Christian *and* women. They are drawing on the wisdom found in their cultural traditions to reenvision the meaning of the Christian *faith for themselves and their people. Because at this time indigenous women collectively have not given a name to the theology in which they are engaged, this project may be designated by the descriptive, generic term *indigenous women's theology*. The original peoples of the North American continent have many distinct languages, cultures, and religions. This rich diversity means that referring to "indigenous women's theologies" may be more precise. Yet there are sufficient commonalities across tribal lines to sketch the outlines of an emergent indigenous women's theology.

Two principal sources for indigenous women's theology are (1) the teachings and ceremonies of their *culture and (2) their experience as indigenous women living in two worlds, that of their own people and that of dominant society. The third major source is the Jewish and Christian *tradition, beginning with the way it has been transmitted through the missionary enterprise. For many women, particularly within Protestant denominations, the Bible has been a primary source of *authority. Much of the critical work done by indigenous women is that of exposing how *doctrine and scripture have been used to impose a *patriarchal social order that pacifies indigenous people, suppresses their culture, and subjugates women.

Along with gender, *race, and class, culture is a central category for both the *deconstructive and reconstructive tasks of indigenous women's theology. The social location of indigenous women offers a unique vantage point from which to critique the dominant Euro-American worldview. Indigenous women may discern distortions and oppressive potentialities in theologies, theories, and practices that those more *inculturated into the modern Western world are unable to perceive. An example of this is the problem of how much of even feminist academic reflection is shaped by linguistic thought patterns that are the legacy of patriarchal Greco-Roman culture. Women viewing the world from cultures with different basic assumptions about the universe can draw on that *difference for analytical purposes of comparison and critique, as well as for the articulation of an alternative vision.

Aboriginal spirituality is at the heart of indigenous women's theology. Creation is understood to be inherently spiritual, with the dynamic life force of spirit moving through and connecting plants and animals, sun, moon, and stars, the elements of earth, air, fire, and water. The *dualisms of natural and supernatural, sacred and spiritual, are irrelevant to the indigenous worldview, wherein all that is created is sacred, death is a part of life, and spirit animates even rocks and the earth, which are themselves living entities.

Widespread among the indigenous peoples of North America has been the spiritual awareness of a Creator who, with the help of other spirit beings, brought into being this Mother Earth and all that she sustains. This original source is known by different names, in some languages by names connoting Great Mystery and the All Spirit. Ascertaining the extent to which missionary teachings have influenced indigenous understandings of a Creator is difficult. However, the ancient *creation stories and other oral traditions point to the awareness of a Great Spirit long predating missionary contact.

In a number of cultures the genetrix is female. The prominent role played by female figures in creation and other stories of many cultures provides a rich resource for indigenous women's theology.

Each people has its communal stories and ceremonies that provide wisdom about and ways of communing with the spirit world. In the present revival of aboriginal spirituality, increasing numbers of women are taking part in traditional women's *rituals such as the moon ceremony. In many places women also participate in the sweat lodge ceremony, which in most cultures was previously open only to men. Some traditional elders explain that in today's society, women are facing the same pressures as men, consequently needing the *healing and restoration that come from prayer time in the sweat lodge.

Because not all indigenous customs and beliefs contribute to the well-being of women, in indigenous women's theology these need to be evaluated. How did they function originally in the life of the people? How do they function in today's world? Respect for culture is a fundamental value but does not preclude critique. Cultural wisdom and practice that restore wholeness to women and men and harmony to *community and the wider creation are reclaimed. Healing of *body, mind and spirit, particularly for oppressed people, is a central goal of aboriginal spirituality.

Native spiritual teachings are also foundational for indigenous women's theology. The branding of those traditional teachings as *pagan and evil has been absorbed by generations of missionized people, resulting in ongoing turmoil and conflict for individuals and communities. Consequently, for women raised in Christian traditions, the recovery of indigenous beliefs and customs can be an arduous process of unlearning and relearning.

Charges of syncretism tend to accompany any "mixing" of Christianity and native ways. For indigenous women's theology, this raises the issue of *gospel and culture. Since gospel, by necessity, always is mediated through culture, from the indigenous viewpoint the question about syncretism needs to be addressed to those cultures into which Christianity has been inculturated, namely, Greco-Roman culture and its Euro-American successors. The more relevant task for indigenous women's theology is that of evaluating how Christian teachings and practices have functioned in the life of their people. What is life-giving to indigenous women? What genuinely is good news for the people? What has disempowered them? Indigenous women's theology is grounded in women's daily struggle for *survival for themselves, their children, people, and land. Given this commitment, the critical question is: What can be reclaimed as life-giving from the Christian tradition?

One primary method of theological discernment is the exploration of ground shared by Christian and indigenous traditions. Common areas include belief in a Creator, an afterlife, prophecy, healing; the *ethics of hospitality, sharing, stewardship, love, walking a good path, the common good; practices such as fasting, feasting, and *prayer. Indigenous ceremonies such as the sun dance have elements of self-giving and intercession for the people that parallel Christian observances. The redemptive role of Jesus has its counterparts in aboriginal traditions, in which are found images of Jesus, such as healer, teacher, and spirit guide, that are more liberative for indigenous people than the exclusively male, monarchical image of Christ the King.

Indigenous women's theology also can draw comparisons of indigenous practices and values with those of the feminist movement, where there is much common ground. Both tend to see the world in terms of *relationship and interconnection, to value egalitarian modes of decision making over *hierarchical, to choose the circle as a symbol and a model for communal life. The *ecofeminist movement shares many values with indigenous people, including respect for the earth and her creatures. Identifying this common, sacred ground will be a valuable contribution of indigenous women's theology.

Allen [1992]; Brant [1988]; Fife [1993]; Gossen [1993]; Green [1984]; Tinker [1993]; Wall [1993]

JANET SILMAN

Theology, *Mujerista* Latina women living in the United States, keenly aware of how *sexism, ethnic prejudice, and economic *oppression subjugate them and willing to struggle against such oppression, call themselves *mujeristas. Mujerista* theology identifies their explanations of their *faith and its role in their struggle for *liberation. As a name created by Latinas for their theological *praxis, "*mujerista* theology" provides a conceptual framework, a point of reference, a mental construct based on their own interpretations of *reality that they use in thinking, understanding, and relating to persons, ideas, movements.

A *mujerista* is someone who makes a *preferential option for Latina women and for their struggle for liberation. *Mujeristas* understand their struggle for liberation as a communal praxis. They understand that their task is to gather their people's hopes and expectations about *justice and peace. They believe that in them, though not exclusively so, God's image and likeness shines forth. *Mujeristas* are called to gestate new women and new men, Latino people willing to work for the good of the people, knowing that such work requires the denunciation of all destructive self-abnegation.

Mujerista theology is a liberative praxis: reflective action that has as its goal liberation. As a liberative praxis, *mujerista* theology is a process of enablement for Latina women. It insists on the development of a strong sense of moral *agency: clarification of the importance and value of who they are, what they think, and what they do. As a liberative praxis, *mujerista* theology seeks to impact on mainline theologies, those theologies that support what is normative in church and, to a large degree, in society. *Mujerista* theology engages in this two-pronged liberative praxis in the following three ways:

First, *mujerista* theology works to enable Latinas to understand the many oppressive structures that greatly control their daily lives. It enables them to understand that the goal of their struggle should be not to participate in and to benefit from these structures but to change them radically. In theological and religious language, this means that *mujerista* theology helps Latinas discover and affirm the presence of God in the midst of their communities and the *revelation of God in their daily lives. Latinas seek to understand the reality of structural *sin and find ways of combating it, because it effectively hides God's ongoing revelation from them and from society at large.

Second, *mujerista* theology insists on and aids Latinas in defining their preferred future: What will a radically different society look like? What will be its values and norms? In theological and religious language, this means that *mujerista* theology enables Latinas to understand the centrality of *eschatology in the life of every Christian. Latinas' preferred future breaks into the present oppression they suffer in different ways. Latinas work to make those eschatological glimpses become their whole horizon.

Third, *mujerista* theology enables Latinas to understand how much they have already bought into the prevailing systems in society, including the religious systems, and thus internalized their own oppression. It helps Latinas see that radical structural change cannot happen unless radical change takes place in each and every one of them. In theological and religious language, this means that *mujerista* theology assists Latinas in the process of *conversion, helping them to see the reality of sin in their lives. Further, it enables them to understand that to resign themselves to what others tell them is their lot and passively to accept *suffering and self-effacement is not necessarily virtuous.

There are two other important *methodological elements in *mujerista* theology. First, the source of *mujerista* theology is the lived experience of Latinas: experience of which they are conscious, experience they have reflected on. Here *mujerista* theology follows Anselm's understanding of theology as faith seeking understanding. It is the faith of Latinas, which historically has proven to be a resource in their struggles for liberation, that is at the heart of *mujerista* theology. This does not preclude church teaching and *traditions or classical biblical understandings. But it actively includes religious understandings and daily religious practices labeled "*popular religion." These are mainly a mixture of Roman Catholic elements with African religions among Latina groups with Caribbean roots and Amerindian religions among Latinas of Central and South American origin. In *mujerista* theology, all of these religious-theological elements are looked at through the lens of Latinas' struggle for liberation. Second, *mujerista* theology is communal theology: materials developed in this theology are gathered mostly during reflection sessions of groups of Latinas meeting in different parts of the U.S.A.

The first publication dealing with *mujerista* theology (then called Hispanic women's liberation theology) appeared in 1987. Therefore, because of its newness and because of the small number of academically trained Latina theologians at present, *mujerista* theology is but a small daughter born of the hope of Latina women for their liberation and the liberation of all peoples.

Isasi-Díaz [1993]; Isasi-Díaz/Tarango [1988/1993]; Isasi-Díaz et al., *JFSR* [1992]

ADA MARÍA ISASI-DÍAZ

Theology, Process For nearly two thousand years, Christian *philosophy and theology were constructed on the substructure of Greek philosophy. The basic category derived from the Greeks was "substance," or the notion that the ideal of reality was that which needed nothing other than itself in order to exist. Given the primacy of substance, corollary values such as "immutability" and "*transcendence" were given high status and were applied eminently to notions of God.

Twentieth-century physics has radically changed the basic understanding of reality. Relations considered accidental in substance philosophy are now considered constitutive and therefore essential to every existent reality. The former ideal of substance is now considered groundless, for "existence," as relation, and "substance," as that which needs nothing other than itself, are contradictory concepts.

It is no exaggeration to say that all twentieth-century theology reflects this fundamental shift in the understanding of how reality is constructed. There are far-reaching implications, particularly with regard to a *doctrine of God. Under substance-dominated theology, God as the ideal substance was logically required to be immutable, incapable of other than intellectual feeling, and essentially transcendent. Under relationally influenced theology, change is no longer inimical to God, the *suffering of God is introduced, and the *immanence of God plays as strong a role as the transcendence of God. Indeed, transcendence is itself qualified: God and the world transcend each other, and God and the world are immanent within each other.

While all twentieth-century theologies reflect relational suppositions about reality, only process theology and, to some extent, feminist theology have been intentional about explicating not only the theological results of the shift from substance to relation but the nature of the shift itself. Process theologians explore the *metaphysics of relations, develop doctrinal implications, and also (particularly in the writings of John B. Cobb, Jr.) give attention to the social and ethical implications of an interdependent, relational world. Feminist theologians tend to assume rather than to explore the shift, but they explicitly apply relational categories to new social, ethical, and theological understandings of human *community, women's *realities, and the relation between God and the world.

The major text for process theologians is Alfred North Whitehead's 1929 volume *Process and Reality.* Here Whitehead asks the question: What must fundamental reality be like to support the relational nature of things revealed through relativity and quantum physics? His suggested answer is that at its quantum level, reality is an event, not a substance. This event is the process whereby a becoming bit of reality actively receives influences from its entire past, integrating those influences into the new thing that is itself. Its existence is a "coming into being" through the process of responding to the energy it has received from its past. In this highly dynamic process, the becoming event aims at its own self becoming *and* toward its influence beyond itself, when it, in turn, adds its own energy to its successor events. Just as it must internally integrate the energies received from its past actual world, its successors must integrate its own energy.

This dynamic process is repeated infinitely throughout existence. Even though it applies as a model to microscopic existence, the countless permutations and interconnections that are achieved create the macroscopic world of the universe, and the middle world of rocks, trees, animals, and humans that we call "earth" and "society." But, whether one discusses the macroscopic, microscopic, or middle realm, one is talking about the effects of relations weaving connections among all things. A relational world is an interdependent world, created in and through the dance of energy and influence.

The greatest impact of such a worldview theologically is its reconstruction of the notion of God. If all existence is relational, and if God exists, then God must also be relational. Whereas an earlier age would have claimed the notion of "*Trinity" as a way of preserving relation and self-sufficiency, this is no longer possible. Selfhood, even for God, is created as external relations are drawn into the inner constitution of the self. Thus it is not possible to posit an existent reality that is not essentially related to a world outside itself. Whitehead sketches this in part 5 of *Process and Reality,* and most process theologians expend considerable energy critically expanding these suggestions. Their efforts explicate the grounds for arguing that God feels the world and hence participates in the world's suffering. God integrates the world within the divine becoming and hence redeems and transforms the world. God also continuously influences the world and hence is a constant creative and providential force in the world's continuous becoming.

Value in a process world cannot be confined either to deity or to humanity but extends throughout existence. If the basic element in all things, and not simply humans, is a decisive experience of a past in terms of how that past can be integrated in the becoming event, then everything has value, both intrinsically within itself and extrinsically in terms of its effects on others. The ethical effect of this is an increased value for all existent things, not simply with regard to their usefulness in the human community but with regard to themselves and their essential *interdependence with others within their environmental location. A process view leads to an ecologically sensitive view. Feminist theologies share this implication, since feminist theologies also build on sensitivity to the interdependence of all things.

Several feminists, such as Sallie McFague and Catherine Keller, have intentionally incorporated aspects of process metaphysics into their constructions of feminist theology, and nearly all feminists acknowledge the compatibility between feminist and process views of the world. Process thinkers also acknowledge their affinity with feminist theory. In an interdependent, relational universe, there is promising ground for critical and constructive *dialogue through the interface between feminist and process theology.

Case-Winters [1990]; Cobb/Griffin [1976]; Keller [1986]; McFague [1993]; Suchocki [1982/1989]

MARJORIE HEWITT SUCHOCKI

Theology, Queer Insights, stories, and reflections based on the *experiences of *lesbian, gay, bisexual, and transgendered people form the basis of what is called "queer theology." Thus far, it is a primarily male and not necessarily feminist phenomenon. But some lesbian scholars are starting to give feminist content to it. The term derives from the previously derisive word *queer,* used in a hostile *culture to describe homosexual persons. As part of a strategy of *liberation, some people have begun to appropriate the pejorative term *queer* in a positive, strategic, politically empowering way.

"Queer" in this sense includes all whose sexual identities and practices fall beyond the parameters of "hetero-patriarchy," all that is normative heterosexuality. It also implies that sexualities can and will change over a lifetime and that ethical reflections need to take these matters into account. This is the term of choice for many young lesbian, gay, bisexual, and transgendered people to signal their collectivity and *solidarity. The right wing mounts efforts to label all theologies done by or in solidarity with lesbian, gay, bisexual, and transgendered people as queer in the negative sense. But there is to be no mistake in usage here: what is queer is positive in queer theology.

Queer theology is the third stage of an evolving effort to bring the experiences of lesbian, gay, bisexual, and transgendered people into the theological mainstream on their own terms. The first was *the homosexual stage* (1972–82). It featured theological reflections by courageous writers such as Sally Gearhart and John McNeill who brought insights into same-sex love to the theological conversation. They inspired denominational support and action groups and sparked the creativity of other scholars. Homosexual theology in this period was normatively male, with little attention paid to the particularities of women's experiences. Just as "homosexual" eventually was seen as exclusively male rather than inclusively human, so, too, was homosexual theology eventually understood to be primarily expressing experience via male categories. This was simply inadequate.

The second stage, what is called *the lesbian/gay/bisexual stage* (1982–92), featured attention to the particularities of female and male experiences. Theologians such as Carter Heyward, Virginia Ramey Mollenkott, and Mary E. Hunt lifted up the specific and different contributions of lesbian women. Bisexual experiences were brought to the fore by James Nelson. Gay men's issues were raised by Kevin Gordon and Chris Glaser.

Differences were obvious in both priorities and content. For example, many women stressed *friendships, while many men focused on *sexuality. Many women were concerned to overhaul *patriarchal Christianity using feminist tools of analysis, while many men seemed content to tinker with it, fitting themselves into it as gay men. Ironically, it was lesbian women who led the way on *ordination, pushing their respective denominations to inclusivity.

HIV and AIDS intervened. The growing gap between lesbian women and gay men narrowed of necessity, through shared concern for people in the respective communities who lived with HIV/AIDS and were in need of support. New issues emerged: health care as a human right; belief in the Divine in the face of this health pandemic; how to act in solidarity with people who suffer, especially women of color and their dependent children; *violence, especially gay and lesbian bashing, as a common occurrence. At the same time, increased information and insight emerged about the lives of transsexual people, those who are born one gender but decide that they must, for their own integrity, live another gender experience.

It was in this far more complex context that *the third stage,* that of *queer theology* (1992–), began. Initial ideas include Jesus as gay, a parallel to liberation efforts to call Jesus feminist and black. The effort is to identify Jesus with the most marginalized people, in this case, gay men, and thereby stretch the reach of Christianity.

The "in your face" attitude of the activist group ACT-UP is an important inspiration for the tone of early queer theology. The most problematic issue is the extent to which "queer" is really another way in which male experience is normative, like homosexual and gay before it. However, queer theology with feminist input holds some promise, as well as a more collegial tone. It signals a new way to bring together people, especially young people, from a broad spectrum of "sexual outlaw" positions and invite their theological reflections. While one has always to remember that some are, as it were, "queerer" than others (i.e., queers of color are differently oppressed than European-American queer men), "queer" signals a willingness to recognize and work with those differences.

As young women, many of whom are bisexual, join the theological conversation, new insights will emerge that their older sisters simply never had. Their axiomatic concerns with ecology; sex as a right, not a privilege; and the eradication of violence mark the outline of a promising new theological framework. Its content remains to be filled in. But surely, the shape of the Divine and right relation with the world and its inhabitants will look different through a queer lens.

Goss [1993]; Hunt, in Clark/Stemmeler [1994]

MARY E. HUNT

Theology, Womanist Womanist theology is a Christian theological perspective emerging among African-American women in the United States. It derives its name from the African-American poet and novelist Alice Walker, who coined the word *womanist* in her book *In Search of Our Mothers' Gardens: Womanist Prose* (1983). Walker described a womanist as a black feminist or feminist of color. She emphasized black mother–daughter communication, women's thirst for knowledge, their responsible behavior, and their seriousness. Affirming women's *culture, their right to sexual preference, their emotional flexibility, their love of art, nature, spirit, and self, Walker portrays a womanist as also committed to the *survival of an entire people, male and female (xi–xii).

Informed by this definition, womanist theology owes its initial stage of development to black female scholars teaching theology, Bible, *ethics, sociology of religion, and *ministry in seminaries, colleges, and university religion departments. The goal of these scholars has been to bring black women's experience into the circles of Christian theological interpretation from which it has been excluded. Though most womanist scholars subscribe to this goal, their ways of achieving it differ. For some, *Christology is the avenue into theological discourse. Thus womanist theologian Jacqueline Grant affirms black women's inclusion in the *image of God by identifying Christ as a black woman. Kelly Brown Douglas suggests that the face of Christ gets its countenance from the *liberation struggle of oppressed black women.

Other womanist theologians bring black women's experience into theology by drawing on the African-American Christian community's traditions of biblical appropriation. Delores S. Williams proposes a prototype relation between the historical experience of African-American women and the biblical Hagar, whom the African-American community has appropriated for more than one hundred years. From an analysis of this prototypical relation, Williams arrives at issues for theological reflection. These issues are black women's surrogacy, survival, and quality-of-life experiences.

Though womanist theology is in its infancy, its pioneers are coursing through some of the most complex theological territory. The problems of *evil and *suffering as these have related and do relate to black women's history are explored by M. Shawn Copeland, Jamie T. Phelps, Cheryl A. Kirk-Duggen, Karen Baker-Fletcher, and biblical scholar Clarice Martin. These explorations are contained in Emilie Townes's edited work *A Troubling in My Soul: Womanist Perspectives on Evil and Suffering* (1993).

In *biblical studies, womanist scholars use unique *methodological strategies to translate the insights of their disciplines into the sociocultural language of black women. Renita Weems employs storytelling strategies to interpret biblical texts. Apparently her intention is to speak first to an audience of black churchwomen and then to the academy. Clarice Martin, a Christian testament scholar, has also taken seriously the audience of churchwomen as she gives attention to gender issues in the household codes in the Christian testament. These womanist biblical scholars began their careers establishing accountability with African-American churches.

In Christian ethics, womanists have focused on a variety of subjects. Marcia Y. Riggs considers black women's struggle with regard to the interstructured character of *racism, *sexism, and *classism. Katie G. Cannon and Jacqueline Carr-Hamilton make visible black women's historical and moral *agency in liberation struggle. Emilie Townes provides insight into womanist spirituality as social witness.

Through the work of womanist theologians and ethicists, the Christian *community is discovering the theological import of the liberation activity of some leading nineteenth-century African-American women. These women were vital to the development of the black Civil Rights movement in the United States. Theologian Karen Baker-Fletcher's work on the intellectual activist Anna Julia Cooper and ethicist Emilie Townes's work on Ida B. Wells have contributed to this discovery. In addition to the attention given to individual black women, there has also been womanist concern for the theological and ethical significance of the liberating character of African-American women's organizations. Marcia Y. Riggs has lifted up black women's club movement activity in the late nineteenth and early twentieth centuries. Cheryl Townsend Gilkes, a leading womanist sociologist of religion, focuses on gender issues in the life of African-American religious institutions and culture. She has done outstanding scholarship on black women in the Pentecostal tradition.

Womanist theology owns its kinship with black theology and white feminist theology. However, womanist theologians are critical of what they have identified as sexist elements in black liberation *theology and racist elements in white feminism. Jacqueline Grant exposed the absence of black women's experience in black liberation theology. Delores Williams traced racism in white feminism. Nevertheless, womanists emphasize that their movement is not separatist, except when black women's health is at stake. Therefore they welcome *dialogue with women and men who harbor a variety of perspectives and are aligned with many other theological schools of thought.

In theological circles, in grass-roots organizations, and among black churchwomen, womanist consciousness is developing rapidly. When womanist thought in theology, ethics, and biblical studies is introduced to black churchwomen, they gravitate toward it in large numbers. This is partly because womanists raise women's issues in a collective context, also inclusive of black men and children. Womanists have clearly stated that they understand their women's experience to be inclusive of women's work both with black men in the black Civil Rights movement and in community building and with other women building the women's movement and women's community. However, the womanist theological enterprise, like the white feminist theological enterprise, is not without opposition in both church and society. But each year, more and more black women enroll in seminaries across the United States, anxious to study womanist theology.

Many women continue to contribute to the development of womanist thought and action. Along with those womanist thinkers previously mentioned, there are some other significant scholars associated with the birth and development of womanist theology. These are Joan Martin, Toinette M. Eugene, Imani Sheila Newsome, Annie Ruth Powell, Joan Speaks, Joy Bostic, Ann Elliott, JoAnne Terrell, and Sallie Cuffee.

Baker-Fletcher [1994]; Cannon [1988]; Douglas [1994]; Grant [1989/1992]; Riggs [1994]; Sanders [1995]; Townes, ed. [1993]; Townes [1995]; Weems [1988]; Williams [1993a]

DELORES S. WILLIAMS

Third World The term *third world* was introduced by Alfred Sauvy, a French demographer who in 1952 compared the emergence of previously colonized countries with the move for independence of the third estate in France at the time of the French Revolution (Fabella). Many use the term in a geopolitical sense to indicate countries not understood to be in the *first world*, where "first" indicates noncommunist Europe, North America, Japan, Australia, and New Zealand. Some use *second world* to refer to countries in Europe previously referred to as "Communist bloc" nations.

In theological circles, the term has moved beyond geographic criteria. The Ecumenical Association of Third World Theologians (EATWOT), uses the term to describe a "social condition characterized by *poverty and *oppression: massive poverty surrounding small pockets of affluence with an oppressed majority facing a powerful elite" (Fabella, 3). For EATWOT, this designation includes parts of the first world where groups of people form an oppressed minority. While some advocate for the term *two-thirds world* to indicate the numerical superiority of those referred to as third world, others insist that the emphasis should be on the perspective offered by those from the "underside" rather than on numerical superiority.

Critiquing the use of the term is Shiva Naipul, who objects to the *imperialist West imposing the term on a large section of the world and thereby lumping together many disparate people (Thistlethwaite/Engel, 3). Others challenge those who would decide the "third-worldness" of a group or nation in a world where economic or political alliances can create dramatic shifts in the quality of life. Still others use "so-called" as a qualifier for these designations (i.e., "so-called third world"), indicating the tentativeness and the problems involved in such terminology. For centuries, men have expressed dominance by claiming to name their world, and women in that world. *Naming and claiming are sacred tasks that ought to be undertaken with care and respect.

Fabella [1993]; Fabella/Oduyoye [1988]; Fabella/Torres [1983]; Thistlethwaite/Engel [1990]

J. SHANNON CLARKSON

Tradition In classical Christian *doctrine, tradition referred to the beliefs, practices, and texts considered authoritative for Christian *faith and practice. Feminist discussion of tradition has centered on the question: Does the Christian tradition offer insights and practices liberating to women, or is the tradition unredeemably patriarchal? Judith Plaskow and Carol Christ distinguish between *revolutionary* feminists, who reject the Christian tradition as inextricably patriarchal, and *reforming* feminists, who argue that the tradition offers liberating insights crucial to the formulation of authentic theologies and practices (10).

Reformers typically identify some essential aspect of Christianity that can be used to critique and redress its many patriarchal expressions. Revolutionaries like Mary Daly deny the significance of this "essence" and urge women to look to their own experience, not to the past, to create a religious *philosophy that avoids the *sexism implicit in a tradition based on God the Father.

Reformers debate among themselves the content of the liberating essence of Christianity. Letty Russell distinguishes the patriarchal process by which Christianity developed from the theological principle that is the tradition's norm: that in Christ there is a *new creation. Rosemary Radford Ruether also designates a theological message as the essence of Christianity. For her, the prophetic call to *justice and *liberation is both the crux of the biblical message and the standard by which contemporary Christian thought and practice are to be guided.

Elisabeth Schüssler Fiorenza rejects theological tenets as the essence of Christianity, pointing instead to the life and *ministry of Jesus, as well as to the egalitarianism of the early "Jesus movement," as the locus of *revelation. Though the early church eventually came to mirror the *patriarchy of the larger society, at its beginning, a historical community of equals inspired by Jesus constituted Christianity. Schüssler Fiorenza contends that historical reconstruction of the Jesus movement, not appeals to theological principles, is the best way to use tradition as a source for theology.

Christ/Plaskow [1979]; Daly [1973]; Ruether/Russell, in Russell [1985a]; Schüssler Fiorenza [1983/1994]

VALARIE H. ZIEGLER

Transcendence This term was used in classical theism to designate the monarchical model of a disembodied, all-powerful God who exercised control over humanity, dwelling "above" in a *cosmos without connection to the world. Emphasizing the "otherness" of God, this oppressively powerful, dualistic view of divine–human relations in *patriarchal *stereotypes has led some to create parallel dualisms of male over female and transcendence over *immanence.

Among others, feminist theologians critique such traditional theological constructions, radically redefining and transforming the direction, shape, and character of God's relations to humanity and all *creation. Most feminists are critically suspicious of describing God as "wholly other," as such definitions have been used to keep women oppressively other-directed. The concrete issue raised by feminist ethicists is that transcendence–immanence *dualism distorts human moral *agency into passivity, inactivity, or *domination in the face of an "almighty Other."

In terms of God's relation to the cosmos, in an early feminist reconstruction Nelle Morton reclaimed women's spiritual revolution as both organic and transcending, redeeming a prepatriarchal history inclusive of women and of the earth. Sallie McFague, constructing models of God that organically address nuclear and ecological crises, advocates the "radicalization of divine transcendence," envisioning the universe metaphorically as God's body, where "God is present to us." McFague joins *ecofeminist Anne Primavesi in reintegrating divine transcendence with creation.

Redefining transcendence in human–divine relations, Carter Heyward claims transcendence is "crossing over," literally, making connections among humanity, all created order, and the fullness of the divine. For Heyward, and for ethicist Beverly Harrison (1985), transcendence is a *power shaped through religious intuition and spiritual resourcefulness, a power that overcomes alienation from others, affirming mutual relation as creative and redemptive.

Heyward and feminist theologian Elizabeth Johnson alike stress God's transcendent immanence. More recently, Johnson has aligned divine transcendence and the classical emphasis on divine incomprehensibility by speaking of the Spirit/Sophia, "She Who" transcends and enfolds reality. These and other Christian feminist theologians speak conceptually of divine immanence and transcendence as correlative and simultaneous.

The concept of transcendence and traditional views of God as "wholly other" will continue to pose challenging theological questions, particularly in interreligious *dialogues, feminist and womanist *ethics, and moral theory.

Heyward [1984]; Johnson [1992]; McFague [1993]; Morton [1985]

FREDRICA HARRIS THOMPSETT

Translation Translation is the art of transporting a message from one language to another. It is a communication process and involves interpreting the meaning of the message from the source language to the receptor language. Underlying the process of translation is the fact that the transfer involves analysis. Because such analysis takes place in someone's brain, the personal *experiences of that individual become part and parcel of the new message.

For countless generations, women have been absent from both the interpretation and the translation of the Bible. More recently, women biblical scholars have suggested that some of the existing Bible translations are loaded with biases of male authorship, both in the language used and in the meaning given to particular passages. An American abolitionist, Sarah Grimké, in 1937 advised women to be trained in biblical scholarship and involved in analysis of the biblical text. The first major women's translation was *The Woman's Bible* (1895), which was the work of twenty suffragists under the leadership of Elizabeth Cady Stanton.

Many women missionaries to "*third-world" countries have been involved in Bible translations in local languages, but they have not always been self-conscious about reading the Bible with the eyes of women. In many African cultures, for example, the name and concept of the deity are often female. It is also women who are responsible for the intervention between people and the deity. This concept was foreign to early missionary Bible translators, and most translations changed the word for God to adapt it to the Western, male God name. These kinds of translations, now accepted by churches, have helped to reverse the status of women in religious spheres, both in the church and in the local *cultures.

The present availability of scores of articles and books on the Bible written by women is raising new consciousness on biblical texts that will help new translations. The New Revised Standard Version is the most up-to-date translation which takes into account the participation and scholarship of both women and men. The translation team sought to reexamine the original Hebrew and the Greek text with gender consciousness. Changes in the language for humans have been made where necessary. Other translations, such as *An Inclusive-Language Lectionary,* have paid more attention to the God-language in the text, avoiding as many male pronouns as possible. However, it should be noted that it is not only the pronouns that determine people's perception of God. The whole socialization affects the way people think, even as it affects the way they transfer messages into other media.

Among the books that have attracted translations by women is the book of Genesis. Women have reexamined the language used for the *creation story in order to find the source of the interpretation that often puts the blame of the *Fall on women, as well as subordinating women because of the order of creation and the naming of Eve by Adam. For instance, the NRSV has restored the phrase "who was with her" that was left out of the RSV translation of Gen. 3:6. In the Hebrew text, both Adam and Eve are present for the conversation with the serpent. A topic of debate for Bible translators is always how to remain faithful to the meaning of the ancient texts while making it possible for modern readers to understand and relate to the message of the *gospel.

AILL [1983–85]; Metzger/Coogan [1993];

Newsom/Ringe [1992]; Nida/Taber [1974]; Stanton et al. [1895/1974]

MUSIMBI R. A. KANYORO

Trinity The traditional Christian *doctrine of the Trinity drew from Greek and Hebrew sources. From the Greeks, early Christian theologians derived the philosophical categories of immutability, substance, and total self-sufficiency; from the Jews and from the Christian experience of salvation, they drew on the religious categories of God interacting creatively, redemptively, and sustainingly with the world. The Greek sources issued into the notion of God as transcendent, omnipotent, omniscient, and omnipresent. The fundamental function of these categories was to provide an answer to the question of the world's existence. The Jewish sources and the Christian notion of God's action for us in Jesus Christ introduced the notion of God's relation to humanity, primarily answering the question of the human predicament of *evil and *sin.

The tension between the philosophical and religious categories was addressed through the classical notion of God as triune. The seeds of the doctrine stem from the philosopher Plotinus, who envisioned an absolute Deity of transcendent oneness that emanated into a dyadic principle of nous, or wisdom, which emanated again into the more complex world-soul. Christians condensed the triple emanations into an eternally triadic unity, God. Within this concept, God is everlastingly generating an "other" within God's self that perfectly reflects the generating God and therefore *is* God. The unity between God as generating (called "Father") and God as generated (called "Son") is also a perfect expression of God's being and hence is the third aspect of the Trinity (called "Spirit"). This description of the internal life of God was called the *immanent Trinity.*

This complex notion was then used to explain the actions of God in the world, under the supposition that as God is, so God acts. God as acting outside God's self was called the *economic Trinity,* or the external expression of the immanent Trinity. The internally generating God became externally creative, bringing the world into being. The internally generated God became externally incarnate, even while remaining transcendent within the inner life of God. As incarnate, God worked in the world for the world's salvation. The internally unifying Spirit completes the *redemptive work by unifying the redeemed world with God through Christ and with one another in the church. Thus the transcendent and immutable God is also the incarnate, relational God, and both together reflect the immanent and economic triune nature of God.

A major challenge to feminist theologians is to extricate male terms from the Christian *naming of God as Trinity. If maleness were simply attributed to God as one way among others of talking about God, the issue would be simpler, but as it is, "Father" and "Son" have become expressive of that which is uniquely Christian about the notion of Trinity. As Mary Daly noted in *Beyond God the Father,* "If God is male, then the male is God" (1973, 13).

Barbara Brown Zikmund, Marjorie Hewitt Suchocki, Catherine LaCugna, Sallie McFague, and Elizabeth Johnson go beyond simply rejecting the masculinity inherent within the notion of Trinity by retrieving the fundamental relationality of the doctrine for feminist use. Zikmund notes that the feminist valuation of relationality might find a strong grounding in the deep relationality of God as triune, often depicted in the Christian *tradition through imagery of "perichoresis," or mutual coinherence in what might be called the "dance of God." Suchocki notes that trinity bespeaks an irreducible diversity as necessary to unity in such a way that it could be used to lead to the valuation rather than rejection of "otherness" in human community. LaCugna examines the communal notion of the Trinity as a mandate for more communal ways of being human together. McFague highlights the metaphorical nature of all language, particularly in relation to God, and uses the terms *mother, lover,* and *friend* as *metaphors for God. Johnson, in a full-scale development of a feminist *appropriation of the Trinity, emphasizes not only its relationality but also its deep connection with the ancient female notion of *Sophia. Like McFague's, Johnson's metaphorical use of language points beyond the human context. Under this thesis, one could theoretically use male as well as female imagery in reference to the Trinity, but Johnson argues that only when female and male metaphors enter equally into Christian discourse for God can the normativeness of male language be overcome. Until such a time, female or neutral God-language is the best corrective to the prevalent *androcentrism. Therefore, she uses *spirit, wisdom,* and *mother* for the triadic naming of God.

In all of the above, the transformation of the Greek-inherited philosophical categories takes place either implicitly or explicitly, *immanence plays a stronger role than *transcendence, and the total self-sufficiency of God is overshadowed by the superlative relationality of God. In place of the immutability of God, there is emphasis on the vulnerability of a God who feels our situation. Finally, the deep androcentrism of the Trinity is radically undercut.

Johnson [1992]; LaCugna [1991]; McFague [1987]; Suchocki [1982/1989]; Zikmund, *CCent* [1987]

MARJORIE HEWITT SUCHOCKI

Truthfulness The term *truthfulness,* which by etymology and meaning belongs to the same family as *truth,* should not be confused with that term, for each has a shade of meaning that differs in important ways from the other. Truth is the fit or correspondence between reality and understanding. The horizon on which it moves is that of knowledge. Deviation from the truth is either error or falsehood.

Truthfulness consists rather of the fit or correspondence between what is said and the person who says it, the coherence of thought and action. The horizon on which it moves is that of *ethics and behavior, of living itself. Deviation from truthfulness is either deceit or a lie. Truthfulness has two levels: A person can be truthful with herself or himself, a behavior of which the opposite is self-deception. A person can also be truthful with others, acting before others as one in fact is, without duplicity.

Truth and truthfulness are inseparable. The search for truth on the plane of knowledge must bring one to truthfulness as an existential attitude. The first leads to the second, and the second is supported by the first. The inseparability of these two terms has broken down, however, in traditional theological reflection, where the search for truth on the nonethical plane predominates over the coherence of theory and practice, and the "intellectualist" dimension predominates over the existential. The starting point has not been a lived *faith (that is to say, a faith coherent with life) but rather a faith that is merely thought or, better still, rationalized.

Feminist theology attempts to overcome the rupture between these two dimensions and seeks their harmonization, placing the accent on truthfulness. One of the tasks to be accomplished in order to carry out that harmonization is to analyze critically, by appeal to a *hermeneutic of suspicion, the biblical texts that present women as lying and malicious—in sum, as not truthful. At the same time, feminist theology must recover those texts where women are seen testifying to the truth with their lives (which is the very meaning of truthfulness).

Christ/Plaskow [1979]; Farley [1986]; Rich [1976/1986]; Sakenfeld [1985]; Vivew [1986]

MARGARITA PINTOS
(TRANS. SHARON H. RINGE)

Unity and Diversity The search for unity commonly refers to the goal of the *ecumenical movement for one church of Jesus Christ, articulated in such phrases as "that all may be one" and "our oneness in Christ." The traditional view has held that though the goal we seek is unity, the unity we seek already exists—God's gift to us, symbolized in the *Trinity.

A statement of the Lambeth Conference of 1920 gives the classical definition: "It [the unity] is in God, who is the perfection of unity, the one Father, the one Lord, the one Spirit who gives life to the one Body." And again, in 1990: "The faithful as the body of Christ participate in the Trinitarian life of communion and love . . . a *koinonia* [community] rooted in and sustained by the communion of Father, Son and *Holy Spirit" (*Church and World* 1990, 23).

Three attributes traditionally point to a united church: the common confession of the apostolic *faith; the full and mutual recognition of *baptism, the *Eucharist, and the *ministry; and common ways of decision making and teaching authoritatively. Feminist theologies question whether such a vision of ecclesiastical unity can be regarded seriously in our day, when painful divisions of *race, gender, and class deny full participation to many. The church, in upholding the values of *orthodoxy and *purity, support of the status quo, and a uniformity of belief, ignores the experience of the diverse community.

In contrast, feminist theologies seek to build *community through a unity that incorporates *difference and is enriched through mutual respect for difference that celebrates uniqueness. In examining the Trinitarian formula as a basis for unity, feminist theologies call for an exploration of the classical male formulations of the Trinity, which emphasize gender over relationship. Is "Father, Son, and Holy Spirit" adequate to incorporate the *experience of women? Is not the unity of God denied in the failure to incorporate the female experience? And, feminists ask, what about Jesus? Does his significance as the basis for unity lie in being created a man or in being the Christ? Does his maleness point to the nature of God, or does the significance of the *incarnation event rest on Jesus' humanness, making possible an identification with all humankind and not just males?

The traditional view of Spirit is called into question as well, for *rûaḥ* is a feminine noun in Hebrew and related languages and thus brings a diverse dimension to the unifying Trinity. What about *Sophia/Wisdom as a dimension of the Creator God? God as mother? Thus only as reformulated can the Trinity be said to express the unity we seek.

What, then, constitutes a common confession? If there is tension between truth and diversity, how is truth or revelation defined, and by whom? Are there limits to diversity in theological imagination? to doctrinal diversity? to social diversity? Further, there is the call for genuine interaction between theology and other disciplines: sociology, *psychology, *philosophy, and science. Rather than two separate entities, church and world are to be viewed as *interdependent contexts. *Ecofeminism seeks a spirituality based on reverence for all *creation as the dynamic arena for the Creator's presence and activity. Further, feminist theologies call for interfaith *dialogue, with mutual respect among religions.

And, again, what about ministry? Can unity be realized when women are still denied *ordination in some churches? Can the Eucharist be a sign of unity when Christ's representative in serving it must be ordained, and in some bodies that means "male"? Finally, feminist theologians seek diversity through reforms that would call for not only full representation in leadership roles but also a process that would allow for more open and varied decision making, reflecting cultural and ethnic variety.

Kinnamon [1988]; May [1989; 1991]; Russell [1988]

MARY ANN LUNDY

Vegetarianism Vegetarianism is a diet of grains, vegetables, fruits, nuts, and seeds, with or without eggs and dairy products. While in recent years the term has, at times, been widened to include the eating of some dead bodies (most frequently fish or chicken), the term is not that elastic, as the meaning includes an objection to the direct destruction of life to enable consumption.

Traditionally viewed as the diet in paradise, given in Gen. 1:29, the practice of vegetarianism has a long history. Vegetarianism was often associated with progressive movements that sought to lib-erate slaves and workers, women, and animals (seen in eighteenth-century England, in nineteenth-century England and the United States, and in contemporary activism). Vegetarianism may be an expression of a spirituality committed to enhancing the individual and the world. In the developed countries, it is often a boycott of a form of animal-based agriculture (factory farming) that is seen as particularly cruel. In addition, many vegetarians reject the *violence they see as inherent in meat eating.

Feminist theology has only recently begun to examine the argument that a *patriarchal worldview recalls itself symbolically through meat eating. In fact, cosmologies and theologies can be seen as either reifying or challenging meat eating. For instance, the Christian *Eucharist derives its central symbolism from meat eating, specifically the eating of lambs (cf. Adams/Procter-Smith). Religious concepts of alienation, brokenness, and separation are being extended to include our treatment of animals. Ethical issues include recognizing that eating animals is a form of institutional violence and addressing whether *solidarity with the oppressed includes oppressed animals. Eating animals, it is now argued, is an existential expression of our estrangement and alienation from the created order. Would a body-affirming theology include the eating of animals? Feminist vegetarian theology argues that autonomous, antipatriarchal being is clearly vegetarian.

Adams [1990; 1994]; Adams/Procter-Smith, in Adams [1993]; Dombrowski [1984]

CAROL J. ADAMS

Violence, Institutionalized Violence is most commonly understood as physical force that produces injury or harm, but violence is not always physical force. The term *violence* may be applied equally to overt physical force or to covert structures of repression. What is common to both understandings, overt and covert violence, is *compulsion.*

New Theories of Violence. Feminist and womanist analyses, as well as *third-world *justice movements, have introduced the critical dimension of *power inequalities into the understanding of violence. Women, for example, have tried to understand their situation in society and to recognize the specific harms done to them. *Sexism, *racism, and *classism have come to be understood as violent because they exercise a kind of prior restraint that is coercive but which does not necessarily, in the moment of its exercise, employ overt physical force. This type of violence is called *institutionalized violence.*

The threat of force, as in the case of domestic violence, is always present, however. This threat or the actual exercise of force maintains the power inequalities, as in *patriarchal marriage or in sexual *violence. "Rape is a particular kind of human violence which carries powerful meanings in any culture, ancient or modern. In our own time, rape signals the asymmetrical relations of power between men and women in which women's bodies, always implicitly subject to male possession, are objectified, fetishized, and freely violated. The threat of rape appears for us as a perpetual assault upon woman's *autonomy, power and personhood" (Keefe, 79).

Hannah Arendt has written that the "extreme form of violence is One against All." She noted that "even slavery, the most despotic *domination we know of," did not require that the masters outnumber the slaves but that the masters have "a superior organization of power" (41). This was the model of South Africa under apartheid, where an elite minority of whites maintained a despotic system of economic, social, and political rights over the black majority by a superior organization of power as domination. The more power is organized unequally, the more violent the system.

When power is understood and defended as control or domination, overt physical force is then the *response* to a threat to that control. This is as true in patriarchal marriage as it is in the nature of war. War and its modern equivalents in "low-intensity warfare" or the "national security state" are, according to Quaker peace activist Jo Vellacott, responses of fear of the loss of control: "I am a dictator, yet I cannot force you to think as I want you to; I fling you in jail, starve your children, torture you" (in McAllister, 32).

Feminist and womanist analyses of power in a patriarchal society have pushed Christian thinking on violence out of the centuries-old, traditional paradigms of pacifism, just war, and crusade. While pacifism remains a strong and viable feminist position, it, too, as noted above in Vellacott, has broadened from its earlier roots in the individual conscience to a larger social analysis. "Just war" and "crusade" have been found to reify structures of power as domination. This is particularly true of the just-war emphasis on "right authority" as one of the principles of *jus ad bello,* the necessary principles to be enacted for war to be waged justly. Mary Potter Engel illustrates this in her unearthing of a "just *battering" tradition. Engel, in analyzing European, primarily French, medieval folktales and popular Christian *doctrine, found a group of criteria justifying the battering of wives that paralleled the just-war criteria. "Right *authority" for the battering of wives existed, for example, in the male headship in the household; the principle of the restraint on the use of force was represented in the injunction to husbands not to beat their wives "to death" or "permanently" injure them (in Engel/Wyman, 51–75).

Only recently has it been recognized that women themselves could constitute "right or competent authority" in just-war theory. This argument has been made in a recent attempt to put just-war theory at the service of thinking about *abortion (Steffen, 79–83).

Why Are Human Beings Violent? One of the most important contributions of feminist and womanist theology has been the reconsideration of the doctrines of *sin and *evil. The history of Christian thinking on violence has rested precisely on the view that the world is fallen and wholly sinful. This view holds that violence is inevitable because human beings are fallen and therefore depraved. Human violence belongs to the order of sin. Therefore, the appropriate response of the Christian would be to resist this evil by separation into personal holiness (the older pacifism), to work practically with the secular powers to restrain evil (just war), or actually to defeat the forces of sin (crusade).

A new paradigm, grounded in the civil rights struggle and the women's movement, called "just peace," offers an alternative to these paradigms that rest on a resignation to human evil and therefore justify the continued existence of violence. It is not, according to just-peace theory, inevitable that human beings, while sinful, fallen, and prone to conflict, will go to war out of that fallenness. How human societies regard war is a product of our social reflections. Human violence is not inevitable; it is the result of social and political systems that justify or repudiate certain forms of violence. This is well illustrated in Peggy Sanday's cross-cultural analysis of "rape-prone" or "rape-resistant" societies.

This is where a difference in feminist reflection has emerged, however. Some feminists regard women's nature as more essentially peaceful than men's. Mary Daly, in her important work *Gyn/Ecology: The Metaethics of Radical Feminism* (1978), makes the point that female energy is essentially biophilic, life-loving, and men's nature is essentially violence-prone, life-hating. However, an essential definition of women's nature as peaceful betrays a *race, class, and national bias, and it gives us few insights into why women are violent. A division into "patriarchal equals violence" and "feminism equals peace" may produce an *ideological blindness to women's participation in different kinds of violence (Brown, 199).

Arendt [1970]; Brown, in Kalven/Buckley [1984]; Engel, in Engel/Wyman [1992]; Keefe, in Camp/Fontaine [1993]; Plaskow [1980]; Sandy, *Journal of Social Issues* [1981]; Stanko [1990]; Steffen [1994]; Thistlethwaite [1989]; Townes, ed. [1993]; Vellacott, in McAllister [1982]; Villa-Vicencio [1988]

SUSAN BROOKS THISTLETHWAITE

Violence, Sexual Sexual violence is a broad category of behavior describing the sexual violation of one person by another, which may include rape, child sexual abuse, and sexual harassment. The conduct may be physical and/or verbal sexual contact or sexualized behavior, against the will of the victim or in a context in which authentic consent is not possible (e.g., child sexual abuse).

Definitions. A definition of *rape* begins with the Latin root *rapere*, "to seize." The focus in English is "to seize and carry away by force" or "to force another person to engage in sexual intercourse." The contemporary legal and applied definitions are gender-neutral and clearly indicate that rapist and victim can be of either or the same gender. Thus rape is the forced penetration of the mouth, anus, or vagina by a penis or an object, regardless of gender. However, because of the social inequities imposed due to gender, *race, age, and sexual orientation, the most likely victims of rape are women and children of all races and nondominant men.

Rape can be categorized according to the relationship between the rapist and victim. Stranger rape, the least common, occurs when a rapist attacks someone who is a stranger. (This would also include acts of rape carried out in wartime as acts of terror against a community.) Acquaintance rape, the most common, describes an assault on someone who is known to the assailant, usually friend, coworker, neighbor, etc. Date rape specifically describes an assault against one's dating partner. Marital rape describes an assault against one's *marriage partner or intimate.

Generally, *child sexual abuse* is divided into incestuous abuse, in which a child is sexually abused by a member of her or his *family, and child molestation, in which a child is sexually abused by a friend, an acquaintance, or a stranger. This abuse may involve an adult or older teen touching the child sexually or getting the child to touch the adult or teen sexually. It may also include taking photos of the child in sexualized poses (which often is linked to the child *pornography industry) or prostituting the child (i.e., forcing a child into *prostitution for the commercial benefit of the adult). Child prostitution is a very serious problem in many Asian countries, where the popularity of sex tourism combined with the fear of *AIDS creates a high demand for child prostitutes.

Sexual harassment generally refers to conduct that takes place in the workplace between a supervisor and employee or between coworkers. It is "the use of one's *authority or *power, either explicitly or implicitly, to coerce another into unwanted sexual relations or to punish another for his or her refusal; or the creation of an intimidating, hostile or offensive working environment through verbal or physical conduct of a sexual nature" (U.S. Federal Equal Employment Opportunity Commission, 1990).

Historical Discussion of Sexual Violence. Traditionally, sexual violence committed against women and children was regarded as a property crime against the husband or father of the victim. Hence laws focused only on the possibility of male assault on an adult female or child; the assault on an adult male by a male was often confused with homosexuality.

Historically, theological discussion about sexual violence has been minimal. Hebrew Scripture discusses rape as a property crime in the Deuteronomic passages and describes acts of sexual violence in the stories of the rape and murder of the unnamed concubine in Judges 19, the rape of Dinah in Genesis 34, and the incestuous abuse of Tamar in 2 Samuel 13. The issue of false accusation of rape is described in the story of Joseph and Potiphar's wife in Genesis 39. The threat of rape against men is described in Judges 19 and Genesis 19 (and subsequently is misinterpreted as homosexuality); in both of these stories, the men seek protection by offering virgin daughters to the assailants.

The understanding of sexual violence in the Christian *tradition perpetuated a tendency to blame the victim and not to find the offender culpable for his actions. From the *Malleus Maleficarum* (sixteenth century) to the canonization of Maria Goretti (twentieth century), *misogyny and the lack of accountability of men prevented addressing the ethical or theological implications of rape. Augustine discussed rape in the context of the question of whether or not suicide is an appropriate action for a victim of rape. The only contemporary theological discussion of sexual violence emerged from feminist theologians, beginning in the early 1980s (Fortune).

Theological and Ethical Discussion. Sexual violence must be understood theologically and ethically as *sin, i.e., as the physical, psychological, and spiritual violation of a person by another person that, as such, violates the bodily integrity of the victim as well as shatters any possibility of right relationship between the victim and abuser. Any form of sexual violence can destroy trust in the other person (when an acquaintance or family member) or in the basic security of one's world (when a stranger). So the secondary effect is to isolate or cut the victim off from her or his *community.

Because, traditionally, males have presumed to have sexual access to women and children, their acts of sexual violence have been minimized as normal male behavior ("Boys will be boys") and often overlooked by the legal system, religious communities, and the community in general. Victims of sexual violence have often been blamed for their own victimization: What was she wearing/doing/thinking? Seldom have men been held accountable for their acts of sexual violence against others.

The rhetoric of the 1970s brought with it new awareness: "Rape is violence, not sex," i.e., acts of sexual violence are not the result of "uncontrollable male sexual urges toward attractive women." The traditional understanding had meant that sexual violence was "sexual" and therefore natural and acceptable. The shift in understanding asserted that sexual violence is an act of violence and aggression in which sex in used as a weapon. While this was an important insight at the time, it failed to comprehend the eroticization of violence in the dominant *patriarchal *culture that led sexual violence to be understood as sexual. The 1990s bring even further awareness: in a culture in which violence is eroticized and *sexuality is largely defined by what men choose to do sexually, there is an inevitable blurring of the line between sexual activity and sexual violence. This understanding presents a particular challenge to those who want to make a qualitative distinction between sex and sexual violence (Adams/Fortune).

Theologically, our understanding of rape reflects our understanding of God and of the nature of persons. If the world as we know it is the created order intended by God, then one might conclude that God created two categories of people, victims and victimizers, and these categories are generally gender specific. But there are societies in which sexual violence does not exist; the people, male and female, do not comprehend the concept as described by anthropologists (Benderly; Ligo). What is most interesting about these societies is the way in which their gender *relationships are organized: women are respected, share power equally with men, participate fully in religious leadership that involves a female deity and/or a male/female deity, and the community seeks harmony with the environment. Thus sexual violence is unnatural, not part of the created order or the nature of humans and not ordained by God as inevitable.

Within Western cultures today, to assert that sexual violence is unnatural and unacceptable runs counter to the dominant norms. Yet this assertion is consistent with the portrayal of God in Hebrew and Christian scriptures as one who stands with the vulnerable and powerless and speaks *judgment against those who choose to use their power in ways that harm others. This assertion also makes it possible to distinguish between sexual violence and sexual activity, condemning the first and affirming the second. To make this distinction, one must assert an ethical norm for sexual relationships that affirms shared power, *equality, authentic consent, and shared *responsibility. This context precludes coercion, aggression, physical force, and *domination and seeks to protect those who are vulnerable due to particular life circumstances (e.g., age). Condemning sexual violence requires assertion of justice making in its aftermath: support for victims/survivors and accountability for offenders within both religious and secular communities.

Adams/Fortune [1995]; Benderly, in *Science* [1982]; Fortune [1983]; Ligo *IGI* [1993]; Trible [1984]

MARIE M. FORTUNE

Virgin Birth In white, Western, male-oriented theology, one interpretation of the Christian *tradition of Jesus' birth from the Virgin Mary is focused on Catholic dogma, which, since the Lateran Synod of 649, venerates Mary as "forever virgin." The other is focused on interpretation according to the "History of Religion" school, namely, that the Marian legends in Matthew 1 and Luke 1—2 were influenced by Hellenistic *mythologies and—because they are tied to a particular time—no longer have significance for *faith.

Two different ways of reinterpreting this Christian tradition have crystallized in feminist theologies: (1) rejection of the virgin birth as an *androcentric Christian myth that supports *patriarchy and denigrates women, and (2) feminist reinterpretation of the virgin birth as the "beginning of the end of the patriarchal order" (Chung). Feminist rejection of the tradition of Mary's virginal childbearing is based primarily on the contrast, inimical to sexuality and women, between sinful Eve and virginal Mary. In this contrast, sexuality is negative and women are defined and degraded as seductresses and seducible (by Satan).

Feminist reinterpretations refer positively to women's traditions of Marian veneration in popular devotional practices. For example, the Virgin of Guadalupe, in her theophany to an Indian, becomes a partisan of Indian peoples against the white man; she speaks their language and affirms their value against the colonial rulers, associating herself with the people's *goddess (Bingemer/Gebara). For some feminists, virginity represents independence from patriarchal role assignments and thus women's *freedom from *marriage; it does not necessarily mean sexual *asceticism. Mary's virginal childbearing is also seen as exclusion of the masculine from the birth of a new humanity (cf. *Mariology).

In feminist interpretation of Matthew 1 and Luke 1—2, other perspectives on virginity emerge. The NT texts reveal God taking the side of a rejected and endangered woman and her child, because they show that the historical Mary was seduced or raped (Schaberg). In contrast, the texts can be read as legends of a birth without masculine begetting, a fatherless birth with no notion of god as begetting; a notion which would subject virgin birth to the patriarchal myth of begetting. Mary's miraculous pregnancy expresses the exaltation of the lowly and the *liberation of oppressed people (Schottroff). In biblical tradition, *rûaḥ* (cf. *pneuma,* Luke 1:35) is a feminine creative power, and Israel's idea of God rejects any notion of a God who begets. In any case, the NT knows nothing of a virginal birth in the sense of later church dogma. The fact that *parthenos* bears the child Jesus (Matt. 1:23; Luke 1:27) means that Mary was an unmarried woman, probably about twelve and one-half years old, just at the age when women usually married.

Bingemer/Gebara [1989]; Chung [1990]; Schaberg [1987]; Schottroff [1995]

LUISE SCHOTTROFF

Virtue Virtue is a disposition or habitual inclination to act in conformity with a given account of human flourishing (or what is sometimes called "the human good").

In a virtue-based ethical theory, the "good" or "moral" person is one who has developed dispositions conducive to appropriate behavior or, more broadly, to good living. In this context, the term *virtue* implies traits of character rather than of personality; that is, they are learned or acquired (not inborn) dispositions. A virtue ethic may emphasize a number of desirable virtues (e.g., courage, magnanimity, temperance, wisdom, and patience); a smaller set of primary or "cardinal" virtues (e.g., fortitude, temperance, prudence, and *justice); or even a single unifying virtue (such as justice or practical wisdom). Certain classical theories (e.g., Aristotelian) maintain a distinction between intellectual and moral virtues; the truly good person possesses virtues of both kinds, but they govern different human capacities. Intellectual virtues (such as prudence) orient the powers of the mind toward the good, while moral virtues (such as fortitude, temperance, and justice) orient the powers of the will. To the traditional table of cardinal virtues, religious thinkers such as Thomas Aquinas add *faith, hope, and charity. Acquired through divine initiative, these theological virtues serve to orient the *soul toward God as the ultimate human good. Virtue-based theories differ in their account of the source and nature of the virtues, but they are generally characterized by a view of the moral life as a developmental or educative process occurring within and with reference to particular communities.

It is this emphasis on the communal and the particular that explains, at least in part, the recent resurgence of interest in virtue *ethics. Increasing dissatisfaction with Kantian-influenced moral thinking, with moralities that are predicated on reason's grasp of universalizable and objective principles, has inspired a return to frameworks that assume a more complex moral *psychology and can accommodate diverse and culturally specific understandings of the human good. Not surprisingly, some contemporary feminists find the language of virtue helpful for shaping an alternative, women-centered "morality of connection." Both Nel Noddings (1984) and Sarah Ruddick (1989) ground the moral life in those *relationships and human practices, such as mothering, through which the dispositions necessary for sustaining intimacy are formed. Overturning the standard agent-oriented virtues (such as courage), these authors lift up relational virtues, e.g., "caring," "reciprocity," and "attentive love." Anne Baier (1994) also modifies traditional virtue theory, supplementing long-standing emphases on *justice with communitarian virtues such as "appropriate trust." Efforts of this sort aim not at articulating a "morality for women" but at incorporating women's life-embracing herstory into the social narratives from which character ideals are drawn.

But other feminists urge caution. Traditional paradigms of theological and moral virtue have both ignored and distorted women's experience. Too often the virtues held out to women have described not the "good person" but the "elite man" or have enjoined feminine dispositions of servility: modesty, selflessness, long-suffering, meekness, and domesticity. Moreover, in equating virtue with self-control, the most influential theories assumed the opposition of *reason and *emotion; the virtuous person moderates his or her passions, chooses well the mean between extremes. Critical retrieval, they insist, must carefully avoid the mere replication of enshrined dualities: the rearticulation of feminine versus masculine virtue or the substitution of new versions of virtuous self-diminishment for old. To be truly transformative, a feminist virtue ethic must rest on an adequate anthropology (one that celebrates passionate rationality), promote gender-integrated ideals of character, and presuppose that questioning the virtue of whatever virtues women are asked to accept is a moral responsibility (Daly, 264).

Baier [1994]; Daly [1978]; Noddings [1984]; Ruddick [1989]; Tong [1993]

MAURA A. RYAN

Virtue, Womanist In the African-American community, the aggregate of the qualities that determine desirable ethical values regarding the uprightness of character and soundness of moral conduct must always take into account the circumstances, the paradoxes, and the dilemmas that constrict blacks to the lowest range of self-determination.

In *Black Womanist Ethics* (Cannon 1988), virtue is the moral wisdom that women of African ancestry live out in their existential context which does not appeal to the fixed rules or absolute principles of the white-oriented, male-structured society. African-American women's appraisal of what is right or wrong and good or bad develops out of the various coping mechanisms related to the conditions of their own cultural circumstances. In the face of this, black women have justly regarded *survival against tyrannical systems of *race, sex, and class *oppression as a true sphere of moral life.

Fundamentally, virtue is inseparable from three principles: "invisibility dignity," "quiet grace," and "unshouted courage." *Invisibility dignity* is the self-celebration of survival against great odds. Living with the tension of the irrational facticity of life, women of African ancestry learn how to deal with insults and humiliations of the larger society so that they do not make the wrong step or give the wrong response, which could jeopardize their lives. *Quiet grace* is the search for truth. It is defined as looking at the world with one's own eyes, forming judgments and demythologizing whole bodies of so-called social legitimacy. *Unshouted courage* is a virtue evolving from the forced *responsibility of black women. In its basic sense, it means the quality of steadfastness, akin to fortitude, in the face of formidable oppression. The communal attitude is far more than "grin and bear it." Rather, it involves the ability to "hold on to life" against major opposition. Virtue is thus the practical attitudes and habits adopted in obedience to these three principles.

KATIE GENEVA CANNON

Whore of Babylon The whore of Babylon appears in the book of Revelation 17 and 18. Traditionally, she represents the *evil, imperial government (usually the Roman Empire). Revelation tells the story of the splendor and final *judgment of the whore in great detail. The whore wears fine linen and jewels and rides a great scarlet beast with "seven heads and ten horns." She carries "a golden cup full of abominations and the impurities of her fornication; and on her forehead was written a name, a mystery: 'Babylon the great, mother of whores and of earth's abominations.'" The name of the whore exposes her evil practices: *prostitution, sexual promiscuity, and *idolatry, but also blasphemy and imperial wealth. Her beauty is horrific; she wears finery but rides a monster and is drunk with the blood of believers in Jesus; she is monstrous.

The judgment on the whore of Babylon is a violent death. Those who profit from her evildoing (kings, merchants, and sailors) will turn against her, stripping, eating, and burning her. Her followers will, in turn, be eaten by the birds of midheaven in Revelation 19. The whore is the great city that is overthrown by God. The believers are called to come out of her, and a great litany celebrates the death of the whore: "Fallen, fallen is Babylon the great!" In liberation readings of the text, the whore is the oppressive, demonic political power that is conquered by God for the liberation of the people of God. Some recent feminist readings question the liberatory value of the representation of evil in a female body and character and the connection of evil with female *sexuality.

Boesak [1987]; Collins [1984]; Garrett, in Newsom/Ringe [1992]; Pippin [1992]

TINA PIPPIN

Wicca / Neopaganism Wicca is a branch of modern neopaganism consisting of the revival of religious practices believed to date to pre-Christian times and centered on nature worship, magic, seasonal rituals, and the invocation of goddesses or a single *goddess. Neopaganism has its recent roots in England in the 1950s and was popularized in the United States primarily in the 1970s and 1980s. There has been considerable controversy within the neopagan community over whether it is the revival of a preexisting religion or the creation of a new one. Some neopagans believe they are reconstructing the dominant religion of pre-Christian Europe, relying on folk religious survivals or on purported lineages of "authentic" *witchcraft. But especially in North American neopaganism, most practitioners borrow religious elements from the so-called major *world religions (particularly Eastern ones) and from tribal religions around the globe.

Wicca, often called "witchcraft," sticks closer to its European roots than do other branches of modern neopaganism (though it may not insist on folk survivals or direct transmission in constructing its religious practices). Very shortly after its immigration to (and independent invention in) America, Wicca became intensely interesting to feminists, and uniquely feminist forms of belief and ritual were developed. In particular, feminist Wicca worshiped female deities to the exclusion of gods, practiced in female-only groups, developed rituals geared to women's life-cycle events, and, indeed, defined Wicca as a religion by and for women. Feminist and nonfeminist Wicca continue today but are overshadowed by more broadly conceived spiritual movements (again, both feminist and nonfeminist) that borrow freely from non-European religions. White feminist Wiccans frequently claim that Wicca is the only appropriate religious option for white women who wish to avoid cultural *imperialism, while those who borrow religious resources from non-European sources regard Wicca as overly narrow and Eurocentric.

Adler [1986]; Eller [1993]; Jade [1991]; Starhawk [1989]

CYNTHIA ELLER

Widows A widow is a woman whose husband has died. In some parts of the early church, "the widows" were an order of *ministry. The Jerusalem church apparently supported widows in its midst (Acts 6). First Timothy 5:9–16 (early second century) shows the existence of an order of widows, with specific requirements given for "enrollment," especially age (over sixty) and reputation. Second-century writers mention the widows; Polycarp calls the widows "an altar of God" and tells them to pray ceaselessly for the church. This image is often used later, with changing meanings: Tertullian (ca. 204) opposed second marriages (for everyone) and admitted into "the widows" a woman only twenty years old. Tertullian also argued that penitents seeking restoration to the community should prostrate themselves before the widows and the presbyters. Did both groups sit in special seats in worship?

By the late third century, the *Didascalia apostolorum* elaborates and diminishes: widows should be carefully selected, and the bishop should accept money for their support only from honorable donors, for whom they will pray. Widows should, like the altar of God, stay put and not be gadding about, asking or answering questions, or baptizing anyone. Widows cannot teach or baptize because Jesus sent only men out as "the Twelve," and had it been lawful, he would have been baptized by Mary. Perhaps some widows were teaching and baptizing, and a clerical *hierarchy in an increasingly imperialized church needed to stop this.

Commentators have assumed that the "widow as altar" image meant widows were passive recipients of the community's support. Recent feminist analyses argue the widows had an active ministry of *prayer that was gradually reduced in favor of the deaconesses, a group more easily managed by the bishop. Knowing about the widows both reveals some arguments still used today to deny ministry to women and undercuts others.

Osiek, *Second Century* [1993]; Thurston [1989]

NADIA M. LAHUTSKY

Wilderness *Wilderness* (Heb *midbar)* in the Bible is fundamentally a geophysical term applied to agriculturally unexploited areas, areas immediately bordering settlements, or arid zones that lie completely outside of human domination. It is thus a place of desolation, exile, danger, and death. Because it is closely identified with nature, it is perceived as indomitable, unpredictable, and destructive. Conversely, wilderness can also be a place of refuge and *revelation.

Wilderness takes on mythical significance in the Bible and in Jewish and Christian theological *tradition, representing the forces of chaos, the antithesis of **shalom,* often portrayed as "paradise" or the "Promised Land." Restoration of shalom (paradise) is sometimes expressed in terms of a conquering or transformation of chaos (nature/wilderness; Isa. 11:6–9; 35:1–10). Wilderness also typifies exile and *judgment, as well as the temporary, transitional aspect of the journey toward *freedom and fulfillment, based on the exodus paradigm.

Women have found in wilderness a potent symbol to express a variety of religious *experiences and theological beliefs. Many draw analogies from the story of Hagar (Gen. 16:1–16; 21:8–21). Womanist theology in particular views Hagar in the wilderness as a prototype of African-American women's experience, representing "a near-destruction situation in which God gives personal direction to the believer and thereby helps her make a way out of what she thought was no way" (Williams 1993a, 108).

Feminist liberation *theology identifies closely with the Israelite wilderness experience, finding in it a paradigm of women's own journey amid continued *oppression, having been technically set free yet still longing for and moving toward the Promised Land of full *equality and harmony. *Ecofeminism affirms the linking of women and nature and maintains that *patriarchalism is responsible for the oppression of both. For ecofeminists, "wilderness" signifies the wasted condition of planet Earth under patriarchal domination. They assert that women are uniquely suited to and called to lead the way in averting complete global destruction and moving humankind toward Earth's restoration.

Adams [1993]; Ruether [1975]; Williams [1962]; Williams [1993a]

CHERYL ANNE BROWN

Witchcraft Witchcraft has been considered the use of magical practices and sorcery in order to cause harm *(maleficium)* to people, animals, and objects. In the Christian West, the notion of witchcraft assumes collaboration of individuals (usually old or single women, "witches") with the devil, which empowers them to use supernatural powers to accomplish *evil. The church originally treated witchcraft as superstition, but in the thirteenth century it became a crime and was associated with *heresy. The inquisitors Heinrich Kramer (Henricus Institoris) and James Sprenger compiled in 1487 the "Hammer of Witches" *(Malleus Maleficarum)*, which became the legal and theological guide for forensic practices, including torture and denunciation. Persecutions of witches reached a peak in the sixteenth century, when up to one hundred thousand witches were tried and as many as sixty thousand executed, 80 percent of them women. Under torture, many admitted to attending witches' sabbaths, copulating with the devil, and signing a pact with him to cause harm. Such confessions further reinforced the belief in witchcraft and in women's culpability.

*Misogynist attitudes of medieval clerics helped to create the legal view of women as dangerous and lustful. But at the village level, where most denunciations took place, accusations had less to do with learned views of witchcraft than with local rivalries. Interestingly, women often denounced other women. This could be attributed to conformism in a *patriarchal society, to competition among women for social standing within the community, or to women's prominent role as healers. *Widows, who were economically poor and outside patriarchal control, were especially vulnerable to denunciation. Most historians therefore agree that the charge of witchcraft was sex-related (even if not sex-specific).

Egyptologist Margaret Murray and some feminist scholars have argued that witchcraft was a survival of women-centered, pre-Christian religion and folk beliefs and that witches were healers and midwives who were persecuted by male competitors. These views have been largely discredited. However, some of the modern neopagan feminist groups such as *Wicca refer to themselves as witches and adopt practices that they believe to be remnants of pre-Christian witchcraft.

Ankarloo/Henningson [1990]; Barstow [1994]; Karlsen [1987]; Larner [1983]; Thomas [1971]

MOSHE SLUHOVSKY

Womanist Voice One of the effects of *patriarchy is the subjugation of women's voices. Women who have resisted *sexism have been vocal in demanding sociopolitical, religious, and economic *justice. The voices of women of color have been silenced or ignored by sexist sociopolitical structures and by racist ones, giving rise to a distinctive understanding of "voice" among historical and contemporary black women who have challenged sexism and *racism. Contemporary womanists challenge interlocking systems of *oppression: racism, *classism, homophobia, and ecological abuse.

In the 1830s, Maria Stewart, a self-taught black woman intellectual who felt inspired by God to challenge socioeconomic structures of slavery and racial and gender inequality, was the first woman in America to raise a political argument before a mixed audience of women and men. In 1859, Sojourner Truth delivered her "Ain't I a Woman" speech, asserting humanity and womanhood in response to a white male heckler who questioned both. In 1892, Anna Cooper described the voices of black Americans as "one muffled strain" and as "a jarring cadenza" that startled those who heard it. Within that chord, the "one mute and voiceless note" was that of the "sadly expectant Black woman" (Baker-Fletcher, 132–50, 189–95).

Such imagery recalls more violent images than Cooper presents: the binding, whipping, rape, and gagging of black women who dared to assert their humanity and liberty under slavery and Jim Crow. Sometimes the very tongues of runaway slaves were cut out upon recapture. "Mute" refers to black women's subjugation. Resistant to a history of silencing, Cooper argued that black women speak on their own behalf. No one else can speak for them.

Likewise, contemporary theologian Jacquelyn Grant defines a womanist as "one who has developed *survival strategies in spite of the oppression of her *race and sex in order to save her *family and her people. . . . Black women speak out for themselves." She warns against the "deadly consequence of silence." "Black women," she explains, "must speak up and answer in order to validate their own experience" (213). Delores Williams, examining the biblical story of Hagar, who finds a God who provides vision for survival, points out that Hagar is the only woman in the Bible who *names* God. Linking Hagar's story with the social-historical experiences of ordinary black women, she suggests the voices of such women possess *power to name their experience and their God.

Emilie Townes warns that white feminist theologians must wrestle with sisters of color and agree to disagree rather than require conformity to one theological or ethical perspective. Relevance of diverse worldviews, she argues, does not take place in a monologue. She proposes the "ring shout," a traditional black religious practice, as a *metaphor for *equality of diverse voices. The ring shout, unlike a monologue or a chorus, she explains, is not performance-oriented and does not focus on harmony. "There are no observers, only pilgrims in the ring" (1–2). Each pilgrim gives voice to her or his *faith story and shares it with others. Cooper described *freedom and equality as a "singing something" within humankind, traceable to the Creator. Her metaphor suggests a call for prophetic response to God's message of freedom and equality (Cooper 1945; Baker-Fletcher, 4–5].

As Townes warns, such prophetic response must be diverse. This is vital not only for feminists in relation to womanists but for womanists in relation to one another. The faith stories of black women are many, revealing diverse strategies for survival, *liberation, and wholeness.

Baker-Fletcher [1994]; Cooper [1945]; Cooper, in Washington, [1988]; Grant, in Wilmore [1989]; Townes, *The Womanist* [1994]; Williams [1993a]

KAREN BAKER-FLETCHER

Women-Church Women-Church is a global movement of feminist base communities and ad hoc women's groups engaged in redefining "church" through creative ritual, mutual support, and a newly emerging spirituality. Originating in the United States as an alternative to *patriarchal religious practice, Women-Church grew out of the Women's Ordination Conference and was formally recognized and named at a major conference titled "Woman Church Speaks" in Chicago in 1983. Two subsequent conferences, "Women-Church Convergence: Claiming Our Power" in Cincinnati (1987) and "Women-Church: Weavers of Change" in Albuquerque (1993), confirmed that the proliferation of grassroots women's groups constituted a genuine movement of the Spirit within and beyond the institutional church, giving visibility to its practices and purpose. Consequently, numerous local groups that seek to support one another in living out of their own *faith experience, together with a coalition of feminist organizations, have come to be known as Women-Church.

Women-Church is *ecumenical in its self-understanding and unconcerned about denominational boundaries, despite its predominantly Catholic beginnings. Open to women of all faiths and to those with no explicit affiliation, Women-Church is committed by its very nature to the power of *unity within diversity and to *justice for women everywhere, beginning with the church. Organizationally, it consists primarily of spontaneous initiatives that are locally based and unconnected. This phenomenological network has no designated central organization, no permanent leadership, and no formal membership, although WATER (Women's Alliance for Theology, Ethics, and Ritual) in Maryland functions as a resource for encouraging new initiatives and for keeping an ongoing directory of groups that choose to be listed there. Because groups are always coming into and going out of existence, and because most groups prefer to remain invisible or unregistered, the list is always fluctuating and gives no indication of the extent of the movement's growth.

Women-Church embraces not only those communities who self-identify as such but also groups that reflect Women-Church characteristics, whether or not they know it. It also includes individuals who no longer belong to a local group yet remain committed to its values, and those who are seeking such a group but are unable to find one. Women-Church is international, with communities in North America, Latin America, Europe, Korea, Australia, and New Zealand. The first public Womanchurch was founded in Seoul, Korea, in 1989 and pastored by the Reverend Young Kim. A journal titled *Women-Church* and coedited by Erin White and Hilary Carey was first published in Sydney, Australia, in 1987.

Theologically, Women-Church sees itself as an exodus community coming out of exile, a Spirit-church within the *tradition. It has enabled many women to remain in the church even as they struggle to transform it. For some, it is an alternative way of "being church"; for others, it is an alternative to church, a parallel tradition rooted in women's wisdom as revealed by the Spirit within. It was conceived not as a separatist movement ultimately exclusive of men but as an interim strategy for women's growth and for their full *liberation.

At the heart of Women-Church is the phenomenon of women's awakening. In small, intimate gatherings, women tell their *stories. As they find their voices and are affirmed, they become aware of their own *oppression, affirm themselves, claim their *power, and are mobilized to seek change. Through innovative *liturgies, *rituals, symbols, and songs, through an experience of genuine community and a holistic spirituality that truly nurtures and inspires, women are envisioning a just world where we and our children are fully included, humanely treated, and free to image and worship God in the truth of our own experience.

Neu/Hunt [1993]; Ruether [1985]; Winter, *CCent* [1989]; Winter/Lummis/Stokos [1994]

MIRIAM THERESE WINTER

Women's Organizations North American Christianity has been profoundly shaped by women's organizations. Many Protestant congregations owe their survival to Ladies Aid societies. Large-scale denominational efforts were organized and financed by women's missionary societies. The Roman Catholic *mission to America depended on women in religious orders.

Ladies Aids were indispensable to many congregations, particularly those on the frontier. Ladies Aids raised money by charging members small monthly dues, selling handmade goods at bazaars, and hosting suppers and socials. The money was used for church expenses, innovative programs such as Sunday schools, and new building requirements such as church parlors and kitchens. Women's altar guilds prepared the communion meal and decorated the altar.

By 1830, Protestant women organized a large number of local reform societies dedicated to the eradication of Sabbath-breaking, intemperance, slavery, sexual immorality, *poverty, crime, and disease. Women also began to build educational institutions for female Christian workers; the first was Mount Holyoke Female Seminary in 1836.

After the Civil War, Protestant women organized regional and national federations, the largest dedicated to home or foreign missions and temperance. The interdenominational Woman's Union Missionary Society of America for Heathen Lands was founded in 1861, the Women's Christian Temperance Union in 1874. The Woman's Foreign Missionary Society of the Methodist Episcopal Church was the first denomination-wide women's organization, in 1869. Northern Presbyterians organized in 1879, Episcopalians in 1874, Southern Methodists in 1878, Augustana Lutherans in 1891, National Baptists in 1900, and so on. Women's missionary societies raised millions of dollars, supported thousands of missionaries, built hundreds of institutions at home and abroad, and published what were at that time the best educational materials on foreign cultures and domestic social problems. They were also important avenues toward social respectability and self-improvement for African-American women and a safe place in which immigrant women could experiment with "Americanization." Women found *friendship and mutual understanding in their church groups.

Roman Catholic women have had several options for organized *religious life in North America. The first convents were founded in Mexico in the mid-sixteenth century. These were usually cloistered and were centers of spirituality and *prayer and places for the protection and *education of elite women. Because convents did not have room for all who wanted to take vows, other options were made available. The *beateros* allowed women to make simple vows to live a devout and chaste life; *recogimientos* were self-secluded groups of women who lived together under the guidance of a priest or friar. Traditional religious orders were expanded by third orders, which were branches for laywomen who made simple, revocable vows. Sodalities, or confraternities, are lay organizations dedicated to fostering the cult of a patron saint and to mutual aid.

In the 1700s French nuns brought with them to the New World the missionary zeal of the Counter-Reformation. They established houses of European orders and organized hospitals and schools. The first noncloistered religious community for women in the New World, the Congregation of Notre Dame, was founded in Montreal in 1657.

Female activism within the Roman Catholic Church reached a zenith in the 1800s. Women's orders dedicated to helping new Catholic immigrants and to solving other social ills sprang up everywhere—119 in all. Nuns served in city, frontier, and Civil War hospitals and opened schools in town after town. There were far more nuns in the United States than priests, and the bulk of the *work fell on female shoulders. Despite the rigors of the work, religious orders gave women *freedom from *marriage, opportunity for meaningful work and leadership roles, and communities of friendship and *care.

Higginbotham [1993]; Hill [1985]; Mooney [1990]; Prelinger [1992]; Zikmund, in Carroll/Roof [1993]

BETTY A. DEBERG

Work When the topic of work is discussed in traditional theology, it is usually to articulate a theology of work. Although orders such as the Benedictines valued manual labor as part of the Christian life, prior to the Protestant Reformation work (both productive and reproductive) was viewed theologically as little more than a curse (Genesis 3). Martin Luther reappropriated the concept of vocation, which had been limited to the monastic life, to give theological value to labor in the workaday world. Max Weber (1968), among others, observed that the Protestant work ethic which developed from the theological insights of Luther and Calvin contributed to the rise of capitalism. Dorothee Soelle is one of few feminist theologians to critique this ethic, examining its contribution to the development of alienated labor and comparing such labor to *prostitution. Self-expression, social-relatedness, and reconciliation with nature are Soelle's theoretical principles for good work.

In dominant theologies, work is understood as productive labor, paid work, performed by men, not women's reproductive labor or unpaid domestic work. Feminist theologians such as Clare Fischer draw on feminist theory to analyze the sexual division of labor, the separation of the spheres of home and work, and occupational segregation of "men's jobs" and "women's jobs" as dynamics contributing to discrimination against and devaluation of women and their work. Feminist theory deconstructs the assumed naturalness of gendered divisions of labor. Womanist, *mujerista,* and some feminist theologies also point to the role of *race, class, age, and sexual preference in constructing unjust divisions of labor.

Feminist theologies differ somewhat on goals and strategies for redressing discrimination against women and devaluation of women's work. Some want women's maternal, domestic roles valued more highly and advocate child or *family allowances as one way of doing this. Others want *equality between women and men at work and at home. They advocate equal educational and employment opportunity, and possibly affirmative action, to overcome the occupational segregation of women into traditional women's jobs such as clerical work. Pay equity or comparable worth is advocated by some to redress the lower wages paid to women in such jobs. Others advocate radical social transformation that replaces *hierarchical relations of *domination and *oppression with more egalitarian social relations as necessary to good work for both women and men.

Some feminist theologians question traditional definitions of work and value and assert the value of caring labor, which is essential to human well-being. Bonnie Miller-McLemore calls for a fundamental reevaluation of definitions of work and value, and a revaluing of the essentiality of caring labor. She argues that psychological notions of generativity must be reconceptualized to include processes of birth and child rearing. She advocates that men share in caring labor, for community accountability through social policies that support caring activities, and restructuring workplaces to make shared *responsibility possible. For some feminists, shared domestic work and child care are essential to women's achieving equality in the workplace.

Many feminists contend that sole responsibility for domestic work is a significant factor in women's oppression. María Pilar Aquino's argument that Latinas' "double oppression resides in their *double workload*" (p. 22) is applicable to other doubly or triply oppressed women. In addition to wage work, "in generally more disadvantaged conditions than men" (p. 22), many women are also solely responsible for domestic work in their own home. Some feminists argue that the unremunerated character of domestic work contributes to the maximization of profit and thus is exploitative. Aquino calls for a new historical order based not on capitalist patriarchal ethics but on fullness and wholeness of life rooted in a vision of the reign of God (p. 24).

Aquino [1993]; Fischer, in Weidman [1984]; Miller-McLemore [1994]; Soelle/Cloyes [1984]

PAMELA K. BRUBAKER

Work, Womanist Work (labor) is a primary reality of human existence and comprises the major expenditure of human time and energy in daily *survival. Through work, the activity of meeting our basic creaturely needs and building the infrastructures of *family and *community life, humans interact with the *creation and construct our world. Recently, feminist, antiracist, and environmental movements have begun to recognize the creation and its creatures *at work* as the foundation for human work, sustaining life on the planet in processes of generation, decay, and regeneration. Because both the creation and humanity engage in this cycle of *interdependence, work is fundamentally social in nature.

Generally speaking, in all of creation, most life-forms participate in some dimension of the social division of labor, both necessary and procreative. As part of this large context, theology and *ethics see work as a means of loving God and serving the common good.

The relation of women to work is historically embedded in *patriarchal, *racist, and *classist understandings that the essential biological, emotional, and spiritual nature of woman defines the nature of her labor. This is generally true in three interrelated aspects of social life: the so-called public world, the community, and the home (the domestic or "private world"). In the public world, the work that women of diverse backgrounds and socially constructed groups undertake is nearly always poorly rewarded financially in proportion to that of all socially constructed groups of men; in the community, it is seen as voluntary "service"; and in the home, it is unpaid work of no monetary value to a nation's gross national (economic) product and is often subject to conflicting and hypocritical moral valuation. Nonetheless, work is understood as necessary for life's social fabric. Specifically, Christian *doctrines and practices originating in the West have traditionally held this view of women and work.

"Womanist" work pertains to "Mama, I'm walking to Canada and I'm taking you and a bunch of other slaves with me. . . . [Daughter,] it wouldn't be the first time" (Walker, xi). In unpacking the meaning of work in African-American women's lives, the emphasis is placed within the context and struggle for *freedom and survival of the whole people. Characteristics of work from a womanist perspective emerge, beginning in slavery and inclusive of the post-Emancipation history to the present: (1) black women's theological and ethical understanding of the relation of God to slavery and freedom; (2) black women's witness to the consistent, transgenerational, work-related activity by their *mothers, sisters, aunts, fathers, brothers, uncles, and the extended enslaved and free community for legal emancipation and full civil and human rights; (3) black women's struggle for control of their own bodies and *sexuality, including the reproduction of children; and (4) black women's own work-related attitudes of self-reliance, voluntary self-sacrifice, and excellence of learned craft and skill. Defined as a "work ethic," this motivating vision of human meaning through livelihood, i.e., the creation and use of intuition, skills, and practices, allows for the sustaining of self and family and contributes to the process of *liberation from *oppression for one's community of accountability, inclusive of the creation. Together, these four characteristics suggest that the nature and meaning of work itself is found in the quest and struggle for concrete freedom and human wholeness in the face of humanly constructed oppression and *evil.

In articulating a womanist understanding of work, labor is inclusive of asserting the nature of persons and the creation as workers with a right to their labor. Further, womanist work underscores this right as a theological and ethical given, free from exploitation. As such, freedom and responsible community are at the heart of the human activity of work, allowing for the development of full human and creational potential.

Grossman/Chester [1990]; Jones [1985]; Schüssler Fiorenza/Carr [1987]; Soelle/Cloyes [1984]; Walker [1983]

JOAN M. MARTIN

Working Poor The category of the "working poor" is ambivalent, since differing definitions reflect *ideologies in conflict. At the simplest level, the term refers to persons with full-time jobs who still find their incomes to be below the official U.S. *poverty line. Outside this official categorization, there are a large number of working-class families who, in spite of full-time labor of all adult members of the household, live "a paycheck away" from poverty. The size of both of these groups has increased over the past decade.

Implicit in the use of the term *working poor* is the idea of the "nonworking poor," a morally laden contrast that usually rests on *racist and *sexist images. In recent political debates over health care and welfare provisions, conservatives and many liberals have used "working poor" to indicate those worthy of sympathy and, possibly, some consideration for public financial support, in contrast to nonworking "freeloaders" (implicitly or explicitly construed as teenage African-American single mothers). Radicals (and some liberals), by contrast, use the term *working poor* to indicate the inability of the capitalist system to provide jobs offering a living wage, arguing that the existence of *working poor* challenges the powerful U.S. mythology that anyone who is willing to work hard can get ahead.

The category *working poor* can be meaningfully evaluated only in relation to the shift from an industrial to a service economy marked by significant unemployment. Much of the predominantly white, male working class has been forced out of relatively well-paid, skilled labor into minimum-wage, unskilled, service-sector labor, putting these workers into a new kind of competition for scarce jobs with female and minority workers and decreasing the employment possibilities for the "nonworking poor."

Bluestone/Harrison [1982]; Copeland [1994]; Lefkowitz/Withorn [1986]; Levitan/Shapiro [1987]

ELIZABETH M. BOUNDS

World Religions The study of world religions is essentially pursued from the perspective of the *history of religion,* that is, the historical unfolding of a *tradition in relation to social, economic, ecological, and political changes, or from the perspective of *comparative religion,* which maintains that different religions can be fruitfully compared (Sharpe, 1975). These approaches may overlap. Both have been guilty of framing their research within a univocal conception of religion and, when explicitly comparative, have been justly criticized for (1) the part they have played in the colonial agenda of Western societies; (2) the assumption that Western notions—for instance, the idea of the *soul—mean the same thing in radically different cultures; and (3) the presumption that one religion is truer, more evolved or higher, than another. When utilized with respect for *difference, however, the study of world religions provides a basis for *dialogue across faiths and a healthy recognition of the cultural limits of one's own *faith. The main point is that if you know only one faith, you know none.

A world religion is a religion that has successfully taken root in different cultural areas. While such a definition excludes living tribal religions, such as those practiced by a variety of Native Americans, Africans, Pacific peoples, and so on, as well as living national religions such as Shinto and dead religions such as Manicheism, it does include Judaism, *Hinduism, *Buddhism, *Confucianism, *Taoism, Christianity, and *Islam. A strong missionary impulse is helpful but not completely necessary in establishing a world religion. An emphasis on universal salvation is, however, essential, even if complete access to such salvation is limited to men of certain classes.

Studying religions from the perspective that there are many different religions, rather than only one true religion, allows feminist scholars and theologians to recognize consistent patterns in seemingly antithetical religions with regard to the religious status of women (Gross/Falk; Young 1993). For instance, an important common factor of Judaism, Christianity, and Islam (in fact, their primary theological link) is the envisioning of a single, all-powerful, male god. Some feminist scholars have criticized this conceptualization of the divine as authorizing a pervasive pattern of female suppression, both through the historical record, which shows their suppression of *goddess religions, and through their limiting women's access to positions of prestige in the religious cult: e.g., historically women were not allowed to be rabbis, priests, or imams. On the other hand, recent work by feminist scholars has uncovered or highlighted the feminine side of the gods of different religions, thereby providing women with a theological basis to be full participants in their religions.

The study of women in world religion has raised questions about exactly how we look at the universal phenomenon of religion. One primary element of analysis has been the division into separate spheres of the sacred and the profane, an idea promulgated by Mircea Eliade, though Emile Durkheim was the first to formulate it. Western feminist scholars of religion such as Mary Daly (1978) and Serinity Young (1993) have challenged this view, suggesting that what is sacred is what men do while what is profane is what women do (cf. Penelope Magee's thoughts on this fundamental binary opposition, in King). This is more than a challenge, because it also calls for a rethinking of how religion gets looked at, giving women's religious experience a full voice alongside the historically dominant male perspective (Gross/Falk).

Another important innovation in the study of religion has been the surge of work on domestic rites. This confronts the sacred–profane dichotomy head on, because the domestic sphere is most often that of women. Further, it brings out the private (female) versus the public (male) enactment of religion. The domestic sphere is of deep importance to religious traditions: think of the kosher laws of Judaism where, while male rabbis are asked for advice, women have had knowledge and control of this essential part of Jewish religious life. In Hinduism it could be argued that the center of the cult is in the home, rather than in the temples and texts.

Feminist interpretations of the comparative study of women in world religion are quite diverse, even though most of the interpreters are, like myself, white, Western feminist women. Diana Eck and Devaki Jain focused on the relation of various religions to the social-change projects and struggles of women around the world. Two-thirds of the papers in their edited book are by non-Western women. Yvonne Haddad and Ellison Findly examined the relationship of religion to social change in the formative periods of religions, in the institutions of religions, in modern revolutionary movements, and in nineteenth-century America. Nancy Falk and Rita Gross, in their 1980 edition, focused on women's religious experience, particularly case studies of non-Western cultures. Consequently, many, but not all, of the essays in their edited volume were written by anthropologists and focused on contemporary situations. The second edition was expanded to include essays on Western religions. Arvind Sharma chose essays by scholars trained in the various traditions that provide a necessary historical perspective. Serinity Young emphasized texts, both oral and written, as an accessible category for comparative study. Susan Starr Sered cut across cultural boundaries and focused on lesser-known (at least in the West) religions where women have traditionally been leaders, religions that occur in matrifocal societies, are characterized by a this-worldly orientation, and emphasize spirit possession, such as Afro-Caribbean religions, shamanism, and so on. Ursula King balanced essays between theoretical and philosophical issues with those on empirical and historical matters. Her contributors are from an international range of developed countries.

The forthcoming *Encyclopedia of Women and World Religion,* edited by Young, will bring together recent and not readily available feminist interpretation of Western and non-Western religions by international scholars in order to develop a comparative and relational understanding of the richness of women's religious experience. Such a feminist perspective on the comparative study of women in world religions challenges prior univocal views and instead seeks to ensure coverage that is balanced by gender, *race, and class. For instance, when women's *ordination is discussed from a feminist perspective based on the history and *experiences of Buddhist, Jewish, and Christian women, one is able to see a pattern of limiting women's access to roles of religious *authority that cuts across religious differences, as well as the complexity of issues within individual traditions. It is hoped that such an understanding of both the general and the particular realities will engender dialogue.

Eck/Jain [1987]; Gross/Falk [1989]; Haddad/Findly [1985]; King [1995]; Sered [1994]; Sharma [1987]; Sharpe [1975] Young [1993; forthcoming]

SERINITY YOUNG

World Religions and Christianity

Christian theologians have often taken an exclusive attitude toward other religions. Today, Christianity is being challenged everywhere by the existence of religious and cultural *pluralism. Faced with the presence of other religions and the experience of cross-cultural encounter, Christian theologians are developing a new theology of religions and interfaith *dialogue, but women have had little part in this so far.

Feminist theologians are critiquing the *patriarchal framework of different world religions and are recovering women's own voices and contributions, their religious roles and *rituals, and the feminine images and *metaphors used for describing the Divine. Women from different *faith communities are now increasingly getting in touch with each other to share their experiences of *oppression as well as their visions of *liberation. The feminist critique of religion has been furthest advanced in Christianity and Judaism, but women from other religions (*Hinduism, *Buddhism, *Islam, Sikhism; Chinese, Japanese, African religions; or other religious traditions) are now applying feminist analyses to their respective faiths. Thus women from different faiths are working on the transformation of world religions from within their own traditions by critiquing the *androcentric assumptions of their scriptural and doctrinal heritage and by recovering muted female voices and experiences from the past.

Women from different faiths are in dialogue with each other, but when looking at contemporary interfaith dialogue from a critical gender perspective, it is evident that feminism is, by and large, a missing dimension of dialogue. Christian women around the world are frequently very active in dialogue groups at the grass-roots level, but they are hardly ever visible as official spokespersons of interfaith dialogue. Nor has Christian feminist theology done much work so far on the encounter between Christianity and other world religions. This is an area in need of further development.

Cooey/Eakin/McDaniel [1991]; Eck/Jain [1987]; Mollenkott, ed. [1988]; O'Neill 1990

URSULA KING

Yin–Yang Traditional Chinese religious systems have understood the *cosmos as shaped and continually influenced by, among other processes, the interplay of the two forces of yin and yang. The earliest extant texts in which the terms appear date to the early fourth century B.C.E., although evidence dating back to the Shang dynasty suggests awareness of fundamental *dualisms in the mid-second millennium B.C.E.

The terms are not presented in the early texts as existing in absolute binary opposition; yin and yang are complementary rather than antagonistic. As a formal system, yin–yang theory attempts to grasp the internal contradictions of things while viewing the cosmos as an organic whole. The terms originally referred to the shaded (yin) and sunlit (yang) sides of a mountain or a river, the orientation for each of which was not identical. Yang indicated the south side of a mountain, the side that receives sunlight, but it connotes the north side of a river, as the light on the river is reflected to that side. During the Han dynasty (second century B.C.E.–second century C.E.), the terms were extended by association to include all observable complementary forces of the universe.

Designations of yin and yang are not static; moreover, they emphasize context and processes of change: a man stands in yang relationship to his wife's yin but exists in yin relationship to his parents, elders, and ruler; with his peers, the balance of yin–yang relationality shifts according to circumstance. During the Han process of synthesis and systematization, however, the superiority of yang over yin was advanced. As the correlations of everything from seasons, numbers, and military ranks to either yin or yang were established in Confucian *orthodoxy, things and persons associated with yin were vulnerable to definition as inferior.

Central to contemporary feminist analyses of *Confucianism is the undoing of the casual category collapse of woman into yin. In any context, yin-associated qualities of weakness, passivity, emotionality, inauspiciousness, the feminine, and/or what is female must be perceived as discrete, and yin must be identified in terms of a dynamic balance of constant change and reconfiguration.

Baldrian, in *Encyclopedia of Religion* [1987]; Lee/Chung, *Ching Feng* [1990]; Pang Pu, in *Social Sciences in China* [1985]

VIVIAN-LEE NYITRAY

Bibliography of Works Cited

Abraham, D., et al., eds. 1989. *Asian Women Doing Theology: Report from Singapore Conference, November 20–29, 1987*. Hong Kong: Asian Women's Resource Center for Culture and Theology.

Achtemeier, E. 1976. *The Committed Marriage*. Philadelphia: Westminster Press.

Acker, J. 1992. "From Sex Roles to Gendered Institutions." *Contemporary Sociology* 21 (September): 565–69.

Ackermann, D. 1985. "Liberation and Practical Theology: A Feminist Perspective on Ministry." *Journal of Theology for Southern Africa*, no. 52:30–41.

ACT UP/New York Women and AIDS Book Group. 1990. *Women, AIDS and Activism*. Boston: South End Press.

Adams, C. J. 1990. *The Sexual Politics of Meat: A Feminist-Vegetarian Critical Theory*. New York: Continuum.

———. 1994a. *Neither Man nor Beast: Feminism and the Defense of Animals*. New York: Continuum.

———. 1994b. *Women-Battering*. Minneapolis: Fortress Press.

———, ed. 1993. *Ecofeminism and the Sacred*. New York: Continuum.

Adams, C. J., and J. Donovan, eds. 1995. *Animals and Women: Feminist Theoretical Explorations*. Durham, N.C.: Duke University Press.

Adams, C., and M. Fortune. 1995. *Violence against Women and Children: A Christian Theological Sourcebook*. New York: Continuum.

Adams, D., and D. Apostolos-Cappadona, eds. 1985. *Art as Religious Studies*. New York: Crossroad.

Adler, M. 1986. *Drawing Down the Moon: Witches, Druids, Goddess-Worshippers, and Other Pagans in America Today*. 2d ed. Boston: Beacon Press.

Adler, R. 1983. "I've Had Nothing Yet So I Can't Take More." *Moment* 8 (September): 22–26.

Adler, R. 1993. "Feminist Folktales of Justice: Robert Cover as a Resource for the Renewal of Halakhah." *Conservative Judaism* 45 (spring): 40–55.

Ahmed, L. 1992. *Women and Gender in Islam: Historical Roots of a Modern Debate*. New Haven, Conn.: Yale University Press.

Albert, M., and R. Hahnel. 1978. *Unorthodox Marxism*. Boston: South End Press.

Albert, M., et al. 1986. *Liberating Theory*. Boston: South End Press.

Allen, P. G. 1992. *The Sacred Hoop: Recovering the Feminine in American Indian Traditions*. Boston: Beacon Press.

———, ed. 1989. *Spider Woman's Granddaughters: Traditional Tales and Contemporary Writing by Native American Women*. Boston: Beacon Press.

Allione, T. 1984. *Women of Wisdom*. London: Routledge & Kegan Paul.

Alt, F. 1989. *Jesus—Der erste neue Mann*. Munich: Piper Verlag.

Altekar, A. S. 1959/1983. *The Position of Women in Hindu Civilization from Prehistoric Times to the Present Day*. Reprint. Delhi: Motilal Banarsidass.

Amott, T., and J. Matthaei. 1991. *Race, Gender, and Work: A Multicultural Economic History of Women in the U.S.* Boston: South End Press.

Anderson, B. W., ed. 1984. *Creation in the Old Testament*. Philadelphia: Fortress Press.

Anderson, S. R., and P. Hopkins. 1991. *The Feminine Face of God: The Unfolding of the Sacred in Women*. New York: Bantam Books.

Anderson, V. C. 1991. *Prayers of Our Hearts in Word and Action*. New York: Crossroad.

Andolsen, B. H. 1981. "Agapē in Feminist Ethics." *Journal of Religious Ethics* 9, 1:69–93.

———. 1986. *Daughters of Jefferson, Daughters of Bootblacks*. Macon, Ga.: Mercer University Press.

Andolsen, B. H., C. Gudorf, and M. D. Pellauer, eds. 1985. *Women's Consciousness, Women's Conscience: A Reader in Feminist Ethics*. Minneapolis: Winston Press.

Andrews, L. 1988. "Feminism Revisited: Fallacies and Policies in the Surrogacy Debate." *Logos* 9:81–96.

Ankarloo, B., and G. Henningson, eds. 1990. *Early Modern European Witchcraft: Centers and Peripheries*. Oxford: Clarendon Press.

Anzaldúa, G., ed. 1990. *Making Face, Making Soul—Haciendo Caras: Critical and Actual Perspectives by Women of Color*. San Francisco: Aunt Lute Books.

Aquino, M. P. 1988. *Aportes para una teología desde la mujer*. Madrid: Biblia y Fe.

———. 1993. *Our Cry for Life: Feminist Theology from Latin America*. Trans. Dinah Livingstone. Maryknoll, N.Y.: Orbis Books.

———. 1994. *La teología, la iglesia y la mujer en América Latina*. Bogotá: Indo-American Press.

Arendt, H. 1970. *On Violence*. New York: Harcourt Brace Jovanovich.

Ariarajah, S. W. 1985. *The Bible and People of Other Faiths*. Maryknoll, N.Y.: Orbis Books.

Arras, J. D., and B. Steinbock, eds. 1994. *Ethical Issues in Modern Medicine*. 4th ed. Mountain View, Calif.: Mayfield.

Aspergen, K. 1990. *The Male Woman: A Feminine Ideal in the Early Church*. Uppsala, Sweden: Uppsala University Press.

Atkinson, C. W. 1983. *Mystic and Pilgrim: The Book and the World of Margery Kempe*. Ithaca, N.Y.: Cornell University Press.

———. 1991. *The Oldest Vocation: Christian Motherhood in the Middle Ages*. Ithaca, N.Y.: Cornell University Press.

Atkinson, C. W., C. H. Buchanan, and M. M. Miles, eds. 1987. *Shaping New Vision*. Ann Arbor: University of Michigan Press.

Atkinson, C. W., et al., eds. 1985. *Immaculate and Powerful: The Female in Sacred Image and Social Reality*. Boston: Beacon Press.

Bahemuka, J. M. 1993. *Our Religious Heritage*. Walton-on-Thames, Surrey: Thomas Nelson & Sons.

Baier, A. C. 1994. *Moral Prejudices: Essays on Ethics*. Cambridge, Mass.: Harvard University Press.

Baker-Fletcher, K. 1994. *A Singing Something: Womanist Reflections on Anna Julia Cooper*. New York: Crossroad.

Baldrian, F. 1987. "Taoism: An Overview." In *The Encyclopedia of Religion*, 14:288–306. New York: Macmillan.

Baldwin, L. V. 1984. "'A Home in Dat Rock': Afro-American Folk Sources and Slave Visions of Heaven and Hell." *Journal of Religious Thought* 41, 1:38–57.

Balka, C., and A. Rose, eds. 1989. *Twice Blessed: On Being Lesbian or Gay and Jewish*. Boston: Beacon Press.

Bar On, B.-A., ed. 1994a. *Engendering Origins*. Albany: State University of New York Press.

———, ed. 1994b. *Modern Engendering: Critical Feminist Readings in Modern Western Philosophy*. Albany: State University of New York Press.

Barrett, M. 1988. *Women's Oppression Today: The Marxist-Feminist Encounter*. Rev. ed. New York: Verso.

Barrett, M., and A. Phillips, eds. 1992. *Destabilizing Theory: Contemporary Feminist Debates*. Stanford, Calif.: Stanford University Press.

Barstow, A. L. 1994. *Witchcraze: A New History of the European Witchhunts—Our Legacy of Violence against Women*. San Francisco: HarperCollins.

Barth, K. 1956, 1957. *Church Dogmatics*. Vols. I/2, II/2. Edinburgh: T. & T. Clark.

Bartky, S. L. 1990. *Femininity and Domination: Studies in the Phenomenology of Oppression*. New York: Routledge.

Bartlett, K. T., and R. Kennedy. 1991. *Feminist Legal Theory: Readings in Law and Gender*. Boulder, Colo.: Westview Press.

Bass, D. C. 1985. "The Reformation Heritage of the UCC and Its Meaning for Twentieth Century Christians." *CTS* 75, 2:3–13.

Baum, G. 1994. "Religious Pluralism and Common Values." *Journal of Religious Pluralism* 4:1–15.

Bea, T. K., and D. M. Gunn, eds. Forthcoming. *Theorizing the Biblical*. London: Routledge.

Beardsley, E. L. 1973–74. "Referential Genderization." *Philosophical Forum* 5:285–93.

Bechtel, L. M. 1991. "Shame as a Sanction of Social Control in Biblical Israel: Judicial, Political, and Social Shaming." *JSOT* 49 (February): 47–76.

Bekkenkamp, J., F. Droes, and A. M. Korte, eds. 1986. *Of Sisters, Maidens and Women—Ten Years of Feminism and Theology at Faculties and Colleges in the Netherlands.* IIMO (Interuniversitair Instituut voor Missiologie en Oecumenica) Research Pamphlet no. 19, Leiden-Utrecht.

Bell, D., P. Caplan, and W. J. Karim, eds. 1993. *Gendered Fields: Women, Men and Ethnography.* London: Routledge.

Bell, R. M. 1985. *Holy Anorexia.* Chicago: University of Chicago Press.

Bellis, A. O. 1994. *Helpmates, Harlots, Heroes: Women's Stories in the Hebrew Bible.* Louisville, Ky.: Westminster John Knox Press.

Bem, S. L. 1993. *The Lenses of Gender: Transforming the Debate on Sexual Inequality.* New Haven, Conn.: Yale University Press.

Benderly, B. L. 1982. "Rape Free or Rape Prone." *Science* (October): 16–22.

Benhabib, S. 1992. *Situating the Self: Gender, Community and Postmodernism in Contemporary Ethics.* New York: Routledge.

Berger, J. 1972. *Ways of Seeing.* London: BBC and Penguin Books.

Bernstein, R. 1983. *Beyond Objectivism and Relativism: Science, Hermeneutics, and Praxis.* Philadelphia: University of Pennsylvania Press.

Berry, P., and A. Wernick, eds. 1992. *Shadow of Spirit: Postmodernism and Religion.* London: Routledge.

Berryman, P. 1987. *Liberation Theology.* New York: Pantheon Books.

Betz, H. D. 1992. "Apostle," *ABD* 1:309–11.

Bingemer, M. C., and I. Gebara. 1989. *Mary Mother of God, Mother of the Poor.* Maryknoll, N.Y.: Orbis Books.

Bird, P. 1982. *The Bible as the Church's Book.* Philadelphia: Westminster Press.

———. 1988. "Translating Sexist Language as a Cultural and Theological Problem." *USQR* 42, 1/2:89–95.

———. 1989. "The Harlot as Heroine in Biblical Texts: Narrative Art and Social Presupposition." *Semeia* 46:119–39.

———. 1994. "The Authority of the Bible," *NIB* 1:33–64.

Bluestone, B., and B. Harrison. 1982. *The Deindustrialization of America.* New York: Basic Books.

Boddy, J. 1989. *Womb and Alien Spirits: Women, Men, and the Zar Cult in Northern Sudan.* Madison: University of Wisconsin Press.

Boesak, A. A. 1987. *Comfort and Protest: The Apocalypse from a South African Perspective.* Philadelphia: Westminster Press.

Boff, L. 1994. "La postmodernidad y la miseria de la razón liberadora." *Pasos* 54 (July–August): 11–15.

Bonino, J. M. 1987. "Nuevas tendencias en teología." *Pasos,* no. 9:18–23.

Bons-Storm, R. 1996. *The Incredible Woman: Listening to Women's Silences.* Nashville: Abingdon Press.

Boucher, S. 1993. *Turning the Wheel: American Women Creating the New Buddhism.* Boston: Beacon Press.

Brant, B., ed. 1988. *A Gathering of Spirit: A Collection by North American Women.* Toronto: Women's Press.

"Breaking the Silence." Preparatory paper for the EATWOT Asian Women's Commission meeting, Dec. 1990.

Bridenthal, R., A. Grossmann, and M. Kaplan, eds. 1984. *When Biology Became Destiny.* New York: Monthly Review Press.

Brock, R. N. 1988/1992. *Journeys by Heart: A Christology of Erotic Power.* New York: Crossroad.

Brock, R. N., P. Cooey, and A. Klein. 1990. "The Questions That Won't Go Away: A Dialogue about Women in Buddhism and Christianity." *JFSR* 6, 2:87–120.

Broner, E. M. 1993. *The Telling.* San Francisco: Harper & Row.

Brooten, B. J. 1996. *Love Between Women: Early Christian Responses to Female Homoeroticism.* Chicago: University of Chicago Press.

Brotherton, A., ed. 1992. *The Voice of the Turtledove: New Catholic Women in Europe.* New York: Paulist Press.

Brown, J. C., and C. R. Bohn, eds. 1989. *Christianity, Patriarchy, and Abuse: A Feminist Critique.* New York: Pilgrim Press.

Brown, L. M., and C. Gilligan. 1992. *Meeting at the Crossroads: Women's Psychology and Girls' Development.* Cambridge, Mass.: Harvard University Press.

Brownmiller, S. 1975. *Against Our Will: Men, Women and Rape.* New York: Simon & Schuster.

Brueggemann, W. 1978. *Prophetic Imagination.* Philadelphia: Fortress Press.

Brumlik, M. 1991. *Der Anti-Alt.* Frankfurt am Main: Eichborn Verlag.

Brundage, J. A. 1987. *Law, Sex, and Christian Society in Medieval Europe.* Chicago: University of Chicago Press.

Buddhist-Christian Studies Journal. 1980–. Honolulu: University of Hawaii Press.

Burke, J., ed. 1983. *A New Look at Preaching*. Dublin: Veritas.

Burawoy, M., et al. 1991. *Ethnography Unbound: Power and Resistance in the Modern Metropolis*. Berkeley: University of California Press.

Bussert, J. 1986. *Battered Women: From a Theology of Suffering to an Ethic of Empowerment*. Philadelphia: Lutheran Church in America, Division for Mission in North America.

Butler, J. 1990. *Gender Trouble: Feminism and the Subversion of Identity*. New York: Routledge.

Bynum, C. W. 1982. *Jesus as Mother*. Berkeley: University of California Press.

———. 1987. *Holy Feast and Holy Fast: The Religious Significance of Food to Medieval Women*. Berkeley: University of California Press.

———. 1991. *Fragmentation and Redemption: Essays on Gender and the Human Body in Medieval Religion*. New York: Zone Books.

Cady, S., M. Ronan, and H. Taussig. 1989. *Wisdom's Feast*. San Francisco: Harper & Row.

Cahill, L. S. Forthcoming. *Sex, Gender, and Christian Ethics*. Cambridge: Cambridge University Press.

Cameron, A. 1981. *Daughters of Copper Woman*. Vancouver: Press Gang.

Camp, C. V. 1985. *Wisdom and the Feminine in the Book of Proverbs*. Sheffield: JSOT.

———. 1988. "Wise and Strange: An Analysis of the Female Imagery in Proverbs in Light of Trickster Mythology." *Semeia* 42:14–36.

Camp, C. V., and C. R. Fontaine, eds. 1993. *Women, War, and Metaphor: Language and Society in the Study of the Hebrew Bible*. Semeia 61. Atlanta: Scholars Press.

Campbell, J. 1990. "The Feminine as Omitted, Optional, or Alternative Story: A Feminist Review of the Episcopal Eucharistic Lectionary." *Proceedings of the North American Academy of Liturgy*, 59–67.

Cannon, K. G. 1988. *Black Womanist Ethics*. Atlanta: Scholars Press.

———. 1989. "Slave Ideology and Biblical Interpretation." *Semeia* 47:9–23.

———. 1993. "Appropriation and Reciprocity in the Doing of Womanist Ethics." *Annual of the Society of Christian Ethics:* 189–96.

———. 1995. *Katie's Canon: Womanism and the Soul of the Black Community*. New York: Continuum.

Cannon, K. G., and E. Schüssler Fiorenza, eds. 1989. *Interpretation for Liberation*. Atlanta: Scholars Press.

Card, C., ed. 1991. *Feminist Ethics*. Lawrence: University Press of Kansas.

Carman, J. B. 1994. *Majesty and Meekness: A Comparative Study of Contrast and Harmony in the Concept of God*. Grand Rapids: Wm. B. Eerdmans Publishing Co.

Caron, C. 1993. *To Make and Make Again: Feminist Ritual Thealogy*. New York: Crossroad.

Carr, A. E. 1988. *Transforming Grace: Christian Tradition and Women's Experience*. San Francisco: Harper & Row.

Carr, A., and E. Schüssler Fiorenza, eds. 1989. *Motherhood: Experience, Institution, and Theology*. London: T. & T. Clark.

———, eds. 1991. *The Special Nature of Women?* Philadelphia: Concilium/Trinity Press International.

Carroll, J., and W. C. Roof, eds. 1993. *Beyond Establishment: Protestant Identity in a Post-Protestant Age*. Louisville, Ky.: Westminster John Knox Press.

Carson, A. 1992. *Goddesses and Wise Women: The Literature of Feminist Spirituality 1980–1992. An Annotated Bibliography*. Freedom, Calif.: Crossing Press.

Case-Winters, A. 1990. *God's Power*. Louisville, Ky.: Westminster John Knox Press.

Castelli, E., et al. 1990. "Special Section on Feminist Translation of the New Testament." *JFSR* 6, 2:24–86.

Cheeler, B., and E. Farley, eds. 1991. *Shifting Boundaries: Contextual Approaches to the Structure of Theological Education*. Louisville, Ky.: Westminster John Knox Press.

Chen, E. M. 1969. "Nothingness and the Mother Principle in Early Chinese Taoism." *International Philosophical Quarterly* 9:391–405.

———. 1974. "Tao as the Great Mother and the Influence of Motherly Love in the Shaping of Chinese Philosophy." *History of Religions* 14, 1(August): 51–64.

Chenu, M. T. v. L. 1993–94. "Violente l'Eglise? Violente envers les femmes?" *Forum Bulletin* (winter): 7–8.

Chopp, R. 1987. "Feminism's Theological Pragmatics: A Social Naturalism of Women's Experience." *Journal of Religion* 67 (April): 239–56.

———. 1989. *The Power to Speak: Feminism, Language, God*. New York: Crossroad.

———. 1995. *Saving Work: Feminist Practices of Theological Education*. Louisville, Ky.: Westminster John Knox Press.

Chopp, R. S., and M. L. Taylor, eds. 1994. *Reconstructing Christian Theology*. Minneapolis: Fortress Press.

Christ, C. P. 1980. *Diving Deep and Surfacing: Women Writers on Spiritual Quest*. Boston: Beacon Press.

———. 1987. *Laughter of Aphrodite: Reflections on a Journey to the Goddess*. San Francisco: Harper & Row.

Christ, C. P., and J. Plaskow, eds. 1979. *Womanspirit Rising: A Feminist Reader in Religion.* San Francisco: Harper & Row.

Chung, H. K. 1990. *Struggle to Be the Sun Again: Introducing Asian Women's Theology.* Maryknoll, N.Y.: Orbis Books.

———. 1991. "Welcome the Spirit; Hear Her Cries: The Holy Spirit, Creation, and the Culture of Life." *C/C* 51 (July 15): 220–23.

Church and World: The Unity of the Church and the Renewal of Human Community. 1990. Faith and Order Paper no. 151. Geneva: World Council of Churches.

Clark, E. A. 1983. *Women in the Early Church.* Wilmington, Del.: Michael Glazier.

———. 1986. *Ascetic Piety and Women's Faith: Essays on Late Ancient Christianity.* Lewiston, N.Y.: Edwin Mellen Press.

Clark, E., and H. Richardson, eds. 1977. *Women and Religion: A Feminist Sourcebook of Christian Thought.* San Francisco: Harper & Row.

Clark, J. M., and M. L. Stemmeler, eds. 1994. *Spirituality and Community: Diversity in Lesbian and Gay Experience.* Las Colinas, Tex.: Monument Press.

Clark, L., M. Ronan, and E. Walker. 1978. *Image-Breaking/Image-Building.* New York: Pilgrim Press.

Clarkson, J. S. 1989. *In the Beginning Was the Word: Implications of Inclusive Language for Religious Education.* Ann Arbor, Mich.: University Microfilms.

Clines, D. 1990. "What Does Eve Do to Help? and Other Irredeemably Androcentric Orientations in Genesis 1—3." *JSOT* (Supplement) 94:29–48.

Coakley, S. 1994. *Christ without Absolutes: Study of the Christology of Ernst Troeltsch.* Oxford: Oxford University Press.

Cobb, J. B., Jr., and D. R. Griffin. 1976. *Process Theology: An Introductory Exposition.* Philadelphia: Westminster Press.

Code, L. 1991. *What Can She Know? Feminist Theory and the Construction of Knowledge.* Ithaca, N.Y.: Cornell University Press.

Cohen, N. 1995. *Self, Struggle and Change: Family Conflict Stories in Genesis and Their Healing Insights for Our Lives.* Woodstock, Vt.: Jewish Lights Publishing.

Collins, A. Y. 1984. *Crisis and Catharsis: The Power of the Apocalypse.* Philadelphia: Westminster Press.

———, ed. 1985. *Feminist Perspectives on Biblical Scholarship.* Atlanta: Scholars Press.

Collins, P. H. 1991. *Black Feminist Thought: Knowledge, Consciousness and the Politics of Empowerment.* New York: Routledge.

Collins, S. D. 1974. *A Different Heaven and Earth: A Feminist Perspective on Religion.* Valley Forge, Pa.: Judson Press.

Comblin, J. 1979. *The Church and the National Security State.* Maryknoll, N.Y.: Orbis Books.

Commission on Theological Concerns of the Christian Conference of Asia (CCA), ed. 1981. *Minjung Theology: People as the Subjects of History.* Maryknoll, N.Y.: Orbis Books.

Comstock, G. D. 1991. *Violence against Lesbians and Gay Men.* New York: Columbia University Press.

Condren, M. 1989. *The Serpent and the Goddess: Women, Religion and Power in Celtic Ireland.* San Francisco: Harper & Row.

Cone, J. H. 1975. *God of the Oppressed.* New York: Seabury Press.

Consultation on Asian Women's Theology. 1985. *Who Is Mary?* Manila: Ecumenical Association of Third World Theologians (EATWOT).

———. 1989. *Mariology.* Singapore: Asian Women Doing Theology.

Cooey, P. M. 1994. *Religious Imagination and the Body: A Feminist Analysis.* New York: Oxford University Press.

Cooey, P. M., W. R. Eakin, and J. B. McDaniel, eds. 1991. *After Patriarchy: Feminist Transformations of the World Religions.* Maryknoll, N.Y.: Orbis Books.

Cooey, P. M., S. A. Farmer, and M. E. Ross, eds. 1987. *Embodied Love: Sensuality and Relationship as Feminist Values.* San Francisco: Harper & Row.

Cook, R. J. 1993. "Women's International Human Rights Law: The Way Forward." *Human Rights Quarterly* 15:230–61.

Cooper, A. J. 1945. *Equality of Races and the Democratic Movement.* Washington, D.C.: privately printed pamphlet.

Copeland, W. 1994. *And the Poor Get Welfare: The Ethics of Poverty in the United States.* Nashville: Abingdon Press.

Corea, G. 1992. *The Invisible Epidemic: The Story of Women and AIDS.* New York: HarperCollins.

Corre, A. 1975. *Understanding the Talmud.* New York: Ktav.

Corrington, G. P. 1992. *Her Image of Salvation.* Louisville, Ky.: Westminster John Knox Press.

Cott, J. 1984. "The Biblical Problem of Election." *Journal of Ecumenical Studies* 21 (spring): 199–228.

Countryman, L. W. 1988. *Dirt, Greed, and Sex: Sexual Ethics in the New Testament and Their Implications for Today.* Philadelphia: Fortress Press.

Couture, P. D. 1991. *Blessed Are the Poor? Women's Poverty, Family Policy and Practical Theology*. Nashville: Abingdon Press.

Craven, T. 1983. *Artistry and Faith in the Book of Judith*. Chico, Calif.: Scholars Press.

Crawford, J., and M. Kinnamon, eds. 1983. *In God's Image*. Geneva: World Council of Churches.

Crownfield, D., ed. 1992. *Body/Text in Julia Kristeva: Religion, Women and Psychoanalysis*. Albany: State University of New York Press.

Cruikshank, M. 1982. *Lesbian Studies, Present and Future*. New York: Feminist Press.

Daly, L. K., ed. 1994. *Feminist Theological Ethics: A Reader*. Louisville, Ky.: Westminster John Knox Press.

Daly, M. 1968. *The Church and the Second Sex*. New York: Harper & Row.

———. 1973a. *Beyond God the Father: Toward a Philosophy of Women's Liberation*. Boston: Beacon Press.

———. 1973b. "Post-Christian Theology." In J. A. Romero, ed., *Women and Religion*. Tallahassee, Fla.: American Academy of Religion.

———. 1978. *Gyn/Ecology: The Metaethics of Radical Feminism*. Boston: Beacon Press.

———. 1984. *Pure Lust: Elemental Feminist Philosophy*. Boston: Beacon Press.

Dane, B. O., and C. Levine, eds. 1994. *AIDS and the New Orphans: Coping with Death*. Westport, Conn.: Auburn House.

D'Angelo, M. R. 1990a. "Women in Luke-Acts: A Redactional View," *JBL* 109:441–61.

———. 1990b. "Women Partners in the New Testament." *JFSR* 6, 1:65–86.

———. 1992a. "Abba and 'Father': Imperial Theology and the Traditions about Jesus." *JBL* 111, 4:611–30.

———. 1992b. "Abba and 'Father': Theology in Mark and Q." *HTR* 85:149–74.

———. 1992c. "Re-Membering Jesus: Women, Prophecy and Resistance in the Memory of the Early Churches." *Horizons* 19, 2:199–218.

Davaney, S. G., ed. 1981. *Feminism and Process Thought: The Harvard Divinity School/Claremont Center for Process Studies Symposium Papers*. Lewiston, N.Y.: Edwin Mellen Press.

Davidman, L. 1991. *Tradition in a Rootless World: Women Turn to Orthodox Judaism*. Berkeley: University of California Press.

Davidman, L., and S. Tenenbaum, eds. 1994. *Feminist Perspectives on Jewish Studies*. New Haven, Conn.: Yale University Press.

Davis, A. 1981. *Race, Class, and Sex*. New York: Random House.

Davis, D. S. 1991. "Rich Cases: The Ethics of Thick Description." *Hastings Center Report* 21, 4:12–16.

Day, P. L., ed. 1989. *Gender and Difference in Ancient Israel*. Minneapolis: Augsburg Fortress.

de Beauvoir, S. 1971. *The Second Sex*. Trans. H. M. Parshley. New York: Alfred A. Knopf.

Decrow, K. 1974. *Sexist Justice*. New York: Vintage Books.

Delphy, C. 1984. *Close to Home: A Materialist Analysis of Women's Oppression*. London: Hutchinson & Co.

DeMallie, R. J. 1984. *The Sixth Grandfather: Black Elk's Teachings Given to John G. Neihardt*. Lincoln: University of Nebraska Press.

Demers, P. 1992. *Women as Interpreters of the Bible*. New York: Paulist Press.

de Romilly, J. 1979. *La Douceur dans la pensée grecque*. Paris: Les Belles Lettres.

Derrida, J. 1981. *Dissemination*. Trans. Barbara Johnson. Chicago: University of Chicago Press.

Devall, B., and G. Sessions. 1985. *Deep Ecology: Living as if Nature Mattered*. Layton, Utah: Gibbs M. Smith.

Diamond, I., and G. F. Orenstein, eds. 1990. *Reweaving the World: The Emergence of Ecofeminism*. San Francisco: Sierra Club Books.

Dietrich, G. 1988. *Women's Movement in India: Conceptual and Religious Reflections*. Bangalore, India: Breakthrough Publications.

Dillard, A. 1982. *Teaching a Stone to Talk*. New York: Harper & Row.

Disability Rag/Resource. 1993– . Advocado Press, P.O. Box 145, Louisville, KY 40201.

Dombrowski, D. A. 1984. *The Philosophy of Vegetarianism*. Amherst: University of Massachusetts Press.

Donovan, D., and A. Marlatt eds. 1988. *Assessment of Addictive Behaviors*. New York: Guilford Press.

Donovan, J. 1988. *Feminist Theory*. New York: Continuum.

Donovan, J., and C. J. Adams, eds. 1996. *Beyond Animal Rights: A Feminist Caring Ethic for the Treatment of Animals*. New York: Continuum.

Donovan, M. A. 1989. *Sisterhood as Power: The Past and Passion of Ecclesial Women*. New York: Crossroad.

Douglas, K. B. 1994. *The Black Christ*. Maryknoll, N.Y.: Orbis Books.

Douglas, M. 1966. *Purity and Danger*. London: Routledge & Kegan Paul.

Douglass, J. D. 1985. *Women, Freedom and Calvin*. Philadelphia: Westminster Press.

Droge, A., and J. Tabor. 1989. *A Noble Death: Suicide and Martyrdom among Ancient Jews,*

Christians, Greeks and Romans. San Francisco: Harper & Row.

Dronke, P. 1984. *Women Writers of the Middle Ages: A Critical Study of Texts from Perpetua (d. 203) to Marguerite Porete (d. 1310).* Cambridge: Cambridge University Press.

Dubose, E. R., R. Hammel, and L. J. O'Connell, eds. 1994. *A Matter of Principles? Ferment in United States Bioethics.* Valley Forge, Pa.: Trinity Press International.

Duchrow, U., and G. Liedke. 1989. *Shalom: Biblical Perspectives on Creation, Justice and Peace.* Geneva: World Council of Churches Publications.

Duck, R. C. 1991. *Gender and the Name of God: The Trinitarian Baptismal Formula.* New York: Pilgrim Press.

Dunfee, S. N. 1982. "The Sin of Hiding." *Soundings* 65, 3:25–35.

Dussel, E. 1991. *History of the Church in Latin America: Colonialization to Liberation (1492–1979).* Grand Rapids: Wm. B. Eerdmans Publishing Co.

Dyke, D. J. 1991. *Crucified Woman.* Toronto: United Church Press.

EATWOT (Ecumenical Association of Third World Theologians) and Working Commission on Church History. 1985. *Towards a History of the Church in the Third World: Papers and Report of a Consultation on the Issue of Periodisation.* Bern: Evangelische Arbeitsstelle Oekumene Schweiz.

EATWOT, Asian Women's Commission Meeting. 1990. "Breaking the Silence: Indian Wom-en Speak Out." Preparatory paper for the December 1990 meeting in New Delhi, India.

Eboussi-Boulaga, F. 1984. *Christianity without Fetishes: An African Critique and Recapture of Christianity.* Maryknoll, N.Y.: Orbis Books.

Eck, D. L., and D. Jain, eds. 1987. *Speaking of Faith: Global Perspectives on Women, Religion, and Social Change.* Philadelphia: New Society Publishers.

Ehrenberg, M. 1989. *Women in Prehistory.* Oxford: Oxford University Press.

Eisland, N. 1994. *The Disabled God.* Nashville: Abingdon Press.

Eisler, R. 1987. *The Chalice and the Blade: Our History, Our Future.* San Francisco: Harper & Row.

Elam, D. 1994. *Feminism and Deconstruction: Ms. en Abyme.* New York: Routledge.

Eliade, M., ed. 1987. *The Encyclopedia of Religion.* 16 vols. New York: Macmillan.

Elkins, H. M. 1994. *Worshipping Women: Reforming God's People for Praise.* Nashville: Abingdon Press.

Ellacuría, I., and J. Sobrino, eds. 1993. Mysterium Liberationis—*Fundamental Concepts of Liberation Theology.* Maryknoll, N.Y.: Orbis Books.

Eller, C. 1993. *Living in the Lap of the Goddess: The Feminist Spirituality Movement in America.* New York: Crossroad.

Embree, L., ed. 1972. *Metaarchaeology.* Dordrecht: Kluwer.

Emerson, S. 1989. "Toni Morrison's Tar Baby: A Resource for Feminist Theology." *JFSR* 5 (fall): 64–78.

Encyclopaedia Judaica. 1971. Jerusalem: Keter Publishing House.

Engel, M. P., and W. E. Wyman, Jr., eds. 1992. *Revisioning the Past: Prospects in Historical Theology.* Minneapolis: Fortress.

England, P., M. Herbert, B. Kiloune, L. Reid, and L. Megdal. 1994. "The Gendered Valuation of Occupations and Skills: Earning in 1980 Census Operations." *Social Forces* 73 (September): 65–100.

Erickson, V. L. 1993. *Where Silence Speaks: Feminism, Social Theory, and Religion.* Minneapolis: Fortress Press.

Esser, A., and L. Schottroff, eds. 1993. *Yearbook of the European Society of Women in Theological Research.* Vol. 1. Kampen, Netherlands: J. H. Kok Pharos.

Eugene, T. M. 1992. "On 'Difference' and the Dream of Pluralist Feminism." *JFSR* 8, 2:91–98.

Fabella, V. 1993. *Beyond Bonding: A Third World Women's Theological Journey.* Manila: Ecumenical Association of Third World Theologians and the Institute of Women's Studies.

Fabella, V., and M. A. Oduyoye, eds. 1988. *With Passion and Compassion: Third World Women Doing Theology.* Maryknoll, N.Y.: Orbis Books.

Fabella, V., and S.A.L. Park, eds. 1989. *We Dare to Dream: Doing Theology as Asian Women.* Maryknoll, N.Y.: Orbis Books.

Fabella, V., and S. Torres, eds. 1983. *Irruption of the Third World: Challenge to Theology.* Maryknoll, N.Y.: Orbis Books.

"Facts about Women and AIDS." Centers for Disease Control, Atlanta, Ga., February 13, 1994, pp. 1–2.

Faderman, L. 1981. *Surpassing the Love of Men: Romantic Friendship and Love between Women from the Renaissance to the Present.* New York: William Morrow & Co.

Falk, M. 1987. "Notes on Composing New Blessings: Toward a Feminist-Jewish Reconstruction of Prayer." *JFSR* 3, 1 (spring): 39–53.

———. 1996. *The Book of Blessings: New Jewish Prayers and Rituals for Daily Life, the Sabbath, and the New Moon Festival.* San Francisco: Harper SanFrancisco.

Falk, N. A., ed. 1994. *Women and Religion in India: An Annotated Bibliography of Sources in English.* Kalamazoo: Western Michigan University.

Fanon, F. 1965. *The Wretched of the Earth.* New York: Grove Press.

Farley, M. 1986. *Personal Commitments: Beginning, Keeping, Changing.* San Francisco: Harper & Row.

———. 1993. "A Feminist Version of Respect for Persons." *JFSR* 9 (spring–fall): 183–98.

Farley, W. 1990. *Tragic Vision and Divine Compassion: A Contemporary Theodicy.* Louisville, Ky.: Westminster John Knox Press.

Farmer, D. A., and E. Hunter, eds. 1990. *And Blessed Is She: Sermons by Women.* San Francisco: Harper & Row.

Farmer, K. 1991. *Who Knows What Is Good?* Grand Rapids: Wm. B. Eerdmans Publishing Co.

Farnham, C., ed. 1987. *The Impact of Feminist Research in the Academy.* Bloomington: Indiana University Press.

Feiloaiga, T. 1992. "Herstory: The Struggle of Pacific Women in Ministry." *Pacific Journal of Theology* 2, 7:31–34.

Felder, C. H., ed. 1991. *Stony the Road We Trod: African American Biblical Interpretations.* Minneapolis: Fortress Press.

Ferguson, E., ed. 1990. *Encyclopedia of Early Christianity.* New York: Garland.

Fetterman, D. 1989. *Ethnography Step by Step.* Newbury Park, Calif.: Sage.

Fife, C., ed. 1993. *The Colour of Resistance: A Contemporary Collection of Writing by Aboriginal Women.* Toronto: Sister Vision Press.

Fine, M., and A. Asch, eds. 1988. *Women with Disabilities: Essays in Psychology, Culture and Politics.* Philadelphia: Temple University Press.

Finson, S. D. 1985. "On the Other Side of Silence: Patriarchy Consciousness and Spirituality—Some Women's Experiences of Theological Education." Ph.D. diss., Boston University.

Firestone, S. 1970. *The Dialectic of Sex: The Case for Feminist Revolution.* New York: Bantam Books.

Flack, H. E., and E. D. Pellegrino, eds. 1992. *African-American Perspectives on Biomedical Ethics.* Washington, D.C.: Georgetown University Press.

Foley, N., ed. 1983. *Preaching and the Non-Ordained: An Interdisciplined Study.* Collegeville, Minn.: Liturgical Press.

Foner, P. S., ed. 1972. *The Voice of Black America: Major Speeches by Negroes in the U.S., 1797–1971.* New York: Simon & Schuster.

Fonow, M. M., and J. A. Cook. 1991. *Beyond Methodology: Feminist Scholarship as Lived Research.* Bloomington: Indiana University Press.

Forman, C. 1982. *The Island Churches of the South Pacific: Experience in the Twentieth Century.* Maryknoll, N.Y.: Orbis Books.

Fortune, M. M. 1983. *Sexual Violence: The Unmentionable Sin.* New York: Pilgrim Press.

———. 1987. *Keeping the Faith: Questions and Answers for the Abused Woman.* San Francisco: Harper & Row.

———. 1989. *Is Nothing Sacred? When Sex Invades the Pastoral Relationship.* San Francisco: Harper & Row.

Foucault, M. 1980. *Power/Knowledge: Selected Interviews and Other Writings, 1972–1977.* New York: Pantheon Books.

Frank, A. G. 1969. *Latin America: Underdevelopment or Revolution?* New York: Monthly Review Press.

Frankenberry, N. 1987. *Religion and Radical Empiricism.* Albany: State University of New York Press.

Freedman, D. N. 1987. "Yahweh of Samaria and His Asherah." *BA* 1 (December): 241–50.

Freedman, D. N., et al., eds. 1992. *Anchor Bible Dictionary.* New York: Doubleday.

Freire, P. 1970. *Pedagogy of the Oppressed.* New York: Herder & Herder.

Friedan, B. 1963. *The Feminine Mystique.* New York: W. W. Norton & Co.

———. 1993. *The Fountain of Age.* New York: Simon & Schuster.

Friedman, S., and A. Irwin. 1990. "Christian Feminism, Eros, and Power in Right Relation." *C/C* 40, 3:387–405.

Frye, M. 1983. *The Politics of Reality: Essays in Feminist Theory.* Freedom, Calif.: Crossing Press.

Frymer-Kensky, T. 1992. *In the Wake of the Goddesses: Women, Culture, and the Biblical Transformation of Pagan Myth.* New York: Free Press.

Fulkerson, M. M. 1994. *Changing the Subject: Women's Discourses and Feminist Theology.* Minneapolis: Fortress Press.

Furnish, V. P. 1985. *The Moral Teaching of Paul: Selected Issues.* 2d ed. Nashville: Abingdon Press.

Gaard, G., ed. 1993. *Ecofeminism: Women, Animals, Nature.* Philadelphia: Temple University Press.

Gadon, E. W. 1989. *The Once and Future Goddess.* San Francisco: Harper & Row.

Ganley, A. L. 1985. *Court-Mandated Counseling for Men Who Batter: A Three Day Workshop for Mental Health Professionals.* Washington, D.C.: Center for Women's Policy Studies.

Garry, A., and M. Pearsall, eds. 1989. *Women, Knowledge and Reality: Explorations in Feminist Philosophy.* Boston: Unwin Hyman.

Gebara, I. 1987. *La opcion por el pobre como opcion por la mujer pobre.* Concilium.

———. 1989. *Levanta-te e anda: Alguns aspectos da caminhada da mulher na America Latina.* São Paulo: Ediçoes Paulinas.

———. 1990. *As incomodas filhas de Eva na igleja da America Latina.* São Paulo: Edições Paulinas.

———. 1994a. *Trindade, coisas velhas e novas—Uma perspectiva ecofeminista.* São Paulo: Edições Paulinas.

———. 1994b. "O gemido da criacao e nossos gemidos. *RIBLA* 21:16–22.

Gill, S., et al., eds. 1994. *Religion in Europe: Contemporary Perspectives.* Kampen, Netherlands: J. H. Kok.

Gilligan, C. 1982. *In a Different Voice.* Cambridge, Mass.: Harvard University Press.

Gilson, A. B. 1995. *Eros Breaking Free: Interpreting Sexual Theo-Ethics.* Cleveland: Pilgrim Press.

Gimbutas, M. 1982. *Gods and Goddesses of Old Europe.* Berkeley: University of California Press.

———. 1991. *The Civilization of the Goddess: The World of Old Europe.* San Francisco: HarperCollins.

Girard, R. 1981. *Violence and the Sacred.* Baltimore: Johns Hopkins University Press.

Glaz, M., and J. S. Moessner, eds. 1991. *Women in Travail and Transition: A New Pastoral Care.* Minneapolis: Fortress.

Gnanadason, A. 1989. "Women and Spirituality in Asia." *IGI* (December): 15–18.

———. 1993. *No Longer Secret: The Church and Violence against Women.* Geneva: World Council of Churches.

———, ed. 1986. *Towards the Theology of Humanhood: Women's Perspectives.* New Delhi: All India Council of Christian Women and ISPCK (Indian Society for the Promotion of Christian Knowledge).

Goldenberg, N. R. 1986. "Anger in the Body: Feminism, Religion and Kleinian Psychoanalytic Theory." *JFSR* 2, 2:39–49.

———. 1987. "The Return of the Goddess: Psychoanalytic Reflections on the Shift from Theology to Thealogy." *Studies in Religion/Sciences religieuses* 16, 1:37–52.

Goldenson, R. M., ed. 1970. *The Encyclopedia of Human Behavior, Psychology, Psychiatry and Mental Health.* Garden City, N.Y.: Doubleday & Co.

Goldin, B. D. 1995. *Bat Mitzvah: A Jewish Girl's Coming of Age.* New York: Viking.

Gonsalvez, A. 1994. "Violence and Women in Asia: The Bangladesh Context." *Voices* 17, 1:70.

González, J. L., and C. G. González. 1994. *The Liberating Pulpit.* Rev. ed. Nashville: Abingdon Press.

Goodfriend, E. A. 1992. "Prostitution, Old Testament." *ABD* 5:505–10.

Goss, R. 1993. *Jesus Acted Up: A Gay and Lesbian Theological Manifesto.* San Francisco: HarperCollins.

Gossen, G. H., ed. 1993. *South and Meso-American Native Spirituality: From the Cult of the Feathered Serpent to the Theology of Liberation.* New York: Crossroad.

Gössmann, E., et al., eds. 1991. *Wörterbuch der feministischen Theologie.* Gütersloh: Gütersloher Verlagshaus Gerd Mohn.

Gottner-Abendroth, H. 1987. *Matriarchal Mythology in Former Times and Today.* Freedom, Calif.: Crossing Press.

Graham, L. K. 1992. *Care of Persons, Care of Worlds.* Nashville: Abingdon Press.

Graham, E., and M. Halsey, eds. 1993. *Life Cycles: Women and Pastoral Care.* London: SPCK.

Gramsci, A. 1971. *Selections from the Prison Notebooks.* Ed. and trans. Quintin Hoare and Geoffrey Nowell Smith. New York: International Publishers.

Grant, J. 1989/1992. *White Women's Christ and Black Women's Jesus: Feminist Christology and Womanist Response.* Atlanta: Scholars Press.

Graves, R. 1948/1966. *The White Goddess: A Historical Grammar of Poetic Truth.* Reprint. New York: Farrar, Straus & Giroux.

Green, R., ed. 1984. *That's What She Said: Contemporary Poetry and Fiction by Native American Women.* Bloomington: Indiana University Press.

Greenberg, B. 1981. *On Women and Judaism: A View from Tradition.* Philadelphia: Jewish Publication Society.

Grey, M. 1989. *Redeeming the Dream: Feminism, Redemption and Christianity.* London: SPCK.

———. 1993. *The Wisdom of Fools? Seeking Revelation for Today.* London: SPCK.

Griffen, V. 1989. *Women, Development and Empowerment: A Pacific Perspective.* Suva, Fiji: Star Printery.

Griffin, S. 1981. *Pornography and Silence: Culture's Revenge against Nature.* New York: Harper & Row.

———. 1982. *Made from the Earth: An Anthology of Writings.* New York: Harper & Row.

Grimshaw, J. 1986. *Philosophy and Feminist Thinking.* Minneapolis: University of Minnesota Press.

Griscom, J. L. 1992. "Women and Power: Definition, Dualism, and Difference." *Psychology of Women Quarterly* 16:389–414.

Gross, R. M. 1978. "Hindu Female Deities as a Resource for the Contemporary Rediscovery of the Goddess." *JAAR* 46, 3:269–91.

———. 1986. "Roundtable Discussion: Feminist Reflections on Separation and Unity in Jewish Theology." *JFSR* 2, 1:127–30.

———. 1993. *Buddhism after Patriarchy: A Feminist History, Analysis and Reconstruction of Buddhism.* Albany: State University of New York Press.

Gross, R. M., and N. Falk. 1989. *Unspoken Worlds: Women's Religious Lives.* San Francisco: Harper & Row.

Grossman, H. Y., and N. L. Chester, eds. 1990. *The Experience and Meaning of Work in Women's Lives.* Hillsdale, N.J.: Lawrence Erlbaum Associates.

Grosz, E. 1994. *Volatile Bodies: Toward a Corporeal Feminism.* Bloomington: Indiana University Press.

Gudorf, C. E. 1994. *Body, Sex and Pleasure: Reconstructing Christian Sexual Ethics.* Cleveland: Pilgrim Press.

Guisso, R. W., and S. Johannessen, eds. 1981. *Women in China: Current Directions in Historical Scholarship.* Youngstown, N.Y.: Philo Press.

Gunew, S., ed. 1990. *Feminist Knowledge: Critique and Construct.* New York: Routledge.

Gutiérrez, G. 1973/1988. *A Theology of Liberation.* 15th anniversary edition. Maryknoll, N.Y.: Orbis Books.

———. 1983. *The Power of the Poor in History.* Maryknoll, N.Y.: Orbis Books.

———. 1990. *Teología de la liberación: Perspectivas.* Salamanca, Spain: Ediciones Sigueme.

Haaken, J. 1993. "From Al-Anon to ACOA: Codependence and the Reconstruction of Caregiving." *JWCS* 18, 2:321–45.

Haddad, Y. Y., and E. B. Findly. 1985. *Women, Religion and Social Change.* Albany: State University of New York Press.

Hallman, D. G., ed. 1989. *AIDS Issues: Confronting the Challenge.* New York: Pilgrim Press.

Halperin, D. M., J. J. Winkler, and F. I. Zeitlin, eds. 1990. *Before Sexuality: The Construction of Erotic Experience in the Ancient Greek World.* Princeton, N.J.: Princeton University Press.

Hampson, D. 1990. *Theology and Feminism.* Cambridge, Mass.: Basil Blackwell.

———. 1995. *After Christianity.* Philadelphia: Trinity Press International.

Hardacre, H. 1989. *Shinto and the State, 1868–1988.* Princeton, N.J.: Princeton University Press.

Hardesty, N. A. 1984. *Women Called to Witness: Evangelical Feminism in the Nineteenth Century.* Nashville: Abingdon Press.

Harding, S. 1991. *Whose Science? Whose Knowledge? Thinking from Women's Lives.* Ithaca, N.Y.: Cornell University Press.

Harrison, B. W. 1983. *Our Right to Choose: Toward a New Ethic of Abortion.* Boston: Beacon Press.

———. 1985. *Making the Connections: Essays in Feminist Social Ethics.* Boston: Beacon Press.

Hartman, J. E., and E. Messer-Davidow, eds. 1991. *(En)Gendering Knowledge—Feminists in Academe.* Knoxville: University of Tennessee Press.

Hartsock, N. 1983. *Money, Sex and Power.* London: Longmans, Green & Co.

Harvey, E. D., and K. Okruhlik, eds. 1992. *Women and Reason.* Ann Arbor: University of Michigan Press.

Hassan, R. 1985. "Made from Adam's Rib: The Woman's Creation Question." *Al-Mushir* 27, 3:124–55.

Hastings, A. 1973. *Christian Marriage in Africa.* London: SPCK.

Haugk, K. C. 1988. *Antagonists in the Church.* Minneapolis: Augsburg.

Hau'ofa, E. 1993. *A New Oceania: Rediscovering Our Sea of Islands.* Suva, Fiji: Star Printery.

Hayes, J. H., and C. R. Holladay. 1987. *Biblical Exegesis: A Beginner's Handbook.* Rev. ed. Atlanta: John Knox Press.

Heinemann, M. 1986. *Gender and Destiny: Women Writers on the Holocaust.* New York: Greenwood Press.

Hensman, P., B. Silva, and M. Perera. 1992. "A Hermeneutic Circle for Doing Women's Theology in Asia: A Sri Lankan Experience." *Voices* 15, 2:143–44.

Herlihy, D. 1985. *Medieval Households.* Cambridge, Mass.: Harvard University Press.

Hershey, L. 1994. "Choosing Disability." *Ms.* 26, 7 (July–August).

Hewlett, S. A. 1986. *A Lesser Life: The Myth of Women's Liberation in America.* New York: William Morrow & Co.

———. 1991. *When the Bough Breaks: The Cost of Neglecting Our Children.* New York: Basic Books.

Heyward, C. 1982. *The Redemption of God: A Theology of Mutual Relation.* Lanham, Md.: University Press of America.

———. 1984. *Our Passion for Justice: Images of Power, Sexuality and Liberation.* New York: Pilgrim Press.

———. 1989a. *Touching Our Strength: The Erotic as Power and the Love of God.* San Francisco: Harper & Row.

———. 1989b. *Speaking of Christ: A Lesbian Feminist Voice.* New York: Pilgrim Press.

———. 1995. *Staying Power.* Cleveland: Pilgrim Press.

Higginbotham, E. B. 1993. *Righteous Discontent: The Women's Movement in the Black Baptist Church 1880–1920.* Cambridge, Mass.: Harvard University Press.

Hill, P. R. 1984. *The World Their Household: The American Woman's Foreign Mission Movement and Cultural Transformation, 1870–1920.* Ann Arbor, Mich.: University Microfilms.

Hines, D. C., ed. 1986. *The State of Afro-American History: Past, Present, and Future.* Baton Rouge: Louisiana State University Press.

Hinkelammert, F. 1988. *La deuda externa en America Latina.* San José, Costa Rica: DEI.

Hinze, C. F. 1992. "Power in Christian Ethics: Resources and Frontiers for Scholarly Exploration." *Annual of the Society of Christian Ethics:* 277–90.

Hirschmann, N. J. 1992. *Rethinking Obligation: A Feminist Method for Political Theory.* Ithaca, N.Y.: Cornell University Press.

Hirshfield, J., ed. 1994. *Women in Praise of the Sacred: Forty-three Centuries of Spiritual Poetry by Women.* New York: HarperCollins.

HIV/AIDS Ministries Network. *HIV/AIDS Ministries Network Focus Papers,* 1989–1995. The United Methodist Church, Room 350, 475 Riverside Drive, New York, NY 10115; (212) 870–3909.

Hoekendijk, J. C. 1952. "The Church in Missionary Thinking." *IRM* 43:324–36.

Hoffman-Ladd, V. J. 1987. "Polemics on the Modesty and Segregation of Women in Contemporary Egypt." *International Journal of Middle East Studies* 19, 1:23–50.

———. 1992. "Mysticism and Sexuality in Sufi Thought and Life." *Mystics Quarterly* 18, 3:82–93.

Holland, N., ed. 1995. *Feminist Interpretations of Derrida.* University Park: Pennsylvania State University Press.

Holland, S., and K. Peterson. 1993. "The Health Care TITANIC: Women and Children First?" *Second Opinion* 18, 3 (October):11–29.

Holmes, H. B., and L. M. Purdy. 1992. *Feminist Perspectives in Medical Ethics.* Bloomington: Indiana University Press.

Homer, *The Homeric Hymns.* 1914. London: G. Allen.

hooks, b. 1984. *Feminist Theory: From Margin to Center.* Boston: South End Press.

———. 1989. *Talking Back: Thinking Feminist/Thinking Black.* Boston: South End Press.

———. 1990. *Yearning: Race, Gender, and Cultural Politics.* Boston: South End Press.

———. 1992. *Black Looks.* Boston: South End Press.

Hopfe, L. M., ed. 1994. *Uncovering Ancient Stones: Essays in Memory of H. Neil Richardson.* Winona Lake, Ind.: Eisenbrauns.

Hough, J. J., and B. G. Wheeler, eds. 1988. *Beyond Clericalism: Congregation as a Focus for Theological Education.* Atlanta: Scholars Press.

Huefner, B., and S. Monteiro. 1992. *"Mulher e Profecia" en O que esta Mulher esta fazendo aqui?* São Bernardo do Campo, Brazil: Imprensa Metodista.

Hunt, M. 1991. *Fierce Tenderness: A Feminist Theology of Friendship.* New York: Crossroad.

Hunter, A. M. 1992. "Numbering the Hairs of Our Heads: Male Social Control and the All-Seeing Male God." *JFSR* 8, 2:7–27.

Irigaray, L. 1987. *Sexes and Genealogies.* Trans. Gillian C. Gill. New York: Columbia University Press.

Inclusive-Language Lectionary: Readings for Years A, B, C., An. 1983–85. New York: Cooperative Publication Association.

Isasi-Díaz, A. M. 1993. *En la lucha (In the Struggle): Elaborating a Mujerista Theology.* Minneapolis: Fortress Press.

———. Forthcoming. "Un poquito de justicia—A Little Bit of Justice: A Mujerista Account of Justice." In A. M. Isasi-Díaz and F. Segovia, eds. *Hispanic/Latino Theology.* Minneapolis: Fortress Press.

Isasi-Díaz, A. M., E. Olazagasti-Segovia, et al. 1992. "Mujeristas: Who We Are and What We Are About." *JFSR* 8, 1:105–25.

Isasi-Díaz, A. M., and Y. Tarango. 1988/1993. *Hispanic Women, Prophetic Voice in the Church: Toward a Hispanic Women's Liberation Theology.* Reprint. Minneapolis: Fortress Press.

Jade. 1991. *To Know: A Guide to Women's Magic and Spirituality.* Oak Park, Ill.: Delphi Press.

Jaggar, A. 1983. *Feminist Politics and Human Nature.* Totowa, N.J.: Rowman & Allanheld.

Jaggar, A. M., and S. R. Bordo, eds. 1989. *Gender/Body/Knowledge: Feminist Reconstructions of Being and Knowing.* New Brunswick, N.J.: Rutgers University Press.

James, S. M., and A.P.A. Busia, eds. 1993. *Theorizing Black Feminisms: The Visionary Pragmatism of Black Women*. New York: Routledge.

Janeway, E. 1981. *Powers of the Weak*. New York: William Morrow & Co.

Jantzen, G. 1984. *God's World, God's Body*. Philadelphia: Westminster Press.

Jardine, A., and P. Smith, eds. 1987. *Men in Feminism*. New York: Methuen.

Jay, K., and J. Glasgow, eds. 1990. *Lesbian Texts and Contexts: Radical Revisions*. New York: New York University Press.

Jay, N. 1992. *Throughout Your Generations Forever: Sacrifice, Religion and Paternity*. Chicago: University of Chicago Press.

Jeffrey, D. L., ed. 1992. *A Dictionary of Biblical Tradition in English Literature*. Grand Rapids: Wm. B. Eerdmans Publishing Co.

Jeremias, J. 1967. *The Prayers of Jesus*. Philadelphia: Fortress Press.

Jewett, P. K. 1975. *MAN as Male and Female*. Grand Rapids: Wm. B. Eerdmans Publishing Co.

John Paul II. 1983. "Considerando che" (Charter of rights of the family). *The Pope Speaks* 29 (October): 78–85.

Johnson, E. A. 1990. *Consider Jesus: Waves of Renewal in Christology*. New York: Crossroad.

———. 1992. *She Who Is: The Mystery of God in Feminist Theological Discourse*. New York: Crossroad.

———. 1993. *Women, Earth and Creator Spirit*. New York: Paulist Press.

Johnson, E. E. 1992. "Ephesians," in *The Women's Bible Commentary*, ed. Newsome and Ringe.

Jones, J. 1985. *Labor of Love, Labor of Sorrow: Black Women, Work and the Family from Slavery to the Present*. New York: Random House.

Jones, N. 1994. *Power of Raven, Wisdom of Serpent: Celtic Women's Spirituality*. Edinburgh: Floris Books.

Jones, S. 1995. *Calvin and the Rhetoric of Piety*. Louisville, Ky.: Westminster John Knox Press.

———. Forthcoming. *Feminist Theory and Theology*. Minneapolis: Fortress Press.

Jordan, J. V., et al. 1991. *Women's Growth in Connection*. New York: Guilford Press.

Joseph, G. I., and J. Lewis. 1981. *Common Differences: Conflicts in Black and White Feminist Perspectives*. New York: Anchor Books, Doubleday & Co.

Joshi, P., ed. 1988. *Gandhi on Women: Collection of Mahatma Gandhi's Writings and Speeches on Women*. New Delhi: Centre for Women's Development Studies.

Joy, M., and P. Magee, eds. 1994. *Claiming Our Rights: Studies in Religion by Australian Women Scholars*. Adelaide: Australian Association for the Study of Religion.

Kalven, J., and M. I. Buckley, eds. 1984. *Women's Spirit Bonding*. New York: Pilgrim Press.

Kanongata'a, K. 1992. "A Pacific Women's Theology of Birthing and Liberation." *Pacific Journal of Theology* 7, 2:3–11.

———. 1994. "Pacific Women and Theology." Paper presented at EATWOT (Ecumenical Association of Third World Theologians) Consultation, Suva, Fiji (September).

Kanyoro, M. 1994. "Cultural Hermeneutics." World Council of Churches Consultation on Women in Dialogue, Bossey Ecumenical Institute, Geneva, May 1–10. Unpublished paper.

Karlsen, C. 1987. *The Devil in the Shape of a Woman: Witchcraft in Colonial New England*. New York: W. W. Norton.

Katoppo, M. 1980. *Compassionate and Free: An Asian Woman's Theology*. Maryknoll, N.Y.: Orbis Books.

Katsuno, L., K. Keay, and O. Ortega, eds. 1994. *God Has Called Us: A Report from the Ecumenical Workshop for Women Theological Educators*. Geneva: World Council of Churches Publications.

Katznelson, I., and A. R. Zolberg, eds. 1986. *Working Class Formation: Nineteenth-Century Patterns in Western Europe and the United States*. Princeton, N.J.: Princeton University Press.

Kaufman, L., ed. 1989. *Feminism and Institutions: Dialogues on Feminist Theory*. Cambridge, Mass.: Basil Blackwell.

Kay, J. W. 1994. "Politics without Human Nature? Reconstructing a Common Humanity." *Hypatia* 9, 1:21–52.

Keck, L., ed. 1994. *New Interpreter's Bible*. Nashville: Abingdon Press.

Kehoe, M. 1989. *Lesbians over 60 Speak for Themselves*. New York: Harrington Park Press.

Keller, C. 1986. *From a Broken Web: Separation, Sexism, and Self*. Boston: Beacon Press.

———. Forthcoming. *Apocalypse Now and Then: A Feminist Approach to the End of the World*. Boston: Beacon Press.

Kelly, J. 1984. *Women, History and Theory*. Chicago: University of Chicago Press.

Kim, C.W.M., S. M. St. Ville, and S. M. Simonaitis, eds. 1993. *Transfigurations: Theology and the French Feminists*. Minneapolis: Fortress Press.

Kim, Y.-B. 1992. *Messiah and Mining: Christ's Solidarity with the People for New Life*. Singapore: Christian Conference of Asia, Urban Rural Mission.

———, ed. 1981. *Minjung Theology: People as the Subjects of History*. Singapore: Christian Conference of Asia.

King, K. L., ed. 1988. *Images of the Feminine in Gnosticism*. Philadelphia: Fortress Press.

King, U. 1989. *Women and Spirituality: Voices of Protest and Promise*. New York: New Amsterdam.

———, ed. 1991. *Liberating Women: New Theological Directions*. Bristol: European Society of Women in Theological Research, Bristol University.

———, ed. 1994. *Feminist Theology from the Third World: A Reader*. Maryknoll, N.Y.: Orbis Books.

———, ed. 1995. *Religion and Gender*. Cambridge, Mass.: Basil Blackwell.

Kinnamon, M. 1988. *Truth and Community: Diversity and Its Limits in the Ecumenical Movement*. Grand Rapids: Wm. B. Eerdmans Publishing Co.

Kinsley, D. R. 1986. *Hindu Goddesses: Visions of the Divine Feminine in the Hindu Religious Tradition*. Berkeley: University of California Press.

Kinukawa, H. 1994. *Women and Jesus in Mark: A Japanese Feminist Perspective*. Maryknoll, N.Y.: Orbis Books.

Kittay, E. F., and D. T. Meyers, eds. 1987. *Women and Moral Theory*. Totowa, N.J.: Rowman & Littlefield.

Kittel, G., and G. Friedrich, eds. 1964–76. *Theological Dictionary of the New Testament*. Grand Rapids: Wm. B. Eerdmans Publishing Co.

Kitzinger, C. 1993. *The Social Construction of Lesbianism*. Beverly Hills, Calif.: Sage.

Klein, A. C. 1994. *Meeting the Great Bliss Queen: Buddhists, Feminists and the Art of the Self*. Boston: Beacon Press.

Knox, J. 1967. *The Humanity and Divinity of Christ*. Cambridge: Cambridge University Press.

Komonchak, J. A., M. Collins, and D. Lane, eds. 1987. *The New Dictionary of Theology*. Wilmington, Del.: Michael Glazier.

Kraemer, R. 1992. *Her Share of the Blessings: Women's Religions among Pagans, Jews, and Christians in the Greco-Roman World*. New York: Oxford University Press.

Kramarae, C., and D. Spender, eds. 1992. *The Knowledge Explosion: Generations of Feminist Scholarship*. New York: Teachers College Press.

Kristeva, J. 1977. *About Chinese Women*. Trans. Anita Barrows. London: Marion Boyars.

———. 1984. *Revolution in Poetic Language*. Trans. Margaret Waller. New York: Columbia University Press.

Kuhn, T. 1970. *Structure of Scientific Revolutions*. Chicago: University of Chicago Press.

Kumari, R. 1989. "Brides Are Not for Burning: Dowry Victims in India." New Delhi: Radiant Publishers.

Kwok, P.-l. 1992. *Chinese Women and Christianity, 1860–1927*. Atlanta: Scholars Press.

———. 1995. *Discovering the Bible in the Non-Biblical World*. Maryknoll, N.Y.: Orbis Books.

LaCugna, C. M. 1991. *God for Us: The Trinity and Christian Life*. San Francisco: HarperCollins.

———, ed. 1993. *Freeing Theology: The Essentials of Theology in Feminist Perspective*. San Francisco: Harper & Row.

Lammers, S., and A. Verhey, eds. 1987. *On Moral Medicine: Theological Perspectives in Medical Ethics*. Grand Rapids: Wm. B. Eerdmans Publishing Co.

Lampe, P. 1992. "Junias." *ABD* 3:1127.

Landry, D., and G. MacLean. 1993. *Materialist Feminisms*. Oxford: Basil Blackwell.

Lang, B. 1987. "The Sexual Life of the Saints: Towards an Anthropology of Christian Heaven." *Religion* 17 (August): 149–71.

Larner, C. 1983. *The Enemies of God: The Witch-Hunt in Scotland*. Oxford: Basil Blackwell.

Larsson, B. 1991. *Conversion to Greater Freedom? Women, Church and Social Change in North-Western Tanzania under Colonial Rule*. Uppsala, Sweden: Acta Universitatis Upsaliensis.

Lebacqz, K. 1987. *Justice in an Unjust World: Foundations for a Christian Approach to Justice*. Minneapolis: Augsburg.

Lebacqz, K., and R. Barton. 1991. *Sex in the Parish*. Louisville, Ky.: Westminster John Knox Press.

Leddy, M. J. 1990. *Reweaving Religious Life: Beyond the Liberal Model*. Mystic, Conn.: Twenty-Third Publications.

Lederer, L., ed. 1980. *Take Back the Night: Women on Pornography*. New York: William Morrow & Co.

Lee, J. Y., ed. 1988. *An Emerging Theology in World Perspective: Commentary on Korean Minjung Theology*. Mystic, Conn.: Twenty-Third Publications.

Lee, P.K.H., and H. K. Chung. 1990. "A Cross-Cultural Dialogue on the Yin-Yang Symbol." *Ching Feng* 33, 3:136–57.

Lee-Park, S. A., ed. 1985–present. *In God's Image*. Asian Women's Resource Centre for Culture and Theology, 134–5 Nokbun-Dong, Eunpyong-Ku, Seoul, 122–020 Korea.

LeFevre, P. D. 1982. "Liberation Theology." *CTS* 72, 2:33–39.

Lefkowitz, R., and A. Withorn, eds. 1986. *For Crying Out Loud: Women and Poverty in the United States.* New York: Pilgrim Press.

Leopold, A. 1966. *A Sand County Almanac, with Essays on Conservation from Round River.* New York: Ballantine Books.

Lerner, G. 1986. *The Creation of Patriarchy.* New York: Oxford University Press.

———. 1993. *The Creation of Feminist Consciousness.* New York: Oxford University Press.

Leslie, J., ed. 1991. *Roles and Rituals for Hindu Women.* London: Pinter.

Levenson, J. D. 1988. *Creation and the Persistence of Evil.* San Francisco: Harper & Row.

———. 1993. *The Death and Resurrection of the Beloved Son: The Transformation of Child Sacrifice in Judaism and Christianity.* New Haven, Conn.: Yale University Press.

Levin, J., and W. C. Levin. 1980. *Ageism.* Belmont, Calif.: Wadsworth.

Levine, H. G. 1978. "The Discovery of Addiction: Changing Conceptions of Habitual Drunkenness in America." *JSA* 39, 1:143–74.

Levine, M. 1994. *Pantheism.* London: Routledge.

Levitan, S., and I. Shapiro. 1987. *Working but Poor: America's Contradiction.* Baltimore: Johns Hopkins University Press.

Levitt, L. 1992. "Covenantal Relationships and the Problem of Marriage: Toward a Post-Liberal Jewish Feminist Theology." Paper for the Annual Meeting of the American Academy of Religion, San Francisco, Nov. 20, 1992.

Lewis, C. S. 1962. "Bluspels and Flananferes," in *The Importance of Language,* ed. M. Black. Englewood Cliffs, N.J.: Prentice-Hall, 47.

Lewis, I. M. 1971. *Ecstatic Religion: An Anthropological Study of Spirit Possession and Shamanism.* West Drayton, Middlesex: Penguin Books.

Ligo, A. 1993. "Banahaw Women's Religiosity." *IGI* 12, 3:16–22.

Liturgy Training Program. 1995. *The Psalter: International Commission on English in the Liturgy.* Chicago: Liturgy Training Publications.

Lloyd, G. 1984. *The Man of Reason: 'Male' and 'Female' in Western Philosophy.* Minneapolis: University of Minnesota Press.

Loades, A., ed. 1990. *Feminist Theology: A Reader.* Louisville, Ky.: Westminster John Knox Press.

Long, A. 1992. *In a Chariot Drawn by Lions.* London: Women's Press.

Long, G.D.C. 1993. *Passion and Reason.* Louisville, Ky.: Westminster John Knox Press.

Lorber, J., and S. Farrell. 1991. *The Social Construction of Gender.* Newbury Park, Calif.: Sage.

Lorde, A. 1984. *Sister Outsider: Essays and Speeches.* Trumansburg, N.Y.: Crossing Press.

Loth, B., and A. Michel, eds. 1951–77. *Dictionnaire de théologie Catholique.* 3 vols. Paris: Letouzey & Ané.

Lovelock, J. 1988. *The Ages of Gaia.* New York: W. W. Norton.

Luke, C., and J. Gore, eds. 1992. *Feminisms and Critical Pedagogy.* New York: Routledge.

Luker, K. 1984. *Abortion and the Politics of Motherhood.* Berkeley: University of California Press.

Luntley, M. 1990. *The Meaning of Socialism.* La Salle, Ill.: Open Court.

MacDonald, B., and C. Rich. 1991. *Look Me in the Eye: Old Women, Aging, and Ageism.* San Francisco: Spinsters Book Co.

MacDonald, D. R. 1983. *The Legend and the Apostle: The Battle for Paul in Story and Canon.* Philadelphia: Westminster Press.

Mack, P. 1992. *Visionary Women: Ecstatic Prophecy in Seventeenth-Century England.* Berkeley: University of California Press.

Mackin, T. M. 1982. *What Is Marriage?* New York: Paulist Press.

MacKinnon, C. A. 1987. *Feminism Unmodified: Discourses on Life and Law.* Cambridge, Mass.: Harvard University Press.

Maimela, S. S. 1994. *Culture, Religion and Liberation.* Pretoria: University of South Africa.

Mainstream Magazine. 1994– . Exploding Myths, Inc., P.O. Box 370498, San Diego, CA 92137-0598.

Malina, B. J. 1981/1993. *The New Testament World: Insights from Cultural Anthropology.* Rev. ed. Louisville, Ky.: Westminster John Knox Press.

Malson, M. R., J. F. O'Barr, S. Westphal-Wihl, and M. Wyer, eds. 1989. *Feminist Theory in Practice and Process.* Chicago: University of Chicago Press.

Mananzan, M. J., ed. 1987/1991. *Essays on Women.* Rev. ed. Manila: Institute of Women's Studies.

Mananzan, M. J., et al., eds. 1996. *Women Struggling against Violence: A Spirituality for Life.* Maryknoll, N.Y.: Orbis Books.

Marable, M. 1983. *How Capitalism Underdeveloped Black America.* Boston: South End Press.

Marcus, E. 1993. *Is It a Choice? Answers to Three Hundred of the Most Frequently Asked Questions about Gays and Lesbians*. San Francisco: Harper & Row.

Marcus, G. E., and M.M.J. Fischer. 1986. *Anthropology as Cultural Critique: An Experimental Moment in the Human Sciences.* Chicago: University of Chicago Press.

Marshall, P. 1984. *Praisesong for the Widow.* New York: E. P. Dutton.

Marshall, S., ed. 1989. *Women in Reformation and Counter-Reformation Europe: Public and Private Worlds.* Bloomington: Indiana University Press.

Martin, C. J. 1990. "Womanist Interpretations of the New Testament: The Quest for Holistic and Inclusive Translation and Interpretation." *JFSR* 6, 2:41–61.

Marx, K. 1964. "Theses on Feuerbach," no. 11, in K. Marx and F. Engels, On Religion. New York: Schocken Books.

———. 1977. *Selected Writings.* Oxford: Oxford University Press.

Matter, E. A., and J. Coakley, eds. 1994. *Creative Women in Medieval and Early Modern Italy: A Religious and Artistic Renaissance.* Philadelphia: University of Pennsylvania Press.

Mavor, J. E., ed. 1977. *Traditional Belief and the Christian Faith*. Suva, Fiji: Lotu Pasifika Productions.

Maxwell, M. 1992. "Moral Inertia." *Zygon* 27 (March): 51–64.

May, M. A. 1989. *Bonds of Unity: Women, Theology, and the Worldwide Church.* Atlanta: Scholars Press.

———, ed. 1991. *Women and Church: The Challenge of Ecumenical Solidarity in an Age of Alienation.* New York: Friendship Press.

Mbiti, J. S. 1969. *African Religions and Philosophy.* London: William Heinemann.

McAllister, P., ed. 1982. *Reweaving the Web of Life: Feminism and Nonviolence.* Philadelphia: New Society Publishers.

McFague, S. 1982. *Metaphorical Theology: Models of God in Religious Language.* Philadelphia: Fortress Press.

———. 1987. *Models of God: Theology for an Ecological, Nuclear Age.* Philadelphia: Fortress Press.

———. 1993. *The Body of God: An Ecological Theology.* Minneapolis: Fortress Press.

McGinn, B. 1991. *The Presence of God: A History of Western Christian Mysticism.* New York: Crossroad.

McGoldrick, M., C. Anderson, and F. Walsh, eds. 1989. *Women in Families.* New York: W. W. Norton & Co.

McIntosh, P. 1988. "White Privilege and Male Privilege." Working Paper No. 189, Wellesley College, Center for Research on Women, Wellesley, MA 02181.

McKinley, J. 1994. "Wisdom the Host?" Ph.D. diss., University of Otago, Dunedin, N.Z.

Merchant, C. 1992. *Radical Ecology: The Search for a Livable World.* New York: Routledge.

Metzger, B. M., and M. D. Coogan, eds. 1993. *The Oxford Companion to the Bible.* Oxford: Oxford University Press.

Meurer, S., ed. 1991. *The Apocrypha in Ecumenical Perspective.* New York: United Bible Societies.

Meyers, C. 1988. *Discovering Eve: Ancient Israelite Women in Context.* New York: Oxford University Press.

———. 1992. "The Contributions of Archaeology." In *The Oxford Study Bible,* New York: Oxford University Press, 48–56.

Meyers, C., T. Craven, and R. Kraemer, eds. Forthcoming. *Dictionary of Women in Scripture: Named and Unnamed Women in the Hebrew Bible, Apocrypha, and New Testament.* Boston: Houghton Mifflin Co.

Meyers, D. T. 1989. *Self, Society , and Personal Choice.* New York: Columbia University Press.

Mies, M., and V. Shiva. 1993. *Ecofeminism.* Atlantic Highlands, N.J.: Zed Books.

Miles, M. 1988. *Practicing Christianity: Critical Perspectives for an Embodied Spirituality.* New York: Crossroad.

———. 1989. *Carnal Knowing: Female Nakedness and Religious Meaning in the Christian West.* Boston: Beacon Press.

———. 1992. *Desire and Delight: A New Reading of Augustine's Confessions.* New York: Crossroad.

Milhaven, J. G. 1989. *Good Anger.* Kansas City, Mo.: Sheed & Ward.

Miller, A. 1981. *The Drama of the Gifted Child: How Narcissistic Parents Form and Deform the Emotional Lives of Their Talented Children.* Trans. Ruth Ward. New York: Basic Books.

Miller, J. B. 1976. *Toward a New Psychology of Women.* Boston: Beacon Press.

Miller, P. D., et al., eds. 1987. *Ancient Israelite Religion: Essays in Honor of Frank Moore Cross.* Philadelphia: Fortress Press.

Miller-McLemore, B. J. 1994. *Also a Mother: Work and Family as Theological Dilemma.* Nashville: Abingdon Press.

Millet, K. 1970. *Sexual Politics.* Garden City, N.Y.: Doubleday & Co.

Minear, P. S. 1994. *Christians and the New Creation: Genesis Motifs in the New Testament.*

Louisville, Ky.: Westminster John Knox Press.

Minnich, E. K. 1990. *Transforming Knowledge.* Philadelphia: Temple University Press.

Miralao, V., C. Carlos, and A. Santos. 1990. *Women Entertainers in Angeles and Olongapo: A Survey Report.* Manila: WEDPRO (Women's Education, Development, Productivity, and Research Organization) and KALAYAAN (Katipunan ng Katabaihan para sa Kalayaan).

Mitchell, J. 1971. *Woman's Estate.* New York: Vintage Books.

Mitchell, S. 1993. *A Book of Psalms.* New York: HarperCollins.

Mohanty, C. T., A. Russo, and L. Torres, eds. 1991. *Third World Women and the Politics of Feminism.* Bloomington: Indiana University Press.

Mollenkott, V. R. 1987. *Godding: Human Responsibility and the Bible.* New York: Crossroad.

———. 1977/1988. *Women, Men and the Bible.* Rev. ed. New York: Crossroad.

———. 1992. *Sensuous Spirituality: Out from Fundamentalism.* New York: Crossroad.

———, ed. 1988. *Women of Faith in Dialogue.* New York: Crossroad.

Moltmann-Wendel, E. 1978. *Freedom, Equality and Sisterhood: On the Emancipation of Women in Church and Society.* Trans. Ruth Gritsch. Philadelphia: Fortress Press.

———. 1982. *The Women around Jesus* Trans. John Bowden. New York: Crossroad.

———. 1986. *A Land Flowing with Milk and Honey: Perspectives on Feminist Theology.* Trans. John Bowden. New York: Crossroad.

———. 1995. *I Am My Body: New Waves of Embodiment.* Trans. John Bowden. New York: Continuum.

Mooney, C. M. 1990. *Philippine Duchesne: A Woman with the Poor.* New York: Paulist Press.

Morgan, R., ed. 1970. *Sisterhood Is Powerful: An Anthology of Writings from the Women's Liberation Movement.* New York: Vintage Books.

Morley, J. 1988. *All Desires Known: Prayers Uniting Faith and Feminism.* Wilton, Conn.: Morehouse-Barlow.

Morrison, T. 1992. *Playing in the Dark: Whiteness and the Literary Imagination.* Cambridge, Mass.: Harvard University Press.

———, ed. 1992. *Race-ing Justice, En-Gendering Power: Essays on Anita Hill, Clarence Thomas, and the Construction of Social Reality.* New York: Pantheon Books.

Morton, N. 1985. *The Journey Is Home.* Boston: Beacon Press.

Mud Flower Collective. 1985. *God's Fierce Whimsy: Christian Feminism and Theological Education.* New York: Pilgrim Press.

Mulack, C. 1987. *Jesus: Der Gesalbte der Frauen.* Stuttgart: Kreuz Verlag.

Murakami, S. 1991. *Kokka Shinto* (State Shinto). Tokyo: Iwanami.

Musurillo, H. 1972. *Acts of the Christian Martyrs.* Oxford: Clarendon Press.

Nag Hammadi Library in English, 1988. Trans. by members of the Coptic Gnostic Library Project of the Institute for Antiquity and Christianity, Claremont, Calif. San Francisco: Harper & Row. 3d ed., rev.

Namihira, E. 1986. *Kurasi no naka no bunka jinruigaku* (Cultural anthropology of our daily life). Tokyo: Hukutake Shoten.

Nashat, G., ed. 1983. *Women and Revolution in Iran.* Boulder, Colo.: Westview Press.

Nathanson, D. L. 1992. *Shame and Pride: Affect, Sex and the Birth of the Self.* New York: W. W. Norton & Co.

Neal, M. A. 1990. *From Nuns to Sisters: An Expanding Vocation.* Mystic, Conn.: Twenty-Third Publications.

Nelson, J. B. 1979. *Embodiment: An Approach to Sexuality and Christian Theology.* Minneapolis: Augsburg.

Netland, H. A. 1991. *Dissonant Voices: Religious Pluralism and the Question of Truth.* Grand Rapids: Wm. B. Eerdmans Publishing Co.

Neu, D. L., and M. E. Hunt. 1993. *Women-Church Sourcebook.* Silver Spring, Md.: WATERworks Press.

New Revised Standard Version Bible. 1989. New York: Division of Christian Education of the National Council of the Churches of Christ in the U.S.A.

Newsom, C. A., and S. H. Ringe, eds. 1992. *The Women's Bible Commentary.* Louisville, Ky.: Westminster John Knox Press.

Nichols, J. A., and L. T. Shank, eds. 1984–87. *Medieval Religious Women.* Vols. 1–2. Kalamazoo, Mich.: Cistercian Publications.

Nicholson, L. J., ed. 1990. *Feminism/Postmodernism.* New York: Routledge.

Nickelsburg, G.W.E. 1981. *Jewish Literature between the Bible and the Mishnah.* Philadelphia: Fortress Press.

Nickelsburg, G.W.E., and G. W. MacRae, eds. 1986. *Christians among Jews and Gentiles: Essays in Honor of Krister Stendahl on His Sixty-fifth Birthday.* Philadelphia: Fortress Press.

Nida, E. A., and C. R. Taber. 1974. *The Theory and Practice of Translation.* Leiden: E. J. Brill.

Noddings, N. 1984. *Caring: A Feminine Approach to Ethics and Moral Education.* Berkeley: University of California Press.

Northup, L., ed. 1993. *Women and Religious Ritual.* Washington, D.C.: Pastoral Press.

Nussbaum, M., and A. Sen, eds. 1993. *Quality of Life.* Oxford: Clarendon Press.

Ochs, V. 1990. *Words on Fire: One Woman's Journey into the Sacred.* San Diego: Harcourt Brace Jovanovich.

Oden, T. 1983. *Pastoral Theology.* San Francisco: Harper & Row.

Oduyoye, M. A. 1986. *Hearing and Knowing: Theological Reflections on Christianity in Africa.* Maryknoll, N.Y.: Orbis Books.

———. 1990. *Who Will Roll the Stone Away?* Geneva: World Council of Churches.

———. 1995. *Daughters of Anowa: African Women and Patriarchy.* Maryknoll, N.Y.: Orbis Books.

Oduyoye, M. A., and M.R.A. Kanyoro, eds. 1992. *The Will to Arise.* Maryknoll, N.Y.: Orbis Books.

Okoshi, A. 1990. *Seisabetu suru Bukkyo* (Sexism in Buddhism). Kyoto: Hosokan.

OLOC (Old Lesbians Organizing for Change) P.O. Box 980422, Houston, TX 77098.

O'Neill, M. 1990. *Women Speaking, Women Listening: Women in Interreligious Dialogue.* Maryknoll, N.Y.: Orbis Books.

Ormerod, T., and N. Ormerod. 1995. *When Ministers Sin.* Alexandria, New South Wales: Millennium Books.

Ortega, O., ed. 1995. *Women's Visions: Theological Reflection, Celebration, Action.* Geneva: World Council of Churches Publications.

Osiek, C. 1993. "The Widow as Altar: The Rise and Fall of a Symbol." *Second Century* 3 (fall): 159–60.

Outka, G., and J.P.J. Reeder, eds. 1993. *Prospects of a Common Morality.* Princeton, N.J.: Princeton University Press.

Overall, C. 1987. *Ethics and Human Reproduction: A Feminist Analysis.* Boston: Allen & Unwin.

Pagels, E. 1979. *The Gnostic Gospels.* New York: Random House.

———. 1988. *Adam, Eve, and the Serpent.* New York: Random House.

Pang, P. 1985. "Origins of the Yin-Yang and Five Elements Concepts." *Social Sciences in China* 6 (spring): 91–131.

Pardes, I. 1992. *Countertraditions in the Bible: A Feminist Approach.* Cambridge, Mass.: Harvard University Press.

Park, N.-S. K. 1994. *Ideology and Utopia: Taoist and Feminist Theological Responses to the Ideological Structures of Confucianism and Christianity.* Ann Arbor, Mich.: University Microfilms.

Parsons, S. F. 1988. "The Intersection of Feminism and Theological Ethics: A Philosophical Approach." *Modern Theology* 4, 3:251–66.

Parvey, C. F., ed. 1983. *The Community of Women and Men in the Church.* Philadelphia: Fortress Press.

Pathil, K., ed. 1987. *Socio-Cultural Analyses in Theologizing.* Bangalore, India: Indian Theological Association.

Paul, D. Y. 1979. *Women in Buddhism: Images of the Feminine in Mahayana Tradition.* Berkeley, Calif.: Asian Humanities Press.

Pearce, D. M. 1978. "The Feminization of Pov-erty: Women, Work, and Welfare." *Urban and Social Change Review* 1, 11:28–36.

———. 1983. "The Feminization of Ghetto Poverty." *Society* (November–December): 70–73.

Peavey, F. 1990. *A Shallow Pool of Time: An HIV+ Woman Grapples with the AIDS Epidemic.* Philadelphia: New Society Publishers.

Pellauer, M. 1987. "Is There a Gender Gap in Heaven?" *C/C* 47 (March 2): 60–61.

Pellauer, M. D. 1991. *Toward a Tradition of Feminist Theology.* Brooklyn, N.Y.: Carlson.

———. 1993. "The Moral Significance of Female Orgasm: Toward Sexual Ethics That Celebrates Women's Sexuality," *JFSR* 9:1/2 (spring/fall): 147–60.

Pellauer, M., et al., eds. 1987. *Sexual Assault and Abuse: A Handbook for Clergy and Religious Professionals.* San Francisco: Harper & Row.

Perkins, P. 1984. *Resurrection: New Testament Witness and Contemporary Reflection.* Garden City, N.Y.: Doubleday & Co.

———. 1988. "Women in the Bible and Its World." *Int* 42, 1:33–44.

Pero, A., and A. Moro, eds. 1988. *Theology and the Black Experience.* Minneapolis: Augsburg.

Peter-Raoul, M., et al., eds. 1990. *Yearning to Breathe Free: Liberation Theologies in the U.S.* Maryknoll, N.Y.: Orbis Books.

Peters, J., and A. Wolper, eds. 1995. *Women's Rights, Human Rights: International Feminist Perspectives.* New York: Routledge.

Petroff, E. A. 1994. *Body and Soul: Essays on Medieval Women and Mysticism.* New York: Oxford University Press.

———, ed. 1986. *Medieval Women's Visionary Literature.* New York: Oxford University Press.

Pieris, A. 1988. *An Asian Theology of Liberation.* Maryknoll, N.Y.: Orbis Books.

Pippin, T. 1992. *Death and Desire: The Rhetoric of Gender in the Apocalypse of John.* Louisville, Ky.: Westminster John Knox Press.

Plaskow, J. 1980. *Sex, Sin and Grace: Women's Experience and the Theologies of Reinhold Niebuhr and Paul Tillich.* Washington, D.C.: University Press of America.

———. 1990. *Standing Again at Sinai: Judaism from a Feminist Perspective.* San Francisco: Harper & Row.

———. 1991. "Feminist Anti-Judaism and the Christian God." *JFSR* 7, 2:99–108.

———. 1993. "We Are Also Your Sisters: The Development of Women's Studies in Religion." *Women's Studies Quarterly* 21, 1/2: 9–21.

———, ed. 1973. *Women and Religion.* Missoula, Mont.: American Academy of Religion.

Plaskow, J., and C. P. Christ, eds. 1989. *Weaving the Visions: New Patterns in Feminist Spirituality.* San Francisco: Harper & Row.

Pobee, J., ed. 1994. *Culture, Women and Theology.* Delhi: The Indian Society for Promoting Christian Knowledge.

Pobee, J. S., and B. Von Wartenberg-Potter, eds. 1986. *New Eyes for Reading: Biblical and Theological Reflections by Women from the Third World.* Geneva: World Council of Churches.

Pomeroy, S. 1975/1995. *Goddesses, Whores, Wives, and Slaves: Women in Classical Antiquity.* New York: Schocken Books.

Potter, P. 1973. "Christ's Mission and Ours in Today's World." *IRM* 62 (April): 151.

Prelinger, C. M., ed. 1992. *Episcopal Women: Gender, Spirituality, and Commitment in an American Mainline Denomination.* New York: Oxford University Press.

Preminger, A., ed. 1974. *Princeton Encyclopedia of Poetry and Poetics.* Enlarged ed. Princeton, N.J.: Princeton University Press.

Primavesi, A. 1991. *From Apocalypse to Genesis: Ecology, Feminism, and Christianity.* Minneapolis: Fortress Press.

Procter-Smith, M. 1990. *In Her Own Rite: Constructing Feminist Liturgical Tradition.* Nashville: Abingdon Press.

———. 1992a. "Lectionaries: Principles and Problems—Alternative Perspectives." *Studia Liturgica* 22, 1:84–99.

———. 1992b. "The Marks of Feminist Liturgy." *Proceedings of the North American Academy of Liturgy*, 69–75.

Procter-Smith, M., and J. Walton, eds. 1993. *Women at Worship: Interpretations of North American Diversity.* Louisville, Ky.: Westminster John Knox Press.

Purvis, S. B. 1993. *The Power of the Cross: Foundations for a Christian Feminist Ethic of Community.* Nashville: Abingdon Press.

Radtke, L. H., and H. J. Stam, eds. 1994. *Power/Gender: Social Relations in Theory and Practice.* London: Sage.

Ramshaw, G., and J. Walton, eds. 1995. *God beyond Gender: Feminist Christian God-Language.* Minneapolis: Fortress Press.

Rasmussen, L., ed. 1983. *The Annual of the Society of Christian Ethics.* Washington, D.C.: Georgetown University Press.

Ravven, H. 1986. "Creating a Jewish Feminist Philosophy." *Anima* 12 (fall): 96–105.

Raymond, J. G. 1979. *The Transsexual Empire: The Making of the She-Male.* Boston: Beacon Press.

———. 1986. *A Passion for Friends: Toward a Philosophy of Female Affection.* Boston: Beacon Press.

———. 1993. *Women as Wombs: Reproductive Technologies and the Battle over Women's Freedom.* New York: HarperCollins.

Reid, D. 1991. *New Wine: The Cultural Shaping of Japanese Christianity.* Berkeley, Calif.: Asian Humanities Press.

"Report from India: Spirituality for Life: Women Struggling against Violence." 1994. *Voices* 17 (June): 84.

Report of the Commission on Obscenity and Pornography. 1979. New York: Bantam Books.

Rest, J. 1979. *Development in Judging Moral Issues.* Minneapolis: University of Minnesota Press.

Rhode, D. L. 1989. *Justice and Gender.* Cambridge, Mass.: Harvard University Press.

Rhodes, L. N. 1987. *Co-Creating: A Feminist Vision of Ministry.* Philadelphia: Westminster Press.

Rhodes, L. N., and N. D. Richardson. 1986. *Mending Severed Connections: Theological Education for Communal Transformation.* San Francisco: San Francisco Network Ministries.

Rich, A. 1979. *On Lies, Secrets, and Silence: Selected Prose 1966–1976.* New York: W. W. Norton & Co.

———. 1986. *Of Woman Born: Motherhood as Experience and Institution.* 10th anniversary ed. New York: W. W. Norton & Co.

Richardson, H., ed. 1987. *On the Problem of Surrogate Parenthood: Analyzing the Baby M Case.* Lewiston, N.Y.: Edwin Mellen Press.

Ricoeur, P. 1970. *Freud and Philosophy: An Essay on Interpretation*. New Haven, Conn.: Yale University Press.

Riggs, M. Y. 1994. *Arise, Awake, and Act: A Womanist Call for Black Liberation*. Cleveland: Pilgrim Press.

Ringe, S. H. 1985. *Jesus, Liberation, and the Biblical Jubilee: Images for Ethics and Christology*. Philadelphia: Fortress Press.

———. 1987. "Standing toward the Text." *Theology Today* 43, 4:552–57.

Rittner, C., and J. K. Roth, eds. 1993. *Different Voices: Women and the Holocaust*. New York: Paragon House.

Robb, C. S. 1993. "Principles for a Woman-Friendly Economy," *JFSR* 9:1/2 (spring/fall): 147–60.

Robbins, T., and D. Anthony, eds. 1990. *In Gods We Trust: New Patterns of Religious Pluralism in America*. 2d ed. New Brunswick, N.J.: Transaction Publishers.

Roberts, W. P., ed. 1987. *Commitment to Partnership: Explorations of the Theology of Marriage*. New York: Paulist Press.

Rodriguez, R. M. 1994. *Femenino fin de siglo: La seducción de la diferencia*. Barcelona: Anthropos.

Rose, D. (1990). *Living the Ethnographic Life*. Newbury Park, Calif.: Sage.

Rosenau, P. M. 1992. *Post-Modernism and the Social Sciences*. Princeton, N.J.: Princeton University Press.

Ross, A. 1967/1986. *The Pagan Celts*. Updated, expanded, and reillustrated ed. Totowa, N.J.: Barnes & Noble Books.

Ross, S. A. 1989. "'Then Honor God in Your Body' (1 Cor. 6:20): Feminist and Sacramental Theology on the Body." *Horizons* 16, 1:7–27.

Rowbotham, S. 1994. *Dignity and Daily Bread: New Forms of Economic Organizing among Poor Women in the Third World and First*. London: Routledge.

Rudavsky, T. M., ed. 1995. *Gender and Judaism: The Transformation of Tradition*. New York: New York University Press.

Ruddick, S. 1989. *Maternal Thinking: Toward a Politics of Peace*. Boston: Beacon Press.

Ruether, R. R. 1975/1995. *New Woman, New Earth: Sexist Ideologies and Human Liberation*. New York: Seabury Press.

———. 1981. *To Change the World: Christology and Cultural Criticism*. New York: Crossroad.

———. 1983/1993. *Sexism and God-Talk: Toward a Feminist Theology*. Reprint. Boston: Beacon Press.

———. 1985. *Women-Church: Theology and Practice of Feminist Liturgical Communities*. New York: Harper & Row.

———. 1990. "Is Feminism the End of Christianity? A Critique of Daphne Hampson's Theology and Feminism." *Scottish Journal of Theology* 43, 3:390–400.

———. 1992. *Gaia and God: An Ecofeminist Theology of Earth Healing*. San Francisco: HarperCollins.

———, ed. 1974. *Religion and Sexism: Images of Women in the Jewish and Christian Traditions*. New York: Simon & Schuster.

Ruether, R. R., and R. S. Keller, eds. 1981–86. *Women and Religion in America*. 3 vols. San Francisco: Harper & Row.

———, eds. 1995. *In Our Own Voices: Four Centuries of American Women's Religious Writing*. San Francisco: Harper & Row.

Ruether, R. R., and H. J. Ruether. 1989. *The Wrath of Jonah: The Crisis of Religious Nationalism in the Israeli-Palestinian Conflict*. New York: Harper & Row.

Russell, L. M. 1974. *Human Liberation in a Feminist Perspective—A Theology*. Philadelphia: Westminster Press.

———. 1979. *The Future of Partnership*. Philadelphia: Westminster Press.

———. 1981. *Growth in Partnership*. Philadelphia: Westminster Press.

———. 1982. *Becoming Human*. Philadelphia: Westminster Press.

———. 1987. *Household of Freedom: Authority in Feminist Theology*. Philadelphia: Westminster Press.

———. 1988. "Unity and Renewal in Feminist Perspective." *Mid-Stream* 27:55–66.

———. 1991. "Feminism and the Church: A Quest for New Styles of Ministry." *Ministerial Formation*, no. 55: 28–37.

———, ed. 1985a. *Feminist Interpretation of the Bible*. Philadelphia: Westminster Press.

———, ed. 1985b. *Changing Contexts of Our Faith*. Philadelphia: Fortress Press.

———, ed. 1990. *The Church with AIDS: Renewal in the Midst of Crisis*. Louisville, Ky.: Westminster John Knox Press.

———, ed. 1993. *Church in the Round: Feminist Interpretations of the Church*. Louisville, Ky.: Westminster John Knox Press.

Russell, L. M., et al., eds. 1988. *Inheriting Our Mothers' Gardens: Feminist Theology in Third World Perspective*. Philadelphia: Westminster Press.

Ryan, M. 1990. "The Argument for Unlimited Procreative Liberty: A Feminist Critique." *Hastings Center Report* 20, 4 (July–August): 6–12.

Saiving, V. 1960. "The Human Situation: A Feminine View." *Journal of Religion* (April).

Sakenfeld, K. D. 1985. *Faithfulness in Action: Loyalty in Biblical Perspective.* Philadelphia: Fortress Press.

———. 1988. "In the Wilderness, Awaiting the Land: The Daughters of Zelophad and Feminist Interpretation." *Princeton Seminary Bulletin* 9:179–96.

Salkin, J. 1991. *Putting God on the Guest List.* Woodstock, Vt.: Jewish Lights Press, 1991.

Sanday, P. 1981. *Female Power and Male Dominance.* Cambridge: Cambridge University Press.

Sanders, C. J., ed. 1995. *Living in the Intersection: Womanism and Afrocentrism in Theology.* Minneapolis: Fortress Press.

Sands, K. M. 1994. *Escape from Paradise: Evil and Tragedy in Feminist Theology.* Minneapolis: Fortress Press.

Sandy, P. 1981. "The Socio-Cultural Context of Rape: A Cross Cultural Study." *Journal of Social Issues* 37 (April): 5–27.

Sargent, L., ed. 1981. *Women and Revolution: A Discussion of the Unhappy Marriage of Marxism and Feminism.* Boston: South End Press.

Saussy, C. 1991. *God Images and Self-Esteem: Empowering Women in a Patriarchal Society.* Louisville, Ky.: Westminster John Knox Press.

Scannone, J. C. 1976. *Teología de la liberación y praxis popular.* Salamanca, Spain: Ediciones Sigueme.

Scanzoni, L. D., and N. A. Hardesty. 1992. *All We're Meant to Be: Biblical Feminism for Today.* 3d ed. Grand Rapids: Wm. B. Eerdmans Publishing Co.

Scanzoni, L. D., and V. R. Mollenkott. 1994. *Is the Homosexual My Neighbor? A Positive Christian Response: Revised and Updated.* San Francisco: Harper & Row.

Schaberg, J. 1987. *The Illegitimacy of Jesus: A Feminist Theological Interpretation of the Infancy Narratives.* San Francisco: Harper & Row.

Schaef, A. W. 1981. *Women's Reality: An Emerging Female System in the White Male Society.* Minneapolis: Winston Press.

Schaumberger, C., and M. Maassen, eds. 1986. *Handbuch feministische Theologie.* Münster: Morgana Fraenbuchverlag.

Schaumberger, C., and L. Schottroff. 1988. *Schuld und Macht: Studien zu einer feministischen Befreiungstheologie.* Munich: Chr. Kaiser Verlag.

Schiffer, M., ed. 1984. *Advances in Archaeological Method and Theory.* New York: Academic Press.

Schmidt, A. 1989. *Veiled and Silenced: How Culture Shaped Sexist Theology.* Macon, Ga: Mercer University Press.

Schneiders, S. 1991. *Beyond Patching: Faith and Feminism in the Catholic Church.* New York: Paulist Press.

Schor, N., and E. Weed. 1994. *The Essential Difference.* Bloomington: Indiana University Press.

Schottroff, L. 1995. *Lydia's Impatient Sisters: A Feminist Social History of Early Christianity.* Louisville, Ky.: Westminster John Knox Press.

Schuller, E. 1992. "The Psalm of Joseph (4Q372 1) within the Context of Second Temple Prayer." *CBQ* 54:343–70.

Schüssler Fiorenza, E. 1983/1994. *In Memory of Her: A Feminist Theological Reconstruction of Christian Origins.* Reprint. New York: Crossroad.

———. 1984/1995. *Bread Not Stone: The Challenge of Feminist Biblical Interpretation.* Boston: Beacon Press.

———. 1985. *The Book of Revelation: Justice and Judgment.* Philadelphia: Fortress Press.

———. 1992a. *But She Said: Feminist Practices of Biblical Interpretation.* Boston: Beacon Press.

———. 1992b. "Feminist Hermeneutics," *ABD* 2:783–91.

———. 1993. *Discipleship of Equals: A Critical Feminist Ekklesialogy of Liberation.* New York: Crossroad.

———. 1994. *Jesus: Miriam's Child, Sophia's Prophet.* New York: Continuum.

———, ed. 1993. *Searching the Scriptures: A Feminist Introduction.* Vol. 1. New York: Crossroad.

———, ed. 1994. *Searching the Scriptures: A Feminist Commentary.* Vol. 2. New York: Crossroad.

Schüssler Fiorenza, E., and A. Carr, eds. 1987. *Women, Work and Poverty.* Edinburgh: Concilium/T. & T. Clark.

Schüssler Fiorenza, E., and M. Collins, eds. 1986. *Women—Invisible in Theology and Church.* Philadelphia: Fortress Press.

Schüssler Fiorenza, E., and M. S. Copeland, eds. 1994. *Violence against Women.* Vol. 1. Maryknoll, N.Y.: Concilium/Orbis Books.

Scott, K., and M. Warren, eds. 1983. *Perspectives on Marriage: A Reader.* New York: Oxford University Press.

Sehested, N. H. 1986. "Women and Ministry in the Local Congregation." *Review and Expositor* 83, 1:71–79.

Seifert, D. J. 1991. "Gender in Historical Archaeology." *Historical Archaeology* 24, special issue.

Selvidge, M. J. 1990. *Women, Cult and Miracle Recital: A Redactional Critical Investigation of Mark 5:24–34*. Lewisburg, Pa.: Bucknell University Press.

Sennett, R. 1981. *Authority*. New York: Vintage Books.

Sered, S. S. 1994. *Priestess, Mother, Sacred Sister: Religions Dominated by Women*. New York: Oxford University Press.

Setel, D. 1986. "Feminist Reflections on Separation and Unity in Jewish Theology." *JFSR* 2, 1 (spring): 113–18.

Shange, Ntozake. 1977. *for colored girls who have considered suicide/when the rainbow is enuf*. New York: Collier Books.

Shapiro, S. 1994. "Rhetoric as Ideology Critique: The Gadamer-Habermas Debate Reinvented." *JAAR* 62 (winter): 123–50.

Sharma, A., ed. 1987. *Women in World Religions*. Albany: State University of New York Press.

Sharpe, E. J. 1975. *Comparative Religion: A History*. New York: Charles Scribner's Sons.

Shaw, B., ed. 1994. *The Ragged Edge: The Disability Experience from the Pages of the First Fifteen Years of the Disability Rag*. Louisville, Ky.: Advocado Press.

Shaw, M. 1994. *Passionate Enlightenment: Women in Tantric Buddhism*. Princeton, N.J.: Princeton University Press.

Sherwin, S. 1992. *No Longer Patient: Feminist Ethics and Health Care*. Philadelphia: Temple University Press.

Shiva, V. 1988. *Staying Alive: Women, Ecology and Development*. London: Zed Books.

Shurden, W. B., ed. 1993. *The Priesthood of All Believers*. Macon, Ga.: Smith & Helwys.

Siegele-Wenschkewitz, L., ed. 1988. *Verdrängte Vergangenheit die Uns bedrängt: Feministische Theologie in der Verantwortung für die Geschichte*. Munich: Chr. Kaiser Verlag.

Silvers, A. 1995. "Reconciling Equality to Difference: Caring (F)or Justice for People with Disabilities." *Hypatia* 10, 1:30–55.

Sjoestedt, M. L. 1982. *Gods and Heroes of the Celts*. Trans. Myles Dillon. Berkeley, Calif.: Turtle Island Foundation.

Sloan, R. B., Jr. 1977. *The Favorable Year of the Lord: A Study of Jubilary Theology in the Gospel of Luke*. Austin, Tex.: Schola.

Sly, D. 1990. *Philo's Perception of Women*. Atlanta: Scholars Press.

Smith, C. M. 1989. *Weaving the Sermon: Preaching in a Feminist Perspective*. Louisville, Ky.: Westminster John Knox Press.

———. 1992. *Preaching as Weeping, Confession, and Resistance: Radical Responses to Radical Evil*. Louisville, Ky.: Westminster John Knox Press.

Smith, D. E. 1987. *The Everyday World as Problematic: A Feminist Sociology*. Boston: Northeastern University Press.

Smith, P., ed. 1993. *Feminist Jurisprudence*. New York: Oxford University Press.

Snitow, A., C. Stansell, and S. Thompson, eds. 1989. *Powers of Desire: The Politics of Sexuality*. New York: Monthly Review.

Sobrino, J. 1978. *Christology at the Crossroads: A Latin American Approach*. Trans. John Drury. Maryknoll, N.Y.: Orbis Books.

Soelle, D. 1975. *Suffering*. Philadelphia: Fortress Press.

———. 1977. "Beyond Mere Dialogue: On Being Christian and Socialist." Paper for the Earl Lectures at the Pacific School of Religion, Berkeley, Calif. (spring).

———. 1995. *Creative Disobedience*. Cleveland: Pilgrim Press.

———, ed. 1990. *Gott denken. Einführung in die Theologie*. Stuttgart: Kreuz Verlag.

———, ed. 1990. *Thinking about God: An Introduction to Theology*. Philadelphia: Trinity Press International.

Soelle, D., and S. Cloyes. 1984. *To Work and to Love: A Theology of Creation*. Philadelphia: Fortress Press.

Solomon, A. 1990. *Songs for the People: Teachings on the Natural Way*. Toronto: North Canada Press.

Soskice, J. M. 1985. *Metaphor and Religious Language*. Oxford: Clarendon Press.

"Special Section on Feminist Translation of the New Testament." 1990. *JFSR* 6, 2:24–86.

Spelman, E. V. 1988. *Inessential Woman: Problems of Exclusion in Feminist Thought*. Boston: Beacon Press.

Spicq, C. 1947. "Bénignité, Mansuétude, Douceur, Clémence." *Revue biblique* 54:321–39.

Spiegel, M. C., and D. L. Kremsdorf, eds. 1987. *Women Speak to God: The Poems and Prayers of Jewish Women*. San Diego: Woman's Institute for Continuing Jewish Education.

Spretnak, C. 1992. *Lost Goddesses of Early Greece: A Collection of Pre-Hellenic Myths*. Boston: Beacon Press.

"Sri Lanka Report." 1994. "Spirituality for Life: Women Struggling against Violence." *Voices* 17, 1:84.

Stanko, E. 1990. *Everyday Violence: How Women and Men Experience Sexual and Physical Danger*. London: Pandora.

Stanton, E. C., and the Revising Committee, eds. 1895/1974. *The Woman's Bible*. Seattle: Coalition Task Force on Women and Religion.

Stanworth, M., ed. 1987. *Reproductive Technologies: Gender, Motherhood, and Medicine.* Cambridge, England: Polity Press.

Starhawk. 1989. *The Spiral Dance: A Rebirth of the Ancient Religion of the Great Goddess.* 2d ed. San Francisco: Harper & Row.

Steffen, L. 1994. *Life/Choice: The Theory of Just Abortion.* Cleveland: Pilgrim Press.

Stendahl, B. 1985. *The Force of Tradition: A Case Study of Women Priests in Sweden.* Philadelphia: Fortress Press.

Stowasser, B. F. 1994. *Women in the Qur'an, Traditions, and Interpretation.* New York: Oxford University Press.

Strayer, J. R., ed. 1987. *Dictionary of the Middle Ages.* New York: Charles Scribner's Sons.

Strottmann, A. 1991. *Mein Vater Bist Du (Sir 51, 10): Zur Bedeutung der Vaterschaft Gottes in kanonischen und nichtkanonischen frühjüdischen Schriften.* Frankfurt am Main: Verlag Josef Knecht.

Suchocki, M. H. 1982/1989. *God–Christ–Church: A Practical Guide to Process Theology.* Rev. ed. New York: Crossroad.

———. 1994. *The Fall to Violence: Original Sin in Relational Theology.* New York: Continuum.

Suh, D. K. 1991. *The Korean Minjung in Christ.* Hong Kong: Christian Conference of Asia.

———, ed. 1988. *The Story of Han.* Seoul: Bohree Press.

Sullivan, D. 1994. "Women's Human Rights and the 1993 World Conference on Human Rights." *American Journal of International Law* 88, 1:152–67.

Sultzman, J. 1989. *An Integrated Theory of Stability and Change.* Chicago: Sage.

Swidler, A., and W. E. Conn, eds. 1985. *Mainstreaming: Feminist Research for Teaching Religious Studies.* Lanham, Md.: University Press of America.

Swidler, L. 1971. "Jesus Was a Feminist." *Catholic World* (January): 177–83.

Swidler, L., and A. Swidler, eds. 1985. *Women Priests: A Catholic Commentary on the Vatican Declaration.* New York: Paulist Press.

Swimme, B., and T. Berry. 1993. *The Universe Story.* San Francisco: Harper & Row.

Tamez, E. 1987. *Against Machismo.* Oak Park, Ill.: Meyer-Stone Books.

———. 1989. *Las mujeres toman la palabra.* San José, Costa Rica: DEI.

———. 1990. *The Scandalous Message of James: Faith without Works Is Dead.* New York: Crossroad.

———. 1993a. "God's Election, Exclusion, and Mercy: A Biblical Study of Romans 9–11." *IRM* 82 (January): 29–37.

———. 1993b. *The Amnesty of Grace: Justification by Faith from a Latin American Perspective.* Trans. Sharon H. Ringe. Nashville: Abingdon Press.

———, ed. 1989. *Through Her Eyes: Women's Theology from Latin America.* Maryknoll, N.Y.: Orbis Books.

Tanner, K. 1992. *The Politics of God: Christian Theories and Social Justice.* Minneapolis: Fortress Press.

Tepedino, A. M. 1990. *As Discipulas de Jesus.* Petrópolis, Brazil: Vozes.

Thistlethwaite, S. B. 1983. *Metaphors for the Contemporary Church.* New York: Pilgrim Press.

———. 1989. *Sex, Race, and God—Christian Feminism in Black and White.* New York: Crossroad.

Thistlethwaite, S. B., and M. P. Engel, eds. 1990. *Lift Every Voice: Constructing Christian Theologies from the Underside.* San Francisco: Harper & Row.

Thomas, J. M., and V. Visick, V. 1991. *God and Capitalism: A Prophetic Critique of Market Economy.* Madison, Wis.: A-R Editions.

Thomas, K. 1971. *Religion and the Decline of Magic.* New York: Charles Scribner's Sons.

Thomas, S. L. 1994. *Gender and Poverty.* New York: Garland Publications.

Thompson, W. I. 1987. *Gaia: A Way of Knowing.* Great Barrington, Mass.: Lindisfarne Press.

Thurston, B. B. 1989. *The Widows: A Women's Ministry in the Early Church.* Philadelphia: Fortress Press.

Tinker, G. 1993. *Missionary Conquest: The Gospel and Native American Cultural Genocide.* Minneapolis: Fortress Press.

Tolbert, M. A., ed. 1983. "The Bible and Feminist Hermeneutics." *Semeia* 28:113–26.

Tong, R. 1989. *Feminist Thought: A Comprehensive Introduction.* Boulder, Colo.: Westview Press.

———. 1993. *Feminine and Feminist Ethics.* Belmont, Calif.: Wadsworth Publishing Co.

Torjesen, K. J. 1993. *When Women Were Priests: Women's Leadership in the Early Church and the Scandal of Their Subordination in the Rise of Christianity.* San Francisco: Harper & Row.

Townes, E. M. 1993a. *Womanist Justice, Womanist Hope.* Atlanta: Scholars Press.

———. 1993b. " 'Introduction': Appropriation and Reciprocity in the Doing of Feminist and Womanist Ethics." *Annual of the Society of Christian Ethics:* 187–88.

———. 1994. "Voices of the Spirit: Womanist Methodologies in Theological Disciplines." *The Womanist* 1 (summer): 1–2.

———. 1995. *In a Blaze of Glory: Womanist Spirituality as Social Witness*. Nashville: Abingdon Press.

Townes, E. M., ed. 1993. *A Troubling in My Soul: Womanist Perspectives on Evil and Suffering*. Maryknoll, N.Y.: Orbis Books.

Traina, C. L. 1992. "Developing an Integrative Ethical Method: Feminist Ethics and Natural Law Retrieval." Ph.D. diss., University of Chicago.

Trible, P. 1973. "Depatriarchalizing in Biblical Interpretation." *JAAR* 41:30–48.

———. 1978. *God and the Rhetoric of Sexuality*. Philadelphia: Fortress Press.

———. 1984. *Texts of Terror: Literary-Feminist Readings of Biblical Narratives*. Philadelphia: Fortress Press.

———. 1989. "Bringing Miriam Out of the Shadows." *BR* 5 (February): 14–25, 34.

———. 1994. *Rhetorical Criticism: Context, Method, and the Book of Jonah*. Minneapolis: Fortress Press.

Tsomo, K. L., ed. 1988. *Sakyadhita: Daughters of the Buddha*. Ithaca, N.Y.: Snow Lion.

Turner, T., and B. Ferguson, eds. 1994. *Arise Ye Mighty People! Gender, Class and Race in Popular Struggles*. Trenton: Africa World Press.

Uhr, M. L. 1988. "The Portrayal of Women in the Lectionary." *St. Mark Review* 135:22–25.

UNICEF (United Nations Children's Fund). N.d. *The Invisible Adjustment: Poor Women and the Economic Crisis*. Santiago: UNICEF Americas and the Caribbean Regional Office.

Unterberger, G. L. 1990. "Through the Lens of Feminist Psychology and Feminist Theology: A Theoretical Model for Pastoral Counseling." Ph.D. diss., School of Theology at Claremont, Calif.

Valcárel, A. 1991. *Sexo y filosofía: Sobre mujer y poder*. Barcelona: Anthropos.

Valverde, M. 1985. *Sex, Power, and Pleasure*. Toronto: Women's Press.

van Braght, T., ed. 1951. *The Bloody Theater or the Martyr's Mirror*. Scottdale, Pa.: Herald Press.

Van der Toorn, K. 1992. "Prostitution, Cultic." *ABD* 5:510–13.

Van Leeuwen, M. S., ed. 1993. *After Eden: Facing the Challenge of Gender Reconciliation*. Grand Rapids: Wm. B. Eerdmans Publishing Co.

Vetterling-Braggin, M., et al., eds. 1977. *Feminism and Philosophy*. Totowa, N.J.: Littlefield, Adams & Co.

Villa-Vicencio, C., ed. 1988. *Theology and Violence: The South African Debate*. Grand Rapids: Wm. B. Eerdmans Publishing Co.

Vischer, L., ed. 1982. *Church History in an Ecumenical Perspective: Papers and Reports of an International Ecumenical Consultation held in Basel, October 12–17, 1981*. Bern: Evangelische Arbeitsstelle Oekumene Schweiz.

Vivew, J. 1986. *El secuestro de la verdad: Los hombres secuestran la verdad con su injusticia*. Santander, Spain: Sal Terrae.

von Kellenbach, K. 1994. *Anti-Judaism in Christian-Rooted Feminist Writings*. Atlanta: Scholars Press.

von Wartenberg-Potter, B. 1987. *We Will Not Hang Our Harps on the Willows*. Geneva: World Council of Churches.

Wadud-Muhsin, A. 1992. *Qur'an and Woman*. Kuala Lumpur: Penerbit Fajar Bakti Sdn. Bhd.

Walker, A. 1982. *The Color Purple*. New York: Washington Square Books.

———. 1983. *In Search of Our Mothers' Gardens: Womanist Prose*. New York: Harcourt Brace Jovanovich.

Wall, S. 1993. *Wisdom's Daughters: Conversations with Women Elders of Native America*. New York: HarperCollins.

Wall, S., and H. Arden. 1990. *Wisdomkeepers: Meetings with Native American Spiritual Elders*. Hillsboro, Ore.: Beyond Words Publishing.

Waring, M. 1988. *If Women Counted: A New Feminist Economics*. San Francisco: Harper & Row.

Warne, R. R. 1989. "Toward a Brave New Paradigm: The Impact of Women's Studies on Religious Studies." *Religious Studies and Theology* 9, 2/3:35–46.

Wartenberg, T. E. 1990. *The Forms of Power*. Philadelphia: Temple University Press.

Washbourn, P. 1977. *Becoming Woman: The Quest for Wholeness in Female Experience*. New York: Harper & Row.

Washington, M. H., ed. 1988. *A Voice from the South*. New York: Oxford University Press.

Weaving. 1994– . Newsletter of the Weavers: Women and Theological Education, South Pacific Association of Theological Schools (SPATS), P.O. Box 2426, Government Buildings, Suva, Fiji.

Weber, M. 1968. *Economy and Society*, ed. G. Roth and C. Wittich. New York: Bedminster Press.

Weems, R. 1988. *Just a Sister Away: A Womanist Vision of Women's Relationships in the Bible*. San Diego: Lura Media.

Weidman, J. L., ed. 1984. *Christian Feminism: Visions of a New Humanity*. San Francisco: Harper & Row.

———, ed. 1985. *Women Ministers: How Women Are Redefining Traditional Roles.* New York: Harper & Row.

Weiler, K. 1988. *Women Teaching for Change: Gender, Class and Power.* South Hadley, Mass.: Bergin & Garvey.

Weitzman, L. 1985. *The Divorce Revolution: The Unexpected Social and Economic Consequences for Women and Children in America.* New York: Free Press.

Welch, S. D. 1985. *Communities of Solidarity and Resistance: A Feminist Theology of Liberation.* Maryknoll, N.Y.: Orbis Books.

———. 1990. *A Feminist Ethic of Risk.* Minneapolis: Fortress Press.

Welsing, F. C. 1970. *The Cress Theory of Color-Confrontation and Racism.*

Westenholz, J. G. 1989. "Tamar, *gedesa, gadistu* and Sacred Prostitution in Mesopotamia." *HTR* 82, 3:245–65.

Wetherilt, A. K. 1994. *That They May Be Many: Voices of Women, Echoes of God.* New York: Continuum.

Whitehead, A. N. 1929/1978. *Process and Reality.* Corrected ed., edited by D. R. Griffin and D. W. Sherburne. New York: Free Press.

Whitford, M., ed. 1991. *The Irigaray Reader.* Cambridge, Mass.: Basil Blackwell.

Wickland, R. A., and J. W. Brehm. 1976. *Perspectives on Cognitive Dissonance.* Hillsdale, N.J.: Lawrence Erlbaum Associates.

Wiethaus, U., ed. 1993. *Maps of Flesh and Light: The Religious Experience of Medieval Women Mystics.* Syracuse, N.Y.: Syracuse University Press.

Williams, D. S. 1986. "The Color of Feminism: Or Speaking the Black Woman's Tongue." *Journal of Religious Thought* 42, 1:42–58.

———. 1993a. *Sisters in the Wilderness: The Challenge of Womanist God-Talk.* Maryknoll, N.Y.: Orbis Books.

———. 1993b. "A Crucifixion Double Cross?" *Other Side* (September–October): 25–27.

Williams, G. H. 1962. *Wilderness and Paradise in Christian Experience.* New York: Harper & Brothers.

Williams, R. 1983. *Keywords: A Vocabulary of Culture and Society.* Rev. ed. New York: Oxford University Press.

Wilmore, G. S., ed. 1989. *African American Religious Studies.* Durham, N.C.: Duke University Press.

Wilson, K. M. 1988. *Hrotsvit of Gandersheim: The Ethics of Authorial Stance.* Leiden: E. J. Brill.

Wilson-Kastner, P. 1983. *Faith, Feminism, and the Christ.* Philadelphia: Fortress Press.

Wink, W. 1984. *Naming the Powers: The Language of Power in the New Testament.* Philadelphia: Fortress Press.

———. 1986. *Unmasking the Powers: Discernment and Resistance in a World of Domination.* Philadelphia: Fortress Press.

Winter, M. T. 1989. "The Women-Church Movement." *CCent* 106 (March 8): 258–60.

———. 1991. *Womanword.* New York: Crossroad.

Winter, M. T., A. Lummis, and A. Stokes, eds. 1994. *Defecting in Place: Women Claiming Responsibility for Their Own Spiritual Lives.* New York: Crossroad.

Wire, A. C. 1990. *The Corinthian Women Prophets: A Reconstruction through Paul's Rhetoric.* Minneapolis: Fortress Press.

Withers, B. A., ed. 1984. *Language and the Church: Articles and Designs for Workshops.* New York: Division of Publication Services, National Council of the Churches of Christ in the U.S.A.

Wittberg, P. 1994. *The Rise and Fall of Catholic Religious Orders: A Social Movement Perspective.* Albany: State University of New York Press.

Wolf, M. 1992. *The Thrice Told Tale: Feminism, Modernism and Ethnographic Responsibility.* Stanford, Calif.: Stanford University Press.

Wolff, H. 1981. *Neuer Wein, alte Schlauche.* Stuttgart: Radius.

Wolkstein, D., and S. N. Kramer. 1983. *Inanna: Queen of Heaven and Earth. Her Stories and Hymns from Sumer.* New York: Harper & Row.

"Women and AIDS: Agenda for Action." Background document for the Fourth World Conference on Women, Beijing, September 1995. Published by the World Health Organization (http://gpawww.who.ch/beijing/agenda.htm).

"Women Bhakta Poets." 1989. *Manushi: Tenth Anniversary Issue* (January–June): 50–52.

Wright, C. 1980. *God's People in God's Land: Family, Land, and Property in the Old Testament.* Grand Rapids: Wm. B. Eerdmans Publishing Co.

Wright, E. O. 1985. *Classes.* London: New Left.

Wylie-Kellerman, J., ed. 1993. "Godly Sex: Gender, Power, Intimacy and Ethics." *Witness* 76 (May): 5–26, 28, 30–32.

Yamane, D., and M. Polzer. 1994. "Ways of Seeing Ecstasy in Modern Society: Experi-